GEOFFREY KHAN, Ph.D. (1984) in Semitic Languages, School of Oriental and African Studies, London, is Professor of Semitic Philology at the Univeristy of Cambridge. He has published in the field of Hebrew and Semitic philology.

DIANA LIPTON wrote her Ph.D. on dreams in Genesis at Cambridge University under the supervision of Robert Gordon (1996). She was a Fellow of Newnham College Cambridge and latterly Reader in Hebrew Bible and Jewish Studies at King's College London.

Studies on the Text and Versions of the Hebrew Bible in Honour of Robert Gordon

Supplements

to

Vetus Testamentum

VOLUME 149

Robert Gordon

Studies on the Text and Versions of the Hebrew Bible in Honour of Robert Gordon

Edited by

Geoffrey Khan and Diana Lipton

BRILL

LEIDEN • BOSTON
2012

This book is printed on acid-free paper.

Library of Congress Cataloging-in-Publication Data

Studies on the text and versions of the Hebrew Bible in honour of Robert Gordon / edited by Geoffrey Khan and Diana Lipton.
p. cm. — (Supplements to Vetus Testamentum ; v. 149)
Includes bibliographical references.
ISBN 978-90-04-21730-0 (hardback : alk. paper) 1. Bible. O.T.—Criticism, Textual. 2. Bible. O.T.—Criticism, interpretation, etc. I. Gordon, R. P. II. Khan, Geoffrey. III. Lipton, Diana.

BS1136.S78 2012
221.6'6—dc23

2011034525

ISSN 0083-5889
ISBN 978-90-04-21730-0

PRINTED BY DRUKKERIJ WILCO B.V. - AMERSFOORT, THE NETHERLANDS

CONTENTS

PREFACE

Editing this volume in honour of Robert Gordon has been a privilege. Without exception, the potential contributors we contacted expressed unqualified enthusiasm about the project. The contributors include former students, past and present colleagues, and general admirers of an honouree who has left his mark, professional and personal, on many lives.

The contributions to this volume represent a wide range of academic interests. That we have been able to elicit papers on these varied aspects of biblical exegesis, translation, versions and commentary is not particularly noteworthy. Of great note, however, is that they all reflect the scholarship of Robert himself. Age may or may not wither him but, as is evident from a glance at his bibliography (let alone the publications of those he has taught, encouraged and inspired), his infinite variety is multiply attested and at no risk of growing stale.

Alongside the many books and articles Robert has written himself, his bibliography includes several edited volumes. Scholars privileged to have papers included in these collections will understand that we anticipate with happiness and fear combined the moment when Robert opens the present volume. He has a much sharper eye than us for misplaced commas.

Those personally acquainted with Robert Gordon will know him as an immensely modest man who neither seeks nor enjoys praise or even due recognition. There is indeed a chance that he would have been happier without a Festschrift in his honour, but we hope that at the very least this modest volume, delivered without fanfare but with affection and admiration, will not embarrass him unduly.

Geoffrey Khan
Diana Lipton

ABBREVIATIONS

AHw	Soden, W. von 1959–*Akkadisches Handwörterbuch* (3 vols.; Wiesbaden: Harrassowitz).
ANET	Pritchard, J.B. 1969 *Ancient Near Eastern Texts Relating to the Old Testament* (Princeton: Princeton University Press, 3rd edition).
Ant.	Josephus' *Antiquitas Judaeorum (Antiquities of the Jews)*
Ap.	Josephus' *Contra Apionem (Against Apion)*
B.J.	Josephus' *Bellum Judaicum (Jewish War)*
Brenton	Brenton, L.C.L. 1844 *The Septuagint Version of the Old Testament* (London: Bagster).
CIS	Corpus Inscriptionum Semiticarum (Paris, 1881ff.).
Gen. Rab.	Genesis Rabbah
Hatch Redpath	Hatch, E., and H.A. Redpath 1897 *A Concordance of the Septuagint* (Oxford: Clarendon Press).
Jastrow	Jastrow, M. 1903 *A Dictionary of the Targumim, the Talmud Babli and Yerushalmi, and the Midrashic Literature* (London: Luzac).
KAI	Donner, H., and W. Röllig 1966, 1968, 1969 *Kanaanäische und Aramäische Inschriften* (2nd. ed.; 3 vols.; Wiesbaden: Otto Harrassowitz).
L.A.B.	Liber Antiquitatum Biblicarum (Biblical Antiquities)
LCL	Loeb Classical Library
Legat.	Philo's *Legatio ad Gaium*
LSJ	Liddell, H.G., R. Scott and H.S. Jones 1948 *A Greek-English Lexicon* (9th edn; Oxford: Clarendon Press).
LSJ.Suppl.	Barber, E.A. 1968 *Greek-English Lexicon: A Supplement* (Oxford: Clarendon Press).
MH	Mishnaic Hebrew
MP	Minor Prophets
Mur	Milik, J.T. 1961 'Textes hébreux et araméens', in *Les Grottes de Murabbaʿât: Texte* by P. Benoit, J.T. Milik and R. de Vaux (Discoveries in the Judaean Desert, 2; Oxford: Clarendon Press) 67–205; Yardeni, A. 2000a *Textbook of Aramaic, Hebrew and Nabataean Documentary Texts from the Judaean Desert and*

	Related Material. A. The Documents (Jerusalem: The Ben-Zion Dinur Center for Research in Jewish History) and 2000b *Textbook of Aramaic, Hebrew and Nabataean Documentary Texts from the Judaean Desert and Related Material. B. Translation, Palaeography, Concordance* (Jerusalem: The Ben-Zion Dinur Center for Research in Jewish History).
NETS	Pietersma, A., and B.G. Wright (eds.) 2007 *A New English Translation of the Septuagint* (New York/Oxford: Oxford University Press).
P.Yadin	Yadin, Y., J.C. Greenfield, A. Yardeni and B.A. Levine 2002 *The Documents from the Bar Kokhba Period in the Cave of Letters: Hebrew, Aramaic and Nabatean-Aramaic Papyri* (Judean Desert Studies; Jerusalem: Israel Exploration Society).
TADAE	Porten, B., and A. Yardeni 1986, 1989, 1993, 1999 *Textbook of Aramaic Documents from Ancient Egypt* (4 vols.; Jerusalem: Department of the History of the Jewish People, the Hebrew University).
WDSP	Gropp, D.M. 2001 'The Samaria Papyri from Wadi Daliyeh', in *Wadi Daliyeh II and Qumran Cave 4. XXVIII* by Douglas M. Gropp and others (Discoveries in the Judaean Desert, 28; Oxford: Clarendon Press) 3–116.
XḤev/Se	Yardeni, A. 1997 'Aramaic and Hebrew Documentary Texts', in *Aramaic, Hebrew and Greek Documentary Texts from Naḥal Ḥever and other sites* by H.M. Cotton and A. Yardeni (Discoveries in the Judaean Desert, 27; Oxford: Clarendon Press) 9–129.
4QVisions of ʿAmram^{c} ar	Puech, É. 2001 *Qumrân Grotte 4. XXII: Textes araméens, première partie, 4Q529–549* (Discoveries in the Judaean Desert, 31; Oxford: Clarendon Press) 331–349.

PUBLICATIONS OF ROBERT P. GORDON

1970 'Isaiah liii 2', *Vetus Testamentum* 20: 491–492.

1971 'Inner-Syriac Corruptions', *Journal of Theological Studies* NS 22: 502–504.

1974 'The Targum to the Minor Prophets and the Dead Sea Texts: Textual and Exegetical Notes', *Revue de Qumrân* 8: 425–429.

'Sperber's Edition of the Targum to the Prophets: A Critique', *Jewish Quarterly Review* 64: 314–321.

'Deuteronomy and the Deuteronomic School', *Tyndale Bulletin* 25: 113–120.

'Targumic Parallels to Acts XIII 18 and Didache XIV 3', *Novum Testamentum* 16: 285–289.

arts. 'Aramaic', 'Chronicon Edessenum', 'Cook (Stanley Arthur)', 'Coptic', 'Hebrew', 'Old Syriac Versions of the New Testament', 'Palestinian Syriac Text of the New Testament', 'Syriac', 'Syriac Versions of the Bible', in *The New International Dictionary of the Christian Church* (ed. J.D. Douglas; Exeter: Paternoster), 62, 225, 261, 262, 455–456, 725, 743, 948–949.

1975 '*KAI TO TELOS KURIOU EIDETE* (Jas. v 11)', *Journal of Theological Studies* NS 26: 91–95.

'An Inner-Targum Corruption (Zech. i 8)', *Vetus Testamentum* 25: 216–221.

'The Second Septuagint Account of Jeroboam: History or Midrash?', *Vetus Testamentum* 25: 368–393.

'The Citation of the Targums in Recent English Bible Translations (*RSV, JB, NEB*)', *Journal of Jewish Studies* 26: 50–60.

'Targum Variant Agrees with Wellhausen!', *Zeitschrift für die Alttestamentliche Wissenschaft* 87: 218–219.

1976 'On BH *tôb* "Rain" ', *Biblica* 57: 111.

'Source Study in 1 Kgs. XII 24a-nα', *Transactions of the Glasgow University Oriental Society* 25: 59–70.

'Targum Onkelos to Genesis 49:4 and a Common Semitic Idiom', *Jewish Quarterly Review* 66: 224–226.

1978 'Micah vii 19 and Akkadian *kabāsu*', *Vetus Testamentum* 28: 355.

'The Targumists as Eschatologists', in *Congress Volume: Göttingen 1977* (ed. J.A. Emerton; Supplements to Vetus Testamentum., 29; Leiden: Brill) 113–130.

'Aleph Apologeticum', *Jewish Quarterly Review* 69: 112–116.

1979 'The Ancient Versions', *Exodus, Leviticus*, in *A Bible Commentary for Today* (ed. G.C.D. Howley, F.F. Bruce, H.L. Ellison; London: Pickering and Inglis) 30–39, 170–237.

'Versions Old and New', *Harvester* 58: 233–235.

1980 'David's Rise and Saul's Demise: Narrative Analogy in 1 Samuel 24–26', *Tyndale Bulletin* 31: 37–64.

'Exorcism in a Dead Sea Scroll', *Harvester* 59: 2–3.

arts. 'Abimelech', 'Abner', 'Armour and Weapons', 'Army', 'Captain', 'Guard', 'Horesh', 'Ichabod', 'Jeshimon', 'Kabzeel', 'Legion', 'Papyri and Ostraca (Hebrew, Aramaic and Greek)', 'War', in *The Illustrated Bible Dictionary* (ed. J.D. Douglas, N. Hillyer; Leicester: Inter-Varsity Press), 4, 5, 111–117, 251–252, 595, 660, 676, 760, 845, 894, 1143–1147, 1628–1631.

1981 'A Problem in the Odes of Solomon XXIII. 20', *Journal of Theological Studies* NS 32: 443–447 (with J.A. Emerton).

'A Syriac Exposition of Psalm 15', *Le Muséon* 94: 231–233.

1982 '*Terra Sancta* and the Territorial Doctrine of the Targum to the Prophets', in *Interpreting the Hebrew Bible: Essays in Honour of E.I.J. Rosenthal* (ed. J.A. Emerton, S.C. Reif; Cambridge: Cambridge University Press) 119–131.

art. 'Holy Place', in *The International Standard Bible Encyclopedia* (revd.) (ed. G.W. Bromiley; Grand Rapids: Eerdmans), vol. 2, 729–730.

Review of C. McCarthy, *The Tiqqune Sopherim and Other Theological Corrections in the Masoretic Text of the Old Testament* (Orbis Biblicus et Orientalis 36; 1981), in *Vetus Testamentum* 32: 358–362.

Review of G.T. Sheppard, *Wisdom as a Hermeneutical Construct* (Beihefte zur Zeitschrift für die Alttestamentliche Wissenschaft, 151; 1980), in *Vetus Testamentum* 32: 374–378.

Review of P.K. McCarter, *I Samuel: A New Translation with Introduction, Notes and Commentary* (Anchor Bible, 8; 1980), in *Journal for the Study of the Old Testament* 24, 109–112.

1983 'Loricate Locusts in the Targum to Nahum III 17 and Revelation IX 9', *Vetus Testamentum* 33: 338–339.

'Did Moses Write "Second Isaiah"?', *TSF News and Prayer Letter* (Summer Issue): 3–4.

‘A Igreja em Tessalônica’, *Vigiai e Orai* 59: 2–4, 17; 60, 14–15, 17.

1984 *1 and 2 Samuel* (Old Testament Guides; Sheffield: JSOT Press).
‘Christianity under the Cloud’, *Harvester* 63, 4–5.
‘A Igreja em Tessalônica’, *Vigiai e Orai* 61, 14, 16–17.

1985 ‘The *Gladius Hispaniensis* and Aramaic *‘ISPĀNÎQÊ*’, *Vetus Testamentum* 35: 496–500.
‘A Igreja em Tessalônica’, *Vigiai e Orai* 62: 5–7.
‘Easter in Durham’, *Harvester* 64: 8–9.
Review of J. Blenkinsopp, *A History of Prophecy in Israel* (1984), in *Journal of Theological Studies* NS 36: 408–410.

1986 *1 and 2 Samuel: A Commentary* (Exeter: Paternoster).
Theology and Religious Studies in UK Universities, Polytechnics and Colleges (CRAC Degree Course Guide 1986/7; Cambridge: Hobsons).
‘The Ancient Versions’, *Exodus*, *Leviticus*, in *The International Bible Commentary* (ed. F.F. Bruce; London: Marshall Pickering), 14–23, 149–213 (revd edn; see 1979).
art. ‘Most Holy Place’, in *The International Standard Bible Encyclopedia* (revd.) (ed. G.W. Bromiley; Grand Rapids: Eerdmans), vol. 3, 426.

1987 ‘Saul’s Meningitis According to Targum 1 Samuel xix 24’, *Vetus Testamentum* 37: 39–49.
Review of D.M. Golomb, *A Grammar of Targum Neofiti* (1985), in *Journal of Theological Studies* NS 38: 469–470.
Review of E. Qimron, *The Hebrew of the Dead Sea Scrolls* (1986), in *Journal of Theological Studies* NS 38: 470–471.

1988 *Theology and Religious Studies: Guide to First-Degree Courses at UK Universities, Polytechnics and Other Institutions* (CRAC Degree Course Guide 1988/9; Cambridge: Hobsons).
art. ‘Rabbinic Theology’, in *New Dictionary of Theology* (ed. S.B. Ferguson, D.F. Wright; Leicester: Inter-Varsity) 555.
‘Targum as Midrash: Contemporizing in the Targum to the Prophets’, in *Proceedings of the Ninth World Congress of Jewish Studies. Panel Sessions: Bible Studies and Ancient Near East* (ed. M. Goshen-Gottstein; Jerusalem: Magnes Press) 61–73.
‘Simplicity of the Highest Cunning: Narrative Art in the Old Testament’,
Scottish Bulletin of Evangelical Theology 6: 69–80.
Review of J. Barton, *Oracles of God: Perceptions of Ancient Prophecy in Israel after the Exile* (1986), in *Vetus Testamentum* 38: 486–488.

1989 *The Targum of the Minor Prophets* (The Aramaic Bible, 14; ed. K.J. Cathcart, R.P. Gordon; Wilmington: Michael Glazier).

'Targumic ^{c}*DY* (Zechariah xiv 6) and the Not So Common "Cold"', *Vetus Testamentum* 39: 77–81.

1990 art. 'Samuel', in *A Dictionary of Biblical Interpretation* (ed. R.J. Coggins, J.L. Houlden; London: SCM) 608–609.

'Word-Play and Verse-Order in 1 Samuel xxiv 5–8', *Vetus Testamentum* 40: 139–144.

'Covenant and Apology in 2 Samuel 3', *Proceedings of the Irish Biblical Association* 13: 24–34.

Review of P.B. Dirksen, M.J. Mulder (eds.), *The Peshitta: Its Early Text and History* (1988), in *Journal of Semitic Studies* 35: 318–319.

1991 'Better Promises: Two Passages in Hebrews against the Background of the Old Testament Cultus', in *Templum Amicitiae: Essays on the Second Temple Presented to Ernst Bammel* (Supplements to Journal for the Study of the New Testament, 48; ed. W. Horbury; Sheffield: JSOT Press) 434–449.

'Compositeness, Conflation and the Pentateuch', *Journal for the Study of the Old Testament* 51: 57–69.

1992 *Theology and Religious Studies in UK Universities, Polytechnics and Colleges* (CRAC Degree Course Guide 1992/93; Cambridge: Hobsons).

'Inscribed Pots and Zechariah xiv 20–21', *Vetus Testamentum* 42: 120–123.

'Foreword to the Reprinted Edition', in *The Bible in Aramaic* I (ed. A. Sperber; Leiden: Brill) i–vi.

'"Isaiah's Wild Measure": R.M. McCheyne', *Expository Times* 103: 235–237.

'The Interpretation of "Lebanon" and 4Q285', *Journal of Jewish Studies* 43: 92–94.

'The Problem of Haplography in 1 and 2 Samuel', in *Septuagint, Scrolls and Cognate Writings: Papers Presented to the International Symposium on the Septuagint and Its Relations to the Dead Sea Scrolls and Other Writings (Manchester, 1990)* (SBL Septuagint and Cognate Studies 33; ed. G.J. Brooke, B. Lindars; Atlanta: Scholars Press) 131–158.

'The Meaning of the Verb *ŠWY* in the Targum to 1 Samuel V–VI', *Vetus Testamentum* 42: 395–397.

'K/KÎ/KY in Incantational Incipits', *Ugarit-Forschungen* 23: 161–163.

arts. 'Hophni and Phinehas', 'Horns of Altar', in *A Dictionary of Biblical Tradition in English Literature* (ed. D.L. Jeffrey; Grand Rapids: Eerdmans) 361–362.

Review of G. Van Groningen, *Messianic Revelation in the Old Testament* (1990), in *Vetus Testamentum* 42: 425–426.

1993 'The Two Minorities', *Priests and People* 7: 10–13.

'From Mari to Moses: Prophecy at Mari and in Ancient Israel', in *Of Prophets' Visions and the Wisdom of Sages: Essays in Honour of R. Norman Whybray on his Seventieth Birthday* (Supplements to Journal for the Study of the Old Testament, 162; ed. H.A. McKay, D.J.A. Clines; Sheffield: JSOT Press) 63–79.

'The Variable Wisdom of Abel: The MT and Versions at 2 Samuel xx 18–19', *Vetus Testamentum* 43: 215–226.

Review of L. Alonso Schoekel (ed.), *Diccionario bíblico hebreo-español,* Fasciculo 1 (1990), in *Vetus Testamentum* 43: 125–126.

Review of W.T. Koopmans, *Joshua 24 as Poetic Narrative* (Journal for the study of the Old Testament supplement series, 93; 1990), in *Vetus Testamentum* 43: 571–572.

1994 *Studies in the Targum to the Twelve Prophets: From Nahum to Malachi* (Supplements to Vetus Testamentum, 51; Leiden: Brill).

'Dialogue and Disputation in the Targum to the Prophets', *Journal of Semitic Studies* 39: 7–17.

'Alexander Sperber and the Study of the Targums', in *The Aramaic Bible: Targums in their Historical Context* (ed. D.R.G. Beattie, M.J. McNamara; Supplements to Journal for the Study of the Old Testament,166; Sheffield: JSOT Press) 92–102.

'Who Made the Kingmaker?: Reflections on Samuel and the Institution of the Monarchy', in *Faith, Tradition, and History: Old Testament Historiography in Its Near Eastern Context* (ed. A.R. Millard, J.K. Hoffmeier, D.W. Baker; Winona Lake: Eisenbrauns) 255–269.

'In Search of David: The David Tradition in Recent Study', ibid. 285–298.

art. 'Targums' in *The Oxford Companion to the Bible* (ed. B.M. Metzger, M.D. Coogan; Oxford: Oxford University Press) 754–755.

Review of S.L. McKenzie, *The Trouble with Kings: The Composition of the Book of Kings in the Deuteronomistic History* (Supplements to Vetus Testamentum, 42; 1991), in *Vetus Testamentum* 44: 135–136.

1995 *The Place Is Too Small For Us: The Israelite Prophets in Recent Scholarship* (Sources for Biblical and Theological Study, 5; ed. R.P. Gordon; Winona Lake: Eisenbrauns).

Wisdom in Ancient Israel: Essays in Honour of J.A. Emerton (ed. J. Day, R.P. Gordon, H.G.M. Williamson; Cambridge: Cambridge University Press)

'Introduction', ibid. 1–13.

'A House Divided: Wisdom in the Old Testament Narrative Traditions', ibid. 94–105.

'Where Have All the Prophets Gone?: The "Disappearing" Israelite Prophet Against the Background of Ancient Near Eastern Prophecy', *Bulletin for Biblical Research* 5: 67–86.

'Variant Vorlagen and the Exegetical Factor: Response to Y. Maori', in *The Peshitta as a Translation:Papers Read at the II Peshitta Symposium, held at Leiden, 19–21 August 1993* (Monographs of the Peshitta Institute 8; ed. P.B. Dirksen, A. van der Kooij; Leiden: Brill) 121–125.

1996 'Translational Features of the Peshitta in 1 Samuel', in *Targumic and Cognate Studies: Essays in Honour of Martin McNamara* (Supplements to Journal for the Study of the Old Testament, 230; ed. K.J. Cathcart, M. Maher; Sheffield: Sheffield Academic Press) 163–176.

1997 articles in *New International Dictionary of Old Testament Theology and Exegesis* (ed. W. VanGemeren; Grand Rapids: Zondervan).

'arar', 524–526 (vol. 1).

'tov', 353–357 (vol. 2).

'Babel', 428–430.

'Curse', 491–493.

'David', 505–512.

'Eli', 570–572.

'Samuel, Theology of', 1168–1177 (vol. 4).

1998 *The Old Testament in Syriac according to the Peshitta Version*, IV, 2: *Chronicles* (The Peshitta Institute; Leiden: Brill)

'The Syriac Old Testament: Provenance, Perspective and Translation Technique', in *Interpretation of the Bible: International Symposium on the Interpretation of the Bible on the Occasion of the Publication of the New Slovenian Translation of the Bible* (ed. J. Krašovec; Sheffield: Sheffield Academic Press) 355–369.

'A Reading in 4QSam[a] and the Murder of Abner', *Textus* 19: 75–80 (with E.D. Herbert).

1999 '"Converse Translation" in the Targums and Beyond', *Journal for the Study of the Pseudepigrapha* 19: 3–21.

2000 *Hebrews: A Commentary* (Readings; Sheffield: Sheffield Academic Press).

2001 'The Legacy of Lowth: Robert Lowth and the Book of Isaiah in Particular', in *Biblical Hebrew, Biblical Texts: Essays in Memory of Michael P. Weitzman* (Supplements to Journal for the Study of the Old Testament, 333; ed. A. Rapoport, G. Greenberg; Sheffield: Sheffield Academic Press) 57–76.

'Book List', *Vetus Testamentum* 51: 115–139.

2002 Chinese edition of *1 and 2 Samuel* (Old Testament Guides; see 1984).

'Book List', *Vetus Testamentum* 52: 427–434.

2003 'Gibeonite Ruse and Israelite Curse in Joshua 9', in *Covenant as Context: Essays in Honour of E.W. Nicholson* (ed. A.D.H. Mayes, R.B. Salters; Oxford: Oxford University Press) 163–190.

'The Ephraimite Messiah and the Targum(s) to Zechariah 12.10', in *Reading from Right to Left: Essays on the Hebrew Bible in Honour of David J.A. Clines* (Supplements to Journal for the Study of the Old Testament, 373; ed. C.J. Exum, H.G.M. Williamson; London: Sheffield Academic Press) 189–200.

'A Warranted Version of Historical Biblical Criticism?: A Response to Alvin Plantinga', in *'Behind' the Text: History and Biblical Interpretation* (Scripture and Hermeneutics Series, 4; eds. C. Bartholomew, C.S. Evans, M. Healy, and M. Rae; Carlisle: Paternoster) 79–91.

'Book List', *Vetus Testamentum* 53: 562–575.

2004 *Holy Land, Holy City: Sacred Geography and the Interpretation of the Bible* (Didsbury Lectures 2001; Carlisle: Paternoster).

'The Ideological Foe: The Philistines in the Old Testament', in *Biblical and Near Eastern Essays: Studies in Honour of Kevin J. Cathcart* (Supplements to Journal for the Study of the Old Testament, 375; eds. C. McCarthy and J.F. Healey; London: T. and T. Clark International) 22–36.

1 and 2 Samuel: A Commentary (repr. Carlisle: Paternoster; see 1986).

2005 *The Old Testament in its World: Papers Read at the Winter Meeting, January 2003, The Society for Old Testament Study, and at the Joint Meeting, July 2003, The Society for Old Testament Study and Het Oudtestamentisch Werkgezelschap in Nederland en België* (Oudtestamentische Studiën 52; ed. R.P. Gordon and J.C. de Moor; Leiden: Brill).
ibid., '"Comparativism" and the God of Israel', 45–67.

2006 *Hebrew Bible and Ancient Versions: Selected Essays of Robert P. Gordon* (Society for Old Testament Study Monographs; Aldershot: Ashgate).

2007 *The God of Israel* (ed. R.P. Gordon; Cambridge: Cambridge University Press).
ibid., 'Introducing the God of Israel', 3–19.
ibid., 'Standing in the Council: When Prophets Encounter God', 190–204.
'Messianism in Ancient Bible Translations in Aramaic and Syriac', in *Redemption and Resistance: The Messianic Hopes of Jews and Christians in Antiquity* (Fs W. Horbury; ed. M. Bockmuehl, and J.C. Carleton Paget; London: T. and T. Clark) 262–273.
'When Prophets Emote: Prophetic First-Person Statements in Targum Jonathan', in *Targum y Judaísmo: Homenaje al profesor J. Ribera Florit en su 70º Aniversario*; ed. L. Díez Merino, and E. Giralt-López; Barcelona: Publicacions i Edicions) 159–168.
'The Week that Made the World: Reflections on the First Pages of the Bible', in *Reading the Law: Studies in Honour of Gordon J. Wenham* (Library of Hebrew Bible/Old Testament Studies 461; ed. J.G. McConville, and K. Möller; New York: T. & T. Clark) 228–244.

2008 *Hebrews: A Commentary* (2nd ed.; Sheffield: Phoenix).
ibid., 'Introduction to the Second Edition', 36–53.

2009 'The Gods Must Die: A Theme in Isaiah and Beyond', in *Isaiah in Context: Studies in Honour of Arie van der Kooij on the Occasion of his Sixty-Fifth Birthday* (Supplements to Vetus Testamentum, 138; ed. Michaël N. van der Meer, Percy van Keulen, Wido van Peursen, and Bas ter Haar Romeny; Leiden: Brill) 45–61.

2010 'The Ethics of Eden: Truth-Telling in Genesis 2–3', in *Ethical and Unethical in the Old Testament: God and Humans in Dialogue* (ed. K.J. Dell; Library of Hebrew Bible/Old Testament Studies 528) 11–33.

RPG

Andrew A. Macintosh[1]

The editors of this volume have thought fit to commission an account of the career and achievements of Robert Gordon. It is their hope that he may be content with this decision, 'and even if he is not…'. This concessive formula, 'and even if…', is a familiar element of Robert Gordon's humour and will be recognized immediately by his pupils and others who have attended his lectures: 'X, would you please read the next verse, if you don't mind—and even if you do…?' The interrogative is, of course, an imperative, and the imperative is strengthened by the concessive clause. The whole may be said to convey a courteous insistence, tempered by humour, a sense of progress to be initiated and impelled by reasoned integrity. It captures an important aspect of the man—his firm commitment to his core beliefs, his willingness to teach and to lead, and his understanding that humour facilitates all these endeavours.

Robert Patterson Gordon was born in Northern Ireland in 1945 to evangelical Christian parents who 'set an example of faithful Christian living that I have cherished all through my life'. They ensured that he was fed into the excellent Grammar School tradition of the Province, and, in particular, to Methodist College, Belfast. Here, building on interests kindled by his father, he studied classics, and in those same days made the acquaintance of Professor David Gooding of Queen's University, with whom he took his first informal steps in Hebrew. Such was Gooding's contribution to his formation that RPG, when later elected Regius Professor of Hebrew, was able to tell his mentor that he 'owned at least a leg of his chair'.

In 1964 RPG arrived in Cambridge to read Hebrew and Aramaic as a member of St. Catharine's College, of which David Winton Thomas,

[1] The author has from RPG the nickname 'the Station Master' by reason of his long association with the neo-Gothic chapel of St. John's College, Cambridge, whose architect, Sir Gilbert Scott, designed the similar and more famous St. Pancras Station in London. The indignity was compounded when he was elected President of St. John's in 1995: then he became, for the time being, the Fat Controller, which owes more to 'Thomas the Tank Engine' than to Gilbert Scott.

then Regius Professor, was a professorial Fellow. There being no teaching Fellow in Hebrew at St. Catharine's, the young Ulsterman was sent to Father Sebastian Bullough, O.P., for Hebrew grammar and composition, and experienced for the first time the inside of a monastery. In the Faculty of Oriental Studies, he encountered Alan Goodman (Aramaic and Syriac), Erwin Rosenthal (Hebrew Texts and Israelite History), Jacob Teicher (Rabbinics), and David Diringer (Epigraphy) in addition to Winton Thomas. Later, Sebastian Brock was to arrive on the scene. Winton Thomas' lectures on Isaiah 40–55, as well as his classes on Hebrew composition, kindled a lifelong interest in Semitic philology, as also in turning English (usually) texts into classical Hebrew.

Placed consistently in the first class of the Oriental Studies Tripos and with a string of University awards and prizes, RPG resolved to read for the Ph.D. degree, settling eventually upon the Targum of the Twelve Prophets under the supervision of the newly elected Regius Professor, J.A. Emerton. It was a happy decision, and he was to recall the comment of J.B. Segal that it is good to cut one's teeth on texts at one remove from the Bible, rather than carve up the biblical text for the limited exercise of a Ph.D. dissertation. Of John Emerton, RPG has the highest regard. As a scholar he was simply 'formidable', setting consistently rigorous standards, not least in the writing of English. It is, perhaps, a result of this regime that RPG has been accustomed to annotate his students' writings, where necessary, with the thermonuclear warning UKSTA/NASTI, which, being interpreted (*pace* Fowler), means 'the United Kingdom split the atom; North America splits the infinitive'.

His Ph.D. dissertation recently begun, RPG was appointed to his first teaching post in October 1968. In the University of Glasgow he found himself bilocated, teaching Old Testament in the Divinity Faculty and Biblical Languages with ancient Near Eastern history in the Department of Hebrew and Semitic Languages. His colleagues here included John Mauchline and John Macdonald, and a fellow-Irishman in Robert Carroll. Here he juggled the composition of lectures and the finishing of his thesis, as well as commitments to church meetings and the organizing of a Sunday School football team in the village of Neilston, Renfrewshire, in the interests of keeping young lads off the streets. Supremely important was his marriage to his beloved wife Ruth, which his appointment to a secure post made possible in December 1970.

1979 saw RPG's appointment as a Lecturer in the Faculty of Divinity in Cambridge. At this stage of his career he was much preoccupied in commentary writing and other work on 1 and 2 Samuel, as well as with the editing of 1 and 2 Chronicles for the Leiden Peshitta project. In respect of the latter, the rule changes emanating from Leiden caused RPG some bemusement, in that the less he did the more progress he seemed to make. A major commitment during the 1980's was a two-year stint as Secretary to the Faculty Board of Divinity, which felt at the time like a life-sentence. In 1995 RPG was elected Regius Professor of Hebrew (the chair was founded by Henry VIII in 1540) in succession to John Emerton. At this point, and in respect of RPG's routine lectures for undergraduates, it is worth recording that your correspondent, with extensive knowledge of undergraduates, knows of two OT courses within a period of thirty years which particularly received their commendation: one was RPG's course on early Genesis for Divinity and Oriental Studies.

Moving from the Faculty of Divinity to the Faculty of Oriental Studies (now renamed Asian and Middle Eastern Studies), he served a term as chairman of the Faculty Board in 1997–1998, and he has recently demitted as chairman of the faculty's Degree Committee after nine years. During the second half of his Cambridge career, RPG has happily been a Fellow of St. Catharine's, his own undergraduate college. When he first returned from Glasgow, however, he was accommodated elsewhere. Showing an admirable commitment to principle, with others he resigned his Fellowship following an internal College dispute. It was, as he reports, one of the sadder moments of his career. A second such difficult time was in 2007, when he and his colleagues were obliged to fight for the status of Hebrew as a main subject, threatened in the process of the reorganization of the Faculty of Oriental Studies.

RPG serves on a number of editorial boards, including *Vetus Testamentum*, the journal of the International Organization for the Study of the Old Testament. He was its Book List editor from 1997 to 2010, and also acted as Secretary of the IOSOT from 2001–4. He edits the monograph series 'The Hebrew Bible and its Versions', and has served on panels for three modern translations of the Bible into English. He was President of the Society for Old Testament Study, 2003.

RPG is a dedicated family man. Ruth and he have three children, now grown up: Graham works in marketing, Claire is a medic, and

Alasdair works in a constituency office in Westminster. If none of the children has inherited his particular interests, they have 'made for improvements in their parents' education'. RPG's gratitude to his wife is 'immense', and not least for her willingness loyally to follow him in a career which took her out of her beloved homeland of Northern Ireland. Commitment to church work (Christian Brethren) gives rein in RPG to a strong sense of pastoral responsibility; a fair amount of time over the years has been spent working with and encouraging students living away from home and happy to enjoy Ruth's and his hospitality. Gentle jogging and private piano playing represent some of his recreational activities.

A list of RPG's extensive and wide-ranging publications is provided elsewhere in this volume, and here it is appropriate simply to furnish an overview of them. His research interests fall into four main categories: (1) Historiography and Narrative in the historical books (especially Samuel) of the OT; (2) The OT in its setting in the ancient Near East; (3) The Ancient Versions; (4) The development of OT themes in the NT and in Jewish and Christian tradition.

1984 saw the publication of his *OT Guide to Samuel* and 1986 his *Commentary* on these books. The duplicates of 1 Samuel 24 and 26 were considered from the perspective of narrative analogy in 'David's Rise' (1980). Resumptive repetition is identified as an important element in the Joab-Abner narrative, in 'Covenant and Apology' (1990). 'Who made the Kingmaker?' (1994) explores the criterion of dissimilarity as a tool for identifying core historical elements in the Samuel tradition.

'From Mari to Moses' (1993) examines OT prophecy in the light of parallel Mesopotamian phenomena, as does his contribution in his edited volume *The Place is Too Small* (1995). The essays support the view that prophets were already in action in eighth-century Israel, and that the notion of the Divine Council is an important interpretative key to a number of texts, and occasionally where its presence has been questioned. 'Compositeness' (1991) adduces a wide body of evidence from both Israel and the ancient Near East to confirm the feasibility of the composite authorship of biblical books. In 2005 RPG co-edited *The OT in its World*, to which he contributed an essay on the question of 'Distinctiveness' in the OT in the context of its recognized affinities with the literature of the Ancient Near East. *The God of Israel* (ed., 2007) represents sixteen essays collected from the Cambridge OT Seminar in the period 2001–4.

RPG's work on the Targums, undertaken for his Ph.D. thesis, put him in a good position to contribute to the Aramaic Bible Project. 1989 saw the publication of *The Targum of the Minor Prophets* (with K.J. Cathcart), the fourteenth volume of the series. *Studies in the Targum to the Twelve Prophets* appeared in 1994. A considerable number of articles on the Targums have also been published. On the Syriac side, RPG prepared the edition of 1 and 2 Chronicles for the Leiden Peshitta Project (1998), but other interests and commitments have so far precluded his making use of the information gleaned in the process. Septuagintal interests have mostly been fulfilled through Ph.D. supervision, but LXX 3 Reigns is the subject of two articles: 'The Second Septuagint' (1975) and 'Source Study' (1976). In 'Converse Translation in the Targums and Beyond' (1999) the importance of 'trans-versional elements'—translational features common to more than one ancient version of the Bible—was explored.

Hebrews: A Commentary (2000; 2nd edn 2008) takes up and explores the issue of supersessionism as a feature of both Judaism and Christianity in respect of the OT, and the importance for dialogue of recognizing this as a feature of both traditions. In the Didsbury Lectures (published as *Holy Land, Holy City: Sacred Geography and the Interpretation of the Bible*, 2004) the OT themes of the 'Land' and 'Zion' are followed through into the NT and further to Jewish and Christian tradition over the centuries.

Under the heading 'work in preparation' is RPG's *Commentary on Amos*, commissioned for the International Critical Commentary series. Already under way, this work awaits the distinct advantages of retirement.

Of particular significance, perhaps, is RPG's essay entitled 'A Warranted Version of Historical Biblical Criticism? A Response to Alvin Plantinga', chapter 14 in *Hebrew Bible and Ancient Versions* (2006). Here, tackling fundamental issues of interpretation in the context of a response to Plantinga's negative evaluation of Historical Biblical Criticism, RPG comes nearest to a published *apologia pro vita sua*. The piece represents a very clear indication of his understanding of the nature of Scripture and scholarly engagement with it.

ANTICIPATIONS OF HOREB: EXODUS 17 AS INNER-BIBLICAL COMMENTARY[1]

Nathan MacDonald

The Wilderness Stories in Exodus 15–18

In the book of Exodus a number of stories occur between the deliverance at the Red Sea and the arrival at Sinai. These narratives belonged, in Noth's judgement, to the theme 'Guidance in the Wilderness', which bridges the gap between the themes of 'Guidance out of Egypt' and 'Guidance into the Arable Land' (1948: 62–63).

> Die Lücke zwischen der Ausführung des Themas 'Herausführung aus Ägypten' und der des Themas 'Hineinführung in das Kulturland' ist zwar kaum geschlossen, aber doch verdeckt worden durch die Einschaltung des Themas 'Führung in der Wüste'. Es ist insofern kein selbständiges Thema, als es nicht wie die anderen Pentateuchthemen seine eigene Wurzel in kultischen Einrichtungen und Begehungen des Kulturlands zu haben scheint, sondern wohl den schon weit entwickelten Ausbau der Pentateucherzählung voraussetzt (Noth 1948: 127).

In Noth's understanding of the formation of the Pentateuch, the wilderness stories found in both Exodus and Numbers originally mediated between exodus and conquest, in a story of Israel's origins that did not include the revelation at Sinai. The form of these stories provided a clue to their original purpose.

Recent scholarship has been more reluctant to assume that the stories found in Exodus were only secondarily related to Sinai. In Van Seters's conception of the Yahwist, Sinai plays a more prominent role and the wilderness stories mediate between exodus and Sinai with

[1] It is a pleasure to offer this essay to my friend and teacher Robert Gordon. With many others I am grateful for the way in which he has modelled both a careful philological scholarship and a gentle Christian piety, always laced with a dry sense of humour. This present research originated as part of an Alexander von Humboldt research fellowship hosted by Christoph Levin in Munich. Thanks to him and also to Rob Barrett and Izaak de Hulster for their insightful comments.

Moses the intercessor receiving prominence (1994: 165–207);[2] Kratz sees the stories as late post-priestly expansions of the priestly itinerary from Egypt to Sinai (2005: 291).[3]

Here as in other respects the current contours of Pentateuchal redaction-criticism are better able to do justice to the present form of the text than earlier scholarship. Nevertheless, Noth was already correct to observe that the wilderness is 'kein selbständiges Thema'. This is apparent to any attentive reader of these stories for, despite the fact that the itinerary markers suggest a steady progression which finally leads to Sinai in 19.1 (cf. Num. 33.8–15), there are various incongruities which suggest the penetration of the Sinai material into these chapters. In Exodus 17–18 the people seem already to have reached Mount Sinai and the narrative sometimes presupposes realities not yet in existence (e.g. 16.33–34). In addition, a location like the 'wilderness of Sin' (16.1) could easily be an artificial creation based on Sinai and there are frequent allusions to the giving of the law (e.g. 15.25–26). This list of problems, which is by no means exhaustive, already suggests that the writer(s) of these chapters are not primarily concerned with the coherent recounting of historical events, but rather with introducing the theological realities associated with the revelation of the law at Sinai.

The illumination that redaction-criticism has shed on Exodus 15–18 tends to suggest that, in large measure, the internal links between these chapters, and between them and the surrounding chapters—the exodus and Sinai material—are superficial. This is not to be understood as a pejorative judgement; it is merely to say that such links do not exist on the level of the 'deep structure' of the stories, but on the surface. It was for this reason that an earlier generation of scholars could proceed with such confidence to isolate the distinct forms of these stories and to speculate about their prehistory. Nevertheless, for the scholar interested in how the present form of Exodus works and how these stories deepen our understanding of the Law and prophetic intercession it is important to gain a sense of how these links were made, however tenuous they may appear.

---

[2] Noth's conception of the wilderness stories as a bridge between Egypt and Canaan is still reflected in Levin's Yahwist (1993: 348–358, 392–393, 422).

[3] For discussion of the wilderness itinerary lists and their priority see Davies (1983).

In this essay I wish to examine the two stories in Exodus 17, the story of the spring at Massah and Meribah (vv. 1–7) and the defeat of Amalek (vv. 8–16). It is not common to consider these stories together. The story of Massah and Meribah is usually interpreted as part of a series of provision stories (15.22–17.7), whilst the story of Amalek 'appears to be…completely isolated from its context' (Coats 1975: 29). Nevertheless, the familiar chapter division rightly combines these two stories. Textually this linkage is achieved by the location of both events at Rephidim (בִּרְפִידִם; vv. 1, 8),[4] and the (final) appearance of the staff of God in Moses's hand (vv. 5, 9). In both instances a strong case has been made that these elements are not original to the story, but are the result of a conscious redactional linkage.[5] There are additional thematic links as Noort has shown. Both stories speak of a mortal threat with YHWH as saviour and Moses playing a principal role (2006). In this essay I will show that both stories anticipate the narratives about the making and breaking of a covenant on Mount Sinai (Exod. 24, 32–34).[6]

---

[4] Noort sees this drawing the two stories closely together (2006: 164); Coats finds nothing more than a loose accommodation to the itinerary framework (1975: 29).

[5] Rephidim is only found at Exod. 17.1, 8; 19.2; Num. 33.15 and is usually thought to be a contribution of the priestly framework (Noth 1958: 110). Levin, however, discerns in v. 1 the original source for the Yahwist (Levin 1993: 357): וַיִּסְעוּ כָּל־עֲדַת בְּנֵי־יִשְׂרָאֵל מִמִּדְבַּר־סִין לְמַסְעֵיהֶם עַל־פִּי יְהוָה וַיַּחֲנוּ בִּרְפִידִים. The names in Exod. 17.1–7 are a particular problem. The existence of four place names usually requires recourse to literary critical means. Horeb is universally recognized as redactional, for not only do we have a Deuteronomic name but it appears prematurely. Yet Massah and Meribah are not unproblematic either. Only here, in Deut. 33.8 and Ps. 95.8 do the two names occur together. Meribah occurs alone in a number of places, but Massah is only found alone in Deut. 6.16 and 9.22. Since v. 7 is sometimes judged a later addition, which has been influenced by Deuteronomy and the poetic pair Massah-Meribah, the story is occasionally stripped of all its names. Fritz's suggestion that none of the four names is original and that the original name may have been lost through the addition of the priestly material is an instance of *reductio ad absurdum*, but illustrates the complexity of the problem (1970: 48). Gertz argues that there the staff-motif is a post-priestly addition and that 'verbindet das Stockmotiv die priesterschriftliche mit der nichtpriesterschriftlichen Plagenerzählung' (2000: 103).

[6] The creation of a relationship between these two stories is driven by a theological concern, and not by a concern for the consistency of the narrative. Van Seters rightly observes that 'The result is a melange that serves his theological interests, even if it sacrifices some of its narrative clarity and consistency' (1994: 194).

Exod. 24 and 32–34 belong closely together despite the insertion of the instructions concerning the Tabernacle. The presence of Moses on the mountain and away from the people presupposes the ascent in Exod. 24. The sin of the Golden Calf is so egregious because it is an assault on the covenant concluded in chapter 24.

The Spring at Massah and Meribah (Exod. 17.1–7)

The story of the spring at Massah and Meribah opens with the Israelites continuing through the wilderness on their way to Sinai. They halt at Rephidim, but do not find there any water (v. 1). In verses 2 and 3 the people twice raise their voices to complain against Moses. On the first occasion Moses rebukes them, identifying their complaint as a test of YHWH. After the second complaint Moses no longer addresses the people, and directs his words to YHWH.

It has long been appreciated that the double complaint creates an excess that can, perhaps, be resolved by literary-critical means. Though verse 2 is most often considered a redactional addition, a better case can be made in my view for vv. 2aβ–3a.[7] Whichever solution is most compelling it is apparent that the motif of testing has now been made to play an important role in the story, as is also the case in the other

[7] It has often been difficult to decide which verse should be judged a redactional addition. Fritz gives no grounds for preferring v. 2 as the original verse: 'In der Geschichte vom Quellwunder in Massa und Meriba ist nur 17,3 als Dublette anzusprechen, da der Konflikt des Volkes mit Mose bereits 17,2 berichtet wird' (1970: 10–11). Aurelius, however, notes that the water-miracle in Numbers 20 lacks לון, which would be a rather unusual omission for a priestly writer should the original story in Exodus 17 have contained v. 3 (1988: 168). Instead, Numbers 20 does have וַיָּרֶב הָעָם עִם־מֹשֶׁה וַיֹּאמְרוּ (v. 3), which is also found in Exod. 17.2. (We cannot, of course, exclude the possibility that the influence between Exod. 17 and Num. 20 has worked in both directions. The same is also true of לָמָּה...הֶעֱלִיתָנוּ מִמִּצְרַיִם לְ in Exod. 17.3.) There are, however, considerations that speak against removing Exod. 17.3 and a number of scholars have argued, instead, that v. 2 should be excised (e.g. Ruprecht 1974: 304; Schart 1990: 167–169). First, we have the theme of testing which occurs in all the wilderness provision stories of Exodus (15.25; 16.4; 17.2, 7), and this element has increasingly been identified with a post-deuteronomistic redaction (see Lohfink 1988). Secondly, as Van Seters observes v. 4 naturally belongs with v. 3: The people thirst, complain against Moses and Moses cries out to YHWH (1994: 191).Verse 2, on the other hand, introduces an exchange between Moses and the people that is form-critically problematic (Schart 1990: 168), as the parallel to Exodus 15 confirms: The people appeal for water, which leads to a rebuke from Moses who, nevertheless, appeals to YHWH. Thirdly, Van Seters also notes that the description of Israel quarrelling with Moses does not fit well with the simple request 'Give us water to drink', but would be appropriate for the people's accusation of Moses in v. 3 'Why did you bring us out of Egypt to kill us…with thirst?' (1994: 192–193). Thus, v. 2 appears to presuppose v. 3 and cannot have existed without it. Fourthly, as Achenbach observes לָמָּה...הֶעֱלִיתָנוּ מִמִּצְרַיִם לְ occurs in both Exod. 17.3 and Num. 20.5 (2003: 303). The problems are generated by assuming that we must accept either v. 2 or v. 3 *in toto*. If we compare Exodus 17 and Numbers 20, then both v. 2aα and v. 3bα belong to the original story, with vv. 2aβ–3a the later development of the story. Such a solution explains Van Seters's observation that the use of וַיָּרֶב in v. 2 is appropriate for the complaint in v. 3, and the absence of לון in Numbers 20.

provision stories (Exod. 15.25; 16.4). One effect of these additions to the basic form-critical structure is to bind Exodus 17 even tighter together with the other wilderness provision stories in Exodus 15–16. They also give the chapter a distinctive role and provide a sense of narrative progression. The lack of food and water in the desert is seen as a test, no longer a test of Israel (15.25; 16.4), but a test of YHWH.[8] YHWH has provided for Israel in her time of need, now she in response to such generosity demands a miracle: תְּנוּ־לָנוּ מַיִם וְנִשְׁתֶּה. This is a trajectory that is far from positive.[9]

In the stories of Marah and the manna the testing motif is clearly linked with obedience to *torah*. The Marah story (Ex. 15.22–27) is not simply about provision in the wilderness, it is also a lesson in obedience. This much is certain, even if the story now has basic incongruities that are not resolved in vv. 25b–26. YHWH gives the people a statute and an ordinance, which is somehow related to testing (15.25).[10] It is possible that part of the stimulus for the interpretation is the description of YHWH directing Moses to a piece of wood (וַיּוֹרֵהוּ יְהוָה עֵץ) with ירה having strong resonances with תּוֹרָה.[11] In the story of the manna YHWH's testing relates either to the collection of the daily provision of the Sabbath or to the double portion on the Sabbath day, or both (16.4–5) (Childs 1974: 286). Either way testing is related to following YHWH's *torah* (v. 4; cf. v. 28). The vocabulary of testing is,

---

[8] The difference between 15.25; 16.4 and 17.2, 7 has naturally raised questions of whether these verses stem from the same hand. Schart attributed the references to testing to two redactional layers. 17.2, 7 is attributed to D_{je} whilst 15.25b–26 is attributed to D_p. Aurelius, on the other hand, sees Exod. 17.1–7 as an artificial construction formed on the basis of the preceding provision stories. Both Schart and Aurelius recognize a distinction between YHWH's testing of Israel and Israel's testing of YHWH, although their judgement of historical priority differs. On the other hand, Van Seters rejects both Schart's and Aurelius's suggestions and attributes all the references to testing to the Yahwist (Schart 1990: 177; Van Seters 1994: 194; Aurelius 1988: 174).

[9] Aurelius (1988: 120–121). Houtman, on the other hand, sees no climax, but only variations on a theme. This is sustained by interpreting וַיִּלֹּנוּ in 15.24 as 'rage' or 'rant' and מַה as a cry of indignation (1995–2002: II, 301, 307). Nevertheless, at Marah the people's complaint is not only legitimate, since they have gone without water for three days, but also phrased as a genuine question 'what shall we drink?'. At Rephidim, on the other hand, the people bring a dispute (וַיָּרֶב) against Moses and accuse him of maliciousness: 'What did you bring us out of Egypt to kill us?' (17.3).

[10] YHWH is probably to be understood as the subject of the verbs שָׂם and נִסָּהוּ (with, e.g., Noth [1958, p. 102]). Moses is never the subject of נסה. Lohfink argues that Moses must be the subject of שָׂם since the singular חֹק וּמִשְׁפָּט is used of Joshua (Josh. 24.25) and David (1 Sam. 30.25) establishing new laws (1988: 43 n. 22).

[11] LXX reads ἔδειξεν and SP *wyr'hw* 'and he showed him'. MT is probably to be preferred as the *lectio difficilior*.

of course, particularly associated with the law in Exod. 20.20. Moses explains the terrifying events at Sinai as a sign of God's testing the people: 'Do not fear. For God has come in order to test you and in order that the fear of him may be before you so that you do not sin'. The test in Exodus 16 as in Exodus 20 is not a testing of whether they have *presently* obeyed the law, but an intimate probing in order to ensure *future* obedience. The thought appears to be similar to that found in Deut. 8.2–5, where such testing is also described as discipline (Schart 1990: 175). Israel suffers need and then receives deliverance in order to discipline her for future obedience to YHWH. Both Exodus 15 and 16, therefore, function as 'eine Art Vorwegnahme der Sinaioffenbarung' (Levin 1993: 351).

In contrast, Exodus 17's 'to test God' is to be disobedient.[12] In its own way this testing is also 'eine Art Vorwegnahme Sinais'. This connection is achieved not by a direct reference to the law, but through the recurrence of the testing motif, and also by the reference in 17.6 to Horeb. In common with vv. 2–3 the premature reference to the mountain of revelation and the distinctive Deuteronomic name have often been taken as signs of redactional activity.[13] Whilst it would be possible to understand Exodus 17 as a narrative that instructs its readers in general about the demanding nature of obedience to YHWH's law, I wonder whether there is an intention to allude especially to the narrative about the making and breaking of the covenant on Mount Sinai (i.e. Exod. 24, 32–34) and especially to the sin of the Golden Calf. Various textual details support this suggestion.[14]

First, as we have seen, the events are said to have taken place at *Horeb*. Horeb is, of course, the mountain of revelation. For the reader of the present-form of Exodus the mention of Horeb is not entirely surprising for although the name is more characteristic of Deuteronomy it is the place of the original revelation to Moses (3.1). The more familiar name 'Mount Sinai' will not appear until 19.11, after which it will dominate the Pentateuchal story until Deut. 1.2. Yet, this will not be the final appearance of Horeb in the Tetrateuch. According to

[12] Cf. Pss. 78.17–18, 40–41, 56; 95.7–9.

[13] Although some would remove just the reference to Horeb, Zenger observed that v. 6aα disturbs the link between the commands 'go' and 'strike'. In addition, Aurelius notes שָׁם is used as in 15.25 to bind this addition to the context, although for the parallel to be exact we might expect שָׁם to be the first word of the addition (Zenger 1982: 59; cf. Aurelius 1988: 168. Note that שָׁם is also found in v. 3aα).

[14] Already Moberly observes some 'interesting links between 33.18–23, 17.1–7 (1983: 206 n. 147).

Exod. 33.6 Horeb is where the worship of the Golden Calf takes place. Interestingly, Sinai is always associated with the giving of the law in the book of Exodus, a pattern shared with the other biblical books. As far as I am aware, it is never associated with the sin of the Golden Calf. Horeb, on the other hand, is *both* the mountain of revelation *and* the place of sinfulness (Exod. 33.6; Deut. 9.8; Ps. 106.19).[15]

Second, whilst YHWH's testing concerns Israel's capacity to obey, Israel's testing of YHWH concerns his presence: 'is YHWH in our midst or not?' (v. 7).[16] The question of YHWH's presence will occur again in Exodus, when YHWH ascends the mountain to receive the law and disappears for forty days. The people demand that gods be fabricated because Moses and his god have disappeared. The issue of presence remains at stake for YHWH initially refuses to go with the people. The dialogues between Moses and YHWH frequently utilize the same language of God's presence in the midst (33.3, 5; 34.9; קרב).

Third, in their complaint the people describe Moses, rather than YHWH, as the one who brought them out of the land of Egypt (לָ֤מָּה זֶּה֙ הֶֽעֱלִיתָ֣נוּ מִמִּצְרַ֔יִם לְהָמִ֥ית אֹתִ֛י וְאֶת־בָּנַ֥י וְאֶת־מִקְנַ֖י בַּצָּמָֽא). Such a complaint is, of course, symptomatic of the murmuring stories (Exod. 16.3; Num. 20.5), but it finds a striking echo in the account of the Golden Calf. There the people attribute their deliverance from Egypt to Moses (32.1, 23), a perspective later affirmed by YHWH when in his anger he disassociates himself from the people: '*Your* people, whom *you* brought up from the land of Egypt' (32.7; 33.1). The rhetorical contexts differ, but the effect is the same—to disassociate YHWH from the exodus event and attribute it solely to Moses. The traditional or canonically approved formula, on the other hand, attributes the deliverance from Egypt to YHWH (Exod. 20.2).

Fourth, the elders of Israel (מִזִּקְנֵ֣י יִשְׂרָאֵ֑ל) appear on a number of occasions in the Pentateuchal narrative.[17] The closest parallel to Exodus 17 is to be found in the Sinai narrative (Exod 24.9–11). In both cases the elders are called outside the camp as part of their juridical

---

[15] Exod. 31.18; 34.2, 4 confirm this observation for, although textually close to the Golden Calf incident, the immediate context is one of revelation.

[16] Verse 7 with its aetiological element is usually seen as a redactional addition (e.g. Childs 1974: 307). The concept of YHWH in the midst is also found in deuteronomistic literature (e.g. Deut. 1.42; 6.15; 7.21; 31.17). Thus, it is with good grounds that this verse has been judged a post-deuteronomistic interpretation. For an attempt to interpret this theme in a historical setting, see Herrmann (1992).

[17] Levin sees the reference to the elders in 17.5, 6 as a redactional addition (1993: 356–358).

role. They are to act as the community's witnesses to YHWH's activity, whose visuality is stressed.[18] As has often been observed, Moses' ascent of Mount Sinai and the conclusion of the covenant in Exodus 24 is presupposed by the account of the sin of the Golden Calf.

Fifth, the people now drink from a stream that flows from Horeb. In the Golden Calf story Moses makes the people drink from water in which the powdered remains of the Calf have been scattered (32.20). The possibility that the two streams are the same should not be pressed too hard, though Propp argues for a connection. 'The springs of Massah and Meribah are really located at the Mountain of Lawgiving itself. They in fact reappear in 32:20, when Moses dissolves the Golden Calf in waters flowing from Horeb' (1998: 605).[19] Certainly in both cases the rebellion of the people leads to their drinking water that flows down from Horeb, though the *hif'il* of (32.20) שׁקה strikes a note of compulsion that is not present in the *qal* of (17.6) שׁתה.

Sixth, Moberly notes the similarities between the rock at Massah and Sinai. 'Interestingly, at Massah Yahweh stands before Moses on the rock (17:6), as Moses stands before Yahweh (33:21; 34:2). Moses passes (*'br*) before the people (17:5), as Yahweh passes (*'br*) before Moses (33:19, 22)' (1983: 206 n. 147). Moberly's first verbal connection is rather loose, for Exodus 17 uses עמד, whilst Exodus 33–34 uses נצב. The second is somewhat stronger. In both cases the 'passing before' seems to be in order to confirm who it is that has acted (cf. Job 9.11).

The Battle with Amalek (Exod. 17.8–16)

The account of the battle with Amalek presents numerous difficulties, many of which appear irresolvable. Amalek, repeated seven times in this passage, is clearly a central focus and the story provides some justification for the eternal enmity between Amalek and Israel. Yet why YHWH should be so opposed to Amalek is unclear (v. 14), nor is it apparent why Amalek attacks Israel in the first place (v. 8). At first blush the story appears to be an aetiology for an altar, but the explanation of the name sits rather loosely at the end of the narrative, and to

[18] In 17.6 this is achieved with a reference to the act occurring before the eyes of the elders: לְעֵינֵי זִקְנֵי יִשְׂרָאֵל.

[19] For his detailed attempt to relate the two streams, see Propp (1987: 61–63).

an otherwise unknown place name is given an opaque explanation.[20] As already observed the story appears rather isolated within the Pentateuch and has its closest parallels with the stories of Joshua's conquest of Canaan and the intercessions of Samuel (1 Sam. 7, 12).

It is perhaps no surprise that literary-critical solutions have been offered for these problems. Most agree that v. 14 reflects Deuteronomic influence, and it is possible that vv. 15–16 are also redactional (Levin 1993: 358). There is no consensus on attempts to find a more extensive literary-critical activity, but concluding with the isolation of vv. 8–13 still seems unsatisfactory to many. In particular, attention is often drawn to the tension between human and divine initiative.[21] At its basic form-critical level the story is an account of an attack by the Amalekites and their defeat by Joshua (vv. 8, 9a, 10a, 13), comparable to what is found in Joshua 10–11.

Again, rather loosely attached at times to the basic story, there are a number of interesting parallels to the making of the Sinai covenant and the sin of the Golden Calf (Exod. 24, 32–34). First, the four main characters of the story are those that will emerge together again in the story of Sinai and the Golden Calf—Moses, Joshua, Aaron and Hur. Joshua appears here for the first time in the Pentateuchal narrative. His appearance owes much to his role as leader of the Israelites during the conquest, for here he will lead the Israelite troops and also receive the promise of God's eternal opposition to the Amalekites (and possibly with it an implied commandment). Joshua will again appear in the story of the Sinai and the Golden Calf as the one who accompanies Moses as he ascends and descends Sinai (24.13; 32.17). This association is particularly noteworthy because Aaron and Hur also reappear in Exod. 24.14. While Moses and Joshua ascend Mount Sinai, Aaron and Hur are left in charge of the people.

---

[20] A particular issue is the relationship between the name of the altar and the explanation given. The altar is named יְהוָה ׀ נִסִּי (v. 15), and yet this appears to be explained by the puzzling כִּי־יָד עַל־כֵּס יָהּ (v. 16). It is simplest to assume either that v. 15 should be emended to יְהוָה כִּסְאִי with the stone to be envisaged as the divine throne (Van Seters 1994: 206) or that v. 16 should be emended to נֵס יָהּ understood as a rallying cry (Childs 1974: 312). Schmitt observes that with the theme of remembrance this is not a proper cult aetiology (1990).

[21] Coats discerned an original tradition with a human activity by Moses and Joshua (vv. 9–13) which was edited so as to emphasise the divine initiative (vv. 14–16) (1975). Zenger offers a more ambitious redactional proposal, which likewise draws on the distinction between Moses-ordained and a YHWH-ordained war. He attributes vv. 8 (בִּרְפִידִים), 10b, 12, 13b–14, 16b to R_p (1982: 76–113).

Second, the unusual vocabulary of ‘prevailing’ (גָּבַר) and ‘defeat’ (וַיַּחֲלֹשׁ) reappears in Exod. 32.18, when Moses replies to Joshua: אֵין קוֹל עֲנוֹת גְּבוּרָה וְאֵין קוֹל עֲנוֹת חֲלוּשָׁה (Van Seters 1994: 199). It is significant not only that we have the same words, but that they are part of an exchange between the two principal characters of Exod. 17.8–16. When reading the present form of Exodus the words of Joshua in 32.17, ‘There is the sound of war in the camp’, most naturally bring to mind Joshua’s prior military experience.

Third, the only occasions on which Moses is said to have built an altar are found in Exod. 17.15 and 24.4.

Fourth, the language of writing, blotting out, and books occurs in both Exodus 17 and 32 in strikingly similar ways. According to Exod. 17.14 YHWH instructed Moses to write down and recite to Joshua YHWH’s judgement against Amalek: ‘Write (כְּתֹב) this as a reminder in the document (בַּסֵּפֶר) and recite it in Joshua’s hearing: I will utterly blot (מָחֹה אֶמְחֶה) out the memory of Amalek from under heaven’. By comparison in Exod. 32 Moses asks to be blotted out of God’s book if he doesn’t forgive the people’s sin: וְאִם־אַיִן מְחֵנִי נָא מִסִּפְרְךָ אֲשֶׁר כָּתָבְתָּ (v. 31). God’s response is that he will punish those who have rebelled against him: מִי אֲשֶׁר חָטָא־לִי אֶמְחֶנּוּ מִסִּפְרִי.

Exodus 17 As Implicit Biblical Commentary

In an early essay Robert Gordon explored the dynamics of the narratives in 1 Samuel 24–26. He observed that

> Hebrew narrative is much more subtle... using a wide range of narrative techniques to perform the functions of the explicit commentaries in the more transparent narrative types. Prominent among these techniques is that of narrative analogy. Narrative analogy is a device whereby the narrator can provide an internal commentary on the action which he is describing, usually by means of cross-reference to an earlier action or speech. Thus narratives are made to interact in ways which may not be immediately apparent; ironic parallelism abounds wherever this technique is applied (1980: 42–43).

As we have seen, the connections with Horeb in Exodus 17 are made via a host of key words and themes.[22] These float rather precariously

[22] These form a contrast, then, with the stories of 1 Samuel 24–26 where the cross-referencing that Gordon discerns is more deeply embedded in the narratives. One

on the surface of the stories. With these connections, the wilderness stories bind together the major narrative complexes of exodus and Sinai, but in addition they also create seemingly loose form of analogies, especially between Exodus 17 and Exodus 24, 32–34. The result is a subtle interaction that following Gordon we might call 'implicit commentary', often exhibiting an 'ironic parallelism'.

The loose and subtle connections to Sinai mean that it is difficult to know what to make of these similarities. Thus, Zenger suggests that the provision of water is being equated with the provision of the law (1982: 74). Certainly the elders of Israel are witness to this act of provision as well as the concluding of the covenant (Exod. 24.1–11), but could such a connection be intended? Is water that comes in response to the complaints of the Israelites a purposeful analogy to YHWH's gracious and unilateral provision of the law?

Assistance should be sought in our observation that both stories in Exodus 17 allude to Horeb, and this should help control the analogies that we discern from dissolving into allegories. Noort's observation that both stories in Exodus 17 speak of mortal threat with YHWH as saviour and Moses playing a principal role is a useful place to begin, for the same dynamics are present in the story of the Golden Calf. In each of the stories Israel faces a threat to its existence. In Exodus 17 these threats are external: thirst and the Amalekites. In Exodus 32 the threat is internal, but no less—and perhaps even more—threatening to Israel's existence. Basic analogies could be drawn between lack of water and idolatry and between military threat and idolatry. The first analogy is found in Jeremiah (2.10–13; 17.13), where it is perhaps a development of earlier prophetic polemic against idolatry and fertility. The second analogy is a well known topos of Deuteronomic literature (e.g. Deut. 7.1–5).

In each of the narratives salvation ultimately stems from YHWH, but Moses plays the central role. The agreement between YHWH and the Israelites that Israel are *Moses*'s people, both distances YHWH from the people, but also beckons Moses towards his mediatorial role. In each of the stories, he is the intercessor. There are crucial differences between the intercession in each of the stories. In the first, Moses' plea is more for himself (17.4); in the second, Moses appears

reason might be that the authors of 1–2 Samuel felt far greater freedom to rewrite the stories. The material in Exodus, on the other hand, is more deeply immersed in the cultic life of Israel and less given to radical alteration.

to be channelling divine power in a mechanical manner that depends on whether his arms are raised or not (17.11–12); in the third, Moses seeks divine favour for the people where wrath is threatened (32.9–14). One consequence of this inner-biblical commentary is that these intercessions are interpreted, even transformed, in light of the others. This is most apparent in the case of the rod in Moses' raised hands. In the exodus story the rod is a means of channelling power in a way that seems to be magical (cf. Exod. 7.8–13). The mechanical relationship between Moses' arms and the course of the battle is some distance from traditional conceptions of prayer, or even the activity of Moses on Horeb. Yet in light of the parallels to Exodus 32 Moses's intercessory activity in both stories in Exodus 17 can appropriately be read as instructive about wrestling in prayer in precisely the way that Jews and Christians have traditionally understood the story (Childs 1974: 316–317).

The inner-biblical commentary also affects our reading of Exodus 32. The story of Moses' tiring hands draws attention to the importance of Moses as mediator. In his weariness will Moses always prevail? As the story of the Golden Calf unfolds in Exodus 32–34 exactly this question is in the reader's mind: will Moses persist with YHWH and can his intercession succeed? The stories leave no doubt about the importance of prophetic intercession for the continued life of Israel.[23]

References

Achenbach, R. 2003. *Die Vollendung der Tora: Studien zur Redaktionsgeschichte des Numeribuches im Kontext von Hexateuch und Pentateuch* (Beihefte zur Zeitschrift für Altorientalische und Biblische Rechtsgeschichte, 3; Wiesbaden: Harrassowitz).

Aurelius, E. 1988. *Der Fürbitter Israels. Eine Studie zum Mosebild im Alten Testament* (Coniectanea Biblica, Old Testament Series, 27; Stockholm: Almqvist & Wiksell).

Childs, B.S. 1974. *The Book of Exodus: A Critical, Theological Commentary* (The Old Testament Library; Philadelphia: Westminster Press).

Coats, G.W. 1975. 'Moses Versus Amalek: Aetiology and Legend in Exod. xvii 8–16', in *Congress Volume: Edinburgh 1974* (Vetus Testamentum, Supplements, 28; Leiden: Brill) 29–41.

Davies, G.I. 1983. 'The Wilderness Itineraries and the Composition of the Pentateuch', *Vetus Testamentum* 23: 1–13.

Fritz, V. 1970. *Israel in der Wüste: Traditionsgeschichtliche Untersuchung der Wüstenüberlieferung des Jahwisten* (Marburger Theologische Studien, 7; Marburg: N.G. Elwert).

[23] For the same dynamics in Gen. 18.16–33, see MacDonald (2004).

Gertz, J.C. 2000. *Tradition und Redaktion in der Exoduserzählung: Untersuchungen zur Endredaktion des Pentateuch* (Forschungen zur Religion und Literatur des Alten und Neuen Testaments, 186; Göttingen: Vandenhoeck & Ruprecht).
Gordon, R.P. 1980. 'David's Rise and Saul's Demise: Narrative Analogy in 1 Samuel 24–26', *Tyndale Bulletin* 31: 37–64.
Herrmann, W. 1992. 'Ex 17,7bβ und die Frage nach der Gegenwart Jahwes in Israel', in *Alttestamentlicher Glaube und Biblische Theologie* (eds. J. Hausmann and H.-J. Zobel; Stuttgart: Kohlhammer) 46–55.
Houtman, C. 1995–2002. *Exodus* (Historical Commentary on the Old Testament; 4 vols.; Kampen: Kok).
Kratz, R. 2005. *The Composition of the Narrative Books of the Old Testament* (trans. J. Bowden; London: T&T Clark).
Levin, C. 1993. *Der Jahwist* (Forschungen zur Religion und Literatur des Alten und Neuen Testaments, 157; Göttingen: Vandenhoeck & Ruprecht).
Lohfink, N. 1988. '"Ich bin Jahwe, dein Arzt" (Ex 15,26): Gott, Gesellschaft und menschliche Gesundheit in einer nachexilischen Pentateuchbearbeitung (Ex 15,25b.26)', in *Studien in Pentateuch* (Stuttgarter Biblische Aufsatzbände, 4; Stuttgart: Katholisches Bibelwerk) 91–156.
MacDonald, N. 2004. 'Listening to Abraham—Listening to Yhwh: Divine Justice and Mercy in Genesis 18:16–33', *Catholic Biblical Quarterly* 66: 25–43.
Moberly, R.W.L. 1983. *At the Mountain of God: Story and Theology in Exodus 32–34* (Journal for the Study of the Old Testament Supplement, 22; Sheffield: JSOT Press).
Noort, E. 2006. 'Josua und Amalek: Exodus 17:8–16', in *The Interpretation of Exodus* (ed. R. Roukema; Contributions to Biblical Exegesis and Theology, 44; Leuven: Peeters) 155–70.
Noth, M. 1948. *Überlieferungsgeschichte des Pentateuch* (Stuttgart: Kohlhammer).
——. 1958. *Das 2. Buch Mose Exodus* (Das Alte Testament Deutsch, 5; Göttingen: Vandenhoeck & Ruprecht).
Propp, W.H.C. 1987. *Water in the Wilderness: A Biblical Motif and Its Mythological Backgrounds* (Harvard Semitic Monographs, 40; Atlanta: Scholars Press).
——. 1999. *Exodus 1–18: A New Translation with Introduction and Commentary* (Anchor Bible, 2; New York: Doubleday).
Ruprecht, E. 1974. 'Stellung und Bedeutung der Erzählung vom Mannawunder (Ex 16) im Aufbau der Priesterschrift', *Zeitschrift für die alttestamentliche Wissenschaft* 86: 269–307.
Schart, A. 1990. *Mose und Israel im Konflikt: Eine redaktionsgeschichtliche Studie zu den Wüstenerzählungen* (Orbis Biblicus et Orientalis, 98; Freiburg: Universitätsverlag).
Schmitt, H.-C. 1990. 'Die Geschichte vom Sieg über die Amalekiter: Ex 17,8–16 als theologische Lehrerzählung', *Zeitschrift für die alttestamentliche Wissenschaft* 102: 335–344.
Van Seters, J. 1994. *The Life of Moses: The Yahwist as Historian in Exodus-Numbers* (Contributions to Biblical Exegesis and Theology, 10; Kampen: Kok Pharos).
Zenger, E. 1982. *Israel am Sinai: Analysen und Interpretationen zu Exodus 17–34* (Altenberge: CIS Verlag).

LEGAL ANALOGY IN DEUTERONOMY AND FRATRICIDE IN THE FIELD

Diana Lipton

The 'rape' laws[1] in Deut. 22.23–29 contain the Hebrew Bible's only example of a legal analogy.[2] A man who lies by force with an engaged woman in the 'field' is subject to the death penalty,[3] but nothing should be done to the woman he raped, since this is *like* the case of a man who rises up against and murders another man (v. 26). In this paper I shall explore the significance of this analogy and its effect upon the law that underlies it. I will suggest that the analogy's interest lies at the intersection of law and narrative; that its literary formulation recalls two cases of fratricide, Cain's murder of Abel (Gen. 4.1–16) and the woman of Tekoa's parable of her two sons (2 Sam. 14.1–20); that the analogy to murder does not clarify but complicates the interpretation and application of the rape law; and (most radical) that it sounds a note of caution about the implementation of the death penalty in relation to this law.

Deut. 22.23–29 sets out and responds to three similar sexual encounters:

---

[1] For the sake of simplicity, I use the term 'rape' to refer to the sexual encounters described in these three Deuteronomic laws. Since I am not concerned with exactly what occurred in each case, or what it signified in its ancient context, this seems to me acceptable, but I am aware that the terminology is problematic, both for the differences it eclipses in these three biblical encounters and for the differences it eclipses between their times and ours. For a discussion of the terminology of rape see Gravett (2004), esp. pp. 279–280.

[2] Num. 15.18–21 includes a quasi-legal analogy: the *ḥallah* that every Israelite is commanded to offer is *like* the offering from the threshing house floor that farmers are obliged to make.

[3] I am grateful to Bernard Jackson (p.c.) for making the crucial point that the rapists in the city and the field deserve the death penalty not because they are rapists, but because they have committed adultery. Yet it seems to me that rape, or the potential for rape, does nevertheless play a significant role of some kind here, as indicated by the differences between these laws and the comparatively straightforward case of adultery with a married woman that precedes them (Deut. 22.22); by the analogy to murder (which is more like rape than it is like adultery); and by the possible allusion I shall discuss below to the case of Amnon and Tamar (rape but not adultery).

22.23 כִּי יִהְיֶה נַעֲרָה בְתוּלָה מְאֹרָשָׂה לְאִישׁ וּמְצָאָהּ אִישׁ בָּעִיר וְשָׁכַב עִמָּהּ׃
22.24 וְהוֹצֵאתֶם אֶת־שְׁנֵיהֶם אֶל־שַׁעַר ׀ הָעִיר הַהִוא וּסְקַלְתֶּם אֹתָם בָּאֲבָנִים
וָמֵתוּ אֶת־הַנַּעֲרָה עַל־דְּבַר אֲשֶׁר לֹא־צָעֲקָה בָעִיר וְאֶת־הָאִישׁ עַל־דְּבַר אֲשֶׁר־
עִנָּה אֶת־אֵשֶׁת רֵעֵהוּ וּבִעַרְתָּ הָרָע מִקִּרְבֶּךָ׃ס 22.25 וְאִם־בַּשָּׂדֶה יִמְצָא הָאִישׁ
אֶת־הַנַּעֲרָה הַמְאֹרָשָׂה וְהֶחֱזִיק־בָּהּ הָאִישׁ וְשָׁכַב עִמָּהּ וּמֵת הָאִישׁ אֲשֶׁר־שָׁכַב
עִמָּהּ לְבַדּוֹ׃ 22.26 וְלַנַּעֲרָהלֹא־תַעֲשֶׂה דָבָר אֵין לַנַּעֲרָה חֵטְא מָוֶת כִּי כַּאֲשֶׁר
יָקוּם אִישׁ עַל־רֵעֵהוּ וּרְצָחוֹ נֶפֶשׁ כֵּן הַדָּבָר הַזֶּה׃ 22.27 כִּי בַשָּׂדֶה מְצָאָהּ
צָעֲקָה הַנַּעֲרָההַמְאֹרָשָׂה וְאֵין מוֹשִׁיעַ לָהּ׃ ס 22.28 כִּי־יִמְצָא אִישׁ נַעֲרָה
בְתוּלָה אֲשֶׁר לֹא־אֹרָשָׂה וּתְפָשָׂהּ וְשָׁכַב עִמָּהּ וְנִמְצָאוּ׃ 22.29 וְנָתַן הָאִישׁ
הַשֹּׁכֵב עִמָּהּ לַאֲבִי הַנַּעֲרָה חֲמִשִּׁים כָּסֶף וְלוֹ־תִהְיֶה לְאִשָּׁה תַּחַת אֲשֶׁר עִנָּהּ
לֹא־יוּכַל שַׁלְּחָהּ כָּל־יָמָיו׃ ס

(22.23) In the case of a virgin who is engaged to a man—if a man comes upon her in town and lies with her, (22.24) you shall take the two of them out to the gate of that town and stone them to death: the girl because she did not cry for help in the town, and the man because he violated another man's wife. Thus you will sweep away evil from your midst. (22.25) But if the man comes upon the engaged girl in the open country, and the man lies with her by force, only the man who lay with her shall die, (22.26) but you shall do nothing to the girl. The girl did not incur the death penalty, for this case is like that of a man who rises up against his neighbour in the field and murders him. (22.27) He came upon her in the open; though the engaged girl cried for help, there was no one to save her. (22.28) If a man comes upon a virgin who is not engaged and he seizes her and lies with her, and they are discovered, (22.29) the man who lay with her shall pay the girl's father fifty [shekels of] silver, and she shall be his wife. Because he has violated her, he can never have the right to divorce her.[4]

The differences between the three laws in this pericope are subtle but significant. In the first case, which I shall call 'sex in the city', the protagonists are a man and a betrothed woman, the location is the city, and both parties are subject to the death penalty. In the second case, which I shall call 'sex in the field', the protagonists are once again a man and a betrothed woman, but the scene is the 'field', and only the man is subject to the death penalty. The third case, which I shall term 'sex before marriage', involves a man and a woman who is not

[4] English translations of biblical texts are taken from *Tanakh* (1999).

betrothed, the location is not specified, but seems to be in the city since they are discovered, and the penalty is payment to the woman's father and marriage without the possibility of divorce.

Bernard Jackson (1993: 142–143) sees the legal analogy embedded in this periscope (v. 26) as confirmation that the woman is indeed a victim:

> This form of analogical argument is, to my knowledge, unique within the biblical legal corpus, and serves as a warning against the imposition of discursive uniformity upon the rationality of Jewish law even in the biblical period. The woman taken in the country is compared to the murder victim; just as we do not blame the latter, so we should not blame the former. But the text proceeds to a second level of justification: the woman is presumed innocent in that any cry for help, in the country, would have been of no avail. This is not the place to explore the text from a literary-historical viewpoint; the uneasy conflation of reasons certainly suggests the amendment of an original text. For present purposes it suffices to note the implication of the final formulation, namely that we are able to justify the comparison between this case and the murder victim: from the circumstances, it is safe to infer that the woman is, indeed, a victim from the fact that the incident occurred in the country. But *why* compare the woman to the murder victim? The reason may perhaps reside in the fact that in both cases we have the use of relatively arbitrary tests in order to resolve a dispute without the need for third party adjudication.

Jackson's closing question—why make this comparison?—preoccupies me too, but while his answer highlights the female victim, mine highlights the male perpetrator. One explanation for the difference between us resides in our different reading of the Hebrew syntax. As Jackson correctly observes, the analogy sits awkwardly with the surrounding text. In addition to the factor he mentions—a conflation of reasons offered for why the woman should not be punished—the subjects alternate confusingly in verses 25–27. The first actor is *the man*, who comes across the woman in the field, seizes her, and sleeps with her (v. 25a). *The man* alone must die (v. 25b). The focus shifts to *the woman*, who did not commit a crime warranting the death penalty (v. 26a), and back to *the man* (not the rapist but his murdering alter-ego) who rose up against his neighbour and killed him (v. 26b). Attention remains with *the man* (now the rapist himself) in the next clause, which reports that he came across her (the woman) in the field (v. 27a), before returning to *the woman*—even had she cried out, there was no-one to save her (v. 27b).

Jackson's reading of the analogy as confirmation that the woman was a victim (and thus has a defense against the accusation of adultery) entails a justified extrapolation from what is written. The text does not explicitly compare the *woman* to the victim of an attack, but rather compares the *man* to someone who attacked another man. It is natural to infer that the comment reflects upon the woman; it follows directly after the statement that she does not merit the death penalty.[5] Yet given the aforementioned shifts between subjects in these verses, we might as plausibly read the assertion that the woman should not be punished as a digression, occurring when it does because it deals with her punishment and the man's punishment has just been mentioned, but interrupting a single train of thought in which the man alone will be killed because he is like a man who rose up against his neighbour and killed him. To be sure, this conceptual repositioning still underlines the woman's status as victim (which was established by the use of the verb 'to seize' in v. 25), but its primary significance is now to comment or elaborate upon the man's punishment, not why the woman *should not* be punished. It is worth noting in addition that, in its actual position, the analogy follows directly after the law's sole direct second person singular address to those who implement justice ('but you shall do nothing to the girl', v. 26, cf. v. 25 which reports only in the third person singular that the man will die). I suggest that it creates for those signified in the verse by 'you' an artful license *not* to kill. This is achieved, I think, by the evocation of two narratives in which men rise up against and kill their brothers in a field but nevertheless avoid the death penalty. Jackson observed that little is gained by comparing the victim of a rape to a murder victim. I hope to show that a great deal may be gained by comparing a rapist to a murderer who is not sentenced to death.[6]

Elsewhere in this volume Nathan Macdonald cites our teacher Robert Gordon (1980: 42–43) on narrative analogy:

> Hebrew narrative... [uses] a wide range of narrative techniques to perform the functions of the explicit commentaries in the more transparent

[5] The same inference is made by many others. See for example Tigay (1996: 208): 'That is, she was a victim, not a participant'.

[6] I am conscious of failing in this paper to engage with the moral dimensions of the subject at hand. How can I write with cool detachment about legal analogies and narrative intertexts as if they were not occasioned by violent or coercive sex? That is a good question to which I have no good answer. I can only say that fortunately others have succeeded where I have failed.

> narrative types. Prominent among these techniques is that of narrative analogy. Narrative analogy is a device whereby the narrator can provide an internal commentary on the action which he is describing, usually by means of cross-reference to an earlier action or speech. Thus narratives are made to interact in ways which may not be immediately apparent; ironic parallelism abounds wherever this technique is applied.

Narrative analogies link two or more narratives by the use of parallels and similarities that invite comparison. The narrator does not call explicit attention to these analogies. Instead, they must be detected by readers using their own knowledge and intuitions. As many scholars have observed, laws too may recall other laws in this allusive way,[7] but my focus here is a single biblical law in which the analogy is explicit in the text. No reader of Deut. 22.26 can doubt the legislator's intention to link rape and murder.

Jackson defines legal analogy as 'justified comparison' (1993: 137). He is not concerned with analogy as it was conceived in rabbinic exegesis—a sophisticated hermeneutic device—but he does see a distinctively Jewish feature of legal analogy, namely its literary basis (1993: 142):

> What appears to me to be characteristic, and distinctive, about the Jewish forms of analogical argument is the fact that the basis of comparison is so often purely linguistic or literary, whereas in secular legal argument, that basis must itself must be substantive.

The analogy in Deut. 22.26 is, for Jackson, notable for its substantive basis. As I read it, it is both literary *and* substantive. By virtue of its precise literary formulation, the analogy evokes two narratives (from Genesis 4 and 2 Samuel 14). Yet the springboard for this literary comparison is substantive, the comparison of two crimes: rape and murder. To understand the analogy's overall effect we must first come to terms with the effect of the substantive analogy at its core.

A legal analogy can be seen as a textual device that resolves ambiguity and limits the range of options available for defining and responding to a particular crime. That is, an analogy could determine that in a given respect X is like Y and is not therefore like A–W or Z. Rape, for example, is like murder and not like theft. Interpreted thus, the analogy could serve to underline a crime's seriousness, or to justify a seemingly harsh punishment by equating an apparently minor misdemeanor with a more serious crime. Yet although a legal analogy can

---

[7] See for example Levinson's (1997) treatment of the relationship between Deuteronomic laws and the Covenant Code.

plausibly be interpreted along these lines, I think it functions here in Deuteronomy in precisely the opposite way, not reducing but expanding the range of available options for defining and responding to the crime in question. On this account, the comparison between X and Y does not limit interpretative options but multiplies them; there are now two cases to consider, as well as the interplay between them. The obvious beneficiaries of this proliferation of interpretative options are those responsible for implementing the law. This observation may sound unconvincingly post-modern when applied to an ancient law, but I hope to show that it is supported by many other aspects of Deuteronomic legislation, as well as by my particular case study.

This emphasis on those implementing the law over the protagonists fits well with Deuteronomy's general thrust where, not surprisingly, judges, magistrates and other guardians of the law are multiply attested. First, even if legislation served in part to notify victims of their obligations and rights, or to discourage criminals from committing crimes, its details and nuances were above all for the benefit of the legislators' natural heirs—those implementing justice. Second, Deuteronomic legislation shows a strong interest in actually doing justice. While judges and juries crave certainty and simplicity when making legal decisions, they are more likely to do justice when they acknowledge the uncertainty and complexity inherent in most serious legal matters. Third, doing justice was a dangerous business in the Deuteronomic world; judges and others were themselves culpable if they failed to punish, and, worse still, they brought blame onto their entire community. I turn now to three separate Deuteronomic manifestations of this latter concern, that is, the imperative to do justice, with all that entails, and the socially and theologically driven need to leave no crime unpunished.

The ritual of the broken-necked heifer (Deut. 21.1–9) allows the town's elders and magistrates (v. 3) to absolve themselves and all Israel from guilt with respect to unsolved murders:

> Then the elders of the town…shall make this declaration: 'Our hands did not shed this blood, nor did our eyes see it done. Absolve, O LORD, Your people Israel whom you redeemed, and do not let guilt for the blood of the innocent remain among Your people Israel (v. 7).[8]

[8] See Barmash (2005: 104–105) for an analysis of this ritual that pays particular attention to the need, even in Deuteronomy, to deal with blood.

The problem addressed by the broken-necked heifer ritual is not that the murderer has escaped from the scene and cannot be found and brought to justice. Rather, this ritual responds to homicides in which the murderer cannot be identified because crucial information *is not known*. Two types of uncertainty are at stake: the murderer's identity and—less discussed but arguably more significant—the area of jurisdiction in which the crime was committed (v. 1). The elders of the town are unable to do justice because they cannot identify the murderer, and because the crime occurred *in the field* (v. 1),[9] and thus outside a recognized area of jurisdiction. The broken-necked heifer represents a *ritual* acknowledgement of both uncertainties, and, proceeding from that, a formal abdication of collective responsibility by the elders and magistrates in the town nearest 'the field' where the corpse was found. To be sure, this abdication is for the benefit of society at large, but it is the elders and magistrates, representing those obliged to punish the criminal, who literally 'wash their hands' of the matter (v. 6).

Evidence of anxiety about doing justice may also be found in the precise terms and structures of Deuteronomy's eleven calls for the death penalty. These calls are patterned on a formula with four components: the nature of the crime, its location, the method of punishment, and the benefit to the community of exacting the punishment. The variations within this basic formula are instructive.

TEXT	CRIME	PLACE	METHOD	BENEFIT
13.6	Dreamers etc	—	—	Remove evil
13.10	Enticement	—	Stoning	Israel fears
17.5	False worship	Your gates	Stoning	Remove evil
17.12	Disregard authority	—	—	People fear
18.20	False prophecy	—	—	—
19.11	Murder	—	Show no pity	It will go well
21.10	Rebellious son	Gates	Stoning	Remove evil and Israel fears
22.21	False virgin	Father's gates	Stoning	Remove evil
22.22	Adulterer	—	—	Remove evil
22.24	Sex in city	City gates	Stoning	Remove evi
22.25	Sex in field	—	—	—

[9] Barmash (2005: 14) describes the field as 'a place often the site of a crime where the infrequency of bystanders complicates the determination of guilt (cf. Deut. 22.25; 2 Sam. 14.6). Tigay (1996: 191) speculates that 'unsolved murders would most often take place outside of towns'.

Of these eleven calls, four (false worship, rebellious son, false virgin, 'sex in the city') specify all four components; two (enticement and murder) specify three components; two (dreamers, disregard authority, adulterer) specify two components; and two (false prophet and 'sex in the field') specify only the crime itself. False prophecy (18.20) explicitly mentions the difficulty of determining guilt ('How can we know that the oracle was not spoken by the LORD?', 18.21). While some prophecies could be proved false by a subsequent event, many prophecies have no sell-by date by which time they can confidently declared to be false, and, depending on their nature and scope, might never be falsifiable. Not only were those responsible for executing justice unable to act immediately, but they could almost never be certain on the day that a death penalty was enacted that it was merited; perhaps the prophecy would be fulfilled later that very day. This is not to suggest that the death penalty was merely notional in the case of false prophecy, but that the near-impossibility of being sure that it was justified may have been a factor in Deuteronomy's abbreviated presentation of the law. The call for the death penalty confirmed the seriousness of the crime, and the absence of practical instructions signalled that, its seriousness notwithstanding, the punishment will rarely be implemented. The similarly abbreviated presentation of 'sex in the field' (only one of four components—the crime itself—is specified) suggests that uncertainty may have been a factor there too. This is all the more plausible when 'sex in the field' legislation is compared with 'sex in the city', which specifies all four components.[10]

Finally, legislative anxiety about implementing the death penalty might reasonably have been provoked by the absence of witnesses. Deut. 17.6 specifies that the death penalty may be applied only on the testimony of two or three witnesses, and not on the word of a single witness. Although this instruction applies to worshippers of other

[10] Another explanation sometimes offered for the abbreviated presentation of 'sex in the field' is that the detailed instructions provided in 'sex in the city' were assumed to carry over to the next law. I find this suggestion unconvincing. First, the field demands instructions that were not needed in the city. Since the physical area of jurisdiction is in doubt, to which gates should the rapist be taken, and who should take him? Second, since false prophecy is nowhere near another call for the death penalty, the 'carrying over' explanation does not work in its case. Third, even the calls for the death penalty that may be said to carry over instructions from the preceding law (e.g., 17.12 cf. 17.5) specify a benefit. 'Sex in the field' and false prophecy are the only death penalty calls that omit a benefit.

gods, there is no reason to restrict it to that case. Applied to 'sex in the field' it raises a serious problem. Since not even a single witness was present to give testimony (Deut. 23.27), on what basis could the rapist be executed? And how could those responsible for bringing the rapist to justice reconcile these apparently conflicting demands?

Even before considering the analogy, then, it is easy to see why a judge, magistrate, elder or other might have had cause for concern when it came to applying the death penalty for 'sex in the field'. The location in the field may indicate that the crime took place beyond the pale of legal oversight; the legislation is scanty, specifying neither where, by whom, or for whose benefit the punishment should be exacted; and a crucial condition was, by definition, not fulfilled: there are no witnesses. I turn now to my literary intertexts to see what light they shed on the matter.

Read in its wider context, the legal analogy in Deut. 22.26 has six main motifs: sex, a man who 'rises up' against another, murder, the field, cry, banishment. The case is likened to the case of a *man who rises up against another and kills him* (v. 26). The analogy's immediate context is a *violent sexual encounter* (v. 25) in *the field* (v. 25), and reference is made to a cry which, had it been uttered, would not have been heard (v. 27). The wider context includes the notion of *banishment*—a man who seizes a non-betrothed woman must marry her and can never divorce her, literally, 'send her away' (v. 29). These motifs evoke two narratives: Gen. 4.1–16 (Cain and Abel) and 2 Sam. 14.1–20 (Tekoa woman).

Gen. 4.1–16 contains all six motifs that feature centrally in Deut. 22.23–29.

4.8 וַיֹּאמֶר קַיִן אֶל־הֶבֶל אָחִיו וַיְהִי בִּהְיוֹתָם בַּשָּׂדֶה וַיָּקָם קַיִן אֶל־הֶבֶל אָחִיו
וַיַּהַרְגֵהוּ׃ 4.9 וַיֹּאמֶר יְהוָה אֶל־קַיִן אֵי הֶבֶל אָחִיךָ וַיֹּאמֶר לֹא יָדַעְתִּי הֲשֹׁמֵר
אָחִי אָנֹכִי׃ 4.10 וַיֹּאמֶר מֶה עָשִׂיתָ קוֹל דְּמֵי אָחִיךָ צֹעֲקִים אֵלַי מִן־הָאֲדָמָה׃
4.11 וְעַתָּה אָרוּר אָתָּה מִן־הָאֲדָמָה אֲשֶׁר פָּצְתָה אֶת־פִּיהָ לָקַחַת אֶת־דְּמֵי
אָחִיךָ מִיָּדֶךָ׃ 4.12 כִּי תַעֲבֹד אֶת־הָאֲדָמָה לֹא־תֹסֵף תֵּת־כֹּחָהּ לָךְ נָע וָנָד
תִּהְיֶה בָאָרֶץ׃ 4.13 וַיֹּאמֶר קַיִן אֶל־יְהוָה גָּדוֹל עֲוֺנִי מִנְּשֹׂא׃ 4.14 הֵן גֵּרַשְׁתָּ
אֹתִי הַיּוֹם מֵעַל פְּנֵי הָאֲדָמָה וּמִפָּנֶיךָ אֶסָּתֵר וְהָיִיתִי נָע וָנָד בָּאָרֶץ וְהָיָה כָל־
מֹצְאִי יַהַרְגֵנִי׃ 4.15 וַיֹּאמֶר לוֹ יְהוָה לָכֵן כָּל־הֹרֵג קַיִן שִׁבְעָתַיִם יֻקָּם וַיָּשֶׂם
יְהוָה לְקַיִן אוֹת לְבִלְתִּי הַכּוֹת־אֹתוֹ כָּל־מֹצְאוֹ׃ 4.16 וַיֵּצֵא קַיִן מִלִּפְנֵי יְהוָה
וַיֵּשֶׁב בְּאֶרֶץ־נוֹד קִדְמַת־עֵדֶן׃

(4.8) Cain said to his brother Abel…*and when they were in the field, Cain rose up against his brother Abel and killed him.* (4.9) The LORD said to Cain, 'Where is your brother Abel?' And he said, 'I do not know. Am I my brother's keeper?' (4.10) Then He said, 'What have you done? *Hark, your brother's blood cries out to Me* from the ground! (4.11) Therefore, you shall be more cursed than the ground,which opened its mouth to receive your brother's blood from your hand. (4.12) If you till the soil, it shall no longer yield its strength to you. *You shall become a ceaseless wanderer* on earth.' (4.13) Cain said to the LORD, 'My punishment is too great to bear! (4.14) Since You have banished me this day from the soil, and I must avoid Your presence and become a restless wanderer on earth—anyone who meets me may kill me!' (4.15) The LORD said to him, 'I promise, if anyone kills Cain, sevenfold vengeance shall be taken on him.' And the LORD put a mark on Cain, lest anyone who met him should kill him. (4.16) Cain left the presence of the LORD and settled in the land of Nod, east of Eden.[11]

Cain rises up against Abel (Gen. 4.8, cf. Deut. 22.26). He murders him (Gen. 4.8 cf. Deut. 22.26). The location is the field (Gen. 4.8 cf. Deut. 22.25). Abel's blood cries out to God (Gen. 4.10 cf. Deut. 22.27). God banishes Cain (Gen. 4.12 cf. Deut. 22.29). The murder follows immediately after an allusion to sexual desire as mentioned in the previous chapter: God's words to Cain, 'Sin couches at the door; its urge is towards you, yet you can be its master (Gen. 4.7)', echo God's words to Eve, 'Your urge shall be for your husband, yet he shall rule over you (Gen. 3.10)', cf., of course, the rape itself (Deut. 22.25).

The parable of the Tekoa woman (2 Sam. 14.1–20), read in its wider narrative context of Amnon's rape of Tamar (2 Sam. 13.1–22) and Absalom's retributive killing of Amnon (2 Sam. 13.23–39), likewise includes all six components of the Deuteronomic analogy.

14.1 וַיֵּ֖דַע יוֹאָ֣ב בֶּן־צְרֻיָ֑ה כִּי־לֵ֥ב הַמֶּ֖לֶךְ עַל־אַבְשָׁלֽוֹם׃ 14.2 וַיִּשְׁלַ֤ח יוֹאָב֙ תְּק֔וֹעָה
וַיִּקַּ֥ח מִשָּׁ֖ם אִשָּׁ֣ה חֲכָמָ֑ה וַיֹּ֣אמֶר אֵ֠לֶיהָ הִֽתְאַבְּלִי־נָ֞א וְלִבְשִׁי־נָ֣א בִגְדֵי־אֵ֗בֶל וְאַל־
תָּס֙וּכִי֙ שֶׁ֔מֶן וְהָיִ֗ית כְּאִשָּׁ֨ה זֶ֚ה יָמִ֣ים רַבִּ֔ים מִתְאַבֶּ֖לֶת עַל־מֵֽת׃ 14.3 וּבָאת֙ אֶל־
הַמֶּ֔לֶךְ וְדִבַּ֥רְתְּ אֵלָ֖יו כַּדָּבָ֣ר הַזֶּ֑ה וַיָּ֧שֶׂם יוֹאָ֛ב אֶת־הַדְּבָרִ֖ים בְּפִֽיהָ׃ 14.4 וַתֹּ֙אמֶר֙
הָאִשָּׁ֣ה הַתְּקֹעִ֔ית אֶל־הַמֶּ֔לֶךְ וַתִּפֹּ֧ל עַל־אַפֶּ֛יהָ אַ֖רְצָה וַתִּשְׁתָּ֑חוּ וַתֹּ֖אמֶר הוֹשִׁ֥עָה

[11] See Barmash (2005: 12–19) for an illuminating discussion of this narrative's contribution to legal thinking about homicide.

הַמֶּֽלֶךְ׃ ס 14.5 וַיֹּֽאמֶר־לָ֥הּ הַמֶּ֖לֶךְ מַה־לָּ֑ךְ וַתֹּ֗אמֶר אֲבָ֛ל אִשָּֽׁה־אַלְמָנָ֥ה אָ֖נִי וַיָּ֥מָת
אִישִֽׁי׃ 14.6 וּלְשִׁפְחָֽתְךָ֙ שְׁנֵ֣י בָנִ֔ים וַיִּנָּצ֤וּ שְׁנֵיהֶם֙ בַּשָּׂדֶ֔ה וְאֵ֥ין מַצִּ֖יל בֵּינֵיהֶ֑ם וַיַּכּ֧וֹ
הָאֶחָ֛ד אֶת־הָאֶחָ֖ד וַיָּ֥מֶת אֹתֽוֹ׃ 14.7 וְהִנֵּה֩ קָ֨מָה כָֽל־הַמִּשְׁפָּחָ֜ה עַל־שִׁפְחָתֶ֗ךָ
וַיֹּֽאמְרוּ֙ תְּנִ֣י ׀ אֶת־מַכֵּ֣ה אָחִ֗יו וּנְמִתֵ֙הוּ֙ בְּנֶ֤פֶשׁ אָחִיו֙ אֲשֶׁ֣ר הָרָ֔ג וְנַשְׁמִ֖ידָה גַּ֣ם אֶת־
הַיּוֹרֵ֑שׁ וְכִבּ֗וּ אֶת־גַּֽחַלְתִּי֙ אֲשֶׁ֣ר נִשְׁאָ֔רָה לְבִלְתִּ֧י שִׂים־לְאִישִׁ֛י שֵׁ֥ם וּשְׁאֵרִ֖ית עַל־
פְּנֵ֥י הָאֲדָמָֽה׃ פ 14.8 וַיֹּ֧אמֶר הַמֶּ֛לֶךְ אֶל־הָאִשָּׁ֖ה לְכִ֣י לְבֵיתֵ֑ךְ וַאֲנִ֖י אֲצַוֶּ֥ה עָלָֽיִךְ׃
14.9 וַתֹּ֜אמֶר הָאִשָּׁ֤ה הַתְּקוֹעִית֙ אֶל־הַמֶּ֔לֶךְ עָלַ֞י אֲדֹנִ֥י הַמֶּ֛לֶךְ הֶעָוֺ֖ן וְעַל־בֵּ֣ית אָבִ֑י
וְהַמֶּ֥לֶךְ וְכִסְא֖וֹ נָקִֽי׃ ס 14.10 וַיֹּ֖אמֶר הַמֶּ֣לֶךְ הַֽמְדַבֵּ֣ר אֵלַ֑יִךְ וַהֲבֵאתוֹ֙ אֵלַ֔י וְלֹֽא־
יֹסִ֥יף ע֖וֹד לָגַ֥עַת בָּֽךְ׃ 14.11 וַתֹּ֡אמֶר יִזְכָּר־נָ֨א הַמֶּ֜לֶךְ אֶת־יְהוָ֣ה אֱלֹהֶ֗יךָ מֵהַרְבַּ֞ת
גֹּאֵ֤ל הַדָּם֙ לְשַׁחֵ֔ת וְלֹ֥א יַשְׁמִ֖ידוּ אֶת־בְּנִ֑י וַיֹּ֙אמֶר֙ חַי־יְהוָ֔ה אִם־יִפֹּ֛ל מִשַּׂעֲרַ֥ת בְּנֵ֖ךְ
אָֽרְצָה׃ 14.12 וַתֹּ֙אמֶר֙ הָֽאִשָּׁ֔ה תְּדַבֶּר־נָ֧א שִׁפְחָתְךָ֛ אֶל־אֲדֹנִ֥י הַמֶּ֖לֶךְ דָּבָ֑ר וַיֹּ֖אמֶר
דַּבֵּֽרִי׃ ס 14.13 וַתֹּ֙אמֶר֙ הָֽאִשָּׁ֔ה וְלָ֥מָּה חָשַׁ֛בְתָּה כָּזֹ֖את עַל־עַ֣ם אֱלֹהִ֑ים וּמִדַּבֵּ֨ר
הַמֶּ֜לֶךְ הַדָּבָ֤ר הַזֶּה֙ כְּאָשֵׁ֔ם לְבִלְתִּ֛י הָשִׁ֥יב הַמֶּ֖לֶךְ אֶת־נִדְּחֽוֹ׃

(14.1) Joab son of Zeruiah could see that the king's mind was on Absalom; (14.2) so Joab sent to Tekoa and brought a clever woman from there. He said to her, 'Pretend you are in mourning; put on mourning clothes and don't anoint yourself with oil; and act like a woman who has grieved a long time over a departed one. (14.3) Go to the king and say to him thus and thus.' And Joab told her what to say. (14.4) The woman of Tekoa came to the king, flung herself face down to the ground, and prostrated herself. She cried out, 'Help, O king!' (14.5) The king asked her, 'What troubles you?' And she answered, 'Alas, I am a widow, my husband is dead. (14.6) *Your maidservant had two sons. The two of them came to blows out in the fields where there was no one to stop them, and one of them struck the other and killed him.* (14.7) Then the whole clan confronted your maidservant and said, 'Hand over the one who killed his brother, that we may put him to death for the slaying of his brother, even though we wipe out the heir.' Thus they would quench the last ember remaining to me, and leave my husband without name or remnant upon the earth.' (14.8) The king said to the woman, 'Go home. I will issue an order in your behalf.' (14.9) And the woman of Tekoa said to the king, 'My lord king, may the guilt be on me and on my ancestral house; Your Majesty and his throne are guiltless.' (14.10) The king said, 'If anyone says anything more to you, have him brought to me, and he will never trouble you again.' (14.11) She replied, 'Let Your Majesty be mindful of the LORD your God and restrain the blood avenger bent on destruction, so that my son may not be killed.' And he said, 'As the LORD lives, not a hair of your son shall fall to the ground.' (14.12) Then the woman said,

'Please let your maidservant say another word to my lord the king.' 'Speak on,' said the king. (14.13) And the woman said, 'Why then have you planned the like against God's people? In making this pronouncement, Your Majesty condemns himself in that Your Majesty does not bring back his own banished one.

The background of Tekoa woman's intervention is a multiply *problematic sexual encounter*, Amnon's rape of his sister Tamar (2 Sam. 13.14, cf. Deut. 22.25). Tamar *cries out* after Amnon has raped her (2 Sam. 13.19, cf. Deut. 22.26). The rape leads to a real *murder*, Absalom's of Amnon (2 Sam. 14.28–29, cf. Deut 22.26), followed by a fictional murder—one of the Tekoa woman's sons kills his brother (2 Sam. 14.6). The murder of Amnon takes place in 'the place where sheep are sheared' (2 Sam. 13.23), presumably in the countryside, if not in a field, and the Tekoa woman's sons fight in *the field* (2 Sam. 14.6, cf. Deut. 22.25). The other princes *rise up* (2 Sam. 13.29, cf. Deut. 22.26) and mount their donkeys as soon as Amnon is killed by Absalom's 'young men'.[12] Absalom is banished (2 Sam. 13.37–39/ 2 Sam. 14.13, cf. Deut. 22.29).

These two narratives complicate the Deuteronomic law that evokes them. In particular, they call into question the punishment specified for the rapist. First, although death is unambiguously the penalty for murder (see Gen. 9.5–6 and Deut. 19.11–13 for statements proximate to our intertexts), Cain and the Tekoa woman's surviving son were not punished by death. This cannot be attributed to judicial incompetence. Abel's blood cries out for justice to God, the Bible's pre-eminent Judge, and yet God banished Cain when he should rightfully have applied the death sentence. David should have insisted on death for the Tekoa woman's surviving son, but instead he offered him protection, and he should likewise have called for Absalom's death instead of allowing him to go into exile. What might explain the apparent failure of God and David to do justice in these two cases where each is approached over a case of fratricide, and neither invokes the death penalty?

One possible explanation concerns extenuating circumstances. Absalom murdered his brother Amnon because Amnon raped their sister,

---

[12] It is curious, though probably insignificant, that the murder of Amnon is carried out by Absalom's 'young men', his נְעָרָיו when Deut. 22.25–27 uses the same term, strikingly but not uniquely (cf. the virgin in Deut. 22.15) in the same gender, for the young betrothed woman.

Tamar. Cain murdered Abel because God (later, his lenient judge) provoked his jealousy by preferring Abel's sacrifice. On the one hand, 'sex in the field' contains no hint of information that, if known, might have affected the outcome of the case. On the other hand, it evokes narratives in which murders have a 'back-story', and that alone may be sufficient to sow the seeds of doubt about whether the death penalty should be applied in this case. A second explanation concerns the high cost to others where the death penalty is implemented. Since the Tekoa woman's husband is dead, she tells David, no substitute child can be conceived and his line will end. Read in isolation, 'sex in the field' is the story of two people, the rapist and his victim. Read alongside the narratives suggested by the analogy, the imaginative lens expands to include other figures, notably the parents of both protagonists, with a particular eye on the costs they would bear through the loss of a child. Is it possible that the Deuteronomic legislation seeks to permit and even encourage those who implement its laws to think beyond the couple standing before them, taking into account possible extenuating circumstances and the impact of punishment on the wider family?

An important component of both 'sex in the city' and 'sex in the field' is the cry for help or lack thereof (Deut. 22.24, 27). The cry seems at first glance to draw attention to the protagonists and the nature of their interaction—did she or did she not resist?[13] A second glance calls this into question. Deuteronomy itself makes it clear that the cry is irrelevant in 'sex in the field'; even if the woman had cried out, she would not have been saved (v. 27). Moreover, consensuality in both laws is more reliably demonstrated by the verb 'to seize', absent in 'sex in the city' and present in 'sex in the field' (v. 25). So what, then, is signified by the cry? The narrative intertexts generate a possible answer.

The cries that feature in Genesis 4 and 2 Samuel 13–1–4 occur not before but *after* the crime has been committed. They are not cries for timely intervention, but cries for justice or retribution. Abel's blood cries out to God from the ground, demanding retributive justice, קוֹל דְּמֵי אָחִיךָ צֹעֲקִים אֵלַי מִן־הָאֲדָמָה (Gen. 4.10). The Tekoa woman asks David for help, הוֹשִׁעָה הַמֶּלֶךְ (2 Sam. 14.4), using the very verb used in Deut. 22.27 in relation to the futile non-cry in the field: צָעֲקָה הַנַּעֲרָה הַמְאֹרָשָׂה וְאֵין מוֹשִׁיעַ לָהּ (cf. מַצִּיל, the verb applied in the continuation of the Tekoa woman's speech (2 Sam. 14.6) to someone who might have intervened at the time to break up the fight between her sons).

[13] See Tigay (1996: 207).

Tamar cries out, וַתֵּלֶךְ הָלוֹךְ וְזָעָקָה (2 Sam. 13.19), long after the rape. (Absalom apparently interprets it as a cry for retribution; he counsels her to keep quiet, while quietly planning his own revenge.) Cries feature prominently in these narratives, then, but none of the victims cries out for help at the time of violation. All the cries occur later, demanding justice of one kind or another. Can the Deuteronomic cry too be interpreted as a cry for justice after the event? I think it can.[14]

For three reasons, I think, what is usually read as a cry for help can as or more plausibly read as a signal to and for those designated to do justice. First, to say that the woman in 'sex in the city' merits the death penalty because she did not seek justice afterwards could be construed as merely another way of saying that the sexual encounter in the city was consensual. There is, however, a difference. A cry in a city is more likely to be heard than a cry in the open countryside, but it is not beyond the realm of possibility that a cry at the time of a violent sexual encounter could go unheard. A 'cry' for legal intervention after the event, less time-bound than a cry for help, is arguably a more reliable indication of non-consensual sex than a cry in the heat of the moment. Second, the omission in 'sex before marriage' of a reference to the cry is odd if it is interpreted as a cry for help. The text reports that the woman was seized (Deut. 22.28), so why not report her response to the attack and thus underline the non-consensuality? One might argue that it makes no difference in this case whether or not she consented—the law is the same either way. But the same objection applies to coercion on the man's part. Why not simply report that a man who has sex with a virgin who is not betrothed must pay her father and marry her? If, however, the cry is interpreted as a cry for justice, its omission in 'sex before marriage' is perfectly clear. The woman did not need to cry out for justice because a legal solution for both parties was already in place that does not involve judges and magistrates: her rapist must pay her father, and marry her with no possibility of divorce (Deut. 22.29). Third, read as a cry for help in the heat of the moment, the reference to the cry in 'sex in the field' is problematic. If the cry is understood as a cry for help, the presence or absence of someone to intervene is immaterial. The fact that she cried should have been sufficient to indicate

[14] Bovati (1994) sees crying out as an essential component of judicial inquiries in the Hebrew Bible, signifying at once a cry for help and a plea for justice directed towards an authorized body (p. 317 and see a table of cases on p. 323).

that the woman did not consent. To be sure, there were no witnesses to confirm it, but neither were there witnesses to confirm that the man seized her or, indeed, any other element of the story. Moreover, the law as usually read is not offering a (weak) psychological explanation for her silence (it was not worth calling out because there was no-one to help), but rather a legal explanation for the cry's irrelevance—there were no witnesses to confirm it. But then why does the texts report that there was no-one to *save* her, rather than reporting that there was no-one to *hear* her? These problems are resolved once the cry is interpreted as a cry for justice after the event. The woman's failure to come forward and seek retribution, for herself and on behalf of the man to whom she was betrothed, cannot be taken as a sign that she was complicit. This is because she, unlike the woman in the city, was violated outside any area of jurisdiction, there is no-one to do justice on her behalf. Consequently, nothing will happen to her or, more to the point, to her attacker. To be sure, he deserves the death penalty (v. 25), but there is no-one to bring him to justice (to save her). The legal analogy drives home this unpalatable point when it evokes two murder victims whose deaths are not avenged and for whom justice is not done. Like the murderers in these cases, the rapist deserved to die, but like them, he will evade the sentence he has earned.

The seeds for this paper were sown during a seminar paper on Gen. 4.7 (sin couching at the door) that Robert Gordon delivered to the Biblical Studies Research Seminar at King's College London. I could not have predicted when I set out to explore links between Gen. 4.1–16 and Deut. 22.23–29 that I noticed for the first time during that seminar that I would eventually find my way back to another paper that began its life in a dialogue (on intercession) with Robert Gordon. In a paper originally delivered at his invitation to the Cambridge Old Testament Seminar, and later published (after many editorial improvements!) in his edited volume *The God of Israel*, I read two biblical texts and two rabbinic midrashim as direct appeals to divine justice (Lipton 2007). One of my two midrashim was *Genesis Rabbah*, a commentary on Cain's murder of Abel in which God is compared to a Roman emperor who allows his athletes (gladiators) to die (ed. T. Albeck, *paraša* 22.):

אמר ר' שמעון בן יוחי קשה הדבר לאומרו ואי איפשר לפה לפרשו, לשני אתליטין שהיו עומדין ומתגששין לפני המלך אילו רצה המלך פירשן, לא רצה לפרשן חזק אחר על חבירו והרגו, והיה צווח ואמר מאן יבעי דיני קדם מלכא כך קול דמי אחיך צועקים אלי מן האדמה.

> [Commenting on Gen. 4.10] Shimon ben Yohai said 'This is a difficult matter to express, barely possible for the mouth to utter': It is like two athletes standing and wrestling before the king. Had the king wanted to separate them, he could have done so. But the king did not wish to separate them. One overwhelmed his partner and killed him. [As he was dying] he cried out 'Who will bring my case before the king?' Thus, *The voice of your brother's blood cries out to me from the ground* (*Genesis Rabbah* 22.9, my translation).

Only while researching the present paper did it occur to me that the author of this midrash probably had in mind the Tekoa woman's parable, as well as Cain and Abel, when he constructed his own. Moreover, the midrash accomplishes for the world's first murder precisely what I have suggested that Deuteronomy's legal analogy accomplishes for its rape law: it shifts attention from the immediate protagonists to the hitherto shadowy figure of the dispenser of justice. Finally, and perhaps most intriguingly, all three texts shift the focus by means of an analogy. The midrashist creates a *mashal* comparing God to a Roman emperor; the Tekoa woman tells a parable likening her sons to David's; and Deuteronomy's rape laws equate a rapist with a murderer. Can it be that, in these texts at least, the notion of analogy is not just instrumental to doing justice, but lies close to its heart?

In this paper, I have offered a re-reading of the Bible's single legal analogy (Deut. 22.25). I have suggested that, alongside its substantive comparison of a rape to murder, it evokes a literary comparison. The man who rapes an engaged woman in the field is likened to a man who rises up against another man in the field and kills him. The analogy's precise wording and wider context call to mind two specific narratives which report precisely this sequence of events: Cain's murder of his brother Abel (Gen. 4.1–16) and the woman of Tekoa's parable about fratricide (2 Sam. 14.1–20). I have suggested that a benefit of evoking these narratives concerns the implementation of the death penalty prescribed for the rapist in the field. Several Deuteronomic texts, notably the ritual of the broken-necked heifer (Deut. 21.1–9) and the eleven calls for the death penalty listed above, exhibit anxiety about implementing the death penalty. At the same time, there are strict rules about applying the death penalty, such as the need for witnesses. The death penalty applied to the rapist in the field, where there were no witnesses, thus presents a problem for the elders and magistrates responsible for doing justice. The analogy is reassuring.

If these two murderers, judged by God and King David, no less, were not executed but banished, then surely there is room here for some lenience. Read thus, Deuteronomy's legal analogy complicates the law that underlies it, providing those responsible for doing justice with room to manoeuver, while limiting the scope for criticism for their failure to punish as prescribed. In the process of advancing this admittedly counter-intuitive reading, I have looked again at several aspects of Deuteronomy's second rape law that other commentators have found problematic, particularly the awkwardly located analogy; the conflation of reasons given for treating the woman as a victim; and the unclear relevance of the cry. While I can by no means claim to have resolved all the difficulties they present, I hope that my re-reading—especially with regard to the cry for justice—has been, at least, suggestive.

I will close with a general observation. Scholarly treatments of Deuteronomic law are often divided between those that see it as a reflection of an ancient society and its legal practices and those that treat it as a literary text whose significance is largely ideological or jurisprudential. My reading bridges the gap between these two approaches.[15] On the one hand, it is grounded in a quintessentially literary reading strategy, intertextuality, but on the other hand it points to a pre-eminently practical concern, the need to keep the law *and* to do justice.

It is a great pleasure to dedicate this paper to my teacher, friend, and erstwhile sparring partner, Robert Gordon.

References

Barmash, P. 2010. *Homicide in the Biblical World* (Cambridge: Cambridge University Press).

Bartor, A. 2010. *Reading Law as Narrative: A Study in the Casuistic Laws of the Pentateuch* (Atlanta: SBL).

Bovati, P. 1994. *Re-Establishing Justice: Legal Terms, Concepts and Procedures in the Hebrew Bible* (trans. M.J. Smith; Sheffield: Sheffield Academic Press).

Gordon, R.P. 1980. 'David's Rise and Saul's Demise: Narrative Analogy in 1 Samuel 24–26', *Tyndale Bulletin* 31: 37–64.

Gravett, S. 2004. 'Reading "rape" in the Hebrew Bible: A consideration of language', *Journal for the Study of the Old Testament* 28, 3: 279–299.

Jackson, B. 1993. 'The Nature of Analogical Argument in Early Jewish Law', *The Jewish Law Annual* 11: 137–168.

[15] For a different approach that bridges this gap, see Bartor (2010).

Levinson, B. 1997. *Deuteronomy and the Hermeneutics of Legal Innovation* (Oxford: Oxford University Press).
Lipton, D. 2007. 'By Royal Appointment: God's influence on influencing God', *The God of Israel* (ed. R.P. Gordon; Cambridge: Cambridge University Press) 73–93.
Tigay, J. 1996. *The JPS Torah Commentary: Deuteronomy* (Philadelphia: JPS).
——. 1999. *Tanakh, The Holy Scriptures* (Philadelphia: JPS).

ARE THERE ANACHRONISMS IN THE BOOKS OF SAMUEL?

Alan Millard

The books of Samuel purport to describe events at the beginning of the history of the kingdom of Israel, which would fall in the decades before and after 1,000 BCE. Yet, according to many scholars, the narratives cannot truly reflect that time because there are anachronisms embedded in them. In a book widely used by students, *Egypt, Canaan and Israel in Ancient Times*, the Egyptologist Donald B. Redford enumerated several apparent mistakes: 'Blatant anachronisms are more numerous than a record with reliable sources should contain: coined money (1 Sam. 13.21), late armor (1 Sam. 17.4–7, 38–39; 25.13), the use of camels (1 Sam. 30.17) and cavalry (distinct from chariotry: 1 Sam. 13.5; 2 Sam. 1.6), iron picks and axes (as though they were common: 2 Sam. 12.31), and sophisticated siege techniques (2 Sam. 20.15)' with a footnote to the last, 'The use of mounds and rams in the southwest, especially by a lesser state, sounds premature' (Redford 1992: 305). The present essay, offered in friendship and admiration to a Christian scholar known for his work on Samuel, among other biblical studies, assesses two of those alleged anachronisms, 'coined money' and 'sophisticated siege techniques'.

Coined Money

Two passages are alleged to refer to coins.

> 1 Sam. 13.21: 'and the charge was a pim for the ploughshares and for the mattocks, and a third of a shekel for sharpening the axes and for setting the goads.'
>
> וְהָיְתָה הַפְּצִירָה פִים לַמַּחֲרֵשֹׁת וְלָאֵתִים וְלִשְׁלֹשׁ קִלְּשׁוֹן וּלְהַקַּרְדֻּמִּים וּלְהַצִּיב הַדָּרְבָן׃
>
> 2 Sam. 18.11–12: 'Joab said to the man who told him, "What, you saw him! Why then did you not strike him there to the ground? I would have been glad to give you ten pieces of silver and a girdle." But the man said to Joab, "Even if I felt in my hand the weight of a thousand pieces of silver, I would not put forth my hand against the king's son."'

וַיֹּאמֶר יוֹאָב לָאִישׁ הַמַּגִּיד לוֹ וְהִנֵּה רָאִיתָ וּמַדּוּעַ לֹא־הִכִּיתוֹ שָׁם אָרְצָה וְעָלַי
לָתֶת לְךָ עֲשָׂרָה כֶסֶף וַחֲגֹרָה אֶחָת׃ וַיֹּאמֶר הָאִישׁ אֶל־יוֹאָב וְלוּא אָנֹכִי שֹׁקֵל
עַל־כַּפַּי אֶלֶף כֶּסֶף לֹא־אֶשְׁלַח יָדִי אֶל־בֶּן־הַמֶּלֶךְ

If these passages do imply coins, they cannot reflect actions in the eleventh or tenth centuries BCE. Coinage began in Anatolia, usually said to be in Lydia, probably a little before 600 BCE, when small lumps of electrum of equal weight were stamped with a design serving as an official or royal guarantee (Schaps 2004). Prior to that, anyone wanting to pay in bullion would weigh the metal, which might be in the form of ingots, or pieces cut off them, or worked metal, plate or jewellery, whole or in fragments. Several examples of hoards of such silver bullion have been unearthed in the Holy Land and adjacent regions, buried during the Iron Age and earlier (Kletter 2003; Thompson 2003). Although late in the third and early in the second millennia BCE Babylonian smiths fashioned long coils of silver from which pieces could be cut to make payment (Powell 1978), nowhere are there any examples of metal lumps of standard weight bearing an official mark of guarantee circulating as money before the late seventh century BCE when Lydian goldsmiths created electrum with a consistent proportion of gold to silver (research by P. Craddock, see Keys 2000). A little earlier in the Near East, certain towns and institutions had standard weights. Examples of bronze weights marked for Hamath are known and the Assyrians reckoned by 'the mina of the land', 'the royal mina' and 'the mina of Carchemish' (Bordreuil 1994: Heltzer 1995; Kwasman 1991) (The oft-quoted passage in which Sennacherib boasts of making large bronze figures, 'I built a form of clay and poured bronze into it, as in making half shekel pieces' (Luckenbill 1927: II, § 391), should not be understood as referring to making half shekel coins. Rather, it parades the ability of the royal smiths to cast enormous bronze figures as easily as very small ones (see Vargyas 2002, in the light of Dalley 1988: 104). Vargyas (2002) observed that scholars who believed the 'aim of the king is to exaggerate his competence in bronze-casting… Regrettably, did not point out parallels for the purportedly metaphoric use of half-shekel' (n. 7). Adequate evidence can now be cited from Neo-Assyrian and other sources that the expression 'half a shekel' indicated a trifling quantity, see CAD *š* 3: 98a.)

In some cases specific amounts of precious metal may have been sealed in small bags. Cuneiform texts from early in the second millennium BCE onwards mention them and sealings and traces of cloth found with a few of the hoards attest them (for references in cuneiform texts, see Silver 2006 and 2004). Joseph's initial generosity to his brothers took that form, a bag of money placed surreptitiously in each man's sack of grain. Here, again, Redford opines 'Genesis 42:35 seems to envisage the meaning "(coined) money" for *keseph*, "silver", kept in a pouch small enough to be stuffed in the mouth of a sack.' Then he adds in a footnote, 'Wenamun 1, 11, refers to silver in a bag, but these were nothing more than small, loose items of a size able to fit in a container and not important enough to be specified' (1992: 426 with n. 156). The passage lists among valuable items stolen from Wenamun, 'a bag of 11 *deben* of silver' (Lichtheim 1997: 90). The *deben* weighed 90–95 grams, so that loss would not have been minor, about 1 kilogram of silver (see Gardiner 1957: 200.) This description of the contents of Wenamun's bag fits well the contents of the hoards and bags attested across the Fertile Crescent and the same description suits Gen. 42.35; coins are not to be envisaged.

Only after the discovery a century ago of small stone weights engraved with the word 'pim' (פִּים), has 1 Sam. 13.21 become intelligible, where the term is used to describe an amount paid. Weighing those stones in conjunction with other weights shows that *pim* (or *payim*) means 'two thirds' of a shekel (Kletter 1998: 20, 78–80). The verse mentions neither shekels nor silver, having only 'the price was two thirds (פִּים)...one third (שְׁלִשׁ)'. Neither does the Hebrew text of the second passage, 2 Sam. 18.11–12, include the word shekel, simply having 'ten of silver' and 'one thousand of silver'. The 'Lucianic' manuscripts insert 'shekels' (σίκλους) which P.K. McCarter would insert into the Hebrew text (1984: 401) and the Septuagint adds it to other passages where it is absent from the Hebrew (e.g. Num. 3.50; 7.85; 2 Sam. 21.16). Yet the ellipsis of a measure is common in many languages, including biblical Hebrew, and so should be understood here (cf. Judg. 16.3; 17.2, 3, 4; 1 Kgs. 10.29 etc., see Gesenius, Kautsch, Cowley 1910: § 134n). It occurs in cuneiform business transactions of the second millennium BCE in the Levant at Alalakh and Ugarit, at the latter site both in Akkadian and in Ugaritic texts (e.g. Wiseman 1953: 13, nos. 66–68, 70–72, 93, 100; Virolleaud 1957: no. 6, lines 13, 14; no. 18, line 21; Nougayrol 1968: no. 27, lines 8, 12ff.; no. 51, lines 9, 12; no. 86, line 16). The shekel being the basic unit of currency across the ancient Near East, there was no need to mention it in every case, it was understood. Larger units, such as the mina and the talent, were named, as in 1 Kgs. 16.24 etc., as were fractions of the shekel, such as the *gera*, apparently one twentieth of the 'holy shekel' (Exod. 30.13, etc.; Kletter 1998: 93–107). The ascription of the weights inscribed in Hebrew with their values, including *pym*, to the time of Hezekiah does not, of course, mean that the shekel and its fractions were not current earlier.

Clearly, payment was made by weighing the silver, as the man expressed to Joab 'even if a thousand shekels were weighed out into my hands…', in the form of bullion that the hoards display. It is for this reason that the verb 'to weigh' (שׁקל) was used in such circumstances (cf. Jer. 32.9). There are no grounds at all for assuming that coinage, which did not appear until the seventh century BCE, was envisaged in either passage in the books of Samuel. To allege that use of fractions implies coined money and so is an anachronism is without any justification at all. Curiously, Redford failed to observe how his assumption about the passages in Samuel contradicted the practice he described in New Kingdom Egypt where 'The use of the word "silver" meaning "money" was established…although prices were usually expressed in weight units of copper, and the terms used indicate units of value rather than coins' (1992: 426 n. 155).

In contrast to the books of Samuel and others relating events during the monarchy, books from the Persian period do have references to coined money, e.g. the drachmas of gold in Ezra 2.69 and Neh. 7.70, 71. 1 Chron. 29.7 reports that the leaders of Israel gave to David 5,000 darics (אֲדַרְכֹנִים) for building the Temple. The gold *daric* and silver *siglos* (= shekel) were coins stamped with the figure of the Persian king usually kneeling as an archer, issued from the reign of Darius I onwards. While the mention of the daric in connection with king David is, strictly, anachronistic, it is intelligible for a book written in the Persian period to use a monetary denomination current at that time (Williamson 1977: 123–126).

Siege Techniques

2 Sam. 20.15 reports, 'And all the men who were with Joab came and besieged him [Sheba] in Abel of Beth-maacah; they cast up a mound against the city, and it stood against the rampart; and they were battering the wall to throw it down' (RSV).

וַיָּבֹאוּ וַיָּצֻרוּ עָלָיו בְּאָבֵלָה בֵּית הַמַּעֲכָה וַיִּשְׁפְּכוּ סֹלְלָה אֶל־הָעִיר וַתַּעֲמֹד בַּחֵל
וְכָל־הָעָם אֲשֶׁר אֶת־יוֹאָב מַשְׁחִיתִם לְהַפִּיל הַחוֹמָה׃

Commentators have seen problems both in the Hebrew of this verse and in the activity portrayed. Robert Gordon wrote, "Standard methods of attacking a besieged city are described. The *mound* was intended to act as a ramp enabling the besieging army to attack the upper section of the wall. A parallel operation to undermine another part of the wall was often undertaken (*cf.* NEB; RSV; NAB, *battering*).” Concerning the next phrase *and it stood against the rampart*, he noted “the exact sense is unclear, witness the ancient versions. NEB (also NAB) transfers the clause to the beginning of the next verse and makes the wise woman the subject: Then a wise woman stood on the rampart…” (Gordon 1986: 295).

The emendation, maintained by NEB, NAB and kept by REB, follows a mainstream opinion adumbrated by Julius Wellhausen (1872: 207), which S.R. Driver clearly stated. He “found the ב before חֵל ‘difficult,” and, after discussing the meaning of ‘rampart’ (חֵל) concluded the phrase rendered by RSV ‘it stood against the rampart’ (וַתַּעֲמֹד בַּחֵל) “must belong, somehow or other, to אִשָּׁה חֲכָמָה in v. 16,” offering two speculative reconstructions, to the effect that the ‘wise woman stood on the wall’ (Driver 1913: 346). Among others, Mauchline (1971: 297) followed Driver in relating ‘it stood against the rampart’ to the wise woman of v. 16, while P.R. Ackroyd explained how “the words were accidentally misplaced” (Ackroyd 1977: 190).

Yet if the subject of the feminine verb ‘it stood’ (וַתַּעֲמֹד) is taken to be the preceding feminine noun, ‘mound’ (סֹלְלָה), which is natural, the need for emendation disappears. H.P. Smith explained ‘it stood with the wall’ as ‘to the same height’ (1904: 371) and H.W. Hertzberg took ‘the mound’ as the subject, rejecting Wellhausen’s proposal as it “would necessitate heavy inroads into the text” (1964: 369). This was accepted by R. de Vaux (de Vaux 1958) and McCarter (1984: 426) and allowed by Ackroyd. In addition, it may be noted, the verb ‘to stand’ is frequently followed by the preposition ‘in, on, at, against’ (Clines 2007: VI. 465). The ‘mound’ evidently enabled the attackers to come close to the town’s defensive wall (‘rampart’ חֵל) to weaken it. The way their action is expressed has also led to the proposal of emendations, partly, as Robert Gordon indicated, because the versions appear to reflect a different wording. S.R. Driver rendered מַשְׁחִיתִם לְהַפִּיל הַחוֹמָה “‘were destroying, to cause the wall to fall,’ i.e. were battering it,” commenting, “the ptcp. here of course implying that the action was only in *process*, and not completed.” He continued, “The expression is, however, a little peculiar” and he was inclined to echo Wellhausen in altering מַשְׁחִיתִם to read מְחַשְּׁבִים (cf. Prov. 24.8; Jon. 1.4) in the light of the Septuagint’s πᾶς ὁ λαὸς ὁ μετὰ ιωαβ ἐνοοῦσαν κατα βαλεῖν τὸ τεῖχος and Targum's מִתְעַשְּׁתִין לְהַבָּלָה שׁוּרָה. More recently, McCarter has "tentatively" taken this course (McCarter 1984: 428).

Considering the circumstances the text describes, it is appropriate to compare the use of the same word when the angels tell Lot 'we are about to destroy this place' (כִּֽי־מַשְׁחִתִ֣ים אֲנַ֔חְנוּ Gen. 19.13) and translate here 'the people were about to destroy the wall,' indicating the situation when the woman called to Joab and so prevented it. There is thus no need to change the text. The Septuagint then spells out the imminent action by expressing the people's intent, 'they proposed to demolish the wall'.

How the wall of Abel was to be breached is the second matter to be elucidated. There were numerous ways for an enemy to bring about the fall of a town in the ancient Near East. Thirty are listed in a recently published Babylonian *tamītu* text, seeking divine answers to problems, which, although preserved in copies made during the first millennium BCE, was apparently composed in the seventeenth century BCE. Overcoming the barrier of a defensive wall was a key one. Among the ways of doing that listed are 'by heaping up earth…by breaching (the walls), by siege tower, by battering-ram, by claw, by ladder, by boring engines, by cutting through the wall, by ramp…' (*ina eperi šapāki…ina nepde ina dimti ina ašipi*[!] *ina ritti ina simmilti ina kalbanāti ina nikis dūri…* Lambert 2007: 26–27, 144–147). The meaning of the Akkadian word rendered 'battering ram', *ašibu, yaši/ubu* or *šub/pû*, is indicated by a passage in the Epic of Gilgamesh (VI 10). A tablet found at Emar on the middle Euphrates, a site destroyed early in the twelfth century BCE, has a complete line partially preserved in slightly different form in later copies: [*y*]*ašubu mu'abbitu dūr abni* 'a battering ram that destroys a wall of stone' (George 2003: 334–335).

Battering rams are mentioned several times in the texts from Mari (*c.* 1750 BCE) and in 'The Siege of Urshu', an Akkadian text from the Hittite area (*c.* 1600 BCE), a king commands, 'Cut a great battering-ram (giš.gud-si-dili) from the mountains of the city of Haššu and let it be put in place! Begin to pile up the earth!' (*ep-ra*[!?]*-am šapāka*, lines 15–17. See Beckman 1995: 24–26; cf. Singer 2008: 50–51). The Sumerian rendered 'battering-ram,' literally a wooden 'bull with one horn,' occurs already in the Ebla tablets of *c.* 2300 BCE (Steinkeller 1987; Lambert 2007: 145). That fits well many of the illustrations of the wheeled vehicles on Assyrian reliefs of the ninth to seventh centuries BCE which modern writers usually designate 'battering-rams'. In most examples, wooden frames covered with wicker shields or leather sheets house a long beam with a head whose purpose was to prise apart and dislodge the masonry of a wall. Reliefs from the palace of Ashurnasirpal at Nimrud, carved in the ninth century BCE, show an axe-like head which might prise the stones or bricks apart, but over a century later, on reliefs from the palaces of Tiglath-pileser III and Sargon II, the beams are tipped with large spear-points. Both might probe to find the weak points of a wall effectively. The best-known examples of the latter type are shown in the attack on Lachish from Sennacherib's palace at Nineveh. The beams were not swung against walls to punch a hole or knock them down as Roman and medieval rams were. Only on the Balawat Gates of Shalmaneser III (858–824 BCE) are there two depictions of a that type of battering ram, wheeled cars with sharp prows, one actually ending in a ram's head, which punch into the walls (for the Assyrian representations, see Yadin 1963: 314–315, with references).

Clearly battering rams of some sort were known in Mesopotamia and beyond from the third millennium BCE onwards, although the heavy battering rams seen on the Neo-Assyrian reliefs may have been an innovation of the time. The Sumerian term could point to a more easily wielded instrument. A recent study has identified as battering-rams wheeled vehicles with protruding poles depicted on cylinder seals of the mid third millennium BCE (Nadali 2009). Some centuries later, Middle Kingdom Egypt supplies another illustration: a wall painting at Beni Hasan, c. 1900 BCE, depicts a group of three soldiers in a shelter prodding the wall of a fortress with a long pole (Yadin 1963: 158–159). A simple device of that sort could surely be improvised anywhere at any time.

In this light, Redford's comment, "The use of mounds and rams in the southwest, especially by a lesser state, sounds premature," may be apt inasmuch as heavy rams in Assyrian style were hardly available to armies in Israel about 1,000 BCE, but that, as shown, is an unnecessary assumption. The English translations of 2 Sam. 20.15, however, seem to have misled readers to assume battering rams were involved. The RV kept AV 'battered' for the participle מַשְׁחִיתִם, the RSV and other translations gave 'battering' (cf. NIV, NKJV). The Contemporary English Version (1995) has become explicit, 'They made a dirt ramp up to the town wall and then started to use a battering ram to knock the wall down.' All these renderings exaggerate the content of the biblical text, for there is no mention of 'rams', only of a 'mound' and a 'rampart'. The participle מַשְׁחִיתִם simply means 'attacking' or 'destroying' without any indication of the means used, which were not limited to battering, as the *tamītu* text reveals.

The assertion about the use of mounds is hard to reconcile with the archaeological evidence for stone walls and earthen banks at sites across the Holy Land, from Neolithic until Roman times. The enormous defences of the Middle Bronze Age, comprising brick walls on stone foundations rising above a plastered glacis are well known. In the early Iron Age the defences may have been less imposing and in some cases the back walls of houses joined to create them. Whatever sort of construction formed the 'rampart' at Abel Beth-Maacah, it would not require any 'sophisticated siege technique' to throw up an earthen bank against it so that the attackers could begin to demolish it with whatever means they had to hand. Commentators have concluded too quickly that the books of Samuel reflect familiar Assyrian-style siege techniques (e.g. Stoebe 1973: 443, 445).

Every ancient document has value as a witness to the past, so to denigrate even one as misrepresenting what it claims to report is a serious matter. It is a charge that surely requires a firm basis, support from other ancient sources and clear argument; a bald assertion should not carry any weight. If no indisputable facts are brought forward, there is a real danger of readers discounting information which could be correct, so diminishing the possiblity of knowledge about an episode in history. Where an anachronism is suspected, it should not be asserted until every possibility that it does not exist has been thoroughly examined and justifiably discarded. While an author may unconsciously reveal his own era by the attitudes or anachronisms he incorporates, there is no reason to suppose authors of any period were unable to write accurately about events or circumstances in generations long past. Repeatedly this has been proved true for Roman and Greek writers, as for Babylonian (see Millard 2002; Potts 2001). Arguments can be brought against all of the alleged 'blatant anachronisms' in Samuel: coined money, late armor, the use of camels and cavalry (distinct from chariotry), iron picks and axes (as though they were common), and sophisticated siege techniques. Some may be stronger than others, but in no case can an anachronism be proved. (The question of 'late armor' has been treated elsewhere, see Millard 2008). This essay has aimed to demonstrate that the writer(s) of Samuel did not imply 'coined money' and 'sophisticated siege techniques' in the Hebrew text and did not create anachronisms.

References

Ackroyd, P.R. 1977. *The Second Book of Samuel* (Cambridge Commentary on the New English Bible. Cambridge: Cambridge University Press).

Beckman, G. 1995. 'The Siege of Uršu Text (*CTH* 7) and Old Hittite Historiography', *Journal of Cuneiform Studies* 47: 23–34.

Bordreuil, P. 1994. 'Métropoles et Métrologies Poliades,' *Semitica* 43–44: 9–20.

Clines, D.J.A. (ed.) *The Dictionary of Classical Hebrew* (Sheffield: Sheffield Phoenix Press).

Dalley, S. 1988. 'Neo-Assyrian Textual Evidence for Bronzeworking Centres,' in *Bronzeworking Centres of Western Asia c. 1000–539 BC.* (ed. J.E. Curtis; London: Kegan Paul).

de Vaux, R. 1958. review of Hertzberg 1956, *Revue biblique* 65: 124–125.

Driver, S.R. 1913. *Notes on the Hebrew Text and the Topography of the Books of Samuel* (Oxford: Clarendon Press, 2nd ed.).

Gardiner, Sir Alan. 1957. *Egyptian Grammar* (London: Oxford University Press, 3rd edn)

George, A.R. 2003. *The Babylonian Gilgamesh Epic* (Oxford: Oxford University Press).

Gesenius, W. 1910. *Gesenius' Hebrew Grammar* (ed. W. Kautzsch, A.E. Cowley; Oxford: Clarendon Press, 2nd edn).

Gordon, R.P. 1986. *I & II Samuel. A Commentary* (Grand Rapids, MI: Zondervan; Exeter: Paternoster Press).

Heltzer, M. 1995. 'Phoenician Trade and Phoenicians in Hamath,' in *Immigration and Emigration within the Ancient Near East. Festschrift E. Lipinski* (eds. K. van Lerberghe and A. Schoors; Leuven: Peeters) 101–105.

Hertzberg, H.W. 1956. *Die Samuelbücher* (Alte Testament deutsch 10.; Göttingen: Vandenhoeck and Ruprecht).

——. 1964. *I and II Samuel. A Commentary* (ETr from 2nd, revised ed., Old Testament Library; London: SCM Press).

Keys, D. 2000. 'Scientists Discover How and Why the First Coins Came to be Invented,' *The Independent*, 19th June.

King P.J. & Stager, L.E. 2001. *Life in Biblical Israel* (Louisville: Westminster John Knox Press).

Kletter, R. 1998. *Economic Keystones. The Weight System of the Kingdom of Judah* (Journal for the Study of the Old Testament Supplement 276; Sheffield: Sheffield Academic Press).

——. 2003. 'Iron Age Hoards of Precious Metals in Palestine—An "Underground Economy"?,' *Levant* 35: 139–152.

Kwasman, T. 1991. *Legal Transactions of the Royal Court of Nineveh*, Part 1 (State Archives of Assyria 6: Helsinki: Helsinki University Press).

Lambert, W.G. 2007. *Babylonian Oracle Questions* (Winona Lake, IN: Eisenbrauns).

Lichtheim, M. 1997. 'The Report of Wenamun' in *The Context of Scripture*, 1 (eds. W.W. Hallo and K. Lawson Younger; Leiden: Brill) 89–93.

Luckenbill, D.D. 1927. *Ancient Records of Assyria and Babylonia* (Chicago: University of Chicago Press).

Mauchline, J. 1971. *1 and 2 Samuel* (New Century Bible; London: Oliphants).

McCarter, P.K. 1984. *II Samuel* (Anchor Bible 9; New York: Doubleday).

Millard, A. 2002. 'History and Legend in Early Babylonia' in *Windows into Old Testament History: Evidence, Argument, and the Crisis of "Biblical Israel"* (eds. V. Philips Long, D.W. Baker, G.J. Wenham; Grand Rapids: Eerdmans).

——. 2008. 'The Armor of Goliath' in *Exploring the* Longue Durée*: Essays in Honor of Lawrence E. Stager* (ed. D. Schloen; Winona Lake: Eisenbrauns) 337–343.

Nadali, D. 2009. 'Representations of Battering Rams and Siege Towers in Early Bronze Age Glyptic Art,' *Historiae* 6: 39–51.

Nougayrol, J. 1968. 'Textes Suméro-accadiens des Archives et Bibliothèques privées d'Ugarit' in *Ugaritica* V (ed. C.F.A. Schaeffer; Paris: Geuthner).
Potts, T. 2001. 'Reading the Sargonic "Historical-Literary" Tradition: Is There a Middle Course? (Thoughts on *The Great Revolt against Naram-Sin*),' in *Historiography in the Cuneiform World, Proceedings of the XLVe Rencontre Assyriologique Internationale*, Pt. 1 (eds. T. Abusch et al.; Bethesda, MD: CDL Press).
Powell, M.A. 1978. 'A Contribution to the History of Money in Mesopotamia prior to the Invention of Coinage', in *Festschrift Lubor Matouš* (eds. B. Hruška, G. Komoróczy; Budapest: Eotvos Lorand Tudomanyegyetem) 211–243.
Redford, D.B. 1992. *Egypt, Canaan and Israel in Ancient Times* (Princeton: Princeton University Press).
Schaps, D.M. 2004. *The Invention of Coinage and the Monetization of Ancient Greece* (Ann Arbor: University of Michigan Press).
Silver, M. 2004. 'Review of David M. Schaps, *The Invention of Coinage and the Monetization of Ancient Greece*,' EH.Net Economic History Services, April 19 2004, URL: http://eh.net/bookreviews/library/0772
——. 2006. '"Coinage Before Coins?": A Further Response to Raz Kletter,' *Levant* 38: 187–189.
Singer, I. 2008. 'On Siege Warfare in Hittite Texts', in *Treasures on Camels' Humps: Historical and Literary Studies from the Ancient Near East Presented to Israel Eph'al* (eds. M. Cogan, D. Kahn; Jerusalem: Hebrew University/Magnes Press) 250–265.
Steinkeller, P. 1987. 'Battering Rams and Siege Engines at Ebla', *N.A.B.U.* no. 27.
Stoebe, H.J. 1973. Das erste Buch Samuelis (Kommentar zum Alten Testament VIII.1; Gütersloh: Mohn).
Thompson, C.M. 2003. 'Sealed Silver in Iron Age Cisjordan and the "Invention" of Coinage,' *Oxford Journal of Archaeology* 22: 67–107.
Vargyas, P. 2002. 'Sennacherib's Alleged Half-Shekel Coins,' *Journal of Near Eastern Studies* 61: 111–115.
Virolleaud, C. 1957. *Texts en cunéiformes alphabétiques des Archives Est, Ouest et Centrales, Palais Royal d'Ugarit* 2 (Paris: Klincksieck).
Wellhausen, J. 1872. *Der Text der Bücher Samuelis* (Göttingen: Vandenhoeck and Ruprecht).
Williamson, H.G.M. 1977. 'Eschatology in Chronicles,' *Tyndale Bulletin* 28: 115–154.
Wiseman, D.J. 1953. *The Alalakh Tablets* (London: British Institute of Archaeology at Ankara).
Yadin, Y. 1963. *The Art of Warfare in Biblical Lands in the Light of Archaeological Discovery* (London: Weidenfeld and Nicholson).

INCONGRUITY IN THE STORY OF SAUL IN 1 SAMUEL 9–15: A METHODOLOGICAL SURVEY

Katharine J. Dell

Scholars have long noted various incongruities in the story of Saul in 1 Samuel 9–15. Incongruities are evident first within the stories themselves, for example the contrast between Saul's looking for lost donkeys and his high calling to become Israel's first king, and second, within the overall theological shape of the text, notably in its juxtaposition of favourable sentiments about Saul's kingship alongside criticism of the institution. Traditional historical-critical scholarship dealt with such incongruities by pointing to different sources in the text or to the work of redactors. Attempts were made to distinguish older stories that might have circulated orally from the concerns of later interest groups as seen in layers of material or sources. More recent scholarship, however, has preferred to read the stories together as a unit and to see incongruities as an expression of irony or tragedy on the part of an author.[1] The text is taken as a whole with little concern about its pre-history. Yet this raises a question: how can these incongruous stories be evaluated both as the accident of oral and source-critical transmission on the one hand, and, on the other, as good, even great, literature containing subtle genres formulated by a clever author or redactor?

The problem is that these curious stories do not really 'work' as 'great literature', in that they appear trivial compared to the high import of the subject matter. The purpose of this article is to look again at these incongruous stories and to provide some kind of evaluation with a particular eye to method. I will ask whether traditional historical-critical readings and recent holistic literary approaches are indeed as incompatible as they at first appear, and I will explore the value of a more 'theological' reading. I shall look at each of the main pericopes of the Saul cycle and discuss different methodological approaches taken by

[1] For example, Exum and Whedbee (1990), whose study of the interplay between the tragic and the comic in the comparable stories of Saul and Samson is of interest.

scholars to these texts. I am particularly pleased to offer this article to Robert Gordon, whom I succeeded in the role of university lecturer in Divinity when he was elevated to the Regius chair of Hebrew. He had regularly lectured on 1 Samuel and this article is a result of my having taken over that mantle and, thanks in large part to his own scholarship (notably Gordon, 1986), discovered afresh this engaging story.

Introducing Saul: Donkeys and Kingship—1 Samuel 9

The beginning of 1 Samuel 9 states that Saul's father was a man of 'wealth'[2] and that Saul was handsome and tall. Saul is introduced while looking for the donkeys of Kish, which had strayed. There an immediate incongruity here—what is the son of a man of wealth doing looking for donkeys? Is this a responsible role for Saul or a trivial task engineered by his father to test his son's abilities? Or is it a deliberate incongruity to highlight the almost comic effect of a boy looking for donkeys being chosen as King of Israel? The quest for donkeys means a long journey before getting to the land of Benjamin and finally to Zuph—the amount of travel and inconvenience seems incongruous with the nature of the task, however valuable a commodity those donkeys were! Saul makes the comment in v. 5 that by now their whereabouts is probably causing concern to his father. Ironically, it is Saul's young companion who now takes the initiative, suggesting that they consult the 'man of God' (אִישׁ־אֱלֹהִים) in the town. They go to meet Samuel on his way to a shrine where the seer is to bless a sacrifice before others eat it (in ironic anticipation of events in 1 Sam. 13, 15 perhaps). This is trivial story—two young men have travelled far and wide to find lost donkeys and decide to go to a seer for help. It does not sound like the beginning of kingship in Israel. In vv. 15–16 there is a kind of flashback—the story relates that only yesterday God had revealed that a man from the land of Benjamin would be sent to Samuel and would be the one to rule Israel. Almost as an aside, the reason is given that on hearing the peoples' pleas for one and because of their suffering, God decided to give Israel a king. When Saul comes into view, Samuel receives a prompt from God that this is the man in question. The incongruity here is striking—Saul has

[2] So NRSV. Overtones of strength and might come in here in the phrase גִּבּוֹר חָיִל.

come to receive wisdom concerning lost donkeys whilst God is telling Samuel of Saul's appointment to the post of king of Israel! On first meeting, Samuel takes control of Saul's life. Having told Saul that the donkeys are found, he hints that a higher purpose is in store for him in a cryptic observation that Israel's desire is fixed on Saul's house and descendants. Saul's response is one of humility—'I am only a Benjaminite' and 'my family is the humblest[3] of all the families of the tribe of Benjamin' (v. 21). There are echoes here of prophetic 'excuses' at the point of calling—such as Jeremiah pleading youth (Jer. 1.6). Saul must have been somewhat taken aback as this is a life-changing moment for him. He is no longer in control of his own destiny. He becomes a pawn in a life predestined by God and executed by Samuel.

In 1 Samuel 10 Samuel anoints Saul with a vial of oil as a sign that God has anointed him ruler (נָגִיד) over Israel. To ratify this promise Saul will meet two men who will tell him that the donkeys have been found, and that his father is indeed worried about him. This takes us straight back to the trivial quest for the donkeys. There is a second sign however—Saul will meet three men on their way to Bethel who will greet him and give him bread. Third, he will meet a band of prophets coming down from a shrine playing music and in a prophetic frenzy. These are signs that God is with him and the frenzy will cause him to be changed. Then Saul is to go to Gilgal to offer sacrifice, waiting seven days before Samuel comes to give him instructions. Samuel already seems to be controlling Saul's life. From wandering around looking for lost donkeys, now his every encounter is meaningful. Furthermore, although God is said to be with Saul, Saul cannot act on his own initiative—he depends upon instructions from Samuel. At this point God gives Saul another heart (לֵב אַחֵר), i.e. a change of mind, suggesting God's control of him. All the signs come to pass, but attention is drawn to the last, the prophetic frenzy which leads people to ask whether the son of Kish is now a prophet. After this Saul returns home and ironically it is his uncle, not his father, who enquires of Saul's activities. Saul keeps the conversation on the level of the trivial, mentioning the donkeys but not the kingship.

An important first question emerges here, in methodological terms, about the categories 'history' and 'story'. Is this material essentially 'history' or is it rather 'story'? If story, it has a historical flavour with

[3] So NRSV. Alternatively 'most insignificant, least' (הַצְּעִרָה).

its references to people, their names, social status and locations—why give such details if there is no historical basis for the events that took place? Of course, stories contain not only facts but also important truths; going beyond the details of place and name, they tell of human reactions and relationships and of interactions with God. Furthermore this material, at least in its final form, seems to be finely crafted, with plot, character development and use of irony, so that 'story' describes best the primary character of the material. There is in addition a key theological dimension. It is interesting that an entirely non-religious event—the lost donkeys—leads on to the central theological point of God's purpose in choosing an unlikely man to be king. This gives the story import within the context of the wider 'history' of the judges, prophets and kings of Israel. The trivial issue of lost donkeys acts as a springboard for more significant events, i.e. God's decision to have a king and his choice of Saul. History may well be enshrined here, but ultimately a theological purpose is the guiding principle of the preservation of the account.

The second methodological question raised is about the origin of this and other stories. Did this pericope originate in oral tradition from early times? This section is pro-Saul, describes his family background and portrays him sympathetically as straightforward and obedient. The original context of such stories could have been an explanation of how this unlikely person came to be king of Israel. This could be evidence of a particular strand of tradition from Saul's home area of Benjamin that saw him as a local hero. If so, how has it arrived in its present position, incorporated into a larger framework? Furthermore, if stories such as this one were originally oral how come they are now so well-crafted in literary terms? How can scholars speak glibly about plot development, irony, structure and deliberate authorial intention? Should they be speaking of inventive authors who reshaped rough stories when they wrote them down, or should they rather speak of clever redactors who pasted the whole together? There is a seeming conflict here between claims that these are old stories, possibly from close to the time of Saul himself, and that the account is a well-crafted literary piece, conceivably shaped a few centuries after the events took place. Although the literary quality of the stories might indicate that they were written from the start, this is countered by evidence of 'sewing together', with duplications and repetitions that clearly indicate the shortcomings of either authors or redactors.

Saul Is Elected—1 Sam. 10.17–27

The next pericope has a very different flavour and was quickly isolated by historical critics as coming from a different layer of the tradition. The most striking aspect is the grudging attitude of God towards having a king, expressed as a rejection of God's own authority. Starting in 10.17, Samuel makes a speech to the people at Mizpah, a historical retrospect about the relationship between God and his people. In v. 19 comes the climax: 'But today you have rejected your God, who saves you from all your calamities and your distresses; and you have said, "No! but set a king (מֶלֶךְ) over us".' The striking incongruity with the previous story is that here Saul is chosen to be king (again) this time by lot. Here, instead of accepting the destiny foisted upon him, he is nowhere to be found as he is hiding amongst the baggage (an irony given his height). Then Samuel announces God's choice of Saul to the people and they accept him, shouting 'Long live the King!' (v. 24). Such incongruities suggest a different layer of tradition, including some duplication of prior material. Once the rights of kings are read out to the people and written down, all is clarified it seems. Everyone goes home, even Saul. However at the end of the section the seed of opposition is sown—some wondered whether Saul was the right person for the role. This sentiment links up with 1 Samuel 8 in which concern is expressed in anti-monarchic mode about the role of king. In contrast to the origin of monarchy as described in 1 Sam. 9.1–10.16, where Samuel anoints Saul at the command of God, now its origin is when the people elect to have a king in direct opposition to God's will. Here Samuel reluctantly consents but holds that a king represents a rebellion against God's purposes for Israel.

Wellhausen (1899) famously isolated two strands or sources in 1 and 2 Samuel, what he called an early stratum (1 Sam. 9.1–10.16; 11; 13; 14)—the most historically reliable and with a favourable view of monarchy—and a late one, from a time well-removed from the events described (enough to be generally devoid of historical value). This source included 1 Sam. 17–27; 12 and 15 and had a suspicious view of the institution of monarchy. Wellhausen saw this view as in keeping with the ideals of the post-exilic community who had no king and found the fulfilment of God's promises in the life of the temple. He noted some Deuteronomic elements in this material but did not build on the idea. Early Samuel studies were heavily influenced by the findings of Pentateuchal criticism and the quest for sources.

Wellhausen saw the original attitude towards the monarchy as having been positive, which changed in time to a negative one, probably due to bad experiences with kings. Source material from both periods was then, he argued, worked together by an author/redactor who realigned material, leading to the contradictions that are apparent.

Saul and the Ammonites—1 Sam. 10.27b–11.15

The next pericope features Saul's defeat of the king of the Ammonites. This is generally regarded as part of the early Saul cycle but is a less sympathetic picture of Saul. Here Saul is infused with God's spirit, but it leads him to an anger that allows him to cut a yoke of oxen in pieces (ironic given his concern for donkeys) and send them out to frighten people into supporting his cause. The message here, in contrast to 10.26, is that it was only fear that made people support Saul. This show of strength on Saul's part seems an overreaction, although it does have the desired effect on the people. Mustering an army allows Saul to challenge the Ammonites and save the inhabitants of Jabesh-Gilead. This victory allows Saul to gain support for his kingship; the people (not Samuel) make him king before God in Gilgal. He is being made king all over again—except that this is presented as a renewal (וּנְחַדֵּשׁ) rather than a first making of a king. How is one to explain the inconsistencies and repetitions here? Although this story may be part of the same historical layer as 1 Sam. 9–10.15 there is still the inconsistency of two different versions of Saul being made king.

This naturally leads, in methodological terms, to a consideration of the oral pre-history of this material.[4] It was noted by scholars that in 1 Samuel stories tend to cluster around key characters, around Saul himself, around Saul and Samuel, Saul and Jonathan, Saul and David. Different narrative cycles of a thematic nature were quickly identified, e.g. the Ark Narrative and the History of David's Rise, and attention (e.g. Rost 1926) tended to be focused on narrative art rather than on oral prehistory, largely because of the literary quality of many of the stories. This raises the oral/literary tension again. However, these stories may have started life as popular legends attracted to particular figures or themes, and this process might explain different versions

[4] According to the form-critical method developed by Gunkel (1933).

of a significant event such as Saul's kingmaking. Weiser believed that disparate traditions about the events of the rise of the monarchy were preserved at different sanctuaries such as Gilgal and Mizpah, and he was opposed to speaking of longer literary sources on Wellhausen's model (Weiser 1962). He saw large and small narrative complexes as brought together, sometimes interwoven, sometimes loosely linked. This shifted scholarly interest into the area of tradition-history, i.e. the question of how smaller units came to form larger ones, and on to issues of redaction.

Samuel's Retrospect—1 Samuel 12

In 1 Samuel 12 there is a different style and subject matter. Samuel has given in to popular demand and provided a king and he is feeling his age. He launches into another historical retrospect, this time concerning the actions of God on behalf of the nation Israel. There follows a reiteration of the people's desire for a king and the requirements of God which contain an element of threat with Deuteronomic overtones: 'If both you and the king who reigns over you will follow the Lord your God, it will be well; but if you will not heed the voice of the Lord but rebel against the commandment of the Lord, then the hand of the Lord will be against you and your king' (vv. 14b–15). The sending of thunder and rain forms a sign of God's wrath at this demand. Samuel has to intercede to reassure the people and remind them of their moral responsibilities. This seems to reflect 10.17–27 in its negative attitude towards the kingship and the emphasis again on the people's demand for a king.

Noth (1957) argued that there are a number of key speeches from the mouths of great men, such as this one by Samuel in 1 Samuel 12, that have a similar style and that have the same structure of retrospect and prospect, with moral demands at the centre of their concern (cf. Joshua 23–24, 1 Kgs. 8.12–61). He found a pattern of apostasy-subjugation-petition-deliverance in each speech. These speeches come at key periods of transition, such as this one from the period of the Judges to that of the Kings, and they have the benefit of hindsight in the way they warn the people about the dire consequences of disobedience. Noth saw these speeches, and the imposing of a style and chronology on the whole of Joshua, Judges, 1 and 2 Samuel and 1 and 2 Kings, as the work of the Deuteronomists, a group working primarily at the Exile when the monarchy was virtually at an end and there was a mood of failure and desolation. A debate about authors or redactors comes in here—were these Deuteronomists simply redactors, cutting and pasting together different stories, or were they authors giving a theological shaping to material, adding to existing material and rewriting to put the whole into a new context? Are they to be identified with the authors of Wellhausen's second layer of an anti-monarchic source? Noth believed that they were (although he spoke of traditions rather than sources), and whilst he saw these compilers as responsible for redactional links and editorial expansions of existing material, he argued that, in authorial mode, they stamped their original viewpoint onto the whole. He believed that the late, anti-monarchical perspective such as found in 1 Sam. 10.17–27 and 12 was the 'free combination' (with theological bias) of the Deuteronomic writer rather than part of an existing tradition. Chapter 12 was the centre of this cycle, with Samuel's farewell address used as a vehicle for the Deuteronomic view of Israel's history of apostasy (cf. also 1 Sam. 13:1; 14:47–51).

Saul, Sacrifice, Disobedience, and the Philistines—1 Sam. 13.2–23

Chapter 13 opens with defeat of the Philistines at Geba, which leads on to a large-scale battle. The Philistines outnumber the Israelites dramatically and this instills fear in the people, who hide. Saul is at Gilgal waiting to offer the sacrifice that is supposed to ensure success in battle. He waits seven days, his support is fading fast, and Samuel does not appear. So Saul offers the burnt offering, on the completion of which Samuel duly arrives and is aghast at what Saul has done. Saul reasonably puts his case that troops were deserting and a large Philistine army was gathering so he thought it best to offer the sacrifice (v. 9). This is his first fatal step—ironically, the first time he takes the initiative he does something wrong. In an incongruous way the punishment seems to outweigh the crime. Samuel tells Saul that this action has cost him the kingship for his descendants and that God has found another candidate. This passage shows the interplay between Saul and Samuel. Although Saul has been made king he is still beholden to Samuel who has the real knowledge of the will of God. Chapter 13 is thought to be part of the earliest Saul cycle, but may not have originally included the rejection of Saul in 1 Sam. 13.7b–15—if added later that would account for the incongruity here. The story of the early sacrifice is relatively trivial compared to the wrath and judgement that ensue from Samuel's mouth. This leads to the question where these verses came from. They could be Deuteronomic, as Noth maintained, but Weiser 1962 isolated a separate strand from the Deuteronomic material which he called the prophetic strand and assigned these verses to it. He found a middle stratum in the text, notably a pro-prophetic source (cf. also McCarter 1980). Weiser argued that a prophetic perspective, suspicious of the institution of the monarchy, was an ancient stream of tradition that existed alongside other traditions more favourable to kingship.[5] This layer deals primarily with Samuel and Saul and may account for the placing of material about Samuel before the story of Saul begins (1 Sam. 1–3; 7), which seems to relativize the importance of Saul. Its purpose is to show the effectiveness of prophetic leadership in the person of Samuel (cf. 1 Sam. 12:1–4), an ideal threatened by the people's demand for a king. The original Saul cycle then could have been reworked by the inclusion of other stories that centre on Samuel and Saul, in order to present the changing role of prophecy in the light of kingship. The prophet is still the spokesman of God, but no longer a political figurehead. The layer is concerned to redefine the prophetic role, but it also wishes to show that the advent of kingship in Israel was a concession to the people, dependent on God's pleasure.

Saul and Jonathan—1 Samuel 14

In chapter 14 the story of the Philistine wars continues. Saul's son Jonathan goes over to the Philistine garrison and gets embroiled in a conflict. Saul knows nothing of this and only discovers he is missing when a role call is made. Events overtake him and his army has to fight to gain a victory. There is then a rather curious story that presents Saul unfavourably. Saul had made an oath that anyone who ate before the evening of the battle being won would be cursed. Because Jonathan knew nothing of the oath, he ate some honey for refreshment. As it is, the troops have taken all the spoil from the battle and eaten cattle, including its blood (which was forbidden). Saul is angry and forces the troops to offer the animals in sacrifice. In fighting mode, he urges a further raid on the Philistines at night, but on asking God's advice

[5] Cf. Fohrer (1970) who speaks of a supplementary stratum and Birch (1976) who speaks of a pre-Deuteronomic edition stemming from prophetic circles.

receives no answer. He realizes that this silence from God is a result of his oath having been broken and so wants to find the culprit. In ironic anticipation of what is to come, Saul rashly swears that even if it is Jonathan who has broken it, he shall die. No one owns up, lots are cast and they fall on Jonathan. Saul fulfils his oath and says to Jonathan that he will have to die, but the people intercede (v. 45). This is a challenge to Saul's authority—just as the people put him on the throne, so they decide to save Jonathan. Saul does not seem to be in charge and once again an incongruous story emerges—God's lack of response to Saul and then Saul's capitulation under pressure from the people stand in contrast to the rather trivial tale about eating honey.

An interest in the Saul narrative as a whole has been a keynote of certain scholars e.g. Good (1965) who, eschewing traditional literary-critical ideas, argues for a narrator who has used techniques of suspense and tragic irony. He sees (p. 58) the theme of the work as the 'theological ambiguity of the establishment of a monarchy and Saul's failure to fit the bill'. He regards (p. 59) the story as revolving around 'those dramatic ironies in which Saul's genuine greatness is played off against his fatal weakness and in which kingship's demands for greatness are played off against the ambiguities of kingship'. He draws out ironies and incongruities in the stories, for example he sees Saul's greatest weakness being that he is 'little in his own eyes' (קָטֹ֤ן אַתָּה֙ בְּעֵינֶ֔יךָ) as Samuel says in 15.17. Twice (9.2; 10.23) Saul is said to stand head and shoulders above the rest of the people and is thus large in everyone else's eyes. But, ironically, he deprecates himself throughout the story, for example, when Samuel tells Saul of his election, Saul questions him in disbelief (9.21); he also hides from his uncle the fact that he has been anointed (10.14). At Saul's election before the people (his moment of glory) he hides in the baggage (10.22). Saul's other weakness (ch. 14) is that he is vain in courting popular acclamation. He is the choice of the people and is concerned with his public image to the detriment of fulfilling God's demands. He in turn chooses the people over God, leading ultimately to his fall from favour.

Saul, Samuel, and God—1 Samuel 15

Here the Samuel/Saul interchange features with Samuel instructing Saul to punish the Amalekites. Saul does as he is told and defeats the Amalekites, sparing the Kenites, King Agag and some animals. But this goes against God's command. God expresses his regret to Samuel that he made Saul king because he does not show strict obedience (v. 10). Saul goes to Carmel to set up a monument in his own honour, an indication of his vanity. Saul seems naively to think that he is obeying God—he tells Samuel just that and orders that the animals are to be sacrificed to God. But Samuel accuses Saul of not heeding God's commands and utters a speech about obedience being more important than sacrifice (ironic in the light of the fuss made over Saul's hastiness at the last sacrifice). Here we have another incongruity—Samuel comes down very heavily on Saul for this relatively minor misjudgement. Saul accepts Samuel's criticism, owns up to listening to the people rather than to God and asks for forgiveness, but Samuel harshly expresses God's rejection of Saul. Saul catches the hem of Samuel's robe as he departs and tears it (v. 27), and this is the opening for Samuel to tell him that God has torn the kingdom from him and given it to another (cf. the tearing of Saul's robe by David in ch. 24, of which this is an ironic anticipation). Saul admits his sin but then asks Samuel to honour him (כַּבְּדֵנִי) before the elders of his people (again, a concern for his popular status) which Samuel does. At this point Samuel seems to take over Saul's leadership role when he asks for Agag and hews him in pieces. Samuel and Saul do not meet again, and it is reiterated that God regretted making Saul king over Israel. Samuel is however sorry for Saul—even he does not entirely agree with God's harsh judgement upon him. In chapter 15 then an anti-monarchical mode dominates, and the issue of prophetic authority is to the fore. There is incongruity in the level of punishment meted out to Saul and there is a sense of predestination in the story in that nothing Saul can do will change God's decision that he was a bad choice for king. This is the beginning of the downhill slope that leads to David's rise and Saul's demise.

Interesting work has been done on the Saul cycle in connection with the genre of tragedy, notably by Gunn (1980, 1981) and Humphreys (1978, 1980, 1982, 1985 [chapter 2]). Gunn emphasizes the power of fate in the story of Saul. He argues that fate equals God and that Samuel is fate's spokesman. He sees the overall narrative theme of the Saul narrative as being about kingship—the people want a king, God grants them their wish and chooses one for them. The king however is subsequently rejected by God, and, after a struggle, a new and acceptable king is established. The element of fate is brought in, he argues, when the dice seem to be loaded against Saul, when obstacles are placed in his path and demands made on him are greater than those made on David (e.g. ch. 14). Gunn asks why David is a favourite and Saul a victim, and suggests that the story was told to highlight the inappropriateness of the people's demand for a king, versus God's choice. Although God seems to respond to the peoples' cry, God in fact demonstrates to the people, through Saul, the weakness of human kingship. A king wholly chosen by God, on the other hand, is the recipient of God's benevolence. Gunn argues that the conclusion is that good and evil are equally at God's disposal—fate can be cruel or kind and there is no moral order to which human beings can appeal. Although Saul's character is flawed he is not an evil man—he is ultimately a victim of fate (i.e. God's purposes) and God's designs are greater than human comprehension. Not all scholars agree with Gunn's emphasis on fate, and many see much of the fault as lying on Saul's side. Although one could say that his mistakes seem trivial, is Saul the tool of forces beyond his control here? Or is he in control but just acting unwisely or overanxiously, trying to impress God and the people, but failing in his efforts? Is fate then simply the will of God or is it a combination of Saul's own character and actions and the will of God? Good (1965) favours the latter—he sees Saul as a tragic figure but sees the tragedy being played out through the character of Saul and his interaction with others as well as through God's dark designs. It is in this context that he draws attention to the irony in particular aspects of Saul's character.

Humphreys (1980) sets out Saul's qualifications for the tragic role—he is of noble birth and heroic stature, he is an appealing figure whose potential is realized when he becomes king, but all the time the real power of speaking for God lies with Samuel. Saul is a man caught at a point of transition between different forms of leadership. He acts hastily and yet he is a victim of events in that God and Samuel turn against him in a manner that his actions have not justified. A great man is thus overtaken by events—his character disintegrates as he is driven into jealousy, virtual madness and despair. This too is as a result of God's action in sending an evil spirit upon him (16.14). Saul is eager to please, but meets with a sharp rebuff, finding himself abandoned by God, his authority withheld by Samuel. Yet, ironically, Saul seeks Samuel and God to the end, even raising Samuel from the dead to consult him (1 Sam. 28). He also finds himself in a position of tension in relation to David that will finally lead to his downfall (1 Sam. 16–31). Humphrey's analysis manages to combine an interest in narrative criticism and genre with a developmental approach. Humphreys sees later groups as first recasting the tragic hero into a villain and God into a strict figure and, second, turning Saul into a foil for David with God as a doting father figure. He thus presents us with an alternative reconstruction of the development of the text based on the thematic concerns of the tragedy of Saul. He divides 1 Samuel 9–31 into three Acts, each with three narrative structures. First the figure of Samuel introduces each Act and the future is announced (9.3–10.16; 10.17–11.15; 13–14). Second, there is a constructive phase in which Saul is successful (15.1–16.13; 16.14–19.10; 19.11–28.2) and third, there is a destructive phase in which gains made are lost and Saul's character disintegrates (28.3–25; 29–31). Humphreys arguably cuts across traditional historical-critical findings in the service of a thematic development, but in fact he shows that the two can be successfully combined.

This raises an interesting question about method. Should readers ignore traditional historical-critical categories and rather focus on literary categories and issues of genre when reading the Saul cycle? Or can the two be combined, as Humphreys has done? Are synchronic and diachronic readings essentially incompatible? Are scholars such as Brueggemann (1989, 1990), who emphasizes beginnings and endings in the final form of the text, ignoring the layering of the text in the service of a unified reading? I suggest that the incongruities in the text do not allow us simply to read it 'flat' and ignore the question of layers. The evidence contradicts readings which overtly disclaim the evidence from historical-critical developmental models. In particular, the pro-monarchic and anti-monarchic sentiments isolated by Wellhausen are strikingly in tension in this text. Moreover, some kind of pro-prophetic and Deuteronomic reworking makes good sense of the incongruities in the text and accounts for some interesting juxtapositions. The issue is whether the subtleties of the text can be appreciated whilst still acknowledging its accreted nature.

The striking factor about the stories in the Saul cycle is that they are actually quite trivial compared to the underlying theological themes being played out of Saul's relationship to God, his suitability for kingship, and the punishment inflicted on him for deeds committed. Our sympathy goes out to Saul because he makes simple mistakes and yet is victimized as a result of them. It is also a strange collection of stories—if you were preserving stories about a king, would this necessarily be your selection? This is perhaps where the oral tradents come in. Stories came down in oral tradition that were positive about Saul as the first king in Israel. Because of the 'trivial' nature of the stories, however, some incongruity entered at the very first level of their initial authorial shaping and then at the second and subsequent levels of the further shaping by different interest groups i.e. the pro-prophetic and Deuteronomic writers. These incongruities then cannot be fully understood without a diachronic reading that takes into account the development of the text, and yet it is interesting that a synchronic reading, in picking up these incongruities, is able to incorporate them into the sense of an overall authorial intention and tragic genre.

Turning to the validity of a theological reading of the Saul cycle. It cannot be denied that it is God who stands at the heart of the tragedy of Saul and at the centre of the enigma of the divine approval of kingship. The actions of the characters are motivated theologically and, at the end of the day, this is literature that witnesses to the action of the God in the lives of the Israelite people. Theological standpoints, whether they are seen in a developmental line or in a final form context, are arguably the most important aspects of the text. The central theological issue in the Saul cycle turns on the relationship between God and the king—in this case Saul. Saul is portrayed as repeatedly disobedient, and as incurring judgement, and yet his disobedience is trivialized by the nature of the incidents. The portrayal of God in 1 Samuel contains some sympathetic elements, the suggestion, for example, that God was hurt by the people's demand for a king and his fallibility in changing his mind. However, the dominant portrayal of God here is somewhat arbitrary and over-judgemental. God's will is absolute and humans must respond in appropriate ways, which Saul ultimately does not do. This story of Saul who suffers rejection by God can seen as an airing of the broader theme of theodicy—the relationship between God and humanity in the light of human suffering at the hand of a seemingly hostile or indifferent God (cf. the picture of God contained in the book of Job).[6]

It is fruitful then to read the Saul narrative on two levels—the stories themselves and the results of critical study. Rather than seeing all incongruities in literary terms as the intention of a clever author, it is more fruitful to see the incongruous juxtapositions of material

[6] See K.J. Dell (2010).

as the result of layering of the text over the centuries. This layering has in turn however contributed even more to the incongruities that are found when the text is read in a synchronic fashion with literary and theological concerns at the forefront of concern. I have argued then that the synchronic and the diachronic can be usefully held together here, as Humphreys does, and that interpretation of the Saul cycle suffers if the value of different methodological stances is not recognized.

References

Birch, B.C. 1976. *The Rise of the Israelite Monarchy: The Growth and Development of I Samuel 7-15* (SBL Diss. Series 27, Missoula: Scholars Press).

Brueggemann, W. 1989. 'Narrative Intentionality in I Samuel 29', *Journal for the Study of the Old Testament* 43: 21–35.

——. 1990 'I Samuel 1: the sense of a beginning', *Zeitschrift für die Alttestamentliche Wissenschaft* 102: 33–48.

Dell, K.J. 2010. 'Does God behave ethically in the book of Job?' in *Ethical and Unethical Behaviour in the Old Testament* (ed. K.J. Dell; Library of Hebrew Bible/Old Testament Studies, 528; London: Continuum) 170–186.

Exum, C. and J. Whedbee 1990. 'Isaac, Samson and Saul: Reflections on the comic and tragic visions', in *On Humour and the Comic in the Hebrew Bible* (ed. Y.T. Radday and A. Brenner, Journal for the Study of the Old Testament Supplement, 92; Sheffield: Almond Press) 117–159.

Fohrer, G. 1970. *Introduction to the Old Testament* (London: SPCK) (German orig.: 1968).

Good, E.M. 1965. 'Saul: The Tragedy of Greatness' in *Irony in the Old Testament* (Philadelphia: Westminster Press) 56–80.

Gordon, R. 1986. *I and II Samuel* (Exeter: Paternoster).

Gunkel, H. 1933. *Einleitung in die Psalmen: Die Gattungen der religiösen Lyrik Israels* (Göttingen: Vandenhoeck & Ruprecht).

Gunn, D.M. 1980. *The Fate of King Saul: An Interpretation of a Biblical Story* (Journal for the Study of the Old Testament Supplement, 14; Sheffield: JSOT Press).

——. 1981. 'A Man Given over to Trouble' in *Images of Man and God: Old Testament Short Stories in Literary Focus* (ed. B.O. Long, Bible and Literature, Series 1; Sheffield: Almond Press) 89–112.

Humphreys, W.L. 1978. 'The Tragedy of King Saul: A Study of the Structure of 1 Samuel 9-31', *Journal for the Study of the Old Testament* 6: 18–27.

——. 1980. 'The Rise and Fall of King Saul: A study of an Ancient Narrative Stratum in 1 Samuel', *Journal for the Study of the Old Testament* 18: 74–90.

——. 1982. 'From Tragic Hero to Villain: A Study of the Figure of Saul and the Development of 1 Samuel', *Journal for the Study of the Old Testament* 22: 95–117.

——. 1985. *The Tragic Vision and the Hebrew Tradition* (Philadelphia: Fortress Press).

McCarter Jr., P.K. 1980. *I Samuel* (Anchor Bible Commentaries, 8; Garden City, New York: Doubleday).

Noth, M. 1957. *Überlieferungsgeschichtliche Studien I* (2nd edn., Tübingen: Max Niemeyer Verlag).

Rost, L. 1926. *Die Überlieferung von der Thronnachfolge Davids* (Beiträge zur Wissenschaft vom Alten und Neuen Testament, 3.6; Stuttgart: Kohlhammer).

Weiser, A. 1962. *Samuel. Seine geschichtliche Aufgabe und religiöse Bedeutung. Traditionsgeschichtliche Untersuchungen zu 1. Samuel 7–12* (Forschungen zur Religion und Literatur des Alten and Neuen Testaments, 81, Göttingen: Vandenhoeck & Ruprecht).

Wellhausen, J. 1899. *Die Composition des Hexateuchs und der historischen Bücher des alten Testaments* (3rd edn., Berlin: B. Reimar).

THE FRIENDSHIP OF JONATHAN AND DAVID

Graham Davies

This is the second of two essays which I have written on the ethics of friendship in the Old Testament, both exploratory rather than definitive. The first dealt with matters of Hebrew terminology and the evidence of the wisdom literature (including Ben Sira), along with some ancient Near Eastern parallels.[1] But, as with other ethical topics within the Old Testament and beyond, the ethics of friendship are displayed in narrative texts as well as in proverbial and other 'instruction' literature. This need not imply that the narratives are primarily didactic in character: the values cherished in a society may emerge naturally in the stories which are told within it. We shall consider here both the biblical accounts of the friendship of Jonathan and David and (more briefly) some non-biblical narratives with a similar theme.

David's own description (if it is his) of his friendship with Jonathan is well known:

> I am distressed for you, my brother Jonathan, very delightful you were to me. Your friendship to me was wonderful, more than the love of women (2 Sam. 1.26).[2]

David of course owed his life to Jonathan, as 1 Samuel 20 in particular spells out at length. The expressions of their friendship are numerous throughout chapters 18–23 (see especially 18.1–4; 19.1–7; 20.1–42; 23.15–18) and episodes which derive from it continue to occur in 2 Samuel (4.4; 9.1–13; 16.1–4; 19.25–31; 21.7). In the former case it is notable that most of the 'one-way' phrases have Jonathan as the subject. True, they together make a covenant, three times (1 Sam. 18.3, 20.16, 23.18), but in the first two cases Jonathan 'makes a covenant with David' (cf. also 20.8). The expressions of friendship are usually Jonathan's: 18.1, 3; 19.1; 20.3, 17, 30. Only 20.41 suggests equality, even that David was the more grieved by the separation. Otherwise, if there is an exemplary

[1] Davies (2010). The general bibliography cited there (though there was not much to cite) is also of relevance to the present study.

[2] Both 'friendship' and 'love' here render Heb. אַהֲבָה, showing the range of its meaning.

friend, it is Jonathan rather than David. There are, of course, unusual features here, including the sworn covenant 'by the Lord' between the two of them (20.8), which gives the friendship a divine guarantor, though this is scarcely the same as the bond in 'the fear of the Lord' that we find in Ben Sira (Sir. 6.16–17; 40.18–27: see Davies 2010: 144–145): it represents the closeness and security of the relationship rather than a spiritual dimension within it. On the other hand, in 2 Samuel after Jonathan's death it is actions of David which naturally come to the fore.

Before proceeding further it needs to be asked whether the passages involved can be given a setting or settings in the earlier accounts (whether oral or written) which most probably underlie the canonical narrative in 1–2 Samuel. The denial of such underlying sources by J. Van Seters (1983: Ch. 8) overlooks a series of duplications in 1 Samuel and some basic differences of outlook between different sections of the narrative, which have led most scholars to envisage as many as four such sources, as well as some other traditions which were probably transmitted independently (e.g. Smith 1904: xv–xxix; McCarter 1980: 23–30; 1984: 4–19; Gordon 1984: 12 and passim; Na'aman 1996; Dietrich 1997: 202–24, 229–57). Van Seters's attribution of most of the narrative text to the Deuteronomistic Historian or a writer dependent on him is most implausible in view of the almost total absence of distinctively Deuteronomistic motifs.

The double account of Saul's death in battle and its aftermath in 1 Samuel 31 and 2 Samuel 1 and the presence in 1 Sam. 28.3–25 of another passage (alongside ch. 31) which practically ignores David (there is a passing reference to him in v. 17) makes it clear that the 'story of Saul' (SS), as might be expected, continued to the end of Saul's life and therefore overlapped with the 'story of David's Rise' (SDR). This provides a ready explanation for the duplications of narrative motifs earlier in 1 Samuel (e.g. David's first encounter with Saul [1 Sam. 16.14–23 vs. 17.55–58] and the occasions where David spares Saul's life [1 Sam. 24 vs. 26]), and these duplicate narratives confirm that, again as one might expect, the later part of the Saul story (which presumably began at 1 Sam. 9.1) included some references to David. It is therefore possible, and even likely, that the friendship of Jonathan and David was described here as well as in the 'story of David's Rise', perhaps with some distinct characteristics. In fact the passages from chapters 18–23 referred to above do display some inconsistency and repetitiveness which suggest the combination of different accounts here. In 20.1–4 (cf. v. 9) Jonathan's protestation that he knows nothing of any intention of Saul to kill David is inconsistent with the account of his conversation with Saul in 19.1–6, and that conversation duplicates the one which Jonathan proposes to have with Saul according to 20.12–13 and actually conducts in vv. 27–34. On the other hand 20.1 does not look like the beginning of David's friendship with Jonathan and v. 8 explicitly refers to an earlier agreement (a בְּרִית יהוה indeed) between them. This makes it likely that 20.1–4 was preceded (not necessarily immediately) by 18.1–4 (cf. the בְּרִית in v. 3), whereas 19.1–7 comes from a different account. 23.15–18 probably also belongs to this latter account, as it introduces the idea of making a covenant (בְּרִית: v. 18) as something new, as Jonathan and David part in the wilderness of Ziph. It is not possible here to present a full analysis of the later chapters of 1 Samuel, but there is good reason to attribute 1 Sam. 18.1–4 and most of ch. 20 to SDR and 19.1–7 and 23. 15–18 to SS. McCarter's view that ch. 20 is not all from one hand is persuasive and it may well be, as he suggests (1980: 344), that vv. 11–17, 23, 40–42 are secondary, perhaps from the compiler of 1–2 Samuel. 2 Samuel 1, with David as its central character, presumably belongs to SDR. The other references to Jonathan in 2 Samuel occur chiefly in the context of the so-called 'Court History of David': the exceptions are 4.4, an awkward digression which prepares the way for the later references to Jonathan's son Mephibosheth (as he is called here), and 21.7, 12–14, which refer both to Mephibosheth and to the reburial of Saul and Jonathan's bones in the tomb of Saul's father Kish and are parts of a now isolated narrative which might once (but might not) have been part of one of the larger works that underlie 1 and 2 Samuel.

It follows from this analysis, first, that the friendship of Jonathan and David was referred to in no less than three of the main narrative sources of Samuel, as well as in the isolated account in 2 Sam. 21.1–14. The memory of this at first sight remarkable relationship was evidently cherished, perhaps precisely because it transcended both dynastic rivalries and the tribal differences which were characteristic of both the time and the tradition. Secondly, the initiative lies very much with Jonathan, no doubt because of his superior status as the son of the king. This is especially apparent in the relatively brief account in the Saul story, which repeatedly emphasises Jonathan's royal status (19.1–4; 23.16–17). But the same expressions also underline the fact that Jonathan is giving the demands of friendship a higher priority than family ties.[3] Thirdly, the language in which the relationship is described varies noticeably from one account to another. In the Saul story Jonathan takes '(great) delight' in David (1 Sam. 19.1: חָפֵץ), an expression also used, disingenuously, by Saul of his own regard for David in 18.22 (and later of supporters of David's general Joab in 2 Sam. 20.11). It can have a sexual sense (e.g. Gen. 34.19), but it need not do so and 1 Sam. 23.17 suggests that for the Saul story at least Jonathan's attitude is primarily political in character. In the SDR this is not so clear, as the recurrent references to 'love' suggest, at least *prima facie*, an intimate personal relationship (18.1, 3; 20.17; 2 Sam. 1.23). A political interpretation has been proposed here too, on the basis of the use of such language elsewhere in the ancient Near East and also in the Old Testament itself (1 Kgs. 5.15). J.A. Thompson has argued that this is implied by other uses of אָהֵב in the narrative (1 Sam. 18.22, 28: cf. 16.21 and 18.16 in what are probably elements of the Saul story) and the political implications of other features in it, such as the gift of armour (18.4: compare Saul's action in 17.38), references to a covenant (or 'treaty': 18.3; 20.8; and 23.18 [but that is from SS]) between Jonathan and David and some other passages (20.30–31; 22.7–8) (1974; citing Moran 1963). However, Thompson seems to overlook the fact that 18.28 (like v. 20) refers to Michal's love for David, where a sexual interpretation is much more likely, and that 20.30–31 and 22.7–8 represent Saul's (mis?)perception of the relationship, which may not be the same as that of the narrator. It is true that the sharing of armour could have political implications, but this is hardly necessary, as the fateful case of Achilleus and Patroclus in *Iliad* 16 (see further below) shows: it may simply be an expression of intimacy between warriors.[4] There remain the references to a covenant between Jonathan and David, but these are not decisive. Even if some uses of 'love' elsewhere in 1 Samuel (16.21; 18.16, 22) have a political connotation (and that is not certain), it is not necessarily what is meant—or all that is meant—in relation to Jonathan.[5]

---

[3] For Clements (1992: 14–27) such an elevation of friendship over the family is a central element of the teaching of Proverbs and a sign of an important social development.

[4] Or, to follow the attractive interpretation of the Iliad episode in Sinos (1980: 42–45), the substitution of one character for the other.

[5] Konstan (1997), passim, is an example of a greater readiness than in the past to recognise a personal dimension to ancient friendship. In Hebrew the technical term for a political ally seems to be רֵעֶה: see Davies (2010: 138, n. 10).

But if the 'friendship' is one of personal intimacy, may it (as Michal's love presumably was) perhaps have been a sexual relationship? This view was worked out at some length by Tom Horner in his book *Jonathan Loved David: Homosexuality in Biblical Times* (1978: Ch. 1–2).[6] According to Horner homosexuality was widespread and generally accepted in the ancient Near East, as it was in ancient Greece, and found literary expression in the relationship of Gilgamesh and Enkidu in the *Epic of Gilgamesh*. This exhibits the 'heroic or noble kind of love' (p. 20) which, for Horner, was also exhibited by David and Jonathan in passages such as 1 Sam. 18.1 and 2 Sam. 1.26.[7] Discussion of this issue has become far too complex for justice to be done to it here. There remains much uncertainty and dispute both about ancient practices, their prevalence and contemporary evaluation of them and about what can be read out of (or into) specific biblical passages. Suffice it to say that one passage which Horner regarded as clear evidence for a sexual relationship is far from being so. This is Saul's outburst in 1 Sam. 20.30–31, which according to Horner shows that Saul 'knows perfectly well what kind of relationship existed between his son and son-in-law' (p. 32: see the whole discussion of these verses on pp. 31–33). Horner's treatment of 20.30–31 as an accusation of a homosexual relationship was at the time novel, as a glance at the commentaries will show, but also mistaken, as detailed examination proves. The description of Jonathan's mother as a 'perverse rebellious woman' (נַעֲוַת הַמַּרְדּוּת) in MT is commonly emended, in the light of LXX and now the Hebrew text in 4QSam[b] (cf. *DJD* XVII, 230, 232–33), to 'a rebellious servant-girl' (נערת המרדות: so S.R. Driver, McCarter and Klein; mentioned as an 'interesting reading' but apparently not adopted in Gordon 1986: 348 n. 61): this identifies Jonathan's offence from the outset even more clearly as conspiracy rather than any sexual misdemeanour. Even the wording of MT carries none of the connotations which 'perverse' may suggest to a modern reader. Secondly, while Horner is right to draw attention to the merits of the LXX alternative to 'choose' of MT (Heb. בֹּחֵר) and to Driver's support for the reading חָבֵר, 'are a companion

[6] The remainder of the book is concerned with other parts of the Old and New Testaments.

[7] See more recently, e.g., Ackerman (2005: ch. 7) and Nardelli (2007: 26–63), with references to other discussions. On the other hand R. Alter (1999: 200) refers to 'repeated, unconvincing attempts to read a homoerotic implication into' 2 Sam. 1.26; cf. Zehnder (1998) and Nissinen (1999).

of' (1913: 171: he is followed by McCarter and Klein ad loc., though unfortunately 4QSam[b] is not extant for the latter part of the verse), this word carries no sexual implications, as an examination of its other occurrences will show. It and its cognates are several times used of a political or military alliance (cf. Judg. 20.11), which fits the context of Saul's accusation well (cf. McCarter 1980: 339, 344: 'in league with', 'conspiracy'; Klein 1983: 209, 'a comrade or ally of David'). Finally, the sense to be given to 'your shame' (לְבָשְׁתְּךָ) and 'the shame of your mother's nakedness' (וּלְבֹשֶׁת עֶרְוַת אִמֶּךָ) is to be determined from the preceding preposition לְ, 'to', and the explanation given in v. 31: it refers to the future consequences of Jonathan's behaviour (the loss of succession to the throne), not to the character of that behaviour. Horner's claim (p. 32) that 'Both "shame" and "nakedness"—the next key word in Saul's outburst—are associated in the mainstream of Israelite patriarchal society with sex, as is illustrated by the Garden of Eden story and in numerous other passages' is quite wrong in the case of 'shame', which hardly ever refers to sexual shame in Hebrew, but rather to 'loss of honour' in a much more general sense, and very misleading in the case of 'nakedness', which (whatever it signifies in the special case of the Eden narrative) must here refer to Jonathan's birth and not to his or anyone else's sexual activity. The expression is a typically vivid way of saying that Jonathan is and will be a disgrace to the mother who bore him, nothing more.

In any case there is a continuation of the story of the friendship of Jonathan and David after the former's death, in the account of David's dealings with Jonathan's crippled son Mephibosheth (or Meribaal, as he seems originally to have been called: 1 Chron. 8.34; 9.40). Apart from the parentheses in 2 Sam. 4.4 and 21.7, these all occur in the Succession Narrative/Court History. Only the first passage, 2 Sam. 9.1–13, refers to Jonathan as Mephibosheth's father (v. 3) and as the reason for David's kindness to him (vv. 1, 7), and even in this passage, as later, Mephibosheth is more often called a 'descendant (literally 'son', בֵּן) of Saul (vv. 7, 9, 10; cf. 16.3, 19.25 and the other references to Saul and his house in these contexts). Still here it is clear that David proposes to act out of חֶסֶד, 'kindness, loyalty', to his deceased friend Jonathan. He does so again in 21.7, where 'the oath of the Lord' is mentioned (שְׁבֻעַת יְהוָה: cf. especially 1 Sam. 20.42, but also 20.8 and 23.18 [בְּרִית, 'covenant']) and Mephibosheth is specifically exempted from the treatment meted out to other descendants of Saul. Such kindness to the son and family of a friend is not specifically commended in Proverbs (though 27.10b comes close to it), and may therefore have been regarded as going beyond what could normally be expected. The two further episodes in which Mephibosheth appears illustrate the complications which can arise when friendship is bestowed and, perhaps, David's wisdom (or lack of it) in dealing with them in the political crisis which followed (cf. 2 Sam. 14.17, 20).[8] In 2 Sam. 16.1–4 David cancels his agreement with Mephibosheth because of reported disloyalty on the latter's part, but in 19.25–31 he partly restores it when they meet face to face, while apparently still giving weight to his informant Ziba's actual recent support (for which see 19.18 as well as 16.1–4). All this recalls the advice given in Proverbs and especially Ben Sira about the need not to be too trusting of one's friends.

To conclude, we may say that in the Saul Story Jonathan's friendship with David is primarily seen as giving David unexpected political security, whereas in the Story of David's Rise it is portrayed more as an intimate personal relationship, comparable but superior to those which David enjoys with women (2 Sam. 1.26). In the Court History and 2 Samuel 21, on the other hand, the emphasis falls on David's responsibilities to the son of his friend and the complications which such responsibilities can raise.

Stories of friendship, like sayings about friendship, also occur in ancient literature outside the Old Testament. The famous examples are the story of the friendship of Gilgamesh and Enkidu (in the *Epic of Gilgamesh*) and the episodes about Achilleus and Patroclus (and Achilleus' other friends) in Homer's *Iliad*. Only a brief account of these is possible here.[9]

Friendship was made into an important subsidiary theme of the Akkadian story of *Gilgamesh* (George 2000: xiii). In the Sumerian tales that lie behind it the theme is not so prominent: Enkidu is described as the 'servant' of Bilgames/Gilgamesh, only very occasionally as his 'friend' or 'companion' in *Bilgames and the Netherworld* (George 2000: 185, 187). Nevertheless the value of joint action is made clear already in *Bilgames and Huwawa* (George 2000: 154–55, cf. 40), anticipating

---

[8] Cf. Whybray (1968: 90–95), where other cases of loyalty and disloyalty to friends in the Succession Narrative are noted.

[9] Among the extensive literature see the recent studies of Konstan (1997: Ch. 1 [esp. pp. 41–42]); Streck (1999: 104–215); Nardelli (2004; 2007); Ackerman (2005: Ch. 1–5); and A.R. George's magisterial works cited below. I am indebted for several of these references (and much encouragement in the preparation of this essay) to Dr Diana Lipton.

the fragmentarily preserved section of the standard epic (vv. 70–77). Enkidu is repeatedly called the friend (*ibru*) of Gilgamesh in the Akkadian version, less often his 'comrade' or 'companion' (*tappu*) (e.g. iii.4–5).[10] Their friendship begins with a fight and mutual admiration (ii.111–15, completed from Old Babylonian tablets: George 2000: 16–17), and their joint exploits against the monster Humbaba and the 'Bull of Heaven' likewise locate their friendship firmly in the world of heroic endeavour. It is, nevertheless, a most unusual relationship, since Enkidu is now a 'wild man' by birth (the Sumerian tales lack this motif: George 2003: 142): if this has some relevance to the author's conception of friendship, rather than only to other aspects of his purpose, it perhaps shows how strong the bonds of friendship are when they can unite such different individuals, as perhaps even more in the case of Etana's friendship with an eagle.[11] Certainly the bond is a very close one, as is shown by Gilgamesh's extreme grief at Enkidu's death (viii passim), which is what inspires his journey to Uta-napishtim in search of the secret of immortality. The closeness of their friendship is expressed in a number of other passages, perhaps most powerfully in i.271, 289, where Gilgamesh's mother Ninsun interprets his dreams (cf. 256, 267, 284) as follows (George 2000: 10–11; cf. e.g. x.244–48 and pars.):

> Like a wife you'll love him, caress and embrace him.

The purpose is that Gilgamesh will have a mighty protector and a good advisor, attributes expected elsewhere of a loyal friend.

It has long been discussed whether the intimacy between Gilgamesh and Enkidu implies a (homo)sexual element in their relationship (so e.g. Horner 1978: 15–20). A.R. George has recently summed up the discussion in the light of a new suggestion that a sexual innuendo based on word-play underlies the account of Gilgamesh's dreams in Tablet I (George 2003: 454 with n. 48 [see in general 452–54]). His conclusion is:

> The debate over the nature of Gilgameš and Enkidu's friendship—homosexual or platonic—still leaves commentators divided. In my view the language of the dream is clear. Gilgameš will love Enkidu as a wife.

---

[10] George (2000: 23). On these terms see briefly Davies (2010: 146, n. 26).

[11] Kinnear Wilson (1985; translation in *COS*, 1, 453–57). A further comparison could be made with the Hittite account of the friendship of Tudhaliya (IV) and Kurunta (*COS*, 2, 100–06), which was established (by an oath) before the former became king (sect. 13).

However, as regards the mechanics of the plot, the nature of the pair's friendship is not important, only the fact of it.

In a footnote he adds:

> ...The repeated use of the verb *ḫabābu* in this connection implies a sexual relationship. If there is any doubt about the significance of this imagery, note also SB VIII 59, where, in death, Gilgameš veils Enkidu like a bride. Graphic evidence for a sexual relationship now comes from SB XII 96–9, as understood in the light of a new manuscript of the text's Sumerian forerunner, BN 250–3.

The *Iliad* comes from a more distant culture, but one whose connections with the literature of the ancient Near East have recently been discussed in detail.[12] Once again the story of friendship concerns elite male figures in a heroic age, in which any historical elements have undergone considerable literary embellishment.[13] But once again it also plays a key role in the plot of the larger epic: it is only Hector's killing of Patroclus which draws Achilleus out of his seclusion to gain vengeance for his beloved friend. The first of many mentions of their friendship is in the very episode that leads to that seclusion: it is Patroclus whom Achilleus sends to bring out his concubine Briseis to be surrendered to Agamemnon's demands (1.345–49).

But this friendship is not an isolated case: the account of the embassy of Odysseus, Aias and Phoenix in Book 9 contains many references to friendship. Nestor proposes that Achilleus be placated 'with words of supplication and with the gifts of friendship' (9.113), indicating that (renewal of) friendship may depend on gifts. But they may not be effective, and Achilleus chides Phoenix for what he sees as a change of loyalty (9.612–15). To Aias Achilleus' refusal is a denial of their friendship:

> He is hard, and does not remember that friends' affection
> wherein we honoured him by the ships, far beyond all others. (9.630–31)[14]

In the end it is Patroclus who responds to the call to arms and he does so clad in Achilleus' armour, as he himself has requested (16.40–43). His going is out of regard for his friend, to 'bring honour to Peleus'

[12] Cf. West (1999, esp. 336–46) on Gilgamesh and Achilleus: West does not deal in detail with the story of David and Jonathan.

[13] See the account of Konstan (1997: Ch. 1, esp. pp. 41–42), and more specifically Sinos (1980: 39–47).

[14] All quotations from the *Iliad* are taken from Lattimore (1951).

son' (16.271): in life Patroclus seems a better example of friendship than Achilleus. He does not know that it is his own death-sentence, as the poet tells us even before he goes (16.45–46) and as Achilleus senses when he warns him not to seek too much glory (16.87–96). Even then Achilleus seems more concerned about his own honour than the welfare of his friend. It is only Patroclus's death which brings out the full extent of Achilleus' affection for his friend: a succession of lamentations punctuate the remaining books of the epic, surrounding Achilleus' terrible vengeance on Hector (18.6–14, 78–93, 324–42; 19.315–37; 23.17–23, 43–53, 221–27; 24.3–13). Most poignant of all is the scene where Patroclus's ghost appears in a dream to Achilleus:

> And I call upon you in sorrow, give me your hand; no longer
> shall I come back from death, once you give me my rite of burning.
> No longer shall you and I, alive, sit apart from our other
> beloved companions and make our plans, since the bitter destiny
> that was given me when I was born has opened its jaws to take me...
>
> Then in answer to him spoke swift-footed Achilleus:
> 'How is it, o hallowed head of my brother, you have come back to me
> here, and tell me all these several things? Yet surely
> I am accomplishing all, and I shall do as you tell me.
> But stand closer to me, and let us, if only for a little,
> embrace, and take full satisfaction from the dirge of sorrow.'
> So he spoke, and with his own arms reached for him, but could not
> take him, but the spirit went underground, like vapour,
> with a thin cry, and Achilleus started awake staring...(23.75–79, 93–101)

There have been suggestions (already in antiquity) that these statements imply an erotic relationship between Achilleus and Patroclus, but that is to misunderstand them: there is nothing to suggest any sexual intimacy between them (see also Konstan 1997: 37–39). But they do exemplify a very special bond of friendship, which goes beyond the expectations (or at least the practice) seen elsewhere in the *Iliad*. It has sometimes been suggested that in the Homeric poems (and indeed elsewhere in the ancient world) friendship was a matter of reciprocal duties rather than affection: 'Homeric "friendship" appears as a system of calculated cooperation, not necessarily accompanied by any feelings of affection'.[15] But, as David Konstan has shown in a detailed discussion, the philological arguments do not justify such a view: although

[15] Millett (1991: 120–22); for further references see Konstan (1997: 24–25).

φίλος is not used specifically of friends in Homer, in combination with ἑταῖρος and ξένος it does identify a relationship that can properly be described as friendship in an emotional as well as a social sense (1997: 28–37). Certainly the account of Achilleus' mourning for Patroclus points to the presence of such an emotional element. At the same time it is worth observing that all the talk of friendship in the *Iliad* occurs in the context of a military campaign, whereas the *Odyssey* with its more peaceful context has little to say on the subject.[16] This may suggest that war, when young men were separated from their families for a time, provided a context within which friendships might develop with particular intensity.

It is remarkable that several motifs recur in all three of these narratives about friendship: a situation of danger, the initial prominence of the devotion of the 'lesser' partner, the death of the latter, and the grief of the survivor.[17] In two cases the friendship overcomes substantial social or political obstacles, though this is not the case with Achilles and Patroclus. One important difference between the story of Jonathan and David and the others just discussed is that it does not record any account of joint exploits of the two friends. This difference highlights the special character of the Jonathan-David story (whatever else it has in common with the others), which arises from the fact that it is part of larger narratives in which David is very much the central focus of attention.

It is a pleasure to dedicate this essay to Robert Gordon, who knows far more about the books of Samuel (and much else) than I ever shall, as a token of gratitude for many years of good friendship and collaboration (see already Davies 1972: 154 n.1), although so far at least neither of us has had to rescue the other from a raging Saul!

References

Ackerman, S. 2005. *When Heroes Love. The Ambiguity of Eros in the Stories of Gilgamesh and David* (New York: Columbia University Press).
Alter, R. 1999. *The David Story* (New York: W.W. Norton).

[16] The brief episodes about Telemachus and Pisistratus in Books 3, 4 and 15 do not tell us much (*pace* Nardelli 2004).

[17] By contrast a homosexual dimension to the relationship is only demonstrable in the case of Gilgamesh and Enkidu.

Clements, R.E. 1992. *Loving One's Neighbour: Old Testament Ethics in Context* (The Ethel M. Wood Lecture 1992; London: University of London).
Davies, G.I. 1972. 'Hagar, el-heğra and the Location of Mount Sinai, with an additional note on Reqem', *Vetus Testamentum* 22: 152–63.
——. 2010. 'The Ethics of Friendship in Wisdom Literature', in *Ethical and Unethical Behaviour in the Old Testament* (ed. K.J. Dell; Library of Hebrew Bible/Old Testament Studies, 528; London: Continuum) 135–150.
Dietrich, W. 1997. *Die frühe Königszeit in Israel: 10. Jahrhundert v. Chr.* (Biblische Enzyklopädie, 3; Stuttgart: Kohlhammer).
Driver, S.R. 1913. *Notes on the Hebrew Text and Topography of the Books of Samuel* (Oxford: Clarendon Press, 2nd edn).
George, A.R. 2000. *The Epic of Gilgamesh. The Babylonian Epic Poem and Other Texts in Akkadian and Sumerian* (translated with an introduction; Penguin Classics; London: Penguin).
——. 2003. *The Babylonian Gilgamesh epic: introduction, critical edition and cuneiform texts* (Oxford: Oxford University Press).
Gordon, R.P. 1984. *1 and 2 Samuel* (OTG; Sheffield: JSOT Press).
——. 1986. *1 and 2 Samuel: A Commentary* (Exeter: Paternoster).
Horner, T. 1978. *Jonathan Loved David: Homosexuality in Biblical Times* (Philadelphia: Westminster).
Kinnear Wilson, J. (ed.) 1985. *The Legend of Etana* (Warminster: Aris and Phillips).
Klein, R.W. 1983. *1 Samuel* (WBC; Waco: Word).
Konstan, D. 1997. *Friendship in the Classical World* (Cambridge: Cambridge University Press).
Lattimore, R. 1951. *The Iliad of Homer* (Chicago: University of Chicago Press, 10th impression 1961).
McCarter, P.K. 1980. *1 Samuel* (AB; Garden City: Doubleday).
——. 1984. *2 Samuel* (AB; Garden City: Doubleday).
Millett, P. 1991. *Lending and Borrowing in Ancient Athens* (Cambridge: Cambridge University Press).
Moran, W.L. 1963. 'The Ancient Near Eastern Background of the Love of God in Deuteronomy', *Catholic Biblical Quarterly* 25: 77–87.
Na'aman, N. 1996. 'Sources and Composition in the History of David', in *Origins of the Ancient Israelite State* (ed. V. Fritz and P.R. Davies; Journal for the Study of the Old Testament Supplement, 228; Sheffield: JSOT Press) 71–86.
Nardelli, J.-F. 2004. *Le motif de la paire d'amis héroïque à prolongements homophiles. Perspectives odysséennes et proche-orientales* (Amsterdam: Adolf M. Hakkert).
——. 2007. *Homosexuality and Liminality in the* Gilgameš *and* Samuel (Amsterdam: Adolf M. Hakkert).
Nissinen, M. 1999. 'Die Liebe von David und Jonatan als Frage der modernen Exegese', *Biblica* 80: 250–63.
Sinos, D.S. 1980. *Achilles, Patroklos and the Meaning of Philos* (Innsbruck: Institut für Sprachwissenschaft der Universität Innsbruck).
Smith, H.P. 1904. *The Books of Samuel* (ICC; Edinburgh: T. and T. Clark).
Streck, M.P. 1999. *Die Bildersprache der akkadischen Epik* (Münster: Ugarit-Verlag).
Thompson, J.A. 1974. 'The Significance of the Verb *Love* in the David-Jonathan Narratives in 1 Samuel', *Vetus Testamentum* 24: 334–338.
Van Seters, J. 1983. *In Search of History: Historiography in the ancient world and the origins of biblical historiography* (New Haven: Yale University Press).
West, M.L. 1999. *The East Face of Helicon: West Asiatic Elements in Greek Poetry and Myth* (Oxford: Clarendon Press).
Whybray, R.N. 1968. *The Succession Narrative. A Study of II Sam. 9–20 and I Kings 1 and 2* (Studies in Biblical Theology, II/9; London: SCM Press).
Zehnder, M. 1998. 'Exegetische Beobachtungen zu den David-Jonathan-Geschichten', *Biblica* 79: 153–179.

A SIGN AND A PORTENT IN ISAIAH 8.18

H.G.M. Williamson

Most of Isaiah chapters 6 and 8 are a first-person account, apparently written by Isaiah himself, concerning his commissioning to the prophetic office and some of his oracles delivered during the so-called Syro-Ephraimite crisis. Near the end there is an account of how he had the document tied up and sealed for the foreseeable future (8.16–17), and there then occurs the following conclusion: 'So now I and the children whom the Lord has given me will become signs and portents in Israel from the Lord of hosts who dwells on Mount Zion' (8.18).

This rendering of the MT is superficially straightforward. There is, however, a variant reading in the A scroll of Isaiah from Qumran to which commentators have paid surprisingly little attention.[1] In place of MT's plural לְאֹתוֹת וּלְמוֹפְתִים, the scroll has the singular לאות ולמופת. Kutscher (1974: 400–1) lists this along with a number of other places where the scroll has a singular form against MT plural, and in several cases he offers a possible explanation. In the present instance, however, he apparently concedes defeat, asking merely 'What was the reason for this change?' Equally, we should note that on pp. 394–400 he discusses an even longer list of passages where the scroll has a plural against MT's singular, so that it would clearly not be possible to ascribe the difference to some characteristic carelessness or *Tendenz* on the part of the scroll's scribe. It looks as though the scroll reading represents a genuine textual variant.

The only comment known to me on this variant is offered by van der Kooij (1988), who ascribes the change to the 'group mentality' of the community responsible for the scroll on the basis of a comparison with 7.11. His suggestion does not seem immediately convincing, however, because it does not even consider the alternative possibility that the MT reading might be secondary and because it jumps too quickly to the supposition that changes in the scroll should be explained without further discussion by the pre-supposed sectarian tendency of the scroll's scribe.

---

[1] This particular verse is not attested in any other of the Qumran fragments.

Approaching the matter from an alternative angle, we may note that the scroll reading is reflected closely in at least two of the ancient versions. The Vulgate *in signum et in portentum*[2] and the Peshitta (ܠܐܬܐ ܘܠܬܕܡܘܪܬܐ) also render as singular. Furthermore, the relevance of LXX's plural rendering, σημεῖα καὶ τέρατα, is blunted by the observation that it also renders the undoubtedly singular combination of these same two words at 20.3 by the same plural forms.[3] Thus the Targum (אתין ומופתין) is the only version which gives reliable evidence for the plural in its *Vorlage* at this point.

If, at least on the face of things, there thus seems to be stronger textual evidence than has usually been recognized for the singular forms here, are there other criteria that may be applied to help adjudicate as to which reading should be preferred? There seem to me to be two or three, all of which point in favour of the priority of the singular.

First, the two nouns in question occur both separately and together quite frequently elsewhere in the Hebrew Bible. When they occur together in the plural as a pair (as here in MT) or in parallel, they appear to be used elsewhere exclusively and without exception of various miraculous phenomena in relation to the Exodus, including but not limited to the plagues;[4] see Exod. 7.3; Deut. 4.34; 6.22; 7.19; 26.8; 29.2; 34.11; Jer. 32.20, 21; Ps. 78.43; 105.27; 135.9; Neh. 9.10. This application may also apply in the case of the words in the plural used on their own (e.g. for אֹתוֹת, see Exod. 4.9, 17, 28, 30; Josh. 24.17; for מוֹפְתִים, see Exod. 4.21; 11.9, 10), but this is not necessarily the case (e.g. for אֹתוֹת, see 1 Sam. 10.7, 9; Isa. 44.25; for מוֹפְתִים, see Joel 3.3; Ps. 105.5 = 1 Chron. 16.12).

The singular of מוֹפֵת has a wider range of application, both when used on its own and when in association with אוֹת. It can again apply to the Exodus complex (Exod. 7.9), but this is rare. More normally it is associated in one way or another with prophecy. In combination with אוֹת, it occurs in Deut. 13.2 and 3 of something that a (false) prophet promises and which comes to fulfilment that may lead the people into following 'other gods'. Their nature is not further specified; they could

[2] In his commentary, however, Jerome renders as plural: *in signa atque portenta*. Is it possible that he was aware of both readings?

[3] For a discussion of some wider aspects of the expression in Greek, see McCasland (1957).

[4] The precise range of allusions is unclear, but the issue is not of importance for our present concerns; see Childs (1967).

be miraculous, but do not seem necessarily to be so. At Isa. 20.3, the combination in the singular is applied to Isaiah himself, his walking naked for three years being explained as a sign and portent against Egypt and Ethiopia—in other words it functions as a sign that points indubitably to (and perhaps as a sign act even helps bring about?) the captivity and exile of those countries by the Assyrians. The only other example of the combined form in the singular is at Deut. 28.46, where it refers to the curses which will 'be among you…for ever' for failure to keep the commandments of God. Used on its own, מוֹפֵת also applies directly to the person of a prophet in Ezek. 12.6, 11; 24.24, 27; here, it refers to him as undertaking strange but not miraculous deeds (rather as with Isaiah), and the use in each chapter of such language as 'as I have done, so shall you do' indicates that these are clearly sign acts, the combination of his and their experiences leading the people to recognize that the Lord is God. The word is also linked to prophetic activity on its three occurrences in 1 Kgs. 13.3 (twice) and 5, at Ps. 71.7 the Psalmist is likewise 'like a portent' to many, and the 'men of portent' in Zech. 3.8 seem to function in a similar manner.[5] The only exception to this general pattern is 2 Chron. 32.24, where 'portent' stands in the same position as 'sign' in 2 Kgs. 20.8, thus suggesting that by that time, at least, the two words had come to be regarded as more or less synonymous.

Though the singular form of אוֹת is used more widely,[6] it can certainly also be used in the context of prophecy, not least in the book of Isaiah, where the prophet offers both Ahaz (7.11, 14) and Hezekiah (38.7, 22) a 'sign' as a stimulus to, or confirmation of, faith.

The upshot of this brief survey is to indicate that MT's plural at Isa. 8.18 is wholly exceptional in referring to something other than the Exodus events; it would, in fact, be unique in that regard. Furthermore, the combined plural form is common and so would have been familiar to anyone with any close knowledge of the biblical text. Conversely, the singular form of מוֹפֵת is most frequently used in association with prophecy and the same circle of ideas is also at least possible in the case of אוֹת. On this showing, we might expect to find the singular in

[5] Meyers and Meyers (1987: 199–201) go so far as to suggest that Zechariah here 'reflects the process of priestly absorption of a function previously associated chiefly with the prophets'.

[6] So far as I am aware, the fullest study remains Keller (1946); for other literature see Helfmeyer (1970; English translation 1977).

Isaiah 8 and equally conclude that the scribal change to plural is more easily understood than the reverse, given the familiarity of the plural form. In addition, given that the subject of the verbless clause is plural ('I and the children'), we could understand the unconscious pressure to substitute a plural for singular, whereas the reverse process would be unlikely. In other words, the 'rule' of *lectio difficilior* favours the singular reading here.

Another feature of the verse on which commentators speak with almost one voice concerns the linking of Isaiah himself with his children[7] as 'signs and portents'. Here I should wish to take issue with the frequently repeated notion that the message is in the names of the children (important though they may be in other respects).[8] What the text says is that the children, not the names, will be a sign and a portent, and furthermore this is prefaced with the emphatic אָנֹכִי, 'I'. While of course it is possible to 'translate' the name Isaiah so as to see in it some sort of message, the fact of the matter is that this is never done in the book, so that it would be expecting rather a lot of the readers to interpret in this way.

If, alternatively, we take seriously the implication that it is the person, not the name, of the prophet with his children that is the sign and portent, our attention should move quickly to Isaiah 20 for a comparison. There, as already mentioned, Isaiah is described in a third-person narrative as walking barefoot and naked for three years in Jerusalem. It is then explained that in this the prophet is acting as 'a sign and a portent against Egypt and Ethiopia' (20.3). In drawing attention to this as the only other passage in the book where our expression occurs, I now want to move on more speculatively to suggest that the connection may be more than coincidental.

[7] הַיְלָדִים must refer to Isaiah's own children. The suggestion that הַיְלָדִים might be a way of referring to the disciples of v. 16 should be discounted (*contra*, for instance, Calvin n.d.: 127; Vitringa 1714–1720, i: 275–76, Budde, 1928: 90; Lindblom 1958: 49–50). As known from the book of Proverbs, to go no further, the pupils in wisdom circles could certainly be addressed as 'sons (בָּנִים)' of their teacher designated as their 'father' (whether this was always biologically the case is unknown but seems unlikely), but they are never styled as 'children' in such a context.

[8] See, for example, Delitzsch (1889; English translation 1894: 232); Procksch (1930: 139). Curiously, Wildberger (1980: 347–48; English translation 1991: 369) draws a distinction in this regard between the children and Isaiah himself (see too, though less forcefully, Gray 1912: 156). There can be no justification for this move, but Wildberger's very unease is a strong indication of the unsatisfactory nature of the usual interpretation.

Isaiah 20 is one of three passages in the first half of the book of Isaiah where we have third-person accounts of the words and deeds of the prophet. The other two are chs. 7 and 36–39. The close connections between the latter two are so strong at the literary level as to make it probable that they were written together in some alternative source about the prophet, since lost to us, and were worked into our present book from there at some indeterminate date. The evidence on which this assessment is based has been frequently rehearsed elsewhere by several scholars of otherwise very different approaches (some, for instance, prefer to think of the two passages as having been written as a diptych for their present position in Isaiah) and reference to them must suffice for the present purpose in view of space constraints; see, for instance, Ackroyd (1982); Smelik (1986); Conrad (1988); Seitz (1991: 89 and 195–196); Williamson (1994: 191–194); Sweeney (1996: 457–459).

Blenkinsopp (2000) deserves the credit for decisively including the narrative in Isaiah 20 in this corpus. In particular he draws attention to a number of what might be called deuteronomistic-like elements which seem to link the passage with chs. 7 and 36–39. This does not, of course, preclude the likelihood that they in turn drew on even earlier historical material (see de Jong 2007: 151–53), but that does not detract from their association with each other in their present form with its consequences for our understanding of the composition history of the book.

In my opinion, there are grounds for believing that Isa. 8.18 was added to vv. 16–17 as a redactional comment, associated with the process of incorporating 7.1–17 into its present position. It is thus likely to have been written by somebody who was particularly familiar with this small corpus of prose narratives about Isaiah. Under the prevailing view that 6.1–8.18 was all part of an original first-person 'memoir' by Isaiah, such a possibility could not have been considered. But much recent work has questioned that view, drawing a distinction between the original first-person account in chs. 6 and 8 and the third-person material in ch. 7.[9] The possibility of other additions associated with this process thus comes into view.

[9] This can hardly be documented in full, but I refer to a few examples by scholars of otherwise quite distinct approaches to justify my otherwise somewhat cavalier statement: Irvine (1992); Barthel (1997: 37–43); Becker (1997: 21–123); Williamson (1998: 73–112). The more traditional view has recently been defended, with modifications, by, for instance, Clements (2000) and Wagner (2006).

The main arguments in favour of distinguishing 8.18 from 8.16–17 are the following. (i) In terms of formal elements, the verse is clearly prosaic, with the use of אֲשֶׁר, the definite article, and no rhythm or parallelism of any kind. By contrast, although vv. 16–17 are hardly high poetry, they do employ parallelism and they lack prose particles; note too the lack of the definite article on תְּעוּדָה and תּוֹרָה. They seem stylistically close to vv. 12–15, where again we may note the use of parallelism but the lack of regular rhythm (admittedly, prose particles also occur in those verses). It would seem strange to have such a prosaic ending as v. 18 as the concluding climax of an originally more poetic form of composition. (ii) Verse 18 makes conscious verbal allusion to Isa. 7:11–14 in several ways (see too, for instance, Dietrich 1976: 73; Barthel 1997: 233). We may note the use of נָתַן אוֹת in 7.14, the use there too of introductory הִנֵּה, and the expression אוֹת מֵעִם יְהוָה in 7.11. Given that the verse clearly has reference to the material which precedes it, these verbal connections seem more than coincidental. This is a style of composition that distinguishes the verse from 8.16–17 but which is characteristic of redactional material in the first part of Isaiah. The particular importance in the present instance is that, if v. 18 is dependent on ch. 7, which we have already seen has been added well after the composition of the first-person material, it must itself also be later. (iii) There is one point of slight tension between vv. 17 and 18 which contributes to the case without, perhaps, being decisive on its own. It is odd to stress God's hiding of his face in v. 17 only then to proceed immediately to speak of him dwelling on Mount Zion in the next verse (cf. Becker 1997: 120). By contrast, the different ways of referring to the audience (house of Jacob in v. 17 and Israel in v. 18) do not seem in any way incompatible. (iv) Although, of course, the use of הִנֵּה does not demand that what follows be a separate element, it is certainly compatible with that conclusion, given that it neither has the conjunction nor is embedded following some other introductory word or phrase, as often elsewhere. Some commentators seem to me to have overplayed this argument, because it is clearly not decisive in itself, but nevertheless it helps by showing that there is no need to explain away any form of syntactical join as a secondary smoothing of the text or whatever. Nor, it may be added conversely, does v. 17 require or lead one to expect any further comment.

These arguments are admittedly of varying strength. The main point is the connections of this verse with ch. 7 and consequently with ch. 20, as previously mooted, for these rule out the presence of v. 18 in the original first-person account. The remaining arguments are supportive and indicate that there is no problem on other fronts to drawing the same conclusion.

There is little need to doubt that the prose narratives in Isa. 7, 20 and 36–39 reflect a movement towards an interest in the person of the prophet beyond that of his words alone and this stands at an early point in a trajectory which continued well into post-biblical times (Blenkinsopp 2006: 55) and which is shared, of course, with many other influential figures from antiquity. By stating that Isaiah and his children would serve as a sign and a portent during the coming days which would be dark in the immediate future but which eventually would see the deliverance of God for his people (v. 17),[10] the redactor sees in them a community of testimony simply by their presence and being, not restrictively by their words or deeds alone. From the redactor's perspective, the words of the prophet have been sealed up, but in the meantime there remains a group which, even if silent, serves as a testimony to what God had said and what the people had rejected. Their presence in Jerusalem is itself a witness, continuing the function that had been adumbrated on a smaller scale in the previous episodes, especially 8.1–4. Thus Procksch (1930: 139) can summarize: 'so dass die Prophetenfamilie zugleich der Kern eines Gottesvolks werden soll' (*pace* Wildberger's reservations), while Beuken (2003: 231) comments forcefully to similar effect: 'es ist neu, dass Jesaja und seine zwei Söhne das Wort JHWHs nicht nur als wahrhaftig verkündigen sollen, sondern dass sie dessen Inhalt auch im eigenen Fleisch und Blut darstellen müssen'; see too (briefly) Rost (1955: 5). It is a theme which we find also picked up in the second half of the book, where, for instance, God's blind and deaf people serve as witnesses in the court simply by virtue of their election and deliverance by God, not because

[10] This positive interpretation of the verbs 'wait' and 'look eagerly' for has occasionally been questioned; Fohrer (1991: 132–33); Steck (1972: 201, n. 33), and Becker (1997: 75), for instance, have suggested that they should be understood negatively in the sense that Isaiah is waiting only for the judgment of God to fall. While it is true that חִכָּה can be used either way (though more usually of hopeful expectation), the verb קִוָּה, here rendered 'look eagerly for', but often more neutrally translated as 'wait for', is virtually always used with a positive, expectant sense, especially when used, as here, with God as its object. The evidence for this has been frequently rehearsed (see, for instance, Westermann 1952–1953; Waschke 1989 [with earlier bibliography]; Lescow 1973: 326; Van Winkle 1985: 448; Barthel 1997: 237). It is attested in particular in the Psalter as part of the lament/confession of trust (Ps. 25, where the verb occurs in vv. 3, 5 and 21, is a good example), and this standard usage amply justifies finding the same sense here (cf. Kaiser 1981: 190–91 [English translation 1983: 197]; Wildberger 1980: 346–47 [English translaton 1991: 368]; Irvine 1990: 209). It is God himself to whom Isaiah looks, not his activity in judgment.

of anything meritorious that they are said to have done (43.10–12 in the context of 8–13).

It will not have escaped Robert Gordon's memory that our passage is cited in the New Testament's epistle to the Hebrews 2.13. Since he has offered his own insightful 'reading' of this epistle (Gordon 2000), it would be an impertinence to comment here in detail. Very much in line with his own exegesis, however, perhaps we may briefly observe that the writer was evidently basing himself on the LXX rendering of Isaiah, as his wording in the first part of the verse, 'I will put my trust in him', for the closing words of Isa. 8.17 makes clear. As Hagner (1983: 31) points out, in the LXX rendering of Isa. 8.17–18, the Tetragrammaton is repeatedly represented, not as κύριος, 'Lord', as might have been expected, but as θεός, 'God', so opening up the text for someone reading christologically to see the words as spoken by 'the Lord' to God; this at least would have been one way of understanding the unnamed subject of the enigmatic καὶ ἐρεῖ, 'and he said', which the LXX translator slips in without Hebrew warrant at the start of v. 17. This then opens the way for the writer of the epistle to reflect by the abbreviated citation of Isa. 8.18 on the close relationship between Christ and 'his children', whom he has already also designated just before as 'his brethren' and with whom, the passage goes on to emphasize, he shared in flesh and blood in order that through his death he might destroy the ultimate enemy.

While it would be possible to expand considerably on these remarks, it is perhaps sufficient for our present purposes to reflect that the emphasis in the passage in Hebrews on the ecclesial identity of the Lord with his people moves very much in line, though in a more exalted manner, with the direction in which I have sought to indicate the 'emended' Hebrew text of Isa. 8.18 was tending. It is only a disappointment that the author of Hebrews did not continue his citation in order to show whether he too would have taken the 'sign and portent' as a singular against MT and LXX plural; it would certainly have suited his theology well at this point if he had.

References

Ackroyd, P.R. 1982. 'Isaiah 36–39: Structure and Function', in *Von Kanaan bis Kerala: Festschrift für Prof. Mag. Dr. Dr. J.P.M. van der Ploeg O.P. zur Vollendung des siebzigsten Lebensjahres am 4. Juli 1979* (eds. W.C. Delsman *et al.*; Alter Orient und Altes Testament, 211; Kevelaer: Butzon & Bercker/ Neukirchen-Vluyn: Neukirchener

Verlag) 3–21; repr. 1987 *Studies in the Religious Tradition of the Old Testament* (London: SCM) 105–20.

Barthel, J. 1997. *Prophetenwort und Geschichte: Die Jesajaüberlieferung in Jes 6–8 und 28–31* (Forschungen zum Alten Testament, 19; Tübingen: Mohr Siebeck).

Becker, U. 1997. *Jesaja—von der Botschaft zum Buch* (Forschungen zur Religion und Literatur des Alten und Neuen Testaments, 178; Göttingen: Vandenhoeck & Ruprecht).

Beuken, W.A.M. 2003. *Jesaja 1–12* (Herders Theologischer Kommentar zum Alten Testament; Freiburg: Herder).

Blenkinsopp, J. 2000. 'The Prophetic Biography of Isaiah', in *Mincha: Festgabe für Rolf Rendtorff zum 75. Geburtstag* (ed. E. Blum; Neukirchen-Vluyn: Neukirchener Verlag) 13–26.

——. 2006. *Opening the Sealed Book: Interpretations of the Book of Isaiah in Late Antiquity* (Grand Rapids and Cambridge: Eerdmans).

Budde, K. 1928. *Jesajas Erleben: Eine gemeinverständliche Auslegung der Denkschrift des Propheten (Kap. 6,1–9,6)* (Gotha: Leopold Klotz).

Calvin, J. n.d. *Calvin's Commentaries*, 3: *Isaiah* (Grand Rapids: Associated Publishers and Authors Inc.).

Childs, B.S. 1967. 'Deuteronomic Formulae of the Exodus Traditions', in *Hebräische Wortforschung: Festschrift zum 80. Geburtstag von Walter Baumgartner* (ed. B. Hartmann *et al.*; Supplements to Vetus Testamentum, 16; Leiden: Brill) 30–39.

Clements, R.E. 2000. 'The Prophet as an Author: The Case of the Isaiah Memoir', in *Writings and Speech in Israelite and Ancient Near Eastern Prophecy* (eds. E. Ben Zvi and M.H. Floyd; Society of Biblical Literature Symposium Series, 10; Atlanta: SBL) 89–101.

Conrad, E.W. 1988. 'The Royal Narratives and the Structure of the Book of Isaiah', *Journal for the Study of the Old Testament* 41: 67–81.

de Jong, M.J. 2007. *Isaiah among the Ancient Near Eastern Prophets: A Comparative Study of the Earliest Stages of the Isaiah Tradition and the Neo-Assyrian Prophecies* (Supplements to Vetus Testamentum, 117; Leiden: Brill).

Delitzsch, F. 1889. *Commentar über das Buch Jesaia* (4th edn; Leipzig: Dörffling & Franke); English translation, 1894 *Biblical Commentary on the Prophecies of Isaiah* (Edinburgh: T. & T. Clark).

Dietrich, W. 1976. *Jesaja und die Politik* (Beiträge zur Evangelischen Theologie, 74; Munich: Chr. Kaiser Verlag).

Fohrer, G. 1991. *Das Buch Jesaja* (3 vols, 3rd edn [1st edn: 1960]; Zürcher Bibelkommentare, Altes Testament, 19.1; Zurich: Theologischer Verlag).

Gordon, R.P. 2000. *Hebrews* (Readings: A New Biblical Commentary; Sheffield: Sheffield Academic Press).

Gray, G.B. 1912. *A Critical and Exegetical Commentary on the Book of Isaiah I–XXVII* (International Critical Commentary; Edinburgh: T. & T. Clark).

Hagner, D. 1983. *Hebrews: A Good News Commentary* (San Francisco: Harper & Row).

Helfmeyer, F.J. 1970. 'אוֹת', *Theologisches Wörterbuch zum Alten Testament* 1: 182–205; English translation, 1977 *Theological Dictionary of the Old Testament* 1: 167–188.

Irvine, S.A. 1990. *Isaiah, Ahaz, and the Syro-Ephraimitic Crisis* (Society of Biblical Literature Dissertation Series, 123; Atlanta: Scholars Press).

——. 1992. 'The Isaianic *Denkschrift*: Reconsidering an Old Hypothesis', *Zeitschrift für die Alttestamentliche Wissenschaft* 104: 216–231.

Kaiser, O. 1981. *Das Buch des Propheten Jesaja, Kapitel 1–12* (5th edn; Das Alte Testament Deutsch, 17; Göttingen: Vandenhoeck & Ruprecht); English translation, 1983 *Isaiah 1–12: A Commentary* (The Old Testament Library; London: SCM).

Keller, C.A. 1946. *Das Wort OTH als "Offenbarungszeichen Gottes": Eine philologisch-theologische Begriffsuntersuchung zum Alten Testament* (Basel: E. Hoenen).

Kooij, A. van der 1988. '*1QIsa*^{a} Col. viii, 4–11 (Isa 8, 11–18): A Contextual Approach of its Variants', *Revue de Qumrân* 13: 569–581.

Kutscher, E.Y. 1974. *The Language and Linguistic Background of the Isaiah Scroll (1QIsa[a])* (Studies on the Texts of the Desert of Judah, 6; Leiden: Brill).
Lescow, Th. 1973. 'Jesajas Denkschrift aus der Zeit des syrisch-ephraimitischen Krieges', *Zeitschrift für die Alttestamentliche Wissenschaft* 85: 315–331.
Lindblom, J. 1958. *A Study on the Immanuel Section in Isaiah: Isa. vii, 1–ix, 6* (Lund: GWK Gleerup).
McCasland, S.V. 1957. 'Signs and Wonders', *Journal of Biblical Literature* 76: 149–152.
Meyers, C.L. and E.M. Meyers. 1987. *Haggai, Zechariah 1–8: A New Translation with Introduction and Commentary* (Anchor Bible, 25B; Garden City: Doubleday).
Procksch, O. 1930. *Jesaia I* (Kommentar zum Alten Testament, 9/1; Leipzig: A. Deichert).
Rost, L. 1955. 'Gruppenbildungen im Alten Testament', *Theologische Literaturzeitung* 80: 1–8.
Seitz, C.R. 1991. *Zion's Final Destiny: The Development of the Book of Isaiah. A Reassessment of Isaiah 36–39* (Minneapolis: Fortress Press).
Smelik, K.A.D. 1986. 'Distortion of Old Testament Prophecy: The Purpose of Isaiah xxxvi and xxxvii', in *Crises and Perspectives: Studies in Ancient Near Eastern Polytheism, Biblical Theology, Palestinian Archaeology and Intertestamental Literature* (ed. A.S. van der Woude; Oudtestamentische Studiën, 24; Leiden: Brill) 70–93.
Steck, O.H. 1972. 'Bemerkungen zu Jesaja 6', *Biblische Zeitschrift* N.F. 16: 188–206.
Sweeney, M.A. 1996. *Isaiah 1–39, with an Introduction to Prophetic Literature* (Forms of the Old Testament Literature, 16; Grand Rapids: Eerdmans).
Van Winkle, D.W. 1985. 'The Relationship of the Nations to Yahweh and to Israel in Isaiah xl–lv', *Vetus Testamentum* 35: 446–58.
Vitringa, C. 1714–1720. *Commentarius in Librum Prophetiarum Jesaiae* (2 vols; Leeuwarden: F. Halma).
Wagner, T. 2006. *Gottes Herrschaft: Eine Analyses der Denkschrift (Jes 6,1–9,6)* (Supplements to Vetus Testamentum, 108; Leiden: Brill).
Waschke, G. 1989. 'קוה', *Theologisches Wörterbuch zum Alten Testament* 6: 1225–34; English translation, 2003 *Theological Dictionary of the Old Testament* 12: 564–573.
Westermann, C. 1952–1953. 'Das Hoffen im Alten Testament: Eine Begriffsuntersuchung', *Theologia Viatorum* 4: 19–70; repr. 1964 *Forschung am Alten Testament: Gesammelte Studien* (Theologische Bücherei, 24; Munich: Chr. Kaiser Verlag) 219–265.
Wildberger, H. 1980. *Jesaja 1–12* (2nd edn; Biblischer Kommentar Altes Testament, 10/1; Neukirchen-Vluyn: Neukirchener Verlag); English translation, 1991 *Isaiah 1–12: A Commentary* (Continental Commentaries; Minneapolis: Fortress Press).
Williamson, H.G.M. 1994. *The Book Called Isaiah: Deutero-Isaiah's Role in Composition and Redaction* (Oxford: Clarendon Press).
——. 1998 *Variations on a Theme: King, Messiah and Servant in the Book of Isaiah* (Carlisle: Paternoster).

JEREMIAH THE HISTORIAN: THE BOOK OF JEREMIAH AS A SOURCE FOR THE HISTORY OF THE NEAR EAST IN THE TIME OF NEBUCHADNEZZAR.[1]

Hans M. Barstad

Background

The Book of Jeremiah was formerly regarded as one of the most important sources for the history of the city state of Jerusalem during the time of Nebuchadnezzar II (604–562 BCE). However, following the recent history aporia in prophetic research, some scholars now claim that the prophetic corpus, similar to the rest of the texts of the Hebrew Bible, is a late literary creation of Persian, or even Hellenistic, times. Furthermore, a few also believe that these late prophetic texts are 'purely literary', and that they have no connections whatsoever with any historical prophetic phenomenon in ancient Israel. Consequently, according to these scholars, the Book of Jeremiah cannot be used for the reconstruction of contemporary historical events.

Even if many of the changes that are taking place within prophetic studies are necessary, we should beware of some of their possible negative consequences. Elsewhere, I have discussed a few of the methodological and theoretical implications of some recent trends in relation to the Book of Jeremiah (Barstad 2009). To reject the importance of the Book of Jeremiah as an historical source is not only unfortunate, but also unnecessary. It represents, indeed, an obvious example of how the baby has been thrown out with the bathwater. The present contribution will attempt to demonstrate why the Book of Jeremiah should still be regarded as one of our most important 'contemporary' sources for the history of the Near East in the 500s BCE.

It is probably superfluous to add that an adequate discussion of what may or what may not be historically correct in the book of Jeremiah would require a whole monograph. This is because of the length

[1] I am happy to present this modest contribution to Robert Gordon; a great scribe and a wise man, as well as a good friend.

and complexity of the sources. For the far less ambitious enterprise at hand it is therefore necessary to choose only a couple of texts from Jeremiah. Furthermore, this is no place to discuss more fully other Jeremiah texts that may throw light upon the few passages that have been selected. Nor can the relationship between the Book of Jeremiah and the histories of the Deuteronomists and the Chroniclers be taken into consideration. Instead, only extra-biblical contemporary sources (together with a few later sources) will be referred to.

The Near East in the First Millennium

The Near East of the first millennium BCE was dominated by the Mesopotamian empires of Assyria and Babylonia, the typical arch enemies. These political giants fought for hegemony assisted by a rich variety of shifting allies (Joannès 2004). It should not be forgotten, however, that throughout the millennium, Egypt is, more often than not, a major player in the international arena, openly and behind the scenes. This position was not only a result of Egypt's antiquity, size and wealth, but it was also based on the country's long standing relations, both diplomatic and commercial, with the Levant. If Egypt is not taken into consideration, a truly scant picture of the Middle East in the first millennium will emerge. Among historians who have discussed, at varying length, Egypt in the 1st millennium BCE, we find: Gozzoli (2006); Grimal (1995: 311–382); Helck (1968: 231–257); James (2000); Lloyd (1994; 2003); and Taylor (2003). For the present purpose, it is the 26th ('Saite') dynasty that is relevant. This study attempts to look at the book of Jeremiah 'from the outside'. For this reason, I do not, with a few exceptions, refer to the vast literature in this area by biblical scholars. Useful references to the Mesopotamian context of the Hebrew Bible in the time of Nebuchadnezzar by a biblical scholar are found in Albertz (2001). As for Egypt, Redford (1992) is much referred to. The most recent book length contribution that I have seen is Schipper (1999).

The Historical Setting of the Book of Jeremiah

One might say, from a historical point of view, that the most important single episode leading to the stories described in Jeremiah is the seizing of the Babylonian throne by the Chaldean Nabopolassar (626–

605 BCE) in 626 BCE (Kuhrt 1995: II, 540–546; Oates 2000: 162–164, 173–189; Albertz 2001: 49–51; Joannès 2004: 122–123).

What happened after this event was, to the best of our knowledge, that the Assyrians made an alliance with Egypt, which was equally interested in solving the 'Chaldean problem'. The Assyrian province Carchemish had allowed Egyptian troops to help out against the Medes and the Babylonians. Apparently, Egyptian forces operated inside Mesopotamia from sometime after 600 BCE. A well preserved tablet in the British Museum (Grayson Chronicle 4) tells the story of the later years of Nabopolassar (Grayson 1975: 97–98). Here, we learn of the activities of the Egyptian army in Mesopotamia, and of how the Egyptians conquered cities and defeated the Babylonians.

One could say that the alliance of Assyrians and Egyptians shows how desperate the situation was. Assyria was no close friend of Egypt. For a very long time indeed the collective memory of Egypt had kept in mind the Assyrian pillages of Thebes in 664 BCE (Gozzoli 2006: 216 and 270–271). Possibly, the official, but quite unhistorical, Egyptian first millennium BCE view that the pharaohs again and again had defeated the Assyrians was helpful in making such alliances with the Egyptians possible (Gozzoli 2006: 214 n. 111). However, the Egyptian army was completely defeated by the Babylonian crown prince Nebuchadnezzar at the battle of Carchemish in 605 BCE (Helck 1980: 340; Lloyd 2003: 372). From a wider perspective, the battle of Carchemish belongs within the larger historical context of the 'Fall of Assyria'. This topic has been dealt with by many, including Oates 2000; Machinist 1995; and Zawadzki 1988.

Jeremiah and the Battle of Carchemish (605 BCE)

An often quoted text in the Book of Jeremiah informs us of the battle of Carchemish. I quote Jer. 46.1–12 (RSV):

> 1. The word of the LORD which came to Jeremiah the prophet concerning the nations. 2. About Egypt. Concerning the army of Pharaoh Necho, king of Egypt, which was by the river Euphrates at Carchemish and which Nebuchadrezzar king of Babylon defeated in the fourth year of Jehoiakim the son of Josiah, king of Judah: 3. Prepare buckler and shield, and advance for battle! 4. Harness the horses; mount, O horsemen! Take your stations with your helmets, polish your spears, put on your coats of mail! 5. Why have I seen it? They are dismayed and have turned backward. Their warriors are beaten down, and have fled in

> haste; they look not back—terror on every side! says the LORD. 6. The swift cannot flee away, nor the warrior escape; in the north by the river Euphrates they have stumbled and fallen. 7. Who is this, rising like the Nile, like rivers whose waters surge? 8. Egypt rises like the Nile, like rivers whose waters surge. He said, I will rise, I will cover the earth, I will destroy cities and their inhabitants. 9. Advance, O horses, and rage, O chariots! Let the warriors go forth: men of Ethiopia and Put who handle the shield, men of Lud, skilled in handling the bow. 10. That day is the day of the Lord GOD of hosts, a day of vengeance, to avenge himself on his foes. The sword shall devour and be sated, and drink its fill of their blood. For the Lord GOD of hosts holds a sacrifice in the north country by the river Euphrates. 11. Go up to Gilead, and take balm, O virgin daughter of Egypt! In vain you have used many medicines; there is no healing for you. 12. The nations have heard of your shame, and the earth is full of your cry; for warrior has stumbled against warrior; they have both fallen together.

The contemporary source for the Battle of Carchemish is the Babylonian Chronicle. The quote below is taken from the Babylonian Chronicle 5 in Grayson's version (Grayson 1975: 99):

> [The twenty-first year]: The king of Akkad stayed home (while) Nebuchadnezzar (II), his eldest son (and) the crown prince, mustered [the army of Akkad]. He took his army's lead and marched to Carchemish which is on the bank of the Euphrates. He crossed the river [*to encounter the army of Egypt*] which was encamped at Carchemish. [...] They did battle together. The army of Egypt retreated before him. He inflicted a [defeat] upon them (and) finished them off completely. In the district of Hamath the army of Akkad overtook the remainder of the army of [Egypt which] managed to escape [from] the defeat and which was not overcome. They [the army of Akkad] inflicted a defeat upon them (so that) a single (Egyptian) man [did not return] home. At that time Nebuchadnezzar (II) conquered all of Ha[ma]th.

Assyriologists agree on dating this event to 605 BCE. This implies that Nebuchadnezzar was still a crown prince when he crushed the Egyptian army at Carchemish. His father, Nabopolassar, who was then in his twenty-first regnal year, was staying in Babylon. Having subsequently overtaken and wiped out the rest of the Egyptian army, Nebuchadnezzar conquered all of Hamath. The name Hamath in the last line of the text above is restored, but, as we see, Hamath does appear in line 7.

When reading this Akkadian text, the historical importance of Jeremiah 46 becomes clear. Even if we are dealing with a late poetic text, reworked and with more than one agenda, it undoubtedly refers to historical circumstances known from extra biblical sources. Thus, there can be little doubt that the historical information found in Jer. 46.2 'About Egypt. Concerning the army of Pharaoh Necho, king of Egypt, which was by the river Euphrates at Carchemish and which Nebuchadrezzar king of Babylon defeated in the fourth year of Jehoiakim the son of Josiah, king of Judah...' refers to a historically true past event.

Other relevant parts of Jeremiah 46 could have been looked into. For instance, we find in this text a remarkable, indirect description of the Egyptian army. Other issues interesting to the historian would be the study of allies in light of other texts from Jeremiah and from other prophetic and historiographical texts of the Hebrew Bible in order to compare them with contemporary Near Eastern sources. Even if the Pharaoh in question is certain, the personal name Necho does not appear is the contemporary Akkadian text quoted above. Here, consequently, Jeremiah gives us a piece of unique historical information. For Necho in the Hebrew Bible, see besides Jeremiah 46 and 27 also 2 Kgs. 23.29; 2 Kgs. 24, 2 Chron. 35.21–22, and 2 Chron. 36. However, the usefulness of any of these latter documents for the historian cannot be taken for granted. Each and every text has to be investigated separately. At the same time, we should not forget that these texts in Jeremiah are not much different from a multitude of other texts in the Hebrew Bible. The prophetic books are full of 'indirect' historical information such as we find in Jeremiah 46. Here, I can mention only a couple of illustrations. One good example is Ezekiel 27. This prophetic word of doom against Tyre in the form of a satirical lament gives us at the same time important historical knowledge of the trade network of Tyre and of Phoenician economy (Liverani 1991). When Amos 1–2 is studied against the background of Neo-Assyrian royal inscriptions, it appears that the names of the foreign city states mentioned in this text do not represent later additions, but refer to a historical coalition against the Assyrians around 770 BCE (Barstad 2007).

Necho in Egyptian Sources

Nekau\Necao\Necho II (Egyptian Wahibre) of the 26th Dynasty ruled from 610–595 BCE. One reason why 'contemporary' Akkadian and Hebrew documents are so important for Necho is that indigenous Egyptian sources are practically non-existent (Redford 1982; Gozzoli 2006). Unfortunately, no military Egyptian texts from the period of

Necho II have reached us. Necho's fragmentary inscription from Elephantine with a list of boats for a possibly Nubian expedition is the only such text that has survived for posterity. As a matter of fact, there are no military records preserved from the 26th dynasty from between the Libyan campaign of Necho's father, Psammetichus I (664–610 BCE) and the Nubian campaign of Psammetichus II (595–589 BCE) (Gozzoli 2006: 101).This unfortunate circumstance is possibly caused by the not unknown phenomenon of a collective *damnatio memoriae* (Gozzoli 2006: 177 n. 98). Since we have no evidence from contemporary Egypt that bears witness to Necho's campaigns, a lot of discussion has gone into the question of Necho's whereabouts before during and after the battle at Carchemish. However, since there are no sources, it goes without saying that some of these reflections may appear as somewhat speculative (Redford 1992: 447–455). One possible clue for this debate was offered by Elmar Edel. He reminds us that the Weidner Chronicle refers not only to king Jehoiachin of Judah as a resident of Babylon, but also to other foreign kings, including Egyptian pharaohs. The name Necho, too, appears in the list (Edel 1978: 18; 1980: 25).

Necho in Herodotus

Information about the battle at Carchemish in 605 BCE is also found in Herodotus (484?–425? BCE). Egyptologists differ in their evaluation of the historical value of Herodotus's writings on Egypt. As for Necho, there seems to be a unanimous view that Herodotus is not very reliable. Herodotus' Egyptian *logoi* are recently and very competently dealt with by, among others, Roberto Gozzoli (Gozzoli 2006: 155–189) and Alan Lloyd (Lloyd 1975–1988). Gozzoli claims that the use of Herodotus as a historical source for ancient Egypt is highly problematic (Gozzoli 2006: 155–189). Lloyd, too, warns throughout his useful commentary about problems with the historical veracity of Herodotus's Egyptian *logoi* (Lloyd 1975–1988: vols. 1–3). However, Lloyd is occasionally more open to drawing historical conclusions from Herodotus.

Considering his relatively long reign (610–595 BCE) and his importance, the references to Necho in Herodotus are relatively brief. He is dealt with in chapters 158–159 of Book II. It is likely that this somewhat short description is caused by an almost complete lack of Egyptian sources for Necho II (see above). Moreover, most of the text in

Herodotus discusses the canal that Necho was supposed to have built. The topic of the canal has been discussed thoroughly, above all by Lloyd (Lloyd 1977, 1988: 149–158).

Most important to us is the following piece of information in II, 159, not dealing with the canal building.

> He then turned his attention to war; he had triremes built, some on the Mediterranean coast, others on the Arabian gulf, where the docks are still to be seen, and made use of his new fleets as occasion arose; and in addition he attacked the Syrians by land and defeated them at Magdolus, afterwards taking Gaza, a large town in Syria (Herodotus 2003: 161).

As we see, this is not a very accurate description of Necho's war activities. For details, one should consult the very thorough commentary by Lloyd (Lloyd 1988: 161–165). The 'Syrians' is a reference to the Chaldeans (Lloyd 1988: 163). Magdolus has wrongly been identified with Megiddo (cf. 2 Kgs. 23:29 and 2 Chron. 35:20–23). However, the information here that Necho killed the Judean king Josiah at Megiddo is found only in the Hebrew Bible (which is also Josephus' source). The identification of Herodotus's Magdolus with Megiddo is simply wrong. As has been demonstrated beyond doubt, most recently by Lloyd (1988: 161–163), Magdolus should be identified with the Egyptian city of Migdol (on Migdol in Jeremiah, see below). This fortified city constituted the boundary towards the north east during the 26th dynasty, and was an important entry into Egypt (Redford 1992: 457).

The most important question in relation to Herodotus's account of Necho concerns his use of sources. From where does he get his information? When there are no reliable sources for him to build upon, he is less interesting to the historian. In the case of Necho, a caveat by Lloyd should be underlined. Lloyd writes about the Necho chapters: 'Although we must make allowance for a dash of autopsy in II, 158, the subject-matter derives pre-eminently from Gk. oral tradition (cf. II, 154, 4) and reflects the selectivity, tendency to exaggeration and the world-attitudes which we would expect of such a source' (Lloyd 1988: 149). Nevertheless, on the whole, we must take care when making statements concerning the value of Herodotus as a historical source. The more one studies Herodotus, the more one realizes that the work does contain a lot of historical information. However, just as when we work with the Hebrew Bible as a history book, here too we should never make sweeping statements. Each and every piece of information in Herodotus has to be looked into separately, and to be compared with other sources. This applies also for the Egyptian *logoi*. Despite their scepticism, both Lloyd and Gozzoli endeavour to reconstruct Necho's 'Asiatic campaigns'. Lloyd makes use (mainly) of the Neo-Babylonian Chronicle, the Hebrew Bible, and Josephus (Lloyd 1988: 159). Lloyd's attempt is masterful. Since he tends to speculate more than Gozzoli, I follow here Gozzoli's 'Lloyd version'. According to Gozzoli (building on Lloyd), Necho's 'Asiatic campaigns' can be assumed to have been the following:

> 610–609 BCE, Necho was an ally of the crumpling Assyrian Empire. He overcame Josiah king of Judah at Megiddo. Following battles between the Egyptians and Chaldeans (607–605 BCE), Necho was defeated by the Chaldean king Nebuchadnezzar at Carchemish in 605 BCE. Following this defeat, the Egyptians lost control of the Levant that had been taken over momentarily by the Chaldeans. The last stage (604–595 BCE) of Necho's campaigns to the Levant was dominated by the growing power of the Chaldeans, and the pharaoh's attempts to make alliances against Nebuchadnezzar with subdued states such as Judah (Gozzoli 2006: 178 n 102, with literature).

Necho in Josephus

Occasionally, Josephus has been brought into the discussion about Necho's campaigns. Ant. 10. 84–87 (Josephus 1937) deals with the battle of Carchemish. The standard commentary on the late period in Josephus is now Begg 2000. However, in this particular case, Josephus is not very useful mainly for two reasons. Begg has shown how Josephus' Josiah story is based exclusively on the biblical texts of Kings and Chronicles (in a Greek version). This means that there is nothing in Josephus that is not also found in the Hebrew Bible. Moreover, due to the fact that Josephus quite freely rewrites his sources in order to create his own Josiah figure, his version of the story becomes too biased to be of much value in relation to the historical Necho (Begg 2000: 493–497).

Jeremiah and the Civil War in Egypt after 570 BCE

Jer. 46.13–28 (RSV):

> 13. The word which the LORD spoke to Jeremiah the prophet about the coming of Nebuchadrezzar king of Babylon to smite the land of Egypt:

> 14. Declare in Egypt, and proclaim in Migdol; proclaim in Memphis (נף) and Tahpanhes; Say, Stand ready and be prepared, for the sword shall devour round about you. 15. Why has Apis fled? Why did not your bull stand? Because the LORD thrust him down. 16. Your multitude stumbled and fell, and they said one to another, Arise, and let us go back to our own people and to the land of our birth, because of the sword of the oppressor. 17. Call the name of Pharaoh, king of Egypt, Noisy one who lets the hour go by. 18. As I live, says the King, whose name is the LORD of hosts, like Tabor among the mountains, and like Carmel by the sea, shall one come. 19. Prepare yourselves baggage for exile, O inhabitants of Egypt! For Memphis shall become a waste, a ruin, without inhabitant. 20. A beautiful heifer is Egypt, but a gadfly from the north has come upon her. 21. Even her hired soldiers in her midst are like fatted calves; yea, they have turned and fled together, they did not stand; for the day of their calamity has come upon them, the time of their punishment. 22. She makes a sound like a serpent gliding away; for her enemies march in force, and come against her with axes, like those who fell trees. 23. They shall cut down her forest, says the LORD, though it is impenetrable, because they are more numerous than locusts; they are without number. 24. The daughter of Egypt shall be put to shame, she shall be delivered into the hand of a people from the north. 25. The LORD of hosts, the God of Israel, said: Behold, I am bringing punishment upon Amon of Thebes, and Pharaoh, and Egypt and her gods and her kings, upon Pharaoh and those who trust in him. 26. I will deliver them into the hand of those who seek their life, into the hand of Nebuchadrezzar king of Babylon and his officers. Afterward Egypt shall be inhabited as in the days of old, says the LORD. 27. But fear not, O Jacob my servant, nor be dismayed, O Israel; for lo, I will save you from afar, and your offspring from the land of their captivity. Jacob shall return and have quiet and ease, and none shall make him afraid. 28. Fear not, O Jacob my servant, says the LORD, for I am with you. I will make a full end of all the nations to which I have driven you, but of you I will not make a full end. I will chasten you in just measure, and I will by no means leave you unpunished.

This text, too, provides us with a lot of important historical information, and quite a few issues could have been looked at in more detail. On the importance of Migdol during the 26th Dynasty (also called the Saite period), see above. The central role of Memphis in that same period (664–525 BCE), is known from contemporary Egyptian sources (Gozzoli 2006: 104). As a whole, Jer. 46.13–28 describes the circumstances on the eve of the civil war that took place in Egypt after 570 BCE, following the death of Pharaoh Apries (Greek form of Egyptian name Haaibra). Apries (589–570 BCE), in Jer. 45.30 called Hophra, was a contemporary of Nebuchadnezzar (604–562 BCE). Formerly an enemy, he later made an alliance with Nebuchadnezzar in order to attack Egypt, and to regain the rule from the usurper Amasis. Apries was killed, however, and Amasis (Ahmose II) was to stay in power for a very long period indeed (570–526 BCE). The main Egyptian source for these events is the Amasis stele from Elephantine, discussed in detail most recently by Gozzoli (Gozzoli 2009: 101–103. See also de Meulenaere 1975; Edel 1978; Spalinger 1979; Leahy 1988; and Redford 1992: 464–469).

Herodotus, too, has a large section on Amasis and Apries and the civil war in Egypt after 570 BCE. According to Gozzoli, this part of Herodotus is the only piece of information regarding the 26th Dynasty that can be called historical. Here, Herodotus is basically retelling the information found on the Elephantine stele of Amasis (Gozzoli 2006: 189, 101–103). One particular matter relates to Nebuchadnezzar's campaign into Egypt, referred to explicitly in Jer. 46.13. This event is referred to in the Book of Jeremiah, the Amasis stele, and in one Neo-Babylonian text. It is not, however, mentioned in Herodotus (Gozzoli 179).

Even if the Babylonian Chronicle for the times of Nebuchadnezzar must have been quite comprehensive, most of it appears, unfortunately, to be lost to posterity. BM 21946 is broken just after introducing Nebuchadnezzar's 11th year campaign into Hatti. We are very lucky therefore that there exists a fragmented text that tells of an attack on Egypt in Nebuchadnezzar's 37th year. Wiseman published new copies of BM 33041, as well as what he thought was a possible related fragment, BM 33053, in his edition of the Babylonian Chronicles (Wiseman 1961: 94–95, Pl. XX, Pl. XXI). Important new insights into this debate were offered by Edel. In a study of the Amasis stele (Edel 1978), he suggests that Apries must have fled to the court of Nebuchadnezzar in Babylon for help. Further evidence for this is to be found in the occurrence of the name of Apries in the 'Weidner Chronicle' (Edel 1980: 22–25).

Conclusion

The present paper discusses Jer. 46.1–12 and Jer. 46.13–28 in order to look into the reliability of the historical information that is found in these two Jeremiah texts. By comparing these documents to contemporary Mesopotamian and Egyptian sources, some important factual observations may be made. It is suggested that Jer. 46.1–12 contains historically accurate facts about the battle of Carchemish in 605 BCE. Likewise, Jer. 46.13–28 and Jer. 45.30 contain valuable historical information about Nebuchadnezzar's invasion into Egypt in his 37th year (568–567 BCE), and about the background for the civil war in Egypt after 570 BCE.

References

Albertz, R. 2001. *Die Exilszeit. 6. Jahrhundert v. Chr.* (Biblische Enzyklopädie, 7; Stuttgart: Kohlhammer).

Barstad, H.M. 2007. 'Can Prophetic Texts be Dated? Amos 1–2 as an Example', in *Ahab Agonistes. The Rise and Fall of the Omri Dynasty* (ed. L.L. Grabbe; Library of Hebrew Bible/Old Testament Studies, 421; European Seminar in Historical Methodology, 6; London: T & T Clark) 21–40.

——. 2009. 'What Prophets Do. Reflections on Past Reality in the Book of Jeremiah', in *Studies in the Book of Jeremiah* (ed. H.M. Barstad and R.G. Kratz; Beihefte zur Zeitschrift für die alttestamentliche Wissenschaft, 388; Berlin: De Gruyter) 10–32.

Begg, C. 2000. *Josephus' Story of the Later Monarchy (AJ 9,1–10,185)* (Bibliotheca Ephemeridum Theologicarum Lovaniensium, 145; Leuven: Leuven University Press).

Edel, E. 1978. 'Amasis und Nebukadrezar II', *Göttinger Miszellen. Beiträge zur ägyptischen Diskussion* 29: 13–20.

——. 1980. *Neue Deutungen keilschriftlicher Umschreibungen ägyptischer Wörter und Personennamen* (Österreichische Akademie der Wissenschaften. Philosophisch-historische Klasse. Sitzungsberichte, 375; Wien: Österreichische Akademie der Wissenschaften).

Gozzoli, R.B. 2006. *The Writing of History in Ancient Egypt during the First Millennium BC (ca. 1070–80 BC). Trends and Perspectives* (Golden House Publications. Egyptology, 6; London: Golden House).

Grayson, A.K. 1975. *Assyrian and Babylonian Chronicles* (Texts from Cuneiform Sources, 5; Locust Valley, NY: J.J. Augustin).

Grimal, N. 1995. *A History of Ancient Egypt* (Translated by I. Shaw; Oxford: Blackwell).

Helck, W. 1968. *Geschichte des alten Ägypten* (Handbuch der Orientalistik. Erste Abteilung. Der nahe und der mittlere Osten, 1:3; Leiden: Brill).

——. 1980 'Karkemisch', in *Lexikon der Ägyptologie* 3 (ed. W. Helck and W. Westendorf; Wiesbaden: Otto Harrassowitz) 339–341.

Herodotus. 2003. *The Histories* (Translated by A. de Sélincourt. Revised with Introduction and Notes by J. Marincola; London: Penguin Books).

James, T.G.H. 2000. 'Egypt: The Twenty-Fifth and Twenty-Sixth Dynasties', in *The Cambridge Ancient History* 3,2 (ed. J. Boardman *et al.*; Cambridge: Cambridge University Press, 2nd edn) 677–747.

Joannès, F. 2004. *The Age of Empires. Mesopotamia in the First Millennium* (Translated by A. Nevill; Edinburgh: Edinburgh University Press).

Josephus. 1937. *Jewish Antiquities, Books IX–XI* (With an English Translation by R. Marcus; The Loeb Classical Library, 6; Cambridge, MA: Harvard University Press).

Kuhrt, A. 1995. *The Ancient Near East c. 3000–330 BC* (2 vols.; London: Routledge).

Leahy, A. 1988. 'The Earliest Dated Monument of Amasis and the End of the Reign of Apries', *The Journal of Egyptian Archaeology* 74: 183–199.

Liverani, M. 1991. 'The Trade Network of Tyre according to Ezek. 27', in *AH, ASSYRIA... Studies in Assyrian History and Ancient Near Eastern Historiography Presented to Hayim Tadmor* (ed. M. Cogan and I. Eph'al; Scripta Hierosolymitana, 33; Jerusalem: The Magnes Press) 65–79.

Lloyd, A.B. 1975–1988. *Herodotus Book II* (Etudes préliminaires aux religions orientales dans l'empire romain (= EPRO), 43; 3 vols.; Leiden: Brill).

——. 1977. 'Necho and the ReedSea: Some Considerations', *The Journal of Egyptian Archaeology* 63: 142–155.

——. 1988. *Herodotus Book II. Commentary 99–182* (EPRO, 63 [3]; Leiden: Brill).

——. 1994. 'The Late Period. 664–323 BC' in B.G. Trigger, B.J. Kemp, D. O'Connor, A.B. Lloyd, *Ancient Egypt. A Social History* (Cambridge: Cambridge University Press) 279–348.

——. 2003. 'The Late Period (664–332 BC)', in *The Oxford History of Ancient Egypt* (ed. I. Shaw; Oxford: Oxford University Press, New paperback edition) 364–387.

Machinist, P. 1995. 'The Fall of Assyria in Comparative Ancient Perspective', in *Assyria* (ed. S. Parpola and R.M. Whiting; Helsinki: The Neo-Assyrian Text Corpus) 179–195.

Meulenaere, H.J. de 1975. 'Apries', in *Lexikon der Ägyptologie* 1 (ed. W. Helck and W. Westendorf; Wiesbaden: Otto Harrassowitz) 358–360.

Oates, J. 2000. 'The Fall of Assyria (635–609 BC)', in *The Cambridge Ancient History* 3,2 (ed. J. Boardman *et al.*; Cambridge: Cambridge University Press, 2nd edn) 162–193.

Redford, D.B. 1982. 'Necho II', in *Lexikon der Ägyptologie* 4 (ed. W. Helck and W. Westendorf; Wiesbaden: Otto Harrassowitz) 369–371.

——. 1992. *Egypt, Canaan, and Israel in Ancient Times* (Princeton, NJ: Princeton University Press).

Schipper, B.U. 1992. *Israel und Ägypten in der Königszeit. Die kulturellen Kontakte von Salomo bis zum Fall Jerusalems* (Orbis Biblicus et Orientalis, 170; Freiburg: Universitätsverlag, Göttingen: Vandenhoeck & Ruprecht).

Spalinger, A.J. 1979. 'The Civil War between Amasis and Apries and the Babylonian Attack against Egypt', in *First International Congress of Egyptology. Cairo, 2–10 October 1976* (ed. W.F. Reineke; Akademie der Wissenschaften der DDR; Schriften zur Geschichte und Kultur des Alten Orients, 13; Berlin: Akademie-Verlag) 593–604.

Taylor, J. 2003. 'The Third Intermediate Period (1069–664 BC)', in *The Oxford History of Ancient Egypt* (ed. I. Shaw; Oxford: Oxford University Press, New paperback edition) 324–363.

Wiseman, D.J. 1961. *Chronicles of Chaldean Kings (626–556 BC) in the British Museum* (London: The British Museum).

Zawadzki, S. 1988. *The Fall of Assyria and Median-Babylonian Relations in Light of the Nabopolassar Chronicle* (Uniwersytet Im. Adama Mickiewicza w Poznaniu. Seria Historia, 149; Poznan: Adam Mickiewicz University Press).

PSALMS, BIBLICAL THEOLOGY, AND THE CHRISTIAN CHURCH

Ronald E. Clements

In his Presidential address to the Society of Old Testament Study on January 2nd 1963 Professor G.W. Anderson chose as his title 'Israel's Creed, Sung Not Signed'. The subject was the Hebrew Psalter and the title was adapted from a phrase popularised by Professor James Denney at a time when doctrinal arguments were greatly hindering moves toward healing rifts within the Scottish churches. Denney himself faced a serious challenge from the Glasgow Presbytery after he was appointed as Professor of Systematic Theology in the United Free Church College in Glasgow in 1897, subsequently being appointed to the New Testament Chair and the Principalship (Denney 1922: ix). The particular charge levelled against him was that of denying the authority of Holy Scripture because he had suggested that King David was not the author of Ps. 110. This was in the wake of earlier dismissals and challenges in the Scottish Free Church Colleges over biblical criticism, the most celebrated being that of W. Robertson Smith in 1881. This case, which ended with Smith's dismissal, was followed by further challenges concerning the appointments of A.B. Davidson, George Adam Smith and Marcus Dods. By the time James Denney came under criticism for his view about the authorship of Ps. 110, he was keenly aware of the disruptive and divisive consequences for the Christian Church if every point of biblical criticism and theological expression was to be challenged in this way. The balance between academic integrity and Church control was not an easy one to keep. For this reason Denney's contention about the value of creeds and doctrines bears significantly and more widely on the relationship between the academic study of the Bible and the Christian Church (Gordon 2007: 358–362; Fleming 1932: 87–110).

1. The Changing Face of Biblical Theology

George Anderson was appointed in 1962 to the Chair of Old Testament Literature and Theology in Edinburgh after James Barr had left for Princeton in 1961. His presidential address to the Society for Old Testament Study was made when difficulties were resurfacing over fresh proposals for Church Reunion in Great Britain, especially affecting the Methodist, Anglican and Church of Scotland communions. These had originated with a proposal from the Methodist Conference in 1955. As a Scottish Methodist the relevance of Denney's shrewd and challenging dictum that 'The Church's confession of faith should be sung, not signed' was evident to George Anderson. It pinpointed the delicate, and often controversial, relationship between the study of theology in an academic setting and the life and worship of the Christian Church (Cheyne 1999: 301). It was also relevant to a number of contemporary publications on the subject of Old Testament theology—a subject in which he was deeply interested. It was appropriate therefore for him to recall in 1963 the celebrated theologian's dictum from more than half a century before since it reflected both on contemporary issues regarding Church reunion and on biblical theology generally. It remains an appropriate point for reflection in the present when new challenges are facing the relationship between the Christian Church and the academic study of theology.

George Anderson was especially and uniquely interested in the Book of Psalms of the Old Testament, since the use of psalms, spoken or sung, held a major place in all branches of the Christian church. In 1962 he published a short commentary on the Old Testament book in the second edition of Peake's one-volume *Commentary on the Bible* (Rowley & Black 1962). Soon after his arrival in Edinburgh he introduced a Saturday morning (10.00am–12.00) reading class on the Psalms in Hebrew for senior students and colleagues which was a memorable feature. It would be quite impossible to draw a line of distinction between the devotional and the academic merit of these classes, since he combined both aspects quite magnificently. Moreover the use of psalms, whether simply recited, chanted or accompanied by music was a recognized feature of Sunday worship for the majority of Christians—certainly in Scotland. In Scottish Churches it was the singing of hymns which had been the more controversial innovation.

This recital of the Old Testament psalms had its origins in the very earliest Christian era. As a consequence they were the part of the Old Testament most familiar to the general worshipper. Most lay persons might have expected this fact to be fully reflected in any Christian theology of the Old Testament. In this context the year of George Anderson's appointment in Edinburgh was fortuitous for a scholar who was so deeply interested in psalms, adding to the sense that his appointment marked a significant turning-point for Old Testament studies in Great Britain. He was the first non-Church of Scotland minister to be appointed as a Professor of Theology to teach in a Scottish university. 1962 happened also to be the year of publication of the English translation of the Norwegian scholar Sigmund Mowinckel's great study of the Hebrew psalms *The Psalms in Israel's Worship* (Mowinckel 1962). For a variety of reasons the book of Psalms had been less than adequately served by modern British scholarship and the publication of Mowinckel's volumes in 1962 marked a welcome step forward.

2. Biblical Criticism and the Psalms

When biblical criticism made its first strong inroads into Old Testament interpretation in Great Britain in the late Victorian era, the study of the Psalms was certainly at the back of the queue. It lagged behind other fields of research both in Great Britain and Germany. The Book of Genesis received most attention, thanks to Charles Darwin, and the Prophets came next. The Psalms were left as an afterthought. However in Germany, from as early as 1904, Hermann Gunkel began to raise fresh interpretive insights, drawing attention to their wider background in the prayers of men and women in the ancient Near East. This older oriental connection was not particularly well received, coming as it did alongside his related claims about their connection with ancient prayers from Babylon. The evident Babylonian connections of some biblical stories had been both exaggerated and misunderstood and gave rise to what came to be described as the 'Bible-Babel' controversy (Hayes 1999: 92). Gunkel's work was followed quickly by Mowinckel's.

The first attempts at a critical approach in England began with Alexander F. Kirkpatrick who took over in 1892 as general editor for the Old Testament volumes of the Cambridge Bible series of commentaries. His revised volumes of commentary on the Psalms replaced the earlier work by the conservative J.J.S. Perowne. Kirkpatrick's contributions originally appeared in three parts between 1895 and 1905, but were subsequently re-issued as a single volume. It remained popular for more than half a century, but held aloof from questions of date and authorship, and owed much of its well-deserved popularity to its retention of the devotional and literary approach of Perowne's earlier volume. The series was originally designed for use in schools, and it was Kirkpatrick who upgraded the series to cover wider critical issues.

Thereafter the progress of Psalm studies in Great Britain during the twentieth century became sharply divided between an acceptance of the late (Maccabean) dating of the Psalms advocated in Germany by Bernhard Duhm and the 'History of Religions' approach popularised by Hugo Gressmann and Hermann Gunkel. Almost nothing of a distinctively British character appeared. The late (Maccabean) dating was adopted by R.H. Kennett (1864–1932), Regius Professor of Hebrew in Cambridge from 1903–1932, who contributed an article on 'The Psalms' for the eleventh edition of *Encyclopedia Brittanica* in 1911. The Gunkel-Gressman 'History of Religions' approach was adopted by W.O.E. Oesterley (1866–1950), who wrote extensively and was Professor of Old Testament Studies at King's College, London from 1927–36. He published two books in 1911, *The Psalms in the Jewish Church* and *Life, Death and Immortality: Studies in the Psalms.* These followed a doctoral dissertation submitted by him in Cambridge in 1907 and published in the following year with the title *The Evolution of the Messianic Idea* (Oesterley 1908). His 'History of Religions' theories are very much evident in his contributions to the volume on *Hebrew Religion: Its Origin and Development* (Oesterley & Robinson 1930, 2nd 1936), where the authorship was shared with T.H. Robinson. This was still a basic textbook for me as a student in the early 1950s, intended to replace earlier Old Testament 'theologies'.

At this period the work of Gunkel, Gressman and Mowinckel was linked to the strong British anthropological interest in the Old Testament which led to the publication of a series of studies in which the relationship of myth and ritual was the primary feature. Pride of place was given to attempts to make extensive use of the Hebrew psalms to reconstruct the course and content of an Israelite New Year festival along these lines, and in particular to show the elevated part played by the king in this festival. In this way the psalms became closely associated with speculative reconstructions of an ancient world of cultic festivals.

The publication in 1962 of Mowinckel's two volumes made available to every student the researches and conclusions of an outstanding scholar who had spent virtually his entire academic life researching and writing on these ancient prayers and praises. During that time his own views had changed and developed quite markedly, initially under the influence of a connection with Frank Buchman, the American evangelical moralist and Church reformer. This made his mature reflections on the subject especially interesting and noteworthy, and George Anderson welcomed without reservation the publication of the translation. The same was not the case, however, with the other great work of Old Testament scholarship which appeared in English translation in 1962, namely the first of the two-volume *Old Testament Theology* by Gerhard von Rad (1901–1971).

As far as I was concerned—just two years into an Assistant Lectureship in Edinburgh—both great works, Mowinckel's *Psalms* and von Rad's *Old Testament Theology*, ranked high above almost everything else published in the previous ten years. Yet whereas George Anderson welcomed Mowinckel's work with unreserved delight and approval, he regarded von Rad's work with considerable caution and reserve. Since I was greatly drawn to von Rad's scholarship, I was initially at a loss to account for the difference. Like the Psalms, the subject of Old Testament theology had passed through a long period of neglect by scholars in Great Britain, and the gap was filled by translations of works by Continental scholars in the 1950s. So why was George Anderson less than overjoyed at von Rad's work? Two considerations are worthy of note.

3. Biblical Theology in Transition

Since the very beginning in the late eighteenth century of historical criticism regarding the Bible's authorship, the particular task of a 'biblical theology' had remained unclear and disputed. By 1962 a full half century of attempts to resurrect the subject as a primary component of theological teaching had stumbled and struggled to gain credibility. In the expectation of many students this was the branch, or sub-division, of Old Testament studies which could be expected to form a bridge between the erudite historical details about Ancient Israel learned in the university and the Old Testament lessons read in Church. Yet the subject had become elusive and, even where it could be found, controversial. As I learned as a teacher of Hebrew in Edinburgh's Faculty of Divinity, many students did not consider learning Hebrew to be time well-spent when the link between the Old Testament and the worship of the Church appeared so tenuous and uncertain. I strongly believed that the publication in English of the volumes of Gerhard von Rad's *Theology of the Old Testament* would provide welcome answers.

But how was this to be achieved? James Denney's contention that he had no interest in a theology that he could not preach took on a new relevance.

Von Rad's work was the latest in a line of publications on the subject published in English in a very short period of time, making up for the earlier neglect. The dearth of suitable works came to an end when translations of the writings of Walther Eichrodt, Edmund Jacob and Th. C. Vriezen were published in the 1950s, and these were now joined by the work of the scholar who was currently attracting large numbers of students to his classes in Heidelberg (Laurin 1970). His opposition to Nazi attempts to control the Church and universities in Germany in the 1930s were known to have been costly for him; his experience showed that Old Testament studies had been seriously remiss in its indifference to Judaism and Jewish understandings of the Hebrew Bible.

Why had not more Old Testament scholars spoken up earlier for Jews and Judaism? British scholars had been less guilty than their German counterparts in this regard, but the same general trend was evident of paying little attention to the history of Jewish interpretation of the Hebrew Bible (cf. Ruderman 2007). Did this fact not illustrate the point that it was possible for biblical scholars and teachers to become so detached from the needs and realities of society at large, and even from the preaching of the Church, that disastrous consequences could follow? The variety of the proposals being canvassed about the subject of Old Testament theology added to the general unease and James Barr's early publications on the subject demanded yet another significant shift of emphasis. Word studies of one kind and another had become the stock-in-trade of a large segment of what counted as 'biblical theology' and Barr's book on *The Semantics of Biblical Language* (Barr 1961) put a firm and abrupt end to this. It also brought to an end the exaggerated attempts to contrast Hebrew with Greek 'thought'. The first Christian Bibles were in Greek, as Barr, an accomplished Classical scholar, had pointed out.

Scotland had a worldwide reputation for producing preachers and teachers who synthesised in an unrivalled way the expertise of the scholar's desk and the homiletic artistry of the pulpit. Nevertheless the advent of biblical criticism had put an end to the allegorising and typology which enjoyed great popularity among Victorian preachers and motivated much popular religious art. In the twentieth century, this methodology was replaced largely by Bible word-studies, going back to the time (1737) of Alexander Cruden's (1699–1770) concordance to the words of the English Authorised Version (KJV 1611). These word-studies became a popular way of linking together the Old and New Testaments, and Bible 'Word-books' (Dictionaries) were readily available. Without Cruden's concordance it would scarcely have been possible for any but the most erudite of scholars to have pursued such studies. James Barr's book on *The Semantics of Biblical Language* showed very clearly that artificial and fallacious conclusions could all too easily be drawn from this approach.

This led to the situation in which the publication in English of the first of von Rad's volumes on the subject of Old Testament theology seemed, in my judgment of the time, to provide a satisfactory bridge between the Old Testament, as read and used in Christian Churches, and the task of the historically oriented scholar. It set out to be an 'Old Testament' theology which took account of a Christian point of view. Moreover, von Rad's speaking out at a critical time for theological study in German universities under a hostile government was a strong commendation for his work. Yet George Anderson remained guarded in his judgment and his choice of subject for his presidential address to the Society for Old Testament Study helps to explain the reason for this.

Von Rad's structural approach to the subject devolved around his isolation of what he called a 'Short Historical Credo' in which the divine initiative in bringing to birth the ancient nation of Israel formed a kind of credal confession. This established the basis of the Pentateuch (or Hexateuch, since the conquest of the land was included) and undergirded the preaching of the Prophets. Psalms and the Wisdom tradition were then relegated to the tail-end of the theology as 'Israel's Response' to the saving acts of God (G. von Rad, I 1962: 356–370). The placing of Wisdom in such a secondary position was subsequently modified by von Rad in a major book on that particular subject, but no such re-alignment regarding the Psalms was forthcoming.

It was this significant relegation of the Psalms that was the focus of George Anderson's dissatisfaction. It neither accorded with the intense human wrestling with the mystery of the divine presence and purpose which shaped the Hebrew Psalter, nor did it correspond with the actual usage of the Christian Church. The Psalms were by far the best-known and most used part of the Old Testament so far as most Christians were concerned, and this was the case from the earliest years of Christianity (Holladay 1993). Moreover the Psalms, with their intense directness and simplicity, spoke readily to all Christians across the familiar barriers of denominations and class.

It was therefore a specific background in a contemporary theological debate which provided the opportunity in 1963 for George Anderson to recall James Denney's comment regarding creeds. Adding to the equation was Charles Wesley's exceptional ability to set out in hymnody the major doctrines of the Christian faith. It is easy to see therefore why, as a Methodist George Anderson was dissatisfied with the structure of von Rad's theology, and why he approved of James Denney's dictum.

4. The Old Testament and the Christian Church

Besides his conviction that von Rad's Old Testament theology did less than justice to the significance of the Psalms in Christian theology and worship, George Anderson had a more immediate reason for concern about the role of doctrinal formularies in Christian life. As a Scottish Methodist he was firmly committed to a relatively small Christian community with a distinctive history and a distinctive spiritual heritage of which he was justly proud. It had nurtured a strong religious vitality among hard-working people, who for the most part were dependent on the demanding industry of North Sea fishing. This tradition valued religious experience highly and, in the wake of several nineteenth-century disputes over doctrinal issues which had racked the different branches of the Scottish national Church its adherents looked askance at the seeming inability of theologians to resolve their differences over uncertainties and obscurities of doctrine. 'Doctrine divides; experience unites' is not too harsh a reflection on several of the disputes that formed the background to Denney's comment.

Within Scotland Methodists were self-evidently a minority religious body, with the national Church of Scotland being the larger and older 'Sister' Church. Discussions were in process in 1962 that looked towards reunion between the major non-Catholic Church communions of Great Britain, while retaining the national boundaries which had exercised a powerful influence in shaping national life. Scottish Methodists were beginning to look decidedly isolated from their fellow Methodists south of the border, and George Anderson was very conscious of this. Hebrew psalmody, with its extraordinary history through two thousand years of Christendom, expressed a degree of 'catholicity' in religious experience which crossed to a remarkable extent national, denominational, and class boundaries. Psalms possessed an inner spiritual dynamic which enabled worshippers to form their own hermeneutic regarding enemies and threats, and promoted trust, integrity and compassion above more outwardly formal designations of membership and doctrinal allegiance. Even the geographical designations of Zion—so frequent in the Psalms—had proved no obstacle towards adopting this out-dated vocabulary of worship in the Christian Church.

Besides this the Hebrew Psalms nurtured a meaningful vocabulary of faith which placed verbal images of God as 'Refuge', 'Rock' and 'Shepherd' above the more abstruse and metaphysical responses of Protestant catechisms and the vocabulary of ritual and sacrifice which savoured of a temple cult. So the many and varied expressions of faith and anxiety described by the psalmists continue to enjoy a special significance; history has shown them to be adaptable to a wide range of political, social and religious contexts (Brueggemann 1995). They give voice to the 'inner dynamics' of faith in a disordered and disorienting world—a perspective which has strong roots in the Methodist tradition. George Anderson was unwilling to subordinate a commitment to a theology which placed great emphasis on the actualities of religious experience to one which gave primary attention to formularies and a credo-like recital of past events. This applied not only to von Rad's theology, but to any theology which appeared artificially constructed and wholly dependent on events and traditions of a long-distant past.

So far as his teaching and personal publications were concerned, George Anderson's best-known writings were a brief introduction to the literature of the Old Testament and a history of the religion of Israel before the Babylonian exile. It was however his unrivalled familiarity with Scandinavian scholarship which gained wide recognition for his work. This field of research had risen significantly in importance in Great Britain, not only in respect of Mowinckel's work, but also on account of a wide range of studies with direct bearing on the Psalms.

In addition to translating Mowinckel's book *He That Cometh* (Mowinckel 1956) on the origin of Israel's messianic hope, Anderson took a close interest in the translation and publication of Johannes Lindblom's study of Old Testament prophecy (Lindblom 1962). He also devoted much time and energy to a project for the British and Foreign Bible Society in producing a handbook for translators of the Psalms

(Anderson 1993) and delivered the Speaker's Lectures on them in the University of Oxford 1974–77. These he left unpublished.

Throughout his publications and in the years when I was his junior colleague in Edinburgh, his deep attachment to the Hebrew Psalms was unmistakeable. He was an unforgettable teacher and a most inspiring colleague who, in his own commitment to the Christian Church and the integrity of academic scholarship embodied the twin ideals which had, from the beginning, shaped the theological teaching of the Scottish universities. Scholarship and preaching belonged together. He fully understood the strong feeling which had brought forth Denney's comments at the beginning of the twentieth century; the fact that they were remembered in conversation rather than being recorded in the minutes of a meeting of a Church Presbytery or Assembly reflect their controversial dimension.

Along with his knowledge of the biblical scholars and scholarship of the 1940s and 1950s, George Anderson was fully committed to the historical-critical method which lay at the very heart of twentieth-century study of the Bible. He was, however, conscious that historical criticism by itself was not a sufficient guarantee of interpreting and commending the Bible in the manner that made it the 'Book of the Christian Church'. A dimension of faith and commitment also belonged to this which implied not that reason and faith were in conflict or contradiction, but rather that they needed to work in respectful dialogue. The Bible was, after all, not simply a book to be studied, but one to be used in worship. Like James Denney he believed that theology, if it was to contribute to national life, had to be preachable.

5. Biblical Studies in Transition

I have suggested that 1963 was a year in which the recollection of James Denney's dictum regarding the role of doctrinal 'confessions of faith' in Church life summed up several important features of the current state of biblical studies and its place in the universities and the Church. The 'historical critical method' was showing its limitations; the publication in 1962 of the second edition of Peake's one-volume *Commentary on the Bible* reflected this waning interest; it could never repeat the impact that the first edition had made. What had been new and challenging in 1920 was ordinary and of less importance in 1962, and by this time many comparable volumes were available. Above all, however, the work which introduced 'biblical criticism' to readers who had little prior knowledge of its methods and aims was now addressing readers for whom it had become a familiar fact. To those whose opinions counted most it was obvious that the Bible had human authors and required to be understood within a particular historical context. This is no criticism of the historical-critical method but recognition that it has limitations and there were new questions in need of answers. The search for the actual authors of the Bible could never become more than a search for probabilities. Critical conclusions about these matters required qualified acceptance.

The larger problem in 1962 concerned awareness that 'Old Testament theology'—a subject from which so much had been expected had simply reached an impasse. It had become a problem in its own right and served no clear agreed agenda. How did the Christian 'Old Testament' relate to the 'Hebrew Bible'? In Great Britain, John Sawyer, who was a student in Edinburgh in 1962, subsequently showed one way forward by recalling the Christian Church's use of the Old Testament with his study of the Christian appropriation of the Book of Isaiah (Sawyer 1996; Childs 2004). Since then a substantial range of studies and publications have drawn attention to the breadth of impact that the reception history of the Old Testament has had on Western culture. It is not only the Church that has used the Bible as a medium of cultural and imaginative creativity, since a wealth of literature has drawn from its writings a variety of personalities, plots, themes and ideas which give insight into the nature of human life and society (Lemon 2009).

These viewpoints found later expression in several important studies indicating that the parameters which scholars had sought to prescribe for the formation of an Old Testament theology were unduly narrow and not particularly helpful (Childs 1970; Brett 1991). The quest for a biblical theology never sat easily alongside historical criticism, not because it was mistaken in its assumptions about the Bible's authors, but because it did not deal with the wider remit of theology beyond purely historical affirmations. This was particularly evident in respect of the Old Testament. With the advent of biblical criticism, the significance of the Old Testament was largely reduced to a 'Preparation' for the coming of Jesus of Nazareth as the Messiah. The well-intended attempts to link it with anthropology and sociology forfeited too much of its spiritual appeal (Wright 1988) The merits of so doing require consideration elsewhere, but the major point was that these were not the primary concerns which had commended the Old Testament to the church life of Scotland since the seventeenth century. Wider focus on politics, social responsibility, education and personal development were all strongly linked to the Old Testament in the Scottish Reformed Church tradition and had been embodied in national life (Wright 1988:65–127). Through preaching and teaching, the stories and figures of the Old Testament had captured popular interest. The biblical critics appeared to have shrunk the Old Testament, and George Anderson felt that it was the task of the serious scholar to restore it to a larger reality.

In some respects the subsequent concern to redress the balance by resorting to a 'canonical' approach to the subject of Old Testament and biblical theology correctly addressed the problem, but laid itself open to too wide a variety of interpretations. It has ultimately raised fresh difficulties. The first concern lay with the necessity for biblical scholarship at an academic level to remain in meaningful dialogue with the methods and conventions of the worship of the Christian Church. The appeal of 'Fundamentalism' which gained ground rapidly in the 1960s rested on its claim to fill the gap between the pulpit and the scholar's desk (Barr 1967).

Reconstructions of the history of Ancient Israel and its religion satisfied the needs of the scholar but all too easily forfeited a direct connection with the Christian Church. There is a constant need to remember that the Old Testament is a book (more strictly a collection of books) of the Christian Church (Barton 1988). Recognition that the New Testament built heavily on the Old Testament became once again an important issue. Perhaps most of all there was a growing awareness of the strangeness in seeking to construct a 'Theology of the Old Testament', or even a 'Theology of the Old and New Testaments' which would be a body of truth that had never before been formulated in this way. The methods and teaching of the early Church Fathers and the great Rabbis of Talmudic Judaism were sufficiently known and accessible to show that they did not possess such a theology. Theology could only be truly 'biblical' by engaging more fully with the actual history of the Bible and its interpretation (Charity 1966 [1987]).

In this setting of a contemporary debate about the nature of Old Testament theology and the way the Bible is read and understood in Churches, the dictum of James Denney remains a topic for reflection. It is not too big a retrospect on the situation that existed for the study of the Bible in British universities in 1963 to claim that it marked a highly significant turning-point. George Anderson's recall of James Denney's comment, coined in the wake of Church controversies, witnesses to the important choices that had to be made at that time regarding scholarship and the life of the Christian Church (Berlinerblau 2005). It is a pleasure to offer these reflections on my own experience in tribute to Robert Gordon who has so expertly and courageously served the needs of both. In doing so I am pleased also to record a deep indebtedness to George Anderson whose example and leadership has remained an inspiration.

References

Anderson, G.W. 1961–1962. 'Recent Biblical Theologies: Th. C. Vriezen's Outline of Old Testament Theology', *Expository Times* 73: 113–116.

Barr, J. 1961. *The Semantics of Biblical Language* (London: Oxford University Press).

——. 1961–62. 'Recent Biblical Theologies. Gerhard von Rad's Theologie des Alten Testaments', *Expository Times* 73: 142–146.

——. 1967. *Fundamentalism* (London: SCM Press).

Barton, J. 1988. *People of the Book? The Authority of the Bible in Christianity* (London: SPCK).

Berlinerblau, J. 2005. *The Secular Bible* (Cambridge: Cambridge University Press).

Brett, M.G. 1991. *Biblical Criticism in Crisis? The Impact of the Canonical Approach on Old Testament Studies* (Cambridge: Cambridge University Press).

Brueggemann, W. 1995. *The Psalms and the Life of Faith* (ed. P.D. Miller; Minneapolis: Fortress).

Charity, A.C. 1967. [1987] *Events and their Afterlife. The Dialectics of Christian Typology in the Bible and Dante* (Cambridge: Cambridge University Press).

Cheyne, A.C. 1999. *Studies in Scottish Church History* (Edinburgh: T & T Clark).

Childs, B.S. 1970. *Biblical Theology in Crisis* (Philadelphia: Westminster Press).

——. 2004. *The Struggle to Understand Isaiah as Christian Scripture* (Grand Rapids: Eerdmans).

Denney, J. 1922. *The Letters of Principal James Denney to his Family and Friends* (ed. J. Moffatt; London: Hodder & Stoughton).

Fleming, J.R. 1933. *The Church in Scotland 1875–1929* (Edinburgh: T & T Clark).

Gordon, J.M. 2007. 'Denney, James (1856–1917)', *Dictionary of Major Biblical Interpreters* (ed. D.M. McKim; Downers Grove: IVP Academic) 358–362.

Hayes, J.H. 1999. *Dictionary of Biblical Interpretation* (2 vols.; Nashville: Abingdon Press).

Holladay, W.L. 1993. *The Psalms Through Three Thousand Years* (Minneapolis: Fortress).

Laurin, R.B. (ed.) 1970. *Contemporary Old Testament Theologians* (Valley Forge: Judson).

Lemon, R. *et al.* (eds.) 2009. *The Blackwell Companion to the Bible in English Literature* (Oxford: Blackwell-Wiley).

Lindblom, J. 1962. *A History of Prophecy in Israel* (Oxford: Blackwell).

Mowinckel, S. 1956. *He That Cometh* (trans. G.W. Anderson; Oxford: Blackwell).

——. 1962. *The Psalms in Israel's Worship* (2 vols.; trans. D.R. Ap-Thomas; Oxford: Blackwell).

Rowley, H.H., and M.H. Black 1962. *Peake's Commentary on the Bible* (2nd fully revised edition; Edinburgh: Nelson & Sons).
Ruderman, D.B. 2007. *Connecting the Covenants. Judaism and the Search for Christian Identity in Eighteenth-Century England* (Philadelphia: University of Pennsylvania Press).
Sawyer, J.F.A. 1996. *The Fifth Gospel. Isaiah in the History of Christianity* (Cambridge: Cambridge University Press).
Wright, D.F. 1988. *The Bible in Scottish Life and Literature* (Edinburgh: The St Andrew Press).

ON THE COHERENCE OF THE THIRD DIALOGIC CYCLE IN THE BOOK OF JOB

V. Philips Long

Introduction

While holistic, or synchronic, approaches to the book of Job seem to be gaining traction in recent Job scholarship, the so-called third cycle of dialogue between Job and his friends (chs 22–27) continues to perplex commentators. Rachel Magdalene, for instance, in her stimulating study of the book of Job in the light of Neo-Babylonian trial law, writes: 'While I attempt to read the bulk of the text synchronically, I believe that theologically driven dislocations and corruptions due to lost material exist from chapter 21 to chapter 28' (Magdalene 2007: 9 n. 32). In the present essay, I want to consider what can be said in favor of the coherence of the third cycle and its relation to its textual surroundings. One of the many convictions I developed while under the doctoral supervision of Robert Gordon is that interpretation should always begin with careful and sustained reading of the extant literary deposit, ever attending to the Hebrew Bible's 'simplicity of the highest cunning' (cf. Gordon 1988). If the Hebrew Bible's *narratives* are 'cunning,' which is Gordon's point in the essay cited, how much more so its *poems*, even if they make no pretence of simplicity. It is with pleasure and gratitude that I dedicate to Robert Gordon the following essay, in which I hope to demonstrate that the extant shape of the third cycle of the dialogues in Job is not as implausible as is often assumed.

I shall begin with a brief rehearsal of key features believed to weigh against the coherence of the third cycle, after which I shall offer some counter observations. This will lead to a consideration of the origin and placement of Job 28 and of the significance of the current shape of the third cycle for our understanding of the complex portrait of Job in the book bearing his name.

Perceived Problems in the Third Cycle

1. The third cycle seems *disjointed*, even ‘thoroughly scrambled’, as Pope puts it (1973: xx). While the preceding dialogues enjoy a measure of coherence and forward movement, of point and counterpoint, the exchanges in the third cycle seem often to miss (or at least to sidestep) the point just made by the previous speaker. How one speech leads to the putative response of the next is not immediately apparent.
2. The third cycle is *truncated*. While the first two dialogic cycles (Job 4–14; 15–21) show a consistent interlocutory pattern with each of the three friends, Eliphaz, Bildad, and Zophar, speaking in sequence, and with Job’s responses to each interspersed, the third cycle lacks any speech by Zophar, and Bildad’s speech is uncharacteristically short (25.1–6).
3. Some of the speeches in the third cycle seem *misascribed*. That is to say, according to the Hebrew Bible’s attribution of the speeches, Job at times espouses viewpoints voiced elsewhere (and earlier) by his friends. Most famously, he articulates in 27.13–23 the certain fate of the wicked and, in so doing, gives eloquent expression to the principle of retributive justice that lay at the heart of his friends’ attacks upon him!
4. As the third cycle draws to an end, we are presented with seemingly *contradictory portraits of Job*. The protesting and combative Job encountered in chs. 26, 27 and again in 29 jars with the more reflective Job of ch. 28—so much so that most commentators assume that ch. 28 must be an interpolation by the poet or someone else.
5. The identical and *distinctive formulae in 27.1 and 29.1*—viz., וַיֹּסֶף אִיּוֹב שְׂאֵת מְשָׁלוֹ וַיֹּאמַר, commonly rendered something like ‘Job again took up his discourse and said’[1]—*are puzzling* with respect to their purpose and meaning and, in any case, differ from the normal formula by which Job’s speeches elsewhere in the book are consistently introduced: ‘and Job answered and said’ (וַיַּעַן אִיּוֹב וַיֹּאמַר in 3.2; 6.1; 9.1; 12.1; 16.1; 19.1; 21.1; 23.1; 26.1).

These are some of the perceived problems in the third cycle. What can be said in response?

[1] Unless otherwise specified, English translations are taken from the *NRSV*.

Arguments in Favour of the Current Shape and Speaker Assignments of the Third Cycle

1. That the third cycle should seem *disjointed* is not surprising when we consider the general trajectory of the dialogues to this point.[2] The increasing sharpness and directness in the friends' challenge to Job is hard to miss, as is Job's growing despair of any meaningful dialogue with them. Very broadly speaking, when the friends' principled defense of *God's justice* in the first round of dialogues and their fervent description of the certain *fate of the wicked* in the second fail to elicit the desired response from Job, Eliphaz moves in the third round to charge Job explicitly with egregious sins: 'Is not your wickedness great? There is no end to your iniquities' (22.5). As the friends' accusatory rhetoric heats up, so does Job's defensiveness until, by ch. 27, Job is ready to quit the conversation with his friends-become-enemies altogether (27.7).

As so often happens in heated arguments, the friends wittingly or unwittingly misrepresent Job's own claims. For instance, in 8.6; 11.4; and 15.14–15, Bildad, Zophar, and Eliphaz, respectively, state or insinuate that Job claims to be 'pure' (זַךְ). But apart from one mundane reference to cleansing his hands with lye (9.30) and a description of his prayer as 'pure' (16.17), Job never uses the term. Bildad returns to the term a second time in his final speech, asking how one 'born of women' can be 'pure' (25.4), again insinuating that this has been Job's claim. Beyond the third cycle, the tendency of Job's interlocutors to 'perfect the enemy' reaches a climax in Elihu's misrepresentation in 33.8–9 of Job's stated position: 'Surely, you have spoken in my hearing, and I have heard the sound of your words. You say, "I am pure (זַךְ), and without transgression (בְּלִי פָשַׁע); I am clean (חַף, a *hapax legomenon*), and there is no iniquity (עָוֺן) in me"' (my translation). As noted, however, Job never in fact claims to be 'pure', nor does he ever claim to be 'without transgression' or to have 'no iniquity'—his plaintive *question* in Job 13:22–24 notwithstanding. Attention to detail suggests that Elihu is somewhat inaccurate (and unfair) also in

[2] For succinct recent analyses of the friends' arguments, see Phillips (2008: 34–35); Timmer (2009: 294–94). More fully, see Engljähringer (2003). Burrell (2008: 27–34) characterizes Eliphaz, Bildad, and Zophar as 'dogmatist', 'jurist', and 'philosopher', respectively.

his characterizations of Job's words in 34.5–6, 9 and 35.3, 15, though space constraints do not allow further comment here.[3]

As the chasm between Job and his friends becomes unbridgeable, the disputants begin 'talking past' one another, and this in turn contributes to the sense that the third cycle is disjointed.

2. The dialogic trajectory just described also helps explain why the third cycle is *truncated*. Both Job and his friends have begun to tire of a debate that is going nowhere. Already by the end of the first round of dialogues, Job seems to have realized two things: first, that his friends have little to offer in terms of consolation or explanation of his suffering—'Look, my eye has seen all this, my ear has heard and understood it. What you know, I also know; I am not inferior to you' (13.1–2); and secondly, that answers, if any are to be found, will have to come from a higher source—'But I would speak to the Almighty, and I desire to argue my case with God' (13.3). This initial impression is confirmed in round after round of debate until the friends simply run out of steam—thus the truncated speech from Bildad (25.1–6) and the absence of Zophar altogether. So, Job is done talking *with his friends* after ch. 27, but he is not done talking. He will not rest his case until he has (metaphorically) signed his defense and challenged the Almighty to answer (31.35). Only then are the words of Job 'completed' (31.40) (תַּ֫מּוּ).[4]

3. If the fact that the third cycle is disjointed and truncated can be explained on contextual grounds, perhaps the same can be said of the speeches that seem misascribed. As noted, the most striking such instance is Job's forceful articulation in 27.13–23 of the principle of

---

[3] For detailed discussion, see Diewert (1991), who, though more favourable than I am towards Elihu, nevertheless concedes that Elihu's characterizations go beyond what Job actually claims: 'The exact wording of these declarations of innocence [in 33.8–9] are not found on Job's lips' (167); 34.5 is 'not taken *verbatim* from one of the earlier speeches' (265) and 34.6 finds 'no precise correlative in the earlier speeches' (267); etc.

[4] Given the importance of the lexeme תמם in the book of Job (e.g., in the Prologue's divine and authorial declarations of Job's 'blamelessness' [1.1, 8; 2.3] and in Job's insistence that he will never set aside his 'integrity' [27.5]), the fact that the writer should employ it here, rather than the more common כלה, evokes a question. Are Job's words not only 'completed' but 'blameless'? 'Perfect' in an absolute sense they are not, for Job will later confess to having spoken of things beyond his understanding and knowledge (42.3). But they have been 'blameless' in the sense of being genuine, relational and honest. In other words, they have had integrity (תֻּמָּה); cf. Wilson (2007: 355).

retributive justice. Surely, this sounds more like something one of Job's friends would say! And, indeed, many commentators would reassign the passage as belonging to Zophar's missing third speech.[5] But Job doesn't deny retributive justice *per se*—recall 'What you know, I also know' (13.2), and see further his words to Bildad, 'Indeed I know that this is so' (9.2); to Zophar, 'Who does not know such things as these?' (12.3); and to Eliphaz, 'I have heard many such things… I also could talk as you do' (16.2, 4).[6] What Job resists (and resents) is his friends' insistence that this principle, and no other, accounts for his present suffering. Indeed, he regards their accusations as tantamount to a lying smear campaign (13.4). Job, like the writer of Psalm 73, is keenly aware that the wicked sometimes prosper and the righteous suffer; his final speech in round two makes this clear enough (ch. 21). If his friends would but look, listen, or travel (21.29), they would know as well as he does of such anomalous situations.[7] Also like the psalmist (see Ps. 73:15–20), Job distances himself from the defiant attitudes that the wicked derive from such anomalies (21.14–16).[8]

Job's nuanced approach to the application of wisdom tenets[9] is utterly lost on Eliphaz, as he launches the third cycle of dialogues. In ch. 22 Eliphaz charges Job with endless iniquity (22.5), of abusing widows, fatherless, and family 'for no reason' (22.6) (חִנָּם),[10] and even

[5] So, e.g., Magdalene (2007: 9 n. 32).

[6] Job's acceptance of the principle of retribution may even be implicit in his threat that his friends should 'fear the sword' themselves (19.29).

[7] Even the book of Proverbs would not subscribe to the kind of woodenly applied retributive justice principle preached by Job's friends; see Fox (2007: 682–683) for an insightful discussion of 'anomaly proverbs'. According to Fox, such proverbs, 'when read in the context provided by the other proverbs, are not 'heretical or ideologically disruptive' but, rather, 'describe a stage before the eventual rectification, whose inevitability is asserted repeatedly'. Is this not the pattern we find also in the book of Job: 'anomalous' (i.e. undeserved) suffering followed by eventual restoration in Job 42.10–17? In this light, to characterize Job's friends as defending 'the standard concepts of the orthodox tradition' (Schmidt and Nel [2003: 83]) and to conclude that 'the author of Job brought into play a new perspective on God that is not part of the traditional theology of wisdom' (ibid., 93) seems misguided.

[8] The proper translation of 21.16b and its parallel in 22.18b is debated. For an alternative to the common rendering (lit. 'far from me'), see Clines (2006: 504 and his discussion on 509–510) who suggests reading 'far from him'.

[9] The key point, implicit in the biblical text and widely recognized by biblical scholars, is that wisdom sayings may be true *in principle* and, indeed, *as principles*, but they are *not equally applicable* in any or every situation; pairings of seemingly opposing proverbs, e.g. Proverbs 26.4–5, prove the point well enough.

[10] This is the fourth and final time that the word חִנָּם occurs in the book of Job, and its use here reminds the attentive reader of the *actual* reasons for Job's suffering, in

of impugning God's perspicacity ('What does God know?' 22.13). Parroting Job's words from 21.16b, Eliphaz 'distances' himself from all such wickedness (22.18). Then picking up on Job's sardonic plea in 21.3 that his friends listen before continuing to 'mock' (לעג), Eliphaz sarcastically remarks that mocking (לעג) is precisely the reaction Job should expect from the innocent, among whom Eliphaz clearly counts himself (22.19). Job's only option, according to Eliphaz, is to repent and return to God (22.21–23). If Job will but abandon his gold and make the Almighty his 'gold' (22.24–25), he will be restored.

Job does not even honour Eliphaz's speech with a direct answer. Instead, he turns his attention towards God, complaining bitterly that God cannot be found (23.1–9). So Job ignores Eliphaz's charges, but he has not missed them, as his double ironic reversal in 23.10 indicates: 'he [God] *knows* the way that I take' (contrast 22.13); 'when he has tested me, I shall come out like *gold*' (recall 22.24–25; my emphases).[11] Though cognizant of his own faithfulness (23.11–12), Job is no more confident of what God may do with him (23.13) than he was back in ch. 21. And so he remains as 'dismayed' or 'terrified' (בהל) in 23.15–16 as he had been in 21.6. Eliphaz's attempt to pin the dread that 'terrifies' (בהל) Job (22.10) on Job's great wickedness (22.5) marks yet another linguistic tie to Job's speeches before and after.[12] But Eliphaz misses the mark with respect to the actual cause of Job's dread, namely, the inscrutability of God's actions; the latter part of Job's first speech in the third round comprises a lengthy description of evil doers (24.1–12) and lovers of darkness (24.13–17), punctuated by remarks on the vexing timing of God's judgement (24.1, 12). That Job concludes with a section describing the *eventual* fate of the wicked (24.18–25) confirms that he is no enemy of the principle of retributive justice, just of its misapplication!

Bildad seems almost at a loss to respond. Perhaps pricked by Job's insinuations that 'just desserts' are not doled out as tidily as one might wish, Bildad insists (rather weakly?) that God does establish 'order' (שָׁלוֹם) in the heights (25.2); his 'light' does shine on everyone (25.3;

contradistinction to Eliphaz's false charges; see the Accuser's charge in 1.9, Yahweh's pronouncement in 2.3, and Job's lament in 9.17.

[11] Further linguistic ties between the speech of Eliphaz in ch. 22 and of Job in chs. 23–24 (e.g., the 'exacting of pledges' in 22.6; 24.3, 9) are too numerous to discuss here, but they are sufficient to suggest that these exchanges, despite their jolting feel, are not misarranged or misassigned.

[12] The only other occurrence of בהל in Job is in Eliphaz's first speech (4.5).

even on 'those who rebel against the light' [24.13]?); and, in any case, it is absurd for man, who is but a maggot, to claim to be 'pure' (זכה), since even the moon and stars cannot claim to be 'pure in his sight' (25.4–6). If all this is meant to challenge Job in some way, it fails, for Job would deny nothing of Bildad's first two points regarding order and light (see comments on 26.5–14 below), and the third is mistargeted since, as we have already noted, Job never claims to be 'pure' (זכה).

So banal is Bildad's tepid speech that Job cannot resist a stingingly sarcastic rejoinder (26.1–4): 'How you have helped the powerless!... What advice you have offered to one without wisdom!... Who has helped you utter these words? And whose spirit spoke from your mouth?' (*NIV*). He then bests Bildad's speech by ringing the changes on the very themes that Bildad introduced and more (26.5–13), concluding with a striking description of the *limits* of human wisdom: 'These are indeed but the outskirts of his ways; and how small a whisper do we hear of him! But the thunder of his power who can understand?' (26.14). Humans are finite in knowledge and in power, but they are not worms! As Job's anger with Bildad subsides and he is caught up in the grandeur of his theme—viz., the power and dominion of One before whom even Death and Destruction (אֲבַדּוֹן) lie naked and exposed (26.6)—it seems as if Job is relaxing his defensive posture and drifting into a more reflective mood.

But if this is so, it doesn't last long, for as ch. 27 opens Job is again in pitched protest against his friends, vehemently refusing to admit that their accusations are founded and adamantly maintaining his 'integrity' (תֻּמָּה v. 5).[13] After invoking a curse on his 'enemy' (his friends?) in 27.7–10, Job announces his intention to teach his friends what they already know full well (27.11–12), namely, the certain fate of the wicked (27.13–23). Putting the proof to his earlier claim that he could speak as they do (16.4), Job declares that, however many the progeny of the wicked (27.14) and however high their heaps of silver (27.16), the power of the east wind will hiss them out of their place (27.23)! By expounding in ch. 27 on what the wicked can surely expect, Job reinstates himself as a sage (cf. Childs 1979: 542) and perhaps also sets the stage for his defence of his own behavior in ch. 29.

[13] Interestingly, תֻּמָּה occurs elsewhere in Job only in the divine commendation of 2.3, the spousal challenge of 2.9, and Job's final challenge to God in 31.6.

But before Job's final defence begins in ch. 29, there is ch. 28. What are we to make of it? Although no new speaker is introduced, most scholars assume that Job cannot be the speaker; the shift in mood and perspective seems just too great. But is it? Consideration of the next perceived difficulty may shed light on this question.

4. What are we to make of the seemingly *contradictory portraits of Job* in the third cycle? If we allow Job the status of a 'rounded character' and take a true-to-life approach, then the real question is, 'What else should we expect?' Are not dramatic swings of emotion and 'outlook' precisely what people suffering great loss or under great pressure experience? Particularly people of faith can find themselves torn between the verities of faith that encourage trust and the experiences of life that cause angst and even anger—witness the lament psalms. I shall have more to say about ch. 28 presently, but first we must consider the question whether the text of Job itself contains any formal markers of Job's swing from one emotional pole to the other. This brings us to the last of the perceived problems mentioned at the start of this essay.

5. I want to suggest that the *distinctive formula* with which chs. 27 and 29 begin may be just the kind of mood-swing or outlook-shift marker we are seeking.[14] As noted earlier, Job's speeches elsewhere in the book are always introduced very simply and consistently: וַיַּ֖עַן אִיּ֣וֹב וַיֹּאמַֽר (lit. 'then Job answered and said'). Why then the distinctive formula in 27.1 and 29.1: וַיֹּ֣סֶף אִ֭יּוֹב שְׂאֵ֥ת מְשָׁל֗וֹ וַיֹּאמַֽר (lit. 'then Job again took up his מָשָׁל and said')? The noun מָשָׁל is best known for its use in wisdom contexts. Indeed, 'Le משל est la forme typique du genre sapientiel, proverbe, parabole ou fable' (Mies 2006: 243). But the term occurs also among the prophets, where it can exhibit 'a further nuance of meaning', often involving warning or admonition (Wilson 1997: II, 1135). Of particular pertinence to our present concern are other instances in the Hebrew Bible where the noun מָשָׁל is combined with the verb נָשָׂא, as here in Job 27.1 and 29.1. In the Latter Prophets, the combination occurs in Isa. 14.4; Mic. 2.4; and Hab. 2.6. How best to render מָשָׁל in these contexts is not obvious, and translations

[14] Whybray (1998: 118) remarks that 'The heading in 27.1 seems to have been intended to indicate a change of direction', viz. 'The debate with the friends is now complete, and the friends do not speak again', but Whybray does not comment on the tonal shift in Job's address.

display a range of options: e.g., discourse, oracle, wisdom, taunt.[15] In any case, given the contexts, something negative or confrontational in tone seems to be in view. Mies understands מָשָׁל in Hab. 2.6 to denote 'un oracle du malheur' and in Isa. 14.4 and Mic. 2.4 to have the sense of 'satire' or 'raillerie' (2006: 244). The *NRSV* chooses 'taunt' in each instance, thus highlighting the negative, contentious character of the pronouncements.[16] Directly relevant to our understanding of the נָשָׂא מָשָׁל formula are the Balaam narratives, where the formula occurs seven times (Num. 23.7, 18; 24.3, 15, 20, 21, 23). The interpersonal dynamic between the Moabite king Balak, who wants Balaam to curse Israel, and Balaam, who finds himself unable to do so, becomes so confrontational that Balak eventually burns with anger against Balaam (Num. 24.10). In this context of disputation, Balaam repeatedly 'takes up' his מָשָׁל and utters precisely what Balak does not want to hear. Thus, as in the three prophetic passages noted above, there is an element of combativeness in Balaam's speeches. Should we read Job 27.1 and 29.1 along these lines?

The introductory formula has perplexed commentators, especially its occurrence in 27.1.[17] Those who have wrestled with the question tend to cite *literary form* as primarily in view. Mies, for instance, noting the particularly parallelistic form of Balaam's speeches, concludes: 'en usant de l'expression נשא משל, le narrateur précise que le discours qui suivra sera poétique, solennel et sapientiel' (2006: 244). Similarly, Habel writes:

> the expression here [in Job] probably refers to the formal oath and imprecation character of the speech which follows. Job is no longer merely responding to his friends, though he does address them in vs. 11–12, but is making a weighty formal public "pronouncement" before the court (1985: 379).

While not wishing to disagree with what these statements affirm, I would argue that something more seems to be involved in Job 27.1

[15] On the range of meaning of מָשָׁל, Beyse (1998: 67) writes: 'Otto Eisfeldt is probably correct in seeing a development from simple, prosaic popular proverbs to taunt songs on the one hand and to poetically framed wisdom sayings on the other.'

[16] This sense is attested also among the Dead Sea Scrolls: e.g., in 1QpHab 8:6 (Pesher to Habakkuk) and in 11Q19 59:2: 'they shall disband them over many lands and they shall be a horror, a byword [משל] and a gibe' (Martínez 1996: 175).

[17] Some regard it as secondary (e.g., Hartley 1988: 368; Gordis 1965: 275–276), others as indicating in one way or another the special character of the speech Job is delivering (e.g., Wolfers 1995: 246–247).

and 29.1. It is not simply that Job continues his 'discourse', however solemn, poetical, or public. In each instance, rather, Job seems to be returning to a more combative, defensive posture after a calmer, more reflective section. In both 26.5–14 and 28.1–28, which immediately precede the formulae in 27.1 and 29.1, Job (if we allow him ch. 28 [see below]) seems to calm down for a time as he ponders God's wisdom and power and the strikingly limited ability of human beings to understand either: 'how small a whisper we hear of him? But the thunder of his power who can understand?' (26.14); 'where does wisdom come from?… It is hidden from the eyes of all living,… God understands the way to it, and he knows its place' (28.20–23 and *passim*). These times of circumspection and reflection are short-lived, however, for soon enough Job again 'takes up his מָשָׁל'; that is, he reassumes his stridently defensive posture.[18] My contention is that Job 27.1 and 29.1 mark these shifts. The first launches Job's final defence before his friends ('Far be it from me to say that you are right', 27.5), while the second his final defence before God ('I cry to you and you do not answer', 30.20; 'Here is my signature! let the Almighty answer me', 31.35). Perhaps renderings such as 'Then Job again took up his defensive protest and said…' or 'Then Job returned to his combative posture and said…' would be about right for both 27.1 and 29.1.[19]

What about Chapter 28 and Beyond?

The problematic of Job 28 is stated plainly by P. van der Lugt: 'The meaning of ch. 28 and its function within the poetic main body of the book of Job is one of the most disputed topics relating to this large-scale composition. It is a fairly common tradition among scholars to take this chapter as an isolated poem' (1995: 521). As suggested already

[18] This nuanced understanding of מָשָׁל in contexts such as Job 27.1 and 29.1 may find some support in Job 13.12, where 'proverbs' and 'defenses' stand in parallel: 'Your maxims are proverbs of ashes, your defenses are defenses of clay' . Whether we are to read 'defenses' (I גַּב) or 'responses' (II גַּב) in the second half of this verse is debated; see Michel 1987: 301–302 . Clines (1989: 282) dismisses the traditional rendering on the basis that 'defenses' 'would be a strange parallel to "proverbs"'. But if our reading of Job 27.1 and 29.1 is roughly on target, then the parallelism is apt. *HALOT*, 'II * גַּב,' suggests a possible wordplay in Job 13.12 with I גַּב.

[19] Pirot (1950: 573) regards Job's מָשָׁל as a complaint ('plainte') marked by black humour ('humour noir').

above, however, ch. 28 can and perhaps should be read as coming from Job.[20] What can be said in support of this position?

First, 'There is nothing in the text...to suggest a break in continuity' (Whybray 1998: 121). Secondly, despite the shift in theme and tone between chs. 27 and 28, certain linguistic subtleties appear to link the two: e.g., the reference to 'silver' in 28.1a recalls the 'silver' of the wicked in 27.16–17, while the 'place' (מָקוֹם) of gold in 28.1b links in catch-word fashion with the 'place', mentioned twice at the end of ch. 27, from which the east wind 'hisses' the wicked (27.21, 23). Thirdly, אֲבַדּוֹן ('destruction, realm of the dead') occurs but three times in the book of Job: in 26.6, 28.22, and 31.12. As the first and last are from the mouth of Job, it would be fitting for the second (28.22) to be from Job as well. Fourthly, ch. 28's sober acknowledgement of the starkly limited character of human understanding is not out of character for Job, as some have supposed. Indeed, the theme of epistemological limitation is anticipated already in Job's speech in 26.5–14. If Job can speak eloquently of God's power and of 'how small a whisper...we hear of him' (26.14), why should he not also be allowed to speak of the hiddenness of wisdom 'from the eyes of all living' (28.21)? Finally—though there is much more that could be said on this topic—if we assume Job to be the speaker of ch. 28, the pattern argued above of Job's vacillating between periods of relative calm and periods of renewed combativeness is reinforced—viz. calm in 26.5–14, combativeness in 27.1–23, calm in 28.1–28, combativeness in chaps 29–31. In chs. 29–31 there is less anger and sarcasm in Job's voice, but this is because, having finished with his friends (enemies) in ch. 27, Job is no longer responding so much to their provocations as to his own misery and his desire for an audience with God.

The effect of recognizing Job as the speaker of ch. 28 is to soften the division between the three cycles of dialogue prior to ch. 28 and the three monologues following ch. 28. As the friends simply run out of words and arguments, Job gains momentum, and this momentum carries him right through to his challenge at the end of ch. 31. The dialogic mode that characterized the debates gives way to a monologic mode (even bordering on soliloquy in ch. 28).

---

[20] Finding advocates of accepting ch. 28 as from the mouth of Job is not as difficult as it once was: see, e.g., Janzen (1985: 187); Magallanes (2004); van der Lugt (1995: 520–29); Wilson (2007: 299–300).

Conclusion

Job is a complex book, 'inviting many competing interpretive perspectives' (Jacobson 2006: 50; cf. Balentine 2002). This very complexity is part of the book's beauty and power. The above study has looked afresh at a couple of the more controversial questions in Joban studies, namely, the integrity and coherence of the third dialogic cycle in Job and the function of ch. 28 in relation to what precedes and what follows. I have attempted to demonstrate that, provided we resist the temptation to reduce Job to a less than three-dimensional character, the third cycle can be read as a coherent conclusion to the preceding dialogues between Job and his friends *and* as a fitting transition to Job's final statement of his case, culminating in his challenge to the Almighty to hear his case and answer him. Job's outpouring of words in the third cycle ranges from profound, almost serene reflection to vehement, defensive challenge, suggesting a commensurate emotional and psychological volatility in Job. This, I have suggested, is neither more nor less than should be expected of a person of deep faith in the midst of severe trial.[21]

References

Balentine, S.E. 2002. 'Have You Considered My Servant Job?' *Review and Expositor* 99: 495–501.

Beyse, K.-M. 1998. 'מָשָׁל', in *Theological Dictionary of the Old Testament* (eds. G.J. Botterweck, H. Ringgren and H.-J. Fabry; Grand Rapids: Eerdmans) vol. 9: 64–67.

Burrel, D.B. with A.H. Johns. 2008. *Deconstructing Theodicy: Why Job Has Nothing to Say to the Puzzle of Suffering* (Grand Rapids: Brazos).

Childs, B.S. 1979. *Introduction to the Old Testament as Scripture* (Philadelphia: Fortress).

Clines, D.J.A. 2006. *Job 21–37* (Word Biblical Commentary, 18a; Nashville: Thomas Nelson).

Diewert, D.A. 1991. 'The Composition of the Elihu Speeches: A Poetic and Structural Analysis', Ph.D. diss., University of Toronto.

Engljähringer, K. 2003. *Theologie im Streitgespräch: Studien zur Dynamik der Dialoge des Buches Ijob* (Stuttgart: Verlag Katholisches Bibelwerk).

[21] Further confirmation of the proposed understanding of the third cycle in its present shape and context would require testing its 'fit' within a larger discussion of the message of the book as a whole, but such discussion moves beyond the limits of the present essay.

Fox, M.V. 2007. 'The Epistemology of the Book of Proverbs', *Journal of Biblical Literature* 126: 669–684.
Gordis, R. 1965. *The Book of God and Man: A Study of Job* (Chicago: The University of Chicago Press).
Gordon, R.P. 1988. 'Simplicity of the Highest Cunning: Narrative Art in the Old Testament', *Scottish Bulletin of Evangelical Theology* 6: 69–80.
Habel, N.C. 1985. *The Book of Job: A Commentary* (Old Testament Library; Philadelphia: Westminster).
Hartley, J.E. 1988. *The Book of Job* (The New International Commentary on the Old Testament; Grand Rapids: Eerdmans).
Jacobson, D.L. 2006. 'God's Natural Order: Genesis or Job?' in *"And God Saw That It Was Good": Essays on Creation and God in Honor of Terence E. Fretheim* (eds. F.J. Gaiser and M.A. Throntweit; Saint Paul Word & World) 49–56.
Janzen, J.G. 1985. *Job* (Interpretation Bible Commentary; Atlanta: John Knox Press).
Magallanes, S.A. 2004. 'The Hymn of Wisdom as an Utterance of Job', M.A.R. dissertation, Azusa Pacific University.
Magdalene, F.R. 2007. *On the Scales of Righteousness: Neo-Babylonian Trial Law and the Book of Job* (Brown Judaic Studies, 348; Providence: Brown Judaic Studies).
Martínez, F.G. 1996. *The Dead Sea Scrolls Translated: The Qumran Texts in English* (Grand Rapids: Eerdmans).
Michel, W.L. 1987. *Prologue and First Cycle of Speeches: Job 1:1–14:22*, vol. 1 in *Job in the Light of Northwest Semitic* (Biblica et Orientalia, 42; Rome: Biblical Institute Press).
Mies, F. 2006. *L'Espérance de Job* (Bibliotheca Ephemeridum Theologicarum Lovaniensium, 193; Leuvan: Peeters).
Phillips, E.A. 2008. 'Speaking Truthfully: Job's Friends and Job', *Bulletin for Biblical Research* 18(1): 31–43.
Pirot, J. 1950. 'Le "mâšâl" dans l'Ancien Testament', *Recherches de Science Religieuse* 37: 564–80.
Pope, M.H. 1973. *Job* (Anchor Bible, 15; Garden City, NY: Doubleday).
Schmidt, N.F. and P.J.U. Nel. 2003. 'The Rhetoric of the Theophany of Job', *Old Testament Essays* 16(1): 79–95.
Timmer, D. 2009. 'God's Speeches, Job's Responses, and the Problem of Coherence in the Book of Job: Sapiential Pedagogy Revisited', *Catholic Biblical Quarterly* 71(2): 286–305.
Van der Lugt, P. 1995. *Rhetorical Criticism and the Poetry of the Book of Job* (Oudtestamentische Studiën, 32; Leiden: Brill).
Whybray, R.N. 1998. *Job* (Readings: A New Biblical Commentary; Sheffield: Sheffield Academic Press).
Wilson, G.H. 1997. 'משׁל', in *The New International Dictionary of Old Testament Theology and Exegesis* (ed. W. VanGemeren; Grand Rapids: Zondervan) vol. 4: 1134–1137.
——. 2007. *Job* (New International Biblical Commentary, 10; Peabody, Massachusetts: Hendrickson).
Wolfers, D. 1995. *Deep Things out of Darkness: The Book of Job, Essays and a New English Translation* (Grand Rapids: Eerdmans).

A FEATURE OF THE DATES IN THE ARAMAIC PORTIONS OF EZRA AND DANIEL

Brian A. Mastin

There are five dates in the Aramaic portions of Ezra and Daniel. They are:

> שְׁנַ֣ת תַּרְתֵּ֔ין לְמַלְכ֖וּת דָּרְיָ֥וֶשׁ מֶֽלֶךְ־פָּרָֽס (Ezra 4.24);
> שְׁנַ֣ת חֲדָ֔ה לְכ֥וֹרֶשׁ מַלְכָּ֖א דִּ֣י בָבֶ֑ל (Ezra 5.13);
> שְׁנַ֨ת חֲדָ֜ה לְכ֣וֹרֶשׁ מַלְכָּ֗א (Ezra 6.3);
> י֣וֹם תְּלָתָ֔ה לִירַ֖ח אֲדָ֑ר דִּי־הִ֣יא שְׁנַת־שֵׁ֔ת לְמַלְכ֖וּת דָּרְיָ֥וֶשׁ מַלְכָּֽא (Ezra 6.15);
> שְׁנַ֣ת חֲדָ֗ה לְבֵלְאשַׁצַּר֙ מֶ֣לֶךְ בָּבֶ֔ל (Dan. 7.1).

In each case, the year is expressed in the form שְׁנַת + a number + ל + either the king's name or מַלְכוּת followed by the king's name + a royal title.

The presence of the preposition ל in these dates has been relied on as an indication of the period in which the Aramaic portions of Ezra and Daniel were written. Rowley (1929: 103–104) states that '[t]he Preposition ל precedes the name of the King (or reign) in dates in Biblical Aramaic, Nabataean, and Sinaitic, but not in Babylonian, Lydian, or Egyptian Aramaic, save once in the last named. In Babylonian Aramaic, in addition to the form without Preposition, in agreement with that of the Papyri and of the Sardis inscription, we find a form with the Preposition ב.' Thus, 'with a single exception, the usage of the Papyri differs from that of Biblical Aramaic, and...the latter agrees with the later usage of the Nabataean inscriptions and the Targums. Moreover, the usage in Babylon in the fifth century B.C. is in disagreement with that of Biblical Aramaic.' Rowley adds that '[i]t is curious...that the single occurrence of the later usage...in the Papyri occurs in what is probably the oldest text of the series'. This is TADAE B5.1, which was written in Egypt in 495 BCE. He emphasizes (p. 108) that this 'was a rare exception in the age of the Papyri'. Charles (1929: lxxvi–lxxvii), like Rowley, refers to TADAE B5.1, but his point is not that the construction with ל is characteristic of one period rather than another, but that it is a distinctive feature shared by Ezra and Daniel which is attested only once in Egyptian Aramaic and not found in earlier Aramaic texts (in which, as it happens, no dates were known to him).

Boutflower ([1931]: 42–43), however, considers the 'rare exception' noted by Rowley a fatal weakness in his argument, and asks, '[i]f this usage occurs once in a papyrus of 495 B.C., may it not occur once, viz. in Dan. 7.1, in the Aramaic portion of a prophetic Book, seemingly written near the end of the reign of Cyrus?' Both Kitchen (1965: 74–75, 78) and Coxon (1977: 113–115, 118, 122) cite texts from Egypt which were discovered after Rowley's book was published, and on this basis Kitchen claims that 'the preposition *l* before a king's name in dates is a mark of *early* date'. He also supposes, perhaps inconsistently, that 'this item in the Aramaic of Daniel...is as likely to be an archaic survival as anything else, and to have found subsequent extension of use in a later day, in Nabataean and Targums'. If I have understood him correctly, Kitchen means by 'an archaic survival' that this is one of the items which 'could be argued to be survivals till the second century BC' (p. 79), since Imperial Aramaic is essentially homogeneous. Further considerations are advanced by Coxon, who believes 'that Rowley is right in pointing to this construction as a piece of important evidence for dating the Aramaic of Daniel because the introductory formula to a king's reign is likely to lie outside the style of a particular writer and reflect a particular stereotyped tradition current in the period to which he belonged'. He maintains, however, that 'Rowley forces the evidence in asserting that the formula in Daniel fits best the period of the Targums', since 'the three early witnesses which contain ל suggest a familiarity of usage in the early period', even though all scholars agree that this 'was not the regular usage in the fifth century B.C.' Coxon also thinks that the construction 'may owe something to Hebrew practice,' and he compares the dates in Hag. 1.1, which he says was composed in 520 BCE, and in Zech. 1.1. He adds, '[t]hat the construction is a common one in classical Hebrew is shown by its repeated occurrence in the historical books of the Old Testament'.

It will be claimed in this article that Coxon is right to hold that the construction with ל is indebted to Hebrew practice, but that it is more satisfactory to go beyond his position and identify it as a Hebraism. It will be argued that evidence from Imperial Aramaic texts is consistent with this conclusion.

In the Hebrew Bible there are ninety-three occasions on which 'year x' in dates is followed either by a king's name (sixty-six times; 1 Kgs. 15.9, 25, 28, 33; 16.8, 10, 15, 23, 29; 22.41, 52; 2 Kgs. 1.17; 3.1; 8.16, 25; 9.29; 12.2; 13.1, 10; 14.1, 23; 15.1, 8, 13, 17, 23, 27, 30, 32; 16.1; 17.1, 6; 18.1, 9, 10[*bis*]; Jer. 1.3; 25.1[*bis*], 3; 32.1[*bis*]; 36.1, 9; 39.1, 2;

45.1; 46.2; 52.29, 30; Hag. 1.1, 15; 2.10; Zech. 1.1, 7; 7.1; Dan. 1.21; 9.1; 10.1; 11.1; Ezra 1.1; 7.7; Neh. 2.1; 5.14; 13.6; 2 Chron. 36.22); by מֶלֶךְ in apposition with a king's name (fifteen times; 1 Kgs. 14.25; 15.1; 2 Kgs. 12.7; 18.9, 13; 22.3; 23.23; 25.2, 8; Isa. 36.1; Jer. 52.5, 12; Esth. 3.7; 2 Chron. 12.2; 13.1); by מֶלֶךְ unaccompanied by a name (once; Ezra 7.8); by מַלְכוּת in the construct before a king's name (eight times; Dan. 1.1; 2.1; 8.1; 1 Chron. 26.31; 2 Chron. 15.10, 19; 16.1; 35.19); or by מַלְכוּתוֹ (three times; Esth. 2.16; 2 Chron. 3.2; 16.12). The various phrases which express 'year x' are always joined to the king's name, the title 'king', or the noun 'reign', by the preposition לְ. Moreover, this is how 'year x' is joined to חַיִּים in the construct followed by a man's name (Gen. 7.11), to גָּלוּת in the construct followed either by a king's name (2 Kgs. 25.27; Jer. 52.31) or by the title הַמֶּלֶךְ + a king's name (Ezek. 1.2), and to גָּלוּת + a pronominal suffix (Ezek. 40.1). The usage is also found in an Aramaic date at Qumran, where לגל[ו]ת̇[ ]י[שראל is restored in 4QVisions of ʿAmram[c] ar 1 a i 3–4.

The sixty-six examples in which 'year x' in dates is followed by a king's name are paralleled by Ezra 5.13; 6.3; Dan. 7.1, just as the eight examples in which it is followed by מַלְכוּת in the construct before a king's name are paralleled by Ezra 4.24; 6.15. The first of these constructions is found four times in Daniel and twice in Ezra, as well as three times in Nehemiah, three times in Haggai, three times in Zechariah, and once in 2 Chronicles, while the second construction is found in Daniel (three times), and in 1 and 2 Chronicles (five times). This last point deserves further consideration.

It is not possible to argue the case in detail here, but it seems most likely that Dan. 1 was written as an introduction when the tales in the first half of the book were collected, and that Dan. 2.1–4a was translated into Hebrew to link the tales written in Aramaic to this Hebrew introduction. This could not have happened before the Hellenistic period, since the fourth empire in Dan. 2 is that of Alexander and his successors. Because the visions of chapters 7–12 reflect the events of Antiochus Epiphanes's reign, but the tales do not, the instances of the construction with מַלְכוּת in Dan. 1.1; 2.1 are to be placed earlier, and that in Dan. 8.1 later, in the Hellenistic period. Williamson (1982: 16) plausibly concludes 'that a date for Chronicles within the fourth century BC is most probable, but that in the circumstances dogmatism is out of the question', and he also argues strongly for a time 'early in the Hellenistic period' for the compilation of Ezra 1–6 (Williamson 1983: 29). Whatever the precise dates at which these documents were composed, other Jewish authors were using the construction with מַלְכוּת in the general period to which Ezra 1–6 belongs.

Mur 18.1, in an Aramaic document from 55/56 CE, employs the preposition ל in the date formula before the name נרון, 'Nero' (Milik 1961: 100–101); Yardeni (2000a: 47) reads שנת ארבע לגאלת ישראל, 'year four of the redemption of Israel', in Mur 22.1, and dates this Hebrew text to 'ca. 69 CE?' (Yardeni 2000b: 27); similarly she assigns Mur 25, which is in Aramaic and was written in שנ]ת̇ תלת לחרות ירו{ו}שלם̇, 'yea]r three of the freedom of Jerusalem', to 'ca. 68 CE?' (Milik 1961: 135; Yardeni 2000b: 22). The last two texts were dated by Milik (1961: 118, 134) to, respectively, 131 and 133 CE, but for present purposes it is not necessary to discuss these different conclusions. The dates of two Aramaic documents from the Cave of Letters, P. Yadin 7 and P. Yadin 8, from 120 and 122 CE respectively, have a ל after 'year x' before the Roman Emperor's titles and name (Yadin, Greenfield, Yardeni and Levine 2002: 73, 109). The other dated Hebrew and Aramaic texts known to come from the Cave of Letters, together with those believed to come from Naḥal Ḥever, are all from the period of the Second Jewish Revolt or the year before it. In the dates 'year x' may be followed by the name Shimʿon, son of Kosiba' (in Hebrew, P. Yadin 44.1; in Aramaic, P. Yadin 47a.3, with the name partially restored); by גא(ו)לת ישראל, 'the redemption of Israel' (in Hebrew, XḤev/Se 49.1–2 [where ל is restored in the damaged space before the phrase]; in Aramaic, P. Yadin 42.1; Wadi Sdeir 1 [Yardeni 2000a: 20]); by חר(ו)ת ישראל, 'the freedom of Israel' (in Hebrew, XḤev/Se 8.8; in Aramaic, XḤev/Se 7.1; 8.1; 8a.1; 13.1); or by הפרכ[יה], 'the Eparch[y] (Provincia Arabia)' (in Aramaic, XḤev/Se 12.11–12). In all these texts, 'year x' is joined by the preposition ל to the following word or phrase. Jews were familiar with this usage, in both Hebrew and Aramaic documents, from 55/56 CE to the time of the Second Jewish Revolt.

For present purposes, it is unnecessary to do more than illustrate Nabataean usage. I have noticed one instance in which the preposition ל may not have been placed before a royal title in a date. The *editio princeps* of P. Yadin 4 restores שנת עשר]ין ותמונא מראנא in lines 10–11 and the editors translate '(of) our lord', though they add ל before מראנא when discussing the text (Yadin, Greenfield, Yardeni and Levine 2002: 251, 245), as does Yardeni (2000a: 293) in her edition of it. It is uncertain whether this example is an exception to standard Nabataean practice. The preposition ל is prefixed to the Nabataean king's name in dates from at least 65 BCE (Yardeni 2000a: 306; 2000b:

100 [= CIS II, §349.5]) until at least 97/98 CE (P. Yadin 2.1, 18; Yadin, Greenfield, Yardeni and Levine 2002: 216); to a Ptolemy's name, and, with 'year x' restored, to מראן ציו אפכלא, 'our master Ṣyw the sage/priest', in an inscription from 77 or 48 BCE (Yardeni 2000a: 307, §A/3.6–8; 2000b: 100); to the title מראנא placed before a Nabataean king's name in line 3 of an inscription from 88/89 CE (Negev 1961: 135–136); to the title 'queen' before the name Cleopatra, and also to the name of, perhaps, a local priest, as well as probably to the name of a Nabataean king, before which a ל has been almost completely lost, in lines 4–7 of an inscription from 37/36 BCE (Jones, Hammond, Johnson and Fiema 1988: 48, 51, 54–55); and to הי/נפרכא, 'the Eparchy (Provincia Arabia)', in an inscription from 126 CE (Yardeni 2000a: 323, §A/48.4; 2000b: 109). The usage in this Aramaic dialect differs from what had become the normal style in Imperial Aramaic.

Similarly in Phoenician date formulae, after 'year x' a ל is prefixed to the titles מלך (KAI 33.1; 39.1; 41.4–5) and אדן מלכם (KAI 40.1; 43.4, 6, 8) placed before a king's name; to royal titles on their own (מלך, Lemaire 1996 §203*.1; אדן מלכם, KAI 18.4–5); to a Ptolemy's name (KAI 19.5); and to eras expressed by אש, 'the people of' (KAI 40.2) or עם (KAI 18.5–6; 19.8 [with restoration of צר]; 60.1) + a city's name.

Most Imperial Aramaic texts, however, are unlike Classical Hebrew, Phoenician and Nabataean texts, and the Aramaic texts from Palestine discussed above, in omitting the preposition ל after 'year x' in dates.

Editions of all the texts included by Schwiderski (2004) have been consulted to ensure that the examination of Imperial Aramaic usage is as complete as possible. Seventy-three texts fall to be considered. No account will be taken of accession year dates, because they have a different structure. Moreover, though the date is repeated in some texts, the figures given here are for the number of texts which contain dates in which the year is expressed, not for the number of dates which they contain, as what is at issue is when and where 'year x' is followed by the preposition ל.

Sixty-three texts have the form year x + king's name, with no ל before the king's name. The earliest of these, KAI 227, which was probably found at Sefire in Syria, is from 571/570 BCE, and in line 5 of the recto the first letter of the name [נ]בוכדרצר is on part of the clay tablet which is missing. There would have been no room for a ל prefixed to the name (Starcky 1960: 99–101). Of the remaining texts, thirty-eight come from Egypt, sixteen from Idumaea, three from Samaria, two from Asia Minor, and one each from Babylon, Afghanistan, and the Shephelah. It will be convenient to begin by listing the texts from Egypt.

The series starts in 483 BCE (TADAE B4.4), there may be a text from 473 BCE (TADAE D1.33), and the other examples are from 471 BCE (TADAE B2.1), 460 or 459 BCE (TADAE B2.3; B2.4), 458 BCE (TADAE D17.1), 456 BCE (TADAE B3.1), 449 BCE (TADAE B3.3), 446 BCE (TADAE B2.7), 440 BCE (TADAE B2.8), 437 BCE (TADAE B3.4), 436/435 BCE (TADAE A5.1), 434 BCE (TADAE B3.5), 427 BCE (TADAE A6.1; B3.6), 420 BCE (TADAE B2.9; B3.7; B3.8), 419 BCE (TADAE A4.1; Segal §27 and p. 4), 416 BCE (TADAE B2.10; B3.9), 415 BCE (Segal §31 and p. 4), 411 BCE (TADAE A6.2), 410 BCE (TADAE B2.11; A4.5, 'or slightly later'), 407 BCE (TADAE A4.7; A4.8), after 407 BCE (TADAE A4.9), ?406 BCE (TADAE D5.38), 404 BCE (TADAE B3.10), 403 BCE (TADAE D2.12; D12.2), 402 BCE (TADAE B3.11; B3.12; B3.13), 401 BCE (TADAE B7.2), and 400 BCE (TADAE B4.6). The Madrid (Abydos) Papyrus (TADAE D24.1) and an inscription on a vase said to be from the region of Memphis (TADAE D24.3) are taken to be forgeries (TADAE 4:299; Folmer 1995: 781–782) and are therefore left out of account. Clearly the concentration of examples towards the end of the fifth century BCE owes much to the accidents of survival, but it shows that by then the construction without a ל had become established in Egypt.

In addition to these thirty-eight examples, it is likely that the inscription on a funerary stela from 482 BCE would belong to this series had a stonemason not reversed the order of 'year 4' and the name of the month by mistake (TADAE D20.3). A graffito from Egypt in which the king is not named, but which is assigned by Porten and Yardeni to the first half of the fifth century BCE, is a further instance of the omission of the preposition ל in dates, this time before the title מלכא (TADAE D22.8 and p. 267).

The preposition ל is not placed before the king's name in dates in twenty-five texts which come from outside Egypt. Apart from the example from Sefire which was noted above, and possibly the Lydian (Sardis) Bilingual to be discussed below, the earliest of these is from Babylon in 421 BCE (Delaporte §79). In another text from Babylon, written in 422 BCE, the preposition ב was probably prefixed by scribal error to the king's name instead of to שנת (cf. Delaporte §§74.3; 93.1). In that case, there would be a twenty-sixth example of this construction from outside Egypt (Delaporte §104 and p. 82). The

Lydian (Sardis) Bilingual (KAI 260) might show that the usage had reached Asia Minor before this. The text is from 455 BCE, 394 BCE, or 348 BCE, depending on which of three kings called Artaxerxes is mentioned (KAI 2:306). Naveh (1971–1976: 57) argues strongly for 348 BCE on palaeographical grounds. The other example from this area, the Xanthos Trilingual, should probably be assigned to 337 BCE (Kottsieper 2002: 209, 233–234). There are further instances from the fourth century BCE from Samaria, from 352/351 BCE (WDSP 2), from 354 BCE (WDSP 7), and in a text in which the numeral is damaged (WDSP 10). Sixteen examples from Idumaea come from the second half of the fourth century BCE (Ephʿal and Naveh 1996 §§13, 56, 96, 97, 108, 111, 112, 128; Lemaire 1996 §38*; 2002 §§19, 87, 88, 91, 92, 93, 94). For present purposes it is unnecessary to discuss the detailed interpretation of these texts, beyond noting that Röllig (1997: 221) identifies the name Antigonus in Ephʿal and Naveh §§56, 108 and 128 and plausibly understands §128.1–2 as a badly damaged date. The series begins in 355 BCE (Ephʿal and Naveh §13), or perhaps in 357 BCE (Lemaire 2002 §19), though this text is usually assigned to 336 BCE (Lemaire 2002: 20 n. 17). If Rosenthal's reading of line 1 of the Second Laghmân Inscription is accepted, this difficult text is evidence for the construction in Afghanistan in 252/251 BCE (Rosenthal 1978: 99*). A draft of an Edomite marriage contract from the Shephelah which was drawn up in 176 BCE contains the most recent known example of the construction (Yardeni 2000a: 342; 2000b: 117), though, if the restoration 'S[eleucos…]' is correct, the reference is to the Seleucid Era, and not to the reign of a particular king (cf. Eshel and Kloner 1996: 5–6). These data are too scanty to permit an assessment of the way in which dates were expressed over the centuries in places where Imperial Aramaic texts are found. It is, however, striking that the preposition ל was omitted before the king's name in dates over such a wide area.

All the texts which have the form year x + ל + a king's name or a royal title come from Egypt, but this may not be significant, since some two-thirds of the Imperial Aramaic documents which include dates were found there. Seven texts have to be considered, four of which are earlier than the first dated document from Egypt in which the ל is omitted. The series begins in 515 BCE with TADAE B1.1, which is the only extant document written by this scribe. The title מלכא is put before, and not after, the king's name. This is followed by TADAE B5.1, from 495 BCE. The name of its scribe is not known.

The third text is a graffito from 493 BCE (TADAE D22.29). In this case the preposition ל is prefixed to the title מלכא (line 4), but it is impossible to read the next word. In the fourth text, TADAE D2.1, which is from 484 BCE, all that survives is the end of the date, together with one word and one letter. There are no further examples until TADAE B3.2 in 451 BCE. The scribe who wrote it is not responsible for any other extant document.

The sixth text is TADAE B7.1, and Porten (1983: 564, 570, 574) argues that it should be assigned to 413 BCE, though 'the year date [is] not absolutely certain' (TADAE 2:141). Porten's transcription (1983: 573), unlike that in TADAE 2:142, has no ל before Darius's name, but the lower part of this letter can be seen in Yardeni's copy of the text (TADAE 2: Foldout 33). Porten and Yardeni (TADAE 2:142–143) restore the name of the scribe as '[Mauziah son of Nathan son of] Anani'. Yardeni (in Folmer 1995: 31 n. 174) says that this and other 'ascriptions are mainly based on the handwriting'. Porten (1983: 569) also relies on the reference to the 'degel commander Iddinnabu', whose name he restores in line 2, since Iddinnabu appears in texts from 446 to 420 BCE (TADAE B6.1:2; 2.9:2) and was Mauziah's contemporary. Four documents written by Mauziah between 434 and 416 BCE (TADAE B2.9; 2.10; 3.5; 3.8) do not have a ל before the king's name in the date. This is one of several reasons given by Folmer (1995: 773–775, 780) for regarding 'the attribution of [TADAE B7.1] to Mauwziah bar Nathan' as 'unlikely'. After twenty years as a scribe, reversion to an older way of expressing dates would be unexpected.

The seventh example is identified as a date by Folmer (1995: 322 n. 257, 774 n. 20) and is part of an isolated line from, presumably, a narrative about Sennacherib found written upside down at the foot of two columns of a customs account, which is itself from 475 BCE (TADAE C3.7 GVEx1; TADAE 3:xx). Porten and Yardeni (TADAE 3:166), however, render ב 4 שנן למרא מלכן ש/סנח]אריב מ[לכא, 'In 4 years of the Lord of Kings Sennach[erib] the [k]ing'. As far as I am aware, the order numeral + שנת/שנן is not attested in any other date. Since so little has survived, it is impossible to determine from the context whether this fragment contains a date. But if it does, the preposition ל is prefixed in it to the royal title מרא מלכן.

The preposition ל is placed before the king's name or title in the dates of a few Imperial Aramaic texts from Egypt, as well as in dates in Classical Hebrew, Phoenician and Nabataean, and is also represented between 55/56 CE and the time of the Second Jewish Revolt in both Hebrew and Aramaic texts. It is necessary to explain why the majority of Imperial Aramaic texts no longer included this feature in what might be expected to have been a stereotyped formula. The key to its absence is provided by Lidzbarski (1908: 212), who comments on TADAE A4.5:2, '[d]ie Jahreszahl ist einfach mit dem Namen des Herrschers verbunden, wie in den gleichzeitigen Keilschrifttexten'. This usage may be illustrated from legal texts published since Lidzbarski wrote. Twelve examples of this construction occur in cuneiform documents found at Nerab, near Sefire. One is from the first year of Nebuchadnezzar II, nine are from the third to the sixteenth years of Nabonidus, and two are from the first and third years of Cambyses (Dhorme 1928: 53; §§1 verso 3; 6 verso 8; 7 verso 8; 9 verso 9; 10 verso 6–7; 11 verso 7; 14 verso 8; 15 verso 8; 16 verso 6; 17 verso 7; 19 verso 6; 20 verso 5). Eight other examples originated in Babylonia and are from the sixth to the twenty-sixth years of Darius I and the fourth year of Xerxes (Joannès and Lemaire 1996: 52–53; §§1.11; 2.19–20; 3.21–22; 4.20; 5.17–18; 6.12, 23–24; 7 recto 6'). All these texts are earlier than TADAE A4.5, which is from the reign of Darius II. Since this usage was current in legal documents written in cuneiform, it is plausible to account for its unexpected appearance in Imperial Aramaic legal texts as a loan translation.

The earliest extant Imperial Aramaic text in which there is no ל prefixed to the king's name in the date was not known to Lidzbarski. It is perhaps significant that it comes from Syria in 571/570 BCE, in the reign of Nebuchadnezzar II, and is written on a clay tablet in a script which 'belongs to a style adapted by cuneiform scribes for writing on clay' (Gibson 1975: 116). The usage is found next in Egypt, then under Persian rule, in 483 BCE, and, if allowance is made for a probable stonemason's error, in 482 BCE, but four dated Egyptian texts written before then, in 515 BCE, 495 BCE, 493 BCE and 484 BCE, all place a ל before the king's name or title. In Egypt there are then six instances of omission of the ל between 473 BCE and 456 BCE, after which the next document with a ל before the king's name was drawn up in 451 BCE, followed by another sixteen until 415 BCE in which the ל is omitted, and the last of the texts which employ ל in 413 BCE. This example is isolated, as there are twenty-three cases between 420 BCE and 400 BCE in which there is no ל prefixed to the king's name. Thus the usage attested in Syria in 571/570 BCE began to be adopted almost a century later in Egypt, and, with only occasional exceptions, it soon replaced the construction with ל.

It is reasonable to assume that the practice of omitting the preposition ל before kings' names and titles in dates entered Imperial Aramaic in Mesopotamia or an adjacent region, and this is corroborated by the evidence from Sefire. Moreover, the construction would not have been employed from Asia Minor to Afghanistan unless it had become established at the centre of the Persian Empire. Its adoption in Egypt after 483 BCE requires its prior acceptance in Mesopotamia, probably at some point during the sixth century BCE.

The dates in Ezra 4.24; 6.15, in which the noun מַלְכוּ is added in the construct before the king's name, have no parallel in non-biblical material. As was noted above, however, there are parallels in the Hebrew Bible from the general period in which the compiler of Ezra 1–6 worked. Both of the examples in Ezra are from the narrative framework of this section of the book, and the compiler may well have been influenced by Hebrew style when he prefixed the preposition ל to מַלְכוּת.

Ezra 5.13 gives the date of one of several events recounted in a letter, but not of the letter itself, which purports to have been written around 520 BCE. The date in Ezra 6.3, which is the first year of Cyrus (539/538 BCE), is said to be that of a memorandum kept at Ecbatana. Because there are no dates in contemporary Aramaic texts from Babylonia or Palestine with which to compare either these dates or that in Dan. 7.1, the conclusion that these verses contain authentic dates from the sixth century BCE cannot be excluded. What Dan. 7.1 describes as the first year of Belshazzar's reign would, however, have been some twenty years, the first year of Cyrus some thirty years, and 520 BCE some fifty years, after the earliest known example of the construction without ל in an Imperial Aramaic text. There is a strong case for holding that this usage would have become current in Babylonia at some point in the sixth century BCE, though precisely when cannot be determined. By contrast, the invariable usage in Classical Hebrew, with which the compiler of Ezra 1–6 and the author of Dan. 7 would have been familiar, was to place the preposition ל before the king's name in dates. Furthermore, the form of the dates in Ezra 5.13; 6.3 may have been influenced by the Hebrew date in Ezra 1.1, which, like them, is the first year of Cyrus. In addition, an author of the Book of Daniel in the sixth century BCE might as readily have used the construction with ל in 7.1 as in 1.21; 9.1; 10.1 and 11.1. If, however, as may plausibly be maintained, Dan. 7 was composed in the second century BCE, when this construction was no longer employed in Imperial Aramaic, the usage in Dan. 7.1 is most satisfactorily understood as a Hebraism. The balance of probability is that this is also the explanation for its occurrence in Ezra 5.13; 6.3.

If the construction in these five verses is a Hebraism, it cannot be used as a criterion for dating the Aramaic of Ezra or Daniel. Moreover, though the Aramaic documents which are quoted in Ezra 4–7 may well be authentic, two of them appear to have been altered in this minor respect by their Jewish editor.

To sum up: There are at most seven dates in extant Imperial Aramaic texts which have the form year x + ל + king's name or royal title. The preposition ל is, however, included in date formulae in Classical Hebrew, Phoenician and Nabataean. On the basis of a comparison with contemporary cuneiform documents, Lidzbarski plausibly claims that the construction without ל in the overwhelming majority of Imperial Aramaic texts is a loan translation. It is likely that it became current in Mesopotamia at some point during the sixth century BCE, and was subsequently adopted in Egypt. The preposition ל prefixed to the king's name in the dates in Ezra 5.13; 6.3; Dan. 7.1 should probably be explained as a Hebraism, as should the ל in the different construction with מַלְכוּ in Ezra 4.24; 6.15, which has no parallel in non-biblical material.

It is a pleasure to dedicate this article to Robert Gordon, who has been a friend for many years, and whose kindness since I came to live in Cambridge has been greatly appreciated.

References

Boutflower, C. [1931]. *Dadda-ʿIdri or The Aramaic of the Book of Daniel* (London: S. P. C. K.).

Charles, R.H. 1929. *A Critical and Exegetical Commentary on the Book of Daniel with Introduction, Indexes and a New English Translation* (Oxford: Clarendon Press).

Coxon, P.W. 1977. 'The Syntax of the Aramaic of *Daniel*: A Dialectal Study', *Hebrew Union College Annual* 48: 107–122.

Delaporte, L. 1912. *Épigraphes araméens: Étude des textes araméens gravés ou écrits sur des tablettes cunéiformes* (Paris: Paul Geuthner).

Dhorme, P. 1928. 'Les tablettes babyloniennes de Neirab', *Revue d'Assyriologie et d'Archéologie Orientale* 25: 53–82.

Ephʿal, I., and J. Naveh. 1996. *Aramaic Ostraca of the Fourth Century BC from Idumaea* (Jerusalem: Magnes).

Eshel, E., and A. Kloner. 1996. 'An Aramaic Ostracon of an Edomite Marriage Contract from Maresha, Dated 176 B.C.E.', *Israel Exploration Journal* 46: 1–22.

Folmer, M.L. 1995. *The Aramaic Language in the Achaemenid Period: A Study in Linguistic Variation* (Orientalia Lovaniensia Analecta, 68; Leuven: Peeters).

Gibson, J.C.L. 1975. *Textbook of Syrian Semitic Inscriptions 2. Aramaic Inscriptions including inscriptions in the dialect of Zenjirli* (Oxford: Clarendon Press).

Joannès, F., and A. Lemaire. 1996. 'Contrats babyloniens d'époque Achéménide du Bît-Abî Râm avec une épigraphe araméenne', *Revue d'Assyriologie et d'Archéologie Orientale* 90: 41–60.

Jones, R.N., P.C. Hammond, D.J. Johnson and Z. Fiema. 1988. 'A Second Nabataean Inscription from Tell esh-Shuqafiya, Egypt', *Bulletin of the American Schools of Oriental Research* 269: 47–57.

Kitchen, K.A. 1965. 'The Aramaic of Daniel', in *Notes on Some Problems in the Book of Daniel* by D.J. Wiseman, T.C. Mitchell, R. Joyce, W.J. Martin and K.A. Kitchen (London: The Tyndale Press) 31–79.

Kottsieper, I. 2002. 'Zum aramäischen Text der "Trilingue" von Xanthos und ihrem historischen Hintergrund', in *Ex Mesopotamia et Syria Lux: Festschrift für Manfried Dietrich zu seinem 65. Geburtstag* (ed. O. Loretz, K.A. Metzler and H. Schaudig; Alter Orient und Altes Testament, 281; Münster: Ugarit-Verlag) 209–243.

Lemaire, A. 1996. *Nouvelles inscriptions araméennes d'Idumée au Musée d'Israël* (Supplement 3 to *Transeuphratène*; Paris: Gabalda).

——. 2002. *Nouvelles inscriptions araméennes d'Idumée* II (Supplement 9 to *Transeuphratène*; Paris: Gabalda).

Lidzbarski, M. 1908. *Ephemeris für Semitische Epigraphik* 2 (Giessen: Alfred Töpelmann).

Milik, J.T. 1961. 'Textes hébreux et araméens', in *Les Grottes de Murabbaʿât: Texte* by P. Benoit, J.T. Milik and R. de Vaux (Discoveries in the Judaean Desert, 2; Oxford: Clarendon Press) 67–205.

Naveh, J. 1971–1976. 'The Development of the Aramaic Script', *Proceedings of the Israel Academy of Sciences and Humanities* 5: 1–69.

Negev, A. 1961. 'Nabatean Inscriptions from ʿAvdat (Oboda)', *Israel Exploration Journal* 11: 127–138.

Porten, B. 1983. 'An Aramaic Oath Contract: A New Interpretation (Cowley 45)', *Revue Biblique* 90: 563–575.

Röllig, W. 1997. Review of Israel Ephʿal and Joseph Naveh, *Aramaic Ostraca of the Fourth Century BC from Idumaea* and André Lemaire, *Nouvelles inscriptions araméennes d'Idumée au Musée d'Israel, Die Welt des Orients* 28: 220–222.

Rosenthal, F. 1978. 'The Second Laghmân Inscription', *Eretz-Israel* 14 (H.L. Ginsberg Volume): 97*–99*.

Rowley, H.H. 1929. *The Aramaic of the Old Testament: A Grammatical and Lexical Study of its Relations with other Early Aramaic Dialects* (London: Oxford University Press).

Schwiderski, D. 2004. *Die alt- und reichsaramäischen Inschriften/The Old and Imperial Aramaic Inscriptions 2. Texte und Bibliographie* (Fontes et Subsidia ad Bibliam pertinentes, 2; Berlin: Walter de Gruyter).

Segal, J.B. 1983. *Aramaic Texts from North Saqqâra with some Fragments in Phoenician* (London: Egypt Exploration Society).

Starcky, J. 1960. 'Une Tablette Araméenne de l'an 34 de Nabuchodonosor (AO, 21.063)', *Syria* 37: 99–115.

Williamson, H.G.M. 1982. *1 and 2 Chronicles* (New Century Bible Commentary; Grand Rapids: Eerdmans; London: Marshall, Morgan & Scott).

——. 1983. 'The Composition of Ezra i–vi', *The Journal of Theological Studies* n.s. 34: 1–30.

Yadin, Y., J.C. Greenfield, A. Yardeni and B.A. Levine. 2002. *The Documents from the Bar Kokhba Period in the Cave of Letters: Hebrew, Aramaic and Nabatean-Aramaic Papyri* (Judean Desert Studies; Jerusalem: Israel Exploration Society).

Yardeni, A. 2000a. *Textbook of Aramaic, Hebrew and Nabataean Documentary Texts from the Judaean Desert and Related Material. A. The Documents* (Jerusalem: The Ben-Zion Dinur Center for Research in Jewish History).
——. 2000b. *Textbook of Aramaic, Hebrew and Nabataean Documentary Texts from the Judaean Desert and Related Material. B. Translation, Palaeography, Concordance* (Jerusalem: The Ben-Zion Dinur Center for Research in Jewish History).

FAT EGLON

James K. Aitken

It has long been recognized that the tale of the judge Ehud defeating the Moabite king Eglon (Judg. 3.15–30) is one of humour and parody.[1] The seemingly successful king is outwitted by Ehud, fooled by a ruse to take him into a private place where he is run through by Ehud's short sword (vv. 21–22), too short for the deep fat of the king, and where his stewards are equally outwitted, thinking the king to be defecating (v. 24). Word-plays and grotesque characterizations abound. The puns, for example, on דְּבַר־סֵ֫תֶר as a secret message or a concealed object (i.e. weapon), and on the verb תקע (the 'thrusting' of the sword in v. 21 prefiguring the 'sounding' of the trumpet in v. 27) contribute to the irony, along with the sexual references of the dagger and the locked doors.[2] Commentators have delighted in the ironic reversals of the story and provided rich retellings that draw out the many subversive elements. It is clear that Eglon is a foreign king who is to be contrasted with the judge Ehud, the local hero for the writer. He conforms to a type of the foolish foreign king or leader (e.g., Pharoah, Exod. 1–2; Balak, Num. 22–24; Sisera, Judg. 4–5; Abimelek, Judg. 9) outwitted by an Israelite hero.[3] Eglon's fate, to be killed in private in a room of dubious function, and to have the 'dirt' exude from him, was not becoming of a person of his stature. And yet, humour as a culturally-bound construct hampers attempts to distinguish between what was considered humorous in ancient Israel from what would be

---

[1] It is a pleasure to offer this to an ever supportive friend and colleague, who is also able to burst any academic pomposity with wit.

[2] These examples are all discussed in Alter (1981: 38–41). The bibliography on the subject of biblical parody and of the Judges narratives is extensive such that we can here only be representative rather than exhaustive. My thanks to Ora Lipschitz for bibliographic assistance. After this article had been submitted, the study of L.G. Stone (2009) appeared touching on similar issues. Although it has not been possible to take his arguments into consideration, they complement the approach taken here.

[3] A full list of examples is compiled by Brenner (1994: 42), who proceeds to discuss some of those in Judges, Esther and Daniel.

today.[4] There are many elements that are indeed intended as ridicule, but not all are necessarily to be put down to a scatological or lewd sense of humour on the part of the author.[5]

The one physical feature that is identified about Eglon is his weight. He is introduced in the following words (Judg. 3.17):

> And he [Ehud] presented the tribute to Eglon king of Moab. Now Eglon was a very fat man (אִישׁ בָּרִיא מְאֹד) (RSV translation)

Features are usually recorded for a purpose, and many commentators have seen this descriptive element, placed so prominently in parenthesis in the introduction of Eglon, as essential to the narrative (e.g., Moore 1895: 93; Budde 1897: 29; Lindars 1995: 142; Schneider 2000: 49–51). The author is at pains to provide as much information as possible, and only Genesis 22 and 2 Samuel 18 in the Hebrew Bible, as Halpern notes (1988: 40), lavish as many details in their accounts of killings. In the case of his corpulence, Budde sees it as a particularly personal and realistic feature to draw attention to ('ein besonders individueller und realistischer Zug', 1897: 29). The fact that Eglon was fat indeed prepares for the description of Ehud's sword being lost in the folds of flesh, allowing the author a phonetic word-play on הַחֶרֶב 'sword' and הַחֵלֶב 'fat' (v. 22). Nevertheless, in recent years, commentators have increasingly read the reference to Eglon's fat as an indicator that he is a humorous or incompetent character. Lindars's is one of the first commentaries to draw attention to the fact that the description is 'intentionally comic' (1995: 142). And such an understanding of the humorous nature of fat Eglon has apparently grown in the latter half of the past century, and is becoming a standard reading of his 'fat'. Schneider, for example, sees the weight as signifying that the king is 'fat, slow-moving, and naïve' (2000: 51), while admitting that it prefigures the grotesque description of the blade and hilt of Ehud's dagger being enclosed with fat (2000: 50). Alter believes Eglon's encumbrance of fat will make him an easier target as he awkwardly rises from his seat, but more importantly sees the fat as a 'token of his *physical ponderousness, his vulnerability* to Ehud's sudden blade, and the emblem of his *regal stupidity*' (1980: 155, emphasis mine; cf. Alter 1981: 40–41). Brenner

[4] Point made aptly by Brenner (1994: 41). She also notes that biblical humour is 'serious' humour, namely less joyful as it is aimed at disparagement of opponents.

[5] McCann suggests 'the story quite literally becomes bathroom humor' (2002: 44–45).

infers that the name Eglon, meaning 'big calf', is an allusion to the king's obesity, going so far as to suggest that, '"Obese" is of course a cultural token of stupidity and vulnerability' (1994: 45). In particular she draws attention to the association of obesity with women, noting that Amos 4.1–3 equates fat with the obtuseness and greed of women.[6] For her, the king is thus feminized, and hence politically ineffectual. Guest suggests that Eglon's fat is intentionally over-stressed: 'Not only is Eglon's physical obesity the subject of derision, however, for fatness operates as a cipher for other qualities as well'. She proceeds to list the attributes of gullibility and greed (an uncontrolled hunger), and observes how it functions to feminize him.[7]

The problem for us is whether his weight is a reason for the humour, symbolic of the incompetence and stupidity of the king, or whether the humorous element of obesity is a modern western phenomenon. Our suspicion is raised in the text of Judges by the translation, sometimes noted though rarely commented upon,[8] in the LXX of בָּרִיא 'fat' by ἀστεῖος, an adjective conventionally translated 'pretty, charming' (LSJ: 260). There are very few biblical characters whose physical features are noted, reflecting the fact that features are only mentioned when essential to the narrative. As a result, it is not easy to conclude anything from the fact that few others are described as fat. It either means it is a striking feature of Eglon (and the use of the adjective מְאֹד might be important here), or that fat was not an issue at all and therefore not elsewhere mentioned. Further consideration of fat both in the narrative and in the cultural context are in order. First we should consider why we should not be so ready to see fat as humorous.

---

[6] The feminization of Eglon has been discussed by Alter (1980: 155–56) and others, but is an issue that requires a separate treatment that space does not allow here. An element that is often noted is the phrase used when Ehud goes to meet Eglon in secret, בוא אל 'he went into him' (Judg. 3.20), which can have a sexual connotation implying Ehud is thrusting Eglon with his sword as a man would a woman. Similar phrases elsewhere in Judges are not sexual (e.g., Judg. 6.18), and such an interpretation has been criticized by Brettler (1991: 295). For criticism of other details, see Barré (1991: 7).

[7] Guest (2003: 191–92). It is easy in our language and culture to make allusions to fat in comical ways. In an otherwise sensitive and careful discussion of Eglon, MacDonald characterizes him as 'a man concerned primarily with his belly' and 'constituted by nothing more than fat and faeces' (2008a: 114).

[8] This reading is not noted at all in his textual notes by Moore (1895: 94). Schneider notes it but without elucidation (2000: 49).

The Cultural Significance of Fat

Increasing attention has been paid in recent years to the cultural significance of fat (e.g., Schwartz 1986; Stearns 2002; Gilman 2008). Stearns noted how until the twentieth century plumpness was associated with prosperity and with good health. While there have often been cultural stereotyping of figures such as Shakespeare's Falstaff, this grew with the later representation of Falstaff in opera (Gilman 2008: 85–100). The real change in the nineteenth century in the west came with increased medical knowledge that recognized the dangers of obesity (Pool 2001: 7; Gilman 2008: 4–9), responding to the nineteenth-century opinion that it was healthy to have a few extra pounds (Pool 2001: 21). This was coupled in the 1950s with the view from Freudian psychoanalysts who saw overeating as a psychological disorder (Pool 2001: 7). As a result an increasing negative stereotyping of fat has grown in the west, being associated with ill-health, psychological problems and lack of self-control. By contrast, under the influence of Greek philosophy, accounting for the different attitude in the Talmud to that in the Bible (see Kottek 1996), it became a powerful myth in the West for philosopher-scientists to have a 'lean and hungry look'. While cases of the social stigma of being fat have existed in previous centuries (cf. Gilman 2004: 11–12, 35–39) it has become such a mainstay in the twentieth century, with fat being seen as a cause or symptom of low self-esteem. It is, therefore, difficult for us to appreciate attitudes from other periods.

Given the cultural determinedness of the meaning of fat, it is not immediately apparent whether a stigma would have been attached to being fat in ancient Israel. Indeed, it is also not apparent whether people would have been seen as fat at all. Although in antiquity degenerative joint disease was very common, it is difficult to determine from archaeology whether people were overweight, since the bones would most likely only show signs of deformity from the pressure of weight in the morbidly obese. Mechanical stress on joints leading to deformation of the skeleton or injury to the joints can be caused by obesity, but it could also arise from poor posture (Živanović 1982: 153–154). It is now thought that osteoporosis can be caused by obesity, and the most likely cause of large amounts of new bone formation especially in the spine (vertebral osteophytosis) may be associated with either diabetes or obesity (Julkunen et al. 1971; Mays 1998: 127–128). Since arthritis and other infectious diseases can cause deformities, it is impossible to conclude for definite whether a skeletal remain suffered from obesity.[9] Obesity can, nevertheless, arise from hormonal disturbances (Pool 2001: 3–4), so that as long as those with the hormonal deficiency have sufficient access to food we would expect to find some people in antiquity overweight.

It is generally accepted that the diet was healthy in ancient Israel, implying cases of obesity would have been fewer (Borowski 2004: 96; 2003: 133n.1; accepted by MacDonald 2008b: 6). Where it did exist, though, there might not have been a conscious social significance to the phenomenon. It might even have been a sign of privilege arising from access to plentiful food. If anyone it might well have been the king who was fat, having access to a more varied diet, meat consumption especially, and to foodstuffs not available to the poorer members of society.[10] As such, a sign of both success and health was to be fat, indicating access to plentiful foodstuffs. In Job being heavy of jowl and sides bulging with fat (Job 15.27) seems to be a mark of prosperity, implied too by Deut. 32.15 (Borowski 2004: 96). Could the symbolism of fat, then, as healthy be a sufficient explanation for Eglon's condition?

Fat in Hebrew

Interpretation of the adjective בָּרִיא 'fat' in a positive sense has been noted already by many commentators.[11] It has been well expressed recently by Ryan (2007: 19–20), who proposes as one possibility that the king's constitution 'is to be understood as robust and healthy, a fine specimen of a well-fed manhood' (p. 19). He even cites in support of this reading the LXX (see below). This sense seems in recent years to have been submerged among the humorous readings of the

[9] The standard works on the archaeological study of skeletal remains include Ortner and Putschar (1985); Rogers and Waldron (1995).

[10] On socioeconomic differentiation in ancient Israel, see MacDonald (2008b: 77–79, 93).

[11] Hepner (2004: 291) comes up with his own explanation, that בָּרִיא might denote 'having a big chasm' (if playing on 'בְּרִיאָה creation'), and thus describing Eglon's large anus from which the dirt will be expelled. This interpretation requires a high degree of associative semantics between the two words and then an extension of the sense of the associative word to mean chasm. It is hard to imagine any reader following such a word-play.

passage. בָּרִיא is primarily used with reference to animals—a cow (Gen. 41.2, 4, etc.), cattle (1 Kgs. 5.3), sheep (Ezek. 34.20; Zech. 11.16), sacrificial animals (Ezek. 34.3)—or of foodstuffs—ear of grain (Gen. 41.5, 7), food (Hab. 1.16). It is, however, also used in two other places of people.[12] The psalmist in Ps. 73.4 is envious of the 'fat' bodies of the arrogant, and in Dan. 1.15 it refers to the better appearance of the youths who had been eating the king's food. It appears, therefore, to be positive when applied to humans, and a sign that something is ripe and ready for eating (Hab. 1.16; Zech. 11.16) or sacrificing (Ezek. 34.3) when applied to animals or foodstuffs. Indeed, the sleek and fat cows of Genesis are described in highly positive terms as יָפֶה 'beautiful' in both מַרְאֶה 'appearance' (Gen. 41.2, 4) and תֹּאַר 'form' (41.18).[13]

A positive interpretation then of the adjective בָּרִיא in Judg. 3.17 conforms to its use elsewhere, and fits the cultural presuppositions already outlined above. It also highlights the insufficiency of the glosses provided in many of our Hebrew lexicons.[14] The simple choice of the word 'fat' (e.g., BDB: 135; HAL: 150, 'fett'; Kaddari 2006: 125, שָׁמֵן) and similar terms (Gesenius[18]: 175, 'dick, korpulent, wohlgenährt…ein sehr dicker Man (Jdc 3.17)') can confuse more than clarify. Some lexicons are much more helpful, providing explanatory additional glosses. Clines's definition of 'fat, fleshy, i.e. nourished, healthy' (1995: 263) and Zorell's glosses (128) '*pinguis, bene saginatus, corpulentus*' recognize the potentially healthy sense of the Hebrew, and Alonso Schoekel's typically full list of glosses, 'Cebado, gordo, orondo, obeso; sustancioso, granado' (117) includes this sense.[15] Alonso Schoekel does not make clear which biblical citations should be ascribed to which meaning, but the order of citation suggests the first set of meanings (fat, obese) are intended for Judg. 3.17, even though the second pair (healthy, choice) might in fact be more appropriate.

A positive interpretation of Eglon's fat would make sense in the context. He is the successful king, grown healthy and prosperous on other people's offerings. The irony lies in the fact that it is such

[12] The application of the adjective to humans elsewhere is sometimes downplayed, especially if the instance in Ps. 73.4 is overlooked (e.g., Amit 1999: 76).

[13] The positive sense is also clear from consultation of Rabbinic Hebrew. See Jastrow: 192–193.

[14] On the problem of using glosses rather than definitions in lexicons, see Lee (2003: 15–30).

[15] On the benefits of Zorell's and Alonso Schoekel's multiple glosses, as well as some of the frustrations, see Aitken (2009).

a successful figure that will be defeated so easily by the judge Ehud. His successful fatness serves as a contrast to his eventual downfall. Hence, the identification of this detail about his physical appearance is placed between two references to Ehud's presenting of the tribute (vv. 17 and 18).

Wénin (2008) has recently drawn attention to the point of view expressed for each character, and in this Eglon's weight is judged from the point of view of Ehud. In presenting tribute he sees Eglon as already fatted, perhaps not even needing the tribute. In particular Wénin repeats what has become a standard interpretation of the passage, playing on the name Eglon meaning 'calf' (e.g., Soggin 1989: 96). He sees Eglon as a fat calf, thanks to excess, ready for slaughtering and eating.[16] This still seems to be the most likely reading of the passage, and adopted recently by Butler (2009: 70). While Eglon is fatted from success, it also makes him a juicy specimen for sacrificing. Alter (1981: 38–41) notes the use of ritual words such as הַמִּנְחָה (3.17, 18) and the verb קרב (3.17, 18; see too Amit 1989: 110; Brettler 1991: 294–95; Lindars 1995: 138). To this we might also note the reference to Eglon's fat הַחֵלֶב (3.22), a component in sacrifice. Eglon thus proves to be a well-fed successful monarch comparable to a fatted calf ready for the slaughter. A similar pun is to be found in the description of his troops as שָׁמֵן, both 'stout' and 'fat' troops (Judg. 3.29; see Alter 1981: 41). The key point is that the end result is the same: the monarch is humiliated.

The Versions

As noted above, of the Versions the LXX is of particular note. The Targum (פַּטִּים) and the Vulgate (*crassus*), on the other hand, merely render the Hebrew by equivalents for 'fat'. The Peshitta, to which we will return in a moment, is more complex than Lindars suggests (1995: 142), who wonders whether the Syriac's 'very simple' shows disapproval or a misunderstanding of the comical Hebrew. In both LXX versions (A and B), however, we have the same striking Greek reading:

---

[16] Barré (1991: 7 n. 24) points, perhaps tenuously, to the root *prš*, also used of cattle, in the peculiar word in v. 22.

καὶ Εγλωμ ἀνὴρ ἀστεῖος σφόδρα

Now Eglom was a very handsome man (NETS)

Few have tried to explain the reading of ἀστεῖος 'handsome, urbane' in the LXX.[17] ἀστεῖος is derived from the Greek ἄστυ 'town', and thus the adjective denotes 'urbane', referring both to manner (refined, witty) and appearance (pretty, graceful). Elsewhere in the LXX ἀστεῖος denotes the beautiful appearance of the infant Moses (Exod. 2.2) and of attractive women (Jdt 11.23;[18] Sus. 1.7), in addition to what appears to be a 'root sense' of 'relating to a town' (Num. 22.32; 2 Macc. 6.23). In the LXX of Judges we should be cautious of reinterpreting the Greek in the light of the Hebrew, and therefore we cannot follow without further evidence Engel, who concludes that a semantic change is present in the translation of fat by ἀστεῖος (1985: 91). Lindars makes a desperate attempt to account for the Greek, proposing that the LXX has taken the adjective as a derivative of ברא I 'to create', and therefore understood the meaning as 'well made, handsome' (1995: 142). It is true that there is confusion in our manuscripts between בריה, the noun 'fat', and בריאה 'creation' or 'creature' (Sir. 16.16), such as in 1Q382 105.7 (DJD XIII: 402; Bindi 1998: 3), and between בריא and בריאה in 1QpHab on Hab. 1.16 (van der Woude 1978: 30). However, even if the LXX read the word as a derivative of ברא I this does not lead naturally to the translation ἀστεῖος. בריאה is translated as φάσμα in Num. 16.30.

We must go back to the nineteenth century and citations of much earlier work to find other attempts to explain the Greek. Schleusner translates the phrase in Judg. 3.17 as '*vir valde pulcher*' (1822: 383), but cites Bonfrère's conjecture (presumably from his 1631 commentary on Judges) ἀνηρ σταιτός (*vir pinguedinis*) or σταίτιος (*pinguis et adipatus*). Unfortunately, these adjectives might not exist in Greek, and seem to be conjectural derivatives of σταῖς/σταίς ('dough'; LSJ: 1633), and hence 'doughy' (i.e. fat?). The only appearance of σταίτιος is with the referent bread, and not a person (in Zonaras's 13th-century lexicon, and in the 15th-century writer Gennadius Scholarius). Cassel (1875: 74) suggests the Greek of Judg. 3.17 follows a different interpretation from

[17] Typically, Aquila's πιμελής ('fat') and Symmachus's παχύς ('stout') render the Hebrew literally (Field 1875: 406).

[18] Engel (1985: 92) suggests that the choice of ἀστεῖος is more restrained than καλός, used by Holofernes in Jdt 11.21.

the Hebrew, to be connected with the narrative context of receiving gifts. He sees the LXX as denoting the manner in which Eglon receives the gifts, since ἀστεῖος could mean 'friendly, accessible' (e.g., Plato, *Phaedo* 116d: 'What a *civil* man'). He adds, to account for this, that in the Egypt of the LXX translators it was still a matter of experience that presentation or tribute of gifts to the rulers did not always meet with a gracious reception. This interpretation might make sense of the word in the context, but does not explain why the translators would choose this equivalent for 'fat' in the first place. Another explanation, also derived from the supposed experience in the ancient world, is that by Serarius, who argues that all *urbani* would have had a tendency to become fat owing to their comfortable living (1609: 87, cited by Cassel 1875: 74).

Schleusner (1822: 383) himself, despite citing Bonfrère's conjecture, does not accept it. He notes that fat can be deemed to be beautiful, drawing attention to Gen. 41.2 where fat cows are said to be beautiful in form in the LXX (though translating a different phrase). Here he is following in a line of interpretation already proposed much earlier by Bochart (1646: 534), who takes ἀστεῖος as a description of a handsome man (cited by Cassel 1875: 74).

We might pause at this point and consider the Peshitta. In the family of manuscripts represented by 7a1 from Milan the translation is given of ܓܒܪܐ ܗܘܐ ܕܒܪܝܪ ܠܚܕ understood by Lindars as 'the man was very simple'.[19] MS 9a1 (Florence) and its family, however, has an expanded reading of ܥܒܝܐ ܗܘܐ ܠܚܕ ܘܓܒܪܐ ܗܘܐ ܕܒܪܝܪ 'he was very fat and the man was simple'.[20] This alternative appears to indicate a corrected reading towards the Hebrew, but still preserves the equivalent ܒܪܝܪ, perhaps reflecting the antiquity of this tradition. As already noted, Lindars saw this as an avoidance of the meaning of the Hebrew (1995: 142), although two other possibilities are available. First, בריא could have been misread as בריר and accordingly translated in the Peshitta, although there is no other textual evidence for this. Second, the semantics of ܒܪܝܪ could suggest it is a translation of the Greek ἀστεῖος rather than the Hebrew, or at least represents the same understanding of the Hebrew. For, the adjective can mean, in

[19] For the text of the Peshitta and manuscript readings, see Dirksen (1978: 8).

[20] It is not the place here to discuss the much-vexed question of the relationship of 9a1 to the other families. It is of the nature of this manuscript to reflect a tradition close to that of the Masoretic text.

addition to simple, 'elegant' or 'pure' (Payne Smith 1868–1901: 621, '*mundus, purus*'), a suitable rendering of the Greek ἀστεῖος, as Payne Smith has already recognized. We therefore have two textual attestations, either as independent witnesses or as one witness, to a positive sense of the Hebrew בָּרִיא.

It seems that we may follow Bochart, Schleusner, and most recently Ryan (2007: 19) and Butler (2009: 54), who have all noted, taking their leave from the LXX translation, that 'very handsome' is an appropriate translation for the king's constitution. This would concur with our earlier investigation into the positive sense of Hebrew 'fat' in the narrative. But there is a further issue in the Greek that should be noted, and one that has been overlooked owing to the manner of presentation of data in our Greek lexicons. Modern Greek can often shed light on ancient Greek, and especially Koine, as has been amply demonstrated by Shipp (1979, and literature therein). In this case we find that in modern Greek ἀστεῖος often denotes 'witty' (εὐτράπελος, Kriaras 1968–: III, 274) or even 'ridiculous' (Dematrakos 1937–1955: 1067–68). This sense is not to be found in the biblical lexicons, but it is in the LSJ entry, if buried under other evidence. Certainly, LSJ records the meaning witty in a positive sense, but the negative connotation is subsumed under the definition of a word of praise (i.e. pretty, charming) as 'ironically, ἀ. κέρδος a pretty piece of luck' (LSJ: 260). Here the English semantics has governed the description of the Greek definition. The ironic use of pretty in English has led to its sub-classification under the Greek for 'pretty' rather than it being given a separate classification of meaning.[21] Consultation of ancient Greek sources does indeed indicate that a negative or ironic connotation of ἀστεῖος can be found. In Aesop, for example, the word is collocated with εὐτράπελος 'witty' (*Fable* 93bis version 3, delta line 17) and in a scholion to Aristophanes it is given as an equivalent of γέλοιος 'laughable' (*Scholia in plutum* 697: Dübner 1969). A character in Aristophanes can exclaim:

> μάχαιραν; ἀστεῖόν γε κέρδος ἔλαβεν ὁ κακοδαίμων
>
> Ha! A knife! What a *joke* of a reward the poor bastard received for his decency! (*Clouds* 1064; translated by George Theodoridis).

[21] As a result it is a sense that seems to have been overlooked in *Diccionario Griego-Español* III (1991).

More importantly, the word may refer to persons. Thus the fourth-century comic writer Diphilus has one character exclaim to the other ἀστεῖος εἶ 'you are a wheeze' (*Synoris* fragment 1, line 2; cf. Plutarch, *Demetrius* 42.3; Longinus, *On the sublime* 34.3). It is possible, therefore, that there is a double meaning in the Greek. Eglon is handsome, owing to his portly indicator of wealth and health, but at the same time he is to be seen as something of a witty character. It is notable that the Syro-hexapla, rendering the Greek some centuries later, translates the phrase as ܓܒܪܐ ܗܘܐ ܦܝ ܣܓܝܐ ܦܟܗ 'the man was very jocular' (Rørdam 1861: 76).

Conclusions

While it may be true in modern satire that the excesses 'we laugh at are usually inferior excesses; the fat man, not the strong man' (Feinberg 1967: 6), it does not apply in the case of Judg. 3.17. Our current cultural pre-occupation with fat can mislead in appreciating its significance in biblical times. The increase in attention in the past thirty years to the humorous nature of Eglon's fat might in part reflect these contemporary concerns, although it might also be a by-product of the greater number of literary readings of Judges that focus on the satirical nature of many of the tales. It might seem churlish to deny the more entertaining interpretations of this passage and to return to the view of Eglon as a calf ready for the slaughter, but there is still much in the tale to entertain the ancient Israelite.

Certainly, the weight of someone can be a cause of their downfall. The case of Eli is the best example, although in 1 Sam. 4.18 he is actually said to be heavy (כָּבֵד) rather than fat. Furthermore, his weight is given as an explanation after his death and not as a narrative feature earlier on. Eglon remains a comical character in some respects, a calf ripe for slaughtering. His healthy weight may be too much (מְאֹד) and his success is leading to his downfall. The weight of Eglon is also a problem for Ehud (Amit 1989: 111): we can imagine him wondering how he on earth he will fit his short sword into such a large stomach. One problem for us is the inadequacy of the glosses in dictionaries to convey the nuances of the Hebrew and we can easily misunderstand words that have a different cultural signification from our own. The Septuagint was more sensitive to this problem, and can be our guide. It is only very recently, in the commentaries of Ryan and Butler (2007 and 2009 respectively), although long ago proposed by Bochart (1646), that the LXX has been accepted as a legitimate translation. In this case, though, the LXX has chosen a most flattering word, used only of beautiful women elsewhere in the LXX, and not entirely appropriate for a monarch. As the word can also be used disparagingly of someone who is a wit or the object of wit, it is Greek that has the last laugh.

References

Aitken J.K. 2009. 'Other Hebrew Lexica: Zorell and Alonso Schoekel', in *Foundations for Syriac Lexicography III* (eds. J. Dyk and W. van Peursen; Piscataway: Gorgias Press), 181–201.

Alter, Robert. 1980. 'Sacred History and the Beginnings of Prose Fiction', *Poetics Today* 1.3 (Special Issue: Narratology I: Poetics of Fiction): 143–162.

——. 1981. *The Art of Biblical Narrative* (London: Allen & Unwin).

Amit, Y. 1999. *Judges, with Introduction and Commentary* [in Hebrew] (Tel Aviv: Am Oved).

——. 1989. 'The Story of Ehud (Judges 3:12–30): The Form and the Message', in *Signs and Wonders: Biblical Texts in Literary Focus* (ed. J.C. Exum; SBL Semeia Studies; Atlanta: Society of Biblical Literature) 97–124.

Barré, Michael L. 1991. 'The Meaning of *pršdn* in Judges III 22', *Vetus Testamentum* 41: 1–11.

Bindi, S. 1998. 'בְּרִיאָה', in *Semantics of Ancient Hebrew* (ed. T. Muraoka; Louvain: Peeters Press) 3–10.

Bochart, S. 1646. *Geographia Sacra seu Phaleg et Canaan* (Caen: Typis Petri Cardonelli).

Borowski, O. 2003. *Daily Life in Biblical Times* (Atlanta: Society of Biblical Literature).

——. 2004. 'Drink and Be Merry: The Mediterranean Diet', *Near Eastern Archaeology* 67: 96–107.

Brenner, A. 1994. 'Who's Afraid of Feminist Criticism? Who's Afraid of Biblical Humour? The Case of the Obtuse Foreign Ruler in the Hebrew Bible', *Journal for the Study of the Old Testament* 63: 38–55.

Brettler, M.Z. 1991. 'Never the Twain Shall Meet? The Ehud Story as History and Literature', *Hebrew Union College Annual* 62: 285–304.

Budde, K. 1897. *Das Buch der Richter* (Kurzer Hand-commentar zum Alten Testament, Abt.7; Freiburg: Mohr, 1897).

Butler, T. 2009. *Judges* (Word Biblical Commentary, 8; Nashville: Thomas Nelson).

Cassel, P. 1871. *The Book of Judges, Translated from the German, with Additions, by P.H. Steenstra* (Edinburgh: T&T Clark).

Clines, D. 1995. *Dictionary of Classical Hebrew, Vol. 2: Beth-waw* (Sheffield: Sheffield Academic).

Dematrakos, D.V. 1937–1955. Μέγα Λεξικόν Ὅλης της Ελληνικής Γλώσσης (Athenai: Demetrakos).

Dirksen, P.B. 1978. *The Old Testament in Syriac: according to the Peshiṭta version. Part 2.2: Judges-Samuel* (Leiden: E.J. Brill).

Dübner, F. 1969. *Scholia Graeca in Aristophanem* (Hildesheim: Olms; reprint of Paris: Didot, 1877).

Engel, H. 1985. *Die Susanna-Erzählung: Einleitung, Übersetzung und Kommentar zum Septuaginta-Text und zur Theodotion-Bearbeitung* (Orbis biblicus et orientalis 61; Freiburg: Universitätsverlag; Göttingen: Vandenhoeck & Ruprecht).

Feinberg, L. 1967. *Introduction to Satire* (Ames: Iowa State University Press).
Field, F. 1875. *Origenis Hexaplorum quae supersunt: Veterum interpretum graecorum in totum Vetus Testamentum fragmenta* (Oxford: Clarendon).
Gilman, S.L. 2004. *Fat Boys: A Slim Book* (Lincoln: University of Nebraska).
——. 2008. *Fat: A Cultural History of Obesity* (Cambridge: Polity Press).
Guest, P.D. 2003. 'Judges', in *Eerdmans Commentary on the Bible* (eds. J.D.G. Dunn and J.W. Rogerson; Grand Rapids: Eerdmans) 190–207.
Halpern, Baruch. 1988. *The First Historians: The Hebrew Bible and History* (San Francisco: Harper & Row).
Handy, L.K. 1992. 'Uneasy Laughter: Ehud and Eglon as Ethnic Humor', *Scandinavian Journal of the Old Testament* 6: 233–246.
Hepner, G. 2004. 'Scatology in the Bible', *Scandinavian Journal of the Old Testament* 18: 278–295.
Kaddari, M.Z. 2006. *Dictionary of Biblical Hebrew (Alef-Taw)* [in Hebrew] (Ramat-Gan: Bar-Ilan University).
Kaufmann, Y. 1962. *Book of Judges* [in Hebrew] (Jerusalem: Ḳiryat Sefer).
Kottek, S.S. 1996. 'On Health and Obesity in Talmudic and Midrashic Lore', *Israel Journal of Medical Sciences* 32: 509–510.
Kriaras, E. 1968–. *Λεξικό της μεσαιωνικής ελληνικής δημώδους γραμματείας 1100–1669* (Thessalonica: Royal Hellenic Research Foundation).
Lee, J.A.L. 2003. *A History of New Testament Lexicography* (Studies in Biblical Greek 8; New York/Oxford: Peter Lang, 2003).
Lindars, B. 1995. *Judges 1–5: A New Translation and Commentary* (Edinburgh: T&T Clark).
MacDonald, N. 2008a. *Not Bread Alone: The Uses of Food in the Old Testament* (Oxford: Oxford University Press).
——. 2008b. *What Did the Ancient Israelites Eat? Diet in Biblical Times* (Grand Rapids, MI: Eerdmans).
McCann, J. Clinton. 2002. *Judges* (Interpretation; Louisville: John Knox Press).
Moore, G.F. 1895. *A Critical and Exegetical Commentary on Judges* (Edinburgh: T&T Clark).
Payne Smith, R. 1879. *Thesaurus Syriacus* (Oxford: Clarendon, 1868–1901).
Pool, R. 2001. *Fat: Fighting the Obesity Epidemic* (Oxford: University Press).
Rørdam, T.S. 1861. *Libri Judicum et Ruth: secundum versionem Syriaco-Hexaplarem, quos ex codice musei Britannici nunc primum edidit, graece restituit notisque criticis illustravit* (Havniae: Ottonem Schwartz, typis excudebat J.C. Scharling).
Ryan, R. 2007. *Judges* (Readings, a new biblical commentary; Sheffield: Sheffield Phoenix Press).
Schleusner, J.F. 1822. *Novus thesaurus philologico-criticus: sive, Lexicon in LXX. et reliquos interpretes graecos, ac scriptores apocryphos Veteris Testamenti* (Glasgow: Andreas & Joannes M. Duncan).
Schneider, T.J. 2000. *Judges* (Berit olam; Collegeville, MN: Liturgical Press).
Schwartz, H. 1986. *Never Satisfied: A Cultural History of Diets, Fantasies and Fat* (New York: Free Press / London: Collier Macmillan).
Serarius, N. 1609. *Iudices et Ruth explanati* (Mogvntiæ: E Balthasaris Lippij Typographeo).
Shapin, S. 1998. 'The Philosopher and the Chicken: On the Dietetics of Disembodied Knowledge', in *Science Incarnate: Historical Embodiments of Natural Knowledge* (eds. Steve Shapin and Christopher Lawrence; Chicago, Chicago University Press) 21–50.
Shipp, G.P. 1979. *Modern Greek Evidence for the Ancient Greek Vocabulary* (Sydney: Sydney University Press).
Soggin, J.A. 1989. 'Ehud und Eglon. Bemerkungen zu Richter 3:11b–31', *Vetus Testamentum* 39: 95–100.

Stearns, P.N. 2002. *Fat History: Bodies and Beauty in the Modern West* (New York/ London: New York University Press).
Stone, L.G. 2009. 'Eglon's Belly and Ehud's Blade: A Reconsideration', *Journal of Biblical Literature* 128: 649–663.
Wénin, A. 2008. 'Le «point de vue raconté», une catégorie utile pour étudier les récits bibliques? L'exemple du meurtre d'Églôn par Éhud (Jdc 3,15–26a)', *Zeitschrift für die Alttestamentliche Wissenschaft* 120: 14–27.
van der Woude, A.S. 1978. *Habakuk, Zefanja* (Nijkerk: Callenbach).

PEOPLE AND PLACES IN THE EARLIEST TRANSLATIONS OF NEO-ASSYRIAN TEXTS RELATING TO THE OLD TESTAMENT

Kevin J. Cathcart

The basic decipherment of Akkadian cuneiform script and language by Edward Hincks between 1846 and 1852 paved the way for scholars to start publishing the cuneiform inscriptions and, more importantly from the public's point of view, to prepare translations of them. Hincks, Henry Creswicke Rawlinson, Jules Oppert and Henry Fox Talbot were leaders in this new research (Cathcart and Donlon 1983; Daniels 1994, 2009; Larsen 1996, 1997; Cathcart 2007–2009, 2011). The early translations are usually ignored but, as will become apparent in this paper, an examination of them is often rewarding and frequently a chastening and humbling experience.

In April 1853 Hincks entered into an agreement with the trustees of the British Museum to prepare transcripts ('into English character') and translations of certain cuneiform inscriptions. The trustees requested that he should commence with 'the Nimroud inscription thence passing to those which treat of Sennacherib' (Cathcart 2008: 199–200). Hincks immediately sent them a specimen transcript and translation of some lines from the inscription on Bellino's cylinder, which describe Sennacherib's second campaign (Cathcart 2008: 200–202). The contract with the trustees was for one year from 1 May 1853 and in May 1854 Hincks sent to Henry Ellis, Principal Librarian at the British Museum, his 'transcriptions' and translations which he wrote in two hardcover books.[1] The first book, entitled 'The Inscriptions of Sennacherib', also included the annals of Shalmaneser III, and the second book contained 'The Inscriptions of Assur-yuṣura-bal [Ashurnasirpal II]'. In the latter Hincks gives a translation of the annals found in the inscriptions on the large pavement slabs of the temple

[1] In the British Library the books are catalogued as one manuscript: MS Add.22097. The first book, received on the 6th May 1854, = ff. 1–27 (Hincks numbered the pages 1–53); the second book, received on the 20th May 1854, = ff. 28–56 (Hincks's pages 1–58; due to a mistake during the stitching of the pages, pp. 28 and 31 are out of order: f. 41 = pp. 26–27; f. 42 = pp. 29–30; f. 43 = pp. 28, 31).

of Ninurta at Calah, the royal residence built by Ashurnasirpal II. He omits the beginning of the inscription but provides a complete translation from i.43b to the end. It was the first translation of this very important inscription to be made and another would not appear for twenty years.[2]

The Inscriptions of Shalmaneser III

During the period in which Hincks was preparing the translations for the trustees of the British Museum, he published a translation of the inscription on the Black Obelisk of Shalmaneser III (1853b: 420–426). Rawlinson (1850: 430–449) had already published a translation some years earlier, but Hincks soon found deficiencies and flaws in it. In his introduction, Hincks discusses the deities listed in lines 1–14 and the royal name and epithets in lines 15–21 but does not give a translation of these lines. This was probably due to the uncertainty of the readings of the names. However, he translates remarkably well the greater part of the inscription, beginning with the twenty-second line. For the fourteenth year of Shalmaneser's activity, he gives a translation of the longer account found in the Bull inscription, 'as it is peculiarly interesting'. He also chooses for translation the fuller account of the eighteenth year in the Bull inscription. In presenting the longer accounts where he deems it useful, he is adopting a procedure followed already by Rawlinson (1850: 430–449) and used in modern times by Oppenheim, for example (ANET 277–281). At the end of his article, Hincks describes the contents of the five epigraphs, which record the tribute of the five kings or peoples, but does not translate the epigraphs. The translation of the Black Obelisk which he sent to the trustees of the British Museum in the following year is a slightly revised version and it gives the short accounts of the fourteenth and eighteenth years found in the obelisk. On this occasion he gives a translation of the five epigraphs. He also provides a translation of the annals on the Bull inscriptions that cover the first fifteen years of Shalmaneser III

[2] See, for example, Ménant (1874: 64–92); Rodwell (1874: 37–80). For a modern edition of the text with a translation, see Grayson (1991: 191–223). It is an interesting exercise to compare Hincks's translation with Grayson's.

and adds the account for the eighteenth year (BL MS Add.22097, ff. 12r–23v).[3]

Hincks was particularly interested in the accounts of the events in the sixth, fourteenth and eighteenth years. We can appreciate his remarkable grasp of the language by comparing his translations of the fuller accounts of the fourteenth and eighteenth years with those of Rawlinson (1850: 440–441) and Oppenheim (ANET 280).

Fourteenth year according to the Bull Inscription:

> Rawlinson: In the fourteenth year, I raised the country and assembled a great army; with 120,000 warriors I crossed the Euphrates. Then it came to pass, that Hem-ithra, king of Atesh, and Arhulena, king of Hamath, and the twelve kings of the tribes of the upper and lower country, collected their forces together, and came before me offering battle. I engaged with them and defeated them; their leaders, and captains, and men of war I cast into chains (1850: 440).

> Hincks: In my fourteenth year, I collected the people in multitudes, which were not to be counted [*the whole country beyond counting*].[4] I crossed the Euphrates through deep water [*in its full stream*], with 120,000 of my soldiers. At that time *Ban*idri of Damascus, and Irkhulina of Hamath, with twelve kings from the shores of the Upper and the Lower Seas, collected their soldiers in great numbers [*their large armies*], which were not to be counted. They came to meet me. I fought with them, and defeated them. I deprived them of their chariots, their moving towers, and their implements of war [*Their chariots and their moving towers I broke. Of their implements of war I deprived them*]. They went off to save their lives (1853b: 423; BL MS Add.22097, ff. 22v–23r).

> Oppenheim: In the fourteenth year of my rule, I called up the innumerable (inhabitants) of my vast country and crossed the Euphrates, at its flood, with my army of 120,000 (men). At the same time, Hadadezer of Damascus, Irhuleni from Hamath as well as 12 (other) kings from the shore of the Upper and Lower Sea, called up the(ir) innumerably large army and rose against me. I fought with them and defeated them. I did destroy their chariots (and) their cavalry-horses, taking away from them their battle equipment. To save their lives they dispersed (ANET 280).

---

[3] For a modern edition of the text on the Black Obelisk and a version of the annals of Shalmaneser III reconstructed from inscriptions on the two monumental bulls from Calah and two small fragments of inscribed stone, see Grayson (1991: 42–48; 62–71). The five epigraphs are on pp. 148–151.

[4] Variants from Hincks's revised translation in the manuscript in the British Museum (BL MS Add.22097) are given in italics and placed in square brackets.

Eighteenth Year according the Bull Inscription:

> Rawlinson: In the eighteenth year, for the sixteenth time I crossed the Euphrates. Then Khazakan of Atesh collected his warriors and came forth; these warriors he committed to a man of Aranersa, who had administered the country of Lemnan. Him he appointed chief of his army. I engaged with him and defeated him, slaying and carrying into slavery 13,000 of his fighting men, and making prisoners 1121 of his captains, and 460 superior officers, with their cohorts (1850: 441).
>
> Hincks: In my eighteenth year, I crossed the Euphrates for the sixteenth time. Khazail (i.e. Hazael) of Damascus, relying on the multitude of his soldiers, collected his soldiers in great numbers. He took up a strong position upon Saniru, a mountain range opposite to Libnana (i.e. Lebanon) [*Saniru (Hermon; see Deut. 3.9), a ridge of mountain opposite to Libnana he took for his place of strength*].[5] I fought with him, and defeated him. I slew in battle 16,000 of his warriors [*16,000 soldiers of his line with arrows I slew*], and deprived him of 1,121 of his chariots, 460 of his moving towers, and his camp (1853b: 423–424; BL MS Add.22097, f. 23v).
>
> Oppenheim: In the eighteenth year of my rule I crossed the Euphrates for the sixteenth time. Hazael of Damascus (*Imērišu*) put his trust upon his numerous army and called up his troops in great number, making the mountain Senir (*Sa-ni-ru*), a mountain, facing the Lebanon, to his fortress. I fought with him and inflicted a defeat upon him, killing with the sword 16,000 of his experienced soldiers. I took away from him 1,121 chariots, 470 riding horses as well as his camp. (ANET 280)

Rawlinson and Hincks had difficulty with the signs which today are transliterated ^{d}IM-*id-ri šá* KUR.ANŠE-*šú* and normalized *Adad-idri ša māt imērišu*, 'Hadadezer of Damascus'. Hincks comes close with '*Ban*idri of Damascus', but he expresses doubts about the reading *Ban*. In the notes to his translation of the Black Obelisk prepared for the trustees of the British Library, he seems confident that the signs for Damascus should be read 'Tushu' or 'Tushshu' (*madu sa Tushu*) (BL MS Add.22097, ff. 17v–18r). Hadadezer of Damascus occurs already in the account of the sixth year and Rawlinson, clearly puzzled by the Assyrian text, writes a long note on 'Atesh', which he thinks is the city's name. He comes to the conclusion that it is modern Homs because of 'its uniform association with Hamath' (Rawlinson 1850:

[5] Hincks cleverly identified *Saniru* with Hebrew *Śənīr*, 'Sanir'. According to Deut. 3.9 it is the Amorite name for Hermon. In Ezek. 27.5 it is parallel with Lebanon.

434–435 n. 2). Damascus does not seem to have crossed his mind. Hem-ithra for Adad-idri/Hadadezer is also wide of the mark. He also fails to identify Hazael of Damascus. Hincks points out that Rawlinson has called the king *Khazaqan*, but according to his syllabary the last sign is 'the ideograph for God' and should be read *il*. The identification with Hebrew *Ḥăzā'ēl* was immediately obvious (Hincks 1851: 1385; Cathcart 2008: 73–74). Today we know the writing of the names Hazael of Damascus is [I]*ḫa-za-a'*-DINGIR šá KUR.ANŠE-*šú*, read *ḫaza'il ša māt imērišu*.

In his diary for 21 December 1851, more than a year before he published his translation of the Black Obelisk, Hincks wrote: 'Thought of an identification of one of the obelisk captives with Jehu, king of Israel, and satisfying myself on the point wrote a letter to the *Athenaeum* announcing it' (Cathcart 2008: 74 n. 1). In the letter he says: 'He is called *Ya.u.a* the son of *Khu.um.ri.i*; that is *yehû'* the son of *'omrî*, or according to the English version, Jehu the son of Omri' (Hincks 1851: 1384–1385). Today we know the writing of the name is [I]*Ia-ú-a* DUMU *Ḫu-um-ri-i*, read *Yaua mār Ḫumri*. Rawlinson (1850: 447) read the name as 'Yahua, son of Hubiri' with the comment: 'a prince of whom there is no mention in the annals, and of whose native country therefore I am ignorant'. A week after the announcement of his identification of the name Jehu in the Black Obelisk inscription, Hincks informed the public that he had found the name Menahem of Samaria in a list of kings who paid tribute to Tiglath Pileser III (1852a: 26; Cathcart 2008: 78–79). Tadmor mentions Hincks's discovery in his edition of the inscriptions of Tiglath Pileser III (1994: 12 n. 11).

The Inscriptions of Sennacherib

Hincks presented to the Trustees of the British Museum transcriptions and translations of the following inscriptions of Sennacherib:

1. The short historical text in the Bull inscriptions (= Luckenbill 76–78, §§7–32).
2. Campaigns 1 and 2 in the Bellino cylinder (= Luckenbill 56–60, §§5–33).
3. Campaigns 1 to 4 in the Bull inscriptions (= Luckenbill 66–71, §§3–37).

He completed his work on these inscriptions by adding transcriptions and translations of a selection of epigraphs.[6] He introduced his work with the following remark: 'With respect to the Inscriptions of Sennacherib a great difficulty exists. The complete copy of the Annals of his first eight years is in the possession of the Executors of the late Col. Taylor and access to it is not to be had' (BL MS Add.22097, f. 1r). Hincks saw the Taylor cylinder for the first time in June 1853 but the inscription was not accessible for copying (Cathcart 2008: 207). In 1855 the British Museum purchased the Taylor cylinder for £250 but by this time Hincks's access to the museum's collection of cuneiform inscriptions was severely restricted. It was only in 1861 that Hincks and Talbot were able to publish partial translations of the annals in the Taylor cylinder (Hincks 1861; Talbot 1862). Plates of the inscription were published in the first volume of *The Cuneiform Inscriptions of Western Asia*, prepared by Rawlinson and Norris (1861).

Mitinti of Ashdod and Ṣidqa and Mitinti II of Ashkelon

When Hincks published a translation of the account of Sennacherib's third campaign, which includes the siege of Jerusalem, as found in the Taylor cylinder (ii.37–iii.49), he described it as 'the most interesting passage in an Assyrian inscription which has yet been found' (1861: 87). More recently Cogan has described this particular passage as 'probably the most discussed Neo-Assyrian inscription' (2000: 302). For this reason it would be superfluous to discuss the events surrounding Hezekiah and the siege of Jerusalem. Instead we shall give our attention to the Philistine kings mentioned in this and other inscriptions, namely Mitinti of Ashdod and Ṣidqa and Mitinti II of Ashkelon.

On 18 April 1849, Edward Clibborn, assistant secretary and assistant librarian at the Royal Irish Academy for nearly forty years, sent Hincks a letter in which he had drawn the impression of a seal deposited in the Academy's library for examination (Cathcart 2007: 276–277). He wrote:

> As you now appear to take an interest in antiquities found in Ireland I venture to send you a copy of an inscription, which is written in the

[6] Russell (1999: 289–291) has found Hincks's transcriptions and translations of the epigraphs useful in his research.

'Malta' or Carthage character, sometimes called old Hebrew. It is cut in relief on a very hard pebble rather flat. The letters are all perfectly distinct, and there can be no mistake or difficulty about any of them except one at the left hand corner, where I have externally written A.[7] I sent a copy of this inscription some time since to the Sect of the chief synagogue in London, and he after some time stated that I should have a translation as it appeared to be Hebrew, but I never heard from him since. Should you make it out you are at liberty to do what you please with the reading, but I should prefer your communicating it to the Academy. The stone was found near Dundrum, in the Co. Dublin.[8] It was here for some time on loan but it has been taken away, and a great price put upon it, since I said the inscription appeared to me to be Punic or Hebrew.

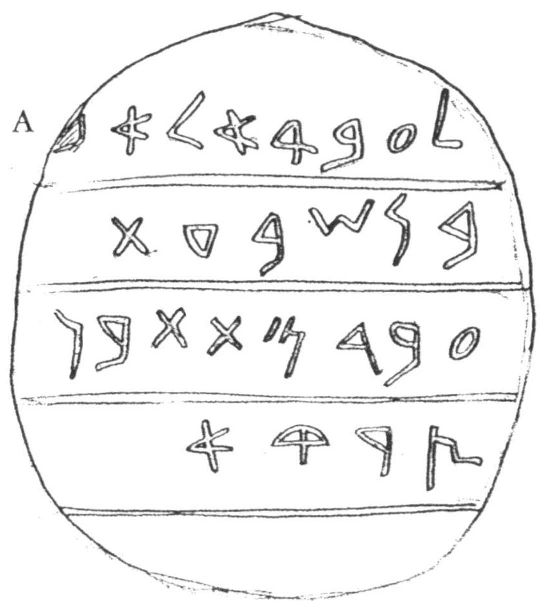

[7] Clibborn wrote A to indicate a note in which he says: 'There is a fault in the stone at this place, but the artist appears to have endeavoured to cut the letter in the hollow or cavity; still there is doubt' (Cathcart 2007: 277).

[8] Rawlinson (1865: 237) reports that the seal 'is said to have been found in Ireland, a relic, it is supposed, of the old Phoenician colonists'. Diringer (1934: 233) says the seal was brought to England by a seafarer. In 1861 the seal was purchased by the British Museum for £5 from its Irish owner, a 'Miss Walsh'. The possibility that 'Miss Walsh' was related to Rev. Robert Walsh (1772–1852), a Church of Ireland clergyman, who lived for a time in Constantinople and travelled widely, deserves investigation. See the entry for him in *Oxford Dictionary of National Biography*.

The seal, which is now in the British Museum, may be Philistine, but the inscription is in Phoenician: *lʿbdʾlʾb bn šbʿt ʿbd mtt bn ṣdqʾ*, 'Belonging to ʿAbd-ʾIlʾib, son of Shibʿat, servant of Mititti, son of Ṣidqa.'[9] There is nothing in Hincks's correspondence or papers to indicate how much attention he paid to this Northwest Semitic inscription. Although he kept Clibborn's drawing of the inscription among his papers, he never made any reference to it in the notes attached to his translations of the Assyrian texts, in which Ṣidqa, king of Ashkelon, and his son Mitinti II, who became king of Ashkelon later, are mentioned. A few years after the seal had been purchased by the British Museum, the inscription appeared in several publications (Bibliography in Cathcart 2007: 278). Rawlinson (1865) includes the inscription in a very poor article on supposedly 'Assyrian-Phoenician bilingual legends'. The 'legends' on the cuneiform tablets are in Aramaic, not Phoenician. This mistaken view led Rawlinson to include the seal discussed here. He does not accept the presence of a letter at the end of line 1 in a damaged part of the stone and reads the line as follows: *l ʿbd-ʾl*, 'belonging to Abdallah' (Rawlinson 1865: 238). However, the letter at the end of the line can be confidently read as *b*: *ʾlʾb*, ''Ilʾib'.[10] Rawlinson is more successful in his interpretation of the remainder of the inscription and astutely observes that the names *mtt* and *ṣdqʾ* might be linked to the names Mitinti and Ṣidqa in the annals of Sennacherib. In his words, 'There is some colour lent to the hypothesis by the association of the names of Mitinta and Zidqa in the account of Sennacherib's campaign, the former being the governor of Ashdod, while the latter ruled in Ascalon' (Rawlinson 1865: 238). The seal possibly belonged to an official or minister serving under Mitinti II. Ṣidqa and his family were exiled to Assyria when Sennacherib conquered Ashkelon in 701 BCE. When his son Mitinti II was king of Ashkelon, he paid tribute to Esarhaddon in 677 BCE and to Ashurbanipal in 667 BCE.

[9] There is a photograph of the seal in Mitchell (1988: 72).

[10] M.A. Levy (1864: 78) quite correctly read [*b*?]. O. Blau (1865: 536) disputed Levy's reading; he read *h* and proposed the name Abdilah, which is not unlike Rawlinson's Abdallah (without *h*).

YADNANA (CYPRUS) AND YAWAN (IONIA)

As early as 1852 Rawlinson found another reason to examine the account of Sennacherib's third campaign in detail. He translated and commented on the first lines of the account as follows:

> 'In my third year', says Sennacherib, 'I went up to the country of the *Khetta* or Hittites (a name used to designate all southern Syria; that is, Phoenicia, Palestine, and the country to the east, as far as the Euphrates). *Luliya*, king of *Sidon* (the Elulaeus of Menander), had thrown off the yoke of allegiance. On my approach from *Abiri* he fled to *Yatnan*, which was on the sea coast.' (*Yatnan* is always spoken of as a maritime city, south of Phoenicia, which formed the extreme limit of the Assyrian territory towards Egypt; it must, therefore, represent the 'Rhinocolura' of the Greeks.) (Rawlinson 1852: 21)

Rawlinson is convinced that the inscriptions of Sargon and Sennacherib show that 'a district at the south-east angle of the Mediterranean, and intermediate between Egypt and Phoenicia, was known to the Assyrians by the name of Yatnan or Atnan' (Rawlinson 1852: 21 n. 1). He also suggests that biblical Hebrew *ʾēṯān* might be 'Yatnan' in Num. 24.21; Ps. 74.15; Jer. 5.15, 49.19 and 50.44. In a lecture to a meeting of the British Association for the Advancement of Science at Belfast in September 1852, Hincks digressed to comment on Rawlinson's views. In his lectures notes, which are preserved in the Griffith Institute, Oxford (MS Hincks 572) he writes:

> We have there [in the Khorsabad inscriptions], after a country which Col. Rawlinson calls Yatnan, the addition 'of the middle of the sea'. Col. Rawlinson says that this Yatnan was Rhinocolura. It was the place to which Luli king of Sidon fled before Sennacherib. His flight is, however, said to have been from Tyre; and it is represented in a bas-relief, as being in large ships. I am not aware that Rhinocolura had a harbour capable of receiving such;[11] and if it had, it would be a most improbable place of refuge for a fugitive by sea from Tyre. Col. Rawlinson seems to have imagined that the flight of Luli was by land. In the inscriptions of Sargon, again, it is said that he was invaded by seven kings of Yatnan, if that was its name, which proves that it was a pretty extensive country; nor was it very near; for these kings are said to have been seven days in crossing the sea.[12] It is evident then, that this country was at least as far

[11] See Rainey's remarks (2001: 60–61).
[12] See the important articles by Naʾaman (1998; 2001).

> as Crete; probably beyond it. According to my view of the matter, it was the Grecian islands, if not the Peloponnesus, to which this name applies. I have good reason for reading the name Yavan, instead of Yatnan.

The passage in Sennacherib, which Hincks and Rawlinson are discussing, is found in the Bull inscription and can be translated as follows: 'In my third campaign I marched against Ḫatti. Luli, king of Sidon, whom the awesome splendour of my lordship had overwhelmed, fled from Tyre to Cyprus (*Yadnana*) in the middle of the sea and perished there'. The account in another Bull inscription does not mention Tyre: 'And Luli, king of Sidon, was afraid to fight me and fled to Cyprus, which is in the middle of the sea, and sought refuge there'; and the account in the Taylor cylinder does not mention Cyprus: 'Luli fled far overseas and perished'.

In a letter to Layard dated 2 August 1852 (therefore before his lecture in Belfast) Hincks writes: 'Yatnan is Asia Minor', but he has also written, then crossed out: 'or Cyprus'. This is unfortunate because Yadnana (Rawlinson's Yatnan) is indeed Cyprus. However, he seems to have had second thoughts, for in the postscript to his article 'On the Assyrio-Babylonian Phonetic Characters', dated 24 Nov. 1852, he writes: 'The place intended is not Rhinocolura, or any country bordering on Egypt, but the isles of Greece, or at any rate Cyprus' (Hincks 1852b: 351). As can be seen in the extract from his Belfast lecture above, Hincks changed his mind still further and proposed to read 'Yavan' for 'Yatnan', but he does not elaborate on his 'good reason' for doing this.[13] Some years later he changed his mind again: 'Luli fled from Tyre to Yavan, i.e. Cyprus or Crete' (Hincks 1861: 88 n.*). So he has returned to the meaning 'Cyprus' but adheres to the reading Yavan for Yatnan! Hincks's original view that *Yatnan/Yadnana* is Cyprus has proven to be correct, and also his idea that *Yawan* and *Yawanaya* are connected to Ionia and the Ionians.

It is worth examining how Hincks arrived at his views on the geographical location of Yadnana and Yawan. As was often the case in his research, a careful analysis of grammar and lexicon lead to secure results. He noticed that in the inscription of Ashurnasirpal II, a list of kings paying tribute, which begins with Tyre and Sidon, ends with 'Arvad which is in the middle of the sea', *arwad ša qabal* ($MURUB_4$)

[13] In his *Report to the Trustees of the British Museum*, dated 31 March 1854, Hincks is far from sure: 'Yatnan (or Yavan) in the middle of the sea' (1854: 9).

tamti (A.AB.BA). Hincks writes: 'I suppose it to be a peculiar description of the last of the cities, Arwad, and to imply that it was "an island."'[14] He further observes that 'though *qabal* has not the signification "middle" in any other language that I am acquainted with I have good reason for giving it this meaning in Assyrian.'[15] He knows the noun *qablu,* 'battle', but he had also come across *qablu* with the meaning 'middle'. He has identified the logogram, to which we now give the value MURUB$_4$, and has placed it in his list of signs. He can give the syllabic writings *qab-lu, qab-li* and *qa-bal* (1852b: 351–352) and in his Belfast lecture he points out that he has met the adjective *qablītu,* 'middle' alongside *elītu,* 'upper' and *šaplītu,* 'lower' in a description of the palace at Kouyunjik.

In recent years there has been extensive discussion and debate about the relations between the Neo-Assyrian Empire and the Greek world (Mayer 1996; Rollinger 1997, 2001; Lanfranchi 2000) and important research has been published on the presence of Greeks in Palestine (Hagedorn 2005). One of the issues debated is the reference to the employment of Ionians (some would say Cypriots) along with Tyrians and Sidonians by Sennacherib. Referring to the account of Sennacherib's maritime expedition in the sixth campaign, Rawlinson (1852: 26) says:

> The mariners and artisans of Tyre and Sidon, and *Yabna* (*Jabneh* of Scripture), rendezvoused at his command upon the Upper Tigris, where they put together rafts or vessels on which they floated down the river to *Beth Yakina.*

Hincks, however, was in no doubt that the sailors were Ionians. He writes in his lecture notes:

> I think, too, that the Yavnay, who are mentioned in conjunction with the Tyrians and Sidonians, as being employed by Sennacherib to navigate his vessels, were Ionians or Grecians; this being the gentile name derived from that of the country; and not as Col. Rawlinson has conjectured, the people of Jabneh, an obscure village in Palestine. The addition 'of the middle of the sea' is appended to the name of these Yavnay, as well as to the country of Yavan (MS: Griffith Institute, Oxford: Hincks 572).

[14] This part of Hincks's lecture at Belfast is found only in the abstract which he prepared for printing in the report of the meeting (Hincks 1853a: 110–112). However, the Assyrian words have been omitted from the printed text, so I cite the form of the text in the MS Griffith Institute, Oxford: Hincks 572.

[15] Haupt (1909: 3) proposes Ar. *qalb,* 'heart, middle', as a cognate of Akk. *qablu,* 'middle'. See also von Soden, AHw 887.

The passage in question reads: 'Syrians, plunder of my bow, I settled in Nineveh. Mighty ships after the workmanship of their land they built dexterously. Tyrian, Sidonian and Ionian sailors, captives of my hand, I ordered down to the bank of the Tigris with them.' The view that the text refers to Cypriot, not Ionian, sailors originated with Luckenbill (1924: 73, 60) who gives the transliteration *ᵐia-ad-na-na-ai*, 'Cyprian', but later says (1926: 145 n. 2): 'Text, *Iadnanai*, but stone seems to have *Iamanai*. The two are however, synonymous.' Salonen (1939: 181) has *ia-am-na-a-a* and Frahm (1997:117), having collated the text, gives two possible readings: KUR.*ia-[am!?]-n[a]-a-a* 'Ionians' and KUR.*ia-[ad]-n[a]-a-a* 'Cypriots'. Lanfranchi (2000: 28) rejects the latter reading, arguing that the gentilic for 'Cypriots' is not found. Although Rawlinson's 'Jabneh' is certainly wrong, it is clear that he did not read *Yadnanay* or *Yadnay* (he would have written *yatnanay* or *yatnay*), and Hincks is sure about *Yavnay*. Hincks's point about the addition of 'the middle of the sea' is well taken because there are several texts, though not the one under discussion, where mention in made of Ionians who live in the midst of the sea. Sargon 'caught the Ionians who live in the midst of the sea like fish' (Fuchs 1994: 64, 76, 262; on the interpretation of the phrase 'in the middle of the sea', see Rollinger 2001: 240).

I have given enough examples to show the usefulness of examining the earliest annotated translations of the Assyrian texts by some of the brilliant pioneers in the field of Assyriology. Robert Gordon has always taken an interest in the study of ancient Near Eastern texts relating to the Old Testament, so it is a pleasure to dedicate my contribution to him, a fellow Ulsterman of admirable scholarship and inestimable humanity, to whom I owe much gratitude for his friendship and kindness over many years.

References

Blau, O. 1865. 'Phönikische Analekten', *Zeitschrift der Deutschen Morgenländischen Gesellschaft* 19: 522–543.

Brinkman, J.A. 1989. 'The Akkadian Words for "Ionia" and "Ionian"', in *Daidalikon: Studies in Memory of Raymond V. Schoder, S.J.* (ed. R.F. Sutton, Jr; Wauconda, Ill.; Bolchazy-Carducci) 53–71.

Cathcart, K.J. 2007–2009. *The Correspondence of Edward Hincks* (3 vols; Dublin: University College Dublin Press).

——. 2011. 'The Earliest Contributions to the Decipherment of Sumerian and Akkadian', *Cuneiform Digital Library Journal* 1: 1–12. Online; http://www.cdli.ucla.edu.

Cathcart, K.J., and P. Donlon. 1983. 'Edward Hincks (1792–1866): A Bibliography of his Publications', *Orientalia* 52: 325–356.

Cogan, M. 2000. 'Sennacherib's Siege of Jerusalem', in *Context of Scripture*, vol. 2 (ed. W. Hallo and K.L. Younger; Leiden: Brill) 302–303.
Daniels, P.T. 1994. 'Edward Hincks's Decipherment of Mesopotamian Cuneiform', in *The Edward Hincks Bicentenary Lectures* (ed. K.J. Cathcart; Dublin: Department of Near Eastern Languages, University College Dublin) 30–57.
——. 1996. 'Methods of Decipherment', in *The World's Writing Systems* (ed. P.T. Daniels and W. Bright; New York and Oxford: Oxford University Press) 141–159.
——. 2008. 'Rawlinson, Henry: ii Contributions to Assyriology and Iranian Studies', in *Encyclopaedia Iranica* Online; http://www.iranica.com.
Diringer, D. 1934. *Le iscrizioni antico-ebraiche palestinesi* (Florence: F. Le Monnier).
Frahm, E. 1997. *Einleitung in die Sanherib-Inschriften* (Archiv für Orientforschung, Beiheft 26; Vienna: Institut für Orientalistik der Universität).
Fuchs, A. 1994. *Die Inschriften Sargons II aus Khorsabad* (Göttingen: Cuvillier).
Grayson, A.K. 1991. *Assyrian Rulers of the Early First Millennium BC I (1114–859 BC)* (The Royal Inscriptions of Mesopotamia. Assyrian Periods, 2; Toronto: University of Toronto Press).
——. 1996. *Assyrian Rulers of the Early First Millennium BC II (858–745 BC)* (The Royal Inscriptions of Mesopotamia. Assyrian Periods, 3; Toronto: University of Toronto Press).
Hagedorn, A.C. 2005. '"Who Would Invite a Stranger from Abroad?": The Presence of Greeks in Palestine in Old Testament Times', in *The Old Testament in Its World* (ed. R.P. Gordon and J.C. de Moor; Old Testament Studies 52; Leiden: Brill) 68–93.
Haupt, P. 1909. 'Some Assyrian Etymologies', *American Journal of Semitic Languages* 26: 1–26.
Hincks, E. 1851. 'Nimrud Obelisk', *The Athenaeum*, no. 1261 (27 Dec. 1851): 1384–1385.
——. 1852a. 'Nimrud Inscriptions', *The Athenaeum*, no. 1262 (3 Jan. 1852): 26.
——. 1852b. 'On the Assyrio-Babylonian Phonetic Characters', *Transactions of the Royal Irish Academy* 22, polite literature: 293–370.
——. 1853a. 'On Certain Ancient Mines', *Report of the Twenty-Second Meeting of the British Association for the Advancement of Science; held at Belfast in September 1852*: 110–112.
——. 1853b. 'The Nimrûd Obelisk', *Dublin University Magazine* 42: 420–426.
——. 1854. *Report to the Trustees of the British Museum respecting Certain Cylinders and Terra-Cotta Tablets, with Cuneiform Inscriptions* (London: Harrison and Sons).
——. 1861. 'Sennacherib and Hezekiah: A Translation from an Assyrian Inscription', *The Museum* 1: 87–89, 215–217.
Lanfranchi, G.B. 2000. 'The Ideological and Political Impact of the Assyrian Imperial Expansion on the Greek World in the 8th and 7th Centuries BC', in *The Heirs of Assyria: Proceedings of the Opening Symposium of the Assyrian and Babylonian Intellectual Heritage Project Held in Tvärminne, Finland, October 8–11, 1998* (ed. S. Aro and R.M. Whiting; Melammu Symposia I; Helsinki: Neo-Assyrian Text Corpus Project) 7–34.
Larsen, M.T. 1996. *The Conquest of Assyria: Excavations in an Antique Land 1840–1860* (London: Routledge).
——. 1997. 'Hincks versus Rawlinson: The Decipherment of the Cuneiform System of Writing', in *Ultra terminum vagari: Scritti in honore di Carl Nylander* (ed. B. Magnusson *et al.*; Rome: Quasar) 339–356.
Levy, M.A. 1864. *Phönizische Studien*, vol. 3 (Breslau: F.E.C. Leuckart).
Luckenbill, D.D. 1924. *The Annals of Sennacherib* (Oriental Institute Publications, 2; Chicago: University of Chicago Press).
Mayer, W. 1996. 'Zypern und Ägäis aus der Sicht der Staaten Vorderasiens in der 1. Hälfte des 1. Jahrtausends', *Ugarit-Forschungen* 28: 463–484.

Ménant, J. 1874. *Annales des rois d'Assyrie* (Paris: Maisonneuve).
Mitchell, T.C. 1988. *The Bible in the British Museum. Interpreting the Evidence* (London: British Museum).
Na'aman, N. 1998. 'Sargon II and the Rebellion of the Cypriot Kings against Shilṭa of Tyre', *Orientalia* 67: 239–247.
——. 2001. 'The Conquest of Yadnana according to Sargon II's Inscriptions', in *Proceedings of the XLV*[e] *Rencontre Assyriologique Internationale, Part 1: Historiography in the Cuneiform World* (ed. T. Abusch et al.; Bethesda: CDL Press) 365–372.
Rainey, A.F. 2001. 'Herodotus' Description of the East Mediterranean Coast', *Bulletin of the American Schools of Oriental Research* 321: 57–63.
Rawlinson, H.C. 1850. 'On the Inscriptions of Assyria and Babylonia', *Journal of the Royal Asiatic Society* 12: 401–483.
——. 1851. 'Memoir on the Babylonian and Assyrian Inscriptions', *Journal of the Royal Asiatic Society* 14: i–civ, 1–16.
——. 1852. *Outline of the History of Assyria, as Collected from the Inscriptions Discovered by A.H. Layard in the Ruins of Nineveh* (London: J.W. Parker).
——. 1865. 'Bilingual Readings—Cuneiform and Phoenician. Notes on Some Tablets in the British Museum, Containing Bilingual Legends (Assyrian and Phoenician)', *Journal of the Royal Asiatic Society* NS 1: 187–246.
Rawlinson, H.C., and E. Norris. 1861. *The Cuneiform Inscriptions of Western Asia.* Vol. 1, *A Selection from the Historical Inscriptions of Chaldaea, Assyria, and Babylonia*, prepared by H.C. Rawlinson and E. Norris (London: R.E. Bowler).
Rodwell, J.M. 1874. 'Annals of Assur-nasir-pal', in *Records of the Past*, vol. 3 (ed. S. Birch; London: Bagster) 37–80.
Rollinger, R. 1997. 'Zur Bezeichnung von "Griechen" in Keilschrifttexten', *Revue d'Assyriologie* 91: 167–172.
——. 2001. 'The Ancient Greeks and the Impact of the Ancient Near East: Textual Evidence and Historical Perspective (ca. 750–650 BC)', in *Mythology and Mythologies: Methodological Approaches to Intercultural Influences: Proceedings of the Second Annual Symposium of the Assyrian and Babylonian Intellectual Heritage Project Held in Paris, France, Oct. 4–7, 1999* (ed. R.M. Whiting; Melammu Symposia II; Helsinki: Neo-Assyrian Text Corpus Project) 233–264.
Russell, J.M. 1999. *The Writing on the Wall: Studies in the Architectural Context of Late Assyrian Palace Inscriptions* (Winona Lake: Eisenbrauns).
Salonen, A. 1939. *Die Wasserfahrzeuge in Babylonien nach šumerisch-akkadischen Quellen* (Studia Orientalia 8/4; Helsinki: Societas Orientalis Fennica).
Tadmor, H. 1994. *The Inscriptions of Tiglath-pileser III King of Assyria* (Jerusalem: Israel Academy of Sciences and Humanities).
Talbot, H.F. 1862. 'Assyrian Texts Translated', *Journal of the Royal Asiatic Society* 19: 135–198.

THE BIBLE, THE SEPTUAGINT, AND THE APOCRYPHA: A CONSIDERATION OF THEIR SINGULARITY

Peter J. Williams

An interesting development within the core vocabulary of biblical studies has been the common evolution of the three terms *Bible, Septuagint*, and *Apocrypha* from plural to singular. Each term has a different story to tell, though there are commonalities. We will begin with *Bible*, which has lost all trace of its plurality, and proceed to *Septuagint*, which now shows only a few signs of plurality, and then turn to *the Apocrypha*, the term which most commonly retains its plurality.[1]

The Bible

As is well known, the English word *Bible* derives from the Medieval Latin word *biblia, -ae*, a feminine singular, which had arisen by reanalysis from a Late Latin neuter plural *biblia, -orum*, a term itself too late to qualify for inclusion in the *Thesaurus Linguae Latinae*. The term *biblia, -orum*, was in turn derived from Greek τὰ βιβλία and generally was used without a singular (i.e. **biblium*),[2] so that already at the time of its creation it would probably have had some collective sense. The change from plural to singular that the form *biblia* underwent is not insignificant since in the singular the sense of a collection is lost and thereby any debate about the extent of the collection of books becomes meaningless. The singular also facilitates focus on the book as a physical object, rather than on a written text. After the conversion of *biblia* to a singular, it becomes possible to create a new plural again,

[1] The section of this paper on the Septuagint formed part of a paper I read in King's College, London, on 15 October 2008. I am grateful to all who attended for the discussion generated and to other scholars, including Jennifer Dines and Peter Gentry, with whom I have had opportunity to discuss these ideas.

[2] Only one occurrence of the singular *biblium* is known, and for the plural the stress is retracted to the antepenultimate syllable in the Latin, whereas the accent was on the penultimate in Greek (Pfister 1997: 1467–68).

but we should observe a general unwillingness to do this among writers of Latin, and note the retention up to the present day of the neuter plural in Latin alongside the feminine singular.[3] Latin titles from at least the sixteenth century sometimes show a studied ambiguity with the use of the term *biblia sacra*, refusing to connect this nominative with a finite verb that would inform us whether the term is singular or plural. However, the use of the genitive and ablative neuter plural in titles remained strong, and the accusative and genitive of the feminine singular were also widely used. The feminine ablative plural is attested too, but only in the sense of physical copies.[4] The feminine genitive plural is virtually never found.

Nevertheless, the extent to which Latin has preserved memory of the plurality of the word is not replicated in other languages. The earliest records in the Romance languages reveal that the word has become singular, and the same applies to Germanic languages,[5] as well as in some Slavic and Baltic ones. More recently, through Bible translation, the singular *Bible* can truly be said to enjoy global usage.

The singular word *Bible* contrasts with early Jewish and Christian plural terms for referring to inspired writings consisting of a number of different books, including γραφαί and γράμματα, usually with some qualifying adjective indicating sacredness,[6] though it is not dissimilar to the later Jewish singulars מִקְרָא and סֵפֶר as terms for the corpus of holy writings.[7] In other languages a singular replaced the plural as well. For instance, in Syriac, when αἱ γραφαί was rendered in the Peshitta, it was generally rendered ܟܬܒܐ,[8] using the same root as the probable

[3] To take just two famous titles exemplifying the plural we may note the *Biblia sacra polyglotta complectentia textus originales* (Walton 1657) and the New Vulgate or *Nova Vulgata Bibliorum Sacrorum Editio* (Libreria Editrice Vaticana 1979).

[4] Cf. the phrase *Bibliis Polyglottis* twice clearly referring to plural Bibles in the 186-word title of Castell (1669). The physical printed Bible is clearly what Castell refers to when he speaks here of errors in Bibles.

[5] Earlier Germanic languages (Gothic, Anglo-Saxon, Old High German) did not have the word *Bible* in any form: '*biblia* sprachlich ursprünglich ein Neutrum pluralis, "die Bücher", erst um die Jahrtausendwende zum Femininum singularis "die Schrift"' (Hoops 1976: II, 487).

[6] The New Testament references to the plural more often have the simple term αἱ γραφαί. See *TDNT*: 1, 751–52. On ἱερὰ γράμματα see Deissmann (1927: 375–376).

[7] מִקְרָא occurs 23 times in the OT, but only in Neh. 8.8 in the sense of 'reading'. The use of סֵפֶר for the Torah may sometimes be an example of a singular being used for a plurality of 'books', but in this case the books are in a single scroll (i.e. book).

[8] Mt. 21.42; 22.29; 26.54, 56; Mk 12.24; 14.49; Lk. 24.27, 45; Jn 5.39; Acts 17.2, 11; 18.28; Rom. 15.4; 16.26[25].

underlying Hebrew term. The problem for us is to know whether the Syriac term was intended as a singular or as a plural, since the number is only distinguished by the additional sign *seyame*. When *seyame* are absent from the Old Syriac manuscripts, which have a tendency to lack them anyway, and when the context does not otherwise tell us, it is difficult to be sure whether the term is singular or plural.[9] At least in one place (Mt. 21.42) the Peshitta has a singular, which may suggest that its translator understood the Old Syriac to have a singular.[10]

The tendency to use a singular rather than a plural term to designate a collection of sacred writings may be observed today by contemporary tendencies in British English to use the term *Bible* at least once for every six times the term *scriptures* is used, and in American English approximately eleven times for every use of the term *scriptures*, as shown in the following table based on numbers of occurrences in large corpora.[11]

	American English		British English	
	sg.	pl.	sg.	pl.
Bible	11009	572	1941	106
Scripture	2399	1005	390	290

Bible, the term which can focus on the physical object, has become the main term, while *scriptures*, with its implication of multiple writings, is receding.[12] One need only go back to the Thirty-Nine Articles to find a very different pattern. There the word *Bible* does not occur at all, whereas the term *Scripture* (often *Holy Scripture*) occurs twelve times, twice in the plural (art. XXV and XXXVII). The term *scripture* does have a qualitative focus absent in *Bible*, but even with the Thirty-Nine Articles there is a peculiarity to consider. When we compare the

[9] We can be confident that the term is plural in the Sinaitic Syriac in Mt. 26.54, 56; Mk 14.49 and Lk. 24.27 and in the Curetonian in Lk. 24.27 and Jn 5.39.

[10] The edition in general use shows no variants giving the plural in Mt. 21.42 (Pusey and Gwilliam 1901).

[11] These data arise from searches on the largest publicly available corpora of texts in British and American English, showing a variety of genres, both written and spoken. The British National Corpus, www.natcorp.ox.ac.uk, contains about 100 million words, and the Corpus of Contemporary American English, www.americancorpus.org, contains over 400 million words. The results from the corpora were taken on 7 May 2010.

[12] It is pleasing to see the title page of the Geneva Bible, which is actually entitled *The Bible and Holy Scriptures conteyned in the Olde and Newe Testament*. It is now, of course, no longer possible for us to think of the Bible being 'contained in' one or both of the Testaments.

Latin edition of 1563,[13] with the English version of 1571,[14] we find that the Latin has a greater tendency to use plural terms. On two occasions (art. VIII, XXII) the plural *scripturae* is rendered with singular *scripture*,[15] while in three instances the plural *sacrae lit(t)erae* (art. XVII, XVIII, XXI; cf. 2 Tim. 3.15) is rendered *holy scripture*. On two further occasions (art. XX and XXVIII) the singular *holy writ* corresponds to a plural in Latin (*divini libri* and *sacrae literae*, respectively). In this small but important text more than half of these designations of sacred writings have been altered from plural to singular during translation from Latin to English.

The tendency towards singularity may have serious implications, since it may involve a movement from an emphasis on a sacred written corpus to a single sacred book. The Qur'ān frequently refers to the *'ahl al-kitāb* 'people of the book' (e.g. 3.64, 112, 199), reflecting the view that the sacred writings of Jews and Christians in the seventh century were best viewed as a singularity. Likewise, to this day, Arabic Christians often call the Scriptures/Bible *al-kitāb al-muqaddas* 'the holy *book*' and there is the tendency in translating αἱ γραφαί not to render its plurality, but simply to render as *al-kitāb* 'the book'.[16]

Of course, there remains a significant awareness internationally of the Bible as being a collection of books. Yet this probably does not receive the prominence it should, and we need to be aware that the tendency towards using a singular word for Bible or related terms has a long and complex history.

---

[13] *Articuli, de quibus in synodo Londinensi anno Domini, iuxta ecclesiae Anglicanae computationem, M.D. LXII, ad tollendam opinionum dissensionem, & firmandum in vera Religione consensum, inter Archiepiscopos Episcoposque utriusque Provinciae, nec non etiam universum Clerum convenit* (London, 1563).

[14] *Articles whereupon it was agreed by the Archbyshoppes and Byshoppes of both Prouinces, and the whole Cleargie, in the conuocation holden at London in the yere of our Lorde GOD, 1562. According to the computation of the Churche of Englande, for the auoyding of the diuersities of opinions, and for the stablishyng of consent touchyng true religion. Put forth by the Queenes aucthoritie* (London, 1571).

[15] The inconsistent capitalization and spelling of words within the Articles is here standardized.

[16] For instance the Arabic translation known as the *Book of Life* (1982) renders γραφαί as singular in Mt. 21.42; 22.29; Mk 12.24; 14.49; Acts 17.2, 11; 18.24, 28; Rom. 15.4; 1 Cor. 15.3, 4. Thus in Acts 17.11 one might imagine the Bereans searching a single bound volume to check whether what Paul said was valid, rather than consulting a number of different scrolls.

The Septuagint

The next term we will consider is *Septuagint*. Nowadays it is possible to buy a convenient copy of the Septuagint—at least that is what we are told. We might purchase Alfred Rahlfs's *Septuaginta: Id est Vetus Testamentum graece iuxta LXX interpretes* (Rahlfs 1935) or 'The Seventy: That is the Greek Old Testament according to the 70 translators'. Many nowadays will simply use the Septuagint or LXX (now often pronounced by spelling out its three 'letters') on their Bible software programme. This enables them to find out how many times a particular word, form, or combination occurs in the whole Septuagint, which they generally recognize has a complex history.

The term *Septuagint*, though superficially an ancient one, has undergone a number of changes through time. It comes of course from the Latin word *Septuaginta* 'seventy', which refers to the pre-Christian account of 70 or 72 translators having rendered Jewish scriptures into Greek during the reign of Ptolemy Philadelphus. In contrast with our own use of the term *Septuagint* as a singular noun, it may seem too obvious to bother noting that the earliest accounts use the number 70 or 72 as a plural. Although the term for *Septuagint* in modern Greek remains a plural, in most other European languages the term has become singular: thus French *Les Septante* has given way to *La Septante*; German *Die Septuaginta* has been reanalyzed as feminine singular rather than as masculine plural.[17] Cognate languages tell similar stories.

Moreover, as we will see, at the earliest stage the word used in Greek referred not to a translation but to *translators*. There was thus no concept of a *version* of the Bible called *the Seventy*, but only a translation or edition *of the seventy [people]*. We can follow changes to the nomenclature through time.

The earliest record we have of reference to these translators is probably the missive (or letter) of Aristeas to Philocrates, which may date from the early first century BCE.[18] This purports to give a contemporary account of the translation of the νόμος or νομοθεσία or νόμιμα of the Jews into Greek, generously sponsored by Ptolemy Philadelphus,

[17] Klappenbach and Steinitz (1976: s.v.) reads 'Septuaginta, die:—"/*ohne Pl.*/"' showing us that even though the German *Septuaginta* has kept the same form as the Latin *seventy* it is, nevertheless, singular.

[18] Hengel (2002: 19) dates the text to the end of the second century BCE.

in order to supply the library in Alexandria, presided over by Demetrius of Phaleron, with a copy of the Jewish holy books. The number of translators in Aristeas is unambiguous: six from each tribe, giving a total of 72. The translators are even named (sections 47–50). This is usually taken to be an account of the translation of the Pentateuch into Greek. The clearest indication of the contents of the books translated is given by discussion of food laws (Leviticus or Deuteronomy) and matters of ritual. The terms νόμος or νομοθεσία or νόμιμα are also very appropriate designations of the Pentateuch.[19] The restriction of translation work to the Pentateuch is made clearer in Babylonian Talmud, Meg. 9a,[20] which speaks of 72 translators, and associates their work with an unnamed translation of the Greek Torah. Josephus *Antiquities* 12.12–118 discusses the translation work, quoting from *Aristeas* at length. Though he speaks of the translation of the νόμος (12.48) by six people from each tribe (12.49), thus logically requiring 72 in total, Josephus is possibly the first writer to abbreviate this to just 70 (12.57, 86).[21] In support of understanding Josephus to be abbreviating the number, we note that Josephus is clearly abbreviating *Aristeas* in the general context and that in *Antiquities* 12.57 he states that he would prefer not to give the list of the names of elders in *Aristeas*. *Aristeas* of course has 72 names, but it is in this very text that Josephus talks of 70. However, in both contexts he speaks of the 'seventy presbyters' (τὰ ὀνόματα τῶν ἑβδομήκοντα πρεσβυτέρων, *Antiquities* 12.57; ἀκούσας Πτολεμαῖος τὴν παρουσίαν αὐτῶν καὶ τοὺς ἑβδομήκοντα τῶν πρεσβυτέρων ἐληλυθότας, *Antiquities* 12.86). The number 70 is not given to the translation, but to the *translators*, and they are never described as 'the seventy' alone, but are described as 'the seventy' in association with a specific noun.

'The seventy' with no accompanying noun does occur early on (e.g. Justin, *Dialogue* 120). However, Irenaeus speaks of 'seventy elders', or even simply the 'elders' (*Adv. Haer.* 3.21). In Eusebius' *Ecclesiastical History* the ἑβδομήκοντα are always personal and we read of 'the

---

[19] Of course the term νόμος is applied in the NT to parts of the OT other than the Pentateuch (Jn 10.34; 15.25; 1 Cor. 14.21; cf. Jn 7.49).

[20] *Antiquities* 1.12: 'for he [Ptolemy] did not immediately acquire all the writings; but those who were sent to Alexandria for translation, handed over only the books of the law.' Cf. Philo, *Life of Moses* 2.25–44, who also understands the translation to consist only of the law.

[21] If a writer like Josephus could indeed abbreviate a number he knew to be 72 to 70, as I argue here, then the use of Patristic evidence to support the number 70 in Lk. 10.1 may need to be re-evaluated.

translation according to the seventy' (5.8.10) or 'others, beside the seventy, who had translated the sacred scriptures' (6.16.1; see also 6.16.4). Jerome talks of the *septuaginta interpretes* or *septuaginta translatores* (*Prologue to Ezra*), and *septuaginta interpretes* can alternate with the term *septuaginta*, which naturally remains plural (*Prologue to Paralipomenon*).

Although there are too many references to be able to tell the entire story, it appears that the personal nature of the reference to the seventy was maintained through the Middle Ages. For instance, Thomas Aquinas used phrases such as *secundum septuaginta*,[22] or *secundum litteram septuaginta*,[23] but when all his usage is examined it is clear that *septuaginta* still refers to people and is plural.[24] He gives no indication that there is a Bible known as 'the Septuagint', nor a 'Septuagint version'.

If we move on to the seventeenth century and the preface to the KJV of 1611 entitled 'The Translators to the Reader', mention of the Seventy refers to people rather than to a version.

> This is the translation of the *Seuentie* Interpreters, commonly so called, which prepared the way for our Sauiour among the Gentiles by written preaching, as Saint *Iohn* Baptist did among the *Iewes* by vocall.

Notice the capitalization of both words, 'Seuentie' and 'Interpreters'. It is these words together that form the title for a group of people not for a translation. Later in the same century, John Owen (1616–1683) was frequently prepared to abbreviate reference to the seventy translators to 'LXX[.]', but his corpus contains phrases showing that the 'LXX[.]' are still often personal, and more often than not he construes 'LXX[.]' with a plural verb.[25]About half a century later, the commentator Matthew Henry (1662–1714) shows further developments. Owen's implicitly personal but cumbersome 'the translation of the LXX' is not

---

[22] *Super Sent.* 4.49.2.7 ad 4; *Super Isaiam* cap. 10, 37, 51. For these and other references from Thomas see www.corpusthomisticum.org.

[23] *Contra Gentiles* 4.16 n. 2; *Summa Theologiae* 2–2.45.1 arg. 3; 2–2.84.3 ad 3; *De potentia* 4.1 ad 7.

[24] *Super Isaiam* 9 l. 1, *propter quod septuaginta subticuerunt et posuerunt loco illorum, magni consilii angelus.*

[25] The following quotation illustrates the personal and plural usage: 'Whereas the Reasons of the *Apostle* for his *Application* of the *Testimonies* used by him in his words and expressions, are evident, as shall in particular be made to appear; so no Reason can be assigned, why the *LXX* (if any such *LXX* there were) who translated the Old Testament, or any other Translators of it, should so render the words of the *Hebrew* Text' (Owen 1674: 52). I am grateful to Lee Gatiss for help with references in Owen.

to be found (Russell 1826: 371, 384, 461, 475, 498, 523, 527), but rather 'the Septuagint translation'.[26] In Henry 'Septuagint' sometimes clearly refers to the translation not to the translators and may be singular.[27] This shows the partial reification of 'the Septuagint', but even at this stage it retained some association with persons. According to the OED (s.v. 'Septuagint') the earliest use of *Septuagint* as a translation is from 1633, though the earliest of its examples that is completely unambiguous is from 1646. Thus there was some overlap between personal and impersonal uses of the term. The sixteenth and seventeenth centuries also according to the OED witnessed a brief spell when the plural 'the Septuagints' was used to refer to the translators, whose personhood was even then an object of focus.

Of course, each language has its own story to tell as to how 'the seventy people' became the reified and singular 'the Seventy translation'.[28] However, it is possible to tell the story of how a range of influential languages came, without coordination, to move together, sometimes at an almost imperceptible pace, to be able to speak of a version called *the Septuagint*.

But simply having the name *the Septuagint* available did not give an immediate guarantee of its success. In the nineteenth and early twentieth centuries the term might still serve merely to qualify the principal words of a book title, which referred to the Old Testament in Greek (Field 1859), or be presented as something rather remote but not necessarily extant (Brooke and McLean 1906), and it was only in the twentieth century that 'LXX' finally bade farewell to its lingering dot.

To summarize, the term *the Septuagint* was simply unavailable as a label for a Greek translation of any scriptures during the period of the Second Temple, New Testament, Rabbis or Church Fathers, and perhaps even far later. Given the mass of data the distinct possibility remains that impersonal occurrences of the term will be found during the Middle Ages. Nevertheless, the absence of the term from

[26] See Henry n.d. on Acts 7.1–16 and Rom. 3.1–18 for the phrase 'the Septuagint translation'.

[27] Commenting on the 70 disciples in Lk. 10.1 Henry talks of other groups of 70: 'They were seventy elders of the Jews that were employed by Ptolemy king of Egypt in turning the Old Testament into Greek, whose translation is thence called the *Septuagint.*'

[28] Jennifer Dines (personal e-mail 7 Feb. 2008) has suggested that the lack of an article in Latin may have assisted in the process of reification of the term in Latin.

early records has consequences for what could have been thought at the time. When we combine this with the observations of differences between the fourth and fifth century Greek uncials (e.g. A B S) and Greek OT texts from Qumran, the use of multiple translation forms in the Second Temple Period,[29] and the fact that there is no explicit statement prior to Justin Martyr that the work of the seventy extended beyond the Pentateuch,[30] we realize how problematic it may sometimes be to talk of a Septuagint version in the Second Temple Period. When a scholar carries out something as innocent as a computer search to find out how many times a word occurs in 'the LXX' or writes of an author adopting 'Septuagintal style', we are dealing with features of a corpus that had no name in the Second Temple Period and consequently would have been hard to identify as a body of literature.

Nor is it merely the lower league of scholars who can stray in terminology. Infelicities of terminology can even occur when in the midst of otherwise nuanced accounts by seasoned scholars, e.g. 'The LXX was the Bible of the authors of the New Testament' (Fernández Marcos 2000: 338) or 'The first Christians quite naturally chose G as their Holy Writ and as the source for additional writings since Greek was their language.' (Tov 2001: 143).[31] Doubtless these authors are clear in their own minds, but such language gives the impression that the Septuagint (or G) was a single identifiable entity, and that books outside the Pentateuch would have been seen as part of that entity. Whether or not translations of books beyond the Pentateuch shared close historical origins with the translations of books of the Pentateuch, we do not know to what degree these translations were *perceived* in the first century of Christianity as having common origins. We have no particular reason to conclude, for instance, that Paul, who was earlier than Josephus, and not much later than Philo, would have thought that a Greek translation of Isaiah was part of the work of the Seventy, though we can at least be sure that he did not refer to it as *the Septuagint*. With books that were not originally composed in Hebrew and would probably not have been known in Hebrew (e.g. Wisdom), or which have a

[29] For further problems with the identifiability of the 'LXX' see Steyn (2008: 697–707).

[30] According to Justin their work included the books of the prophets, such as Isaiah (*First Apology* 31), as well as Ezra, Jeremiah, and the Psalms (*Dialogue with Trypho* 71–73). See further Hengel 2002: 26–35.

[31] He identifies G with the *Septuagint* (Tov 2001: 134).

translator's preface (Ben Sira) it becomes more likely that a Jew with knowledge of Hebrew literature would *not* think of it as part of the work of the Seventy. We also do not know the extent to which users of Greek translations of books in the Hebrew scriptures were aware of different forms of the text, though there are significant differences between what they used and what we now call the Septuagint.[32]

The Apocrypha

The third term we consider is *the Apocrypha*. This is still often construed as a plural and has a relatively active singular *apocryphon*. Moreover, the plurality of the term and its cognates is well preserved in languages that have lost all sense of the plurality of *Bible*. In English there are probably still more than a few scholars who would regard the construal of *the Apocrypha* with a singular verb as a mistake. Nevertheless, there are also significant signs of its ability to function as a singular. No less an authority than W.D. McHardy could write in the Introduction to *The Apocrypha* of the *New English Bible* 'The Apocrypha as here translated *consists* of fifteen books or parts of books' (p. xi; emphasis added). This statement in 1970, in a translation published under the auspices of nine denominations, two Bible societies, and the University Presses of both Oxford and Cambridge, was presumably seen by a number of eyes at the proofing stage and appeared to them unremarkable. Examples of the term as a singular could be multiplied considerably. A second sign that the word has partly developed into a singular is the emergence of a secondary (or double) plural *apocryphas*.[33] After all, how else could one refer to different editions of those books simultaneously?

---

[32] As has long been known; cf. Swete (1914: 395): '...there is a considerable weight of evidence in favour of the belief that the Evangelists employed a recension of the LXX. which came nearer to the text of cod. A than to that of our oldest uncial B. This point has been recently handled in Hilgenfeld's *Zeitschrift f. Wissenschaftliche Theologie* [vol. 36, pp. 97–98], by Dr W. Staerk, who shews that the witness of the N.T. almost invariably goes with codd. ℵ AF and Lucian against the Vatican MS., and that its agreement with cod. A is especially close. It may of course be argued that the text of these authorities has been influenced by the N.T.; but the fact that a similar tendency is noticeable in Josephus, and to a lesser extent in Philo, goes far to discount this objection'.

[33] E.g. Cunningham (2000). Admittedly this article appears to contain a considerable number of neologisms.

The little detail, however, that I wish to consider here is connected to the appearance of the plural and is in fact the definite article. If one consults the *editio princeps* of the KJV in 1611 and of the Geneva Bible in 1560 one will see that the definite article is not to be found on title pages or running headers.[34] In the KJV *Apocrypha* were, it appears, not viewed as a collection, but as books each of which was apocryphal. Though the definite article is attested prior to the Geneva Bible,[35] the translations retain the old practice of not using the article. This is appropriate for the period, since it was only after the Reformation that there had been any gathering together of these books, which, in Old Testament collections prior to the Reformation, were positioned amid those books which were also in the Hebrew Bible. The anarthrous use of the term *Apocrypha* continues today and one can contrast the RSV's many references to *the Apocrypha* with the more recent *The Holy Bible containing the Old and New Testaments with the Apocryphal / Deuterocanonical Books: New Revised Standard Version*,[36] which is probably an attempt to reflect the earlier adjectival use of *Apocrypha*. It is this anarthrous and plural usage surely that gives a deeper sense of the history of the word.

Conclusion

We have considered the voyage of three important terms *the Bible, the Septuagint*, and *the Apocrypha* from plural to singular. They have of course reached different points, in diverse manners and at sundry times. Nevertheless, in each case there are distinct advantages to

---

[34] The KJV was printed in London by Robert Barker. The page of contents for the whole Bible has three major headings: 'The names and order of all the Bookes of the Olde and New Testament, with the Number of their Chapters'; 'The Bookes called Apocrypha'; 'The Bookes of the New Testament'. The page on which 1 Esdras begins is headed 'Apocrypha'. Likewise, whereas books of the Old and New Testament have running headers indicating contents, Apocrypha have the running header 'Apocrypha' on the left and right side of every page. A further feature distinguishing Apocrypha from what is canonical is the absence of the term Apocrypha from the title page, which reads 'The Holy Bible, Conteyning the Old Testament, and the New: Newly Translated…' All these features with regard to Apocrypha are essentially continued from the Geneva Bible.

[35] For examples, as well as a survey of Apocrypha in Early Modern English Bible translations see Westcott (1905: 281–291).

[36] Nashville: Thomas Nelson, 1989. It is also possible to purchase NRSVs with the phrase 'with Apocrypha' or 'with the Apocrypha' on the dust jacket.

reminding ourselves of the original plurality of these terms since the plural can carry with it a rather different and earlier sense. Whatever terminology we choose to adopt, the plurality is significant and needs at times to be reasserted.

References

Bible editions. 1560. *The Bible and Holy Scriptures conteyned in the Olde and Newe Testament* (Geneva: Rouland Hall).

——. 1979. *Nova Vulgata Bibliorum Sacrorum Editio* (Vatican City: Libreria Editrice Vaticana).

Brooke, A.E., and N. McLean. 1906. *The Old Testament in Greek, according to the Text of Codex Vaticanus, Supplemented from Other Uncial Manuscripts, with a Critical Apparatus Containing the Variants of the Chief Ancient Authorities for the Text of the Septuagint* (Cambridge: Cambridge University Press).

Castell, E. 1669. *Lexicon Heptaglotton* (London: Thomas Roycroft).

Cunningham, V. 2000. 'The Best Stories in the Best Order? Canons, Apocryphas and (Post) Modern Reading', *Literature and Theology* 14: 69–80.

Deissmann, A. 1927. *Light from the Ancient East* (London: Hodder and Stoughton).

Fernández Marcos, N. 2000. *The Septuagint in Context: Introduction to the Greek Versions of the Bible* (Leiden: Brill).

Field, F. 1859. *Vetus Testamentum Graece, juxta LXX interpretes* (Oxford: Jacob Wright).

Hengel, M. 2002. *The Septuagint as Christian Scripture: Its Prehistory and the Problem of Its Canon* (London: T&T Clark).

Henry, M. n.d. *Commentary on the Whole Bible* (London: William MacKenzie).

Hoops, J. 1976. *Reallexikon der Germanischen Altertumskunde* (2nd edn; Berlin/New York: de Gruyter).

Klappenbach, R., and W. Steinitz (eds.) 1976. *Wörterbuch der deutschen Gegenwartssprache* (Berlin: Akademie Verlag).

Owen, J. 1674. *Exercitations on the Epistle to the Hebrews... With an Exposition and Discourses on the two First Chapters of the said Epistle to the* HEBREWS (London: Nathaniel Ponder).

Pfister, M. 1997. *Lessico Etimologico Italiano vol. 5: *bassiāre–*birotulāre* (Wiesbaden: Dr. Ludwig Reichert Verlag).

Pusey, P.E., and G.H. Gwilliam. 1901. *Tetraeuangelium Sanctum* (Oxford: Oxford University Press).

Rahlfs, A. 1935. *Septuaginta: Id est Vetus Testamentum graece iuxta LXX interpretes* (Stuttgart: Deutsche Bibelgesellschaft).

Russell, T. (ed.) 1826. *The Works of John Owen*, Vol. 4 (London: Richard Baynes).

Steyn, G.J. 2008. 'Which "LXX" Are We Talking about in NT Scholarship? Two Examples from Hebrews', in *Die Septuaginta—Texte, Kontexte, Lebenswelten* (eds. M. Karrer and W. Kraus; Tübingen: Mohr Siebeck) 697–707.

Swete, H.B. 1914. *An Introduction to the Old Testament in Greek* (Cambridge: Cambridge University Press).

Tov, E. 2001. *Textual Criticism of the Hebrew Bible* (2nd edn; Assen: Van Gorcum).

Walton, B. 1657. *Biblia sacra polyglotta complectentia textus originales* (London).

Westcott, B.F. 1905. *The Bible in the Church: A Popular Account of the Collection and Reception of the Holy Scriptures in the Christian Churches* (London and Cambridge: MacMillan & Co.).

THE LAND IS FULL OF FOREIGN CHILDREN: LANGUAGE AND IDEOLOGY IN LXX ISA. 2.6

Rodrigo de Sousa

Introduction

It is well known that Isa. 2.6 is a challenge for those who try to interpret and translate the book of Isaiah.[1] Over the years, several emendations of the Hebrew text have been proposed and the LXX has often been used as a resource for the clarification of the verse's meaning and textual history.[2] But in the light of recent developments in research, which have indicated that the form of the Hebrew *Vorlage* of LXX Isaiah was indeed very close to MT, a new set of questions can be asked with regard to the relationship between the MT and LXX of Isa. 2.6. Sweeney (1996: 101) is correct in his assessment that the ancient versions 'represent the translator's or scribe's attempts to make sense out of a confusing text'.[3] If the *Vorlage* of the Greek Isaiah is similar to MT, a comparison between the versions opens a window into significant aspects of the LXX translation process.

In the present contribution, I explore the translation technical aspects of LXX Isa. 2.6, focusing on questions of syntax, vocabulary, textual relationship between LXX Isaiah and other LXX texts, and ideological factors behind the rendering.[4] I expect that this contribution

[1] It is a great honour and privilege to offer this contribution in honour of my *Doktorvater*, Robert P. Gordon. In my years as a doctoral student at Cambridge, I learned from Robert Gordon well beyond academic matters.

[2] Some of the proposed emendations have found their way into BHS and modern versions. See the surveys in Barthélemy (1986: 13), and De Waard (1997: 12–13). In this connection the work of Gray (1911; 1912) needs to be highlighted for his strong stance on the superiority of the LXX to MT as a witness to the original text of Isaiah.

[3] See also Sweeney (1988: 139–41).

[4] The notion of textual relationship is used here instead of *intertextuality*, as the latter term involves a series of complex principles and methodological presuppositions related to structuralist and post-structuralist literary criticism, represented by the work of authors such as Kristeva (1969; 1974). While the concept of intertextuality is valid for the study of texts (even within the LXX) it does not apply to the kind of simple relationship of direct influence envisaged here between LXX Isaiah and LXX

will advance our knowledge of the principles that oriented the translation of Isaiah in the LXX.

The LXX Translation of Isa. 2.6

First of all, here is a parallel translation of the MT and LXX of Isa. 2.6:

MT	LXX
כִּי נָטַשְׁתָּה עַמְּךָ בֵּית יַעֲקֹב כִּי מָלְאוּ מִקֶּדֶם וְעֹנְנִים כַּפְּלִשְׁתִּים וּבְיַלְדֵי נָכְרִים יַשְׂפִּיקוּ׃	ἀνῆκε γὰρ τὸν λαὸν αὐτοῦ τὸν οἶκον τοῦ Ισραηλ ὅτι ἐνεπλήσθη ὡς τὸ ἀπ' ἀρχῆς ἡ χώρα αὐτῶν κληδονισμῶν ὡς ἡ τῶν ἀλλοφύλων καὶ τέκνα πολλὰ ἀλλόφυλα ἐγενήθη αὐτοῖς
For you have abandoned your people, the house of Jacob. For they are filled from the east, and sorcerers like the Philistines, and with the children of foreigners they strike.	For he has forsaken his people, the house of Israel. Because *their country*[5] has become filled, as at the beginning, with sorceries like *that* of the foreigners, and many foreign children have been born to them

Modern commentators tend to be bothered by the second person addresses in MT Isa. 2.6 and 9, while third person forms are overall privileged in Isa. 2.6–9. Instead of seeing these two instances as mutually supportive,[6] scholars have sought to reconstruct alternative Hebrew texts. For instance, Duhm (1902: 39–40) argues that נָטַשְׁתָּה[7] possibly springs from a misreading of נטשׁ יה עמו, occasioned by the joining of the first two words and the confusion of ו and ך resulting in the second person possessive suffix we find in MT's עַמְּךָ. For Duhm, this is probably the reading of the LXX *Vorlage*, and the explanation for the third person rendering ἀνῆκε. However, if the translator had a text similar to the one reconstructed by Duhm, one would expect

---

Deuteronomy and Hosea, as we shall see below. For a succinct account of intertextuality, see Elam (1993) and Thiselton (1992: 38–42).

[5] The portions in italics represent additions in the LXX.

[6] As suggested by Williamson (2006: 190).

[7] The *plene* spelling in MT agrees with 1QIsa[a].

a Greek equivalent for יה as subject of the verb. Taking this together with the lack of support for the LXX rendering in other ancient versions, we are left with little evidence of a *Vorlage* different from MT (cf. Wildberger 1991: 99; Williamson 2006: 190).

That being the case, the rendering of נָטַשְׁתָּה by ἀνῆκε in Isa. 2.6 can be seen as the manoeuvre of a translator attempting to to produce a meaningful representation of the verse, taking into account the sense of its immediate context. For the Isaiah translator, the use of third person forms in vv. 7 and 8 could have warranted a shift in v. 6. In his discussion of 'personalization' in LXX Isaiah, Baer (2001: 57–58) has demonstrated that in places like Isa. 14.21 and 51.3, the translator was willing to reconfigure his text by maintaining a consistency of pronouns for homiletical and stylistic reasons. Concerns to maintain an intelligible text flow are consistent with the translator's personalizing and homiletical tendencies.

Verse 5 would also have given grounds for the change. While the structure of Isaiah 2 is a matter of intense debate, most commentators agree to delimit vv. 6–22 as a discrete unit.[8] It is likely, however, that the LXX translator conceived the section as opening in verse 5.[9] The *petuḥa* at the end of 2.4 in MT suggests a very old tradition of breaking the section between vv. 4 and 5. This tradition is also attested in 1QIsa[a] and 4QIsa[b] (fragment 2), both of which have line breaks at this point. The LXX addition of καὶ νῦν in v. 5 could also point in this direction (cf. de Sousa 2010: 20–22).

For the translator then, the textual unit begins with the summons for the house of Jacob to walk in the light of the Lord in v. 5,[10] so instead of having the awkward insertion of an address to the Lord in verse 6, with the second person נָטַשְׁתָּה, it seemed better to proceed directly from the summons to an explanation of why the people are estranged from the Lord and in need of a call to walk in his light. The

[8] Truly, many consider the present arrangement of these verses to be the result of heavy editing, and some do not think that verse 6 originally belongs where it currently stands—see, for instance, Duhm (1902: 39), and Wildberger (1991: 99–106). This is irrelevant for the present study because the LXX Isaiah translator would have before him a textual form similar to MT.

[9] This delimitation is also proposed by Sweeney (1996). Watts (1985) is also in favour of this arrangement but with a very particular understanding of the relationship between verses 5 and 6 (See below).

[10] The rendering of בֵּית יַעֲקֹב by τὸν οἶκον τοῦ Ισραηλ will be discussed later.

use of the third person (ἀνῆκε) created a smooth flowing explanation from verses 6 to 8.

Watts (1985: 32) has a quite peculiar understanding of Isa. 2.5–9. He follows the early witnesses in dividing the text at the beginning of verse 5, but sees an incongruity between the invitation to walk in the light of the Lord (v. 5) and the contents of verses 6 onwards. He argues that the MT of v. 6 negates the invitation with a declaration that the people had been abandoned, and that the LXX attempts to solve this difficulty. He proposes that ἀνίημι does not mean 'to abandon' but 'to approach, pertain to'. He thus translates ἀνῆκε γὰρ τὸν λαὸν αὐτοῦ τὸν οἶκον τοῦ Ισραηλ as 'for it applies to his people, the house of Israel'. While open to the possible retroversion כי נטה את העמו בית יעקב,[11] he is inclined to see here 'a deliberate change with theological motivations'. For him, the LXX operates in consistency with the promises of future blessing in Isa. 2.2–4 and 5 and validates the invitation that the MT seems to deny. He affirms that this shift 'could be interpreted as an open door to Samaritans in later times'.

Several factors speak against the proposal of Watts. If the invitation to walk in the light of the Lord is really at the head of the new section, than it is perfectly reasonable to read it as pressuposing that the people are currently *not* walking in this light but in the sins described in the following verses. Of course, the second person verb in v. 6 feels somewhat dislocated, yet the slight adjustment offered by the LXX helps to clarify the relationship between v. 5 and vv. 6–8. Besides that, if Watts were correct in his interpretation, solving the problem of the relationship between verses 5 and 6 would still generate an incongruency between verses 6 and 7, which list the sins of the people.

Also, his translation of ἀνῆκε is unwarranted. The sense 'to abandon, to forsake' for ἀνίημι is quite justified.[12] More significantly, the kind of openness and universalism suggested by Watts could not be in less agreement with the nationalistic tendencies of the Isaiah translator.[13] In fact, LXX Isaiah 2 has possible indications of an anti-Samaritan polemic.[14]

---

[11] He sees the LXX change of 'Jacob' to 'Israel' as irrelevant.

[12] The meaning 'abandon' probably developed from the classical Greek sense of 'relax, loosen, let loose'. Cf. Euripedes' *Orestes* 94.1; Thucydides 5.9; Herodotus 4.28.

[13] Cf. Seeligmann (1948) and Baer (2001), *passim*.

[14] In LXX Isa 2.18, the 3rd person plural of the verb κατακρύπτω deviates from MT (which reads יַחֲלֹף—3rd person singular), but agrees with 1QIsa[a] and all the most

The discussion above serves to indicate that, on the linguistic level, the near context of a verse influences the translator's choices. The contextual considerations of the translator will also come into play as he deals with the difficulties of the second part of Isa. 2.6. The seemingly peculiar uses of the verb מלא and the preposition מן in the construction מָלְאוּ מִקֶּדֶם have proven to be a challenge to commentators at least since Lowth.[15] The LXX rendering indicates that the translator also struggled with the text and produced a version that differs markedly from MT but which makes sense for him within the overall context of the passage. While these differences suggest to some a LXX *Vorlage* very different from MT, it is possible to reconstruct the trajectory from a Hebrew parent text resembling MT to the LXX.

The rendering of מָלְאוּ as ἐνεπλήσθη suggests that the translator did not have any difficulties with the meaning of the verb as such, but rather with the identification of its subject and object. By ignoring the ו in עֹנְנִים the translator finds his object (what he does with מִקֶּדֶם is discussed below).

The translator also seems to have had difficulty with seeing the 'house of Jacob'—or 'Israel'—as the subject of מָלְאוּ. He thus supplies

---

important ancient versions (Vulgate, Peshitta, Targum). Since haplography could easily explain the reading in MT, it is most likely that LXX reflects a different *Vorlage* at this point. The difference in the meaning of the verbs is also worthy of note. κατακρύπτω carries the ideas *to cover over, hide away, conceal*, and is most frequently associated with the roots טמן (Gen. 35.4; Jer. 13.4,6), סתר (Ps. 30[31].20), and חבא (2 Chron. 18.24; 22.12). חלף means *to pass away, carry*, or *substitute*, and is mostly connected to ἀλάσσω (Gen. 35.2). This is the only instance in the LXX in which the two terms are connected, and the reason for this could be gleaned from reading verses 18 and 19 together. If we connect the aorist participle form εἰσενέγκαντες (from εἰσφέρω, *to carry into*) with τὰ χειροποίητα as an accusative and not as a nominative, we read that men will carry the idols into the caves—*and into the clefts*, with the addition of καὶ εἰς τὰς σχισμὰς possibly influenced by v. 21—of the rocks and hide them there. In LXX Gen. 35.4 where we have the narrative of Jacob hiding (κατακρύπτω) the idols and earrings of his servants under the Terebinth at Shechem, the LXX adds 'and he destroyed them until the present day' (καὶ ἀπώλεσεν αὐτὰ ἕως τῆς σήμερον ἡμέρας). It is possible that the addition in Genesis fits within a later anti-Samaritan polemical tradition, which connects Jacob's hiding of the idols and Mount Gerizim. This tradition is also reflected in texts such as Ant. 18:85–89, Jubilees 31.1, L.A.B. 25.10, and Gen. Rab. 81. See also Harl (1986: 251) and Kippenberg (1971: 250–251). It is conceivable that, under the influence of this tradition, the translator connected Gen. 35.4 and the destruction of the idols in Isa 2.18–19.

[15] Lowth (1868: 149) proposed the reading מקסם מקדם ('*with* divination from the east') instead of MT's מִקֶּדֶם as the original one, with the first word being lost through some form of haplography. This view has enjoyed acceptance by several commentators, such as Kaiser (1972: 31).

a different subject for the verb, namely, ἡ χώρα αὐτῶν. Gray (1912:51–53) does not see ἡ χώρα αὐτῶν as an addition but as a translation of ארצו, present in the *Vorlage* but subsequently lost. He supports this argument by pointing to the distance between the phrase and the verb ἐνεπλήσθη and to the presence of אַרְצוֹ in vv. 7 and 8, noting that it is not unusual for LXX Isaiah to render a singular pronoun referring to a collective noun as plural.

Yet, the distance between the phrase and the verb should not be a problem if the translator were trying to represent a *Vorlage* similar to MT. The use of ἡ χώρα αὐτῶν is in fact related to the presence of אַרְצוֹ in the immediate context, but does not point to an alternative *Vorlage*, rather to the translator's contextual awareness and reading sensibilities. The presence of אַרְצוֹ twice in v. 7 and once in v. 8 suggested to the translator that the passage focused on the *land* and this authorized an addition. This in turn required a change in the verb from plural to singular. Duhm (1902: 39) argues that the singular suffixes of אֶרֶץ in vv. 7 and 8 suggest that the *Vorlage* of LXX Isaiah had a singular form of מלא. This is an unnecessary assumption. A change in verb number to create coherence is quite within the parameters of the translation techniques of LXX Isaiah (e.g. 6.2; 7.1).

Incidentally, the same choice of subject is found in the Targum, which adds ארעכון at this point. While producing quite different renderings,[16] both LXX and Targum seem to have been influenced by the same kind of contextual considerations. That is, the presence of אַרְצוֹ three times in the following verses (twice in verse 7 and once in verse 8) made it possible for the translators to understand the construction in verse 6 as also referring to the land, even if adjustments had to be made.

The perception of the centrality of the land in the passage possibly also lies behind the rendering of מִקֶּדֶם. The translator understands קדם at this point as *beginning, ancient, of old*, and not *East*.[17] He therefore does not see the opposition East-West, represented by פְּלִשְׁתִּים/קֶדֶם

[16] The Targum reads ארי שבקתון דחלת תקיפא דהוה פקיד לכון דבית יעקב ארי אתמליאת ארעכון טעון כיד מלקדמין ועננין כפלשתאי ובמוסי עממיא אזלין ('For you have abandoned the fear of the Strong One who has delivered you, you of the house of Jacob, because your land is filled with idols as from the east, and sorcerers like the Philistines, and they go in the customs of the peoples').

[17] Symmachus, on the other hand, has ἀπὸ τῆς ἀνατόλης. The Vulgate's *olim* agrees with LXX, but it could have been influenced by it; see Barthélemy (1986: 13).

in the Hebrew. This is clear from his use of the phrase ὡς τὸ ἀπ' ἀρχῆς. The phrase is peculiar to LXX Isaiah, occurring only in 1.26, 2.6, and 63.19. In 1.26 it is a somewhat literal translation of כְּבָרִאשֹׁנָה. The context is the divine promise to restore Zion to its former state of glory and righteousness: 'I will set up your judges as in the past and your counsellors *as at the beginning*'.

ὡς τὸ ἀπ' ἀρχῆς in Isa. 63.19 is a free translation of מעולם. The MT of 63.19[a] reads הָיִינוּ מֵעוֹלָם לֹא־מָשַׁלְתָּ בָּם לֹא־נִקְרָא שִׁמְךָ עֲלֵיהֶם ('We have become as those whom you never ruled; upon whom your name has not been called'). The LXX is ἐγενόμεθα ὡς τὸ ἀπ' ἀρχῆς, ὅτε οὐκ ἦρξας ἡμῶν οὐδὲ ἐπεκλήθη τὸ ὄνομά σου ἐφ' ἡμᾶς ('We have become as at the beginning, when you did not rule over us, neither was your name called upon us').[18] The translator conceives of a distant time in the past, before the Lord exerted his rule upon Israel, and uses the temporal expression ὡς τὸ ἀπ' ἀρχῆς to convey this.

In the light of these examples the use of the phrase in 2.6 is also clearly temporal. In this case, the translator conceives of a time, also distant in the past, when 'the country of the house of Israel was filled with sorceries like that of the foreigners'. It is interesting to note that when כַּפְּלִשְׁתִּים is rendered by ὡς ἡ τῶν ἀλλοφύλων, the syntax of the LXX does not draw a comparison directly between the different people groups, as in MT; rather, the *countries*, or *lands*, are compared. This is quite an acceptable shift, since a territory could be conceived as the *locus* of customs or practices, as in 1 Macc. 1.44, which mentions the introduction of 'customs strange to the land' (νομίμων ἀλλοτρίων τῆς γῆς). More significantly, the expression γῆ ἀλλοφύλων appears in 1 Macc. 3.41, 4.22, 5.66, and 68, referring to the land of the Philistines. This suggests that the LXX Isaiah translator could have a specific territory in mind, the coastal area traditionally associated with the Philistines. As argued by Levine (1999: 24), the populations in the coastal areas of Palestine were more susceptible to the process of Hellenization.[19] These thoroughly Hellenized coastal regions were naturally perceived as a threat to the purity of Jewish life, and especially of Jerusalem.

---

[18] The translation of 63.19[b] (64.1) is discussed in detail by Baer (2001: 181–92).

[19] It is noticeable, for instance, that the region of Galilee was not as thoroughly Hellenized as coastal cities such as Cesarea and Decapolis (cf. Chancey 2002; 2006).

The choices of words to represent עֹנְנִים and פְּלִשְׁתִּים also need to be observed. The noun κληδονισμός appears only here and in Deut. 18.14, where it is also connected with ענן. In Deut. 18.10, ענן is rendered by the verb κληδονίζεσθαι. The suggestion of Ziegler (1934: 107) that the translator was influenced by LXX Deut. 18.10 and 14 is taken up by Barthélemy (1986.13) as evidence that this is a peculiar interpretation of MT. The list of pagan magical and religious practices in Deut. 18.10–14 provided the kind of ideological framework that could be used to describe the pagan customs of gentiles, and could be associated with other texts that also deal with similar issues, such as Isa. 2.6.[20]

It is well known that פְּלִשְׁתִּים is rendered as θυλιστειμ in LXX Pentateuch, Joshua, and in the B text of Judges, and with forms of ἀλλόφυλος in the remainder of the LXX books. Different explanations for the phenomenon have been offered, but only two are highlighted here. Seeligmann (1948: 87) suggests that a 'definite historical circumstance' lies behind the rendering. Following Exod. 34.15 as well as 1 and 2 Maccabees, he sees the term as referring to the populations surrounding Palestine who were hostile to Israel during the persecution of Antiochus Epiphanes but who were forcibly converted to Judaism and incorporated into the Jewish state—without becoming 'citizens'—after the Maccabean wars. The difficulty with this view is that it does not fit well Seeligmann's own proposal of dating LXX Isaiah prior to 140 BCE.[21]

A more elaborate and attractive proposal is offered by De Vaux (1972). After tracing some particularities of the historical usage of the term, he points out that it was apparently reserved for the non-Jews living alongside the Jews '*dans la terre promise à Abraham*'—as opposed to the Canaanites, who occupied the land *prior* to the Jews but had been absorbed (p. 190). De Vaux's criticism of Seeligmann's view is pertinent as it is difficult to view this kind of Septuagint evidence as pinpointing a specific historical situation (such as the Maccabean campaigns) and it is methodologically preferable to look for a more general historical context, such as the geographic and political

[20] As we have seen, the non-rendering of the preceding ו alters the syntax of the verse markedly, but was a necessary change to construct a coherent and meaningful Greek verse.

[21] He is aware of the difficulty and entertains the possibility that earlier strata of LXX Isaiah did contain φυλιστειμ (a view for which there is indeed some slight textual support) and this was subsequently replaced by ἀλλόφυλοι.

configuration of people groups in the areas surrounding Palestine. He proposes that ἀλλόφυλος carries the peculiar nuance of designating those who were the propagating agents of Hellenism. The same kind of ideological drive could lie behind the rendering of פְּלִשְׁתִּים as Ἕλληνας in LXX Isa. 9.11(12).

In this connection, I note that in Legat. 30: 200, Philo describes the 'multitude' inhabiting the city of Jamnia as μιγάδες ('mixed'). They are a mixture, the majority of which is made out of Jews, while others are ἀλλόφυλοι from neighbouring countries (πλησιοχώρων), who are a constant distress to the Jewish people for their continuous violation of Jewish customs.

Thus, the rendering ἀλλόφυλα for נָכְרִים later in Isa. 2.6 is also noteworthy. The root נכר is more frequently translated in the LXX with ἀλλότριος (e.g. Gen. 17.2; 31.15; 35.2, 4; Exod. 2.22; Lev. 16.1; Josh. 24.14; Neh. 9.2; 13.26–27; Isa. 28.21; 62.8; Jer. 2.21; 5.19; Zech. 1.8; Mal. 2.11) or ἀλλογενής (Gen 17.27; Exod. 12.43; Lev. 22.25; Isa. 56.3, 6; 60.10; 61.5; Ezek. 44.7, 9[2x]). The use of ἀλλόφυλα for נכר is exclusive to LXX Isaiah, appearing only here and in 61.5, where the Hebrew reads בְּנֵי נֵכָר. The same Hebrew expression is rendered as υἱοὶ ἀλλότριοι in 62.8.[22] It seems that ἀλλόφυλος, ἀλλότριος, and ἀλλογενής had enough semantic affinity to be able to be used somewhat loosely to refer to those who represented the dangers and evils of Hellenism. This fluidity in the use of vocabulary explains why the translator could also use Ἕλληνας in LXX Isa. 9.11(12) to translate a Hebrew word normally rendered by one of these Greek terms. The use of ἀλλόφυλα for נָכְרִים in the last part of Isa. 2.6 could indicate an effort to harmonize the Greek text. Attempting to provide an adequate rendering in Greek the translator opted for the word that would create greater coherence in the context.

The adjectival form ἀλλόφυλα occurs within the rendering of the difficult construction וּבְיַלְדֵי נָכְרִים יַשְׂפִּיקוּ. The Greek καὶ τέκνα πολλὰ ἀλλόφυλα ἐγενέθη αὐτοῖς does not seem to correspond either in syntax or in meaning with the Hebrew construction. Yet again we can conceive of the Greek as a free rendering of a *Vorlage* that was similar to MT.

---

[22] In 1.7, a text with an obvious intertextual relationship to 62.8, we have two occurrences of זָרִים. These are translated as ἀλλότριοι and λαῶν ἀλλοτρίων.

The discussion about the meaning of the Hebrew construction generally centres on the understanding of יַשְׂפִּיקוּ.[23] Commentators and modern translators are usually divided as to whether יַשְׂפִּיקוּ should be understood as derived from the root שׂפק I or שׂפק II. The first carries the meaning 'to strike, clap (hands)'. In Isa. 2.6 it would have been used either as a metaphor for striking bargains, or with connotations of some sort of sorcery.[24] This proposal often requires the emendation of בילדי as בידי.[25]

The root שׂפק II means 'to be enough, suffice'. Barr (1968: 232–233) points to uses in the Hebrew Bible (the verb in 1 Kgs. 20.10, the noun form שֲׂפְקוֹ in Job 20.22), to the existence of several cases in Sirach (with the spelling ספק),[26] and to the familiarity of שׂפק II in later Hebrew, to argue that this is the meaning intended in Isa. 2.6. Besides the merits of Barr's proposal to ascertain the meaning of the verb in its original Isaianic context, it seems to be quite plausible that this understanding does indeed lie behind the LXX rendering (note also the insertion of πολλά, prompted by the translator's attempt to express the sense of the verb clearly).

Several commentators also suggest that the translator has שׂפק II in mind when dealing with יַשְׂפִּיקוּ. Wildberger(1991: 100) argues that the translator deduced from שׂפק II the meaning 'to have an overflow' (in the *hif'il*).[27] For Williamson (2006: 193), the rendering καὶ τέκνα πολλὰ ἀλλόφυλα ἐγενήθη αὐτοῖς could be based on a 'loose interpretation' of שׂפק II (which he translates as 'to suffice, abound') and the ignoring of ב in ילדי.[28]

Somewhat related to this is the proposal of Lowth (1868: 149). He argues for the corruption of יַשְׂפִּיקוּ in MT and points to Michaelis' connection of יִסָּפְחוּ ('they huddle together') in Job 30.7 with the noun סָפִיחַ, noting that it means 'corns springing up, not from the seed regularly sown on cultivated land, but in the untilled field, from the

[23] Several ancient manuscripts (including 4QIsa[b]) read יספיקו.

[24] This seems to underlie Symmachus' translation καὶ μετὰ τεκνῶν ἀλλοτριῶν ἐκποτήσαν.

[25] My own translation of the MT reflects this understanding—without the emendation of בילד—but this is secondary to the issue at hand, namely, how the LXX translator understood the term.

[26] The manuscript evidence attests both השׂפיקו and הספיקו for Sir. 42:17.

[27] Wildberger's own view is that the use in MT reflects שׂפק I.

[28] For Williamson's illuminating discussion of the evidence of later Greek versions and Jerome, see pp. 193–194.

scattered grains of the former harvest'. His contention is that 'the noun, by an easy metaphor, is applied to a spurious brood of children irregularly and casually begotten'. For Lowth this would be the best way of explaining the difficult rendering καὶ τέκνα πολλὰ ἀλλόφυλα ἐγενήθη αὐτοῖς of the LXX, as well as the Vulgate's use of *adhaeserunt*. While this proposal is unique, it is closer to the meaning of שׂפק II.

The reference to the birth of children in the Greek suggests that either an explanation derived from שׂפק II or something along the 'metaphorical' lines proposed by Lowth lies behind the LXX rendering. This brings us to another significant issue. A common feature to the studies of Lowth, Wildberger, Williamson, and Seeligmann is the suggestion of a relationship between LXX Isa. 2.6 and LXX Hos. 5.7, which translates כִּי־בָנִים זָרִים יָלָדוּ ('for they have given birth to foreign children') fairly literally as ὅτι τέκνα ἀλλότρια ἐγεννήθησαν αὐτοῖς ('for alien children have been born to them').[29] The comparison is suggestive because of the similarity in wording between the two Greek versions. The fact that LXX Hos. 5.7 is a more direct rendering leads Seeligmann—and contemporary commentators—to see it as prior to that of LXX Isa 2.6.[30]

Though not argued by any of the commentators cited above, the influence of LXX Hos. 5.7 could also lie behind the change of 'Jacob' to 'Israel' in LXX Isa. 2.6. The expression 'The house of Jacob' (בֵּית יַעֲקֹב) appears in MT in both verses 5 and 6. The LXX renders the occurrence in verse 5 by ὁ οἶκος τοῦ Ιακωβ, but the one in verse 6 by τὸν οἶκον τοῦ Ισραηλ. The lack of textual support in ancient witnesses indicates a *Vorlage* identical to MT. Perhaps the change was effected by literary motivations (to avoid repetition) as something similar happened in the translation of אַרְצוֹ in the following verses.[31]

In Isa. 8.14 we have the reverse phenomenon. There בָּתֵּי יִשְׂרָאֵל is translated by ὁ οἶκος τοῦ Ιακωβ. It is thus likely that the two expressions could simply be used interchangeably without any particular implications. Yet, since the translator could have used either term, something must have steered him in a particular direction. In the light of the

[29] Besides the aforementioned commentaries, see Seeligmann (1948: 72).

[30] Seeligmann's argument (1948: 70–72) is that whenever a deviating LXX rendering agrees with a literal rendering of another passage, the former is to be seen as dependent on the latter. There is no need to disagree with this assessment at this point.

[31] אַרְצוֹ occurs twice in verse 7 and once in verse 8. The first occurrence is rendered by χώρα and the other two by γῆ.

proposed influence of LXX Hos. 5.7, it should be noted that in LXX Hos. 5.1 it is the οἶκος Ισραηλ (בֵּית יִשְׂרָאֵל) that is being addressed. Hos. 5.7 is part of a larger address in which the 'House of Israel' is indicted for its sins. If we have a strong case for the influence of the verse in the rendering of Isa. 2.6, it is conceivable that the whole context of the Hosea passage was in the mind of the Isaiah translator, and this could have prompted the translation of בֵּית יַעֲקֹב by οἶκος Ισραηλ.[32]

That ancient readers took account of larger textual units is abundantly evidenced by the existence of textual division systems in early manuscripts.[33] Also, several recent studies point to the contextual character of the translational decisions of LXX Isaiah.[34] If the ancient competent reader—like *any* competent reader—read and processed texts in larger units and not simply at the individual word and sentence level,[35] we can expect that when a different text was evoked, it could also have been evoked as a whole. That is, the translator could have in view larger contextual units than the simple verse.[36]

Ideological Factors in LXX Isa. 2.6

The strategies used to render Isa. 2.6 and the influence of texts such as LXX Deuteronomy and, especially, LXX Hosea on the translation give us insight on the kind of process operating in the mind of the LXX Isaiah translator. As he attempted to make sense of the difficult

---

[32] It could also be the case that the translator was influenced at this point by the use of לְבֵית יִשְׂרָאֵל in Isa. 63.7. It is conceivable that we have in LXX Isa. 2.6 a glimpse of a tradition which will be developed further in the Targum, where the phrase 'house of Israel' was used as a collective designation of God's chosen, whether in obedience to the Lord or in open transgression of the Law, as in 5.3; 9.1–2; 27.1–4; 28.9, 25; 42.7 (cf. Chilton 1983: 33–37). This tradition could have found its way to the translator's thinking, who disregarded the precise equivalent in the rendering of Isa. 2.6.

[33] See the articles in Korpel and Oesch (2000; 2002).

[34] See especially Van der Kooij (1997; 1998). For a discussion of Van der Kooij's view, see de Sousa (2010: 13–40).

[35] See the distinction made by Barr (1979: 297) between the *input* and *output* sides of the translation process.

[36] One is reminded here of Dodd's well known approach to the issue of the use of the Old Testament in the New Testament. Dodd (1952: 126) affirms that when a certain text was quoted in *testimonia* collections, the full context of the passage cited was in view. While this position has been largely discredited, it still has commendable elements.

Hebrew verse before him he was guided by clues in the text itself, by his knowledge of previous texts, and by ideological factors.

Thematic and ideological parallels between Isaiah 1–4 and the book of Hosea (especially chapter 5) would have easily been perceived by a translator familiar with both texts. The whole of Isa. 2.5–4.6 is dominated by the theme of the cleansing of Zion (Sweeney 2006: 89), where indictments for the sins of the people are combined with promises of restoration. Hosea presents similar features. Hos. 5.1–7, in particular, continues the association between prostitution and idolatry, which dominated the first four chapters (Mays 1969: 82, 84; Wolff 1974: 101; Macintosh 1997: 189–191). The association between foreign cults and sexual immorality is graphically developed in Hosea. Significant examples are 1.2–9; 2.1–13; 4.11–19; 8.5–11. The themes in Isaiah and Hosea could have been combined and appropriated by post-exilic Jewish groups.

The tensions between the Judaism of the 2nd century BCE and the Hellenizing influences to which it was subject, together with traditions developed around the reading of sacred texts provided the kind of ideological material that steered biblical interpretation and translation in particular directions.[37]

For instance, the traditions reflected in Ezra-Nehemiah (e.g. Neh. 13.23–31) associate the marriage between Jews and non-Jews with the snare of idolatry and moral defilement. Klawans (1998: 402–405) demonstrates how these traditions subsequently made their way into diverse texts. The two most significant for the present study are: 4Q381, frg. 69, lines 1–2, which states that the practices of the inhabitants of the land are the cause of its moral defilement; Jubilees 20.19–22, and 30.13–15, which contain strong admonitions against intermarriage, also connecting the practices of foreigners with the defilement and pollution of the land.[38]

Also significant is CD 8.1–13 (cf. 4Q266, frg. 3, col. 4, lines 1–6), which contains an indictment against those who do not adhere to the strict regulations of the group.[39] The indictment is crafted in language

[37] Neh. 13.23–31 speaks of Nehemiah purging the foreign influences on the Israelites, especially with regard to the marriage to foreign women (נָשִׁים נָכְרִיּוֹת / γυναῖκες ἀλλότριαι [LXX]) and having children with them.

[38] It is interesting to note that Jubilees 20.22 describes the idolatrous practices of the Canaanites in language that is akin to Isa. 2.5–22.

[39] That is to say the group behind this specific passage. The composite character of the Damascus Document leads many scholars to believe that several different groups

that combines elements from Deuteronomy, Isaiah, and Hosea. Besides a direct allusion to Hos. 5.10,[40] the text combines motifs present in the book of Isaiah, e.g. the untreatable infirmities of Isa. 1.5–6, and Hosea, e.g. references to 'prostitutions' (זנות), to craft the accusation against the sinners.[41] The section culminates with a citation of Deut. 32.33, relating the Deuteronomic threats and curses to the Hellenizers who were perceived as a menace the community.

Concluding Remarks

Following the common procedure in early Judaism, the translator of LXX Isaiah read scriptural texts with a keen eye to their common features, and perceived in them severe warnings against the dangers of Hellenization and other alien influences. Being immersed in these traditions and ideological milieu, when trying to make sense of the difficult syntactical constructions in Isa. 2.6, he understood יַשְׂפִּיקוּ as related to שׂפק II and perceived in the text references to pagan practices, intermarriage, and the begetting of 'foreign' children. Elements which threatened to contaminate the land of Israel from its vicinity.

The translator of LXX Isaiah certainly belonged to the scribal circles entrusted with the preservation and transmission of prophetic literature.[42] He was most likely endowed with extensive knowledge of scriptural texts, and lived in a context where certain conditions of interpretation were in vogue. These conditions were religious and ideological, stemming from a community which accorded central value to the scriptures, and derived from these texts its values and traditions. In this context, the translation of a particular biblical text was certainly

lie behind the overall composition of the document. See a helpful summary of the discussion in Hempel (2000: 54–56). The difficulty in recovering history from the Damascus texts is highlighted by Grossman (2002), and Metso (2004).

[40] The condemnation is presented as coming upon the leadership of Judah ביום אשר תשפוך עליהם העברה ('on the day in which wrath will be poured upon them'). The MT of Hos. 5.10 reads הָיוּ שָׂרֵי יְהוּדָה כְּמַסִּיגֵי גְּבוּל עֲלֵיהֶם אֶשְׁפּוֹךְ כַּמַּיִם עֶבְרָתִי ('The princes of Judah are like those who remove a boundary; upon them I shall pour my wrath like water').

[41] While focused solely on the Admonition section of the Damascus Document, the study of Campbell (1995), is very helpful in pointing to the pervasive use of scriptural texts, whether as citations or allusions in the composition of the document.

[42] For a discussion of the possible priestly background if LXX Isaiah and its connection with the Oniad dynasty, see de Sousa (2010: 108–113).

carried out with the avowed intent to be faithful to its message, yet also with particular ideological premises giving shape to its interpretation.

References

Baer, D. 2001. *When We All Go Home: Translation and Theology in LXX Isaiah 56–66* (Journal for the Study of the Old Testament Supplement, 318; Sheffield: Sheffield Academic Press).

Barr, J. 1968. *Comparative Philology and the Text of the Old Testament* (Oxford: Clarendon Press).

——. 1979. *The Typology of Literalism in Ancient Biblical Translations* (Mitteilungen des Septuaginta-Unternehmens, 15; Göttingen: Vandenhoeck & Rupecht).

Barthelemy, D. 1986. *Critique textuelle de l'Ancien Testament 2. Isaïe, Jérémie, Lamentations* (Orbis Biblicus et Orientalis, 50.2; Göttingen: Vandenhoeck & Ruprecht).

Campbell, J.G. 1995. *The Use of Scripture in the Damascus Document 1–8, 19–20* (Beihefte zur Zeitschrift für die Alttestamentliche Wissenschaft, 228; Berlin/New York: de Gruyter).

Chancey, M.A. 2002. *The Myth of a Gentile Galilee: The Population of Galilee and New Testament Studies* (Society for New Testament Studies Monograph Series, 118: Cambridge: Cambridge University Press).

——. 2006. *Greco-Roman Culture and the Galilee of Jesus* (Society for New Testament Studies Monograph Series, 134; Cambridge: Cambridge University Press).

Chilton, B. 1983. *The Glory of Israel: The Theology and Provenience of the Isaiah Targum* (Journal for the Study of the Old Testament Supplement, 23; Sheffield: Sheffield Academic Press).

De Vaux, R. 1972. 'Les Philistins dans la Septante', in *Wort, Lied und Gottespruch: Festschrift für Joseph Ziegler* (ed. J. Schreiner; Forschung zur Bibel, 1; Würzburg: Echter Verlag/Katholisches Bibelwerk) 185–194.

de Sousa, R. 2010. *Eschatology and Messianism in LXX Isaiah 1–12* (The Library of Hebrew Bible/Old Testament Studies, 516; London/New York: T & T Clark).

De Waard, J. 1997. *Handbook on Isaiah* (Textual Criticism and the Translator, 1; Winona Lake: Eisenbrauns).

Dodd, C.H. 1952. *According to the Scriptures: The Sub-structure of New Testament Theology* (London: Nisbet).

Duhm, B. 1902. *Das Buch Jesaia* (2nd edn; Göttingen: Vandenhoeck & Ruprecht).

Elam, H.R. 1993. 'Intertextuality', in *The Princeton Encyclopedia of Poetry and Poetics* (ed. A. Preminger and T.V.F. Brogan; New York: MJF Books) 620–622.

Gray, G.B. 1911. 'Critical Discussions—Isaiah 2.6; 25:1–5; 34:12–14', *Zeitschrift für die Alttestamentliche Wissenschaft* 8: 111–126.

——. 1912. *Isaiah I–XXVIII—A Critical and Exegetical Commentary on the Book of Isaiah* (ICC; Edinburgh: T & T Clark).

Grossman, M.L. 2002. *Reading for History in the Damascus Document: A Methodological Study* (Studies on the Texts of the Desert of Judah, 45; Leiden: Brill).

Harl, M. (ed.) 1986. *La Genèse* (La Bible d'Alexandrie, 1; Paris: Cerf).

Hempel, C. 2000. *The Damascus Texts* (Companion to the Qumran Scrolls, 1; Sheffield: Sheffield Academic Press).

Kaiser, O. 1972. *Isaiah 1–12* (Translated by J. Bowden; The Old Testament Library; London: SCM Press).

Kippenberg, H. 1971. *Garizim Und Synagoge: Traditionsgeschichtliche Untersuchungen zur Samaritanischen Religion der Aramaeischen Periode* (Religionsgeschichtliche Versuche und Vorarbeiten, 30; Berlin: de Gruyter).

Klawans, J. 1998. 'Idolatry, Incest, and Impurity: Moral Defilement in Ancient Judaism', *Journal for the Study of Judaism in the Persian, Hellenistic and Roman Period* 29: 391–415.

Korpel, M.C.A., and J.M. Oesch, eds. 2000. *Delimitation Criticism: A New Tool in Biblical Scholarship* (Pericope 1; Assen: Van Gorcum).

——. 2002. *Studies in Scriptural Unit Division* (Pericope 3; Assen: Van Gorcum).

Kristeva J. 1969. *Séméiôtiké: recherches pour une sémanalyse* (Paris: Edition du Seuil).

——. 1974. *La révolution du langage poétique: l'avant-garde à la fin du XIX*[e] *siècle, Lautréamont et Mallarmé* (Paris: Éditions du Seuil).

Levine, L.I. 1999. *Judaism and Hellenism in Antiquity: Conflict or Confluence?* (Peabody: Hendrickson).

Lowth, R. 1868. *Isaiah: A New Translation with a Preliminary Dissertation and Notes* (London: William Tegg).

Macintosh, A.A. 1997. *Hosea: A Critical and Exegetical Commentary on the Book of Hosea* (ICC; Edinburgh: T & T Clark).

Mays, J.L. 1969. *Hosea: A Comentary* (Old Testament Library; London: SCM Press).

Metso, S. 2004. 'Methodological Problems in Reconstructing History from Rule Texts Found at Qumran', *Dead Sea Discoveries* 11: 315–335.

Seeligmann, I.L. 1948. *The Septuagint Version of Isaiah: a Discussion of its Problems* (Ex Oriente Lux; Leiden: Brill). Reprinted in R. Hanhart and H. Spieckermann (2004) *The Septuagint Version of Isaiah and Cognate Studies* (Tübingen: Mohr Siebeck) 119–294.

Sweeney, M.A. 1988. *Isaiah 1–4 and the Post-Exilic Understanding of the Isaianic Tradition* (Beihefte zur Zeitschrift für die Alttestamentliche Wissenschaft, 171; Berlin/New York: de Gruyter).

——. 1996. *Isaiah 1–39—with an Introduction to Prophetic Literature* (The Forms of the Old Testament Literature, 16; Minneapolis: Fortress Press).

Thiselton, A.C. 1992. *New Horizons in Hermeneutics: The Theory and Practice of Transforming Biblical Reading* (Grand Rapids: Zondervan).

Van der Kooij, A. 1997. 'Isaiah in the Septuagint', in *Writing and Reading the Scroll of Isaiah: Studies of an Interpretive Tradition* (ed. C.C. Broyles and C.A. Evans; Supplements to Vetus Testamentum, 70.2; Leiden: Brill) 513–529.

——. 1998. *The Oracle of Tyre: the Septuagint of Isaiah XXIII as Version and Vision* (Supplements to Vetus Testamentum, 71; Leiden: Brill).

Watts, J.D.W. 1985. *Isaiah 1–33* (Word Biblical Commentary, 24; Waco: Word Books).

Wildberger, H. 1991. *Isaiah 1–12* (Translated by T.H. Trapp; Continental Commentaries; Minneapolis, MN: Fortress Press).

Williamson, H.G.M. 2006. *A Critical and Exegetical Commentary on Isaiah 1–27—Volume 1: Isaiah 1–5.* (ICC; London/New York: T & T Clark).

Wolff, H.W. 1974. *Hosea: A Commentary on the Book of the Prophet Hosea* (Translated by G. Stansell; Hermeneia; Philadelphia: Fortress Press).

Ziegler, J. 1934. *Untersuchungen zur Septuaginta des Buches Isaias* (Alttestamentliche Abhandlungen, 12.3; Münster: Verlag der Aschendorffschen Verlagsbuchhandlung).

WHAT WAS AN ὈΠΩΡΟΦΥΛΆΚΙΟΝ?

Jennifer Dines

If you were strolling through the vineyards outside Alexandria on a fine summer's day in 150 BCE and you came across an ὀπωροφυλάκιον, what exactly would you have seen? A shed full of fruit? A watchman's hut? Or something else? The word is attested only in LXX and dependent literature, although it may of course have been in wider circulation. If a coinage, it is so idiosyncratic that one translator probably blazed the trail for the others.[1] My aim is to clarify its meaning(s); it is a pleasure to offer the modest exercise to Robert Gordon, whose interest in LXX, where he cut his scholarly teeth,[2] continues today not least through guidance of an impressive relay of doctoral students, as well as through friendly encouragement of older practitioners like myself.

ὀπωροφυλάκιον and Associated Terms

The compound has two elements: ὀπώρα, 'late summer'/'autumn', and so 'fruit',[3] and φυλάκιον, 'guard-post', 'watch', a predominantly military term.[4] In LXX, ὀπώρα occurs only in Jer. 31(48).32; 47(40).10, 12, rendering קַיִץ, 'summer fruit'; φυλάκιον does not feature anywhere, although cognates such as φυλακή, φύλαξ, φυλάσσω are frequent.

The closest parallels involving ὀπώρα are (i) ὀπωροθήκη, 'fruit store' (Varro, *Res Rustica* 1.59, glossing Latin *pomarium*, 'fruit loft'); this would have been an obvious choice if 'warehouse' was intended in LXX (cf. ἀποθήκη, 'barn', Lk. 12.17–18; σκηνοθήκη, 'tent store', in a

[1] It features in attempts to establish the relative order of translation of Minor Prophets (MP), Isaiah and Psalms (see Seeligmann 1948: 73–74; Aejmelaeus 2003: 512 n. 46); it will not be possible to address this issue here (but see below, n. 34).

[2] Gordon (2006: xxvi).

[3] Cf. Aquila's reading ὀπωρισμός, 'vintage' in Deut. 7.13.

[4] Equivalent to φυλακεῖον (Polybius uses both forms); cf. ὀπωροφυλακεῖον as a textual 'correction' in Jer. 33(26).18 (Ziegler 1957: 334). Both are Hellenistic alternatives to classical φυλακή.

second-century BCE inscription), and (ii) ὀπωροφύλαξ, a 'fruit-guard('s place)', whose methods of discouraging intruders are described by Aristotle (*Problemata* 938a; other occurrences are noted by van der Meer 2010: 192–99); more about this character later.

From its composition, then, ὀπωροφυλάκιον appears to mean 'something, or somewhere, for protecting fruit'. Most scholars, ancient and modern, interpret this as a garden watchman's hut. From its five occurrences in LXX, however, I will propose an alternative, or at least overlapping, meaning.

ὀπωροφυλάκιον in Isaiah 1.8; 24.20; Micah 1.6; 3.12; Ps. 78(79).1[5]

1. *Isaiah 1.8*

> ἐγκαταλειφθήσεται ἡ θυγάτηρ Σιων ὡς σκηνὴ (סֻכָּה) ἐν ἀμπελῶνι καὶ ὡς ὀπωροφυλάκιον (מְלוּנָה) ἐν σικυηράτῳ, ὡς πόλις πολιορκουμένη.
>
> Daughter Sion will be left like a hut in a vineyard and like a fruit-guard('s place) in a cucumber field, like a city besieged.

Within 1.1–9 (the first section of a longer judgement oracle) 1.8 forms the climax. 'The sinful nation' (1.4) is presented as a rebellious child, punished but unrepentant. The metaphor yields in 1.7 to what 'punishment' has meant in real terms: Judah invaded by foreign armies which have devastated the countryside, burned the towns, and are now helping themselves to the produce. In 1.8, Jerusalem is likened to:[6]

(i) a סֻכָּה (a temporary hut made of latticed boughs)[7] in a vineyard, and

(ii) a מְלוּנָה (a night-shelter(?))[8] in a מִקְשָׁה (a cucumber field). That a vineyard should contain a guard-hut is understandable, but why is the parallel a cucumber field? Why not an olive grove, a date-palm plantation, or some other high-profile crop? The only other

[5] In discussing these texts in alphabetical order, I am not suggesting that this was the order in which they were translated.

[6] As the *Vorlagen* of the five passages were all close to MT, the latter can provide a useful framework for comparison and will be included in the discussions.

[7] Cf. Gen. 33.7 (for cattle); 2 Sam. 11.11 (for soldiers); Jon 4.3 (for protection against the sun); Lev. 23.42 (for harvest celebrations). Neh. 8.15 describes the *ad hoc* method of construction.

[8] Found only here and Isa. 24.20. Perhaps coined to match סֻכָּה?

occurrence of מִקְשָׁה comes in Jer. 10.5. Here, the exiles are warned against the lure of Babylonian 'idols' which are 'like a scarecrow (תֹּמֶר, 'upright post')[9] in a cucumber field'. The humble location evidently underlines the futility of the idols, which neither speak nor move. There may be a similarly contemptuous nuance in Isa. 1.8.

But what is in Isaiah's field? From its supposed derivation from לִין, 'spend the night', מְלוּנָה suggests not a scarecrow, as in Jer. 10.5, but a night-shelter. In Isa. 10.29, the cognate מָלוֹן refers to a military arrangement (cf. 10.28; Josh. 4.3). This, like סֻכָּה, in 1.8, suggests a temporary structure. Elsewhere, it designates something more permanent, an 'inn' (e.g. Gen. 42.27). In a cucumber field, it will hardly have been five-star accommodation; nothing more, perhaps, than a shack in which labourers could sleep while working away from home. Modern commentators think of it as provision for a watchman, although this element is not required by the etymology. Nor is the hut's insubstantiality emphasised.

What does the translator make of the two comparisons?[10]

(i) He renders סֻכָּה by σκηνή. This is properly a tent (in LXX it is the normal equivalent for אֹהֶל and מִשְׁכָּן), but it can denote any simple structure, such as a wooden hut (Dio Chrysostom 7.23) or a market-vendor's stall (Aristophanes, *Thesmophoriazusae* 658; Theocritus 15.16). It represents סֻכָּה only here in Isaiah.

(ii) מְלוּנָה is rendered by ὀπωροφυλάκιον. A second structure seems required, but the translator would not necessarily have followed the Hebrew synonymous parallelism. The rendering of סֻכָּה by σκηνή, although unusual, makes sense, but ὀπωροφυλάκιον is a strange choice for מְלוּנָה. If the translator recognised a connection with לִין[11] there were other words he could have used: νυκτοφυλάκιον, 'night guard-post' (the rendering, later, of Symmachus

[9] Cf. תָּמָר, 'date-palm'; the root meaning is presumed to be 'go straight up'; cf. MH תֹּמֶר.

[10] A third comparison, 'like a city watched'(?), is textually problematic, but does not affect this part of the discussion. LXX and Targum interpret as 'besieged'.

[11] He did not recognise מָלוֹן in 10.29, but in 1.21, where לִין occurs, he translates correctly with ἐκοιμήθη, so he did know the verb.

> here);[12] or κατάλυμα, 'inn', 'bivouac' (rendering מָלוֹן in Exod. 4.24). An even better option would have been καλύβη or καλύβιον. These words occur in classical and Hellenistic Greek alike for a simple hut,[13] sometimes specifically in which to spend the night: Theocritus describes one with sides of woven leaves (cf. Neh. 8.15) used by fishermen overnight (21.7.18); Plutarch has the defeated Pompey sheltering overnight in another fisherman's καλύβιον (*Pompey* 73); Symmachus in fact has καλύβη for סֻכָּה in Isa. 1.8. The translator seems, however, to be thinking along quite other lines.

We must return to the 'scarecrow' in Jer. 10.5. LXX and MT diverge here: in LXX, 10.9 MT comes between 10.5a and 10.5b (see Ziegler 1957: 200; Walser 2010: 73; 316–318). LXX has equivalents for neither תֹּמֶר ('post') nor מִקְשָׁה ('cucumber field'), rendering instead ἀργύριον τορευτόν ἐστιν, 'it (the idol) is chased silver'. But there is a telling elaboration of this passage in Ep. Jer. 69: ὥσπερ γὰρ ἐν σικυηράτῳ προβασκάνιον οὐδὲν φυλάσσον, 'like a scarecrow in a cucumber field, guarding nothing.' The insignificance of the location, implied in Jer. 10.5, is here explicit. But it is the 'scarecrow' that startles: a προβασκάνιον is properly an amulet 'hung up outside workshops or in fields' (LSJ), or worn as protection against spells (τὸ βασκαίνειν, Plutarch *Table Talk* 5.681); a βασκάνιον too is a charm or amulet (such as the shell necklaces worn by Troglodyte women, according to Strabo 16.4.17). The object in Ep. Jer. 69 was no Worzel Gummidge; more likely an amulet, perhaps attached to a post, to ward off the evil eye.[14]

Was an ὀπωροφυλάκιον too a magical 'fruit-guard' of a similar kind? An indication that this may be the case is the occurrence of words in the φυλάσσω range with similar connotations, especially φυλακτήριον,

[12] Not mentioned by LSJ, but cf. νυκτοφυλακία, 'night watch' in PCairZen. 329.6; νυκτοφύλαξ, 'night watchman', Xenophon, *Anabasis* 7.2.18; Philo *De Specialibus Legibus* 1.156; *In Flaccum* 120; *Quaestiones in Genesim* 4.228. Aquila has αὐλιστήριον, 'night enclosure (for cattle)', glossed by Hesychius as συοβαύβαλος, 'pigsty'; he also uses this term for מָלוֹן in Isa. 10.29, where Symmachus has αὐλισμός, 'night lodging', yet another option in Isa. 1.8.

[13] E.g. Thucydides 2.52 (hovels erected in Athens by refugees); Diogenes Laertius 4.19 (huts set up by students in the Academy gardens).

[14] According to Hesychius, another word for a scarecrow is κεράμβηλον, also a kind of beetle (κεράμβυξ), apparently fixed to trees to drive off gnats(!); a garbled piece of country lore, which may, however, preserve some genuine prophylactic practice.

a 'guard post', but also an 'amulet'; Plutarch mentions one worn by Isis (*Isis and Osiris* 377B).[15]

But ὀπωροφυλάκιον may have suggested something even more shocking. A passage in Diodorus Siculus which features an ὀπωροφύλαξ gives the game away (4.6.4). Within a wider account of the worship of Dionysus, Diodorus discusses myths relating to Priapus (4.6.1–2). He gives a specifically Egyptian colouring by associating the phallic nature of the Priapus cult with the Osiris myth (4.6.3).[16] He then says:

> Honours are accorded him not only in the city, in the temples, but also throughout the countryside, where men set up his statue to watch over their vineyards and gardens (ὀπωροφύλακα τῶν ἀμπελώνων...καὶ τῶν κήπων) and introduce him as one who punishes any who cast a spell over some fair thing which they possess (πρὸς τοὺς βασκαίνοντάς τι τῶν καλῶν τοῦτον κολαστὴν παρεισάγοντες).[17]

If this is what the translator of Isa. 1.8 was suggesting, he was making a preposterous comparison between doomed Jerusalem and a statue of Priapus, with enormous phallus, ensuring fertility and warding off the evil eye (note βασκαίνω in Diodorus' account).[18] Even if the primary sense of ὀπωροφυλάκιον is a watchman's hut (matching σκηνή), I suggest that a very strong *double entendre* is operating here. But I do not think we need suppose a structure at all: φυλάκιον may not be a form of φυλακεῖον here, but a diminutive of φύλαξ ('guardian'), by analogy with other similar pairs, such as κοράκιον/κόραξ, μειράκιον/μεῖραξ, κυλίκιον/κύλιξ, μαστίγιον/μάστιξ. It is nowhere attested as such, but could easily have existed (or been invented).[19]

Ὀπώρα, 'ripe fruit', may also have sexual overtones: a young boy's youthful beauty is called ὀπώρα in a clearly erotic context (Pindar, *Isthmians* 1.25), and in Aeschylus' *Suppliants*, the daughters of Danaus reassure their father that he need not worry about their 'fruit', i.e. their virginity (1015), following his reminder that 'tender fruit is not

---

[15] Cf. φυλακτηριάζομαι, 'be provided with an amulet', P.Mag.Par 1.789, 2627.

[16] He apparently identifies Priapus with the Egyptian ithyphallic Min; Oldfather (1967: 358 n. 3).

[17] Oldfather (1967: 358).

[18] The continuation of Ep. Jer. 69, 'so are their gods, made of wood and gold...' (NETS), suggests that προβασκάνιον may also refer to a statue.

[19] In any case, a personal sense is attested for φυλάκιον itself; see Polybius 6.33.7, where it designates a 'watch' composed of four men.

at all easy to guard' (998).[20] In this context, Cant. 1.6 might be considered, where the female speaker tells how her angry brothers 'made me keeper of the vineyards, but my own vineyard I have not kept'. This is evidently some kind of disgrace or punishment. LXX renders: ἔθεντό με φυλάκισσαν ἐν ἀμπελῶσιν; if it equates her with a 'scarecrow', it is also an insult.[21]

All in all, it looks as if ὀπωροφυλάκιον may have been a less than innocent word. Modern commentators who understand it as a means of guarding rather than of storing produce are probably right. But I think that, in Isa 1.8, it was a kind of pun, playing on ὀπωροφυλάκιον as both a substitute for ὀπωροφυλακεῖον and a diminutive form of ὀπωροφύλαξ.

2. *Isaiah 24.20*

> ἔκλινε καὶ σεισθήσεται ὡς ὀπωροφυλάκιον ἡ γῆ ὡς ὁ μεθύων καὶ κραιπαλῶν καὶ πεσεῖται καὶ οὐ μὴ δυνήται ἀναστῆναι, κατίσχυε γὰρ ἐπ'αὐτῆς ἡ ἀνομία.
>
> the earth was beginning to lean[22] and will be shaken like a fruit-guard('s place), like a drinker (who is) intoxicated and (who) will fall and be unable to get up again, for lawlessness prevails over it.

This verse comes towards the end of the opening chapter of 24–27, the so-called 'Isaiah Apocalypse'. Instead of disaster falling only on Judah/Jerusalem, as in Isa. 1, the whole world is to be devastated (24.1, 3) for the sins of its inhabitants (24.5, 16). Cataclysmic images of flood and earthquake (24.18) are developed with hyperbolic exaggeration(24.19). Then comes the bizarre, almost ludicrous, image of the earth staggering about like a drunkard and swaying like a מְלוּנָה. This word echoes 1.8, thus implicitly involving Jerusalem. The image of nations staggering drunkenly under catastrophe occurs also in Isa. 19.14; Jer. 25.27; Nah. 3.11. But Isa. 24.20 is surely an anticlimactic example of the commonplace.

[20] Chaeremon 12 refers to ὀπώρα Κύπριδος, i.e. sexual love.

[21] Φυλάκισσα is a *hapax* in Greek, but cf. φυλακίς, a female 'guardian' in Plato *Republic* 457c. For sexual *double entendre* in the vineyard imagery here, see Goulder (1986: 13).

[22] Or 'leant' (aor.). The perfect 'has bent over' (NETS) seems less likely. Brenton has a present, 'it reels'.

LXX covers all the elements of MT, but reverses the Hebrew order (where the earth first 'staggers', then 'sways'), and compresses the two clauses, so that the earth collapses and is tossed about like a 'hut'/'statue' (and) like a drunken carouser. Perhaps it seemed more logical for a drunk to be unable to get up than for a hut/statue, or the earth itself (the subject throughout in Hebrew, less obviously so in Greek). The explanation: 'its lawlessness prevails over it' is then moved to the end of the verse.

As in Isa. 1.8, there is no 'night' element to represent מְלוּנָה. The translator has simply repeated ὀπωροφυλάκιον, although there has been no agricultural imagery since 24.7, 13. If he thought ὀπωροφυλάκιον referred to a hut, it was obviously as something unstable. But a 'scarecrow' might have seemed appropriate here too, especially as Priapus figured in Dionysian 'orgies' and would have reinforced the image of debauchery implied by the staggering drunk (unless, of course, ὀπωροφυλάκιον stood here for a human ὀπωροφύλαξ).

3. *Micah 1.6*

> Καὶ θήσομαι Σαμαρεῖαν εἰς ὀπωροφυλάκιον (לְעִי) ἀγροῦ καὶ εἰς φυτεὶαν ἀμπελῶνος
>
> And I will make Samaria a fruit-guard('s place) in a field, and a planting for a vineyard.

1.6 comes within Micah's opening judgement oracle against Samaria (1.2–7), although the passage starts with an address to the whole earth as the object of God's anger (1.2; cf. Isa. 24). A theophany with cataclysmic effects (1.3–4) is followed by the identification of the 'sin' of Israel (Samaria) and the 'high place' of Judah (Jerusalem) as the causes of God's judgement (1.5). Samaria's punishment is then proclaimed: destruction of the city (1.6) and of its 'idols' (1.7).

In 1.6, ὀπωροφυλάκιον renders a quite different Hebrew word from Isa 1.8; 24.20. עִי, 'heap (of stones/ruins)' occurs in the singular only here, and in the plural only in Mic. 3.12 (עִיִּין); Jer. 26.18; Ps. 79.1 (עִיִּים).[23] Leaving piles of stones was usually a sign of 'an intentional destruction (cf. Josh. 8.28)' (Smith 1984: 19); clearing the rubble to plant vines would then seem contradictory. The juxtaposition of עִי

[23] Job 30.24 is probably corrupt, as is an apparently related noun מְעִי in Isa. 17.1.

and שָׂדֶה is awkward: the razing of hilltop Samaria and the devastation of the surrounding countryside have been telescoped together, mixing rural and urban imagery. The climax comes in 1.7 with the destruction of Samaria's idols and the characterization of Samaria as a prostitute.

LXX represents שַׂמְתִּי...לְ by τίθημι...εἰς. Turning enemy cities into something unpleasant, using this idiom, occurs also in Zeph. 2.13 (ἀφανισμόν, 'annihilation'; cf. Jer. 12.11; 28(51).29).[24] Τίθημι...εἰς ἀφανισμόν is found also in Joel 1.7 (ἀμπελόν) and, indeed, Mic. 1.7 (εἴδωλα), so it is surprising that the Micah translator (probably the same as for the rest of MP) did not produce something similar in 1.6, even if he had to guess the meaning of עִי. Perhaps the agricultural setting (ἀγροῦ, ἀμπελῶνος) led him to speculate on what might have been in the 'field'. A hut would fit, but a sharper image would result if, as I have suggested for Isa. 1.8, he visualised a priapic 'scarecrow'. He might well have thought this appropriate for Samaria, especially given 1.7, where 'idols' (γλυπτά, εἴδωλα) are to be destroyed. It would intensify MT's already negative attitude, and would not be the only place where the MP translator has pagan allusions[25] and displays a marked animus against Samaria.[26]

4. *Micah 3.12*

> Διὰ τοῦτο δι'ὑμᾶς Σιων ὡς ἀγρὸς ἀροτριαθήσεται καὶ Ιερουσαλημ ὡς ὀπωροφυλάκιον (עִיִּין) ἔσται καὶ τὸ ὄρος τοῦ οἴκου εἰς ἄλσος (לְבָמוֹת) δρυμοῦ.
>
> and so, because of you, Sion will be ploughed like a field and Jerusalem will be like a fruit-guard('s place) and the mountain of the house a grove in a wood.

3.12 ends a section that starts with an indictment of Israel's unjust rulers (3.1–4), followed by a condemnation of all the prophets (except Micah himself, 3.5–8). A new apostrophe makes it clear that the judgement is against political and religious leaders (3.9–11). It is because of them that Jerusalem's fate is sealed. The link with 1.6 is clear: Jerusalem will share Samaria's disgrace.

---

[24] Also Isa. 10.6 (κονιορτόν, 'dust'); 25.2 (χῶμα, 'heap'); Jer. 4.7 (ἐρήμωσιν, 'wilderness'; cf. 22.6).

[25] E.g. τετελεσμένοι (Hos. 4.14); ἐγγαστρίμυθος (Hos. 11.6); τελεταί (Amos 7.9); τερατοσκόπος (Zech. 3.8).

[26] E.g. Hos. 10.5–6; Amos 6.1, among a wider range of passages hostile to the Northern Kingdom.

The plural עִיִּין, 'heaps', may be a stylistic variation on the singular in 1.6 (Wolff's suggestion that the *nun* deliberately echoes צִיּוֹן is attractive; McKane 1998: 113). Most understand the form as an Aramaic plural, although the word itself is not attested in Aramaic; the nearest being a verb, עוֹן, 'watch' (Jastrow, 1054; cf. LSJ Suppl., 110). However, although עִיִּין is plural, ὀπωροφυλάκιον is singular, as in 1.6. The translator may have understood the Hebrew noun too as a singular, analogous to MH *עיון, 'guard(ing)'.[27] This is plausible, given the tendency towards singular renderings in the versions.[28] A word taken to mean 'guard' might have suggested φυλάκιον, with ὀπώρα supplied from the context; more likely the rural imagery of the first clause suggested the whole compound, especially if it refers to a 'scarecrow', with φυλάκιον understood as a diminutive of φύλαξ. This would be a shocking comparison for Jerusalem, far worse than for Samaria in 1.6, where the pagan implications may have seemed well deserved. The translator has, however, lessened the impact: unless כְּ was in his source, he has added ὡς before ὀπωροφυλάκιον, turning the metaphor into a simile.

The strange juxtaposition of the two final words (לְבָמוֹת יָעַר), and the unexpected plural, have led to various emendations (Hillers 1984: 47; McKane 1998: 114–115), but LXX presupposes some form of בָּמָה, probably, as in 1.5, a singular, since ἄλσος is also singular.[29]Although the translator uses standard renderings for שָׂדֶה and יַעַר (ἀγρός, δρυμός), ἄλσος for בָּמָה is effectively a *hapax*, since Jer. 33.18, the only other occurrence, is a quotation of Mic. 3.12.[30] It strongly reinforces the pagan implications of ὀπωροφυλάκιον. The 'mountain of the house' clearly refers to the Temple; its fate is to become 'like a grove of a wood'. The tautology results from translating בָּמָה/בָּמוֹת by ἄλσος. In non-biblical texts this word often denotes a sacred grove; one dedicated to Athena near allotments outside the city is described in *Odyssey* 6.291.[31] In LXX, ἄλσος almost always renders אֲשֵׁרָה, 'an

[27] Seeligmann 1948: 74, following Kaminka; cf. Hillers (1984: 47 n. f). Seeligmann wonders why ὀπωροφυλάκιον rendering עִי etc. acquired a curse-like effect. The reason may now be clearer. Theocharous' proposal that עִי was itself an 'offensive' term, toned down by ὀπωροφυλάκιον, is interesting, but may rather reinforce my understanding of the Greek term's scandalous resonance (2011: 109–111).

[28] Λιθολογία (Aquila); ἐρήμωσιν (Theodotion); Symmachus, however, has βοῦνοι. Cf. ἄβατον in Jer. 33.18. See below, n. 35.

[29] Perhaps the *taw* is construed as a feminine singular construct. Cf. ὕψος (Symmachus); βοῦνον (Theodotion); Aquila's rendering is not extant.

[30] The standard equivalent is ὑψηλός.

[31] Cf. *Iliad* 2.506 (Poseidon); Hesiod, *Shield* 99 (Apollo); Herodotus 5.119 (Zeus).

Asherah'.[32] This loaded term sometimes refers to a cultic object, sometimes to a sacred grove; the Hebrew Bible condemns both. Ἄλσος as sacred grove occurs first in Exod. 34.13, heading a list of Canaanite places and objects which must be 'cut down' (ἐκκόπτω) or otherwise destroyed: βωμοί 'altars', στήλαι, 'pillars' and γλυπτά, 'images'. This passage is echoed in Deut. 7.5; 12.3, while Deut. 16.21 forbids planting groves beside altars. In Samaria, a sacred grove is among the 'sins of Jeroboam' (4 Kgdms 13.6; cf. 17.16), and Ahab 'made an Asherah' (ἄλσος; 3 Kgdms 16.33). But the practice is also condemned in Judah: establishing 'groves' as well as 'high places' (ὕψηλα, בָּמוֹת) features among the 'sins of Rehoboam' (3 Kgdms 14.23), while Manasseh put an 'image of the grove' (τὸ γλυπτὸν τοῦ ἄλσους) in the Temple.[33] Of particular interest, given non-biblical usage, is 1 Kgdms 7.4, where הָעַשְׁתָּרוֹת, 'the Astartes', is expanded into τὰ ἄλση Ἀσταροθ, 'the groves (dedicated to) Astarte'; this is the only place where a dedicatee is mentioned. The Micah translator may or may not have known Greek versions of Samuel-Kings, but the Pentateuchal occurrences suffice to show that he was probably aware of the ἄλσος/אֲשֵׁירָה equivalence. Exod. 34.13 is echoed in Mic. 5.13–14(12–13), especially ἐκκόψω τὰ ἄλση σου, 'I will cut down your groves' (אֲשֵׁירֶיךָ, 'your Asherim', 14(13)). In 3.12, the unique, anomalous rendering of בָּמָה as ἄλσος suggests the deliberate choice of a word with idolatrous biblical resonances which also evoked a rural Greek grove/shrine. This creates a powerful partnership between ἄλσος and (if I am right) the equally pagan ὀπωροφυλάκιον. Both 'groves' and 'scarecrows' must often have met the translator's eyes as he walked in the countryside, providing him with daring images for Jerusalem's total degradation.[34]

Before leaving Mic. 3.12, a glance at Jer. 33(26).18 is in order since Mic. 3.12 is quoted there as proof that a true prophet can survive an—apparently—unfulfilled prophecy of doom.

---

[32] 35 of 42 instances in Hatch Redpath. It also renders עַשְׁתֹּרֶת, 'Astarte' (1 Kgdms 7.3, 4) and אָב, 'thicket' (Jer. 4.29; not cultic here).

[33] This literal Kaige rendering shows the ambivalence of 'Asherah' as both sacred pole (?) and grove; cf. 4 Kgdms 23.4–15.

[34] The combination may strengthen the case for Micah being at the origin of the usage.

Jeremiah 33(26).18

Σιων ὡς ἀγρὸς ἀροτριαθήσεται καὶ Ιερουσαλημ εἰς ἄβατον (עִיִּים) ἔσται καὶ τὸ ὄρος τοῦ οἴκου εἰς ἄλσος δρυμοῦ.

Sion will be ploughed like a field and Jerusalem will become uninhabitable and the mountain of the house a grove in a wood.

The only variation from Mic. 3.12 MT is the Hebrew ending of עִיִּים. The only divergence from Mic. 3.12 LXX is that εἰς ἄβατον ('impassable', uninhabitable') replaces ὡς ὀπωροφυλάκιον in some witnesses.[35] Ἄβατον looks like an independent attempt to make sense of עִיִּים. Found first in Lev. 16.22 of the γῆν ἄβατον (גְּזֵרָה) into which the scapegoat is sent, it occurs again in Jeremiah, preceded by εἰς, in contexts similar to 33.18, e.g. 30(49).11 (Idumaea); 31(48).9 (Moab); 49(42).18 (exiles from Jerusalem). It is, therefore, a good choice in 33(26).18, giving a better sense for עִיִּים than ὀπωροφυλάκιον (though still an approximation). Furthermore, ἄβατος occurs throughout LXX Jeremiah for various Hebrew words, accounting for no less than 17 of the 29 occurrences in Hatch Redpath. If he knew Mic. 3.12 LXX, the translator of Jer. 33.18 apparently altered it, perhaps because he understood the Hebrew better, or because he found the Greek shocking. But it would be the only place where he altered his model. Alternatively, the change is the work of an editor who substituted a phrase more typical of LXX Jeremiah; this solution is favoured by various modern commentators and is perhaps more likely. As for the relationship with Mic. 3.12, ἀγρός, ἀροτριάω and δρυμός are standard renderings for שָׂדֶה, חָרַשׁ ('plough'), and יַעַר, but ἄλσος is so unusual for בָּמוֹת/בָּמָה that it is difficult to imagine both translators coming up with it independently: one will have borrowed from the other.

5. *Psalm 78(79).1*

Ὁ θεός, ἤλθοσαν ἔθνη εἰς τὸν ναὸν τὸν ἅγιόν σου, ἔθεντο (שָׂמוּ) Ιερουσαλημ εἰς ὀπωροφυλάκιον (לְעִיִּים).

O God, nations have come into your holy temple; they have made Jerusalem into a fruit-guard('s place).

[35] B, the corrector of S, the Coptic and Ethiopic versions and Symmachus. The hexaplaric evidence for Aquila is uncertain, offering both σωρός (another singular!) and λιθολογία (as for Mic. 1.6; Ps. 79.1), 'heap (of stones)'; either way reinforcing the likelihood that the noun was understood as a singular; see above, n. 28.

This psalm is a national lament which petitions God to take vengeance on the godless nations who have attacked Jerusalem. The scenario—the destruction of city and temple—overlaps with Isa. 1.8; Mic. 3.12, but the plea for vengeance changes the tone radically.

The statement in MT that foreigners have entered the land is reminiscent of Isa. 1.7 (although with different vocabulary), while שָׂמוּ, יְרוּשָׁלַםִ and עִיִּים in the final colon suggest both Mic. 1.6 (שַׂמְתִּי) and 3.12 (עִיִּין, יְרוּשָׁלַםִ). Mic. 1.6 is the closest parallel, even with Samaria as object, since Jerusalem has been the final word of 1.5. The two verses together provide an intertextual link with Ps. 79.1. Linkage with Isa. 1.8 is less compelling: here we find מְלוּנָה, not עִיִּים, and צִיּוֹן, not יְרוּשָׁלַםִ (although the names are obviously synonymous). The defiling of the Temple is not explicit in Isa. 1.8, but is implied in the final words of Mic. 3.12.

LXX presupposes MT; the periphrasis τὸν ἅγιόν σου for קָדְשֶׁךָ occurs again in Ps. 5.8; 137(138).2 (cf. 10(11).4; 27(28).2). The final phrase, ἔθεντο Ιερουσαλημ εἰς ὀπωοφυλάκιον mirrors Mic. 1.6 LXX, with necessary adjustment of verb tense and subject, and substituting Jerusalem for Samaria.

Τίθημι is the standard rendering for שִׂים in LXX; in Psalms the equivalence occurs 27 times out of 65, although τίθημι also renders שִׁית (19 times) and נָתַן (16 times). It is therefore an open question whether ἔθεντο in Ps. 78.1 is prompted by Mic. 1.6 or constitutes an independent choice. It is most unlikely that the translator thought of ὀπωροφυλάκιον by himself. Neither this verse nor the rest of the psalm requires rural imagery, and the picture of the little 'hut' seems inadequate to the horror of the situation; still less is a word with a possible pagan resonance likely to have been chosen or intended. More plausibly, the translator was nonplussed by the unfamiliar Hebrew word and found help from its other appearances in Mic. 1.6 and 3.12, perhaps unaware of the implications.[36] Although ὀπωροφυλάκιον also occurs in Isa. 1.8; 24.20, the Hebrew is different (מְלוּנָה), and therefore unlikely to have been the translator's first port of call. The Hebrew syntax of Mic. 1.6 is also closer to that of Ps. 79.1.

---

[36] If the Psalter was translated in Palestine, there may have been fewer 'hellenized' scarecrows in evidence.

Conclusion: What Was an ὀπωροφυλάκιον?

With no attestations outside LXX, meanings have had to be deduced from the passages in which the term occurs, and from related terminology. If its component parts are taken to be ὀπώρα ('late summer', 'ripe fruit') and φυλάκιον ('guard', guard post'), the compound could suggest 'fruit store', or 'place for garden watchman'. The first option is possible but unlikely since φυλάκιον has predominantly military meanings and does not suggest the storage of fruit or other produce, for which words constructed with -θήκη (ἀποθήκη, ὀπωροθήκη) were available. The second option, 'a guard post for fruit', meaning 'a hut for a garden watchman' is the one most often adopted. Such things certainly existed; writing in the fifth century CE, Cyril of Alexandria remarks that people 'preserve what grows in a field by weaving shelters and sitting in them, thus warding off all harm from it; but when the fruit is gathered the guards cease their labour and go off home after upturning their shelters' (Hill 2008: 188); he is commenting on Mic. 1.6, but has Isa. 1.8 also in mind; the woven shelters suggest σκηνή rather than ὀπωροφυλάκιον. I have suggested a third possibility: ὀπωροφυλάκιον is a 'fruit-protector', understanding φυλάκιον not as an equivalent of φυλακεῖον, but as a diminutive form of φύλαξ, 'guard'. This ὀπωροφύλαξ could simply have been someone hired to chase off wild animals (as in Aristotle), but the biblical contexts do not imply a living person and require something more dramatic. I have proposed that the reference—either directly, or through *double entendre*—is to statues of Priapus, set up, according to Diodorus Siculus, in vineyards and allotments to ensure fertility and ward off the evil eye, like the προβασκάνιον in Ep. Jer. 69. Such statues would have been a familiar sight in Hellenistic Egypt (where Isaiah and Micah, at least, were probably translated). Perhaps by Cyril's time they had vanished from a less pagan countryside, but originally they would have provided a truly shocking image for the punishment of Jerusalem.

References

Aejmelaeus, A. 2003. '"Rejoice in the Lord!" A Lexical and Syntactical Study of the Semantic Field of Joy in the Greek Psalter', in *Hamlet on a Hill* (eds. M.F.J. Baasten and W.Th. van Peursen; Leuven: Peeters) 501–521.

Gordon, R.P. 2006. *Hebrew Bible and Ancient Versions: Selected Essays of R.P. Gordon* (Aldershot: Ashgate).

Goulder, M.D. 1986. *The Song of Fourteen Songs* (Sheffield: JSOT Press).
Hill, R.C. (trans.) 2008. *St Cyril of Alexandria. Commentary on the Twelve Prophets, Volume 2* (The Fathers of the Church; Washington DC: Catholic University of America Press).
Hillers, D.R. 1984. *Micah* (Hermeneia; Philadelphia: Fortress Press).
McKane, W. 1998. *The Book of Micah: Introduction and Commentary* (Edinburgh: T & T Clark).
Van der Meer, M. 'The Question of the Literary Dependence of the Greek Psalter Revisited,' in *Die Septuaginta—Texte, Theologien, Einflüsse* (eds. W. Krauss and M. Karrer; Tübingen: Mohr Siebeck) 162–200.
Oldfather, C.H. 1967. *Diodorus of Sicily* (LCL; London/Cambridge MA: Heinemann/Harvard University Press).
Seeligmann, I.L. 1948. *The Septuagint Version of Isaiah: A Discussion of its Problems* (Leiden: Brill).
Smith, R.L. 1984. *Micah-Malachi* (Word Biblical Commentary; Waco TX: Word Books).
Theocharous, M. 2011. 'Lexical Dependence and Intertextual Allusion in the Septuagint of the Twelve Prophets: Studies in Hosea, Amos and Micah' (University of Cambridge Dissertation).
Walser, G. 2010. *Jeremiah. A Translation and Commentary on Jeremiah in Codex Vaticanus* (Gothenburg: University of Gothenburg).
Ziegler, J. 1957. *Jeremias, Baruch, Threni, Epistula Jeremiae* (Septuaginta. Vetus Testamentum Graecum XV; Göttingen: Vandenhoeck and Ruprecht).

WHAT REMAINS OF THE HEBREW BIBLE? THE ACCURACY OF THE TEXT OF THE HEBREW BIBLE IN THE LIGHT OF THE QUMRAN SAMUEL (4QSAM[A])

David J.A. Clines

The question that begins the title of this paper is one familiar to the recipient of this volume, for he has endured several oral disquisitions upon its theme over lunches he has very kindly entertained me to in his college. If nothing else, this paper adds to the documentary evidence he will need if he is to refute the ideas.

When I gave the Mowinckel lecture in Oslo in 2001, under the title 'What Remains of the Old Testament? Its Text and Language in a Postmodern Age' (Clines 2002), I undertook, among other things, to examine the accuracy of the text of the Hebrew Bible that we now have in the form of the Masoretic text. I was not interested in establishing the superiority of certain textual readings over against other readings, as text critics have been wont to do, or in explaining how such and such readings may have come into existence. I set myself the more limited task of attempting to quantify the number of places in the text of the Hebrew Bible where variant readings exist and therefore have to be evaluated.

I should say that this task was not in the interests of pure research, but had a rather pressing practical implication. For I was writing my commentary on the Book of Job and every day was faced with questions of proposed emendations to the Masoretic text. I realized that if I did not accept (or propose) any emendations to the text, I was silently propounding the view that the Book of Job has been handed down across the centuries in an immaculate form, exactly as its original author had intended it—as well as tying myself in knots trying to create some sort of sense out of apparently meaningless sentences. On the other hand, if I accepted any emendations, where would I stop? There were thousands of proposals. Was there any way of knowing roughly how many places in the Book of Job are likely to have been corrupted, and thus what would be a reasonable quantity of emendations to accept into my commentary? Would 6 be too few, or 200 too many?

I thought of a rather simple exercise I could do, one, moreover, that no one had ever done before, as far as I knew. I could compare passages that occurred twice in the text of the Hebrew Bible (that is, texts in double transmission) and count how many variants the Masoretic text displayed. My showcase example was the rather lengthy psalm found in both 2 Samuel 22 and Psalm 18. If I knew how many variants there existed in one text compared with the other, I could get a sense of whether I was being absurdly conservative or else laughingly liberal in my text-critical decisions for the Book of Job.

2 Samuel 22 Compared with Psalm 18 in the Masoretic Text

There follows a sample of the evidence I was able to present. In the translations, I have shown the differences between the texts with these marks:

Single underline = a plus/minus (words in one text and not in the other)
Double underline = a variant (difference in wording)
Bold underline = difference in word order

(1) Some examples of significant pluses and minuses:

2 Sam. 22.2	And he said, Yhwh is my rock and my fortress…
	וַיֹּאמַר יְהוָה סַלְעִי וּמְצֻדָתִי
Ps. 18.2–3	And he said, I love you, O Yhwh, my strength. Yhwh is my rock and my fortress…
	וַיֹּאמַר אֶרְחָמְךָ יְהוָה חִזְקִי׃ יְהוָה ׀ סַלְעִי וּמְצוּדָתִי

2 Sam. 22.3	I take refuge in him, my shield and the horn of my salvation, my height, and my refuge, my saviour; you save me from violence.
	אֶחֱסֶה־בּוֹ מָגִנִּי וְקֶרֶן יִשְׁעִי מִשְׂגַּבִּי וּמְנוּסִי מֹשִׁעִי מֵחָמָס תֹּשִׁעֵנִי
Ps. 18.3	I take refuge in him, my shield and the horn of my salvation, my height.
	אֶחֱסֶה־בּוֹ מָגִנִּי וְקֶרֶן־יִשְׁעִי מִשְׂגַּבִּי

(2) An example of word order variant:

2 Sam. 22.45	Foreigners came cringing to me; as soon as they heard, they obeyed me.
	בְּנֵי נֵכָר יִתְכַּחֲשׁוּ־לִי לִשְׁמוֹעַ אֹזֶן יִשָּׁמְעוּ לִי

Ps. 18.45	<u>As soon as they heard, they obeyed me</u>; <u>foreigners came cringing to me</u>.
	לְשֵׁמַע אֹזֶן יִשָּׁמְעוּ לִי בְּנֵי־נֵכָר יְכַחֲשׁוּ־לִי

(3) Some examples of significant variants:

2 Sam. 22.11	...and he <u>was seen</u> on the wings of the wind.
	וַיֵּרָא עַל־כַּנְפֵי־רוּחַ
Ps 18.11	...and he <u>flew</u> on the wings of the wind.
	וַיֵּדֶא עַל־כַּנְפֵי־רוּחַ

2 Sam. 22.44	You <u>kept</u> me as head of the nations...
	תִּשְׁמְרֵנִי לְרֹאשׁ גּוֹיִם
Ps 18.44	You <u>made</u> me head of the nations...
	תְּשִׂימֵנִי לְרֹאשׁ גּוֹיִם

These are all interesting and substantial. But my main concern was with the question of *how many* such variants there were. Leaving out of account orthographic and grammatical differences, I was able to construct the following table:

Total Number of Variants between 2 Samuel 22 and Psalm 18 in the Masoretic Text

Pluses	including 13 cases of the word 'and'	49
Word Order		3
Other Variants	including 9 cases of synonyms	52
Total		104

If that seems a large number of variants, consider the significance of the number when set against the number of words in the text. By my count, there are 382 words in 2 Samuel 22, and 397 words in Psalm 18. If 2 Samuel 22 contains 104 words that are at variance with Psalm 18, then slightly more than one in four words is a variant (one in 3.67, to be exact); in each case one text or the other is corrupt. The result is not significantly different if we compare the 104 variant words with the word count of 397 words in Psalm 18 (one in 3.82).

As a preliminary conclusion, I suggested that if the text of 2 Samuel 22 and Psalm 18 is at all typical of the Masoretic text of the Hebrew Bible, *one word in four may be textually corrupt*. Since we cannot know which word in each set of four words is likely to be the corrupt one, we might well find ourselves in a situation of radical doubt about the text of the Hebrew Bible.

2 Samuel 22 (MT) Compared with 4QSam[a]

In an attempt to quantify the number of variants that exist in the text of the Hebrew Bible we are of course not restricted to comparing passages within the Masoretic text. We also can consider the evidence of the ancient versions, making due allowance for readings in the versions that do not reflect a different *Vorlage*. And we should also consider the evidence of the Qumran texts.

Now when I studied this question in 2001 the DJD edition of the Qumran Samuel we were expecting from F.M. Cross was still awaited (Cross 2005), and I promised myself that when it was published I would revisit the whole matter and count how many variants from the Masoretic text 4QSam[a] would prove to have contained. Kyle McCarter had indeed mentioned a number of variants in the Textual Notes to his Anchor Bible commentary on 2 Samuel. He had remarked in the Introduction to his volume on 1 Samuel that 'the MS [4QSam[a]] is unpublished' (McCarter 1980: 6), and no one was to know how fragmentary 4QSam[a] is for 2 Samuel 22 (the text is in Cross 2005: 180–81), nor that McCarter had noted in his commentary, 25 years before the appearance of Cross's edition, all its variances from the MT (except two cases of a variant *waw*, nos. 6 and 7 below).[1] But my project was not completely needless. In my paper, I had noted that 4QSam[a] contains 9 readings not attested in Psalm 18 or ancient versions of 2 Samuel; but now I am able to present all the 18 variants of 4QSam[a] (constituting 24 words of variance) as against the MT. In the first column I have numbered the items of variance, and in the last column I have noted the number of words that are at variance.

[1] In one case McCarter offered a reading of 4QSam[a] different from Cross's: in item 17 (v. 49) he read [ת]נצרני as against Cross's]תנצרני (McCarter 1984: 463]. Ulrich (1978) had also noted a number of the readings of 4QSam[a], but there was no way of knowing from his work how representative his citations were or indeed what the extent of the Qumran text of this chapter was.

Item	Verse	MT	4QSam[a]	Words
1	33	הָאֵל מָעוּזִּי God is my refuge	[...ה]אל מאזרני God who girded me	1
2	36	וַעֲנֹתְךָ and your answering (?), your conquest (?)	ועזרתך and your help	1
3	37	תַּחְתֵּנִי under me	>	1
4		וְלֹא מָעֲדוּ קַרְסֻלָּי and my feet did not slip	ול[א עמדו קמי...] and my enemies did not stand [ולא מ[עדו קרסלי] [supralinear] and my feet did not slip	2
5	39	וָאֲכַלֵּם and I consumed them	>	1
6		וָאֶמְחָצֵם and I thrust them through	אמח[צם...] I thrust them through	1
7	40	תַּכְרִיעַ you made them sink	ותקרע and you made them sink	1
8	41	וָאַצְמִיתֵם and I destroyed them	אצמית[ם] I destroyed them	1
9	43	כַּעֲפַר־אָרֶץ like the dust of the earth	[כעפר על] פני ארח upon the face of the path (cf. Ps. 18.43 עַל־פְּנֵי־רוּחַ before the wind)	2
10		אֲדִקֵּם I crushed them	>	1
11	44	וַתְּפַלְּטֵנִי מֵרִיבֵי עַמִּי תִּשְׁמְרֵנִי and you delivered me from conflicts with my people, you kept me	ותפלט[ני מריבי עמים תשימני...] and you delivered me from conflicts with the peoples, you sct me	
12	45	בְּנֵי נֵכָר יִתְכַּחֲשׁוּ־לִי Foreigners came cringing to me	>	4
13	46	יִבֹּלוּ They lost heart	[...יכחשו לי] they cringed before me	
14		וְיַחְגְּרוּ מִמִּסְגְּרוֹתָם and they girded themselves from their fortresses (?), and they were fettered with their neck collars (?)	לא יחגרו ממסרותם they did not gird themselves with their bonds [?]	3

Table (*cont.*)

Item	Verse	MT	4QSam[a]	Words
15	48	הָאֵ֕ל הַנֹּתֵ֥ן נְקָמֹ֖ת לִ֑י God who gives me vengeance	[...האל] נתן נקמות לי God gives me vengeance	1
16		וּמוֹרִ֥יד עַמִּ֖ים תַּחְתֵּֽנִי and brings down (ירד) peoples beneath me	ומרדד עמים תחתנ[י and beating out (רדד), i.e. subduing, peoples beneath me	1
17	49	תַּצִּילֵ֑נִי you delivered me	תצרני you kept me	1
18	50	יְהוָ֖ה בַּגּוֹיִ֑ם Yahweh among the nations	[...בגויים יהוה...] among the nations Yahweh	
				24

The table shows some 18 items, some with more than one variant word, and so a total of 24 words. In 7 cases (nos. 1, 2, 9, 14, 15, 16, 17) there is a substantive variant. In 4 (nos. 3, 5, 10, 12) the Qumran text has a significant minus compared with the MT, and in 1 a significant plus (no. 14). In 1 (no. 7) the Qumran text has a *waw* where the MT does not, and in 2 (nos. 6, 8) the MT has a *waw* where the Qumran text does not.

There are four other more complicated items. (1) In item 4 (v. 37b), 4QSam[a] offers two readings: after the word צעדי there is, on the line,]ול, and above the line]ולא מא. The former reading is reasonably expanded by Cross to [...ול]א עמדו קמי 'and my enemies did not stand', which is what is presupposed by LXX[L] (καὶ οὐχ ὑπέστησάνμε οἱ ὑπεναντίοι). Above the line, there is, in the same hand, a correction to]ולא מא, which Cross completes as [ולא מ]עדו קרסלי 'my feet did not slip'—which is what we have in the MT. For my purposes, I count these both as the readings of 4QSam[a], and mark the former as a variant of two words from the MT. (2) Item 11 (v. 44) shows in the text as reconstructed by Cross [...ותפלט]ני מריבי עמים תשימני 'and you delivered me from conflicts of the peoples, you set me', as against the MT וַֽתְּפַלְּטֵ֔נִי מֵרִיבֵ֖י עַמִּ֑י תִּשְׁמְרֵ֙נִי֙ 'and you delivered me from conflicts with my people, you kept me', which contains 2 variants. There are no textual grounds for reading עמים 'peoples' as against MT עַמִּ֑י 'my people' (Cross merely thinks it makes a better parallel to גּוֹיִ֔ם later in the verse), and תשימני is presumably adopted on the basis of the reading of LXX[L] ἔθουμε 'you set me'. I have not counted these variants, since they appear only in the reconstructed text. (3) Item 14 (v. 46a) is very complicated, involving a possible dittograph in the MT. Cross suggests that 4QSam[a] had room for the subject בני נכר only once, and that MT יִבֻּ֑לוּ may represent an earlier בל, synonymous with 4QSam[a]'s לא. For my part, because there is no direct equivalent of MT יִבֻּ֑לוּ in 4QSam[a], the words [...יכחשו לי] appearing only in square brackets in the published text, I will not count these words as an attested variant—though it seems improbable that 4QSam[a] ever read the same as MT here. (4) In item 18 (v. 50) MT has יְהוָ֖ה בַּגּוֹיִ֑ם 'Yahweh among the nations', but in Cross's filling of the gap he has supplied [...בגויים יהוה...] 'among the nations Yahweh', presumably because this is the order of the two words in LXX[L]. But we do not know for sure that this is what 4QSam[a] read here, so I have not counted this item among the variants between 4QSam[a] and MT.

To summarize: by my count, there are some 66 words extant in the 4QSam[a] text of 2 Samuel (I have not counted words of which only part remains, unless it is pretty certain that the word must have stood in the manuscript). There are in the table above 24 words that are variants; in only 3 cases is the variant trivial (the presence or absence of a *waw*). 24 variants in a text of 66 words is on average one variant every 2.75 words.

In my previous paper, as I noted above, I found in a comparison of 2 Samuel 22 with Psalm 18 in the Masoretic text one variant for every 3.67 or 3.82 words. The comparison of the MT and the Qumran text of 2 Samuel 22 that I have undertaken here shows an even higher incidence of variants, at one every 2.75 words.

This ratio is close to the one of 1:2.16 I eventually established after I had added all the variants to 2 Samuel 22 and Psalm 18 that I could discover both in the Masoretic text and the ancient versions. I hasten to add now that I will not presume to suggest that the state of the text of 2 Samuel 22 is typical of the Hebrew Bible in general, and in my previous paper I considered a number of factors that could make an increase or a decrease in the ratio plausible. I will not repeat those arguments here, and in any case the actual number of variants in the Hebrew Bible as a whole must remain hypothetical.

My main point, however, is that if the Masoretic text of 2 Samuel 22, either in comparison with the parallel Masoretic text of Psalm 18 or in comparison with the Qumran text of 2 Samuel 22, provides any kind of guide to the presumable quantity of variants in the Hebrew Bible, then the text of the Hebrew Bible is indeed in a state of radical uncertainty. An overriding consideration is that when we are reading a text of the Hebrew Bible for which we possess no variants we cannot assume that there have never been any variants, but simply that we do not now have any. The presumption must be that there have been variants.

To put the matter another way: we know that for every 2.16 words, or every 2.75 words or every 3.67 words, at least and on average, there will have been a variant in the textual evidence that once existed. A specially interesting aspect of this realization is that when the evidence is missing *we do not know which word it is that is the variant*. For most practical purposes, it is as if every single word in the Hebrew Bible was a known variant, and as if we possessed an entirely uncertain text.

Another way of representing the state of affairs is to extrapolate the situation in 2 Samuel 22 to the whole of the Hebrew Bible. If the rest of the Hebrew Bible contained as many variants of the MT compared with the Qumran texts as we have observed for 2 Samuel 22, 24 words out of 66 words, then there would be for the whole of the Hebrew Bible some 111,090 variants (the Hebrew Bible is 305,500 words or thereabouts, according to Andersen and Forbes 1989: 3). Needless to say, the text of Samuel is in much poorer shape than much of the Hebrew Bible, and we should not base a general view of the text of the Hebrew Bible on the evidence of Samuel. Suppose we take the case of Isaiah and compare the number of variant readings (orthographical and grammatical apart) that Eissfeldt could present in the seventh edition of *Biblia Hebraica* (the 1951 edition of what is usually called the third edition of *Biblia Hebraica*, BH^3), viz. 1698 readings in a text of some 16,935 words; extrapolating that ratio, of one variant every 9.97 words, to the whole of the Hebrew Bible we would still reach the figure of 30,630 variants. I have been referring to the number of variants that could be presumed for just one text (or, set of texts) alternative to the Masoretic text. If we included the Hebrew Bible readings we could safely retrovert from the LXX, the number would be much higher.

My larger point here is that, regardless of the actual number of variants that may be supposed or calculated, the indications are that there is an issue here that must not be ignored by Hebrew Bible scholars generally. It is not a small technical matter that can be left to text critics (my sense is that text critics have themselves not come to recognize the size of the problem); it affects the working life of every exegete of the Hebrew Bible.

It might be responded that it hardly matters how many inferior variants exist if we have in our hands, in the shape of the Masoretic text, a pretty sound version of the Hebrew Bible. But we should be cautious in presuming that the MT is in general a better text than the variants. Although the 4QSam[a] manuscript 2 Samuel 22 is admittedly too narrow a base to build a general theory on, it is worthy of note that of the 66 words of this text McCarter judges 4 to be superior to the MT reading (items 1, 10, 16, 17) and 2 others to point the way to a reading superior to the MT's (items 9, 12). This proportion of superior readings, if applied to the whole Hebrew Bible, would imply as many as 27,700 places where the MT text may be judged inferior to a non-Masoretic variant.

I do not mean to say that this state of radical textual uncertainty implies that we no longer have a Hebrew Bible, or that we do not any longer know what the contents and the sequence of materials within the biblical books generally were. Viewed from a perspective of some distance from text-critical enquiries, the text of the Hebrew Bible is reasonably sound; there are, speaking generally, no major lacunae, large-scale disarrangements or wildly variant textual witnesses. For many purposes, therefore, we can say that what remains of the Hebrew Bible is good or good enough; but if our purpose is to say exactly what the content of the Hebrew Bible was, line by line and word by word, then we must admit that in tens of thousands of cases it was likely to have been other than what we hold in our hands as the Masoretic text. We have been blinded to some extent by the remarkable transmissional accuracy of the Masoretic tradition, which cannot be denied. Yet there was for most of the books of the Hebrew Bible a long period available for the creation of textual pluriformity between the composition of the books of the Hebrew Bible and the beginnings of Masoretic solicitude,[2] and it is entirely reasonable that the usual fallible processes of scribal transmission have left their marks on what is now perceived as the received text.

[2] S. Talmon remarks: 'The evidence is that at the very time the Masoretic text was first in the making, the Qumran community was content with a highly pluriform text'. As Talmon says, 'Nothing in their writings reveals a recognition of the phenomenon of textual variation or an apprehension over the great number of variants in their biblical scrolls. Equally, there is no indication whatsoever that they considered variance in the biblical text an issue which divided their community from contemporary mainstream Judaism...Critically, the Community never conceived of the very notion of a unified and stabilized text of the biblical books' (Talmon 2000: 153).

References

Andersen, F.I., and A.D. Forbes. 1989. *The Vocabulary of the Old Testament* (Rome: Pontifical Biblical Institute).

Clines, D.J.A. 2002. 'What Remains of the Hebrew Bible? Its Text and Language in a Postmodern Age', *Studia Theologica* 56: 76–95.

Cross, F.M., D.W. Parry, R.J. Staley, and E. Ulrich. 2005. *Qumran Cave 4.* XII. *1–2 Samuel* (Discoveries in the Judaean Desert, 17; Oxford: Clarendon Press).

McCarter, P.K. 1980. *I Samuel: A New Translation with Introduction, Notes and Commentary* (Anchor Bible, 8; Garden City, NY: Doubleday).

——. 1984. *II Samuel: A New Translation with Introduction, Notes and Commentary* (Anchor Bible, 9; Garden City, NY: Doubleday).

Talmon, S. 2000. 'Textual Criticism: The Ancient Versions', in *Text and Context: Essays by Members of the Society for Old Testament Study* (ed. A.D.H. Mayes; Oxford: Oxford University Press): 141–170.

Ulrich, E.C., Jr. 1978. *The Qumran Text of Samuel and Josephus* (Harvard Semitic Monographs, 19; Missoula, MT: Scholars Press).

THE SOCIAL MATRIX THAT SHAPED THE HEBREW BIBLE AND GAVE US THE DEAD SEA SCROLLS[1]

Charlotte Hempel

Let me begin by outlining a paradox in Dead Sea Scrolls research. On the one hand, scholars have long recognized and emphasized that the 'Bible' did not exist at the period attested by the Scrolls. The term, we are frequently told, is anachronistic at this point in Jewish history (Campbell 2005; Ulrich 1999). Scholars sensitive to this recognition use different terms, such as scriptures (with lower or upper case s), authoritative texts, and even pre-Bible (Brooke 2002). Yet, on the other hand, at several levels of scholarly perception of and methodological approach to the ancient Jewish sources at our disposal, this widely recognized anachronism wields considerable power in all sorts of subtle ways. In short, we are all very capable of reflecting with great subtlety when considering a particular conundrum, or question of definition, only to succumb to a rather unreconstructed approach to a related issue, almost as if caught off-guard after a period of intense scrutiny. One clear example of this is the mainly unselfconsciously anachronistic distinction between the study of biblical and non-biblical texts from Qumran. I am less concerned here with the issue of fringe compositions that are considered scriptural by some and para-scriptural by others, e.g. 4Q(Reworked)Pentateuch (White Crawford 2008: 39–59). Rather, I am keen to stress the lack of dialogue and conceptual overlap in our approaches to Qumran texts that would later become Bible and non-biblical material. For the most part, different scholars plough these apparently different fields. Even if the same scholar ploughs both

[1] Earlier versions of this paper were presented to the Old Testament Seminar at the University of Oxford and the 20th Congress of IOSOT in Helsinki. I am grateful to Profs. John Barton and Raija Sollamo for their invitations, and to the distinguished members of both audiences for their contributions in the ensuing discussion. I would like to single out Prof. Emanuel Tov (Jerusalem), a visitor to Oxford at the time, and Prof. Reinhard Kratz (Göttingen) for their constructive responses to earlier versions of this material. Any remaining shortcomings are to be laid at my feet. It is a pleasure to contribute to the *Festschrift* of Prof. Robert Gordon who exudes learning, wit, and generosity in equal measure.

fields, he or she will often do a quick change-over of mental tools. There are commendable exceptions, such as two excellent treatments of these issues by Brooke and Kratz, the former taking a theoretical approach whereas the latter exemplifies the fluidity of interpretation both within and outside the Hebrew Bible in the Abraham tradition (Brooke 2009; Kratz 2009; see also Kratz 2004: 123–156 and VanderKam 2002: 95–96). To give a more specific example, we have long understood that the so-called biblical texts from Qumran attest a perhaps surprising degree of pluriformity. Yet, when faced with the pluriform textual tradition of the Community Rule since the early 1990s, we are troubled by these multiple textual manifestations of the Rule as if faced for the first time with such a pluriform picture (Metso 2007). I recently argued that the pluriformity of the texts of the emerging scriptures and the pluriformity of the Rule texts are two sides of the same coin and point towards the likelihood that textual fluidity was a hallmark of ancient Jewish texts preserved mid-way through their crystallization (Hempel 2010a). Readers may disagree with my conclusion on this particular issue, but I am convinced that it is high time to look at the evidence across the board without letting anachronistic labels set the agenda—even if only implicitly.

I developed a different aspect of this line of reflection at a conference held at the University of Toronto in 2010. The overall topic of that meeting was the impact of the Dead Sea Scrolls on our understanding of the transmission of traditions and the production of texts. The following will serve as a further illustration of how my thoughts as developed in the remainder of this chapter fit into a broader perspective:

> In light of the evident literary creativity witnessed by the Damascus Document and the Community Rule it would be worthwhile to encourage more dialogue with the current debates on how to understand the phenomena often referred to with the term 'rewritten scripture.' Different ancient Jewish texts are fluid and influencing each other, and as scholars we are caught in the difficult position of trying to trace how the influence operated. It seems certain that comparable processes and activities can be witnessed in the realm of D [the Damascus Document], S [the Community Rule...] and the literature dubbed 'rewritten scripture.' This should not be unexpected since the constituency of people performing such complex learned processes are almost certainly genetically related to one another. If we think of the community or at least its scribal component as learned and engaged in sophisticated dealings with texts and traditions, it is unlikely that they would have made a

> conscious distinction in their approach to re-writing scripture and re-writing Serekh/D-type-traditions when going about their business. (Hempel 2010b: 131)

In other words, the fluidity and creativity we witness in so-called biblical and para-biblical texts from the late Second Temple Period is mirrored by the fluidity and creativity evident in the creation and transmission of non-biblical texts. Moreover, this shared creative approach to texts is most fully appreciated if we disregard the anachronistic distinction between biblical and non-biblical texts in this period.

Now that all the texts from Qumran are available, it is essential that we allow ourselves the intellectual space to stand back and resist the temptation of simply fitting new pieces of evidence into an existing framework. This is particularly necessary since much of the framework we are working with goes back to the initial phase of the discoveries when pioneering scholars needed to make sense of a huge amount of new data: the most natural sifting mechanism was to reach for labels such as biblical/non-biblical and sectarian/non-sectarian. Following the publication of the contents of Cave 4, many more texts emerged that seem to defy straightforward categorisation in one way or another. This in turn poses something of a challenge to the nature of the dominant categories themselves.

A particularly fruitful area of investigation is the light the Scrolls can shed on the processes of ancient Jewish literary activity (Brooke 2005; Carr 2005; Jaffe 2001; van der Toorn 2007; Tov 2004; Vermes 1994: 23). Qumran provides us with more than nine hundred ancient manuscripts from a time when both the text of the Hebrew Bible and the canon were still fluid. Similarly, critical biblical scholarship has worked for centuries in the knowledge that the Hebrew Bible evolved in complex and creative ways. Here again, the evidence of the Scrolls is invaluable in shedding light on the kinds of processes we have long suspected of having left their mark on the final form of the Hebrew Bible (Brooke 2005; Tov 2006).

Moving from texts to social realities behind them, Morton Smith argued already in 1960 that the covenant in Nehemiah 10 involves the first Jewish sect attested. He further emphasized the way in which this sect was defined by 'particular legal interpretations, and consequently to peculiar practices' (Smith 1960: 356). Morton Smith's suggestion that biblical interpretation lies at the heart of early Jewish sectarianism was further developed by Joseph Blenkinsopp in a number of publications (Blenkinsopp 1981; 2009). Similarly Shemaryahu Talmon maintained for that Jewish sectarianism goes back to the fifth and sixth centuries (Talmon 1986; see also Davies 2008; Hultgren 2007).

Turning to the Dead Sea Scrolls, we observe a growing retrospective relevance of much this material. Thus, recent scholarship has demonstrated the importance of this cache of manuscripts for our understanding of Second Temple Judaism much beyond the confines of a small, dissident sect. Alison Schofield has recently referred to earlier models of the Qumran community as 'isolationist' (Schofield 2009: 48). With the full publication of the corpus the sectarian component of the collection emerges as no more than around one third of the collection (Dimant 1995). Even with respect to clearly sectarian texts, a number of scholars now advocate a wider view. On the basis of close study of the rich evidence of the Community Rule both Schofield and Collins now prefer to speak of a YaHad that goes beyond Qumran (Collins 2009; Schofield 2009). The title of Collins's recent monograph encapsulates his view: *Beyond the Qumran Community: The Sectarian Movement of the Dead Sea Scrolls* (Collins 2009), and J. Jokiranta likewise speaks of the 'Qumran movement' in her doctoral dissertation (Jokiranta 2005: 54).

A fascinating next step in tracing the significance of the Qumran Scrolls is the much discussed issue of the social background of the material from a broader perspective. The Scrolls testify to a learned group of Jews engaged in composing, shaping and collecting a very large amount of literature. We know that there were similarly learned Jews engaged in shaping, collecting, and editing another very large amount of literature: the emerging Hebrew scriptures. Since both social spheres share a considerable amount of overlapping material, interests and skills, the connections between both become even more tangible. Thus, Talmon notes with reference to the Scrolls, 'they were written when biblical literary activity was still ongoing' (Talmon 1989: 24), and refers to their 'partial chronological overlap with the end phase of the biblical era' (Talmon 1989: 25). Since literacy, and especially learning at the level required to deal with the material at issue here, was the preserve of a small elite in the Second Temple Period (as elsewhere in the ancient world), it is likely that the same limited stratum of highly educated scribes is the pool responsible for collecting and shaping the emerging Hebrew scriptures *and* the corpus of the Scrolls. The job description of both groups is captured exceedingly well by Kratz's account of the chief duties of the scribe as consisting of 'die Pflege von Wissen und Literatur' (Kratz 2004: 112). The individuals responsible for composing, collecting, redacting, and archiving the material found in the Qumran Caves are every bit as masterful[2] as the circles that gave us the Hebrew Bible. By removing the wedge that accidents of preservation and discovery have placed between both entities the shared literary, cultural, and perhaps also social worlds of both groups can illuminate one another.[3]

I am thinking here less in terms of authorship (a concept somewhat anachronistic for the ancient world) where the chronological gap between the Scrolls and a great deal of the emerging Hebrew Scriptures can be formidable, but rather in terms of the processes of collecting, transmitting, and shaping existing material. In this realm the Scrolls bring us as close as we can get to a priestly Second Temple group. It seems to me extremely unlikely that a dissident group was able to train and establish the highly developed and sophisticated scribal culture we witness in the Dead Sea Scrolls from scratch. It is inevitable that the milieu behind the Scrolls came out of the wider scribal culture, probably associated with the Temple, and a great deal of the cultural background, even if rejected, will have left its mark on the collection. There was a dis-connect not a dis-tinction between both worlds.

In stressing the huge potential of paying close attention to what the Scrolls share with their wider Second Temple Jewish background, it would be foolish to deny the distinctive elements within them. The unique and distinctive component of the Qumran collection is often referred to as the sectarian element. Scholars have grappled with defining sectarian pointers and identifying the sectarian component of the collection ever since it was unearthed—and even before if we consider the struggle to place the Damascus Document found some half century prior to the Scrolls in the Cairo Genizah (Newsom 1990; Hempel 2003; and recently Steudel 2009). Many scholars now shy away from speaking of a neat divide between sectarian and non-sectarian material and acknowledge instead a more gradated scenario. Most recently Brooke proposed a spectrum ranging from 'incipient' to 'full-blown' and 'rejuvenated' sectarianism (Brooke 2011), whereas Florentino García Martínez proposes abandoning the distinctions sectarian/

---

[2] The term 'mastery' is developed by Carr (2005: 190).

[3] On the accidental element in our ancient sources see recently Tov (2010).

non-sectarian and biblical/non-biblical altogether (2008; 2010: 446). In other words, recent scholarship on the Scrolls conceives of the presence of sectarian and distinctive elements in terms of a spectrum rather than a neat divide. An obvious further question that has not received the attention it deserves is: what happens if we go to or approach the end of the spectrum? In other words, how close does the most 'incipient' end of the Qumran material take us to the much debated context of developing sectarianism in the Hebrew scriptures? Whereas emerging sectarianism in the Hebrew Bible has been the subject of scholarly interest for some time (Davies 2008; Hultgren 2007; Smith 1960; Talmon 1986), fresh and exciting new areas for reflection open up if we attempt to connect the dots between this latter and well established line of enquiry and some of the most recent developments in Qumran studies.

As far as the incipient end of the Qumran social spectrum is concerned, my own work has recently looked for fossils of more embryonic[4] states of affairs in otherwise highly developed sectarian texts (Hempel 2007; 2011). In this contribution I would like to explore the potentially extremely exciting *rendezvous* of embryonic sectarianism in the Scrolls and emerging sectarianism in the Hebrew Scriptures.

As far as the Hebrew Bible is concerned, we may draw attention to the great impetus gained by the Qumran discoveries for our understanding of the growth and shape of the Psalter. The debate is well known between those scholars who would argue that 11QPs[a] is a secondary liturgical collection (Goshen-Gottstein 1966; Skehan 1973; Talmon 1966) rather than a Psalms Scroll proper, albeit in a form different from what we would have expected (Sanders 1965; Flint 1997). At present the latter camp seems to be winning the argument and to be much more in tune with the wider recognition of variety and pluriformity attested by the Scrolls.

Recent Psalms scholarship has devoted a great deal of attention to the study of the shape and shaping of the Psalter as a whole. The shape of the Psalter as we have it was still in flux in the Second Temple Period, and there are many indications of gradual growth and compilation in the book itself, perhaps the most clear-cut examples being Ps. 72.20 ('The prayers of David son of Jesse are ended'), the identification of

[4] I owe the helpful terminology 'embryonic' to my colleague Prof. David Chalcraft of the University of Sheffield.

Ps. 151 in the LXX as 'outside the number,' and the presence of a number of duplicate psalms in the collection (Ps. 14=53 / Ps. 40.13–17 = Ps. 70 / Ps. 108 = Ps. 57.7–11+60.5–12. Cf. also Ps. 18 = 2 Sam 22). Whereas Arthur Weiser's preface to the third edition of his commentary could refer to the Psalms as 'pictures without a frame' (Weiser 1962: 9), recent research has very much emphasized the frame, the whole as much as the parts. Just as the variety of themes present in individual Psalms has long been noted—leading Martin Luther to describe the Psalter as 'eine kleine biblia' (Kratz 1996)—so the shape of the whole cannot be determined with surgical precision. The parts and the whole eloquently promote a variety of agendas and themes. Modern scholars have proposed a variety of perceptive readings of the final shape of the Psalter and have identified a dominant framework, variously stressing the Davidic element, the instructional element, the eschatology, or the Zion theology. It seems to me, coming to this as an outsider, that it is precisely the richness of the material, the parts and the whole, and its clearly complex and successive evolution which gives rise to staunchly defended and well argued proposals of such variety. Several different points of view, it seems to me, capture some aspects of the bigger truth. It has often been emphasized that ancient Jewish literary activity promoted its literary heritage by means of creative transmission and supplementation. This seems to be evident in the Psalter as well. Thus, if modern scholars are able to uncover a plurality of emphases, this is because our ancient predecessors left us with such a plurality. Sensitive contemporary readers are able to uncover different parts of the ancient creative mosaic of tradition. A fundamental difference in approach is our compulsion to try and find 'the one' central framework or theological direction, whereas to the ancients several valid frames and directions could be explored side by side. Here, I am sympathetic to Stuart Weeks's conclusion to his study of the category of Wisdom Psalms in the course of which he reminds us that 'all our distinctions and classification are just a poor approximation to a vibrant and complicated literary culture.' (Weeks 2007: 305).

In the remainder of this chapter I would like to offer some tentative reflections on a passage found in Ps. 1.2, Josh. 1.8, and the Community Rule from Qumran. A prominent voice in the search for the shape of the Psalter was the monograph by Gerald Wilson in which he highlights the promise of scrutinizing 'the "seams" between the collections where editorial activity should be most evident' (Wilson

1985: 5). Whatever one's position on the relationship of Psalms 1 and 2 to one another, there is no doubt that Ps. 1 is a major seam in the Psalter. Within the first Psalm verse 2 stands out for several reasons. Although the Psalm draws a contrast between the righteous and the wicked, much more attention is devoted to the wicked. When speaking of the righteous, most of the space is devoted to describing their enviable fate at the time of judgment in verse 6, and the image of the reliably fecund tree is applied to them in verse 3. As part of this contrast, verse 2 stands out in terms of its concrete language in describing the ideal life of a righteous person: his delight is the law of the Lord which he recites (יֶהְגֶּה) day and night.

Another characteristic of Ps. 1.2 is its close relationship to a similar sentiment and formulation in Josh. 1.8. The context of Josh. 1.8 is a divine address to Joshua in the wake of Moses' death (vv. 1–9). Commentators customarily attribute Joshua 1 to the work of the Deuteronomists (Noth 1952: 9, 27; Butler 1983: xxi, 6; Miller and Tucker 1974: 7, 21; Soggin 1972: 27). Moreover, several scholars have noted the resumptive nature of v. 8 which repetitively picks up a number of points raised in the previous verse (e.g., Miller and Tucker 1974: 24). There is little doubt, then, that in Josh. 1.8 we are again dealing with a 'seam' in the Hebrew Bible—to use Gerald Wilson's terminology. Another intriguing connection between Josh. 1.8 and Ps. 1.2 is what Alexander Rofé describes as the 'structural' correspondence' between both passages in the opening lines of a collection of material and intended to direct the reading of what ensues (Rofé 1993: 82).

The close resemblance between Josh. 1.8 and Ps. 1.2 is well known (Gray 1967: 50; Soggin, 1972: 32; Weinfeld 1972: 280), and Boling has described the relationship of both passages in terms of 'the same subject with some of the same vocabulary.' (Boling 1982: 125). Moreover, Rudolf Smend has observed, 'Zwischen unserer Stelle [Josh. 1.8, C.H.] und der Psalmstelle muss ein direkter Zusammenghang bestehen.' (Smend 2002: 149 n. 9). Joshua is often considered the earlier of the two. Smend further assigned Josh. 1.7–9 to a nomistic redaction (Dtr N) that left its mark on the Deuteronomistic history (Dtr H) (Smend 2002). The rather forced ('etwas gezwungen') introduction of Torah piety in an address offering encouragement in military matters was noted by Martin Noth (Noth 1952: 29).[5]

[5] I am grateful to Prof. Reinhard Kratz for drawing my attention to this.

On the basis of the correspondences between Ps. 1.2, Josh. 1.8 and Isa. 59.21 Alexander Rofé has developed a fuller argument than his predecessors (Rofé 1993). In particular, the secondary nature of Josh. 1.8 and its close affinities with Ps. 1.2 and Isa. 59.21 led Rofé to relate all three passages to 'a later Jewish ideal' to be associated with 'the final stages of the compilation of the Canon.' (Rofé 1993: 80–81). Rofé is able to draw out connections in terms of message and terminology between all three passages and speaks eloquently of their 'cognate origin' (Rofé 1993: 83). In what follows I will focus on Josh. 1.8 and Ps. 1.2 in particular because of their close relationship to a particular passage in the Scrolls which I would like to incorporate into the stimulating discussion set in motion by Rofé and others.

Returning for a moment to Smend's analysis of Josh. 1.7–9, he notes the layered or successive nature of the work of the Deuteronomistic redactor(s) at this point and helpfully draws on H.W. Hertzberg's concept of 'Nachgeschichte' (Hertzberg 1962: 70). In the remainder of this article, I will explore a more prolonged 'Nachgeschichte' of this biblical passage in the Scrolls. In two different documents from Qumran we have again, as we will see, 'the same subject with some of the same vocabulary,' to use the phrase coined by Boling (1982: 125).

The thought experiment I would like to conduct in this contribution is whether or not we are able to draw a meaningful comparison between the 'pious conventicles,' to use the old-fashioned phrase, reflected in Josh. 1.8 and Ps. 1.2, and the lowest end of the spectrum of sectarian cohesion in the Scrolls. The passage resembling the ideal set out in Josh. 1.8 and Ps. 1.2 is found in 1QS 6.6b–7a.[6]

ואל ימש במקום אשר יהיו שם העשרה איש דורש
בתורה יומם ולילה תמיד על יפות[7] איש לרעהו

> And in every place where there are ten there shall be present a person who studies the law continually day and night one replacing the other.[8]

Scholars have frequently pointed to the clear influence of Josh. 1.8 and Ps. 1.2 on the formulation in 1QS 6.6b–7a (so already Brownlee 1951: 24).

---

[6] None of the Cave 4 manuscripts of the Rule preserve these words. The immediate context has survived in 4QS[d] (4Q258) II:10b, but all that can be said on the basis of the size of the lacuna is that this manuscript preserved a considerably shorter text than 1QS (Alexander and Vermes 1998: 99–100, Pl. 12).

[7] Often emended to חליפות.

[8] The rendering 'one replacing the other' is based on an emendation of the Hebrew על יפות to read חליפות frequently adopted by commentators.

By referring to a person who studies the law permanently day and night the stress here seems to be on the constancy of study rather than the identity of the individual who conducts this activity; this is implied also by the notion of rotation. According to the logic of this passage, the individual is exchangeable and almost dispensable. The passage in 1QS 6.6b–7a forms part of a series of disparate statements that stand somewhat incongruously side by side the material that precedes and follows. This was noted already by Michael Knibb who writes of this part of the Rule of the Community that it is 'somewhat miscellaneous in character, and it is plausible to think that material of diverse origin and date has been brought together.' (Knibb 1987: 113). The opening lines of column 6 stand apart from the remainder of the Rule by referring to 'all their dwelling places' and by including two directives on how to conduct business in a place where ten come together. It is this distinctive material that has inspired John Collins's recent re-evaluation of the Qumran *yaḥad* as an 'umbrella organization' of a plurality of communities and as a movement rather than a single, localised community (Collins 2009). Sarianna Metso, on the other hand, has proposed instead that the quorum of ten individuals refers to travelling members of the one *yaḥad* who meet while away from the community centre (Metso 2006). Both views, even though rather different, read the material as indicative of a geographic diversity. I have devoted three articles to this part of the Rule where I take a different approach (Hempel 2003b; 2008; 2011). Rather than interpreting this material as indicative of a geographical spread, I have suggested that the diverse statements preserved in the opening lines 1QS 6 give us a flavour of embryonic beginnings of communal life. I have variously stressed:

(i) the *small scale set-up* of loosely organized groups of like-minded individuals.

(ii) the *grass roots flavour of study* as opposed to other passages that advocate much more restricted access to the correct interpretation of scripture from what is described here, cf., e.g. 1QS 5.8–9, where prospective members are enjoined to 'take upon themselves a binding oath to return to the law of Moses according to all that He has commanded with all (their) heart and all (their) soul according to all that has been revealed from it to the sons of Zadok the priests who keep the covenant [...] and to the multitude of the people of their covenant.' Here the sons of Zadok and the people of their covenant are presented as almost exclusive channels of correct interpretation.

(iii) the *pragmatic colour* of the description which contrasts with the much more ideologically and theologically fine-tuned account of small scale community origins in 1QS 8.1: 'The council of the community shall be made up of twelve (lay) people and three priests, perfect in everything that has been revealed from the whole law.' The 1QS 8 description is clearly theologically motivated representing the twelve tribes plus the sons of Levi according to Num 3.17 (Milik 1959: 100).

(iv) I suggested, moreover, that the reference to the three core activities of meeting to eat together, pray together and exchange council together constitute 'a very basic level of social interaction between like minded Jews' (Hempel 2008: 45). We note that *yaḥad* here occurs as an adverb and not yet as the technical self-designation it was to become—a development perhaps based on its initial adverbial usage in passages like the opening lines of 1QS 6.

In sum, the opening lines of column 6 comprise a mixture of heterogenous material, some of which gives the impression—to me at least—of going back to the earliest and simplest beginnings of communal life. 1QS 6.6b–7a, which closely resembles Josh. 1.8 and Ps. 1.2, portrays continuous study of the law as 'a shared grassroots commodity that characterised the community from its earliest days in small groups.' (Hempel 2003b: 79). Elsewhere in the Rule access to the correct interpretation of the law became restricted to particular interpreters or groups of leading priests. Whereas Steven Fraade would speak of '"elitist" and "egalitarian" Torah ethics' operating side by side in the Qumran community (Fraade 1993: 68), I proposed that both approaches go back to different periods in the development of the community.

If we try to approach both the two late passages from the Hebrew Bible and what, on my reading of the evidence, is a glimpse of an embryonic kernel of communal activity in 1QS 6 without immediately assuming that one is simply quoting the other, both sets of agendas are less distant from one another than one might expect. All three passages stress the need to apply oneself to the Torah continually. It is at least worth considering that the Scrolls passage is not merely alluding to or even quoting the biblical sister passages as objectified source texts, but that there is a shared agenda and maybe even a cognate way of life behind all three passages. Here I would like to draw on what Susan Niditch has called 'traditional referentiality,' as opposed to direct quotation, as a way of accounting for recurring phrases in the Hebrew Bible (Niditch 1996: 18–19). If, as seems likely, a group of pious Torah scholars advocate a lifestyle not too removed from what our passages promote, then it is likely that the language that recurs in all three texts became 'formulaic' in Niditch's terms, something like a mantra, in those circles (Niditch 1996: 18). The increased recognition of orality in the development of ancient Hebrew literature advocated by Niditch and others should make us hesitate in assuming the work of the ancient scholar was reminiscent of our own endeavours in looking for quotes and turning pages followed—hopefully—by conscientious acknowledgments in the footnotes.

Alongside the possibility of a shared outlook over and above the shared language between the late biblical statements and the Scrolls passage, there are subtle differences also, especially the strong *emphasis on study* (דרש) in the Scrolls as opposed to more straightforward recitation (הגה) in the Bible. Both Joshua 1 and Psalm 1 appear confident that the benefits of Torah are freely accessible to Joshua and the righteous one. In the 1QS 6 passage, by contrast, it is necessary to be more searching. Moreover, elsewhere in the Community Rule we notice a progressive narrowing of access to the privilege of arriving at the correct understanding of the law. The element of immediacy is gradually waning. We are reminded also of Neh. 8.7–9 where the simple public reading of the law to the people requires guidance from Ezra and the Levites in order to reach the assembled people (see also Niditch 1996: 124).

Moreover, the pragmatic idea of regulating a rotation of individual members who devote themselves to Torah study introduced in 1QS 6.6–7 is absent from Josh. 1.8 and Ps. 1.2.[9] It is possible also that the activities described by the different verbs (הגה and דרש) are of intrinsically different quality. Lohfink has argued with reference to Ps. 1.2 and Deut. 6.6f. that הגה refers to a type of rhythmic, meditative murmuring:

> Dass man meditierte, indem man, im Rhytmus des Atmens, auswendig gewusste Texte murmelte, wird hier als selbstverständlich vorausgesetzt. (Lohfink 1992: 6)

[9] Cf. also the stipulation for 'the many' to devote a third of the nights to read the book and study the law in 1QS 6.7b and the instruction in Neh. 9.3 for the seed of Israel to confess their sins and read from the book of the law for a fourth of the day.

In the same context he also speaks of 'einem halblauten, rhytmischen Singsang'. If Lohfink is right then it is not inconceivable for devoted individuals to perform such an activity almost constantly.[10]

Turning back to my opening remarks on the common mind-set and milieu of anthologizing, archiving, and updating evident in the Qumran texts and the emerging Hebrew Scriptures, I have tried to suggest that the circles that ultimately gave rise to the Qumran milieu are the heirs of the Torah-disciples identified by Rofé as lying behind the 'winding up of the Hebrew Bible'. If my reading of the opening lines of 1QS 6 as preserving a flavour of embryonic communal life is correct, then these embryonic styles of social organization that foreshadow the fully-fledged *yaḥad*—pre-sectarian or incipit sectarian practices—offer opportunities to bridge the gap back to the circles that shaped the final stages of parts of the Hebrew Bible. Similar suggestions with results compatible with my own have been made by Armin Lange in a pair of studies where he explored the connections of the final redaction of the proto-masoretic Psalter, on the one hand, and of Qohelet, on the other hand, to pre-sectarian Qumran sapiential texts such as Mysteries and 4QInstruction (Lange 1998; 2000). Similarly Reinhard Kratz has shown that the ideal of Jewish learning advocated already in the Hebrew Bible (singling out Deut. 6.4–9; Ps. 1; and Sir 38.34–39.11) continues to find expression in the Scrolls and subsequently in rabbinic literature (Kratz 2004: 154–155; see also with reference to the ideal of Ezra Kratz 2004: 113–118). It is hoped that my own suggestions encourage us to look for such connections even in some less expected places. Finally, Rudolf Smend's former student the late Timo Veijola explored his teacher's Dtr N hypothesis more fully in a study entitled 'Schriftgelehrtentum: Die Deuteronomisten als Vorgänger der Schriftgelehrten. Ein Beitrag zur Entstehung des Judentums' (Veijola 2000). In this study Veijola boldly sets out to identify the late Deuteronomists behind Dtr N—groups of learned exegetes and teachers of the Law—as the predecessors of the post-70 sages: 'eine Vorform

[10] In contrast to my own analysis some have argued that in 1QS 6.6–7 דרש refers to instruction on the part of an expert (e.g., Maier 1996: 115; Jaffee 2001: 33). I suspect that the intriguing statement found in 1QS 6.6–7 is all too often read in light of better known hierarchical passages. This is explicitly the case in a study by A. Schremer (Schremer 2001: 112) where the quotation of 1QS 6.6–7 is followed by an emphatic statement stressing the role of the teacher in such endeavours in the Damascus Document.

des Standes der Rechtsgelehrten' (Veijola 2000: 224). He rightly questions the predominant, and rather unlikely, neat division between what he terms 'Hebraismus' and 'Judentum/Judaismus' and observes: 'Von daher lässt sich nicht sagen, dass es sich bei der Entstehung des klassischen Judentums um einen unvorhergesehenen Betriebsunfall handle…' (Veijola 2000: 239–240). I have tried to argue here that there are good reasons to take a close look at the Dead Sea Scrolls along the way.

References

Alexander, P.S., and G. Vermes. 1998. *Qumran Cave 4. XIX: Serekh Ha-Yaḥad and Two Related Texts* (Oxford: Clarendon).

Blenkinsopp, J. 1981. 'Interpretation and the Tendency to Sectarianism. An Aspect of Second Temple History,' in *Jewish and Christian Self-Definition* (ed. E.P. Sanders; Philadelphia: Fortress) vol. 2: 1–26.

——. 2009. *Judaism the First Phase: The Place of Ezra and Nehemiah in the Origins of Judaism* (Grand Rapids: Eerdmans).

Boling, R.G. 1982. *Joshua: A New Translation with Notes and Commentary* (Garden City NY: Doubleday).

Brooke, G.J. 2002. 'The Rewritten Law, Prophets, and Psalms: Issues for Understanding the Text of the Bible', in *The Bible as Book: The Hebrew Bible and the Judaean Desert Discoveries* (ed. E.D. Herbert und E. Tov; London: The British Library), 31–40.

——. 2005. 'The Qumran Scrolls and the Demise of the Distinction Between Higher and Lower Criticism', in Campbell, Lyons and Pietersen (2005) 26–42.

——. 2009. 'New Perspectives on the Bible and Its Interpretation in the Dead Sea Scrolls', in Dimant and Kratz (2009) 19–37.

——. 2011. 'From Jesus to the Early Christian Communities: Modes of Sectarianism in the Light of the Dead Sea Scrolls,' in Roitman, Schiffman and Tzoref (2011) 413–434.

Brownlee, W.H. 1951. *The Dead Sea Manual of Discipline: Translation and Notes* (New Haven: ASOR).

Butler, T.C. 1983. *Joshua* (*Word* Biblical Commentary, 7; Waco: Word Books).

Campbell, J.G. 2005. '"Rewritten Bible" and "Parabiblical Texts:" A Terminological and Ideological Critique,' in Campbell, Lyons and Pietersen (2005) 43–68.

Campbell, J.G., W.J. Lyons and L.K. Pietersen (eds.) 2005. *New Directions in Qumran Studies* (London: T & T Clark).

Carr, D.M. 2005. *Writing on the Tablet of the Heart: Origins of Scripture and Literature* (Oxford: Oxford University Press).

Collins, J.J. 2009. *Beyond the Qumran Community: The Sectarian Movement of the Dead Sea Scrolls* (Grand Rapids: Eerdmans).

Davies, P.R. 2008. '"Old" and "New" Israel in the Bible and the Qumran Scrolls: Identity and Difference,' in García Martínez and Popovic (2008) 33–42.

Day, J. (ed.) 2007. *Temple and Worship in Biblical Israel* (London: T & T Clark).

Dimant, D. 1995. 'The Qumran Manuscripts: Contents and Significance', in *Time To Prepare the Way in the Wilderness* (ed. D. Dimant and L.H. Schiffman; Leiden: Brill) 23–58.

Dimant D., and R.G. Kratz (eds). 2009. *The Dynamics of Language and Exegesis at Qumran* (Tübingen: Mohr Siebeck).

Flint, P. 1997. *The Dead Sea Psalms Scroll and the Book of Psalms* (Leiden: Brill).
Fraade, S.D. 1993. 'Interpretative Authority in the Studying Community at Qumran,' *Journal of Jewish Studies* 44: 46–69.
García Martínez, F. 2008. '¿Secatario, no-sectario, o qué? Problemas de una taxonomía correcta de los textos qumránicos,' *Revue de Qumran* 23: 383–394.
——. 2010. 'Aramaica Qumranica Apocalyptica?,' in *Aramaica Qumranica: The Aix en Provence Colloquium on the Aramaic Dead Sea Scrolls* (ed. K. Berthelot and D. Stökl Ben Ezra; Leiden: Brill), 435–449.
García Martínez, F., and M. Popovic (eds). 2008. *Defining Identities: We, You, and the Others in the Dead Sea Scrolls* (Leiden: Brill).
Gillingham, S. 2007. 'The Zion Tradition and the Editing of the Hebrew Psalter,' in Day (2007) 308–341.
Goshen-Gottstein, M.H. 1966. 'The Psalms Scoll (11QPs[a]): A Problem of Canon and Text,' *Textus* 5: 22–33.
Gray, J. 1967. *Joshua, Judges and Ruth* (London: T. Nelson and Sons).
Hempel, C. 2003a. 'Kriterien zur Bestimmung "essenischer Verfasserschaft" von Qumrantexten,' in *Qumran Kontrovers: Beiträge zu den Textfunden vom Toten Meer* (ed. J. Frey and H. Stegemann; Paderborn: Bonifatius), 71–78.
——. 2003b. 'Interpretative Authority in the Community Rule Tradition,' in *Dead Sea Discoveries* 10: 59–80.
——. 2008. 'Emerging Communal Life and Ideology in the S Tradition', in García Martínez and Popović (2008) 43–61.
——. 2010a. 'Pluralism and Authoritativeness—The Case of the S Tradition', in *The Authoritativeness of Scriptures in Ancient Judaism* (ed. M. Popović; Leiden: Brill) 193–208.
——. 2010b. 'Shared Traditions: Points of Contact between D and S', in *The Transmission of Traditions and the Production of Texts as They Emerge from the Dead Sea Scrolls* (ed. S. Metso, H. Najman and E. Schuller; Leiden: Brill) 115–131.
——. 2011. '1QS 6:2c–4a—Satellites or Precursors of the Yachad?' in Roitman, Schiffman and Tzoref (2011) 31–40.
Hertzberg, H.W. 1962. *Beiträge zur Traditionsgeschichte und Theologie des Alten Testaments* (Göttingen: Vandenhoeck & Ruprecht).
Hultgren, S. 2007. *From the Damascus Covenant to the Covenant of the Community: Literary, Historical, and Theological Studies in the Dead Sea Scrolls* (Leiden: Brill).
Jaffe, M. 2001. *Torah in the Mouth: Writing and Oral Tradition in Palestinian Judaism, 200 BCE–400 CE* (Oxford: Oxford University Press).
Jokiranta, J. 2005. 'Identity on a Continuum: Constructing and Expressing Sectarian Social Identity in Qumran Serakhim and Pesharim' (University of Helsinki: PhD Thesis).
Knibb, M.A. 1987. *The Qumran Community* (Cambridge: Cambridge University Press).
Kratz, R.G. 1996. 'Die Tora Davids. Ps 1 und die doxologische Fünfteilung des Psalters,' *Zeitschrift für Theologie und Kirche* 93: 1–34.
——. 2004. *Das Judentum im Zeitalter des Zweiten Tempels* (Tübingen: Mohr Siebeck).
Kratz, R.G. 2009. 'Friend of God, Brother of Sarah, and Father of Isaac: Abraham in the Hebrew Bible and in Qumran' in Dimant and Kratz (2009) 79–105.
Lange, A. 1998. 'Die Endgestalt des protomasoretischen Psalters und die Toraweisheit,' in *Der Psalter in Judentum und Christentum* (ed. E. Zenger; Freiburg: Herder), 101–136.
Lange, A. 2000. 'Eschatological Wisdom in the Book of Qohelet and the Dead Sea Scrolls,' in *The Dead Sea Scrolls: Fifty Years After Their Discovery 1947–1997* (ed. L. Schiffman, E. Tov and J. VanderKam; Jerusalem: Israel Exploration Society) 817–825.
Levin, C. 2003. 'Das Gebetbuch der Gerechten. Literargeschichtliche Beobachtungen am Psalter', in *Fortschreibungen: Gesammelte Studien zum Alten Testament* (Berlin: De Gruyter) 291–313.

Lohfink, N. 1992. 'Psalmengebet und Psalterredaktion,' *Archiv für Literaturwissenschaft* 34: 1–22.
Maier, J. 1996. 'Early Jewish Biblical Interpretation in the Qumran Literature,' in *Hebrew Bible/Old Testament: The History of Its Interpretation. Volume I: From the Beginnings to the Middle Ages (Until 1300)* (ed. M. Sæbø; Göttingen: Vandenhoeck & Ruprecht) 108–129.
Metso, S. 2006. 'Whom Does the Term YaHad Identify?' in *Biblical Traditions in Transmission: Essays in Honour of Michael A. Knibb* (ed. C. Hempel and J. Lieu; Leiden: Brill), 213–235.
——. 2007. *The Serekh Texts* (London: T & T Clark).
Milik, J.T. 1959. *Ten Years of Discovery in the Wilderness of Judaea* (London: SCM).
Miller, J.M., and G.M. Tucker. 1974. *The Book of Joshua* (Cambridge: Cambridge University Press).
Newsom, C. 1990. '"Sectually Explicit" Literature from Qumran,' in *The Hebrew Bible and Its Interpreters* (ed. W.H. Propp et al.; Winona Lake: Eisenbrauns) 167–187.
Niditch, S. 1996. *Oral World and Written Word: Ancient Israelite Literature* (Louisville: Westminster John Knox).
Noth, M. 1952. *Das Buch Josua* (2nd ed.; Tübingen: Mohr Siebeck).
Rofé, A. 1993. 'The Piety of the Torah-Disciples at the Winding-up of the Hebrew Bible: Josh. 1:8; Ps. 1:2; Isa. 59:21,' in *Bibel in jüdischer und christlicher Tradition: Festschrift Johann Maier zum 60. Geburtstag* (ed. H. Merklein, K. Müller and G. Stemberger; Frankfurt a. M.: Hain) 78–85.
Roitman, A., L.H. Schiffman and S. Tzoref (eds). 2011. *The Dead Sea Scrolls and Contemporary Culture* (Leiden: Brill).
Sanders, J.A. 1965. *The Psalms Scroll of Qumran Cave 11 (11QPs[a])* (Oxford: Clarendon).
Schofield, A. 2009. *From Qumran to the Yaḥad: A New Paradigm of Textual Development for the Community Rule* (Leiden: Brill).
Schremer, A. 2001. '"[T]he[y] Did not Read in the Sealed Book." Qumran Halakhic Revolution and the Emergence of Torah Study in Second Temple Judaism,' in *Historical Perspectives: From the Hasmoneans to Bar Kokhba in Light of the Dead Sea Scrolls. Proceedings of the Fourth International Symposium of the Orion Center for the Study of the Dead Sea Scrolls and Associated Literature, 27–31 January, 1999* (ed. D. Goodblatt, A. Pinnick and D.R. Schwartz; Leiden: Brill) 105–126.
Skehan, P. 1973. 'A Liturgical Complex in 11QPs[a],' *Catholic Biblical Quarterly* 35: 195–205.
Smend, R. 2002. 'Das Gesetz und die Völker,' in *Die Mitte des Alten Testaments: exegetische Aufsätze* (Tübingen: Mohr Siebeck) 148–161.
Smith, M. 1960. 'The Dead Sea Scrolls in Relation to Ancient Judaism,' *New Testament Studies* 7: 347–360.
Soggin, J.A. 1972. *Joshua: A Commentary* (trans. R.A. Wilson; London: SCM).
Steudel, A. 2009. 'Dating Exegetical Texts from Qumran' in Dimant and Kratz (2009) 39–53.
Talmon, S. 1966. 'Pisqah Be'emṣaʿ Pasuq and 11QPs[a],' *Textus* 5: 11–21.
——. 1986. 'The Emergence of Jewish Sectarianism in the Early Second Temple Period', in *King, Cult, and Calendar in Ancient Israel: Collected Studies* (Leiden/Jerusalem: Brill/Magnes) 165–201.
——. 1989. *The World of Qumran From Within* (Leiden/Jerusalem: Brill/Magnes).
Toorn, K. van der. 2007. *Scribal Culture and the Making of the Hebrew Bible* (Cambridge: Harvard University Press).
Tov, E. 2004. *Scribal Practices and Approaches Reflected in the Texts Found in the Judean Desert* (Leiden: Brill).
——. 2006. 'The Writing of Early Scrolls. Implications for the Literary Analysis of Hebrew Scripture,' *Dead Sea Discoveries* 13: 339–347.

——. 2010. 'The Coincidental Textual Nature of the Collections of Ancient Scriptures,' in *Congress Volume Ljubljana 2007* (ed. A. Lemaire; Leiden: Brill) 153–169.
Ulrich, E. 1999. *The Dead Sea Scrolls and the Origins of the Bible* (Grand Rapids: Eerdmans).
VanderKam, J.C. 2002. 'Questions of Canon Viewed Through the Dead Sea Scrolls,' in *The Canon Debate* (ed. L.M. McDonald and J.A. Sanders; Peabody: Hendrickson) 91–109.
Veijola, T. 2000. *Moses Erben: Studien zum Dekalog, zum Deuteronomismus, und zum Schriftgelehrtentum* (Stuttgart: Kohlhammer).
Vermes, G. 1994. *The Dead Sea Scrolls: Qumran in Perspective* (3rd ed.; London: SCM).
Weeks, S. 2007. 'Wisdom Psalms,' in Day (2007) 292–307.
Weinfeld, M. 1972. *Deuteronomy and the Deuteronomic School* (Oxford: Clarendon).
Weiser, A. 1962. *The Psalms: A Commentary* (London: SCM).
White Crawford, S. 2008. *Rewriting Scripture in Second Temple Times* (Grand Rapids: Eerdmans).
Wilson, G.H. 1985. *The Editing of the Hebrew Psalter* (Chico: Scholars Press).

JOSEPHUS AND 11Q13 ON MELCHIZEDEK

William Horbury

Josephus closes his account of the fall of Jerusalem with the story of the first foundation of the city and the building of the temple (B.J. vi 438; repeated, without an explicit claim about temple-building, in Ant. i 180). The founder (he says) was a ruler of Canaanites called in the ancestral tongue Righteous King; he truly was so, and because of this he first served the God as priest and, being the first to build the temple (*to hieron*), gave the name Hierosolyma—'holy Solyma' or perhaps 'temple of Solyma'—to the place hitherto called simply Solyma.

This narrative of Melchizedek and Jerusalem expands Gen. 14.18. It has been discussed in relation to Josephus' own biblical learning. Did he simply know stories like this when he wrote the *Jewish War*, gaining real knowledge only when he prepared the *Antiquities*?[1] He no doubt then deepened his biblical study, but, just as Philo used material which resembles rewritten bible but also quoted the biblical text itself, so Josephus' seeming allusions to rewritten bible need not preclude that awareness of the biblical books themselves which he does already claim in the *War* (B.J. iii 352, as a priest he was not ignorant of the prophecies in the sacred books).

The present note suggests that his story of the foundation of Jerusalem and the temple, beginning from a paraphrase of Gen. 14.18 on the lines of existing Aramaic and Greek Jewish interpretative tradition, is based on associative exegesis used in rewritten bible; this exegesis would have been linked with a catena of biblical texts on Melchizedek, related to and perhaps illuminating that which lies behind 11Q13 (11QMelchizedek).

Gen. 14.18 in Josephus' Narrative

The story as Josephus gives it seems wholly Hellenic; Hebrew names are omitted or Graecized. At the same time, however, it is bound up

[1] This was argued by Schwartz (1990: 23–35, 43–45).

with Jewish renderings of Gen. 14.18, Aramaic as well as Greek. These seem to depend on exegesis of Gen. 14.18 in association with Ps. 76.3 'at Salem was his tabernacle, and his dwelling in Zion'. In its treatment of Hebrew names the narrative based on this exegesis draws on Aramaic paraphrase translated into Greek, but also on distinctively Greek-language interpretation.

Thus Aramaic interpretation seems ultimately to underlie the treatment of the name Melchizedek itself, which is entirely omitted, and replaced by Righteous King. In the omission the *Jewish War* stands, it is true, in contrast with much Aramaic as well as Greek paraphrase of Gen. 14.18. The Aramaic Genesis Apocryphon from Qumran simply gives the Hebrew name without interpretation, although it notes that Salem is Jerusalem, and identifies the King's Vale with the valley of Beṯ-hak-kerem nearby (1QApGen ar xxii 13–14); this localization, probably already assumed in Genesis 14, is confirmed by the exegesis of Gen. 14.18 through association with Ps. 76.3, discussed below.[2] The king's Hebrew name is there still in Philo on 'Melchizedek' who 'is called Righteous King' (Leg. All. iii 79), the prince of peace (Salem, cf. Ps. 76.3 LXX his tabernacle was in Peace) who feeds the soul and especially as priest represents the Logos (Leg. All. iii 81–2); although elsewhere in Philo, in paraphrase rather than commentary, he is the unnamed 'great priest of the God most great' (Abr. 235). The name survives in Josephus himself in the *Antiquities* on 'Melchizedek, which means Righteous King' (i 180), in Targum Onkelos and, in the Palestinian Targumic tradition, the Fragment-Targums, which leave the Hebrew name without interpretation, paraphrasing 'and Melchizedek king of Jerusalem'.[3]

With 'Righteous King' Josephus and Philo both seem, however, to represent in Greek an assonant Aramaic explanation *malka ṣaddiqa* which is found also in Targum Ps.-Jonathan. These Greek Jewish interpretations probably contrast in linguistic background with that found in the roughly contemporary Epistle to the Hebrews, 'king of righteousness' (Heb. 7.2), a seemingly Hebrew- rather than Aramaic-based explanation. Onkelos and the Fragment-Targums give the Hebrew name without interpretation, as noted already, but in Targum Ps.-Jonathan it is simply replaced with Righteous King, as in Josephus'

[2] On Genesis 14 see Emerton (1990: 45–71).

[3] Berliner (1884: i, 13), Klein (1980: i, 50).

Jewish War; for Gen. 14.18 is rendered 'and Righteous King, that is Shem, son of Noah, king of Jerusalem, came to meet Abram'.[4]

In this paraphrase of the name, then, as Philo confirms, Targum Ps.-Jonathan gives interpretation which was in vogue before the capture of Jerusalem by Titus. Moreover, this Targum stands together with Philo and Josephus in applying the righteousness signified by the name to Melchizedek himself, whereas a perhaps later type of explanation attested in the midrash applies it to Jerusalem; he was a king of a righteous city, or of a city called 'Righteousness' (unattributed interpretations in Gen. Rab. 43.6). Neofiti half-replaces the name, giving the compromise *malka ṣedeq*, perhaps representing the impact of the familiar Hebrew and Onkelos, and maybe also of the midrashic cherishing of *ṣedeq*, on a copyist of a text with *malka ṣaddiqa*.[5]

The interpreted name is linked in Ps.-Jonathan with the rabbinic identification of Melchizedek as Shem, found also in Neofiti and the Fragment-Targums.[6] Josephus himself, however, lacks this possibly later link with Shem and views Melchizedek as non-Jewish, going on to call David the first Jewish king of Jerusalem (B.J. vi 440). Thus, although the name Righteous King reflects Aramaic interpretative tradition, and could have suited the lost Aramaic version of the *Jewish War*, the effect of the replacement of the name Melchizedek in the context of the *War* as we have it is largely to provide a fully Greek version which helps to make the founder of Jerusalem a moral exemplar.

Similarly, in Josephus the Hebrew place-names Salem and Jerusalem survive only beneath the fully Greek forms Solyma and Hierosolyma.[7] Aristotle was said to have found the name *Hierusaleme* 'altogether awkward', πάνυ σκολιόν (according to Clearchus of Soli as quoted by Josephus, Ap. i 179); in this version of the Melchizedek story we have instead a classicizing form, favoured in Josephus' time and long before, which recalls those 'hills of the Solymites' mentioned in Homer's Odyssey (v 283).

---

[4] Rieder ed. (1974: 19).

[5] Le Déaut (1978: 163) notes that the name in Neofiti should perhaps be corrected to the form found in Ps.-Jonathan.

[6] The possibility that the identification with Shem (based on a chronology differing from those followed in Jubilees and Philo) is old is underlined by Hayward (1995: 156; 1996: 67–80).

[7] On these names in Josephus and elsewhere see Smith (1907–1908: i, 259–265), Nodet (1996: 155).

Perhaps the most striking expansion of Gen. 14.18 in the *Jewish War* is the statement that Righteous King was not only the first to officiate as priest, but also the first to build the temple, whence he bestowed the name Hierosolyma. Like the identification of Salem with Jerusalem, the claim that the temple was first built at the time when the city was still called Salem is likely to rest on the association of Gen. 14.18 with Ps. 76.3. The suggested connection of the city-name in the form Hierosolyma with the building of the *hieron* is, however, by contrast with the Aramaic-based interpretation Righteous King, a distinctively Greek-language etymological venture; contrast too the later Hebrew-based explanation of the name Jerusalem as a tactful divine combination of Abraham's 'Jireh' (Gen. 22.14) with Shem/Melchizedek's 'Salem' (Gen. Rab.56.10). Josephus' explanation is paralleled in Greek, with a less ambitious claim for antiquity, in the connection of both Hierusalem and Hierosolyma with Solomon suggested by the second-century B.C. Jewish historian Eupolemus.[8] Here then in Josephus the linguistic setting of the story is Greek; but the occasion for mentioning Solyma and Hierosolyma in the first place is the identification of Salem with Jerusalem found in the Genesis Apocryphon and the Targums, with the claim for a temple in Salem—together based on association of Gen. 14.18 with Ps. 76.3, as argued below.

The names then together suggest a background of Aramaic interpretation translated into Greek, and associative exegesis comprehensible through both Semitic-language and Greek-language forms of biblical text, but a foreground in which distinctively Greek-language interpretation has been used. The claim that the temple was in fact built by the ruler called Righteous King is not found in Eupolemus, Philo, or the Targums; but its emergence from the link between Gen. 14.18 and Ps. 76.3 into a Greek-speaking as well as Semitic-language Jewish milieu probably goes back at least to the time of Samaritan-Jewish controversy in the second century BCE. The story of a public Jewish-Samaritan disputation before Ptolemy Philadelphus is told by Josephus (Ant. xiii 74–9). A Greek outline of the patriarchal history from about this period, ascribed to Eupolemus by Alexander Polyhistor but probably shaped by another author in the Samaritan interest, calls

[8] Eupolemus, fragment 2, quoted from Alexander Polyhistor in Eusebius, P.E. ix 34, 11.

Melchizedek king and priest of mount Gerizim.[9] The Jerusalem version found in Josephus, with the claim that Righteous King built the temple, probably represents a Jewish counterpart.[10]

The story as Josephus gives it, then, is Hellenically presented, and he probably draws here on older Greek Jewish narrative in favour of Melchizedek and Jerusalem, resting on or incorporated in rewritten bible. His claims for the city and the temple would have suited controversy with Samaritans in particular, but are equally adapted to his own broader apologetic needs. Righteous King was a priest-king who truly exemplified righteousness, somewhat as in Philo he was fit to represent the Logos. The Greek name Hierosolyma is explained so as to give the utmost antiquity to the city, the temple, and its cult, and to associate the origins with justice and piety. Yet the Greek story as Josephus tells it is rooted in Aramaic as well as Greek Jewish interpretation of Gen. 14.18, associated with Ps. 76.3.

Josephan Reflections of Associative Exegesis of Gen. 14.18

The interpretation which forms the basis of this story, the location of Melchizedek in a city which became Jerusalem and where he founded the temple, seems then to be bound up with exegesis of the Pentateuch by association with the Psalter. In this exegesis Gen. 14.18 (Melchizedek king of Salem was priest of the most high God) is amplified by association with Ps. 76.3 (2) 'at Salem was his tabernacle, and his dwelling in Zion', LXX 'his place (τόπος) came to be in Peace, and his dwelling in Sion'. Thus in the midrashic tradition Ps. 76.3 comes eventually to be quoted as the proof-text for the identification of Salem with Jerusalem.[11]

Yet this psalm-verse also mentions his 'tabernacle' (סֻךְ 'covert' or 'booth') at Salem; here and at Lam. 2.6 (שֻׂכּוֹ, here spelt with *śin*; LXX σκήνωμα) the Targum renders 'house of his sanctuary'. The LXX

[9] Eusebius, P.E. ix 17, 5–6, again quoting Alexander Polyhistor, who ascribes the passage to Eupolemus; but the identification of Salem with the holy mount Gerizim, not simply with a place in the district of Shechem, suggests a Samaritan source, despite contrary arguments summed up by Gruen (1998: 147–148).

[10] Gianotto (1984: 267–269).

[11] Buber ed. (1894: i, 30) on Gen. 14.18 *And Melchizedek king of Salem*: 'This was Shem son of Noah who was king in Jerusalem, as it is said, *And in Salem was his tabernacle*' (Ps. 76.3).

versions already point in the same direction, given the sacral associations of both τόπος and σκήνωμα (Ps. 132 [131].5). The first temple, then, was at Salem, identified with Jerusalem.

An attempt to retain the identification of Salem indicated by Ps. 76.3 and to be true to the tenor of this verse without retrojecting the temple entirely into the Salem period is seen later in an ingenious midrash probably current in fourth-century Galilee: 'When it was still Salem, the Holy One, blessed be he, made himself a *sukkah* and used to pray within it [Salem], as it is said, *And in Salem was his tabernacle*...' (Gen. Rab. 56.10; more fully, *Midrash Tehillim* 76.3). This interpretation brings out the importance of *ʾelohim* (Ps. 76.2) as the subject of Ps. 76.3.

Josephus' wording suggests that yet one more association with the psalter lies beneath. The etymology which presents Melchizedek as an exemplar of righteousness is developed as follows: 'righteous—for such indeed he was; on this account (διὰ τοῦτο) he was the first to officiate as priest to the God' (B.J. vi 438, followed in Ant.i 180 'righteous—and such he admittedly was, so that for this cause he also became priest of God'). Josephus' eagerness to account for Melchizedek's priesthood stands out, and it has been suggested that this prominent feature of his two narratives depends on tradition.[12] The mention of the ruler's righteousness followed by 'on this account' in fact recalls Ps. 45 (44), verses 7–8 (6–7) 'thy throne O God is for ever and ever: a sceptre of equity is the sceptre of thy kingdom. Thou hast loved righteousness and hated iniquity; therefore (LXX διὰ τοῦτο) God, even thy God, hath anointed thee with the oil of gladness above thy fellows'.

These lines address the righteous king as *ʾelohim*, LXX ὁ θεὸς. They are quoted in the Epistle to the Hebrews (1.8–9) to show the superiority of Christ to the angels, and are often thought to have been drawn by the writer from a testimony-collection.[13] In the second and early third centuries they recur, accompanied by Ps. 110.1 and other texts, in Justin Martyr, Irenaeus and Tertullian, here probably from a testimony-collection grouping passages which suggest that scripture

[12] Franxman (1979: 136) (perhaps overrating the oddity of Josephus' emphasis, but rightly noting its weight), Horton (1976: 83) (tradition is suggested by the agreement of the two narratives and the adverb 'admittedly'; but note that the latter may be meant to indicate the opinion of contemporaries of Melchizedek, not of Josephus).

[13] Harris and Burch (1916–1920: ii, 43–49), Rüsen-Weinhold (2004: 176, 180–182), suggesting that the slight difference of the text quoted from LXX confirms this view.

envisages two divine beings.[14] In their seeming address to a second divine being of the vocative ὁ θεὸς, representing Hebrew *ʾelohim*, Ps. 45.7–8 also recall the much earlier application of *ʾelohim* in the Psalms to Melchizedek in 11Q13, a composition which appears to anticipate aspects of the line of scriptural proof followed in these early Christian writings. The exegesis in Josephus, making Melchizedek's priesthood ensue on his righteousness, thus seems to associate Gen. 14.18 on Melchizedek not only with Ps. 76.3, but also with Ps. 45.7–8. The importance of *ʾelohim* in Ps. 76.3 as well as Ps. 45.7–8 can now be recalled.

The claim that Melchizedek became the first priest, paralleled in Philo (*Cong.* 99), probably reflects his primacy as the first personage in the Pentateuch to be called a priest; it will also presuppose the mention of Melchizedek in Ps. 110.4 'you are a priest for ever after the order of Melchizedek', not clearly alluded to by Josephus. His more distinct echo of Ps. 45.7–8 uses it to answer the implied question, On what account did Melchizedek merit priesthood? These psalm-verses were later used somewhat comparably of Aaron's priestly anointing on account of Moses's righteousness (*Midrash Tehillim* 45.6).

'On what account?' was a widely-used exegetical question in rabbinic interpretation.[15] In an instance resembling that implied in Josephus—On what account did Judah merit kingship?—it was likewise answered by citation of texts which demonstrated virtue.[16] Both the rabbinic and the Josephan answers reflect the exegetical importance of the question-and-answer form, and the need to show that biblical narrative exhibits reason and upholds virtue; but in Josephus—in accord with the rationalizing aspect of his presentation of Jewish tradition—explicit allusion to the scriptural proof is missing, and its presence is betrayed simply by a striking echo.

The narrative in Josephus then seems to be based on association of Gen. 14.18, on Righteous King, with both Ps. 76.3 on Salem and

---

[14] Ps. 45.7–8 in Justin Martyr, Dial. lvi 14 (and, with the same accompanying proof-texts, in Irenaeus, Haer. iii 6, 1; Tertullian, Prax. xiii 1–3), as interpreted by Skarsaune (1987: 126, 209), Bobichon (2003: ii, 737).

[15] Bacher (1899, 1905: i, 113; ii, 116–117); on Hellenic, Jewish and Christian exegesis of this kind, Volgers and Zamagni eds. (2004).

[16] This question was posed in the circle of R. Tarphon, according to Mekhilta, *Be-Šhallaḥ* 2.5, on Exod. 14.22 (ed. H.S. Horovitz and I.A. Rabin [1931], p. 106); *Midrash Tehillim* 76.2.

Ps. 45.7–8 on the anointing of the righteous king. In Ps. 45 the righteous king is addressed as *ʾelohim*, and in Ps. 76 it is *ʾelohim* whose tabernacle was in Salem. These points are now considered in relation with the application of biblical texts using *ʾelohim* to Melchizedek in 11Q13.

ʾElohim in Biblical Quotation in 11Q13 on Melchizedek

In 11Q13, perhaps a hundred and fifty to two hundred years before Josephus, the interpretation 'for the last days' (col. ii, line 4) of Leviticus 25.9–13 on the Jubilee, and the associated law for the year of release, forms a thread running through most of the surviving text. The psalm most fully used in reference to Melchizedek is Psalm 82, although Psalm 7 is also quoted.[17]

Melchizedek thereby emerges as a great angel or divine being, *ʾelohim* (Ps. 82.1) as well as *ʾel* (Ps. 7.9; MT has the tetragram here). At the tenth Jubilee, in the last days, when liberty is proclaimed, as ordained for Israel in Lev. 25.9–10, a passage amplified in Isa. 61.1–3 on the proclamation of liberty to the captives (11Q13, col. ii, lines 2–9), he will restore the captives and carry out the divine judgment (Pss. 7.9, 82.1–2, quoted in 11Q13, lines 9–13). Those who form the 'inheritance of Melchizedek' (11Q13, line 5) are by implication those whom *ʾelohim* 'will inherit in all the nations' (Ps. 82.8).[18] 'The year of good pleasure for the Lord' (Isa. 61.2) becomes in 11Q13, line 9 'the year of good pleasure for Melchizedek and his armies', again probably presupposing *ʾel* where MT has the tetragram.[19] Melchizedek is probably also 'our God' (*ʾelohenu*) in the adjacent phrase 'day of vengeance for our God' (Isa. 61.2), for 'Melchizedek will wreak the vengeance of the judgments of *ʾe*[*l*]' (11Q13, col. ii, line 9).

These points emerge from 11Q13, col. ii, lines 2–14, and for the present purpose there is no need to ask if the messenger or one of the messengers in the following lines is Melchizedek (11Q13, col. ii,

[17] For suggested interpretations see García Martínez (2007) and Knohl (2009).

[18] Emerton (1966), noting (401, n.3) the possible connection between the 'inheritance' and Ps. 82.8.

[19] This, on the analogy of the substitution of *ʾel* in Ps. 7.9 and the preference for *ʾel* in 1QS, 1QM and 1QH, seems to me more likely than the direct representation of the tetragram by Melchizedek assumed for example by Puech (1993: ii, 553).

lines 15–25, interpreting Isa. 52.7).[20] In these later lines it seems clear, however, irrespective of this question, that Zion's *ʾelohim* who reigns (Isa. 52.7), as a messenger declares, is once again Melchizedek (11Q13, lines 16, 23–5).

The recognition of Melchizedek in the *ʾelohim* of Ps. 82.1 is perhaps already presupposed in the sabbath-hymn fragment 4Q401 11, line 3, restored 'Melchi]zedek, priest in the assem[bly of God'.[21] In 11Q13, then, Lev. 25.9–13 on the Jubilee, with which the related prophecy Isa. 61.1–2 has been associated, outlines a liberation to be performed by Melchizedek as *ʾel* and probably also *ʾelohim* (Isa. 61.2). Psalm 82, on *ʾelohim* (Melchizedek) as judge and deliverer, and more briefly Ps. 7.9 on *ʾel* (Melchizedek) as judge, are associated with these two texts, and joined by Isa. 52.7, on the reign of Zion's *elohim* (Melchizedek).

The designation of Melchizedek as *ʾelohim* and *ʾel* stands out. Angels in the plural are not infrequently *ʾelohim* and *ʾelim*, but the honorific application of *ʾelohim* and *ʾel* to a single great angel is striking. This point is recognized when they are interpreted here as references to a divine hypostasis, like the angel of the Lord when seemingly indistinguishable from the Lord (as at Gen. 16.7; 13); or to the high God himself, when 'Melchizedek' would be understood simply as one of his titles, 'King of righteousness'.[22] Yet then, especially in the second case, justice is scarcely done to the coherence of a designation of Melchizedek as *ʾelohim* and *ʾel* with biblical treatments of lesser divine beings, as developed in the Greek and Roman periods.

Thus, not long before the probable time of the composition attested in 11Q13, the biblical affirmations that Moses will be as *ʾelohim* to Aaron, and is made *ʾelohim* to Pharaoh (Exod. 4.16, 7.1) are taken up by Ben Sira in the line 'and he honoured him as *ʾelohim*, and made him strong among the high ones'—mighty among the angels (Sir. 45.2, Genizah MS. B. as restored in the light of the Greek).[23] Another roughly contemporary kindred figure appears in LXX Ps. 110 (109).1–4, where 'my lord', begotten before the day star, and so by implication a senior angel, destined to bear rule among the brightnesses of the holy ones,

---

[20] For discussion of this point see Chester (2007: 259–261).

[21] So Newsom (1985: 24, 37, 134; 1998: 205).

[22] Milik (1972: 125—hypostasis); Manzi (1997: 31–103, 261–265—the high God).

[23] Segal (1958: 309–310). A similar echo of Exod. 7.1 appears in 4Q374, 2 ii 6 'and he set him for *ʾelohim* over majestic ones, and a cause of reeli[ng] to Pharaoh', probably again in reference to Moses; see Newsom (1995: 102–103), Fletcher-Louis (2002: 136–141), Lierman (2004: 232–233).

is a priest after the order of Melchizedek.[24] Later on, probably not long after the reign of Archelaus in Judaea, Moses is described as sacred spirit (*spiritus*) in the Assumption of Moses (11.17).[25]

The early Christian, including Gnostic, continuations of Melchizedek's own place as a great angel, as asserted with the title *'elohim* in 11Q13, are first attested in the Epistle to the Hebrews.[26] Here he is without father, mother, or pedigree, but made like the son of God (Heb. 7.3). The impact of specifically Christian belief suggested by '*the* son of God' does not exclude influence here from Jewish views of Melchizedek as angel.[27] After Hebrews the idea of likeness between Melchizedek and an angelically-envisaged Christ recurs with a different emphasis in the view attributed to Theodotus the banker in early third-century Rome, in which Melchizedek is 'a certain very great power, greater than the Christ' (Hippolytus, *Elenchus*, vii 35–6 [24]). Of particular interest, however, as suggesting a mode in which angelic interpretations of Melchizedek were transmitted, is the statement that the ascetic Hieracas, in Egypt at the beginning of the fourth century, identified the angel of the Holy Spirit, in the Ascension of Isaiah ix 35–6, with Melchizedek (Epiphanius, Haer. lvii 3, 2–4). The reading of apocryphal works evident here also probably lies behind Origen's view of Melchizedek as an angel, known through dissent from it in Jerome, who had been sent a book expressing the Hieracas-like opinion that Melchizedek was the Holy Spirit (Jerome, Ep. 73.2); for Origen supported his own view that John the Baptist was an angelic spirit from the presentation of Jacob as an incarnate angel in the Prayer of Joseph (Origen, Comm. in Joh. ii, 20–31, 180–92, on Jn 1.6).

Hence Jewish biblical paraphrase and expansion, as mingled with Christian comment in Old Testament pseudepigrapha, and perhaps also as developed by contemporary Jews, will have encouraged interpretation of the Epistle to the Hebrews in favour of the angelic nature of Melchizedek. The Christian speculations should not be derived simply from Hebrews, despite the importance of the Epistle, as a

[24] Gianotto (1984: 7–18, following Parente) and Schaper (1995: 101–7, 129).

[25] On ancient Jewish descriptions of Moses as spirit see Horbury (2006: 38–43).

[26] For Christian, including Gnostic, sources see de Jonge and van der Woude (1966: 323–326); more fully, Gianotto (1984: 145–169, 187–262).

[27] As noted by Gordon (2000: 81).

source respected by both sides in Christian debate, in argument for Melchizedek as a spirit.[28]

In the period of these Christian interpretations Jews were likewise ready to connect biblical figures with angels or spirits, as when Resh Laqish in third-century Tiberias is said to identify the divine spirit upon the waters in Gen. 1.2 as the spirit of Adam and the spirit of the Messiah.[29] This background should be envisaged in consideration of the view of Melchizedek suggested by a rabbinic interpretation of Zechariah probably current in early fourth-century Galilee. The four smiths of Zech. 2.3–4 (1.20–21) who will come 'to cast down the horns of the nations' are identified as Elijah, the king Messiah, Melchizedek, and the priest anointed for war.[30] Melchizedek's work here is as described in 11Q13, and silence on his status should not be taken to rule out the possibility that he is still envisaged as angelic.

However this may be, the interpretation of Melchizedek in 11Q13 as a great angelic spirit, called *ʾelohim* in texts which are held to speak of his work, is confirmed by its kinship with roughly contemporary Jewish interpretation of Moses and of the priest-king of Ps. 110, and its continuation in various ways by early Christians. It is also consistent with the focus on and high view of Melchizedek in the older exegesis of Gen. 14.18 and the name Melchizedek reflected in Philo, Josephus, and Hebrews, by contrast with later tendencies to pass his righteousness to Jerusalem or to hide him behind Shem.

In 11Q13, however, the interpretation of Melchizedek as *ʾelohim* appears through texts like Psalm 82 which prima facie have little to do with Melchizedek—a point which has been held to support the view already noted that God himself, rather than Melchizedek, is the subject. How did Jewish exegetes of the Hasmonaean age come to apply these passages to Melchizedek? Josephus seems to indicate an answer.

---

[28] For example in Ps.-Augustine, *Quaestiones Veteris et Novi Testamenti*, cix, arguing for Melchizedek as the Holy Spirit.

[29] *Tanḥuma* (ed. S. Buber), Leviticus, 16b, *Tazriaʿ* 2, on Lev. 12.1–2 (Adam); *Genesis Rabba* 1.4, on Gen. 1.2 (the Messiah), discussed in Horbury (1998: 101–102).

[30] Cant. R. 2.13, 4, *Pesiqta Rabbati* 15.75a, *Pesiqta de-Rav Kahana* 5.9, all with the name Melchizedek, attribution to R. Isaac (early fourth-century Tiberias and Caesarea, with a visit to Babylonia), and identification of the four with the 'flowers' of Cant. 2.12; cf. Babylonian Talmud, Sukka 52b, with the name Cohen Zedek and no link to Cant. 2.12, quoted in *Yalquṭ Šimʿoni* on the Prophets, no. 569, on Zech. 2.3.

Josephus in Relation to 11Q13

Two groups of biblical texts linked with Melchizedek have emerged. Gen. 14.18, with Pss. 76.3, 45.7–8, both using *ʾelohim*, in Josephus, stand beside Lev. 25.9–13, with Isa. 61.1–2 (*ʾel* and probably *ʾelohim*), Ps. 82.1–2; 8 (*ʾelohim*), Ps. 7.9 (*ʾel*) and Isa. 52.7 (*ʾelohim*), in 11Q13. The unusual designation *ʾelohim* is the most prominent link between the groups, although it is not brought to the fore by Josephus himself.

In each case a Pentateuchal text has had non-Pentateuchal texts associated with it. Only in Josephus, however, is Melchizedek named in the Pentateuchal text. In 11Q13 Lev. 25.9–13 has become linked with Melchizedek, probably through its existing association with Isa. 61.1–2 on the Jubilee liberty to come in the future. Similarly, in 11Q13 it is assumed that *ʾelohim* in Psalm 82 and other passages refers to Melchizedek; only in Josephus is there a clearer link, through the names Salem and Melchizedek, between Melchizedek and psalm-passages using *ʾelohim*.

The two psalms underlying the Josephan narrative in fact suggest a bridge to 11Q13. Psalm 76.3 is linked with Gen. 14.18 by Salem, but it is *ʾelohim* whose tabernacle is there, and the whole psalm, especially in verses 9–13, describes a judgment and deliverance by *ʾelohim* closely resembling that carried out by *ʾelohim* in Psalm 82. Then Ps. 45.7–8 is linked with Gen. 14.18 by its address to a king (Ps. 45.2) who loves righteousness, but here he is called *ʾelohim*. The title *ʾelohim* then emerges for Melchizedek (Righteous King) from this verse somewhat as it emerges for Moses from Exod. 4.16; 7.1.

It may be suggested, then, that Josephus, although later by far than 11Q13, attests an older group of proof-texts on Melchizedek. These, through their verbal connections with Gen. 14:18, provide the basis on which Melchizedek is designated *ʾelohim* and regarded as a judge and deliverer. This step in turn permits Psalm 82 and other texts with *ʾelohim* in judgment and deliverance to be linked with Melchizedek, as in 11Q13.[31]

[31] It is a pleasure to offer this note to Robert Gordon, in admiration and with gratitude for friendship and kindness over many years.

References

Bacher, W. 1899–1905. *Die exegetische Terminologie der jüdischen Traditionsliteratur* (2 vols.; Leipzig: Hinrichs; repr. in one vol., Darmstadt: *Wissenschaftliche Buchgesellschaft*, 1965).

Berliner, A. 1884. *Targum Onkelos* (2 vols.; Berlin).

Bobichon, F. 2003. *Justin Martyr, Dialogue avec Tryphon: Édition critique, traduction, commentaire* (Paradosis, 47, 2 vols.; Fribourg: Academic Press Fribourg).

Buber S. (ed.) 1894. *Midrash Agadah* (2 vols.; Vienna).

Chester, A. 2007. *Messiah and Exaltation* (Wissenschaftliche Untersuchungen zum Neuen Testament, 207, Tübingen: Mohr Siebeck).

de Jonge, M., and A.S. van der Woude. 1966. '11QMelchizedek and the New Testament', *New Testament Studies* 12: 301–326.

Emerton, J.A. 1966. 'Melchizedek and the Gods: Fresh Evidence for the Jewish Background of John X. 34–36', *Journal of Theological Studies* N.S. 17: 399–401.

——. 1990. 'The Site of Salem, City of Melchizedek', *Supplements to Vetus Testamentum* 41: 45–71.

Fletcher-Louis, C.H.T. 2002. *All the Glory of Adam* (Studies on the Texts of the Desert of Judah, 42, Leiden: Brill).

Franxman, T.W. 1979. *Genesis and the "Jewish Antiquities" of Flavius Josephus* (Biblica et Orientalia, 35; Rome: Biblical Institute Press).

García Martínez, F. 2007. 'The Traditions about Melchizedek in the Dead Sea Scrolls', in *Qumranica Minora* (ed. E. Tigchelaar; 2 vols.; Studies on the Texts of the Desert of Judah; 63–64; Leiden & Boston: Brill) 95–108.

Gianotto, C. 1984. *Melchisedek e la sua tipologia* (Supplementi alla Rivista Biblica, 12; Brescia: Paideia Editrice).

Gordon, R.P. 2000. *Hebrews* (Sheffield: Sheffield Academic Press).

Gruen, E.S. 1998. *Heritage and Hellenism* (Berkeley, Los Angeles & London: University of California Press).

Harris, R., and V. Burch. 1916–1920. *Testimonies* (2 vols., Cambridge: Cambridge University Press).

Hayward, C.T.R. 1995. *Saint Jerome's Hebrew Questions on Genesis* (Oxford: Clarendon Press).

——. 1996. 'Shem, Melchizedek, and Concern with Christianity in the Pentateuchal Targumim', in *Targumic and Cognate Studies: Essays in Honour of Martin McNamara* (eds. K.J. Cathcart and M. Maher; Journal for the study of the Old Testament supplement series, 230; Sheffield: Sheffield Academic Press) 67–80.

Horbury, W. 1998. *Jewish Messianism and the Cult of Christ* (London: SCM).

——. 2006. *Herodian Judaism and New Testament Study* (Wissenschaftliche Untersuchungen zum Neuen Testament, 193; Tübingen: Mohr Siebeck).

Horton, F.L. 1976. *The Melchizedek Tradition: a Critical Examination of the Sources to the Fifth Century A.D. and in the Epistle to the Hebrews* (Society for New Testament Studies Monograph Series, 30; Cambridge: Cambridge University Press).

Klein, M.L. *The Fragment-Targums to the Pentateuch According to their Extant Sources* (Analecta Biblica, 76; 2 vols.; Rome: Biblical Institute Press).

Knohl, I. 2009. 'Melchizedek: A Model for the Union of Kingship and Priesthood in the Hebrew Bible, 11QMelchizedek, and the Epistle to the Hebrews' in *Text, Thought and Practice in Qumran and Early Christianity: Proceedings of the Ninth International Symposium of the Orion Center for the Study of the Dead Sea Scrolls and Associated Literature* (ed. R.A. Clements and D.R. Schwartz; Studies on the Texts of the Desert of Judah, 84; Leiden: Brill) 255–266.

Le Déaut, R. 1978. *Targum du Pentateuque: traduction des deux recensions palestiniennes complètes avec introduction, parallèles, notes et index par Roger Le Déaut, avec*

la collaboration de Jacques Robert, tome 1, Genèse (Sources Chrétiennes, 245: Paris: Éditions du Cerf).
Lierman, J. 2004. *The New Testament Moses* (Wissenschaftliche Untersuchungen zum Neuen Testament. 2. Reihe, 173; Tübingen: Mohr Siebeck).
Manzi, F. 1997. *Melchisedek e l'angelologia nell' Epistola agli Ebrei e a Qumran* (Analecta Biblica, 136; Rome: Biblical Institute Press).
Milik, J.T. 1972. 'Milki-sedeq et Milki-resaʿ dans les anciens écrits juifs et chrétiens', *Journal of Jewish Studies* 23: 95–144.
Newsom, C. 1985. *Songs of the Sabbath Sacrifice: a Critical Edition* (Harvard Semitic Studies, 27; Atlanta, Georgia: Scholars Press).
——. 1995. *Qumran Cave 4.14, Parabiblical Texts, Part 2* (eds. M. Broshi, C. Newsom et al.; Discoveries in the Judaean Desert, 19; Oxford: Clarendon Press).
——. 1998. *Qumran Cave 4.6, Poetical and Liturgical Texts, Part 1* (eds. E. Eshel, C. Newsom et al.; Discoveries in the Judaean Desert, 11; Oxford: Clarendon Press).
Nodet, E. 1996. *Le Pentateuque de Flavius Josèphe* (Paris: Éditions du Cerf).
Puech, E. 1993. *La croyance des esséniens en la vie future: immortalité, résurrection, vie éternelle?* (2 vols.; Paris: Gabalda).
Rieder, D. (ed.) 1974. *Pseudo-Jonathan: Targum Jonathan ben Uziel on the Pentateuch, copied from the London MS (British Museum Add. 27031)* (Jerusalem: Salomon).
Rüsen-Weinhold, U. 2004. *Der Septuagintapsalter im Neuen Testament* (Neukirchen-Vluyn: Neukirchener).
Schaper, J. 1995. *Eschatology in the Greek Psalter* (Wissenschaftliche Untersuchungen zum Neuen Testament, 2.76; Tübingen: Mohr Siebeck).
Schwartz, S. 1990. *Josephus and Judaean Politics* (Columbia Studies in the Classical Tradition, 18; Leiden: Brill).
Segal, M.H. 1958. *Sefer Ben-Sira ha-šalem* (2nd edn; Jerusalem: Bialik).
Skarsaune, O. 1987. *The Proof from Prophecy: a Study in Justin Martyr's Proof-text Tradition, Text-type, Provenance, Theological Profile* (Supplements to Novum Testamentum, 56; Leiden: Brill).
Smith, G.A. 1907–1908. *Jerusalem: the Topography, Economics and History from the Earliest Times to A.D. 70* (2 vols.; London: Hodder and Stoughton).
Volgers, A., and C. Zamagni (eds.) 2004. *Erotapokriseis: Early Christian Question-and-Answer Literature in Context* (Leuven: Peeters).

JOSEPHUS, ONKELOS, AND JONATHAN: ON THE AGREEMENTS BETWEEN JOSEPHUS' WORKS AND TARGUMIC SOURCES

Arie van der Kooij

I

The purpose of this contribution is to discuss the issue of concurrences between Josephus' works (Ant. in particular), on the one hand, and Targum Onkelos (Law) and Targum Jonathan (Prophets), on the other.[1] Scholars like Thackeray, Rappaport, and Marcus have listed a number of agreements between Josephus' Ant. and Tg Jon. The agreements do raise of course the question of how to evaluate the evidence. It has been suggested by several scholars that Josephus made use of an Aramaic version which, as stated by Marcus, was 'practically identical with the traditional Targum of Jonathan'.[2] Others, however, doubt whether the evidence is strong enough for such an assumption. According to Attridge 'the evidence...for the use of *targum* is slender at best' (Attridge 1984: 211).[3] In this contribution to the Festschrift in honour of Robert Gordon I would like to investigate this issue a little further, especially since this is in line with one of his own comments on the whole matter: 'the full extent of Josephus' acquaintance with Aramaic and, in particular, Targumic sources is a subject worthy of further investigation' (Gordon 1994: 22).[4]

First of all I will present examples of agreements between Josephus and the targumic sources, Tg Jon in particular, examples which in my

[1] This contribution is the revised version of a paper presented at the Vth Congress of the International Organization for Targumic Studies, held on 12–13 July 2007 in Lubljana.

[2] Marcus (1966: x). See also Thackeray (1929: 82); Rappaport (1930: xx); Brownlee (1956: 182); Schalit (1967: xxxi); Piovanelli (1992: 32). Feldman (1988: 458) seems to refer to the oral targum in the synagogue.

[3] In his dissertation (Attridge 1976: 31f.) he states that in 'only a few passages he may have had a written Aramaic source'.

[4] As indicated I will concentrate on Tg Onk and Tg Jon, leaving out of consideration the issue of agreements between Josephus and other targumic versions (on this matter, see Feldman 1988: 459–460).

view are the most significant ones. Then the question will be dealt with whether these agreements point to the use of an Aramaic version, or not. Finally, I will add some comments on the milieu of both Josephus and the authors of the Aramaic version, ascribed to Onkelos and Jonathan, examining whether they may share a common background.

II

A. *First, Examples of Specific Terms in Aramaic*

1. According to Exod. 28.39–40, the 'girdle' (אַבְנֵט) is part of the vestments for Aaron and his sons. Josephus: 'Moses gave it the name of abaneth (ἀβανήθ), but we have learnt from the Babylonians to call it hemian (ἐμίαν)' (Ant. 3.156). The latter word is the equivalent found in Tg Onk (המין).[5]

2. Other examples are the well-known cases of 'chaanaeae' (χααναίας) in Ant. 3.151, meaning 'the priests', a Hellenized form of Aramaic כהניא, and 'anarabaches' (ἀναραβάχης), ibid., signifying 'the high priest' (Aramaic כהנא רבא).

3. There is yet another term, to be found in Ant. 8.95 (and see B.J. 5.226, 228), which has not been discussed in this connection so far: γείσιον or γείσον. It refers to a parapet surrounding the temple, having a height of three cubits. It was built in order to keep the multitude from entering the court of the priests. Josephus tells us that it was called *geision* 'in the native tongue' (Ant. 8.95; 'and θριγκός by the Greeks'). The latter carries the meaning 'fence of any sort'. According to Maier the term *geision* is to be understood as being derived from the root חצה 'to divide' (Maier 1997: 153, 155). It seems to me more plausible, however, to regard *geision* as a Hellenized form of the Aramaic גויתא, which is part of the expression דרתא גויתא in Tg Ezek. 44.17, 'the inner court', i.e. the court of the priests.

4. In Ant. 3.252 it is stated that the Hebrews call the fiftieth day after the period of the forty-nine days of the 'Weeks', asartha (ἀσαρθά).

[5] The same is true for Tg Neof, but not for Tg PsJon.

Josephus then explains that this term, which is to be considered Aramaic, denotes 'fiftieth'. At first sight this may seem strange, but his remark is fully understandable because the word refers to the fiftieth day after Pesach, i.e. the concluding feast of the Pesach festival. This term, used this way, is also found in Tg Onk Num. 28.26. It reads 'On the day of the first fruits, when you present a new offering before the Lord at your *festive gathering* (עצרתא; MT: 'feast of weeks'); it should be a sacred occasion for you'. It here denotes a specific day, the day after having completed seven weeks (cf. PsJon). Notably, the equivalent in Hebrew (עֲצֶרֶת) can have the same meaning as is for example clear from a passage in the Mishnah (Hag. 2.4).

5. 1 Kgs. 4.7
In the section dealing with the provincial governors of Solomon (cf. 1 Kgs. 4.7), Josephus uses the Greek στρατηγός (Ant. 8.35). The same word, being borrowed from the Greek,[6] is employed in Tg 1 Kgs. 4.7: Solomon had twelve 'officers' put in charge of all Israel. The same term (אסטרטיג) also occurs at other places (e.g. verse 5; 5.7, 30; 9.23; 22.48).

B. *The Following Examples Are of an Exegetical Nature*

6. Josh. 2.1
Ant. 5.7–8: The spies went to Jericho, and retired to 'the inn' of Rahab;
Tg: the spies went to Rahab, 'the innkeeper' (MT: Rahab, 'the harlot').

Both share the same interpretation, based on the view that hostesses, keepers of public houses, were at the same time 'harlots'. However, in the case of the two harlots in 1 Kgs. 3.16 Josephus, speaking of 'harlots' like in MT, does not agree with the Tg ('innkeepers').

7. 1 Sam. 1.15
Ant. 5.345: 'But, on her replying that she had drunk but water and that it was for grief at lack of children that she was *making supplication* to God'.
Tg: 'Hannah: …I have not drunk. And I have told the sorrow of my soul *in prayer*' (MT: 'And I poured out my soul').

[6] Cf. Tal (1975: 178).

8. 1 Sam. 2.22
Ant. 5.339: 'the women who came for worship';
Tg: 'the women who came to pray (at the gate of the tent of meeting)' (MT: 'the women who were serving').

The same interpretation is found in Tg Onk Exod. 38.8.

9. 1 Kgs. 21.27
Ant. 8.362: Ahab went 'with bare feet';
Tg: 'And Ahab...was going about barefoot' (MT: 'softly').

10. 2 Kgs. 9.20
Ant. 9.117: 'Jehu was going along rather slowly and in good order';
Tg: 'Jehu...he is driving with gentleness' (MT: 'in madness').

11. 2 Kgs. 11.14
Ant. 9.151: the king (Joash) 'standing on the platform (ἐπὶ τῆς σκηνῆς)';
Tg: 'the king was standing upon the balcony' (MT: 'by the pillar').

The 'pillar' of MT presumably 'is imagined as supporting a balcony either in the Temple or the King's palace' (Harrington and Saldarini 1987: 310 n. 5). The Aramaic is similar to words used for the Temple portico found in Babylonian Talmud, Pes. 13b. According to Smolar and Aberbach (1983: 107) Tg 2 Kgs. 11.14 (and 23.3) refer to the royal portico in the Herodian temple (see e.g. Ant. 15.411).

The same interpretation is also found in Tg 2 Kgs. 23.3 ('And the king [Josiah] stood upon the balcony'). Cf. Josephus, Ant. 10.63: 'standing on the tribune', though the term used here is different from that in Ant. 9.151 (βῆμα cf. Ant. 4.209).

12. 2 Kgs. 25.18 (par. Jer. 52.24)
Ant. 10.149: 'the officers who guarded the temple';
Tg: 'the three temple-officers/trustees' (MT: 'the three keepers of the threshold').

It is to be noted that the Aramaic used here (pl. of אמרכל) is also the equivalent of the Hebrew phrase at other places in Tg Jon. (see Smolar and Aberbach 1983: 104).

13. Jer. 34.3
Tg: 'and you [Zedekiah] shall be carried to Babylon' (MT: 'you shall come'). The rendering may represent an attempt to harmonize the text

with Ezek. 12.13: MT 'I will bring him to Babylon...; he shall not see it'. The king could not see Babylon because he was blinded (see 2 Kgs. 25.7); hence, the rendering 'carried' in Jer. 34.3 (which, by the way, is not the same verb as in Tg Ezek. 12.13). The contradiction was also recognised by Josephus (Ant. 10.106–107, 141).[7]

14. Jer 31.38–40
The final part of Jer 31 is a prophecy in which the rebuilding of the city of Jerusalem is proclaimed. As has been noted by scholars the Aramaic version of this passage contains two elements which were prominent features of the Herodian city:[8]

Tg v. 38: 'Behold, the days are coming, says the Lord, when the city Jerusalem shall be rebuilt before the Lord, from the tower *of Piqqus* (MT: 'of Hananel')...'
Tg v. 40: 'And every valley...to the Wadi of Kidron, as far as the corner gate, the place of *the king's race-course* (MT: 'up to the corner gate of the horses') eastward, shall be holy for the Lord'

The tower of Piqqus (see also Tg Zech. 14.10) is called Hippicus in Greek. It is one of the towers built by Herod the Great, as we know from Josephus (*War 2.440; 5.161–165*). The second element, the race-course of the king, the hippodrome, is also mentioned by Josephus (B.J. 2.44; Ant. 17.255; see also Tg Onk Gen. 14.17).

There is yet another element in this passage that agrees with information given by Josephus, which seems not to have been noted so far. Tg v. 40 contains the following clause: 'And the whole valley, the place where the corpses of the armies of the Assyrian fell' (MT: 'And the whole valley of the corpses and the ashes'). The location referred to in the Tg is best understood as the place called by Josephus 'the Camp of the Assyrians' (*War 5.303, 504*), the place which was considered to be the site where the forces of Sennacherib were decimated (2 Kgs. 19.35).

15. Jer. 38.7
Ant. 10.122: 'in honour';
Tg: 'a mighty man' (MT: 'eunuch').

[7] See Hayward (1987: 143 note).
[8] See e.g. Hayward (1987: 35, 135).

16. Nah. 2.9–14
Informing the reader about the prophet Nahum, Josephus offers a paraphrase of a particular passage from the book of this prophet (Ant. 9.239–241), a paraphrase which is fairly close to the wording of the Hebrew text (Nah. 2.9–14). Scholars have noted that his reading of this passage contains two elements which are in line with the interpretation as found in the Targum.[9]

(a) Nah. 2.9 (final clause): 'but none turns back' (MT)
Ant. 9.239: 'But there will be no one willing' (that is to say, to stop and remain in order to seize gold and silver);
Tg: 'But there is no one who turns back and halts'.

Both share the same interpretation of the underlying Hebrew text, Tg being closer to it. For the plus 'and halts' in Tg, see Tg Jer. 46.5.[10]

(b) Nah. 2.11 (final clause): 'all faces grow pale' (MT)
Ant. 9.240: 'and their faces will be darkened with fear';
Tg: 'and all their faces are covered with a coating of black like a pot'.

Both have the idea of darkness, blackness of faces in common, based on the interpretation of Hebrew פָּארוּר equals פָּרוּר 'pot'. Notably, the expression in Tg also occurs in other places (Jer. 8.21; 14.2; Joel 2.6), partly based on the root (קדר in Jer. 8.21 and 14.2), partly on a Hebrew reading as in Nah. 2.11 (Joel 2.6).[11]

(c) Interestingly, there seems to be a third instance where Josephus and Tg go together, namely in v. 14 (MT: 'and the sword shall devour your young lions'):
Ant. 9.240: 'and no more shall lions go forth from thee to rule the world';
Tg: 'and the sword shall slay your princes'.

The (young) lions are understood as a metaphor for princes (Tg), as rulers of the world (Josephus), the difference being that Tg, as usual, renders the image word for word by its meaning, whereas Josephus makes the meaning explicit by adding the phrase 'to rule the world'.

[9] See Begg (1995: 5–22, and the literature cited there).
[10] As noted by Cathcart and Gordon (1989: 137).
[11] As noted by Cathcart and Gordon (1989: 137).

17. Hab. 1.16
MT: 'Therefore he sacrifices to his net and burns incense to his seine';
Tg: 'Therefore they sacrifice to their weapons and burn incense to their standards'.

Tg refers here to the Roman practice of *signa*-worship (Cathcart and Gordon 1989: 148). Although we do not know the way this text was understood by Josephus, there is clear evidence that this Roman practice was known to him. In B.J. 6.316 he tells about an event when, having captured the Jerusalem temple, the Romans 'carried their standards into the temple court and, setting them opposite the eastern gate, they sacrificed to them'.[12] Interestingly, the word used for 'standards' in both sources is the same since the Aramaic term (סימא) has been borrowed from the Greek (σημαία).[13]

In addition it may be noted that, as has been observed by scholars, 1QpHab. 6.3–5 offers an interpretation which is very much the same: 'they offer sacrifices to their standards and their weapons are the object of their worship'. There is a difference though, since in the Qumran pesher the choice of 'standards' represents an explanation of 'net' in the first part of the sentence, whereas in Tg the second part of the verse has been interpreted that way ('standards' for 'seine'). It is an interesting case of agreement between this writing of Qumran and Tg, but it does not seem to require the idea of Tg being dependent here on this text of Qumran, or the other way around.[14]

III

It should now to be asked whether the agreements presented above[15] do point to the use of a written Aramaic version by Josephus, as has been argued by scholars. To cite Brownlee, '[t]he evidence drawn from Josephus, well distributed through the historical books of the Prophetic canon, proves the existence of a targum in Josephus' day which

[12] Cf. Cathcart and Gordon (1989: 148).
[13] Cf. Hayward (1987: 19).
[14] See Cathcart and Gordon (1989: 149), and more in particular, Gordon (1994: 90–95). For the Semitic background of the Roman practice, see Dirven (2005).
[15] Scholars like Rappaport and Brownlee have noted other examples as well but most of them are less significant.

is organically related to the extant Targum of Jonathan' (Brownlee 1956: 182). This is, however, hardly plausible. First, the knowledge of specific words in Aramaic, such as the ones related to the temple, is best understood as being due to the fact that Josephus was familiar with Aramaic.[16] Second, the remaining cases are more easily explained as due to common exegesis since the evidence is very limited indeed and does not require the assumption of a written Tg. Furthermore, Josephus' version of Nah. 2.9–14 displays agreement with Tg at a few points only, whereas as a whole it is different from Tg.[17]

Moreover, if Josephus was making use of a written Aramaic version this would imply that in case of Tg Onk and Tg Jon these sources would already have been available to him. This too is difficult to accept as it is likely that both targums in written form were produced in the second century AD, and not in the first century AD. True, the dating issue is a complicated one, being based on one's assumptions regarding the type of Aramaic, on the one hand, and the historical allusions, on the other. It is interesting to note, however, that there is a growing consensus for dating these targumim before 200 AD, and that, as far as the language is concerned, scholars tend to date Tg Onk and Tg Jon—at least the body of them—in the first half of the second century (before 135 AD), with Palestine as the place of origin.[18]

IV

As to the idea that the agreements might have been due to common exegetical traditions rather than the use of a written Targumic source, I would finally like to raise the question of whether Josephus and the authors of our Targumic sources shared a particular milieu of Jewish scholarship.[19] If so, this would strengthen the hypothesis formulated above.

---

[16] See Rajak (1983: 174–184, 230–232); Gussmann (2008: 221–223).

[17] Cf. Begg 1995: 13–14.

[18] For an excellent discussion of this issue, see now Kuty 2010.

[19] It has been suggested that Josephus got the exegetical ideas by the oral targum in synagogal services (Feldman 1988: 458). The difficulty with this theory is the underlying idea that Tg Onk and Jon, as written targumim, were based on the practice of the oral targum. For a critical assessment of this view, see Smelik (1995: 35), and Van der Kooij (1999: 207).

The cases presented above, however, are mostly minor elements which do not provide any evidence for this idea. Yet there is a topic of a more general and fundamental significance shared by both Josephus and our Aramaic sources which favours the assumption of a common milieu of expertise and authority—the interpretation of prophecies by applying them to events in their own time.

A telling example concerns the view that the destruction of the city and the temple by the Romans in 70 AD was foretold by the ancient prophets: as to Josephus, see B.J. 6.109–110; Ant. 10.79 and 10.276, and as to Tg Jon, see e.g. Isa. 8.2; 29.1–2, and 32.14.[20] In the passages of Ant. 10 Josephus refers to Jeremiah, Ezekiel, and Daniel respectively. The passage in B.J. however contains a reference which is held to be uncertain (see e.g. Thackeray 1968: 406 n. b). At the end of his speech to John and the Jews, in August 70 AD, when the Romans were going to take the temple area, Josephus in trying to persuade his countrymen to surrender in order to prevent a pending disaster, argues as follows, 'Who knows not the records of the ancient prophets and that oracle which threatens this poor city and is even now coming true' (109). 'For', he continues, 'they foretold that it would then be taken whensoever one should begin to slaughter his own countrymen. And is not the city, aye and the whole temple, filled with your corpses?' (110). One wonders which 'records' and 'oracle' Josephus might have had in mind. I would suggest that he is referring here to 2 Kgs. 21. As to the 'records' one might think of v. 16 ('Manasseh shed very much innocent blood, till he had filled Jerusalem from one end to another'), and as to the 'oracle', it would make sense if one assumes that he thought of vv. 12–13 of the same chapter, which contain a prediction of the destruction of Jerusalem.

As to the suggestion of a common milieu, it is interesting to note that our sources—Josephus' works and Tg Jon—clearly indicate that this type of reading prophecies was the privilege of particular persons in early Judaism.

As is well known, for Josephus there is a strong relationship between prophets, prophecy and priesthood.[21] In Ant. 10.80 it is said, with some emphasis, that the prophets Jeremiah and Ezekiel were priests. As has been pointed out by scholars, Josephus being a member of an

[20] See Van der Kooij (1981: 170–173); Chilton (1987: 57, 63).

[21] See e.g. Mason (1991: 267–272); Gussmann (2008: 240–249, 297–304).

illustrious priestly family, saw himself as a prophet, in line with the ancient prophets, and in particular with Jeremiah.[22] 'As a priest', so he tells us in B.J.3.352, he was familiar with the interpretation of dreams and prophecies. In this connection he presents himself as follows: 'a priest himself and of priestly descent, he was not ignorant of the prophecies in the sacred books'.[23] The distinction made here, between being 'a priest' and being of priestly descent, is of great interest. This distinction is also found in the passage on Jeremiah and Ezekiel, referred to above (Ant. 10.80). Both prophets are said to be 'priests by birth', but unlike Ezekiel, Jeremiah had something extra as he 'lived in Jerusalem'. This seems to add to the authority of this prophet. This sheds light on the statement of Josephus: he was not only priest by birth, but also 'a priest', that is to say, 'a priest from Jerusalem' (*War 1.3*; cf. *Life 1–8*). In dealing with the issue of this distinction made by Josephus, Schwartz came to the conclusion that to be a priest from Jerusalem for Josephus 'was a matter of potential'.[24] This is true, but in my view it is possible to be more specific. To be a priest from Jerusalem was a matter of prestige and authority. The priests who were living in Jerusalem are likely to be seen as members of the priestly aristocracy, the milieu of the 'chief priests' (ἀρχιερεῖς) who held a most prominent position in the temple hierarchy. In distinction to other priests officiating in the temple, the chief priests had a *permanent* position,[25] and it, therefore, is understandable that they and their families were living in the city. Although we do not know whether Josephus himself ever was a member of the ruling body of chief priests, it seems clear that he belonged to the priestly nobility in Jerusalem.[26]

But what about the scholars who were responsible for Tg Onk and Tg Jon? Tg Jon in particular contains evidence that points to a close relationship between the type of interpretation referred to above and priesthood. To begin with, it is important to note that just as with Josephus, Jeremiah is presented in Tg Proph as a priest living in Jerusalem. Tg Jer. 1.1. reads thus:

---

[22] See e.g. Mason (1991: 271); Gussmann (2008: 295–296).

[23] See e.g. Mason (1991: 270). As to 'dreams and prophecies' compare Dan. 1.17 ('dreams and visions').

[24] Schwartz (1981: 135).

[25] See Jeremias (1976: 178–179).

[26] See Gussmann (2008: 203–205).

> The words of the prophecy of Jeremiah the son of Hilqiah, one of the heads of the service of the priests, of the temple officers who were in Jerusalem (...)

According to this text, the prophet Jeremiah belonged to the body of the 'chiefs of the service of the priests, the temple-officers' (pl. of אמרכל). Interestingly, the phrase 'the priests' in MT has been interpreted here as a reference to the leading priests in the temple. The designation 'the chiefs of the service of the priests' is to be equated with the phrase 'the chiefs of the priests' as attested in writings from Qumran (see e.g. 1QM 2.1). These leading priests are also called, in our text, 'the temple-officers'. As I have argued elsewhere these 'officers' are best understood as the priests who in sources of the time are designated as ἀρχιερεῖς 'chief priests'.[27] Thus, unlike MT, Jeremiah is seen here as belonging to the leading priests of the temple (see above). Presumably, this is based on the view that Hilqiah was considered to be the same as the high priest at the time of king Josiah (2 Kgs. 22.8). In the light of our discussion about Josephus being a priest from Jerusalem, the final clause in the Aramaic version, 'who were in Jerusalem', is significant. Tg attests the idea that the leading priests were the ones who lived in the city. In comparison to Josephus, it seems that Tg is slightly more specific since it says that Jeremiah was not only a priest living in Jerusalem, but also someone who belonged to the body of the chief priests of the temple. Be this as it may, the view of Jeremiah as a most important priest is just another case of agreement between Josephus and Tg Jon. Both try to enhance the authority of Jeremiah by claiming that he belonged to the priestly aristocracy of Jerusalem.

The term 'prophet' is, however, not only used for a prophet in the past, like Jeremiah. It is also used for someone who is able to 'interpret' prophecies as is clear from Tg Isa. 21.11b:

> He calls upon me from the heavens:
> Prophet, interpret for them the prophecy;
> Prophet, interpret for them what is about to come

The prophet is the one who by interpreting prophecies can tell what is 'about to come'. Both Aramaic versions, Onk and Jon, are marked by this type of interpretation. Examples are to be found in Gen. 49; Judg. 5; 1 Sam. 2, and 2 Sam. 23, and of course in the books of the ancient

[27] Van der Kooij (1981: 201–202).

prophets (Isaiah, Jeremiah, Ezekiel, and the Twelve). By telling what is about to come he announces, among other things, the 'consolations' to the people, more in particular to the righteous (see e.g. Tg Isa. 8.2; 18.4; 40.1; 62.12). The good news to be told by the prophet/interpreter is that Jerusalem 'is about to be filled with people of her exiles' (Isa. 40.2), or as Tg Isa. 54.1 put it:

> Sing, O Jerusalem who was a barren woman who did not bear; shout in singing and exult, [you who were] as a woman who did not become pregnant! For the children of desolate Jerusalem will be more than the children of inhabited Rome, says the Lord.[28]

Since the Targumic versions testify to this type of interpretation, it is reasonable to assume that their authors were 'prophets'.

This leads to the question of who are these 'prophets'. This is a complex issue as far as our Targumic sources are concerned, but the following brief discussion may suffice for the sake of argument. To begin with, it is important to note that in Tg Jon the prophets are clearly distinguished from the 'scribes'. So for instance in Tg Isa. 29.10:

> the prophets, the scribes, and the teachers

This listing of authorities reflects a hierarchy of scholars. The 'prophet 'is the one who has the ability and authority of the interpretation of prophecies, something which as far as Tg Jon is concerned does not apply to the 'scribe', the latter being the teacher of the written Law (cf. e.g. Tg Judg. 5.9). Of the 'teachers it is said in our text that they 'were teaching you the teaching (אולפן) of the Law', that is to say, it was their task to teach the oral Law.[29]

The 'prophets' apparently are to be regarded as the highest rank of scholars, thus carrying the highest authority. As Tg Jer. 1.1 suggests there is reason to believe that the 'prophets' are to be equated with the chief priests, the 'temple officers' in the terminology of the targum.[30] This is actually the way they are presented in the Didache (13.3): 'the prophets, for they are your chief priests'. This sheds light on the fact that in all instances where MT refers to 'priests and prophets' in the

[28] See also Tg 1 Sam. 2.5b!

[29] See Van der Kooij (1981: 199). For a comparable listing of authorities from a rabbinic perspective, see m.Sot. 9.15. This passage distinguishes, in descending order, between 'sages', 'scribes/teachers', and 'pupils' (variant: 'synagogue-servants').

[30] See Van der Kooij (1981: 197–200).

temple, Tg Jon always offers the rendering 'priests and *scribes*' (see e.g. 2 Kgs. 23.2; Jer. 6.13; 14.18; 18.18). The term 'priest' here is parallel to the term 'prophet' in the list appearing in Tg Isa. 29.10 quoted above, yielding the following correspondences:

'priests' and 'scribes'
'prophets' and 'scribes'.

It thus seems that 'priest' and 'prophet' were taken as persons of the same rank, namely, as the ones making up the body of the leading priests of the temple. Notably, this is in line with the expression 'the chief priests and the scribes' to be found in the New Testament (see e.g. Mt. 20.18; 21.15; Mk 10.33). This picture explains, in my view, why the term 'prophet' as found in the expression 'priests and prophets' in MT has been translated 'priests and scribes' in Tg Jon.[31] Several suggestions have been made as to the rendering 'scribe' for 'prophet' in a number of passages in Tg Jon,[32] but without taking into account the issue of the hierarchy involved.

All in all, Josephus and the authors responsible for Tg Jon—and Tg Onk as well, in my view—belonged to the milieu of the leading priests, scholars who were able and authorized to interpret prophecies by applying them to their own time. They were considered the appropriate authorities for this way of reading the ancient prophecies, very much so as with another figure of great authority—the priest designated as Teacher of Righteousness in the writings of Qumran. This common milieu may help explain the common features—Aramaic terminology, exegetical ideas—between both sources discussed in this paper.

References

Attridge, H.W. 1976. *The Interpretation of Biblical History in the Antiquitates Judaicae of Flavius Josephus* (Missoula: Scholars Press).

——. 1984. 'Josephus and his works', in *Jewish Writings of the Second Temple Period. Apocrypha, Pseudepigrapha, Qumran Sectarian Writings, Philo, Josephus* (ed. M.E. Stone; CRINT Section Two, II; Assen: Van Gorcum; Philadelphia: Fortress Press) 185–232.

Begg, C. 1995. 'Josephus and Nahum Revisited', *Revue des Études Juives* 154: 5–22.

[31] Cf. Hayward (1987: 36–37).

[32] See Van Staalduine-Sulman (2002: 150 and the literature cited there).

Brownlee, W.H. 1956. 'The Habakkuk Midrash and the Targum of Jonathan', *Journal of Jewish Studies* 7: 169–186.

Cathcart, K.J., and R.P. Gordon. 1989. *The Targum of the Minor Prophets. Translated, with a Critical Introduction, Apparatus, and Notes* (The Aramaic Bible, 14; Edinburgh: T. & T. Clark).

Chilton, B.D. 1987. *The Isaiah Targum. Introduction, Translation, Apparatus and Notes* (The Aramaic Bible, 11; Edinburgh: T. & T. Clark).

Dirven, L. 2005. 'ΣΗΜΗΙΟΝ, SMY', SIGNUM. A Note on the Romanization of the Semitic Cultic Standard', *Parthica* 7: 119–136.

Feldman, L.H. 1984. *Josephus and Modern Scholarship (1937–1980)* (Berlin: de Gruyter).

——. 1988. 'Use, Authority and Exegesis of Mikra in the Writings of Josephus', in *Mikra. Text, Translation, Reading and Interpretation of the Hebrew Bible in Ancient Judaism and Early Christianity* (ed. M.J. Mulder, executive editor H. Sysling; Compendia Rerum Iudaicarum ad Novum Testamentum, Section Two, I; Assen/Maastricht: Van Gorcum; Philadelphia: Fortress Press) 455–518.

Glessmer, U. 1995. *Einleitung in die Targume zum Pentateuch* (Texte und Studien zum antiken Judentum, 48; Tübingen: Mohr Siebeck).

Gordon, R.P. 1994. *Studies in the Targum to the Twelve Prophets. From Nahum to Malachi* (Supplements to Vetus Testamentum, 51; Leiden: Brill).

Gussmann, O. 2008. *Das Priesterverständnis des Flavius Josephus* (Texte und Studien zum antiken Judentum, 124; Tübingen: Mohr Siebeck).

Harrington, D.J., and A.J. Saldarini. 1987. *Targum Jonathan of the Former Prophets. Introduction, Translation and Notes* (The Aramaic Bible, 10; Edinburgh: T. & T. Clark).

Hayward, R. 1987. *The Targum of Jeremiah. Translated, with a Critical Introduction, Apparatus, and Notes* (The Aramaic Bible, 12; Edinburgh: T. & T. Clark).

Jeremias, J. 1976. *Jerusalem in the Time of Jesus. An Investigation into Economic and Social Conditions during the New Testament Period* (third impression; London: SCM Press).

Kuty, R.J. 2010. *Studies in the Syntax of Targum Jonathan to Samuel* (Ancient Near Eastern Studies Supplement Series, 30; Leuven: Peeters).

Maier, J. 1997. *Die Tempelrolle vom Toten Meer und das "Neue Jerusalem"* (3. Aufl.; Uni-Taschenbücher, 829; München, Basel: Ernst Reinhardt).

Marcus, R. 1966. *Josephus in Nine Volumes V: Jewish Antiquities, Books V–VIII* (reprint of 1934; Loeb Classical Library, 281; London: Heinemann Ltd; Cambridge, Massachusetts: Harvard University Press).

Mason, S. 1991. *Flavius Josephus on the Pharisees. A Composition-Critical Study* (Studia Post-Biblica, 39; Leiden: Brill).

Piovanelli, P. 1992. 'Le texte de Jérémie utilisé par Flavius Josèphe dans le Xe livre des Antiquités Judaïques', *Henoch* 14: 11–33.

Rajak, T. 1983. *Josephus. The Historian and His Society* (London: Duckworth).

Rappaport, S. 1930. *Agada und Exegese bei Flavius Josephus* (Frankfurt am Main: Kaufmann).

Schalit, A. 1967. *Introduction to the Hebrew Translation of the Antiquities* (Jerusalem: Mosad Bialik).

Schwartz, D.R. 1981. 'Priesthood and Priestly Descent: Josephus, *Antiquities* 10.80', *Journal of Theological Studies* 32: 129–135.

Smelik, W.F. 1995. *The Targum of Judges* (Oudtestamentische Studiën, 36; Leiden: Brill).

Smolar, L., and M. Aberbach. 1983. *Studies in Targum Jonathan to the Prophets, and Targum to the Prophets by P. Churgin* (Library of Biblical Studies; New York and Baltimore: Ktav and The Baltimore Hebrew College).

Tal (Rosenthal), A. 1975. *The Language of the Targum of the Former Prophets and its Position within the Aramaic Dialects* (Texts and Studies in the Hebrew Language and Related Subjects, 1; Tel Aviv: Tel Aviv University).
Thackeray, H.St.J. 1929. *Josephus, the Man and the Historian* (New York: Jewish Institute of Religion Press).
——. 1968. *Josephus in Nine Volumes, III: The Jewish War, Books IV–VII* (reprint of 1928; Loeb Classical Library, 210; London: Heinemann Ltd.; Cambridge, Massachusetts: Harvard University Press).
Van der Kooij, A. 1981. *Die alten Textzeugen des Jesajabuches. Ein Beitrag zur Textgeschichte des Alten Testaments* (Orbis Biblicus et Orientalis, 35; Freiburg: Universitätsverlag; Göttingen: Vandenhoeck & Ruprecht).
——. 1999. 'The Origin and Purpose of Bible Translations in Ancient Judaism: Some Comments', *Archiv für Religionsgeschichte* 1: 204–214.
Van Staalduine-Sulman, E. 2002. *The Targum of Samuel* (Studies in the Aramaic Interpretation of Scripture, 1; Leiden: Brill).

THE TARGUMS: TEL-LIKE CHARACTER AND A CONTINUUM

Martin McNamara

In choosing a subject for an essay in the Festschrift in honour of Robert Gordon I opt for the Targums, in view of Professor Gordon's major contributions to this field of research and to fruitful cooperation with him over a number of years. One of Robert's major contributions to Targum research is his work on the Targum of the Twelve Prophets, from Nahum to Malachi, first as his doctoral dissertation (1973) and later (1994) in book form. This was an ideal preparation for his work, in conjunction with Kevin J. Cathcart, for the annotated translation of the Targum of the Minor Prophets in *The Aramaic Bible* series (Cathcart and Gordon 1989). In his review of this volume, and critical of the earlier volumes of the *Aramaic Bible* series, Stephen Kaufman (1992), wrote:

> The authors demonstrate great familiarity with the (non-Hebrew) secondary literature. A survey of quite a few randomly selected passages failed to reveal any serious errors of translation, even in heavily augmented passages, though minor syntactic distinctions are regularly ignored. In short, this is the first volume of the series that I intend to keep on my reference shelf. I hope the remaining volumes of the series can approach its level!!

In this essay I propose to follow up on work done and suggestions made by Robert, in keeping with my own work and interest in Targum study, which has been and is predominantly the possible bearing of the Targums on the understanding of the New Testament. In this I intend to pay attention to the 'tell-like structure' of Targums, works with possible snippets of interpretations from different ages set side by side. At the same time I will try ascertain whether in some, or in a number of, cases a line of continuity can be traced for traditions and interpretations.

Targumic study is currently in a flourishing state, with no particular interest, however, in their bearing on the New Testament. In 1992 an international conference on 'The Aramaic Bible: Targums in their Historical Context' was held in Dublin, at the Royal Irish Academy. At the end of this conference a resolution was passed to explore the possibility of setting up an international organization for Targum study, with regular meetings, and the task was given to Ernest Clarke, Emeritus Professor of the University of Toronto, to explore what possibilities there were for this. This he did very effectively with the executive of the International Organization for the Study of the Old Testament (IOSOT), and at the next meeting of this body, at Cambridge, in 1995 the International Organization for Targumic Studies (IOTS) was formally erected at Fitzwilliam College, and Ernest Clarke was elected by acclamation as its first president. Death was to take him two years later. The new organization (IOTS) meets every three years in conjunction with IOSOT, and reads papers concerned with various aspects of Targum study, and discusses plans for critical editions of Targums.

Emphasis on what aspect of the Targums is being studied can vary from one period to another. In the thirties, forties, fifties, sixties and in part the seventies of the last century it was the Palestinian Targum of the Pentateuch and its presumed bearing on the language spoken by Jesus and on the interpretation of the New Testament. This Targum and its form of Aramaic were presumed to represent the language and cultural situation of New Testament and Galilee. Matters changed later, particularly after the Qumran Aramaic finds, and as already mentioned, less attention is now paid to the New Testament connection by many scholars.

Those who do so must present a methodology justifying their use of this material. Two scholars in particular have clearly expressed opinions of this matter: Bruce Chilton and Geza Vermes. The former has written extensively on the Targums (particularly the Targum of Isaiah) and the New Testament, and due to his work the value of targumic evidence even for studies on the historical Jesus is recognized.[1] An obvious requirement in a contemporary study of the issue is a clear indication of the methodology being used. All agree that it is not a question of the New Testament being dependent on the Targums (or rabbinic tradition) but rather both being witnesses to an earlier Jewish tradition. Chilton and Vermes each present their understanding of the approach to be taken. In 1994 Bruce Chilton published an essay with eight theses on the use of Targums in interpreting the New

[1] E.g. by Evans (2001: 155–181).

Testament.[2] In these he stresses strongly the late, post-New Testament, date of the Targums. In thesis (1) he notes that the Targums generally were composed after, and without reference to the paramount concerns of, the New Testament. They are post-135/136 CE. The destruction of the Temple (definitively in 135–136 CE) and the consequent crisis in eschatological hope in the restoration of Israel caused the Aramaic interpreters, as representatives of rabbinic Judaism, to confront afresh what the choice of Israel, the Davidic promise, the Temple itself, the coming of the messiah, the predictions of the prophets, and the commands of Torah might mean; (2) the targumic agenda is essentially rabbinic. Rabbis were concerned with how scripture was rendered in the synagogues, and were in the end responsible for the Targums as they can be read today, instancing the presentation of Genesis 22 in the Palestinian Targumim as providing an instance of exegesis comparable to the rabbinic understanding of the passage; (3) within early and Rabbinic Judaism, the provenience and programme of the Targumim are variegated (from Onqelos to Targum Esther); (4) there are no 'Palestinian', 'pre-Christian' Targumim. Elements within the Targumim may arguably antedate, or be contemporaneous with, documents of the New Testament, but such a case remains always to be made, and may not be assumed; (5) a targumic approach to the New Testament is to be distinguished from an Aramaic approach. In view of their history, the Targums are of less moment for reconstructing the dialect of Jesus than are the discoveries at Qumran, Naḥal Ḥever and Murabbaʿāt; (6) a Targum of a date later than the New Testament might, on occasion, represent a tradition which was current in the period of the New Testament, albeit not in a targumic context (instancing Pseudo-Jonathan Lev. 22.18 and Lk. 6.36 ('be merciful…'); (7) on rare occasions, a Targum might provide us with a tradition which was—at the time of the New Testament—already of an exegetical nature (instancing Targum Isa. 6.9, 10 in relation to Mk. 4.12). His final thesis (no. 8) is that the Targums instance not only traditions which may be reflected in the New Testament, but a process of conveying these traditions which might be illuminating. Once the history of targumic development is reckoned with, it becomes obvious that their greatest use for the student of the New Testament lies in their provision, not of antecedents, but analogies.

[2] Chilton (1994: 305–315). See also Chilton (2000).

In 1982 Geza Vermes contributed a major essay on reflections and methodology regarding Jewish literature and New Testament exegesis.[3] In the course of this essay Vermes gives his reaction to Joseph Fitzmyer's contention that Qumran Aramaic (and the Aramaic of first century CE tomb and ossuary inscriptions) 'must be the latest Aramaic that should be used for philological comparison of the Aramaic substratum of the Gospels and Acts' (Vermes 1982: 364–368), including consideration of κορβᾶν, μαμωνᾶς, and ὁ υἱὸς τοῦ ἀνθρώπου. He then passes on to the question of methodology. Vermes outlines four possibilities for explaining the similarities between the New Testament and Jewish Literature: (1) coincidence, (2) rabbinic borrowing from the New Testament, (3) New Testament dependence on the Targum or midrash, and (4) a New Testament passage and a targumic/rabbinic text have their source in 'Jewish traditional teaching' (Vermes 1982: 372–373). Vermes prefers the fourth option, namely, that convergences between the New Testament and the Targum reflect a common Jewish tradition. Vermes believes that instead of looking at the New Testament as an independent unit set against a background of Judaism, we have to see it as part of a larger environment of Jewish religious and cultural history (Vermes 1982: 374–375).

Dating Targums and Targumic Traditions

A balanced approach to the question of a relationship between targumic tradition and the New Testament requires close cooperation between New Testament scholars and specialists in the field of Targum study, each working, as is indicated, according to the principles of their own field of specialization. One major question throughout any such enquiry is whether a given Targum, or targumic tradition, can be assigned a pre-70 CE date, or appears to be later.

With regard to the Targum of the Prophets (specifically that of the Minor Prophets) we have a model in the researches of Robert Gordon in his *Studies in the Targum to the Twelve Prophets from Nahum to Malachi* (Gordon 1994), evidence presented anew with exceptional clarity and an economy of words in his annotated translation, in conjunction with Kevin J. Cathcart, of the *Targum of the Minor Prophets*

[3] Vermes (1982).

(Cathcart and Gordon 1989). In the first of these works Gordon studies various aspects of the Targums in question in the course of ten chapters and in a final chapter gives a summary and prospectus. He examines historical allusions in seven texts in Tg Twelve Prophets (chapter 2) and makes a detailed study of the Land and the *Shekinah* in the same Targum (chapter 9). In his summary he notes that the main chapters in this monograph reflect in a variety of ways on the origin and development of Tg Twelve Prophets. It is perhaps also to be expected, he remarks, that the majority of the historical indicators fall on this side of the 70 CE divide. Most of the seven texts examined in ch. 2 are compatible with a dating in the Tannaitic [to 200 CE]/ Amoraic period(s). He also notes that there are clear expressions of a post-70 CE diaspora perspective in certain texts which deal with the topics of land and *Shekinah* (ch. 9) (Gordon 1994: 150–51).

In their introduction to the translation of the Targum in the *Aramaic Bible* series, Kevin Cathcart and Robert Gordon express the same position more forcefully, in the section devoted to 'Dating' (Cathcart and Gordon: 16–18). They write:

> Even if, as is often assumed, *Tg.* Prophets had an oral prehistory, it obviously assumed literary form at some point, and, no matter what elements may survive from the prehistory, it is the historical circumstances in which the literary crystallization occurred that we should expect to find most truly reflected in the text. It is indeed possible to point to occasional features of *Tg.* Minor Prophets which seem to be more satisfactorily explained on the basis of a pre-AD 70 date of origin, as when, for example, some have attempted to make out a case from the midrashic equating of 'Lebanon' with 'nations' in Zech 11:1, or as might be concluded for Mal 3:6, which is more than a little redolent of the sectarian controversies in the late Second Temple period. Such claims, however, can seldom, if ever, be demonstrated with anything approaching absolute certainty, and the same has to be said of attempts to show the dependence of the Qumran Habakkuk Commentary (lQpHab) upon an early version of *Tg.* Habakkuk. The pursuit of SecondTemple elements in *Tg.* is a legitimate one, but it is important that enthusiasm for 'early' features should not be allowed to distort the overall picture.
>
> There are, on the other hand, fairly clear indications of a post-AD. 70 origin for various *Tg.* references, especially in relation to the two topics of the *Šekinah* and 'the land'.

They conclude the section on the date of the Targum as follows:

> To conclude this section: unless the short survey above is unrepresentative of *Tg.* Prophets as a whole, the preponderance of evidence points

> to the period after AD 70 as that when significant work of composition or editing of *Tg.* Prophets was carried out. There is indication enough of compositional, or at the least redactional, activity after AD 70: how much evidence is there to suggest the same for the earlier period?

Tel-Like Character of Targums

In the 'Prospectus', after his final summary, Robert Gordon takes note of some recent developments and makes suggestions as to possible profitable new approaches (Gordon 1994: 151–153). The relationship of Tg Twelve to the remainder of Tg Prophets, and indeed the relationship of individual books within Tg Twelve Prophets to one another and to other parts of Tg Prophets, may also prove worthy of investigation, the multiple signs of interconnectedness among various Targums notwithstanding. He notes the observations of some scholars on the distinctiveness of Jeremiah and Ezekiel among the Major Prophets. He goes on to remark that some differences between the lexical stock of Tg Former Prophets and that of Tg Latter Prophets have been observed by A. Tal, while in the very specific case of the targumic rendering of the Hebrew *nws* ('flee') Bernard Grossfeld has pinpointed a significant difference between these divisions of Tg prophets in that the verb *ʾpk*, which occurs frequently (50 times) in Tg Former Prophets as a translation of *nws*, is not found at all in Tg Latter Prophets. Grossfeld's explanation is that Tg latter Prophets is older than its stable-mate, and that *ʾpk* had not yet begun to replace *ʿrq* ('flee') by the time of its completion. Gordon notes that while there is definite promise in the lexical approach, *a sensitivity to the tel-like character of Tg is required in such investigation, since the extant text probably includes stratified elements representing as much as several centuries of Targumic development* (Gordon 1994: 152).

This is a very important insight with regard to Targums, an acknowledgement that there may be a deeper dimension in a targumic tradition than redactional features, lexical phenomena or others. The principle of tel-like character, one may observe, will probably not hold for any Targum in general, but for specific texts within it, not apparently for sections of targums that are plain translations of the Hebrew text. In a tel there are layers from various ages, sometimes deposited in chronological sequence but occasionally with disturbed stratification. When applying the principle to Targums it may be best to take each Targum as we now have it. Some elements of this may represent anonymous hermeneutical activity, whose origins can no longer be traced. Other elements will be regarded, at least by some scholars, as due to redactional activity and intentional additions after the basic Aramaic translation had been made. Some of the additions are often regarded as developments from an already expanded targumic paraphrase.

In this context it may be well to note that a tel-like character should not be restricted to Targums alone. It can be regarded as applicable to any hermeneutical and exegetical tradition, whether it be oral or written. The Targums originated and were given their present form in such a tradition. Most of this tradition continued to develop in rabbinic and other circles, to emerge later in writing in extra-biblical and the rabbinic works. For this reason it may well be that additions made to a completed Targum need not necessarily be later in time than this Targum. They may be early exegetical traditions, even if added later to the targumic work or text.

A tel-like character of a Targum need not surprise us. We find it already in the Hebrew Bible, more noticeable in some books than in others. The Book of the Prophet Isaiah is apparently built up of texts and blocks of material dating from the time of the eighth-century prophet to about 400 BCE if not later. A first division (Isa. chs. 1–39) has material dealing with the named prophet Isaiah; a second (chs. 40–55) is from late exilic times, and a third (chs. 56–66) comprises collections from post-exilic times. And yet the first section has material (ch. 35) that properly would belong to the second, Deutero-Isaiah. And it may well be that the 'sealed book' spoken of in Isa. 29.11–12 refers to the entire book of Isaiah itself as a whole, or at least to that book in whatever shape it existed at the time of writing (Blenkinsopp 2006: 12).

In a work such as Targum Prophets, with only a single text to work on, tel-like texts are less easy to identify. I believe we have one in Tg Hos. 6.2, where the Hebrew text 'After two days he will revive us, on the third day he will raise us up that we may live before him' (rendering of NRSV) is translated in the Targum (expansions denoted by italics):

> He will give us life *in the days of consolation that will come; on the day of the resurrection of the dead* he will raise us up and we shall live before him.

In the text of Hosea 'after two days' and 'on the third day' are intended to express a short space of time. The targumist paraphrases these as the future days of consolation and of the resurrection, rendering 'after two days' as 'in the days of consolation that will come', and translating 'on the third day' as 'on the day of the resurrection of the dead'. In Tg Hosea the biblical text is simply paraphrased from what must be Jewish tradition. The expected future is referred to as 'the determined time of blessing and consolation' in the Palestinian Targums (Gen. 49.1). Interpretation of 'the third day' as that of the resurrection may have been helped by the immediate context of Hosea with mention of 'showers', 'spring rain', terms which recall 'dew', understood in rabbinic tradition as an indication of the resurrection (see Isa. 26.19). It must have also been helped by rabbinic reflection on the various occurrences of the words 'third day' in the Bible, all of which were seen to have been salvific: thus Gen. 22.4; 42.17; Exod. 19.6; Josh. 2.16; Hos. 6.2; Jon. 2.1; Esth. 9.2.

In Tg Hos. 6.2 the biblical text has vanished, being replaced by what was most probably reckoned as the original meaning. It may be in this form that it was known and used in New Testament times. This would explain how in the New Testament Christ is said to have been raised on the third day *in accordance with the scriptures* (1 Cor. 15.3–4). It was written that the Christ was to suffer and to rise from the dead *on the third day* (Lk. 24.46).[4]

There is another Targum text in which the Hebrew text as known to us completely disappears to be replaced by paraphrase. It is the Palestinian Tg Num. 21.17–18 where a series of place names is replaced by the midrash of the well that was said to follow Israel during the desert wanderings. It is a well-attested Jewish tradition, referred to by Paul (1 Cor. 10.4), apparently a very early literary artefact preserved in the tel of targumic and early Jewish tradition (McNamara 2010a: 416–418 = McNamara 2011: 507–509).

Returning to Tg Prophets, we may well have very early elements in the mention of the 'second death' in Tg Isa. 22.14, 65.5–6, 65.15 and in Tg Jer. 51.39 (and in all the Tgs of Deut. 33.6). The phrase also occurs in the New Testament: Rev. 2.11; 20.6,14; 21.8 (McNamara 2010b: 223–227).

[4] See further McNamara (2010a: 414–416; 2010b: 206–208).

The Targums of the Pentateuch present a greater opportunity for the study of development and redaction of a Targum tradition, by reason of the multiplicity of texts (Onqelos, Pseudo-Jonathan, Neofiti, Fragment Targums, Genizah Palestinian Targum texts, Targumic Toseftot). It is not always clear whether with regard to extant Palestinian Targum texts we have to do with the formation of a tradition, the conscious redaction of an earlier written Targum or some other phenomenon. With regard to Targum Neofiti, for instance, there appears to be more than one level in the text. B. Barry Levy notes that in Neofiti, together with a literal rendition of the text, there are many passages that were added to it in the course of its development and were not part of the original translation, which undoubtedly differed from the present document. The evidence for this claim comes from the literary layering in the text (the seams are, in many cases, still evident) and the linguistic differences evidenced in it. These passages range in size from a word or phrase to a column of text. In his view, while Neofiti may be assumed to contain some older ideas, the bulk of it dates well past the first century CE, and in its final form it appears to be from the Talmudic period (post 200 CE).[5]

The examination of the Palestinian Targum evidence from this point of view will become much easier with the compilation of a synoptic presentation of the Pentateuchal Targums, a task now rendered much easier with the completion of the English translation of all the works.[6] A few examples will illustrate the tel-like character of these texts.

The *'Aqeda* midrash on the 'Sacrifice of Isaac' (on Gen. 22) is an old and probably pre-70 tradition. It is found in the Pal. *Tg.* Gen. 22.10, 14. ending with a prayer to God to remember Israel in their hour of distress. It is recalled again in Pal. *Tg.* Lev. 22.27 (on an ox, a sheep or a goat as an offering), in a paraphrase introduced with the words: 'Recall in our favour our offering which we used to offer and atonement was made for our sins. But now that we have nothing to offer of our flocks of sheep, atonement can be made for our sins... [T]he lamb was chosen to recall the merit of a man, the unique one, who was bound on one of the mountains like a lamb for a burnt offering upon

[5] Levy (1986) and Levy (1987). For a summary of his position see Levy (1986: viii–ix).

[6] See McNamara (2002: 3–27).

the altar…'. The tradition and prayer as presented here seem to have a definite post-70 CE setting.

Part of the prayer ending the *'Aqeda* midrash is a plea to God to remember Israel in her 'hour of distress'—the word rendered 'distress' translating any of three distinct Aramaic terms. This expression, 'hour of distress' is also found in Tamar's prayer in a midrash in Tg Gen. 38.25. The phrase is found in all texts of the Palestinian Targums in these two passages. It is found in Neofiti alone seven times outside of these midrashim, once (Nf Deut. 20.19) in relation to a tree under siege. These occurrences may represent additions in Tg Neofiti.[7]

We have a clearer instance of an addition at Gen. 38.35 (again in the midrash on Tamar) where all the Pal. *Tg.* texts simply say that Tamar asked for the three witnesses but could not find them. Two Cairo Genizah Targum texts (MS X and MS FF; both paper manuscripts, mid-11th to late 14th century) add to this: '(She sought the three witnesses but did not find them;) for Samael [= Satan or Angel of Death] had come and concealed them from her'.[8] Doubts can immediately be raised as to whether these texts belong to the original Palestinian Targum since Samael is not otherwise mentioned in the Targums of the Pentateuch and does not appear within rabbinic literature until after the fifth century. This particular tradition on Samael is quite similar to that found in *b. Sot.* 10b, suggesting that this appears to be a later addition to the Palestinian Targum tradition. This becomes all the more probable when it is recognized that the two Genizah manuscripts do not represent Palestinian Targum proper, but rather targumic Toseftot.[9]

More examples of additions to the Palestinian Targum, whether of single words, phrases, or entire traditions (e.g. the midrash on the tree, *'Ešel*, Abraham planted at Beersheba, Gen. 21.33) could be added, but I believe sufficient texts have been given to illustrate the tel-like character of the targumic tradition.

---

7 See further McNamara (2010a: 418–422; 2010b: 215–219).

8 Aramaic texts and English translation in Klein (1986: 90–91).

9 See Klein (1986: vol. 1, xxvi–xxvii; xxxvii) regarding dating.

A Continuum: Targums and Formation of Late Second Temple Judaism

(i) *Parallels and Parallelomania*

In 1961 Professor Samuel Sandmel gave the Presidential Address at the annual meeting of the Society of Biblical Literature and Exegesis on the topic 'Parallelomania'. This was duly published under the same title (Sandmel 1962) and has remained a very influential treatment of the topic and the dangers inherent in drawing parallels between Jewish writings and the New Testament. For his purpose Sandmel defines parallelomania as 'that extravagance among scholars which first overdoes the supposed similarity in passages and then proceeds to describe source and derivation as if implying literary connection flowing in an inevitable or predetermined direction' (Sandmel 1962: 1). He confines his observations to the areas of rabbinic literature and the gospels, Philo and Paul, and the Dead Sea Scrolls and the New Testament. His restrictions with regard to the use of rabbinic parallels have to do in good part with the material assembled by Strack-Billerbeck and its use. In relation to Paul and rabbinic texts Sandmel asks us to assume that at no less than 259 places, Paul's epistles contain acknowledged parallels to passages in the rabbis, but goes on to deny that this hypothetical situation implies that Paul and the rabbis are in thorough agreement. He acknowledges that it was right for the scholarship of two hundred and a hundred years ago to have gathered the true and the alleged parallels, but today it is a fruitless quest to continue to try to find elusive rabbinic sources for everything which Paul wrote.

The points made by Sandmel were well taken when first made, and are still timely. They do not, however, take from the need of pursuing parallels between a Jewish writing and a New Testament text in the interest of seeing how genuine they are, and, if genuine, seeking an explanation for the parallels, without in any way implying direct influence and without denying due differences between the two bodies of literature.

(ii) *Idea of a Continuum*

We have seen above the approaches of Bruce Chilton and Geza Vermes on the relation of Targum to the New Testament. Other writers express the same idea in slightly different terminology. Thus Craig S. Keener in his recent work on John's Gospel devotes an entire excursus to a discussion of the value of rabbinic texts for Johannine study (Keener 2003: vol. 1, 185–194). In a review of the minimalist and maximalist positions he notes that a minimalist position necessarily excludes much data that reflect a general cultural continuum valuable for such studies as those of the Johannine tradition (Keener 2003: vol. 1, 190). A view expressed by rabbis can be used provided it is a view that the rabbis could have derived from the broader continuum of early Judaism. He notes that in his commentary rabbinic literature is treated as one useful strand of evidence by which we seek to reconstruct the broader cultural and social milieu of early Judaism—not as if implying that the New Testament borrows from rabbinic tradition, but that notable commonalities probably reflect a common source in early Judaism or at times in the generally Pharisaic movement of scholars that coalesced into rabbinic Judaism (Keener 2003: vol. 1, 188–187). He also wisely observes that 'if sayings or ideas rapidly became the property of the community, their sources could be more ancient than the specific rabbis who first cited them or to whom they were attributed (from whom those reporting them first heard the account)' (Keener 2003: vol. 1, 189).

In what follows I intend to examine some passages in which parallels between New Testament texts and targumic or rabbinic tradition seem best explained through the continuum of tradition we are considering.

(iii) *Ephesians 4.8 and Targum Psalms 67(68).19*[10]

In Eph. 4.7–8 the author explains to the Christian church in Asia how the unity of the Church is the gift of Christ. Reigning in heaven after his ascension the Risen Saviour grants to the Church the gifts that are necessary for unity in diversity. The author of the letter first cites a text from an unidentified source ('he/it says', λέγει) and then proceeds to gloss and to explain it as referring to Christ.

> (verse 7) But each of us was given grace according to the measure of Christ's gift. (8) Therefore it is said (literally: it/he says, λέγει): '*When he ascended on high he made captivity itself captive; he gave gifts to men*' (ἔδωκεν δόματα τοῖς ἀνθρώποις). (9) When it says, 'He ascended', what

[10] See McNamara (1966: 78–81; 2010b: 234–235) and Le Déaut (2002).

> does it mean but (literally 'what is this but') that he had also descended into the lower parts of the earth? (10) He who descended is the same one who ascended far above all the heavens, so that he might fill all things. The gifts he gave were that some might be apostles, some prophets...

It is clear that the text cited and commented on in this passage is a form of Ps 67(68).19, one, however, which is not that of the Hebrew text or of the Septuagint. The Hebrew has a very obscure text in verse 17(18)c: אֲדֹנָי בָּם סִינַי בַּקֹּדֶשׁ literally 'The Lord among them Sinai in the holy (place)' (NRSV: 'The Lord came from Sinai into the holy place'), rendered in the Greek as: 'The Lord is among them, in Sinai into the holy place'. This is followed by words addressed to an unnamed person: 'You ascended on high; you took captivity captive; your received (from the root *lqḥ*) gifts for men' (with the singular/collective 'man', בָּאָדָם; or 'among men'). The ending is rendered more or less literally in the Septuagint: '...you have received gifts for (or: among) man' (ἔλαβες δόματα ἐν ἀνθρώπῳ). The text in Ephesians understands the Psalm passage as 'giving, distributing' rather then 'receiving', probably reading a Hebrew root *ḥlq* ('divide, distribute') instead of *lqḥ*. This is the understanding and rendering of the passage we find in the Targum of Psalms, which is also that of the rabbinic commentary on this book. Several of the midrashic and haggadic additions in Targum Psalms have parallels in *Midrash Tehillim*. They may draw on a common body of haggadic reflections. In the text that interests us both Targum and midrash seem influenced by the reference to Sinai immediately preceding. The unnamed person addressed ('You ascended') is Moses. The verse is rendered in Targum Psalms (italics indicate additional paraphrase):[11]

> (v. 19). You ascended to *the firmament, O prophet Moses*, you took captives, *you taught the words of the Law, you gave them as gifts to the sons of man*; even among the rebellious *who are converted and repent* does the Šeḵinah of the glory of *the LORD God dwell.*

As David Stec has noted: for the tradition represented by this text of Targum Psalms we can confer the rabbinic commentary on Psalms *Midrash Tehillim* 68.11:

> *Thou hast gone up on high, thou hast led the captivity captive; thou hast received gifts for men* (Ps. 68.19). These words are to be read in the light

[11] In the translation of Stec (2004: 131).

> of what scripture says elsewhere: *A wise man goeth up to the city of the mighty, and bringeth down the strength wherein it trusteth* (Prov. 21:22). This *wise man* is Moses, of whom it is said, 'And Moses went up unto God' (Ex. 19:3); the words *thou hast received gifts for men* refer to the Torah which was bestowed upon Israel as a gift, at no cost.[12]

Targum Psalms is generally regarded as a late composition. Its language is considered by some as virtually the same as the of Targum Job and Pseudo-Jonathan. It is variously dated from the fourth to the seventh century. The relation of this paraphrase to that of the Epistle to the Ephesians would be a good instance of the continuum in exegetical tradition.

(iv) *Zechariah Son of Barachiah: Matthew 23.35 (Luke 11.51) and Targum Lamentations 2.20*[13]

Matthew and Luke record condemnation by Jesus of the scribes (lawyers) and Pharisees, but in different contexts. Both, however, end with a warning that on the current generation would come punishment for their sins and for the infidelity of their forefathers. Matthew's text runs (Mt. 23.34–36): 'Therefore I send you prophets, sages, and scribes, some of whom you will kill and crucify...(35) so that upon you may come all the righteous blood shed on earth, from the blood of the righteous Abel to the blood of Zechariah son of Barachiah, whom you murdered between the sanctuary and the altar. (36) Truly I tell you, all this will come upon this generation'. Luke's text (Lk. 11.49–52) lacks 'son of Barachiah'. The Zechariah in question seems clearly to be the Zechariah son of the priest Jehoiada of 2 Chron. 24.21–22. During the apostasy of king Joash, God sent prophets among the people to bring them back to the Lord, but they would not listen (2 Chron. 24.19). 'Then the spirit of God took possession of Zechariah son of Jehoida the priest who stood above the people and said to them: "Thus says God: Why do you transgress the commandments of the Lord, so that you cannot prosper? Because you have forsaken the Lord, he has also forsaken you". But they conspired against him and by command of the king they stoned him to death in the court of the house of the

[12] In the translation of Braude (1976: vol. 1, 545).

[13] See the earlier treatment in McNamara (1966: 160–163); revised in McNamara (2010b: 231–234).

Lord.... As he was dying, he said: "May the Lord see and avenge"' (24.20–22).

Two differences between the texts of Luke and Matthew and that of 2 Chronicles are to be noted. One is the place of the murder in the Temple (house of the Lord): between the sanctuary and the altar (Matthew), in Luke 'between the altar and the house' (οἴκου), the term 'house' being variously understood and rendered: 'sanctuary' (NRSV), 'Temple' (NJB), 'temple building' (NAB), while 2 Chronicles simply has 'in the court of the house of the Lord'. Another difference is in the connection in the New Testament between the shedding of the blood of Abel and Zechariah and the punishment for these crimes to come 'on this generation' of the scribes (lawyers) and Pharisees.

There is a further difference in Matthew's text in that Zechariah is called the son of Barachiah. There are three Zechariahs mentioned in the Hebrew Scriptures: Zechariah, the son of Jeberechiah (Isa. 8.2), rendered in the Septuagint as 'son of Barachias', the person already mentioned in 2 Chron. 24.20–22 and, the third the eleventh of the Twelve Minor Prophets, in the Book of Zechariah bearing the full title: 'Zechariah the son of Berechiah the son of Iddo' (Zech.1.1). He is nowhere called by the short form 'Zechariah son of Berechiah'. He is mentioned three times in the Old Testament, and identified through his grandfather's name: 'Zechariah the son of Iddo'. Matthew's text is most probably to be explained by the identification of the Zechariah of 2 Chronicles with the Minor Prophet.

A text in the Targum of Lamentations (Tg Lam. 2.20c) throws light on Matthew's text, and on the Jewish setting of both Matthew and Luke. In the Targum, Zechariah of Chronicles is identified with the Minor Prophet, but under his usual name 'Zechariah son of Iddo'. When situated in the broader rabbinic context a fuller meaning of both Targum and New Testament texts is revealed. The Hebrew Text of Lam. 2.20c says: 'Should the priest and the prophet be slain in the temple of the Lord?' This is part of the author of Lamentation's complaint against the Lord on account of the destruction of Jerusalem and the profanation of the Temple. In the preceding portion of the verse the poet complains: 'Look, O Lord, and consider! To whom have you done this? Should women eat their offspring, the children they have borne?' The targumist lets the first part of the people's complaint stand. In the paraphrase of v. 20c he has the Lord (under the designation 'The Attribute of Justice') answer the complaint (italics designate additional paraphrase to the Hebrew Text):

> *The Attribute of Justice answered, and thus said*: 'Is is *fitting* to murder in the House of the Sanctuary of the Lord the priest and the prophet, *as you murdered Zechariah the son of Iddo, the high priest and faithful prophet, in the House of the Sanctuary of the Lord on the Day of Atonement, because he admonished you not to do that which was evil before the Lord?*'[14]

The central point of the Targum's paraphrase is that the destruction of Jerusalem by Nebuzaradan (2 Kgs. 25.8–12) is linked with the earlier murder of Zechariah (son of Barachiah) son of Iddo, and the blame for this is laid on the generation of the destruction. There are some differences between the Targum and the account of this in 2 Chronicles. Zechariah is explicitly called 'prophet', implicit in Chronicles. He is also called 'high priest', which need not surprise as 'priests' of the earlier biblical texts are often described as 'high priests' in the targums (Melchizedek, Gen. 14.18 and others),[15] and in any event Josephus (*Ant.* 9.166), so designates Zechariah's father. The murder is also said to have taken place on the Day of Atonement, which adds to the gravity of the crime. The Targum's link of the Temple's destruction with the much earlier (252 years earlier!) murder of Zechariah of Chronicles is best understood when set in the context of rabbinic tradition, within which our present text of this Targum originated. As Philip S. Alexander puts it in his note to the English translation of chapter 2.20 of this Targum: 'The idea that the murder of Zechariah was a major cause of the destruction of the first Temple is an old and deeply embedded element in the tradition. According to a widespread rabbinic aggadah, the murdered Zechariah's blood never dried, but continued to seethe until Nebuzaradan, Nebuchadnezzar's general, slaughtered young priests to appease it'.[16] The apocryphal *Lives of the Prophets* (chapter 23. 'Zechariah son of Jehoiada'), probably of the first century CE, of Palestinian origin, and contemporary with Matthew and Luke, does not have the rabbinic legend on this Zechariah, but

[14] In the translation of Alexander (2008: 141).

[15] See McNamara (2000: 22–26).

[16] Alexander (2008: 141, note 73), with many rabbinic references, including one to Targum Lamentations 4.13 where there is mention again of the murder of Zechariah and its consequences for the destruction of the Temple. '*The Attribute of Justice answered and thus said*: *None of this would have happened but for* the sins of her prophets…and the iniquities of her priests,… and they are the ones who caused the blood of the righteous to be shed in her midst' (in the translation of Alexander, 2008: 170).

records the belief of the disastrous consequences of his murder: 'From that time visible portents occurred in the Temple, and the priests were not able to see a vision of angels of God or to give oracles from the *Debeir*, or to inquire by the Ephod, or to answer the people through Urim as formerly.'[17]

The targumic and rabbinic traditions seem to illustrate the connection made by Jesus between the murder of Zechariah (and others) and the impending punishment to come on the 'this generation'. The New Testament, and Matthew's text, can be taken as indicating an early date for this particular tradition, preserved in rabbinic literature and in the Targum of Lamentations, itself probably to be dated towards the end of the fifth century CE. The relevance of this text for an understanding of a New Testament passage would be another instance of the continuum—the continuation of a tradition through the centuries.

(v) *Father in Heaven in Matthew and Rabbinic Judaism*[18]

In Matthew's Gospel Jesus speaks of God some twenty times as 'Father who is in the heavens' ('My, thy, our, your Father who is in the heavens', πατήρ μου[σου, ἡμῶν, ὑμῶν] ὁ ἐν τοῖς οὐρανοῖς): Mt. 5.16,45, (48, in a variant reading); 6.1,9; 7.11,21; 10.32,33; 12.50; 16.17; 18. (10,) 14,19; (23.9, a variant reading).

As a variant Matthew has also '(your/my) heavenly Father'—ὁ πατὴρ ὑμῶν ὁ οὐράνιος (Mt. 5.48; 6.14,26,32; 23.9); ὁ πατήρ μου ὁ οὐράνιος (Mt. 15.13; 18.35). It seems fairly clear that this is a Greek presentation of an original 'Father who is in the heavens'. We may then accept it that 'Father who is in the heavens' was current phraseology in the Matthean community.

The expression is also found in Mk. 11.25: 'And whenever you stand praying, forgive, if you have anything against anyone; so that your Father who is in the heavens (ἐν τοῖς οὐρανοῖς) may also forgive you your trespasses'. The parallel passage to this in Mt. 6.14 (in the Sermon on the Mount) has 'your heavenly Father'. This form of the phrase in Matthew, as already noted, is a secondary formulation. Mark is here a representative of early Palestinian Christian language.

---

[17] See translation by Hare (1985: 398).

[18] See further, McNamara (2010a: 403–411; 2010b: 177–186; 2011: 496–503); and earlier McNamara (1972: 115–119).

Luke does not have the expression, but in 11.13 he has a text from the Q source clearly dependent on the original Palestinian formula. Lk. 11.13 has: 'If you then, who are evil, know how to give good gifts to your children, how much more will the Father who is from heaven (ὁ πατὴρ ὁ ἐξ οὐρανοῦ) give the Holy Spirit to those who ask him!' The parallel text from Q in Mt. 7.11 reads: '…how much more will your Father who is in the heavens give good things to those who ask him!'

From all this it is clear that the expressions 'Father who is in the heavens' was current in the Matthean community, in the community from which Mark's Gospel ultimately emerged, and in the original form of the Q source. This eminently Semitic expression was, under Greek influence, changed in part in Matthew's Gospel to become 'heavenly Father', and further in Luke's presentation of the Q source. It is an open question to what extent, if at all, Jesus himself used this expression. It was one of a number of ways of referring to the loving and caring God.

The corresponding Hebrew phrase אב שבשמים *ʾab̲ še-be-šamayim* is attested in rabbinic sources for a period from the end of the first century CE onwards.[19] 'Israel and its Father in heaven' is a particularly common form, but even the individual 'my Father in heaven' is put on the lips of R. Yochanan b. Zakkai (died *ca.* 80 CE). A common phrase is 'Before the Father in heaven'. Another favourite expression is: 'To direct one's prayer to the Father in heaven'. 'To do the will of the Father in heaven' is a common mode of expression in rabbinic Judaism.[20]

The phrase 'Father who is in the heavens (אב שבשמים *ʾab̲ še-be-šamayim*) occurs five times in the Mishnah.[21] It occurs three times in *m. Sot.* 9.15 in the form 'our Father who is in the heavens' (אבינו שבש־מים *ʾab̲inu še-ba-šamayim*), twice on the state of depression resulting from the destruction of the Temple, once on the turmoil to come 'with the footprints of the Messiah'. Thus: 'R. Eliezer the Great (ben Hyrcanus; *ca.* 120 CE) said: 'Since the day the Temple was destroyed the sages began to look like school teachers…On whom shall we stay ourselves? On our Father who is in the heavens''.[22] In *m. Yoma* 8.9 we

[19] See Schrenk (1967: 979–981).

[20] See Schrenk (1965: 54).

[21] See Kosovsky (ed. 1967: 4). I wish to express my thanks to Prof. Dr. Liliane Vana, Paris, for indicating the presence of the expression in the Mishnah to me.

[22] See the translation in Danby (1933: 306); Neusner (1988: 465–466).

have the form 'Your Father who is in heaven'. 'R. Aqiba (put to death 135 CE) said: 'Blessed are ye, O Israel. Before whom are you made clean and who makes you clean? Your Father who is in heaven...' (citing Ezek. 36.25).[23] In *m. R. ha-Sh.*3.8, Exod. 17.12 and Num. 21.8 are interpreted with the note that victory did not come automatically by Moses raising his hands, nor healing by gazing on the bronze serpent, but rather because 'the Israelites directed their thoughts on high and kept their heart in subjection to the Father who is in the heavens, otherwise they suffered defeat (or: pined away')'.[24]

In the Palestinian Targums of the Pentateuch alone among the targums do we find the designation of God as 'Father in heaven'. As in the New Testament, it is never found alone, but is always accompanied by a qualifying pronoun, 'your', 'their', 'our' ('Father who is in heaven'). Like most of the New Testament occurrences of the expression, in the targums too it is found chiefly in certain definite contexts, i.e. in reference to prayer, merit or divine will.

I have found a total of thirteen occurrences of the expression 'Father in heaven' in the Palestinian targums: three in Pseudo-Jonathan, seven in the Fragment Targums and three in Neofiti, The texts are as follows: Gen. 21.33 (Fragment Targums, manuscripts PVNL); Exod.1.19 (Pseudo-Jonathan and Fragment Targums manuscripts P,V, B_2 and in Neofiti); Exod. 17.11 (Fragment Targums, manuscript P; cf all other Frg. Tgs texts); Lev. 22.28 (Pseudo-Jonathan, variant); Num. 20.21 (Fragment Targums, manuscript V, Second *Biblia Rabbinica*, Neofiti); Num. 21.9 (Fragment Targum, manuscript V, Second *Biblia Rabbinica*); Num. 23.23 (Fragment Targum, manuscript V, Second *Biblia Rabbinica*, P); Deut, 28.32 (Fragment Targum, manuscript V, Second *Biblia Rabbinica*, manuscript P); Deut. 32.6 (Fragment Targum, manuscripts V, P); Deut. 33.24 (Neofiti).

In only one instance (Exod. 1.19; prayer to Father in heaven) do all three representatives of the Palestinian Targum carry this particular designation of God. As in the Gospel evidence, we may ask: in which texts is it original and in which added? Is its absence or presence due to the date of composition or to later editorial work? Perhaps, like 'holy spirit', שכינה *Šeḵinah*, דיברה *Dibberah* and בת קול *Bat Qol* in

[23] See the translation in Danby (1933: 172); Neusner (1988: 279).
[24] See translation in Danby (1933: 192); Neusner (1988: 304–305).

rabbinic texts, 'Father in heaven' was another of the expressions which could easily be replaced by a synonym.

'Father in heaven', as a designation of God, was a well-established expression in the community within which the Gospel of Matthew originated. The same can be said with regard to the Gospel of Mark. We may presume that it formed part of the language of Jesus.

It is attested for Rabbinic Judaism for the late first century CE. The question arises whether it was current in Palestinian Judaism in the time of Jesus, or whether its use in rabbinic Judaism is to be explained through influence from the Christian community. Both existed side by side in Palestine and in theory the influence could have been in either direction.[25] Given the expression itself in both the Gospels and rabbinic texts, and its combination in other phrases, e.g. 'before the Father in heaven', 'good will before your/our Father in heaven' etc., it seems preferable to assume that the expression was basically a Jewish one, pre-dating Christianity, but used by Jesus and the early Christian community, who would have infused new meaning into it by reason of the person and mission of Jesus.

(vi) *The Sheḵinah (m. Abot 3.3, 6;ARN B, ch. 34, p. 74) and Mt. 18.20: 'I am there among them'*

We have already spoken of the Sheḵinah of the Lord, and noted that a number of scholars believe that its use in the Targums, together with references to possession of the land, are indications of a post-70 CE date for texts. The theme *Sheḵinah* has been extensively studied. My intention here is not to go over these again but rather to present a slightly different approach to the topic, one in keeping with the theme of this essay.[26]

The Hebrew noun שכינה *šeḵinah* (in Aramaic in the emphatic singular שכינתא *šeḵinta*) is an abstract noun from the verb שכן *šaḵan* (root in Hebrew and Aramaic *škn*),[27] 'to dwell, rest'. It is a central

[25] See Schrenk (1967: 979–980).

[26] It is a topic which I treat of elsewhere; seeMcNamara (2010b: 147–153).

[27] The verb *škn* with the sense of 'inhabit', 'dwell' occurs in Official Aramaic, in Biblical Aramaic, in Samaritan Aramaic and in Syriac: of birds on trees (Dan. 4.18); 'the God Iahu who dwells in Yeb' (Brooklyn Papyrus, 12,2); God who made his name

term and concept in rabbinic literature, expressing God's presence in the Temple and with his people. It is also very common in the various targums of the Pentateuch and of the Prophets, with differences, however, in the manner in which it is used in Onqelos, the Palestinian Targums (in particular Neofiti) and the Targums of the Prophets. Since the present work is not merely on the Targums, but rather on the Targums and the New Testament it is indicated that examination of the matter begin with consideration of the possible early use of the term and concept in Judaism.

Whereas the verb *šak̲an* and terms from the root *škn* occur in the Hebrew Scriptures, and while the term *šek̲inah/šek̲inta* is extremely common in rabbinic literature and the targums, no occurrence of it is attested in pre-rabbinic literature. It is not found in the Qumran texts. This might lead one to believe that the term and concept originated after the fall of Jerusalem in 70 CE, or after New Testament times. However, an indication of its earlier use may be seen in 2 Macc. 14.35 (in a work completed before the Roman conquest, 63 BCE). In a prayer for the safety of the Temple the priests remind God: 'You were pleased that there should be a temple for your habitation (ναὸν τῆς σῆς σκηνώσεως) among us'. The abstract noun σκηνῶσις corresponds closely in meaning and form to *šek̲inah*, probably indicating that this term was already in liturgical use by 50 BCE.

There are also early rabbinic texts indicating early use of the concept and term. The term *Šek̲inah* occurs only twice in the Mishnah, once in words ascribed to Rabbi Hananiah ben Teradyon (probably executed 135 CE): 'If two sit together and the words between them are of the Torah, then the *Šek̲inah* is in their midst' (*m. Aboth* 3.3). Again in *m. Avot* 3.6: 'R. Halafta b. Dosa [latter half of the second century] said: 'If ten men sit together and occupy themselves with the Law, the *Šek̲inah* rests among them''. A similar saying, with broader connotation, is attributed to R. Halafta of Sepphoris (R. Hananiah's contemporary) who speaks of the presence of the *Šek̲inah* with any 'two or three who sit together in the market place and the words between them are of the Torah' (*Avot de Rabbi Natan* B, ch. 34, p. 74). These texts are naturally compared with Mt. 18.20: 'Where two or three are gathered together in my name there am I in their midst'. The difference between the

---

dwell there' (words of Darius on the Jerusalem Temple) (Ezr 6.12). The verb *škn* in this sense is not found in the Targums, where the usual term for 'dwell', 'rest' is *šrʾ*.

two contexts must be borne in mind. Matthew's text speaks of Jesus, rather than God's *Šeḵinah*, being present, which is in keeping with the New Testament, where Jesus is spoken of as Immanuel. It is recognised that Mt. 18.20 may be related to the Jewish traditions, Matthew's relation to rabbinic tradition being generally accepted. While it is possible that the Jewish tradition depends on Matthew, it is more probable that the Jewish rabbinic theology and terminology on the *Šeḵinah* were already a reality in the first century and that Matthew moulded this in keeping with New Testament christology.

The foregoing research on the date of the use of the concept *Šeḵinah* in Judaism was made by Professor Joseph Sievers of the Biblical Institute, Rome.[28] In his first study in English Sievers notes that the references to the *Šeḵinah* in Targum Onqelos as well as in the various recensions of the Palestinian Targum are numerous. Although the Targumim contain much earlier material, he continues, they were not redacted in final form before the third century. Therefore, they are of little help in establishing the origin of the term *Šeḵinah*. He omits all references to the targums in the revised form of the essay in German.

With regard to this one may observe that a concept and term of this nature if current, or used, in rabbinic Judaism of New Testament times (and earlier) can be presumed to have also been used in liturgical, or 'popular' Aramaic translations of the Bible. And in point of fact we find it freely used in all the Targums of the Pentateuch (Onqelos and the Palestinian Targums) and of the Prophets. There is a tendency to date the Targums of Onqelos and the Prophets before 135 CE. The precise manner in which the term *Šeḵinah* is used in the various targums differs from one to the other, and there should be no question of trying to ascertain which targumic usage is the oldest. In the use of the concept and term there was probably an inner-targumic development. Here as elsewhere the targumists were not free to introduce the term at will. Their primary purpose was to translate the Hebrew text. They insert reference to the *Šeḵinah* in places where the Hebrew speaks of God 'dwelling/resting' in the Temple or with his people.

(vii) *Other Texts*

In the texts given above I have adduced some instances where I believe there has been continuity in the targumic tradition before and after the

[28] Sievers (1990) and Sievers (2005), a revision of his earlier essay (1990).

70 CE divide. Other theological themes and phrases could be added to these, some of which are the subject of intense study today: for instance *Memra* (or Word) of the Lord,[29] good works, rewards, merit in heaven, being merciful as Our Father in Heaven is merciful and others besides. I believe that sufficient evidence has been presented to indicate that the theme of continuity in the targumic exegetical tradition merits attention.

Conclusion

Methodology will continue to remain a concern for scholars wishing to use the targumic evidence in New Testament or first century CE studies. My conviction is that sensitivity to the tel-like character of Targum, to which Professor Robert Gordon has drawn our attention, together with an awareness of the presence of continuity in the targumic exegetical tradition, can play useful rules in future research in this area. While we identify markers suggesting or proving a post-70 date for a text or tradition, it might be well to examine whether these are limited in number, whereas much in the tradition, or at least traditions within it, are little, if at all, connected with the 70 CE disaster.

References

Alexander, P.S. 2008. *The Targum of Lamentations. Translated, with a Critical Introduction, Apparatus and Notes* (The Aramaic Bible, 17B; Collegeville, MN: Liturgical Press).

Blenkinsopp, J. 2006. *Opening the Sealed Book. Interpretations of the Book of Isaiah in Late Antiquity* (Grand Rapids, MI & Cambridge, UK: Eerdmans).

Braude, W.G. 1976. *The Midrash on Psalms*, (2 vols; Yale Judaica Series, 13; New Haven: Yale University Press, 3rd edition).

Cathcart, K.J., and R.P. Gordon. 1989. *The Targum of the Minor Prophets. Translated, with a Critical Introduction, Apparatus, and Notes* (The Aramaic Bible, 14; Wilmington, Delaware: Michael Glazier).

Chilton, B.D. 1994. *Judaic Approaches to the Gospels* (Atlanta GA: Scholars Press for the University of South Florida).

——. 2000. 'Four Types of Comparison between the Targumim and the New Testament', *Journal for the Aramaic Bible* 2: 163–188.

Danby, H. 1933. *The Mishnah. Translated from the Hebrew with Introduction and Brief Explanatory Notes* (Oxford: University Press; London: Geoffrey Cumberlege).

[29] Among the more recent studies on this these see Ronning (2010).

Evans, C.A. 2001. *Jesus and his Contemporaries. Comparative Studies* (Boston & Leiden: Brill).

Gordon, R.P. 1994. *Studies in the Targum to the Twelve Prophets. From Nahum to Malachi* (Leiden: Brill).

Hare, D.R.A. 1985. 'The Lives of the Prophets (First Century AD)' in *The Old Testament Pseudepigrapha* (ed. J.H. Charlesworth; vol. 2; London: Darton, Longman & Todd) 379–400.

Kaufmann, S. 1992. Review of Cathcart and Gordon (1989), *Catholic Biblical Quarterly* 54: 108.

Keener, C.S. 2003. *The Gospel of John. A Commentary* (2 vols; Peabody, MA: Hendrickson).

Klein, M.L. 1986. *Genizah Manuscripts of Palestinian Targum to the Pentateuch. Vol. 1* (Cincinnati: Hebrew Union College Press).

Kosovsky, C.Y. (ed.) 1967. *Otsar leshon ha-Mishnah. Thesaurus Mishnae: Concordantiae verborum que in sex Mishnae ordinibus reperiuntur* (revised edition; Tel-Aviv: Massadah Publishing).

Le Déaut, R. 2002. 'Targum', in *Supplément au Dictionnaire de la Bible.* vol. 13: cols. 308*–309*.

Levy, B.B. 1987. *Targum Neofiti 1: A Textual Study. Vol. 2. Leviticus, Numbers, Deuteronomy* (Lanham, Md., New York & London: University Press of America).

Levy, B.B. 1986. *Targum Neofiti 1: A Textual Study. Vol. 1. Introduction, Genesis, Exodus* (Lanham, Md., New York & London: University Press of America).

McNamara, M. 1966. *The New Testament and the Palestinian Targum to the Pentateuch* (Analecta Biblica, 27; 27A; Rome: Biblical Institute Press; reprint 1978).

——. 1972. *Targum and Testament. Aramaic Paraphrases of the Hebrew Bible: A Light on the New Testament* (Shannon, Ireland: Irish University Press & Grand Rapids: Eerdmans).

——. 2000. 'Melchizedek: Gen. 14, 17–20 in the Targums, in Rabbinic Literature and Early Christian Literature', *Biblica* 81: 1–31. Reprinted in McNamara (2011: 289–317).

——. 2002. 'Towards an English Synoptic Presentation of the Pentateuchal Targums', in *Targum and Scripture. Studies in Aramaic Translations and Interpretation in Memory of Ernest G. Clarke* (ed. P.V.M. Flesher; Studies in the Aramaic Interpretation of Scripture, 2; Leiden & Boston: Brill): 3–27. Reprinted in McNamara (2011: 132–160).

——. 2010a. 'Targum and Testament: A Revisit', in *The New Testament and Rabbinic Literature* (ed. R. Bieringer, F. García Martínez, D. Pollefeyt and P.J. Tomson; Supplement to Journal for the Study of Judaism, 136; Leiden: Brill) 385–425. Reprinted in McNamara (2011: 480–517).

——. 2010b. *Targum and Testament Revisited: Aramaic paraphrases of the Hebrew Bible* (Grand Rapids/Cambridge: Eerdmans).

——. 2011. 'Targums and New Testament, A Way Forward? Targums, Tel-Like Character, a Continuum', in M. McNamara, *Targum and New Testament. Collected Essays* (Tübingen: Mohr Siebeck): 518–530.

Neusner, J. 1988. *The Mishnah. A New Translation* (New Haven and London: Yale University Press).

Ronning, J.L. 2010. *The Jewish Targums and John's Logos Theology* (Peabody: Hendrickson Publishers).

Sandmel, S. 1962. 'Parallelomania', *Journal of Biblical Literature* 81: 1–13.

Schrenk, G. 1965. '*thelema*' in *Theological Dictionary of the New Testament*, vol. 5 (Grand Rapids: Eerdmans) 54.

——. 1967. '*patêr*', in *Theological Dictionary of the New Testament*, vol. 5 (Grand Rapids: Eerdmans) 974–1002.

Sievers, J. 1990. '"Where Two or Three...". The Rabbinic Concept of Shekinah and Matthew 18:20', in *The Jewish Roots of Christian Liturgy* (ed. E.J. Fisher; New York & Mahwah: Paulist Press) 47–61.

——. 2005 '"Wo zwei oder drei..." Der rabbinische Begriff der Schechina und Matthäus 18,20', in *Das Prisma: Beiträge zu Pastoral, Katechese & Theologie* 17,1: 18–29.

Stec, D.M. 2004. *The Targum of Psalms. Translated, with a Critical Introduction, Apparatus, and Notes* (The Aramaic Bible, 16; Collegeville: Liturgical Press).

Vermes, G. 1982. 'Jewish Literature and New Testament Exegesis: Reflections and Methodology', *Journal of Jewish Studies* 33: 361–376.

MULES, ROME, AND A CATALOGUE OF NAMES: GENESIS 36 AND ITS ARAMAIC TARGUMIM

Robert Hayward

To the casual reader, the forty-three verses which make up Gen. 36 appear to be nothing but a tedious inventory of persons and places associated with Esau who is Edom. The narrative of Genesis up to this point related the tragic death of Rachel, Reuben's misadventure with Bilhah, the names of Jacob's sons, and an account of Isaac's death (Gen. 35.16–29). These are episodes full of human interest, which leave the reader wanting to know more; and more is given with the opening of Gen. 37 and its introduction to the story of Joseph, surely one of the most engaging in the Hebrew Bible. The narrative pace of these stories is unambiguously slowed by Gen. 36; and the not-so-casual reader will notice that the chapter is remarkably self-contained both in form and content. It begins and ends with deictic formulae, 'These are the generations of Esau' (Gen. 36.1), and 'These are the chiefs of Edom' (Gen. 36.43); and contains nothing but information about Esau, his descendants, their territories, and their rulers. Consequently, modern commentators sense that the chapter's structure and position in the larger narrative sequence require explanations, and hasten to supply them.[1]

Ancient students of the Bible sometimes perceived in this chapter an allusion to a bitter conflict between Esau and Jacob. Esau had sworn to kill his brother (Gen. 27.41), yet following Isaac's death (Gen. 35.29) Esau seems not to have acted on this oath. Careful attention to Gen. 36.6, however, reveals that Esau had journeyed to 'a land from before Jacob his brother' after Isaac's death; and the author of the Book of

[1] For representative interpretations, see Westermann (1986: 568–569), who notes that the chapter repeats in genealogical format the development of society from family, through tribe, to monarchy recorded elsewhere in the Bible; and Sarna (5479/1989: 246–253), who isolates seven units of tradition which, he suggests, may represent different, overlapping traditions about Esau's family. He also provides an important Excursus on the king list (5479/1989: 408–410). Note also the pertinent comment of Berlin and Brettler (1999: 72–73), that this chapter suggests a fraternal feeling for Esau which is absent in much post-biblical literature.

Jubilees chapter 37 seems to have understood these biblical reports as indicating that on Isaac's death Esau had, indeed, attacked Jacob, with the assistance of his descendants who are named in the preceding five verses; that he had been defeated; and that he had therefore gone away, in flight, 'from before' Jacob his brother.[2] Philo, by contrast, drew attention to the presence of Amalek, Israel's deadly enemy, among Esau's descendants: his name Philo understood as 'a people which licks up', signifying passion which licks up and destroys all things. In similar fashion the name of Eliphaz, the son of Esau, is taken by Philo to mean 'God has scattered me', indicating the banishment of the soul of that man from the divine Presence.[3] Eliphaz, according to Philo, has both a wife who produces wickedness as offspring, and a concubine who produces passion: the latter is Timna, and this name signifies an eclipse which causes the soul to fail.[4] Of all these persons, Esau is the progenitor: his name means 'an oak', or 'a thing made', the former designation pointing to his stubborn folly, the latter to his vacuous, tragic-comic character.[5] The generally dark and negative portrayal of Esau and his descendants in the exegesis of Second Temple times is alleviated somewhat, however, by the famous epilogue to the book of Job preserved in the Septuagint, which refers explicitly to Gen. 36 and designates Job as a grandson of Esau, identifying him with the Jobab of Gen. 36.33 and including him in the list of Edomite kings.[6] A similar tradition was evidently known to Aristeas the Exegete, who reports that Job was the son of Esau by his wife Bassara, and was born in Edom: the ultimate source of this information seems to be a particular understanding of Gen. 36.31–39; and the same chapter appears to have provided Aristeas with the basis for other items about Job's

[2] See Kugel (1998: 371–372). The traditions informing the author of Jubilees 37 are discussed in detail by Brin (2002: 17–24) and Himmelfarb (2006: 75–77).

[3] See Philo, *De Congressu* 54–56. The Scriptural verse under consideration here is Gen. 36.12.

[4] See Philo, *De Congressu* 59–60. According to *TanḥumaWayyešeḇ* 1, Eliphaz married his daughter, who was none other than this Timna. In some sources, however, Timna is presented in a much better light, as recognizing Abraham's nobility, seeking to marry into his family, and accepting her own ineligibility for full membership of Israel's polity: see Gen. Rab. 82.14.

[5] See Philo, *De Congressu*, 61–62.

[6] For the Greek text of this epilogue, see Rahlfs (1935: vol. 2: 844–845): this is reproduced, with an English translation, by Holladay (1983: 274–275).

family which he also transmits.[7] Alone among the Aramaic Targumim of Gen. 36, Pseudo-Jonathan mentions Job, informing us that Eliphaz son of Esau was his colleague.[8]

None of this, however, prepares us for a major inference which many rabbis drew from this chapter, with its tangle of names and leaders and kings: many of Esau's children, they held, were the product of incest and other illicit relationships. Already in the first century CE Josephus had signalled that Esau's family was unsatisfactory, informing us that Amalek was a bastard born to Esau of a concubine.[9] The first comment on this chapter offered by *Genesis Rabbah* cities Gen. 36.4, and leaves the reader in no doubts:

> And Oholibamah bore Jeush, *etc.* (Gen. 36.4). This refers to what is written, how 'I have stripped Esau' (Jer. 49.10). R. Simon said, I have peeled him like onions. Why so? 'I have disclosed his secrets' (Jer. 49.10), to reveal the bastards who are among them. And how many bastards did he beget? Rav said, three; R. Levi said, four; R. Benjamin in the name of R. Levi said, The Korah of this passage was a bastard.[10]

The comment immediately following suggests that Esau was more concerned for his women folk than for his sons: this comes as little surprise, given that the Bible has repeatedly mentioned Esau's marriages to women not approved by his father long before the reader reaches this point in the narrative.[11] The underlying hint, that Esau and his family are engaged in irregular sexual conduct, is made explicit by the midrash when the character ʿAnah appears, first at Gen. 36.20 as son of Seir, that is, son of Esau; then at Gen. 36.24 as son of Zibeon, the latter described elsewhere in another fashion, as son of Seir (Gen. 36.20). Gen. Rab. 82.13 is quite clear in its explanation of this state of affairs: there was only one ʿAnah, and the Scriptural information about his origins is taken to mean that Zibeon, who was son of

[7] The one surviving fragment of Aristeas's work is preserved by Eusebius, *Praeparatio Evangelica* IX.25.1–4, the Greek text of which may be conveniently consulted, along with an introduction, English translation, and commentary, in Holladay (1983: 261–273). See also Doran (1985: 855–858) and Schürer (1986: 525–526).

[8] See Pseudo-Jonathan of Gen. 36.12; and for further observations on the relationship between Esau and Job in antiquity, see H. Jacobson (1996: vol. 2: 391–393). Quotations from this Targum (hereafter PJ) are taken from Clarke, Aufrecht, Hurd, and Spitzer (1984).

[9] Josephus, Ant.ii.5.

[10] Gen. Rab. 82.12.

[11] See Gen. Rab. 82.13; and see also Gen. 26.34–35; 28.8–9.

Seir-Edom, slept with his mother and produced ʿAnah: in this sense it is said that ʿAnah was both son of Zibeon and son of Seir.[12] The Babylonian Talmud (Pes. 54a) lends its authority to this explanation, and its report on this matter will be discussed presently.

The Aramaic Targumim of Gen. 36, with the exception of Targum Pseudo-Jonathan (PJ), have little to say directly about these sexual irregularities, although Targum Onqelos (TO), given its well known affinity with wider Rabbinic tradition, was almost certainly aware of them. Targum Neofiti (TN) has no rendering of Gen. 36.22–30; and verses for which it offers translation and comment do not engage with the irregularities of Esau's family. The Fragment Targums (FT) are extant only for Gen. 36.39. This is not to say, however, that the Aramaic versions pay no attention to the problems of Esau's wives; rather, they prefer to discuss them with reference to other chapters of Scripture, leaving Gen. 36 generally untouched by this matter, and thus potentially open to discussion of other concerns.[13] Such other concerns, however, do not generally make themselves felt. The Targumim of Gen. 36 do offer some limited interpretation of the Hebrew text; and most of these comments are taken up into PJ's version, which is exceptional in presenting us with exegesis which, like the chapter itself, appears self-contained, consistent, and homogeneous. It is to PJ, therefore, that this essay will principally be addressed.

1. Some People and Places

We begin where it seems that the book of Jubilees began, with Gen. 36.6 and its note that Esau took his family and possessions, moved from

[12] See also Rashi's commentary on Gen. 36.24, and his earlier remarks commenting on Gen. 36.2 about the illegitimacy of Oholibamah (she was Zibeon's daughter by his daughter-in-law, ʿAnah's wife). *Tanḥuma Wayyešeḇ* 1 gives a detailed account of ʿAnah's parentage.

[13] Gen. 26.35 describes Esau's wives as מֹרַת רוּחַ to Isaac and Rebekah, which TO understood as meaning that they were 'rebellious and agitating against the authority of Isaac and Rebekah': so Grossfeld (1988: 98–99). PJ, TN, and FT of this verse offer the same general criticism of the wives, adding that they were idolaters; and PJ of Gen. 28.9 briefly defines Basemath's relationship to Nebaiot which is again mentioned at PJ of Gen. 36.3 without further comment. See also Rashi's commentary on Gen. 28.9. Quotations from TO are drawn from Sperber (1959); those from TN are taken from Díez Macho (1968), and FT is cited from Klein (1980). All translations are mine unless otherwise noted.

the land of Canaan, 'and went to a land from before Jacob his brother'. This last, somewhat cryptic sentence PJ explained as meaning that Esau 'journeyed to another land, because the awe of Jacob his brother had been thrown down upon him'. Both TO and TN agree with PJ that Esau moved to *another* land, but neither Targum gives a reason for his journey.[14] The reason which PJ offers is multi-layered, and may be understood with reference to at least three aspects of Scripture. First, the 'awe', Aramaic אימתיה, of Jacob which had been thrown down (דהות רמיא), on Esau, recalls the words of PJ's expansion of Gen. 15.12. In that verse, we learn that Abraham during the covenant ceremony 'between the pieces' of sacrificial animals fell into a stupor, 'and behold great dark awe (Hebrew אֵימָה) was falling upon him'. PJ interpreted these words as alluding to four future world empires, the word אֵימָה signifying Babylon, while 'falling' signifies 'Edom which is destined to fall and is not to be raised up'. A further link between Gen. 36.6 and Gen. 15.12 in PJ is the repetition of the notion of something *thrown down*: in the former it is a question of Jacob's awe cast upon Esau; in the latter, the stupor in which Abraham is granted his vision is something thrown down (Aramaic מתרמיית) on him.[15] The departure of Esau for Seir might, therefore, imply for PJ the beginnings of a future promised to Abraham, a world where Edom is incapacitated.

That this is exactly what PJ has in mind is indicated by the second Scriptural allusion latent in the Targum's expression. We speak here of Exod. 15.15–16, part of Israel's great song of victory following the Exodus, which declares: 'Then were the chiefs of Edom (אַלּוּפֵי אֱדוֹם) terrified; as for the strong ones of Moab, trembling seized them; all the inhabitants of Canaan melted'. The chiefs of Edom explicitly form the subject matter of Gen. 36.15–19; and Exod. 15.16 goes on to tell how 'awe and fear fell upon them, תִּפֹּל עֲלֵיהֶם אֵימָתָה וָפַחַד.[16] PJ of

[14] The Hebrew worried the LXX translators, who rendered it as 'and he went out of the land of Canaan from the face of Jacob his brother': see Wevers (1993: 592–593) and Harl (1994: 255). The Syriac states that 'he went to the land of Seir', thus anticipating the information given at Gen. 36.8.

[15] The presence of this kind of literary allusion, in which the verb 'throw down' (*rmy*) is used of both Abraham and Esau but in contrasting ways (in a good sense in Abraham's case, in a disastrous manner in Esau's) is strengthened by our further observations.

[16] The Hebrew imperfect form תִּפֹּל may be translated as 'shall fall', suggesting a future fright for Edom; and the whole song after the departure from Egypt might refer to the future, if we were to translate the first words of Exod 15.1 as 'Then Moses

Exod. 15.15 speaks of the chiefs of Edom as רברבני אדום, the same expression as is used in PJ of Gen. 36.15–19, and notes how (Exod. 15.16) the 'awe' (אימתא) of death shall fall on them'. The allusion to all the inhabitants of Canaan in Exod. 15.15 is also relevant to interpretation of Gen. 36, given the context. PJ evidently understood Esau's journey, motivated by awe engendered by his brother Jacob, as a prelude to what would happen when Israel came victoriously out of Egypt, when awe fell upon the terrified leaders of the Edomites.

An allusion to a third passage of Scripture is to be discerned in the 'other land' to which Esau journeyed, though not in PJ of Gen. 36.6 itself. We must advance two verses, to Gen. 36.8 where the Bible names this place as Seir: PJ gives it as Gabla, the usual identification of Seir in this Targum.[17] This place name is particularly significant for PJ as the home of aboriginal aristocrats. At Gen. 36.20 and 21, where the Bible speaks of the sons of Seir the Horite and the chiefs of the Horites the sons of Seir, PJ refers to 'the sons of Gebal, the nobles who formerly were inhabitants of that land', and 'the chiefs of the nobles, the sons of Gebal'.[18] Now the name Gebal is listed in Ps. 83.8 along with Edom (Ps. 83.7), the prime concern of Gen. 36, and two other nations whose names are found in that chapter of Genesis: Moab in Ps. 83.7 and Gen. 36.35; and Amalek in Ps. 83.7 and Gen. 36.12, 16. These nations the Psalm depicts as confederate in a vicious and concerted attack on Israel, and prays that God will destroy them. Along with them are 'the sons of Lot' (Ps. 83.9); and their land, we are told by Deut. 2.9–10, was once inhabited by a people described as הָאֵמִים, 'the awesome ones'. More will be said about these 'awesome ones' later. For the present, however, let us note that all three of the Scriptural allusions implied in PJ's version of Gen. 36.6, 8 include notions of Esau's complicity with others in attacks on Israel; a sense that Esau's departure to Seir was the result of Jacob's 'awe' affecting him; and the hint that the ultimate overthrow of Edom announced to Abraham is adumbrated in

---

and the sons of Israel shall sing this song to the Lord', following ancient precedent: see Rabbi's comment on Babylonian Talmud San. 91b; and *Mekhilta de R. Ishmael* Shirta 1.1–10.

[17] See McNamara (1972: 194), who notes the same identification in 1QapGen XXI.29 and Josephus, Ant. ii. 6, among other sources.

[18] See also PJ of Gen. 36.30. On the Targum's translation of Horites as 'nobles', see further below.

that same departure of Esau for 'another land', although that land is associated with enemies of Israel.

It will be helpful here to note that PJ's exegesis of Gen. 36.6 contrasts with other interpretations preserved in the midrashim. Gen. Rab. 82.13 reports two reasons for Esau's departure to Seir. R. Eleazar declared that it was because of the 'note of indebtedness' (שטר חוב), an allusion to God's decree that Abraham's children should be sojourners in a land not theirs (Gen. 15.13). Esau thus fled to Seir to side-step God's plans: he was apparently aware of these plans, but unlike his brother Jacob he seeks to evade the difficulties of loyalty to the Almighty. R. Joshua b. Levi states that he went to Seir out of shame: by this the Rabbi may mean that Esau was ashamed of his illegitimate offspring, or of having sold his birthright.[19] PJ presents quite different reasons for Esau's departure: his awe of Jacob is emphasised, and the language employed has strong military connotations, with allusions to Israel's victories.

We must now return to Gabla and the people associated with it. As noted earlier, Gen 36.20 speaks of 'the sons of Seir, the Horites, the inhabitants of the land', and the following verse mentions 'the chiefs of the Horites, the sons of Seir in the land of Edom'. The Horites (הַחֹרִי) are named also at Gen. 36.29, 30; and PJ alone of the Targumim takes the designation not as a people, but as an aristocratic title, translating with גנוסיאי, 'the nobles'. PJ doubtless had in mind the Hebrew word חוֹר 'noble' and its Aramaic cognate;[20] but the Targum has used a Greek loan-word to translate it. The Greek word in question is most likely εὐγενής, which means 'nobly born'; but the orthography this word assumes in Aramaic, גנוסיא, is in the singular form identical with the Aramaic representation of another quite different Greek term, γενέσια, meaning 'birthday'.[21] The latter is a term with strong links to Roman imperialism, with its regular, public celebrations of

[19] The same exegesis is found again at Gen. Rab. 84.2, where it is provided with a *petiḥa*, Prov. 28.1 being cited in Hebrew, 'The wicked one flees, but no-one pursues: but the just is confident like a young lion' and is at once followed by an Aramaic version of the first half of the verse; and see also Rashi's comment on Gen. 36.6. For the notion of fear engendered in Esau by his abdication of the birthright, see the comment on Gen. 36.7 in *ʾAggadat Berešit* 58.

[20] See (e.g.) 1 Kgs. 21.8, 11; Neh. 2.16; 6.17; and especially Isa. 34.12, where Edom is under discussion. The word is found in Aramaic in the Elephantine Papyri, Papyrus 30, line 19: see Cowley (1923: 112).

[21] See Krauss (1964: vol. 2: 180), who gives the spelling of both Greek loan-words in the singular as Aramaic גנוסיא.

the birthdays of past and present emperors and members of the imperial family.[22] The nobles in all societies under Roman rule played a prominent role in these politically significant celebrations and, as PJ will eventually tell us directly, Rome is genetically linked to Esau who is Edom, who lives in Seir which is Gabla, with its 'nobles'. PJ's choice of language is, to say the least, suggestive, and will remain so throughout the chapter, as the next item for discussion will show.

2. The Mules in the Desert

Gen. 36.24 records the sons of Zibeon, including that man ʿAnah whom we had occasion to notice earlier.[23] The verse further defines him: 'That was ʿAnah who found *hayyēmīm* (הַיֵּמִם) in the desert when he was pasturing the he-asses of his father Zibeon'. The word not translated in this verse is transliterated here as the Masoretes have vocalized it: in this form, it is *hapax legomenon*, and led the ancient exegetes to differing explanations. The LXX, along with Aquila, Symmachus, and Theodotion, resorted to transliterations.[24] The Peshitta, however, rendered the word as 'waters', either by vocalizing the Hebrew consonants to read הַיַּמִּם *hayyammīm*, 'the seas', or by re-arranging the consonants to yield הַמַּיִם *hammayim*, 'the water'. Eusebius of Emesa (died *ca.* 359 CE) cites 'the Hebrew' as indicating that the word means 'water', an opinion shared by some other Greek Christian writers.[25] A related translation is 'spring, well', attributed to 'the Syrian'.[26] Jerome's translation of the word as *aquas calidas*, 'hot waters', bears a family

[22] These birthdays and their observances were intimately linked to the notion that the Roman Emperor was a god: see Rives (2007: 148–153). Jews would not have been strangers to royal birthdays. From long before the Roman period, 2 Macc. 6.7 alludes to monthly celebrations of Antiochus IV's birthday. Some influence of Ptolemaic royal custom is discernible here, according to van Henten (2007: 273–274). See also Goodman (2007: 243–245, 306–307).

[23] Unlike Gen. Rab. 82.13, however, the LXX of this verse seems concerned to distinguish carefully this ʿAnah from the ʿAnah of verses 2 and 20 by adopting a different spelling for his name: see Wevers (1993: 601).

[24] LXX, Symmachus, and Theodotion put ιαμιν, while Aquila has ιμειμ: see Wevers (1993: 601), although Field (1875: vol. 1: 52) records also for Theodotion the reading ιαμειμ, and for Symmachus ημιν. With these transliterations, Aquila and Symmachus use the plural definite article τους, while LXX and Theodotion have the singular τον. LXX seem to have regarded the word as a proper noun, Yamin (Harl 1994: 256).

[25] See Ter Haar Romeny (1997:56–57, 379–383).

[26] See Field (1875: vol. 1, 53). On the identity of 'the Syrian', see extended discussion by Weitzman (1999: 143–147).

resemblance to these renderings.[27] TO, however, translated it as גבריא, 'the mighty ones, giants', and in so doing draws our attention back to the notion of awe and awesome people noted earlier (pp. 4–5).[28] This interpretation of a single Hebrew word is a vital clue in discerning TO's understanding of the whole chapter; but before it can be properly appreciated, PJ's expansion of Gen. 36.24 needs to be explored.

PJ offers details of ʿAnah and *hayyēmīm* as follows: 'That was ʿAnah who hybridized wild asses (ערדיא) with she-asses (אתני); and after a time he found the female mules (כודנייתא) which had gone forth from them, when he was pasturing the he-asses of his father Zibeon'. Several rabbinic sources understand *hayyēmīm* to be mules, and discuss the cross-breeding of horses and asses used to produce them.[29] But PJ's mules, it should be noted, are not the offspring of horses and asses: they are rather the progeny of wild creatures mated with domestic animals. The law of Mishna Kil. 8.6 is explicit: the ערוד *ʿarod* belongs to the category of wild beasts, and consequently may not be mated with domestic animals. ʿAnah the Edomite has thus done what no observant Jew could lawfully carry out, the crossing of wild with domestic animals resulting in hybrids. Given the discussion elsewhere in Rabbinic texts about these mules, it would seem that the Targum wishes to emphasize particularly the illicit mixing of the wild with the domestic, and the resulting production of female mules, which are incapable of reproduction. This explicit foregrounding of the mating of wild and domestic animals is not apparent in other sources which discuss Gen. 36.24, and its significance is not altogether clear.

---

[27] Jerome was aware of different translations of the word, and of various Jewish traditions about its meaning, even though he finally opted for the sense 'hot waters' in his Vulgate. It is evident that he did not find the LXX and other transliterations helpful: see Hayward (1995: 74–75, 217–218).

[28] Some Syriac commentators were aware of this translation through the so-called ʿEbraya ('the Hebrew'): see on this term Weitzman (1999: 139–142), and especially p. 140, where Gen. 36.24 is discussed.

[29] See Babylonian Talmud Pes. 54a; Hul. 7b; Tosefta Ber. 5: 4; Gen. Rab. 82.14; Palestinian Talmud Ber. 8.5. Mules may result either from crossing a he-ass with a mare, or from mating a stallion with a she-ass, as is plain from the debate in Gen. Rab. 82.14. The laws of *kilʾayim* at Lev. 19.19 forbid Jews from breeding such animals, although their use is nowhere forbidden (see 2 Sam. 13.29; 18.9; 1 Kgs. 10.25 for examples of biblical references to use of mules occasioning no comment). Philo, De Spec. Leg. iii.47–50 is scathing in his criticism of those who produce mules from specially bred he-asses and mares, and understands the law of Lev. 19.19 as an admonition against illicit sexual intercourse between human beings; but he does not explicitly relate this reference to Esau's family.

What led PJ and other authorities to translate the word הַיֵּמִם in Gen. 36.24 as mules? One explanation might be that the Hebrew word sounds similar to the Greek ἡμίονος, which Rabbinic Hebrew borrowed to designate the mule, and which is indeed used in Gen. Rab. 82.14 and Palestinian Talmud Ber. 8.5 in discussions about this verse.[30] While this may be so, it raises another, obvious question: since Hebrew has a perfectly good and well known word for mule (פֶּרֶד), why should a different, foreign word be used in discussions about Gen. 36.24? What is special, if anything, about these particular beasts? This very question, 'why are they called *yēmīm*?' was asked by R. Joshua b. Levi, and he provided the answer: 'because their awe (אימתם) is thrown over the creatures' (Babylonian Talmud Hul. 7b). In other words, the rabbi interprets the obscure יֵמִם as being related to, and comprehensible through, the common Biblical Hebrew word אֵימָה 'awe, terror'. The central significance of this word in the interpretation of Gen. 36 is now becoming clear: the element of danger is to the fore. The notion that mules, or certain sorts of mule, may be very dangerous, is clearly stated on the same page of the Talmud: R. Hanina reports that no-one had ever enquired of him about a wound caused by a white mule (פרדה לבנה) and had recovered. When an objection is raised to this, R. Hanina explains that he is talking specifically about a mule with white legs.

A similar kind of conversation about dangerous mules, providing extra information about this discussion in the Babylonian Talmud, features in Gen. Rab. 82.14 and in Palestinian Talmud Ber. 8.5; and both treatments of the subject are very similar in character. They both begin by noting that although fire and hybrids (כלאים) had not been brought into being during the six days of creation, they had nonetheless entered into the divine plan during those days; and the discourse then turns to consider when hybrids had in fact been created.[31] The answer, as we might by now expect, is to be found in Gen. 36.24 and הַיֵּמִם, which R. Judah b. R. Simon explains through the Greek loan word ἡμίονος 'mule', and the rabbis with reference to another Greek word ἡμίσυ, 'half', signifying a creature of mixed parentage, half horse

[30] See for details Krauss (1964: vol. 2: 229) and Sarna (5479/1989: 251).

[31] Gen. Rab. 82.14 and Palestinian Talmud Ber. 8.5 mention ʿAnah alone as creator of the mule; butBabylonian Talmud Pes. 54a records a discussion in which Adam is named as the inventor of both fire and the mules.

and half donkey or ass.[32] The 'signs' of this creature are then given. R. Jonah in Gen. Rab., R. Judah according to the Palestinian Talmud, state that mares as dams and he-asses as sires produce mules with small ears, whereas female asses as dams and stallions as sires produce mules with big ears. R. Mannah states his preference for the small-eared sort; and then the question is asked what ʿAnah (Gen. Rab.) or Zibeon and ʿAnah together (the Palestinian Talmud) actually did in respects of the mules? We are told that he brought a she-ass and mated it with a stallion, and a she-mule (פרדה) came forth from this union. The Almighty then declared that he had not created a thing which causes damage; and vowed in return to create something that really would cause damage! Thus we hear that God, by cross-breeding a הכינא with a הרדון, produced a חברבר, some kind of reptile, from whose bite no-one has ever recovered, just as no-one has ever survived from a wound inflicted by the kick of a white mule. Both Gen. Rab. 82.14 and Palestinian Talmud Ber. 8.5 are emphatic on two key points: ʿAnah brought something into the world which was extremely dangerous, proximity to which would prove lethal; and that by doing so ʿAnah was indirectly responsible for the introduction into the created order of yet another deadly animal whose bite is incurable.

These sources assert that certain types of mule are very dangerous. But the mules PJ has in mind, produced through crossing wild asses with the domestic variety, are called כודנייתא, and none of the vocabulary used in the Rabbinic discussions we have noted is to be found in this Targum. The Hebrew word associated with the mules of Gen. 36.24 in Babylonian Talmud Hul. 7b is אימה 'awe', and it evidently informs rabbinic discussion of these beasts at every turn. At this point we should recall that TO translated הַיֵּמִם as גבריא 'mighty ones, giants', and add to this the information that גבריא is the word which TO used consistently to translate רְפָאִים 'the Rephaim', an ethnic group dwelling in Canaan in the time of the Patriarchs.[33] Deut. 2.11 informs us that the Moabites called these people אֵמִים 'awesome ones'. It would seem that TO of Gen. 36.24 has reasoned that Hebrew

[32] Various spellings of the latter are found, including המיסו and היימיס; see Krauss (1964: vol. 2: 229–230), and Levy (1867: 355) under כודנתא.

[33] Forthe translation of Rephaim as גבריא, see TO of Gen. 14.5 (where the *ʾemim* are associated with them: the following verse mentions Horites and Seir, whose names are found frequently in Gen. 36); 15.20; Deut. 2.11. 20; 3.13. In Targum Jonathan of the Prophets, all occurrences of the word Rephaim are translated as גבריא. The Samaritan Pentateuch at Gen. 36.24 reads not הַיֵּמִם but האימים 'the ʾEmim'.

הַיֵּמִם is to be explained with reference to אֵמִים, a term synonymous with Rephaim, for which this Targum has invariably used the designation 'mighty ones, giants', גבריא.[34] TO thus stands shoulder to shoulder with R. Joshua b. Levi's explanation of the word recorded in Babylonian Talmud Hul. 7b, as signifying something awesome and terrible; and we may further deduce that, in using this particular interpretation of the word, the Targum expects the intelligent student to be aware of the discussions attendant on the interpretation of הַיֵּמִם as 'the awesome ones'. For TO these creatures are a people, not mules; but it is important to note that if TO were at any stage to be read in the light of discussions about mules, then the Targum might be taken to mean that the Rephaim had been products of a mixed ancestry.

A brief stock-taking exercise may be helpful at this stage. Gen. 36.24 was widely understood by ancient Jewish exegetes to refer to the origin of mules, specifically white mules, whose kick was held to be lethal. This understanding was possible because the verse contains a *hapax legomenon*, the baffling word הַיֵּמִם, which the exegetes associated with a common Hebrew word meaning 'awe, terror'. Sources which discuss this verse emphasise the dangerous quality of these mules, which are the first hybrids. Like Esau's own family, they are progeny of illicit unions;[35] and we have briefly reviewed some of the interesting and colourful discussions arising out of a difficult verse of Scripture. As often, TO with a single word hints at knowledge of wider discussion which is taken for granted. By contrast, PJ talks of the mules using vocabulary which differs entirely from that used in the Rabbinic discussions reviewed, and offers an account of their origin which seems to be *sui generis*. Most striking of all, PJ does not yoke the mules to the notion of 'awe'. Nevertheless, 'awe' is a quality prominent at the start of PJ's interpretation of Gen. 36. It is brought to our attention not in respect of the mules, but with regard to 'the awe of Jacob' which had fallen upon Esau, the ancestor of ʿAnah, and had brought about his departure to Seir. This 'awe of Jacob' is not dangerous: indeed, it is the very opposite of dangerous, in that it will protect Jacob's children from Esau's malice and determination to attack his brother.

A further peculiarity of PJ's interpretation of Gen. 36.24 is revealed by closer inspection of its treatment of the original Hebrew. This

[34] Note also that TO also describes as גבריא the Nephilim, and the Gibborim of Gen. 6.4, the 'giants' whose wickedness brought about the Flood in Noah's days.

[35] This point is made most tellingly at Babylonian Talmud Pes. 54a.

mentions ʿAnah as the one 'who found *hayyēmīm* in the desert': it will be recalled that PJ makes two co-ordinate clauses out of this one statement. Thus the Targum notes first that this was ʿAnah 'who hybridized wild asses with she-asses.' and reports second that 'after a time he found the female mules which had gone forth from them'. In this Targumic paraphrase, all mention of 'in the desert', Hebrew בַּמִּדְבָּ֔ר, has apparently disappeared. A possible explanation of this state of affairs might lie to hand if one envisages the Targumist as somehow having discerned in this common phrase the notion of hybridization. How so? By examining the unvocalized consonants of the Hebrew word במדבר, the exegete might have perceived in them a form of the common root דבר 'speak', in a rare form of that root, understanding it as an infinitive construct *hitpaʿel* with prefixed preposition *b-* to yield בְּמִדַּבֵּר, signifying 'by conversing together, congressing', that is, by cross-breeding.[36] Then, quite naturally, the Targumist can go on to tell how ʿAnah found the mules, Hebrew מָצָא being generally employed to describe the discovery of something that already exists. If this explanation of PJ's exegetical procedure is correct, it would indicate that the Targum's interpretation is rooted in the perceived meaning of a particular word in the Hebrew text, not in some other principle or point of exegesis deriving from outside the Bible. This is an important observation, given that Babylonian Talmud Pes.54a records a significant difference of opinion on the matter of the mules. Rabban Simeon b. Gamliel states that mules came about in the days of ʿAnah, and cites Gen. 36.24 as proof; but then we learn that the *dorše ḥamurot* used to say that because ʿAnah was *pasul*, 'ritually unfit', in like manner he brought *pasul* into the world, citing as proof Gen. 36.20, 24a and going on to discuss the illegitimate and scandalous nature of his ancestry: the hybrid ʿAnah is responsible for producing the hybrid mule.[37] PJ evidently turns its back on this interpretation: there is nothing in this Targum's version of Gen. 36 to indicate directly that Esau's family was illegitimate, and the episode of the mules is consequently quite separate from any such consideration. We shall need to return to this point.

---

[36] The *hitpaʿel* form of root דבר is rare, though it is attested with the sense of 'converse together': see Koehler and Baumgartner (1958: 200) and Waltke and O'Connor (1990: 431).

[37] The identity of the *dorše ḥamurot* is unknown, although it seems that they offered an allegorical or symbolical interpretation of Scripture.

3. Riches, Possessions—and Rome

The presence of wicked people among Esau's descendants is not denied by PJ. At Gen. 36.28 the Hebrew gives the name of one of the sons of Dishan as Aran, which PJ understands as Aram, who gave his name to the homeland of the wicked Balaam: unsurprisingly, this villain appears in PJ of Gen. 36.32 as the Targum's interpretation of the personal name given in Hebrew as Bela. PJ Numb. 22.5; 31.8 identifies Balaam with Laban the Aramean, and here his Edomite affiliations are made explicit.[38] The complex of names appearing in Gen. 36.39 attracted the Targumists, such that this is the only verse in the entire chapter to which Fragment Targum survives. The particular point of interest was the Edomite king named as Hadar and his wife. Her name is given as Mehetabel, 'daughter of Matred daughter of Me-zahab'. TO understood the final name in this list to mean 'refiner of gold': this terse interpretation may, as we shall see, assume a certain amount of knowledge on the hearer's or reader's part. PJ and FT offer similar, extended interpretations. We give PJ's as the example:

> ...the daughter of Matred. He was the man who was working with the hunting-spear and the net; and when he had become rich and had acquired possessions, he again became haughty, saying, What is silver? and What is gold?

The arrogance of Matred could hardly be more trenchantly expressed.[39] In PJ, as we approach the end of the long list of personnel descended from Esau, we pass from the 'nobles' with their Romano-imperial associations, through Aram and the villain Balaam, to a wielder of spear and snare whose riches are so great that he can express open contempt for them. Riches and possessions have already featured at Gen 36.6–7 in the Bible and the Targums as abundantly significant for Esau and his family: the increase in these things in some way assists in understanding Esau's journey to another land, away from

---

[38] See also Babylonian Talmud San. 105a for Balaam's identity as Laban, and Gen. Rab. 57.4, where the name Qemuel is applied to Laban who is Balaam. In postbiblical exegetical writings, Balaam is generally represented as a villain seeking to destroy Israel: see G. Vermes (1973: 127–177); Baskin (1983); and Greene (1992).

[39] See further Shinan (1979: vol. 1: 101–102), and variations of this interpretation at Gen. Rab. 83.4–5; Targum 1 Chron.1.50. TN gives a more muted interpretation, according to which Matred became rich 'and knew what was silver and what was gold', suggesting, perhaps, an arrogance tempered, or exacerbated, by the fastidious knowledge of the connoisseur.

his brother Jacob. Matred's riches, however, are of a quite different order, equalled only by his simple-minded pride in the possession of them. And this brings us, finally, to Rome. The last verse of the chapter (36.43) lists chief Magdiel and chief 'Iram, concluding with the note that these are the chiefs of Edom according to their settlements in the land of their possession: 'he is Edom, the father of the Edomites'. The first of these chiefs PJ identifies further: 'Chief Magdiel: he was called Magdiel on account of the name of his city, the strong tower (מגדל תקיף), that is, Rome the sinful'. The description of Rome as 'the strong tower' may well be intended to indicate its status as blasphemer. PJ has here expounded the name Magdiel with reference to the Hebrew words מִגְדָּל 'tower' and אֵל 'God' understood in the sense of 'the strong, powerful one'. The resultant expression 'strong, mighty tower' evokes in the mind of the reader or hearer both Ps. 61.4, with its urgent prayer that the Lord be a 'strong tower' for the petitioner in the face of his enemies; and Prov. 18.10, which declares that the Name of the Lord is a strong tower into which the just person runs and is secure. Furthermore, PJ's interpretation of the poem *Ha'azinu* (Deut. 32) consistently translates 'rock' as a title of the Almighty in that text with the word 'strong' (תקיף).[40] PJ thus by implication presents Rome as the blaspheming city, claiming divine status. Quite simply, it is 'the sinful Rome'.[41]

This last verse of Gen. 36 was interpreted in Gen. Rab. 83.4–5 with reference to the future. This text records a vision of R. Ammi, in which it is revealed to him that 'Magdiel' had become king on the day of Diocletian's accession. The rabbi's reaction to this vision is a declaration that only one more king remains of Edom's imperial dynasty. In this midrash Edom is equated, as often, with Rome; and the remainder of this chapter of Gen. Rab. looks forward to the coming of Messiah, and the nations' acceptance that the world was created for Israel's sake.[42] On the subject of the future, the coming of redemption, and the place

---

[40] See PJ of Deut. 32.4, 15, 18, 30, 31.

[41] See also PRE 38. This was probably the description of Rome given also at PJ of Num. 24.19, part of Balaam's prophecy which predicts the destruction of Constantinople (?) following the rout of the sons of Gabla with their riches (Num. 24.28). See le Déaut (1979: 236–237). For discussion of these verses in TN and PJ, see McNamara (1995: 140–141, 260–261).

[42] On the Rabbinic equation of Esau-Edom with Rome, see Cohen (1967: 19–48); Zeitlin (1969: 262–263); and Feldman (1988–1989: 130–133).

of the nations in time to come, however, all the Targumim of Gen. 36 including PJ are silent.

4. A Distinctive Perspective for Targum Pseudo-Jonathan

Targum PJ of Gen. 36 emerges from this investigation as presenting a remarkably distinctive exegetical trajectory. If we begin by considering the point just noted, that Rabbinic texts frequently equate Esau-Edom with Rome, PJ's stance begins to emerge. The Targum is evidently aware of this equation, and indeed makes use of it in expounding Gen. 15.12; Lev. 26.44; and Deut. 32.24; but in its exegesis of Gen. 36 the reference to Rome is saved up until the very end of the chapter, and is then associated with a particular descendant of Esau whose name can be linked to a powerful city and to blasphemy against the Almighty. This seems to be the goal towards which the Targum's exegesis of this chapter is slowly but inexorably working.[43] The beginning of PJ's exegesis, however, might in other circumstances be considered properly as the end of the story: we have heard in PJ of Gen. 36.6 of 'the awe of Jacob' which 'had been thrown down' on Esau, compelling him to move to another land; and we have examined the implications of that phrase 'the awe of Jacob his brother'. In fine, PJ's exegesis of Gen. 36 opens with allusions to the ultimate overthrow of Esau, which this Targum perceived as already having begun in his departure 'to another land'. This approach to Gen. 36 differs considerably from other sources we have examined. From the outset, PJ seems to regards Gen. 36 as a catalogue of persons who, however mighty they might become, are all gathered under 'the awe of Jacob', which is cast over them from the very beginning.

These persons are many in number; and, like the Bible, PJ treats Gen. 36 which lists them as a self-contained sense-unit. The first verse in the Hebrew speaks of 'Esau: he is Edom', which PJ makes precise with the rendering 'Esau, *who is called* Edom'. The last verse of the

[43] This suggestion is strengthened by the Targum's failure to provide an exegesis of the name 'Iram, which follows that of Magdiel in Gen. 36.43, and which is carefully explained by Gen. Rab. 83.4 (R. Hanina of Sepphoris) with reference to the future heaping up (עתיד לערום) of treasure for the use of the coming messianic king. This provides a suitably triumphant conclusion to the treatment of Gen. 36 in this midrash. PJ's note of triumph in this verse is muted, and finds fullest expression in its exposition of Gen. 36.6.

chapter mentions in the Hebrew chief Magdiel *tout court*, while PJ provides a boundary recalling its own beginning of the chapter by noting 'chief Magdiel: *he was called* Magdiel because of the name of his city'. Within these boundaries we find names of Israel's enemies. Unlike other Rabbinic sources, however, PJ is not unduly interested in their scandalous parentage. Rather, the Targum interprets particular names, such that attention is drawn to Gabla, the biblical Gebal which Ps. 83 sets in a catalogue of Israel's enemies, and 'nobles' representing the Horites: in this last instance, a Greek loan word of somewhat ambiguous character is used, possibly carrying with it overtones of Roman imperial birthday celebrations and cult. Then (Gen. 36.24) we meet ʿAnah and his mules. Once more, these are familiar from other Rabbinic texts; but in PJ they appear in a quite different guise. The notion of 'awe' signifying danger, central to most Rabbinic treatments of the mules, is nowhere to be found explicitly in PJ, which in contrast to other sources has already mentioned 'awe' at the beginning of the chapter in relation to Jacob. From the perspective of the Talmud and the Midrash, this 'awe' has been displaced from the mules onto Jacob: a transformation of exegesis has taken place, and those texts, in their turn, do not speak of Jacob's awe in expounding this chapter. PJ's mules are happy to be Aramaic mules: the Greek loan words used to speak of them in other sources are lacking. They are hybrids of wild and domestic animals, and PJ seems to have derived directly from the Scriptural text of Gen. 36.24 the means by which they were produced: the Targum conveys no suggestion that the 'mixed' parentage of Esau's family is comparable to the 'mixed' parentage of the mules, or has anything to do with it. Next, PJ is happy to list Aram and the wicked Balaam among Esau's descendants, and to transmit, in common with other interpreters, a damning account of Matred's character: then, at last, Rome is directly named, the sinful city, the 'strong tower' whose name seems designed to challenge the Almighty with its blasphemous connotations.

From the point of view of the other Rabbinic texts we have discussed here, PJ's interpretation appears not only self-contained, but also somewhat counter-intuitive. The absence of invective against the sexual antics of Esau's family; the failure explicitly to identify Edom with Rome; the prominence of Gabla and nobles; the very distinctive account of ʿAnah's mules; the Targum's sense that the origin of those mules can be derived directly from the Hebrew of Gen. 36.24 without the help of extra-biblical tradition, however colourful; and the absence of any explicit reference to the days to come certainly distinguish PJ's interpretation of this chapter from Rabbinic texts we have surveyed. That said, the Targum's account of Matred, and its note about Eliphaz and Job, find their exact counterparts in Talmud and midrash. What, then, might be PJ's objectives in interpreting Gen. 36 in this unusual manner? We might note the following points. First and foremost, Jacob has nothing to fear from Esau. Quite the reverse: once, long ago, Esau had moved his dwelling *because of the awe of Jacob which had fallen upon him*, and that same awe was still operative when Israel came out of Egypt and sang a song about it, a song which may also be sung at the final redemption. Second, Esau is not *simply* the equivalent of Rome. From Esau came forth many and varied enemies of Israel: their exact origin is of little importance, despite their numbers and their power. Some of them (like Balaam) no longer exist, and others (like those listed also in Psalm 83) are under God's judgement. The last of them to be named is Rome, who is also the strongest and most terrible; but Rome, too, will be thrown down, falling never to rise: its 'awe', which Abraham had seen when the deep sleep had 'been thrown down' upon him, will disappear, just as Jacob's 'awe' made Esau depart from him. PJ thus appears to be reflecting upon the received traditional interpretations of a number of key biblical texts, and drawing conclusions from them, because Gen. 36 represents the last occasion in the book of Genesis when Esau and his family will be the subject of narrative.[44]

As for ʿAnah and his Aramaic mules, the Targum may be concerned to draw a lesson from these hybrids by implication. They are engendered from the wild and the domestic, and without discoursing on the character of the wild ass, PJ may perhaps be inviting a particular conclusion. No foreign term is needed to describe them, unlike the Horite 'nobles'; and they do not spring from different species of quadruped. They represent the same species which has 'gone off the rails', as it were; ʿAnah, whose ancestry is not openly disparaged in this Targum, brought them into being. In Esau's family, then, there are 'mixtures' of different sorts, and Israel should perhaps be conscious of this. But it is striking that it is this particular instance of the mixing of diverse kinds which the Targum chooses particularly to highlight, though its reasons for doing so are no longer obvious to us.

---

[44] See Sarna (5479/1989: 246).

References

Baskin, J.R. 1983. *Pharaoh's Counsellors: Job, Jethro and Balaam in Rabbinic and Patristic Tradition* (Chico: Scholars Press).
Berlin, A., and M.Z. Brettler. 1999. *The Jewish Study Bible* (Oxford: Oxford University Press).
Brin, G. 2002. 'The Idea and Sources of Esau's Speech in Jubilees 37 according to 4QPapJubilees[h], Unit 2, Col. IV', in *Studies in Bible and Exegesis VI: Yehuda Otto Komlosh—In Memoriam* (eds R. Kasher and M.A. Zipor; Ramat-Gan: Bar-Ilan University Press) 17–24 [in Hebrew].
Clarke, E.G. 1995. *Targum Pseudo-Jonathan: Numbers* (The Aramaic Bible, 4; Edinburgh: T. & T. Clark).
Clarke, E.G., with W.E. Aufrecht, J.C. Hurd, and F. Spitzer. 1984. *Targum Pseudo-Jonathan of the Pentateuch: Text and Concordance* (Hoboken, NJ: Ktav).
Cohen, G.D. 1967. 'Esau as Symbol in Early Medieval Thought', in *Jewish Medieval and Renaissance Studies* (ed. A. Altmann; Cambridge, MA: Harvard University Press) 19–48.
Cowley, A.E. 1923. *Aramaic Papyri of the Fifth Century BC* (Oxford: Clarendon Press).
Díez Macho, A. 1968. *Ms. Neophyti 1 Tomo 1 Génesis* (Madrid-Barcelona: Consejo Superior de Investigaciones Científicas).
Doran, R. 1985. 'Aristeas the Exegete', in *The Old Testament Pseudepigrapha*, vol. 2 (ed. J.H. Charlesworth; London: Darton, Longman and Todd) 855–858.
Feldman, L.H. 1988–1989. 'Josephus' Portrait of Jacob', *Jewish Quarterly Review* 79: 100–151.
Field, F. 1875. *Origenis Hexaplorum Quae Supersunt*, 2 vols (Oxford: Clarendon Press).
Goodman, M. 2007. *Rome and Jerusalem. The Clash of Ancient Civilizations* (London: Allen Lane).
Greene, J.T. 1992. *Balaam and His Interpreters: A Hermeneutical Study of the Balaam Traditions* (Atlanta: Scholars Press).
Grossfeld, B. 1988. *The Targum Onqelos to Genesis, Translated, with a Critical Introduction, Apparatus and Notes* (The Aramaic Bible, 6; Edinburgh: T. & T. Clark).
Harl, M. 1994. *La Bible d'Alexandrie 1 La Genèse* (Paris: Éditions du Cerf).
Hayward, C.T.R. 1995. *Jerome's* Hebrew Questions on Genesis *Translated with an Introduction and Commentary* (Oxford: Oxford University Press).
Himmelfarb, M. 2006. *A Kingdom of Priests. Ancestry and Merit in Ancient Judaism* (Philadelphia: University of Pennsylvania Press).
Holladay, C.R. 1983. *Fragments from Hellenistic Jewish Authors Volume 1: Historians* (Chico: Scholars Press).
Jacobson, H. 1996. *A Commentary on Pseudo-Philo's* Liber Antiquitatum Biblicarum *With Latin Text and English Translation*, 2 vols (Leiden: Brill).
Klein, M.L. 1980. *The Fragment Targums of the Pentateuch according to their Extant Sources*, 2 vols (Rome: Biblical Institute Press).
Krauss, S. 1964. *Griechische und Lateinische Lehnwörter im Talmud, Midrasch und Targum*, 2 vols (reprinted Hildesheim: Georg Olms).
Kugel, J. 1998. *Traditions of the Bible. A Guide to the Bible as it was at the Start of the Common Era* (Cambridge, MA: Harvard University Press).
le Déaut, R. 1979. *Targum du Pentateuque III Nombres* (Paris: Éditions du Cerf).
Levy, J. 1867. *Chaldäisches Wörterbuch über die Targumim* (Leipzig: Baumgärtner's Buchhandlung).
McNamara, M. 1972. *Targum and Testament. Aramaic Paraphrases of the Hebrew Bible: A Light on the New Testament* (Shannon, Ireland: Irish University Press & Grand Rapids: Eerdmans).

Rahlfs, A. 1935. *Septuaginta*, 2 vols (Stuttgart: Württembergische Bibelanstalt).
Rives, J.B. 2007. *Religion in the Roman Empire* (Oxford: Blackwell).
Sarna, N. 5479/1989. *The JPS Torah Commentary. Genesis* (Philadelphia–New York-Jerusalem).
Schürer, E. 1986. *The History of the Jewish People in the Age of Jesus Christ*, vol. III.1 (eds. G. Vermes, F. Millar, and M. Goodman; Edinburgh: T and T Clark).
Shinan, A. 1979. *The Aggadah in the Aramaic Targums to the Pentateuch*, 2 vols (Jerusalem: Makor) [in Hebrew].
Sperber, A. 1959. *The Bible in Aramaic I The Pentateuch According to Targum Onkelos* (Leiden: Brill).
Ter Haar Romeny, B. 1997. *A Syrian in Greek Dress. The Use of Greek, Hebrew and Syriac Biblical Texts in Eusebius of Emesa's Commentary on Genesis* (Louvain: Peeters).
Van Henten, J.W. 2007. 'Royal Ideology: 1 and 2 Maccabees and Egypt', in *Jewish Perspectives on Hellenistic Rulers* (eds. T. Rajak, S. Pearce, J. Aitken, and J. Dines; Berkeley: University of California Press).
Vermes, G. 1973. 'The Story of Bala'am—The Scriptural origins of Haggadah', in *Scripture and Tradition in Judaism* (2nd rev, ed.; Leiden: Brill) 127–177.
Weitzman, M.P. 1999. *The Syriac Version of the Old Testament* (Cambridge: Cambridge University Press).
Westermann, C. 1986. *Genesis 12–36* (London: SPCK).
Wevers, J. 1993. *Notes on the Greek Text of Genesis* (SBL Septuagint and Cognate Studies Series, 35; Atlanta: Scholars Press).
Zeitlin, S. 1969. 'The Origin of the Term Edom for Rome and the Christian Church', *Jewish Quarterly Review* 60: 262–263.

THE CONDEMNED RULERS IN TARGUM ISAIAH'S ESCHATOLOGICAL BANQUET

William D. Barker

As Robert Gordon has rightly pointed out, the Targumists were as much 'eschatologists' as they were biblical expositors (Gordon 1978: 113).[1] While the Targumists' development of such eschatological concepts as resurrection, Messianism, and final reward (or final retribution) has been explored, relatively little has been said about the Targumists' interpretation of one of the Second Temple period's prominent eschatological concepts: the final banquet.[2] In both the MT and the Targums, the foundational text about the banquet is Isaiah 25.6–8. An examination of this text in the Targum tradition can provide some insight into the early interpretation of the book of Isaiah, as well as serve as a case study for some of the translation techniques of the Isaiah Targumist. However, perhaps the most valuable aspect of the passage for understanding the Targumist's eschatological concerns is revealed in his conception of Israel's two great enemies and their fate as seen in Tg. Isa. 25:7.

[1] Two important areas of Robert Gordon's research have been the ancient versions of the Hebrew Bible and studies in the book of Isaiah. In keeping with these subject areas, and mindful of his significant contributions to the field of biblical studies, this essay is offered in his honour. The innumerable students, colleagues, and friends who have benefitted from Robert Gordon's scholarship as well as his kindnesses over the years will also see a tribute to him in the banquet theme since he and his family have humbly welcomed so many to their own table—a veritable foreshadowing of the blessings of the eschatological feast in every way.

[2] In terms of the development and prominence of this theme in the eschatology of the late inter-testamental period, in addition to Tg. Isa. 25.6–8, one thinks of such passages as 4 Ezra 6.48–52; 2 Baruch 29.4; 1 Enoch 60.7–10, 24; Tg. Cant. 8.2; and Tg. Ezek. 39.16–20. Of course this banquet motif continued developing as a part of Jewish eschatological thought in various communities, as reflected in such later texts as Babylonian Talmud B.B. 74b–75a and also the New Testament.

I. The Two Unidentified Enemies in Tg. Isa. 25.7

A variety of Targum translation techniques account for most of the changes in meaning from MT Isa. 25.6–8 to Tg. Isa. 25.6–8 (e.g. the use of stock phrases, the consoling vengeance motif, converse translation, *gezerah shavah* and perhaps the reminiscence of other Targum texts).[3] However, there is one enigmatic translation in the Targum passage that is not so readily explained. Whereas MT 25.7 refers to the swallowing of הַלּוֹט and הַמַּסֵּכָה, in the hands of the Targumist פְּנֵי־הַלּוֹט becomes אפי רבא ('the face of the great one') and הַמַּסֵּכָה becomes אפי מלכא דשליט על כל מלכותא ('the face of the king who rules over all the kingdoms'). This alteration in the Targum takes the MT's discussion of a covering and a veil (generally understood as garments used for mourning, symbolic of death itself) and transforms it into a condemnation of two unidentified but apparently antagonistic rulers. It is possible that these two kings of Tg. Isa. 25.7 are meant to represent death, since death could be conceived as the final ruling authority over mortals and this would be in keeping with the meaning of the MT. Both the grammar and the theme of the passage in the MT clarify the imagery of the veil and the curtain as death. However, these clarifications are missing in the Targum, and with their absence it seems highly improbable that the Targumist envisaged the singular personified death as the two rulers mentioned in 25.7. Consequently, elucidating the identity of these rulers is necessary for understanding Tg. Isa. 25.7 and the Targumist's conception of the eschatological banquet.

A. *The Collective but Undefined Enemies of Israel*

One interpretive option is that 'the great one' and 'the king who rules over all the kingdoms' do not refer to any specific individuals. In this case, the Targumist may have understood 25.7 as a collective but undefined reference to the enemies of Israel and their rulers whom YHWH would overthrow at the inauguration of his kingdom on Mount Zion—thus a general polemic against the leaders of Israel's enemies, but nothing more specific. Targum Isa. 54.15b and 56.9 speak of the destruction of 'the kings of the peoples that gather to oppress'

[3] For the 'interpretive principle of *gezerah shavah*' and its relationship to the Targums, see Gordon (2001: 70).

Jerusalem. Both verses also declare that these 'kings of the peoples' will meet their end in Jerusalem (Chilton 1983: 25). Such imagery, connected to an eschatological event in Jerusalem, could, at first glance, appear to be a fitting interpretation of the rulers who meet their end in Tg. Isa. 25.7. However, the problem with this interpretation is that only in the phrase 'kings of the peoples' do the kings appear to be undefined, eschatological enemies of YHWH who are more symbolic of the end of evil human rule than they are particular historical figures. The singular forms of רבא and מלכא in Tg. Isa. 25.7, and the fact that the forms are emphatic, suggest that the Targum is speaking of specific individuals or entities in this instance. In fact the substantival רב is used often by the Isaiah Targumist as an epithet for a specific human leader or a particular earthly power about to come under YHWH's judgement (e.g. Tg. Isa. 3.3, 6–7; 31.3; cf. 30.25; 36.13). Targum Isa. 25.7 uses רב to refer to a ruler 'over all peoples…the king…' who will be 'devoured' as part of YHWH's vengeance. Such use in 25.7 is in keeping with these wider connotations of the term in Targum Isaiah.

So, while the conceptual and lexical bonds between 56.9–12 and 25.6–8 are strong, such affinities do not require that the passages be interpreted in identical fashion. A universal judgement of all evil kings is the emphasis of 56.9–12 and is likely assumed in the context of 25.6–8. By contrast, however, 25.6–8 cannot be limited to a general, universal judgement, since the emphatic forms of 25.7 appear to be concentrated on YHWH's condemnation of specific, and perhaps supreme, offenders.

B. *Rome*

A more specific identification is proposed by Chilton, who suggests that 25.7 is a reference to a Roman emperor (Chilton 1987: 49, n. 25:1–25:12).[4] In this case, both the phrases in question (i.e. 'the face of the great one' and 'the king who rules over all the kingdoms') would represent two references to one ruler, rather than singular references to two different rulers. According to Tg. Isa. 56.9–12, among the key victims at the Mount Zion judgement will be the kings who have oppressed Jerusalem. In the light of 56.9–12, then, 25.7 seems to suggest that no earthly king will escape YHWH's wrath, least of all

[4] Cf. the identification of the Roman emperor as one of the kings in both Tg. Isa. 25.7 and 27.1 by van der Kooij (2000: 189).

the ultimate offender. The identity of such an ultimate offender could, theoretically, have been a Roman emperor, or a personification of Rome and its oppression of Israel.

C. *Gog—Rome*

A third possibility for the identification of one of the rulers in 25.7 is Gog. A number of Targums identify Gog as the mighty leader of the nations that will assemble themselves against YHWH and Jerusalem.[5] This eschatological event ends with the death of Gog and the annihilation of his armies, followed by the scattering of their bodies and armaments, and the burial of their remains on the mountains of Israel. The many accounts of Gog in the Targums seem to fit well with the setting of Tg. Isa. 25.6–8, and nothing in the Gog accounts precludes a Gog identification in 25.7.

Further bolstering this argument, there are four characteristics of the Gog assault that are clearly paralleled in the banquet of Tg. Isa. 25.6–8. First, both events are eschatological and mark the beginning of YHWH's reign by the return of YHWH's faithful followers to Mount Zion and the judgement of YHWH's enemies in the same locale. Secondly, in the Gog judgement and Tg. Isa. 25.6–8 the enemies of Israel come expecting to receive wealth or glory, but, surprisingly, find judgement and death instead. Thirdly, both narratives feature a powerful ruler who will be condemned in Jerusalem. Jerusalem as the locus of eschatological judgement is characteristic of the Isaiah Targum and the Gog references, and Jerusalem is the centre of events in 25.7 as well. Fourthly, the two morbid vignettes describe deadly feasts. Tg. Isa. 25.6–8 speaks of a feast of plagues and the devouring of 'the face of the great one…the king who rules over all the kingdoms…'. The references to the Gog judgement (e.g. Tg. Ezek. 38–39; Tg. Isa. 33.22–24; Tg. Ps.-J. Exod. 40.11; Num. 11.26; 24.17; Tg. Neof. Num. 11.26; Tg. Cant. 8.4) describe more fully than the Isaiah passage the dark, eschatological banquet, by specifying that beasts and birds will feed on the flesh and blood of the evil leader, Gog, and his armies.

The association of Gog and one of the kings of 25.7 introduces the entire corpus of Targum references to Gog into 25.6–8; such an understanding of Isaiah's eschatological banquet continues the tendency of

---

[5] E.g. Tg. Ezek. 38–39; Tg. Isa. 33.22–24; Tg. Ps.-J. Exod. 40.11.

early and rabbinic Judaism to interpret the feast as an event in which a messiah was in some way a participant. Concerning the messianic figure, the Targums are unique, but not unanimous, in their interpretation, as there are four opposing views concerning the role of a messiah in vanquishing Gog. First, there are some texts that speak of the fall of Gog before 'the King Messiah' (Tg. Ps.-J. Num. 24.17 and Tg. Neof. Num. 11.26).[6] Secondly, Tg. Ps.-J. Exod. 40.11 is more specific than the 'King Messiah' citations, stating that the Messiah, son of Ephraim (rather than Messiah, Son of David) '[will] be victorious over Gog and his associates at the end of days'. Thirdly, and in direct opposition to the second view, is the marginal reading of Tg. Zech. 12.10 found in Codex Reuchlinianus, in which the Messiah, son of Ephraim, is slain by Gog at the gate of Jerusalem. Finally, Tg. Ps.-J. Num. 11.26 maintains solidarity with Tg. Isa. 25.6–8 in that only YHWH is mentioned as the enactor of divine judgement. These views of the final end of Gog and the role of a messianic figure are not explicit in Tg. Isa. 25.6–8, but any of the Gog judgement passages could be seen to fit within the events of 25.6–8; such possibilities for interpretation are made more interesting by other Jewish traditions specifying the presence of a messiah at the eschatological banquet concurrent with the defeat of Israel's enemies (e.g. 2 Bar. 29–30; Rev. 19). In fact, in the New Testament, Revelation 19 goes so far as to include such similar elements as the appearance of a messianic figure, a feast reminiscent of the Gog judgement accounts in Ezek. 38–39, and the destruction of two antagonistic figures—'the beast' and 'the false prophet' (Rev. 19.19–20)—making it appear as though the author of Revelation had at least some awareness—if not some dependence—on the eschatological banqueting tradition in Tg. Isa. 25.6–8.

If Gog is identified as one of the two kings of Tg. Isa. 25.7, then there is an important implication: Gog as the devoured king of 25.7 likely lends support to Chilton's argument that the king is to be understood as Rome. In the history of the interpretation of Gog and Magog, Gog has often been identified as a symbol of Rome (Bøe 2001: 192–193,

[6] MS. Parma 3235 (Rossi 42/1) Tg. Esth. II 5.1 might possibly also be understood in this light, even though there is no explicit mention of a messianic figure. The peripheral mention of the role of YHWH during 'the days of Gog and Magog' does not exclude the possibility that there would be a messianic figure involved in the defeat of Gog; it may be that the reference simply fails to give sufficient detail about the manner in which YHWH will defeat Gog.

198; Chilton 1987: 49; Levey 1987: 109).[7] Such a Gog-Rome interpretation may be part of 25.7, especially if we understand Gog-Rome as 'the king who rules over all the kingdoms'. If this view is correct, then there would still need to be an interpretation of 'the great one' in 25.7.

D. *Sennacherib*

Whether the Gog-Rome interpretation of 'the king who rules over all the kingdoms' is accurate or not, it is possible to understand the king of Assyria as 'the great one' of 25.7. Targum Isa. 10.12, 16, 26 emphasize that the king of Assyria was a figure believed to one day be the principal object of YHWH's wrath. In this respect, it seems a reasonable conjecture that the Targumist may have been recalling 10.12, 16–27 and YHWH's judgement upon Assyria when translating 25.6–8. Several additional supports for this view may be cited. First, יסופון is used often in Targum Isaiah to refer to the death of the wicked or the death of idol worshippers (Tg. Isa. 1.31; 2.18; 10.19; 34.4; 66.17). Secondly, this term is also used to describe the final annihilation of the armies of the king of Assyria in Tg. Isa. 10.19, and in 25.6 to describe the end of 'all peoples' at the mountainside feast. Thirdly, both Tg. Isa. 10.16, 26 and 25.6 speak of the מחא ('of YHWH') as the means by which great numbers of people will die in judgement. In fact, the banquet of 25.6–8 is introduced in verse 6 as a 'feast of strokes' (מחא). Fourthly, 25.7 states that 'the great one' will be destroyed בטורא הדין. This location is very likely the mountain of YHWH in Jerusalem, in keeping with the MT locus of the eschatological banquet. Similarly, in Tg. Isa. 10.32 it is precisely על טור בית מקדשא דבציון ועל עזרתא דבירושלם that Sennacherib makes his final assault before being destroyed by YHWH (cf. 10.33). The two texts indicate that the location of the destruction of Sennacherib is identical with the location of the destruction of the 'great one' in the eschatology of the Targumist. Finally, as noted in the comments above, רב can be used in Targum Isaiah as the epithet of a human leader or earthly power about to come under YHWH's judgement. רב is used, apparently in this regard, when describing the coming judgement of the king of Assyria in Tg. Isa. 36.13. There is obvious significance in the fact that the same term is used to describe both the king of Assyria and the ruler of 25.7.

[7] Cf. Tg. Ezek. 39.11, 15–16.

E. *Gog and Sennacherib As a Polemic against Foreign Oppressors and Idolatry*

A final possibility is that Tg. Isa. 25.7 refers to Sennacherib, the king of Assyria, as 'the great one' and Gog-Rome as 'the king who rules over all the kingdoms'.[8] As noted above, Targum Isaiah seems to associate Assyria and its king with idolatry. Gog, and its association with Rome, may have been representative of those nations and kings which oppressed Israel. As J. Ådna notes, 'There were groups within early Judaism whose eschatology reckoned with a plurality of saving mediator figures...In such an eschatological conception the functions were distributed among the various figures' (Ådna 2004: 222–223). This same plurality of personality and function also appears to be present with evil figures, as evidenced here in Tg. Isa. 25.7. In this case, the two malevolent kings would collectively represent the arch-enemies of Israel and YHWH, their final assault on Mount Zion, and their subsequent destruction outside of Jerusalem. The personalities represented would be Gog (Rome) and Sennacherib (Assyria) and their functions appear to represent the foreign oppression of Israel through presumably military means (in the case of Rome) and the foreign oppression of Israel through idolatry (in the case of Assyria).[9]

This same plurality of enemies and their collective condemnation is found explicitly in the Isaiah Targum's translation of MT Isa. 27.1. In Tg. Isa. 27.1 three kings—Pharaoh, Sennacherib and 'the king as strong as the sea'—are destroyed by YHWH (van der Kooij 2000:189). Consequently, the interpretation of Tg. Isa. 25.7 presented here seems even more likely since 'the king as strong as the sea' in Tg. Isa. 27.1 has been identified as representing Rome (e.g. see Chilton 1987: 53, n. 27:1–27:13). Thus, 27.1 is expanding on this idea of collective condemnation first found in 25.7, with two of the rulers—Sennacherib and Gog (or Assyria and Rome)—already present, and adding a third—Pharaoh, as representative of Egypt.

---

[8] Interestingly, P. Grelot found another connection between Gog and Sennacherib in the Isaiah Targum on the basis of his research on Tg. Isa. 10.32–34; see Grelot (1983: 22).

[9] This condemnation of internal and external enemies can also be seen in the Isaiah Targumist's reference to either the destruction of 'rebellious Israelites', the destruction of 'Gentile oppressors' or, quite possibly, both in Tg. Isa. 33.14; see Gordon (1978: 125).

In addition to the evidence listed above, there is further support for this interpretation. Targum manuscripts Brit. Mus. Or. MSS. 2211 and 1474 contain a marginal reading of Tg. Isa. 10.32, whereas Codex Reuchlinianus and Codex Socin 59 incorporate the same reading as part of the main text of 10.32 (Stenning 1949: 227–228; Chilton 1983: 26). Describing Sennacherib's military approach to Jerusalem, this variant links Sennacherib's march against Jerusalem with the coming march of Gog and Magog upon Jerusalem כד ישלים עלמא קציה לאת־ פרקא. The import of this reading of 10.32 is that, taken with 10.33, it implies that the judgement of the king of Assyria is either a forerunner pointing towards a greater eschatological event involving Gog, or that the judgement of the Assyrians and Gog will occur together in a single eschatological event. Further, whether the events are interpreted as a simultaneous judgement or similar but different judgements, this reading of 10.32–33 envisions the death of the king of Assyria and the battle of Gog in the same location as the judgement and death of 'the great one' in Tg. Isa. 25.6–8.As part of the context for 10.32–33, the previously mentioned smiting of YHWH's enemies that takes place in Tg. Isa. 10.26 also seems to point towards the parallel between Tg. Isa. 10 and Tg. Isa. 25.6–8.

Consequently, it appears that the most likely identification of 'the great one' and 'the king who rules over all the kingdoms' in Tg. Isa. 25.7 is Sennacherib and Gog, or, stated another way, Assyria and Rome. Gog appears to have primarily represented Rome as a symbol of the oppressors of Israel. Sennacherib appears to have primarily represented Assyria as a symbol of idolatry and the idolatrous leaders of foreign nations. Together in 25.7, these two figures, then, collectively represent those whom the Isaiah Targumist, and perhaps his community, believed to be the arch-enemies of Israel and YHWH. They also represent the Targumist's condemnation of idolatry and Israel's oppressors—thus serving as a polemic against Israel's internal enemies (when idolatry was adopted from within) as well as her external enemies.

II. Tg. Isa. 25.7 and the Eschatology of the Isaiah Targumist

Insofar as the early interpretation of Isaiah is concerned, if the understanding of Tg. Isa. 25.7 set forth here is accurate, then it would appear the Isaiah Targumist perceived the two greatest enemies of Israel to be foreign oppression and the practice of idolatry. Others may debate the setting(s) that gave rise to the Isaiah Targumist's own eschatological concern for these foreign oppressors to be defeated and idolatry to be eliminated. However, such discussions should also note that Targumic concerns with idolatry and foreign entanglements are also maintaining thematic fidelity (even when the grammar, through such devices as converse translation, does not) to the MT Isaiah tradition.

Concerning the perception of the eschatological banquet in the Isaiah Targum, this interpretation of the rulers in 25.7 is in keeping with the rest of the Targum understanding of the banquet as a 'feast of strokes' and judgement, more akin to the MT Ezekiel 38–39 macabre *fête noir* than the celebratory tone in MT Isa. 25.6–8.[10] This also allows for continuity with both the converse translation technique and the consoling vengeance motif that appear to have been employed throughout the Isaiah Targum.

As seen with respect to the two condemned rulers in 25.7, one additional translation technique employed by the Isaiah Targumist may have been the use of collective representations, not only of Israel's messianic figures, but also of Israel's eschatological enemies. When there was such a collective representation of these enemies, there was also an accompanying collective condemnation. In the case of these antagonists, as with the messianic figures, there was a distribution of their respective functions of leadership, with one condemned ruler representing foreign oppression and the other signifying the practice of idolatry. In this way, the Isaiah Targumist included a polemic against both these enemies of Israel, while also expressing the eschatological hope for their ultimate demise and final ruin.

[10] In MT Isa. 25.6–8 there is an absence of the judgement, as evidenced by the dregs-free wine that is often symbolic of God's wrath in the Hebrew Bible (e.g. MT Psa. 75.9; cf. Tg. Isa. 51.17), on all but personified death. The verses are more concerned with the final blessings upon Israel rather than the final judgement of her enemies. In contrast, Tg. Isa. 25.6–8 emphasizes the banquet as a 'feast of strokes' upon Israel's enemies, without any further attention to additional blessings for Israel. Again, this type of converse translation and consoling vengeance motifas translation techniques run throughout the translation of Targum Isaiah.

References

Ådna, J. 2004. 'The Servant of Isaiah 53 as Triumphant and Interceding Messiah: The Reception of Isaiah 52:13–53:12 in the Targum of Isaiah with Special Attention to the Concept of the Messiah', in *The Suffering Servant, Isaiah 53 in Jewish and Christian Sources* (eds. B. Janowski and P. Stuhlmacher; Grand Rapids: Eerdmans), 189–224.

Bøe, S. 2001. *Gog and Magog* (Wissenschaftliche Untersuchungen zum Neuen Testament, 2, Reihe 135; Tübingen: Mohr-Siebeck).

Chilton, B.D. 1983. *The Glory of Israel: Theology and Provenience of the Isaiah Targum* (Journal for the Society of the Old Testament Supplement Series, 23; Sheffield: University of Sheffield).

——. 1987. *The Isaiah Targum* (The Aramaic Bible, 11; Wilmington, Delaware: Michael Glazier, Inc.).

Gordon, R.P. 1978. 'The Targumists as Eschatologists' in *Congress Volume, Göttingen 1977* (ed. J.A. Emerton; Supplements to Vetus Testamentum, 29; Leiden: Brill) 113–130.

——. 2001. 'The Legacy of Lowth: Robert Lowth and the Book of Isaiah in Particular' in *Biblical Hebrew, Biblical Texts* (eds. Ada-Rappoport-Albert and Gillian Greenberg; Journal for the Society of the Old Testament Supplement Series, 333; Festschrift Michael P. Weitzman; Sheffield: Sheffield Academic Press) 57–76.

Grelot, P. 1983. 'Le Targoum d'Isaïe, X, 32–34 Dans Ses Diverses Recensions', *Revue Biblique* 90: 202–228.

Levey, S.H. 1987. *The Targum of Ezekiel* (The Aramaic Bible, 13; Collegeville: Michael Glazier, Inc.).

Stenning, J.F. 1949. *The Isaiah Targum* (Oxford: Oxford University Press).

van der Kooij, A. 2000. 'The Cities of Isaiah 24–27 According to the Vulgate, Targum and Septuagint' in *Studies in Isaiah 24–27* (eds. H.J. Bosman, H. van Grol, *et al.*; Old Testament Studies, 43; Leiden: Brill) 183–198.

TARGUM PROVERBS AND THE PESHITTA: REFLECTIONS ON THE LINGUISTIC ENVIRONMENT

John F. Healey

The Proverbs Targum (TgProv) is probably the oddest in the whole targumic canon.[1] It contains very few of the kind of expansions and interpretative interventions which make the targumic literature interesting to us. Those who have written on this targum have drawn attention to a handful of places where the text departs significantly from what is found in the Hebrew and in the other versions. The following are the main examples, often cited (e.g. by Mangenot: 1911: col. 2006):

Prov. 24.14

> MT: 'Know that wisdom is such for your soul; if you find it, there will be a future and your hope will not be cut off'.
> Tg: 'So have wisdom in your soul, for if you find it at first, a later time comes which is better than it and your hope will not cease'.

Prov. 28.1

> MT: 'The wicked flee when no one pursues, but the righteous are secure as a lion'.
> Tg: 'The wicked flee when there is nobody pursuing them, but the righteous are like a lion which looks out for its food, hoping for wisdom'.

There are many other very minor departures from the MT, usually clarifying the obvious meaning, occasionally introducing circumlocution (e.g. in 29.18 avoiding the implied failure of prophecy). The other side of this literalism is the fact that other known haggadic interpretations of verses of Proverbs (e.g. in 1.8–9; 25.19; 26.4–5) are completely ignored by TgProv (Healey 1991: 7).

[1] There is a need for a critical edition of the text. The text edited by P. de Lagarde (1873: 118–45) (here L) remains the readily available one, though there appears to be considerable variety in the textual tradition. The Alfonso de Zamora manuscript edited by L. Díez Merino (1984: 173–202) (here Z) is occasionally cited in what follows. The Syriac is provided by di Lella in the Leiden Peshitta (1979).

As a result of this general adherence to the standard text, interest among scholars has focused on the impact that the main ancient versions may have had on TgProv. An extensive study of the text in relation to the LXX (Kaminka 1931–1932) led to the conclusion that TgProv often reads the text in the same way as the LXX, going against the MT (Kaminka 1931–1932: 171–4). Kaminka concluded that this indicates (in a targum which is generally very literal) that the targumist was using a different Hebrew *Vorlage* from the Hebrew of the MT. This would have dating implications (below). However, some of these cases of following the LXX are paralleled in the Peshitta and a possible conclusion might be that both TgProv and the Peshitta were each directly or indirectly influenced by the LXX. However, this brings us to the other great peculiarity of TgProv, the fact that its text is closely linked with that of the Peshitta, but in a way that is not easily explained.

The introduction to the volume of the *Aramaic Bible* project containing the Targum of Proverbs attempted to summarize debate over this relationship between the Targum and the Peshitta version of the book (Healey 1991: 1–2). What follows is a review of some of the issues involved and adds some reflections on dating and linguistic environment. (A more complete survey of earlier views, with fuller explanations of them, has been published more recently by R.J. Owens [1998]; see also the summaries of Alexander 1992: 326–7; de Waard 2008: 10*–11* and McNamara 2010: 320.)

Since the 18th century scholars have been aware of the fact that there is a close connection between the TgProv and the Peshitta version of the book. J.A. Dathe's *De ratione consensus versionis Chaldaicae et Syriacae Proverbiorum Salomonis* (Leipzig 1764) demonstrated the connection and this led eventually to a scholarly consensus that the Syriac had been used in the creation of the Targum. According to Kaminka's figures 300 of the 915 verses of the Book of Proverbs are identical in the two versions (Kaminka 1931–1932: 171). Melammed (1972: xii) had different figures, though making the same point. He identified 410 verses as being effectively identical (sixty literally identical), with a further 150 showing strong similarity. Though reaching a different conclusion about TgProv's dependence on the Peshitta, D.C. Snell (1998) calculated that 72% of the words in the two are shared. Thus, as most have argued, a Jewish targumist had based his targum text on the Christian Syriac. Those who agreed with Dathe also included H. Pinkuss (1894: 109–13) and Díez Merino (1984: 307). This view is reflected also in most of the secondary literature (see Healey 1991: 2–3).

There have, however, been some scholars who found the idea of a Jewish borrowing of the Peshitta surprising. Matthew Black (1967: 25) could not imagine 'the indebtedness of the Synagogue to the Christian Church for its Targum'. Apart from socio-religious considerations of this kind, there had earlier been some dissidents whose views were based on detailed examination of the texts, notably S. Maybaum (1871; see also Segal 1955: III, 972), who argued for the priority of TgProv. This brought an immediate response from Th. Nöldeke (1872), who was categorical in his own assessment that the only way to explain the Syriacisms in TgProv was to assume dependence on the Peshitta. Much more recently D.C. Snell (1998: 73) also, using his statistical evidence, found 'that there is no special and direct dependence of the Targum on the Peshiṭta'. He particularly noted the places where the Peshitta follows the LXX but these readings do not appear in TgProv (1998: 73).

Most recently the late Michael Weitzman (1999: 109–10; Weitzman's earlier comments on this matter are reviewed in Owens 1998: 205–206) firmly endorsed what is now the established consensus view, that TgProv was composed on the basis of the Peshitta text. It is interesting that, while Weitzman had no hesitation in accepting the broad consensus, he felt it necessary to cite historical evidence to show that Jewish borrowing of the Christian text was plausible, specifically demonstrating (a) that the targums of the Hagiographa had no official status (and were thus free of restrictions which might have applied, e.g., to Pentateuchal targums, a point made already by Nöldeke [1872: 249]) and (b) that such Jewish dependence on Christian sources is attested historically. He mentions two pieces of evidence, the fact that Hai Gaon (939–1038) in a *responsum* clearly indicated that the Targums of the Hagiographa had no official status and the fact that Hai sent a messenger to the Nestorian Catholicos to consult him on an obscurity in Ps. 141.5b (sources cited in Weitzman 1999: 110 nn. 133, 134). He concludes that there was Jewish demand for translations of the Hagiographa in Hai's time and that Jews regarded biblical translation, at least in regard to the Hagiographa, as common ground between Christians and Jews. Jews had no difficulty in principle in consulting a Christian authority. Weitzman's endorsement of the view that Tg made use of the Peshitta seems at first sight to settle the matter.

The issue of dating comes into this discussion, as noted earlier. Peshitta dependence on the Targum (the minority view) would have implied a very early date for the Targum. Kaminka, another of the dissenters from the consensus (1931–1932), noted, as we have seen, the evidence in TgProv of a non-Masoretic Hebrew *Vorlage* and proposed to date it as early as the 3rd century BCE. Such a dating goes hand in hand with the view that the Targum was the source of the Peshitta rather than *vice versa*. Obviously the consensus view (that the Targumist based his work on the Peshitta) dates the Peshitta of Proverbs before TgProv: E. Mangenot (1911: col. 2006) dated the Targum to the 8th/9th centuries CE and Weitzman too implies a very late date (1999: 110).[2]

There is nothing, however, in the Targum's text to indicate a late *or* an early date: conclusions about dating cannot be reached independently of these issues of interdependence. Accounts of attitudes at the time of Hai Gaon give context to the use of the Peshitta by the targumist and make it easier to overcome the difficulty felt by Black (above), but they do not, of themselves, settle the issue of the origins of TgProv. Nor do they address in detail the linguistic peculiarities of TgProv (first fully reviewed by Maybaum 1871; resumé in Owens 1998: 196–198), except on the assumption of a rather wooden (and incompetent) copying of a Peshitta *Vorlage*, or do justice to the complexity of the underlying linguistic situation of north Mesopotamian Aramaic in the first millennium CE. All theories should, in my view, be evaluated in the light of this linguistic situation.

What are the *linguistic* peculiarities in TgProv? The language of the text was regarded by Nöldeke as a *Mischsprache* containing elements of Syriac and Jewish Aramaic. It was not, in his view, a real language which was spoken by anyone, not an Aramaic dialect which could contribute to our understanding of the history of the language, but the product of a scholarly exercise of revision or translation by someone who was careless about linguistic details (Nöldeke 1872). The evidence of this mixing of forms is exemplified by the following:

> (i) appearance side by side of 3rd person imperfect forms with *y*- and *n*- (Maybaum 1871: 75—*n*- 149 times, *y*- 79 times; both appearing in TgProv 9.11 [L only], where the Peshitta is identical, though with *n*- in both instances)

[2] On dating note Díez Merino (1984: 163–167).

(ii) rare appearances of specifically Syriac features such as the use of the particles *gyr* (29.19, where Tg and Peshitta are identical) and *dyn* (17.16, where the Peshitta does not have *dyn* [nor does Z])

It is difficult to evaluate these linguistic features of TgProv, but it is noteworthy that the compiler of TgProv, who according to the theory of TgProv dependence on the Peshitta was converting a Classical Syriac text into a Jewish Aramaic dialect, saw no difficulty in including significant linguistic forms which *we* regard as foreign to his dialect. But if he *did* find them acceptable, then they must have been familiar at least in the form of Aramaic which he normally used. He and his audience must have been able to read his final text without serious difficulty, in which case the *n*- prefix and *gyr/dyn* must have been more or less acceptable in his dialect.

The alternation of *y*- and *n*- prefixes for imperfects is one of the characteristic features of the early Syriac inscriptions and it may reflect dialectal variation within the Edessa region (Healey 2008: especially 225–226). Hence the variability in TgProv might be explained as arising from the linguistic background of a compiler or editor or reviser of TgProv who lived in northern Mesopotamia and was familiar with Syriac.

Note may also be made of the frequent appearance in TgProv of *l*- as object marker (e.g. 1.12; 3.12; 5.22; 13.21; 28.1), but very rare occurrence of *yt*, which appears just a few times (23.11; 25.8; 7.21; 30.17 [the last two only in Z]). *yt* is the normal usage in Targumic Aramaic. However, while it is true that *l*- became the universally used form in Classical Syriac, *yt* does appear in the Peshitta as a calque on Hebrew *ʾeṯ* (see Gen. 1.1, etc.) and *yt* is known in Palmyrene Aramaic (Healey 2009: no. 33: 4 and discussion p. 44). Both appear also in the literary Aramaic of Qumran, so that it is difficult to argue that either form was exclusive to one or other of the dialects.[3]

A fourth peculiarity, masculine plural noun-ending *-y* for /*-ē*/ (Maybaum 1871: 72–73—294 times, against 42 instances of *-yʾ*), is only a matter of orthography. Although this spelling is odd, it is also the case that this nominal ending was spelled in a variety of ways in Mesopotamian Aramaic, as we can see from Palmyrene and Hatran (Healey 2009: 44, 48). Indeed, different spellings, *-yʾ* and *-ʾ*, both representing /*-ē*/, occur side by side in the same line in the Palmyrene Tariff (Healey

[3] See also on this Díez Merino (1984: 168).

2009: no. 37 i 7), while in Hatran Aramaic it is common to spell the masculine construct plural with -ʾ rather than *-y*. All these spellings represented /*-ē*/ and the compiler of TgProv presumably did not see any problem here.

We may note also certain choices of vocabulary which are unexpected from a Targumic point of view. Thus *nmwsʾ* appears nine times for *tōrā* (1.8; 3.1, etc.), while *ʾwryytʾ* appears three times (28.7, 9; 29.18) (see Melammed 1972: 19; Díez Merino 1984: 39). Of some theological interest is the use of *ʾlhʾ* instead of the tetragrammaton (Díez Merino 1984: 38–39). Melammed's claim that this is to avoid *mryʾ*, 'the Lord', because the latter is a homograph of the name of Mary, the mother of Jesus, seems to me far-fetched and in any case there would be no homograph, since Mary's name in Aramaic is *Maryam* (Melammed 1972: 24). In general vocabulary choices there is a tendency for TgProv to agree with the Peshitta (Díez Merino 1984: 110–11).

Although these peculiarities of language can be accounted for in simple terms as the result of Syriac influence mediated by the use of the Peshitta of Proverbs as a base-text by the targumist, there is another more complex way of looking at the situation. But we should first consider the complexity of the linguistic background.

I have discussed elsewhere (Healey 2008) the fact that the earliest 'Syriac' inscriptions reveal considerable dialectal variation. Some are specifically labelled 'Syriac' on the quite flimsy basis of the fact of being written in the Syriac script. To take a more or less contemporary analogy, it is equally true that the Nabataean Aramaic script was used long after the demise of the Nabataean kingdom for the writing of other Aramaic dialects and for the writing of Arabic. This would obviously not justify the labeling of these later inscriptions as 'Nabataean Aramaic' from a linguistic point of view (see Macdonald 2003; Healey 2009: 28). So far as the Syriac case is concerned, the point is that there was considerable variety in the Aramaic of northern Mesopotamia and 'Syriac' is only one of the various dialects. Thus, for example, the existence of both *y*- and *n*-prefix imperfects in the early Syriac inscriptions (above).

Even the so-called 'Classical Syriac' of the earliest Syriac literature is by no means uniform linguistically, as van Rompay (1994), Joosten (1999) and Brock (2003) have noted. It is easy to forget that Classical Syriac is mainly known to us as a literary language which, after the translation of the Bible and the promulgation of the Peshitta, came to be regarded as a special form of Aramaic, a 'high' language, used most obviously in the international, interregional discourse of the Syrian Orthodox Church and the Church of the East. Priests and bishops and other learned folk had to know Classical Syriac in order to read it correctly in the church and be able to enter into dialogue of an elevated kind with co-religionists from distant places.

The issue of whether this Classical Syriac was used as a vernacular and in other non-literary contexts is not at all clear. There is an extreme paucity of surviving evidence for vernacular language. Suggestive of use in the legal context is the survival of Syriac legal texts from the third century CE, though some oddities in these texts may be explained by the influence of a spoken dialect different from Classical Syriac (Drijvers and Healey 1999: nos P1–3). More recently there have been published a few business documents of the 9th century CE from northern Iraq in 'Classical Syriac', though again there are grammatical forms which suggest a different linguistic register from that of the classical language (Harrak 2009).[4]

While Classical Syriac is itself varied, there is also evidence that it could be written in non-Syriac scripts. At Edessa in the first centuries CE, alongside the pagans and early Christians, there was a *Jewish* community carving inscriptions. Some of these inscriptions have been preserved (Pognon 1907: nos 40, 41, 43; Noy and Bloedhorn 2004: 128–32) and have linguistic features identical with those of early Syriac inscriptions and Classical Syriac, despite the fact of being written in the Jewish form of the Aramaic script (thus Pognon 1907: 78, though he regarded them as Palestinian Aramaic; note also ter Haar Romeny 2005: 28–9). The most obvious linguistic feature marking two of these inscriptions as Syriac is the use of *hnʾ* as the masculine singular near demonstrative, rather than any of the other available forms known in the Aramaic associated with Jews. The appearance of *by* for *byt* in one of these texts (no. 43: 1, *byʿlmʾ*) is not unique in north Mesopotamian Aramaic, since it is found in another of the Old Syriac inscriptions (Drijvers and Healey 1999: no. As59: 3, *bqbwrʾ*) and the same apocopated form appears in two fifth/sixth-century Syriac inscriptions (Briquel Chatonnet and Desreumaux 2008: line 6, *bshdʾ*; Littmann 1934: no. 52: *bshdʾ*; also in Hatran, Healey 2009: 90, on no. 70: 3, *byldh*). It

[4] Later there was, of course, a Classical Syriac revival, continuing down to the present day, with some Syrian Orthodox families speaking Classical Syriac in the home, though this revival is not relevant to our present concern.

seems to be a north Mesopotamian characteristic and the implication is clear: the script of the Pognon inscriptions is Jewish (i.e. the square Hebrew/Aramaic script) but the language is early Syriac. The inscriptions are in 'Judaeo-Syriac'.[5]

The mixing of Aramaic dialects, with local varieties having an impact on an Aramaic *koiné* used by Jews, Christians and pagans, is reflected also in the Aramaic- and Syriac-script incantation bowls and the Babylonian Talmud, where archaizing also played a role (cf. Harviainen 1981; Healey 2008: 225–6).

We thus have a very complex linguistic situation. There was a variety of Aramaic dialects as well as a kind of *koiné* and, emerging as a prestige language of scripture, Classical Syriac. Although the latter is specifically associated with Christians, there were Jews who spoke and wrote in a form of Aramaic very close to Syriac, but normally using the Jewish Aramaic script. We may remind ourselves that almost a third of the text of TgProv can be simply read as Classical Syriac (though it is easier to do this if one converts the script).

This series of linguistic factors could be considered as simply setting the scene for the consensus view that the Targum depends on the Peshitta, but a number of scholars have thought that both the Peshitta and TgProv depend on a common source in a Syriac-like dialect. We may quote W. Bacher (1906: 62):

> the Targum to Proverbs was derived from the same sources as the Peshiṭta..., the Syriac version itself being based on a translation originally intended for Jews who spoke the Syriac dialect.

A very similar hypothesis was also adopted very recently by Brock (2006: 27):

> ...the Peshitta translation of Proverbs is also likely to have been the work of Jews in northern Mesopotamia: it subsequently came to be taken over by Syriac-speaking Christians and by later Jews (who lightly modified the dialect).

This kind of hypothesis has the advantage of avoiding the assumption of a simple Jewish borrowing of a Christian text, and of bringing into the discussion a consideration of the complexity of the linguistic situation in northern Mesopotamia. It was for these reasons that it

[5] They should be added to the list of Old Syriac inscriptions, the number of which has expanded considerably since the publication of Drijvers and Healey (1999). See, e.g., Healey (2006).

was advocated in Healey (1991: 8–10). Such a hypothesis also fits well with Díez Merino's important point that there may have been Peshitta *influence* on the Targum, even if the latter had an *independent origin* (Díez Merino 1984: 167).

We can thus not exclude the possibility that our targumist was using not simply the Christian Peshitta, but an older Judaeo-Syriac targum which he was trying to adapt to a more normal targumic form. This would have involved adjusting the language and at least glancing at the Hebrew. Reworking of the older text would take account of the MT and perhaps the LXX (though it seems unlikely that he would have known Greek) or another Hebrew text, while Christian reworking to produce the Peshitta took account of the LXX. The targumist may have used the Peshitta additionally as a guide.

It must be admitted, however, that this is a highly speculative suggestion, not supported by any concrete evidence and serves mainly to resolve the problem voiced by Black, the implausibility of a Jewish translator using the Christian version as his starting point, when he could have used the Hebrew (or possibly even the LXX).

If we do accept the *consensus* view (TgProv adapted from the Peshitta), it too should be viewed in the light of the linguistic situation. A Jewish scholar who spoke a form of Aramaic which was almost identical with Classical Syriac may have tried to fill the need for a Jewish version of the Book of Proverbs by using the available Christian version which was written in a script which was not usually used by his own community (being by this time specifically Christian). To a large extent all he had to do was to change the script (300+ verses), but he also took the opportunity to correct the Christian version by keeping his eye on the Hebrew. His end-product was a little unsatisfactory, since it was not based on a careful linguistic consideration of the features which distinguished Classical Syriac from other local forms of Aramaic: indeed he may have been scarcely aware that there was any difference between Classical Syriac and his own dialect.[6]

Nöldeke was adamant that the language of TgProv could never have been the real spoken language of any group, since it combines

[6] One is reminded of the fact that modern Arabic-speakers often claim to be speaking *fuṣḥā* or even 'the language of the Qur'ān' and modern Aramaic-speakers to be speaking Classical Syriac or even 'the language of Jesus', when neither group is doing anything of the kind. Native-speakers of languages rarely have an accurate perception of where their own idiolect fits into the wider picture.

forms which belong to different dialects and places them side by side. It would thus have been a product of the scholar's study (conjuring up images of College rooms in Cambridge!). However, the variety of linguistic forms represented in the text may come from a very localized area in northern Mesopotamia, where various dialects were used side by side.

One must agree above all with Owens (1998: 204, 207) that little further progress can be made on these issues until we have a critical edition of TgProv.

References

Alexander, P.S. 1992. 'Targum, Targumim', in *The Anchor Bible Dictionary* 6 (ed. D.N. Freedman; New York: Doubleday) 320–331.

Bacher, W. 1906. 'Targum', in *The Jewish Encyclopedia XII* (ed. I. Singer; New York/London: Funk and Wagnalls Co.) 57–63.

Black, M. 1967. *An Aramaic Approach to the Gospels and Acts* (3rd edn; Oxford: Clarendon Press).

Briquel Chatonnet, F. and A. Desreumaux. 2008. 'L'inscription syriaque', in *Le martyrion Saint-Jean dans la moyenne vallée de l'Euphrate: Fouilles de la Direction Générale des Antiquités à Nabgha au nord-est de Jarablus* (Documents d'archéologie syrienne XIII; Damascus: Ministère de la Culture, Direction Générale des Antiquités et des Musées) [joint authors: R. Sabbagh, F. Ayash, J. Balty, F. Briquel Chatonnet and A. Desreumaux] 23–30.

Brock, S.P. 2003. 'Some Diachronic Features of Classical Syriac', in *Hamlet on a Hill: Semitic and Greek Studies Presented to Professor T. Muraoka on the Occasion of his Sixty-Fifth Birthday* (eds. M.F.J. Baasten and W.Th. van Peursen; Orientalia Lovaniensia Analecta, 118; Leuven: Peeters) 95–111.

——. 2006. *The Bible in the Syriac Tradition* (Gorgias Handbooks, 7; Piscataway, NJ: Gorgias Press).

Dathe, J.A. 1764. *De ratione consensus versionis Chaldaicae et Syriacae Proverbiorum Salomonis* (Leipzig: Officina Langenhemia).

Díez Merino, L. 1984. *Targum de Proverbios. Edición Principe del Ms. Villa-Amil no. 5 de Alfonso de Zamora* (Bibliotheca Hispana Biblica, 11; Madrid: Consejo Superior de Investigaciones Científicas Istituto 'Francisco Suárez').

Drijvers, H.J.W., and J.F. Healey. 1999. *The Old Syriac Inscriptions of Edessa and Osrhoene* (Handbuch der Orientalistik, I/XLII; Leiden: Brill).

Haar Romeny, R.B. ter. 2005. 'Hypotheses on the Development of Judaism andChristianity in Syria in the Period after 70 CE', in *Matthew and the Didache: Two Documents from the Same* Jewish-Christian Milieu? (ed. H.W.M. van de Sandt; Assen: Van Gorcum/Minneapolis: Fortress Press) 13–33.

Harrak, A. 2009. 'Was Classical Syriac a Business Language?", in *The Volume of the Fourth Syriac Language Conference* (eds. Sh. I. Khoshaba, R. Bet Shmuel *et al.*; Dohuk: Beth Mardotha) 87–93.

Healey, J.F. 1991. 'The Targum of Proverbs', in *The Aramaic Bible 15* [Job, Proverbs, Qohelet] (eds. M. McNamara *et al.*; Collegeville: The Liturgical Press) [separate pagination].

——. 2006. 'A New Syriac Mosaic Inscription', *Journal of Semitic Studies* 51: 313–327.

——. 2008. 'Variety in Early Syriac: the Context in Contemporary Aramaic', in *Aramaic in its Historical and Linguistic Setting* (eds. H. Gzella and M.L. Folmer; Veröffentlichungen der Orientalischen Kommission, 50, Akademie der Wissenschaften und der Literatur, Mainz; Wiesbaden: Harrassowitz Verlag) 221–229.

——. 2009. *Aramaic Inscriptions and Documents of the Roman Period* (Textbook of Syrian Semitic Inscriptions, IV; Oxford: Oxford University Press).

Kaminka, A. 1931–1932. 'Septuaginta und Targum zu Proverbia', *Hebrew Union College Annual* 8-9: 169–191.

Lagarde, P. de. 1873. *Hagiographa Chaldaice* (Leipzig: B.G. Teubner).

Lella, A.A. di. 1979. *The Old Testament in Syriac according to the Peshiṭta Version II/5* (Leiden: Brill).

Littmann, E. 1934. *Syriac Inscriptions* (Publications of the Princeton University Archaeological Expeditions to Syria in 1904–1905 and 1909. Division IV. Section B; Leiden: Brill).

Macdonald, M.C.A. 2003. 'Languages, Scripts, and the Use of Writing among the Nabataeans', in *Petra Rediscovered: the Lost City of the Nabataeans* (ed. G. Markoe; London: Thames & Hudson) 36–56.

Maybaum, S. 1871. 'Ueber die Sprache des Targum zu den Sprüchen und dessen Verhältniss zum Syrer', in *Archiv für Wissenschaftliche Erforschung des Alten Testamentes II/i* (ed. A. Merx; Halle: Verlag der Buchhandlung des Waisenhauses) 66–93.

Mangenot, E. 1911. 'Targums', in *Dictionnaire de la Bible V (fasc. xxxvii)* (ed. F.G. Vigouroux; Paris: Letouzey et Ané) cols. 1995–2007.

McNamara, M. 2010. *Targum and Testament Revisited: Aramaic paraphrases of the Hebrew Bible* (Grand Rapids MI/Cambridge: W.B. Eerdmans) (revised edition; original 1972).

Melammed, E.Z. 1972. 'The Targum on Proverbs', *Bar-Ilan Annual* 9 *(i)* (H.M. Shapiro Memorial Volume): 18–91[in Hebrew], English xi–xii.

Nöldeke, Th. 1872. 'Das Targum zu den Sprüchen von der Peschita abhängig', in *Archiv für Wissenschaftliche Erforschung des Alten Testamentes II/ii* (ed. A. Merx; Halle: Verlag der Buchhandlung des Waisenhauses) 246–249.

Noy, D. and H. Bloedhorn. 2004. *Inscriptiones Judaicae Orientis. III Syria and Cyprus* (*Texts and Studies in Ancient Judaism 102*; Tübingen: Mohr Siebeck).

Owens, Jr., R.J. 1998. 'The Relationship between the Targum and Peshitta Texts of the Book of Proverbs: *status quaestionis*' in *Targum Studies, Volume Two: Targum and Peshitta* (ed. P.V.M. Flesher; South Florida Studies in the History of Judaism, 165; Atlanta, GA: Scholars Press) 195–207.

Pinkuss, H. 1894. 'Die syrische Uebersetzung der Proverbien textkritisch und in ihrem Verhältnisse zu dem masoretischen Text, den LXX und dem Targum untersucht', *Zeitschriftfür die Alttestamentliche Wissenschaft* 14: 65–141, 161–222.

Pognon, H. 1907. *Inscriptions sémitiques de la Syrie, de la Mésopotamie et de la région de Mossoul* (Paris: Imprimerie Nationale).

Rompay, L. van. 1994. 'Some Preliminary Remarks on the Origins of Classical Syriac as a Standard Language: the Syriac Version of Eusebius of Caesarea's Ecclesiastical History', in *Semitic and Cushitic Studies* (eds. G. Goldenberg and Sh. Raz; Wiesbaden: Harrassowitz) 70–89.

Segal, M.Ts. 1955. *Mebō ha-Miqrā* (4 vols.; Jerusalem: Qiryat Sefer).

Snell, D.C. 1998. 'The Relation between the Targum and the Peshiṭta of Proverbs', *Zeitschriftfür die Alttestamentliche Wissenschaft* 110: 72–74.

Waard, J. de. 2008. *Proverbs* (*Biblia Hebraica Quinta 17*; Stuttgart: Deutsche Bibelgesellschaft).

Weitzman, M.P. 1999. *The Syriac Version of the Old Testament* (University of Cambridge Oriental Publications, 56; Cambridge: Cambridge University Press).

ON SOME CONNOTATIONS OF THE WORD *MAʿASEH*

Stefan C. Reif

Some forty years ago, Robert Gordon and I—academic novices both—shared an office at the University of Glasgow. The building in which it was situated was occupied by the staff of the closely associated departments of Hebrew and Semitic Languages and Old Testament Language and Literature. I had been appointed to a lectureship in the former and he joined me when taking up a similar post in the latter. Alas, by the necessary order of such things, many of those who were our colleagues in that building have gone to their eternal rest while, equally sadly but by a somewhat less necessary order laid down in the name of academic progress (*so genannt*), such university departments have long been consigned to the *genizah* of educational history. I soon appreciated that Robert loved all manner of scholarly fare but always sought to season it with generous sprinklings of humour and even a soupçon of irreverence. Teaching for him essentially meant giving of himself and on many occasions assigning priority to students over his own ambitions and interests. While deeply committed to the critical study and sound analysis of primary sources, he never felt that this precluded him from personal commitment and institutional involvement in the religious sphere. I found myself in awe of his deep, emotional attachment not only to the Hebrew Bible but also to the land of Israel. And so it was that from our first meeting we discovered that we shared not only a professional place of work but a definition of what kind of scholarly *esprit de corps* we wished to adopt and encourage. To our minds, the maintenance of honesty and integrity was much to be desired and promoted in scholarly circles. Since those early days in our academic careers until the present time in Cambridge, when we somehow appear to have acquired a seniority at least of years, we have enjoyed being friends, exchanging confidences, supporting some fairly harmless forms of iconoclasm, and even, I daresay, indulging in a degree of mutual admiration. There is no scholar in the realm of Biblical Hebrew studies more worthy of recognition, admiration and respect and I am delighted to be able to offer my modest contribution to a volume that is intended to bring him at least part of the honour that he richly deserves.

A problem that often confronts teachers and students of Hebrew, especially in its Biblical and early post-Biblical forms, is the tendency of the language to use a limited number of verbs and nouns for a great variety of meanings, rather than to develop a more extensive vocabulary (Sáenz-Badillos 1993: 74–75). Whether this is an innate characteristic of a language with a simple triliteral root system that inevitably has its limitations, or a phenomenon that should not be unexpected in the language's earlier, and therefore more primitive, forms, will not here concern us. What has often intrigued me is the degree to which the verb עָשָׂה and the noun מַעֲשֶׂה exemplify the problem and consequently present a challenge to translators and exegetes alike. The topic I specifically propose to address is whether, in the case of the word מַעֲשֶׂה, the lexicographers have provided adequate guidance as to its semantic range and variety of nuances, and whether the translations and comments provided for its occurrences in a wide range of Biblical Hebrew verses do adequate justice to the meaning being conveyed in each instance. Given the editorially imposed limit (certainly a wise precaution!) on the size of each essay in this collection, I shall obviously not be able to deal with every relevant verse but I hope to provide enough examples to be able to illustrate the problem and to suggest that there may be some cases in which renderings and annotations might be improved.

Firstly, then, what is noted by the lexicographers about any special senses of the word מַעֲשֶׂה? Given the major contribution he made to the development of Hebrew grammatical studies in the Middle Ages, it is not inappropriate to begin with the views of one of the most distinguished and insightful Jewish scholars of Hebrew in eleventh-century Spain, Jonah (ʾAbū al-Walīd Merwan) Ibn Janāḥ. In his comments on the root עשה (Ibn Janāḥ, 388), he points to the sense of 'property' sometimes carried by the word מַעֲשֶׂה and goes on to champion an explanation that this derives from the basic agricultural sense of 'collecting and storing up produce'. He cites Ezek. 28.4 for the verbal use but, more pertinently to the current analysis, makes reference to Jer. 48.7 in which Moab is accused of trusting in בְּמַעֲשַׂיִךְ וּבְאוֹצְרוֹתַיִךְ, and to the rendering by Targum Jonathan which finds precisely such a sense in the word בְּמַעֲשַׂיִךְ, translating it as באוצרך ('your riches') and the subsequent word as בבית גנזך ('your treasure house'). David Qimḥi of twelfth-century Provence, and therefore still very much under the Spanish influence, follows Ibn Janāḥ in his definition of the basic sense of מַעֲשֶׂה but he himself offers a slight expansion, suggesting that the word means 'acquisition, collection and treatment' (הקנין האסיפה והתיקון). He cites (Qimḥi, 281) with approval the view of Judah Ḥayyūj (ed. Nutt, 90) that the various meanings of the root עשה represent essentially one overall sense and notes that the context dictates precisely which nuance is to be preferred. Both Ibn Janāḥ and Qimḥi cite numerous verses where slightly varying senses pertain but their overall definitions cover all these.

The modern dictionaries provide lists of meanings for the root עשה and then move on to treat the noun מַעֲשֶׂה. Ben Yehuda lists thirteen usages for the verb: 'make', 'create/produce', 'prepare food', 'celebrate a festival', 'appoint', 'act justly', 'take action', 'busy oneself', 'deal with', 'conducted/appropriate/suitable' [in the passive mood], 'tarry', 'amount to', 'add up to', noting, in addition, the abbreviated עש for עשה in medieval Hebrew poetry (Ben Yehuda, 4765–4772). Nine senses are listed for the noun: 'work', 'act/action', 'occupation', 'character', 'creation by a human', 'story/event', 'activity', 'achievement/behaviour', 'performance' (Ben Yehuda, 3202–3208). It would therefore seem that BY is slightly at variance with Ibn Janāḥ and Qimḥi, opting rather for a basic sense of 'doing', 'making', with variations on this theme, but not stressing any agricultural origin for the various usages, or any central sense of 'collection'.

For its part, Brown, Driver, Briggs divides the root into two general headings covering the two senses of 'do' and 'make'. Under the first of these headings are listed sub-divisions that detail who is doing, making or dealing what to, with or for whom. The emphasis here is on the remainder of the phrase or expression and how it qualifies and clarifies the basic meaning. Under the second heading, examples are provided of the root when it bears the senses of 'making', 'producing', 'preparing', 'offering', 'arranging', 'celebrating', 'appointing', 'bringing about' and 'passing time' (BDB, 793–795). Here the lexicographers are stressing that the root occurs as more than an auxiliary and are suggesting that these noted instances demonstrate extensions of its semantic range. BDB lists the senses of the nominal form מַעֲשֶׂה under the two main headings of 'deed' and 'work'. The first list is sub-divided into: 'work', 'labour', 'business', 'pursuit', 'undertaking', 'enterprise', 'achievement', 'deeds', 'works'; while the second list notes the three senses of 'work': 'thing made by man', 'work done by God', 'product' (BDB, 795–796). Effectively, then, BDB adheres closely to the meaning of 'activity' in defining the word מַעֲשֶׂה and is again interested in defining who is carrying out the action in each case, especially whether human beings or God, and in what circumstances.

The comprehensive and extensive dictionary of the Israeli educator and writer, Avraham Even-Shoshan, identifies six basic senses of the root עשה, namely (in my translations): 'make'/'carry out work'/'actively engage in preparing something', 'produce'/'yield', 'behave'/'bring about', 'appoint', 'spend time', 'complete'/'achieve'. When used as an auxiliary, it yields the meanings 'execute', 'arrange' and 'perform' (Even-Shoshan, 2012). For the noun מַעֲשֶׂה, Even-Shoshan offers three headings. The first covers the senses of 'activity', 'work', 'business' and 'execution'. The definition given under the second is 'the manner in which something is made, constructed or formed' while the third lists instances of the word bearing the sense of 'occurrence', 'happening' or 'fact' (Even-Shoshan, 1451–1452). Here, the basic sense is 'performing', 'creating' and 'effecting'.

Fifteen basic meanings are given for the verb in the revised English edition of the Koehler and Baumgartner Lexicon: 'make/ manufacture', 'attach', 'make for/with', 'create', 'give effect to/do', 'acquire', 'prepare', 'make', 'carry out/perform', 'perform' (in a forensic context), 'perform labour', 'act/behave', 'behave' (in various ways), 'do/treat', 'enjoy oneself' (KBL, II, 890–892). The substantive מַעֲשֶׂה is translated as 'work', 'labour', 'accomplishment', 'works and deeds of God', 'human achievement', and 'deal with someone' (KBL, II, 616–617). The general stress is on 'activity'.

The Dictionary of Classical Hebrew, edited by David Clines, treats the verb under the nineteen headings of 'work/perform', 'be active', 'create', 'produce/yield/ procreate', 'bring about', 'make/proclaim a decree/ conclude an agreement', 'appoint', 'acquire', 'achieve', 'prepare', 'offer sacrifice', 'attend to', 'use for', 'cultivate', 'make a journey', 'spend time', 'comprise', 'violate (sexually)', 'be carried out' (Clines, VI, 569). As regards the noun, the two main senses are given as 'work' and 'making' and these are followed by the five standard meanings of 'deed'/'action', 'deeds'/'activity'/'behaviour', 'product'/'produce'/'work'/'manufacture', 'labour'/'occupation'/'trade'/'business', and 'creation'/ 'creature'/ 'created being'. Three other meanings, which occur in later Hebrew, especially in the language of the Dead Sea Scrolls, cover 'object of mockery'/'substance'/'cultic apparatus', 'sexual intercourse', and 'event'/'episode'/'story' (Clines, V, 416). These latter senses, as well as the inclusion of a variety of renderings in the earlier list appear to indicate an awareness of some connotations that are less than obvious and may easily be missed.

Helmer Ringgren aims for a greater degree of precision and lists, in the case of the verb, twelve broadly described and discussed senses, among which there are some overlaps. For our purposes, these may be summarized as: 'make'/'hold (a feast)'/'prepare or 'offer' (a sacrifice)', 'make (gods and idols)' which are then described as מַעֲשֵׂה יְדֵיהֶם, 'make' (specifically to describe creative activity by God), 'produce' and 'yield' (that is, food and drink), 'create/acquire (wealth/reputation)', 'bring about'—as with God's bringing about great deeds/wonders/justice/revenge and punishment, 'practise (justice, mercy and kindness)', 'do good or evil', 'carry out (an instruction)', 'bring about (war, peace)' and 'commit (evil, wickedness or sin)', 'do (something for someone else)' or 'make into/cause to become', 'act (on the part of God in bringing about his wishes in the process of history)'. He also notes various locutions making use of עשה, such as with מָה or with כֹּה (Ringgren 2001: 389–398). For the noun, Ringgren lists 'work of human hands' (approved or disapproved), 'idols'/'wealth', 'fruit'/'produce', 'pattern'/'design', 'God's work', 'deed', 'conduct', 'continuing action/behaviour', 'deeds of mortals', 'labour'/'occupation'/'business', 'general activity including achieving great things', 'God's activity in history', and 'divine providence'. Ringgren claims that Qumran has little new to offer and identifies the primary renderings in the Septuagint as ποιεῖν for the verb (with eight other, less common translations) and ἔργων for the noun. In the case of the latter there is also the occasional employment of ποιήμα, ποιήσις, and ἐργασίς. Interestingly, then, Ringgren includes with the usual 'creation' and 'activity' such notions as 'wealth', 'produce' and 'behaviour' (Ringgren 2001: 399–403).

The question now to be addressed is how some of the major medieval and modern commentators relate to the meaning of the word מַעֲשֶׂה in a number of contexts where it may be less than obvious. While lexicographers are generally constrained by the extensive nature of their commitment to provide a brief definition and translation, exegetes have the opportunity of expanding on the contextual meaning of a word or expression. They may therefore be in a better position to detect and note a nuance—especially a less than usual one—that may have escaped the writer of a dictionary. Contexts and phraseology often provide the clues to such ranges of meaning. 'Acts' in English may, among other things, be parliamentary, divine or theatrical but no

English speaker would for a moment expect such epithets to apply if the phrase in question were 'indecent acts'.

When the pentateuchal legislation demands of the Israelites that they do not do according to the מַעֲשִׂים of the surrounding peoples, what precisely is its intent? There are two verses that might usefully be consulted in this context, Lev. 18.3 and Exod. 23.24.

Lev. 18.3: כְּמַעֲשֵׂ֧ה אֶֽרֶץ־מִצְרַ֛יִם אֲשֶׁ֥ר יְשַׁבְתֶּם־בָּ֖הּ לֹ֣א תַעֲשׂ֑וּ וּכְמַעֲשֵׂ֣ה אֶֽרֶץ־
כְּנַ֡עַן אֲשֶׁ֣ר אֲנִי֩ מֵבִ֨יא אֶתְכֶ֥ם שָׁ֙מָּה֙ לֹ֣א תַעֲשׂ֔וּ וּבְחֻקֹּתֵיהֶ֖ם לֹ֥א תֵלֵֽכוּ׃

The Spanish Jewish exegete, Abraham ben Meir ibn Ezra (1089–1164), expresses the view that the activities of the Egyptians and the Canaanites to which this pentateuchal passage is most opposed are those of idolatry and sexual immorality, which are in any event often closely associated. By way of introduction to this passage (*Torat Ḥayyim*, 159), he refers to his comments on other verses in order to establish the nature of the current context. In his interpretation of Lev. 17.7 he indicates that the reference to 'demons' or 'satyrs' (לַשְּׂעִירִ֕ם) was motivated by Egyptian practices pursued by the Hebrews during their slavery and is a call to avoid being disloyal to God and to true belief in Him (*Torat Ḥayyim*, 155–56). The reference to abominable activities in Lev. 18.26 (*Torat Ḥayyim*, 169) refers back to all the forbidden sexual relationships just listed which were practised by the Canaanites and defiled the land of Israel.

In his comments on Lev. 18.3 itself (*Torat Ḥayyim*, 160), Ibn Ezra appears to use the word משפטים to mean the whole Egyptian way of life, including their legal and religious customs. In his published translation of Ibn Ezra's commentary on Leviticus, which is a commendable piece of work, Jay F. Shachter translates the word as 'Egyptian legal system' (Shachter 1986: 90). Given, however, Ibn Ezra's references to these other contexts of idolatry and sexual immorality, it would appear that he is here using משפטים to mean the religious *and* legal systems, that is to say, their total behaviour. In his comments on Lev. 18.3, he draws a parallel with Exodus 22–23 which certainly includes all manner of practices, not only legal, and in Lev. 18.26 he links the legal aspect with the punishment for transgressing the sexual restrictions just listed.

On Hag. 2.12, in the standard Rabbinic Bible, Ibn Ezra refers to the term קדיש(ה), as in Deut. 23.18, and defines it in a remarkable way, thus shedding further light on his understanding of ancient Egyptian practice. He explains that the humidity of the Nile weakens the

Egyptians so much that by the age of forty they are themselves physically unable to penetrate a virgin. They therefore engage younger Egyptians to commence penetration and take over themselves once the hymen is breached. Such a youngster is known as a קדיש.

Moses Naḥmanides (1194–1270) of Gerona, and later of Jerusalem, greatly admired Ibn Ezra but often took the opportunity of criticizing his work. In this case, he cites Ibn Ezra's interpretation and yet expands on it. He too makes a link between all the forbidden practices associated with idolatry and immorality, indicating that the Egyptians were not simply guilty of the former but also of the latter (*Torat Ḥayyim*, 160). In support he makes reference to a halakhic midrash of the early Rabbinic period (*Sifra* 9.3 and 13.8; 85b–86a), where it is alleged that the Egyptians of the day were steeped in serious, sexual misconduct of various sorts. Naḥmanides also points to the biblical verses in 1 Kgs. 14.24 and Ezek. 16.26 the sexual import of which is linguistically clarified by Ezek. 23.20, Lev. 15.2 and 15.19 where בָּשָׂר ('flesh') is clearly a euphemism for the sexual organ. It may be added that this is another example of a word that carries a special, contextual nuance.

An adjacent *Sifra* passage (9.8; 85b) is most interesting for the present discussion. It comments on the word מַעֲשֵׂה:

> יכול לא יבנו בנינים ולא יטעו נטיעות כמותם ת״ל ובחקותיהם לא תלכו. לא אמרתי אלא בחוקים החקוקים להם ולאבותיהם ולאבות אבותיהם. ומה היו עושים? האיש נושא לאיש והאשה לאשה. האיש נושא אשה ובתה והאישה ניסת לשנים לכך נאמר ובחקותיהם לא תלכו.
>
> [In my English translation:] 'Looking at the word מַעֲשֵׂה on its own, I might have concluded that Israel is here being prohibited from following Egyptian and Canaanite practices in the spheres of construction and agriculture. The context is, however, clarified by the subsequent phrase וּבְחֻקֹּתֵיהֶם לֹא תֵלֵכוּ. What is meant is that Israel should not follow practices that have been ingrained in ancient Egyptian and Canaanite culture for countless generations. What then are the acts they performed that are here prohibited by the word מַעֲשֵׂה? Single sex marriages, both male and female; a man marrying a woman and her daughter; and a woman functioning as a wife with [consorting with?] two men.'

For this early rabbinic midrash, then, the emphasis in the current prohibition is on the sexual aspects of the Egyptian and Canaanite practices, rather than on their more mundane pursuits, the word מַעֲשֵׂה carrying a sexual nuance. For two of the leading medieval Jewish exegetes, the word may best be translated as 'lifestyle' since its semantic range goes well beyond the sexual. These alternative renderings of מַעֲשֵׂה as 'lifestyle' and 'sexual misdemeanour' are reflected in the ancient versions and in the modern translations and commentaries. The Septuagint (Rahlfs, I, 190) renders מַעֲשֵׂה as ἐπιτηδεύματα meaning 'habits, customs, way of life' while the Targum Onqelos remains neutral and uses the Aramaic עובדין which tells us no more than the original Hebrew (*Torat Ḥayyim*, 160). Pseudo-Jonathan, on the other hand, adds an adjective, offering עובדין בישין , thereby understanding the prohibition to be aimed at 'bad behaviour' (Ginsburger 1903: 204). E.S. Hartom is a little more specific, using the modern Hebrew phrase מנהגים מתועבים ('foul habits') and associating this with idolatrous customs, thus adopting the link made by the medieval commentators between idolatry and immorality (Hartom 1964: 58). J. Milgrom refers broadly to 'practices, mores' (Milgrom 1990: 1518) while B. Levine argues that the term implies incest, bestiality and homosexuality (Levine, 118). The NEB ('as they do in Egypt') and JPS ('the practices of the land of Egypt') evidently regard the term מַעֲשֵׂה as non-specific. In sum, a fair number of interpreters see here an allusion to idolatry and sexual immorality, not a nuance that figures prominently in the dictionaries.

Another passage in the Hebrew Bible in which מַעֲשִׂים occurs and where there are clear allusions to both idolatry and sexual immorality is Ps. 106.33–40. There, in a powerful summary of their history, the Israelites are accused of having followed the practices of other nations, serving their idols even at times by way of sacrificing their children, polluting thereby the land of Israel and antagonizing God. Three phrases occur in vv. 35–36. The first, וַיִּתְעָרְבוּ בַגּוֹיִם, refers to non-Israelite influences, and the third, וַיַּעַבְדוּ אֶת־עֲצַבֵּיהֶם, to idolatry. The middle phrase, וַיִּלְמְדוּ מַעֲשֵׂיהֶם, could, in another context, have the general sense of 'following their practices' but, given the phrases which precede and follow it, it seems reasonable to conclude that the reference is to sexual immorality. The Psalmist's criticism of his people is that, having integrated with the Canaanites, they adopted their indecent behaviour and worshipped their gods. Such an understanding of the passage matches well with the overall theme. The word מַעֲשֵׂיהֶם occurs again in v. 39 (וַיִּטְמְאוּ בְמַעֲשֵׂיהֶם וַיִּזְנוּ בְּמַעַלְלֵיהֶם) where the complaint is that the Israelites have defiled with their מַעֲשִׂים and whored with their מַעֲלָלִים. If these two nouns are parallel, they could both be understood as idolatry or as sexual immorality; alternatively, they may each refer to only one of these religious misdemeanours. Either way, מַעֲשִׂים is to be understood as something undoubtedly more precise and nuanced than 'deeds', 'ways' or 'customs'. This appears to have been the way the text was understood by Briggs (1907: 353), Hartom (1964: 235) and *Daʿat Miqra* (290–291).

There are several other verses in which מַעֲשֶׂה may conceivably, even if not convincingly, allude to idolatry and should therefore be noted at this point in the discussion. In the sixth chapter of his prophecies, Micah rails against the people of Israel for their nefarious activities, and in v. 16 he accuses them of maintaining the practices of Omri, and in a parallel expression, of following the מַעֲשֵׂה of the house of Ahab. Which kinds of behaviour are implied by the word מַעֲשֶׂה? Most of the translations and commentaries opt for a general sense of misbehaviour but Hartom (1964: 102) finds a reference here to idolatry and T.K. Cheyne (1921: 54) to the worship of Baal. Ringgren (2001: 400) specifically rejects such a meaning here while Smith, Ward and Bewer in the ICC (1911: 135) regard the word מַעֲשֶׂה here as an allusion to the criminal act of murdering Naboth in order to steal his vineyard. The question in Isa. 66.18 is whether the activities and thoughts being noted are those of the idolaters described in the previous verse. This is the interpretation favoured by *Daʿat Miqra* (695) and Hartom (1964: 193), while J. Skinner (1898: 229) and J. Blenkinsopp (2003: 310), following Bernhard Duhm (1892: 455), remove the doubt by relocating the first phrase of this verse in the idolatrous context of the previous verse. King Jehoshaphat receives praise in 2 Chron. 17.4 for not having subscribed to Baal worship and in the subsequent verse it is stated that he followed the religious traditions of his davidic ancestor, and not מַעֲשֵׂה יִשְׂרָאֵל ('Israelite practice'). *Daʿat Miqra* (687) and Hartom (1964: 120–121) see such practice as idolatry and this is the view taken by E.L. Curtis and A.A. Madsen in the ICC (1910: 392), with a supporting reference from 2 Chron. 11.15, and by W.A.L. Elmslie (1899: 236), with a supporting reference from 2 Chron. 13.8–9.

Exod 23.24, לֹא־תִשְׁתַּחֲוֶה לֵאלֹהֵיהֶם וְלֹא תָעָבְדֵם וְלֹא תַעֲשֶׂה כְּמַעֲשֵׂיהֶם כִּי הָרֵס תְּהָרְסֵם וְשַׁבֵּר תְּשַׁבֵּר מַצֵּבֹתֵיהֶם, carries a message similar to that of Lev. 18.3 which has just been discussed. The Canaanite gods are not be worshipped but they and their altars are to be eliminated in favour of the service of God. Between these two instructions is the prohibition against practising their מַעֲשִׂים. But to which practices is the verse alluding? Ibn Ezra (*Torat Ḥayyim*, 63–64) explains that the intention of all the laws in the Book of the Covenant is to prohibit idolatry. The collection of such laws begins, for him, in Exod. 20.20

where it is forbidden to make silver images even in God's honour and ends in Exod. 23.33 where the instruction is given to rid the Holy Land of all idolaters since they will only lead the Israelites astray. Even if they perform every positive precept of the Torah, their idolatry makes them guilty of every negative precept and damns them in this world and the next. The context for Ibn Ezra is therefore definitely that of idolatry but in this instance he does not define precisely what kind of idolatry is meant by the word כְּמַעֲשֵׂיהֶם in this verse.

Naḥmanides (*Torat Ḥayyim*, 63–64) raises the possibility that the allusion made by the word כְּמַעֲשֵׂיהֶם in this verse may be to magical and superstitious activities, such as are forbidden by the Talmudic rabbis (Babylonian Talmud Shab. 67a) unless they are known to have sound, therapeutic efficacy. The sense here would therefore be similar to that carried by the phrase וּבְחֻקֹּתֵיהֶם לֹא תֵלֵכוּ in Lev. 18.3 which is specifically identified by R. Meir in the *Sifra* (13.9; 86a) as a reference to such magical and superstitious activities. Naḥmanides then expresses his preference for an interpretation of the phrase as a prohibition against idolatry that includes an additional aspect. This constitutes a warning not to follow idolatrous practices even if they are to be carried out in a manner that might be construed by the Israelites as an insult to the gods being worshipped. He cites a midrashic interpretation of Deut 12.30 (Babylonian Talmud, San. 61b and 64a) which sees it as categorically prohibiting just such a kind of practice even if it may be argued that by engaging in it the Jew feels that he is offending the idol. Here, therefore, the word מַעֲשֶׂה is to be construed as a direct reference to idolatry.

An even more precise definition of the word in this context is offered by Levi ben Gershom (Gersonides, 'Ralbag', 1288–1344), philosopher and Bible exegete from the south of France. He claims (Levi ben Gershom, 99v) that the notion is the same as that mentioned in Deut. 12.30 and conveys the idea that the Israelites should not follow the liturgical practices of other nations when they worship God. Such a liturgical sense is also reflected, in different ways, in some modern treatments of the verse. Nahum Sarna (1991: 148) appears to suggest that תַעֲשֶׂה כְּמַעֲשֵׂיהֶם refers to the 'adoption of their cultic practices' while the New English Bible renders 'nor observe their rites', assuming a different sense from that occurring in Lev. 18.3. Arnold Ehrlich (1899: 185–186) innovatively understands the word to refer to the items worshipped and not the worshippers, that is, 'do not construct idols like those of the Canaanites'. This is also the view of August

Dillmann (1897: 282). W.C. Propp (1998: 288–289) cites the possibility that sacrifices are what the verse prohibits but rejects the rendering 'idols', claiming that nowhere else does מַעֲשִׂים have such a sense. In truth, the rendering 'idols' is usually employed for the longer Hebrew compound מַעֲשֵׂה יָד but מַעֲשֶׂה could be an abbreviated form of such a usage, as supported by the phrase וְנִמְחוּ מַעֲשֵׂיכֶם in Ezek. 6.6. This is how the latter verse is understood by A.B. Davidson (1892: 42) and *Daʿat Miqra* (38), while Greenberg (1983: 129, 133) sees here 'illicit forms of worship'.

Further support for a liturgical sense of מַעֲשֶׂה may be adduced from two other verses in Chronicles. The first, in 1 Chron. 23.28, describes part of the service performed by the Levites in the Jerusalem temple as וּמַעֲשֵׂה עֲבֹדַת בֵּית הָאֱלֹהִים, with the first word arguably having the sense of performing or carrying out the cultic procedure. Interestingly, there is a Talmudic passage in which the word appears to have a related sense. In Babylonian Talmud Hor. 13a it is ruled that שיהא ראשון קודם לפר העדה בכל מעשיו, that is to say, that the high priest's bullock should be offered first, preceding that of the assembly in all its procedures, the word מעשיו being used in the sense of 'cultic procedures'. The problem in the Chronicles verse may be side-stepped by emending the text (as Curtis and Madsen in the ICC, 1910: 268) or by adopting a literal and unilluminating rendering such as 'work of the service' (Elmslie 1899: 141) or 'general service' (NEB). Other modern treatments do, however, nod in the liturgical direction. *Daʿat Miqra* (412) and J.M. Myers (1965: 158) see here a reference to the necessary preparation that precedes the sacrifice itself and JPS renders 'and the performance of the service of the house of God'. The second verse is in 2 Chron. 4.6 and describes a rinsing procedure that was followed by the priests in the Jerusalem temple in the case of מַעֲשֵׂה הָעוֹלָה. Rashi, in the Rabbinic Bible, addresses the problem of what precisely is meant by the words מַעֲשֵׂה הָעוֹלָה by paraphrasing as קרבי העולה, 'the body parts of the animal being used as a burnt offering'. Hartom (1964: 91) sees the phrase as a description of the meat being offered (בשר (קרבנות העולה, so that מַעֲשֶׂה is conveying the sense of קרבן ('offering'). To conclude this aspect of the discussion, such liturgical senses are again not of significance to the lexicographers, and Ringgren (2001: 400) specifically rejects it in the case of the Exodus verse.

Both Deut. 3.24, אֲשֶׁר־יַעֲשֶׂה כְמַעֲשֶׂיךָ וְכִגְבוּרֹתֶךָ, and Deut. 11.3, וְאֶת־אֹתֹתָיו וְאֶת־מַעֲשָׂיו אֲשֶׁר עָשָׂה בְּתוֹךְ מִצְרָיִם, refer to the divine power, the first declaring that there can be no equivalent in heaven or on earth, and the second describing the historical manifestations of these in Egypt. In the first instance the word מַעֲשִׂים is being employed as a parallel to גְּבוּרוֹת, just as the phrase יָדְךָ הַחֲזָקָה is parallel to גָּדְלְךָ, earlier in the same verse. In that case it bears the sense of 'great, powerful or impressive acts'. Abraham Ibn Ezra (*Torat Ḥayyim*, 33) and the thirteenth-century French exegete, Hezekiah ben Manoaḥ (*Torat Ḥayyim*, 32), recognize that both these acts are remarkable but distinguish מַעֲשִׂים from גְּבוּרוֹת as acts performed with wisdom rather than with power. JPS prefers to treat the phrase כְמַעֲשֶׂיךָ וְכִגְבוּרֹתֶךָ as a hendiadys, rendering 'powerful deeds' but the NEB opts for a parallelism and offers 'thy works and mighty deeds'. Neither appears to take account of the powerful syntactical case for a parallelism here.

The parallelism in the second verse cited (Deut. 11.3) is between מַעֲשִׂים and אוֹתוֹת so that one is again justified in understanding the word מַעֲשִׂים as 'great, powerful or impressive acts'. This is further supported by the fact that the subsequent verses list the miracles performed for Israel in Egypt and in Sinai. In addition, a similar parallel again occurs here, in the previous verse. The Septuagint (Rahlfs, I, 306) renders καὶ τὰ σημεῖα αὐτοῦ καὶ τὰ τέρατα αὐτοῦ, raising the question of whether they read מוֹפְתִים rather than מַעֲשִׂים since the word τέρατα is used for מוֹפְתִים elsewhere, as in Deut. 6.22 and 7.19. But the verb that occurs with מוֹפֵת, when God is the subject, is usually שים, נתן or שלח, as in Exod. 4.21, with the verb עשה referring to human activity, as in Exod. 11.10 (BDB, 69). Perhaps, then, the Greek translators also had the notion that the word מַעֲשִׂים here carries the nuance being suggested. Ibn Ezra (*Torat Ḥayyim*, 93) and Naḥmanides (*Torat Ḥayyim*, 92–93) differ in the significance they attach to each of these parallel expressions, the former relating each of the phrases to a specific event while the latter argues that they are general messages about the power of God to punish evil. Ibn Ezra explains the first part of v. 3 as especially referring to the miracles that he did at Pharaoh's expense so for him מַעֲשָׂיו apparently means 'wondrous deeds'.

There are four other instances in which a good case may be made for identifying in the word מַעֲשִׂים a sense of 'great, powerful or impressive acts'. In Num. 16.28, Moses is arguing his case against Korah and his followers and declares that God has sent him to do כָּל־הַמַּעֲשִׂים הָאֵלֶּה and they are not his own initiatives. Rashi, his grandson Samuel ben Meir, Ibn Ezra and Hezekiah ben Manoaḥ (*Torat Ḥayyim*, 146)—and, similarly, Milgrom (1990: 137) among modern exegetes—all see in this phrase a reference to specific actions, such as taking the priesthood away from the firstborn and giving it to the levites, and/or testing Korah and his supporters with the incense, that constitute unexpected and innovative acts of leadership on the part of Moses. Naḥmanides (*Torat Ḥayyim*, 146) goes further and regards the phrase as relevant to all his distinguished acts of leadership throughout his career, and not to these events alone. Either way—and regardless of whether one refers the phrase to past events or to the judgement on Korah and his followers that is about to be witnessed by the Israelites—a plausible sense is 'impressive acts'. Three verses in Psalms also testify to such a sense. Ps. 106.13, in the course of describing the powerful acts that God had performed for his people in their journey through the Sinai desert, notes that they soon forgot מַעֲשָׂיו. In a section of his poem that discusses God's power as a healer of the sick, the poet in Ps. 107.21–22 invites those who have derived benefit from this power to praise God for his wonders and to thank him by joyfully relating מַעֲשָׂיו. These can only be precisely such powerful acts as have just been noted. Qimḥi, in the Rabbinic Bible, describes them as 'acts of generosity' while *Daʿat Miqra* (302) and Briggs (1907: 361)—rightly in my view—go further and refer respectively to 'God's miraculous deeds' and 'divine works of deliverance'. The phrase כֹּחַ מַעֲשָׂיו הִגִּיד לְעַמּוֹ in Ps. 111.6 was sufficiently unusual to invite the attention of some of the medieval commentators, as recorded in the new edition of the Rabbinic Bible (Cohen 2003: 142–143).

Rashi quotes a midrash that explains that God, who can give his property to whomsoever he wishes, wrote for Israel the story of the world's creation to strengthen its claim to the land. The paraphrase used by Qimḥi was נפלאותיו ומעשיו הגדולים, 'his wonders and his great deeds', while Menaḥem b. Solomon Meʾiri (1249–1316), from a Provençal family, added the word נפלאותיו to the phrase כֹּחַ מַעֲשָׂיו. *Daʿat Miqra* (331) explains the phrase as an allusion to God's miraculous conquest of the land of Canaan.

It will be recalled that among all the lexicographers, it was only Ringgren who paid some attention to the nuance here being suggested for מַעֲשִׂים but, on the basis of the evidence presented above, it seems fair to say that it appears to be an important enough usage to merit more than a passing attention. I do not believe that in this short study I have exhausted all the possibilities with regard to the semantic range of the word מַעֲשִׂים in Biblical Hebrew nor do I believe that a close study of its occurrences in later Hebrew would prove exegetically uninteresting or devoid of value for the linguist. Perhaps I, or a scholar with similar such interests, will return to the topic at a future date. Meanwhile, Robert exemplifies well Rabbi Shimʿon ben Gamaliel's claim (Mishna Avot 1.17) that לא המדרש עיקר אלא המעשה. It is after all not just study (המדרש) that is at the centre of all that we do, but also—dare I?—impressive behaviour (המעשה).

References

Ben Yehuda, E.E. 1908–1959, 1960. *A Complete Dictionary of Ancient and Modern Hebrew by Eliezer Ben Yehuda of Jerusalem* [in Hebrew] (Jerusalem, New York: Yoseloff).
Blenkinsopp, J. 2003. *Isaiah 56–66: A New Translation with Introduction and Commentary* (New York: Doubleday).
Briggs, C.A., and E.G. Briggs. 1907. *A Critical and Exegetical Commentary on the Book of Psalms* (vol. 2; Edinburgh: T. & T. Clark).
Brown, F., S.R. Driver, and C.A. Briggs. 1906. *A Hebrew and English Lexicon of the Old Testament* (Oxford: Clarendon).
Cheyne, T.K. 1921. *Micah* (Cambridge: CambridgeUniversity Press).
Clines, D.J.A. (ed.) 2001–2007. *The Dictionary of Classical Hebrew* (vols. 5–6; Sheffield: Sheffield Academic Press).
Cohen, M. (ed.) 2003. *Mikraʾot Gedolot Haketer, Psalms* (Part II; Ramat-Gan: Bar-Ilan University Press).
Curtis, E.L., and A.A. Madsen. 1910. *The Books of Chronicles* (Edinburgh: T. & T. Clark).
Daʿat Miqra. 1984. *Isaiah* (commentary by A. Hakham; Jerusalem: Rav Kook).
——. 1985. *Ezekiel* (commentary by Y.Z. Moshcovitz; Jerusalem: Rav Kook).
——. 1987. *Psalms* (vol. 2; commentary by A. Hakham; Jerusalem: Rav Kook).
——. 1986. *Chronicles* (2 vols.; commentary by Y. Kiel; Jerusalem: Rav Kook).
Davidson, A.B. 1892. *The Book of the Prophet Ezekiel* (Cambridge: Cambridge University Press).
Dillmann, A. 1897. *Die Bücher Exodus und Leviticus: kurzgefasstes exegetisches Handbuch zum Alten Testament* (Leipzig: Hirzel).
Duhm, B. 1892. *Das Buch Jesaia übersetzt und erklärt* (Gottingen: Vandenhoeck & Ruprecht).
Ehrlich, A.B. 1899. *Mikrâ ki-Pheschutô* (vol. 1; Berlin: Poppelauer).
Elmslie, W.A.L. 1899. *The Books of Chronicles* (Cambridge: Cambridge University Press).
Even-Shoshan, A. 1980. *Ha-Millon He-Ḥadash* (7 vols.; Jerusalem: Kiryath Sepher).
Ginsburger, M. (ed.) 1903. *Pseudo-Jonathan (Thargum Jonathan ben Usiël zum Pentateuch)* (Berlin: Calvary).
Greenberg, M. 1983. *Ezekiel 1–20: A New Translation with Introduction and Commentary* (Garden City: Doubleday).
Hartom, E.S. 1964. *Sifrey Ha-Miqra* (16 vols.; Tel-Aviv: Yavneh).
Ḥayyūj, Judah. 1870. *Two treatises on Verbs Containing Feeble and Double Letters* (ed. J.W. Nutt; London: Asher & Co.).
Ibn Janāḥ, Jonah (Abulwalîd Merwân Ibn Ganâh). 1896. *Sepher Haschoraschim* (ed. W. Bacher; Berlin: Itzkowski).
JPS = *The Torah* (2nd ed., 1967); *The Prophets* (1978); *The Writings* (1982) (Philadelphia: Jewish Publication Society of America).

Koehler, L., and W. Baumgartner, W. 1995. *The Hebrew and Aramaic Lexicon of the Old Testament* (ed. J.J. Stamm; vol. 2; English translation (Leiden: Brill).

Levi ben Gershom. 1547. *Commentary on the Torah* (פירוש על התורה) (Venice: Bomberg).

Levine, B. 1989. *The JPS Torah Commentary: Leviticus* (Philadelphia: Jewish Publication Society).

Milgrom, J. 1990. *The JPS Torah Commentary: Numbers* (Philadelphia: Jewish Publication Society).

Myers, J.M. 1965. *Chronicles: A New Translation with Introduction and Commentary* (Garden City: Doubleday).

NEB = *The New English Bible: The Old Testament* (1970; Oxford and Cambridge: Oxford University Press and Cambridge University Press).

Propp, W.H.C. 1998. *Exodus 1–18: A New Translation with Introduction and Commentary* (New York: Doubleday).

Qimḥi, David. 1847. *Rabbi Davidis Kimchi Radicum Liber* (eds. J.H.R. Biesenthal and F. Lebrecht; Berlin: Bethge).

Rahlfs, A. (ed.) 1952. *Septuaginta: Id Est Vetus Testamentum Graece Iuxta LXX Interpretes* (5th ed.; New York: American Bible Society).

Ringgren, H. 2001. 'עשה', in *Theological Dictionary of the Old Testament* (eds. G.J. Botterweck, H. Ringgren, and H.-J. Fabry; vol. 11; trans. D.E. Green; Grand Rapids: Eerdmans) 387–403.

Sáenz-Badillos, A. 1993. *A History of the Hebrew Language* (trans. J. Elwolde; Cambridge: Cambridge University Press).

Sarna, N.M. 1991. *The JPS Torah Commentary: Exodus* (Philadelphia: Jewish Publication Society).

Shachter, J.F. 1986. *The Commentary of Abraham ibn Ezra on the Pentateuch. Vol. 3, Leviticus* (Hoboken: Ktav).

Sifra, Commentar zu Leviticus (ed. I.H. Weiss; 1862, Vienna: Schlossberg).

Skinner, J. 1898. *The Book of the Prophet Isaiah, XL–LXVI* (Cambridge: Cambridge University Press).

Smith, J.M.P., W.H. Ward, and J.A. Bewer. 1911. *Micah, Zephaniah, Nahum, Habakkuk, Obadiah and Joel* (Edinburgh: T. & T. Clark).

Torat Ḥayyim. Ḥamišah Ḥumšey Torah (ed. M.L. Katzenellenbogen; 7 vols.; 2004; Jerusalem: Rav Kook).

REFLECTIONS ON THE CHRISTIAN TURN TO THE *HEBRAICA VERITAS* AND ITS IMPLICATIONS[1]

Philip Alexander

In Christian dogma the pre-eminent textual authority is the Bible. The Bible, to be sure, ministers as authority in subtly different ways in different communions. In some forms of Protestantism it is deemed to be the ultimate, and indeed sole, court of appeal on all matters of doctrine and practice. In Catholicism and Orthodoxy its authority is less singular and absolute: tradition, the creeds, the pronouncements of the great ecumenical councils, and promulgations of the popes hedge it about. Anglicans, following Hooker (though he did not himself use the formula), see Scripture, tradition, and reason as forming a three-fold *regula fidei*, to which Methodists would add experience (to form the so-called Wesleyan Quadrilateral). But all venerate the Bible as the word of God, and quote it more than any other text to validate their teachings and to exhort the faithful. The problem is this: which form of the Bible is authoritative? Take the situation in the Latin West in the Middle Ages. Christian scholars were aware then of the existence of three Bibles. First, there was the Latin which they all used (in the multifarious versions commonly called the Vulgate). Second, there was the Greek, both the New Testament and the Old. In the New Testament the Greek was the original, in the Old it was a translation of the Hebrew. Access to the Greek Bible was limited in the West until the later Middle Ages: copies were scarce and knowledge of the Greek language meagre. But the existence of the Greek Bible was well known. And third there was, for the Old Testament, the Hebrew. Somewhat paradoxically Christian scholars had, potentially, more ready access to the Hebrew language and the Hebrew Scriptures than to the Greek, because there was a widespread and learned

[1] It gives me great pleasure to dedicate this little piece to one of the finest Christian Hebraists of his generation, someone I have known since my teenage years in Belfast. It is something of a *jeu d'esprit*, which reflects our shared interests. I should make it clear that though it deals with theological issues I do not write as a theologian, but purely as a historian of religion.

Jewish Diaspora in Europe, and every Jewish community would have had at least one Torah scroll, which some adult males would have been able to read. There was also a sizeable cohort of Jewish scholars well able to teach Christians. Though few Christians availed themselves of this opportunity, they were well aware that the Old Testament had originally been given in that language. So there were three forms of the Bible, but which of them had priority? To put the question more theologically: which was the inspired word of God?

The problem is more than academic. Relying on translations is dangerous, since the translator may not always have got it right. Two well known examples will make the point. Jerome chose to translate the Greek μετανοεῖτε in Mt. 3.2 by *paenitentiam agite*, which was interpreted as meaning 'do penance', and cited as the biblical basis for the doctrine of penances. But, as the Reformers pointed out, this is a misunderstanding of the Greek, which means simply 'repent', literally, 'change one's mind'. And so the Scriptural foundation for one of the sacraments of the Catholic Church disappeared at a stroke. Similarly, Christian writers, starting with the New Testament itself, took the words in Isa. 7.14, 'Behold a virgin shall conceive and bear a son', as a prediction of the virgin birth of Jesus, because they were relying on the Greek version which uses παρθένος to translate the Hebrew עַלְמָה. But, as Jewish scholars long ago noted, the Hebrew עַלְמָה means 'young woman', not 'virgin', for which Hebrew has the unambiguous word, בְּתוּלָה. A 'virgin' may be an עַלְמָה, but an עַלְמָה is not necessarily a virgin. And so the basis of one of the cardinal doctrines of the Catholic faith, and one of the key proof-texts of Christian apologetic, is thrown into doubt.

It would be illogical not to see the Hebrew of the Old Testament and Greek of the New as the Word of God, but what about translations which most, because they do not have the Biblical languages, are obliged to use? On the face of it, the problem of which version to rely on can be quickly solved. A particular translation can be declared by competent ecclesiastical authority to be as inspired as the original. Theologically this is not a difficult position to articulate. It has always been implicit in the Christian doctrine of Scripture that not only was the text given originally under divine inspiration, but that it was preserved by divine providence in a sufficiently pure form to minister God's word to the Church. It is easy to extend this idea of providence to certain translations of the Bible. The claim that a translation of the Bible may be as inspired as the original has a long pedigree. Though the Letter of Aristeas accords great honour to the Septuagint, it does not itself, when closely read, claim inspiration for this version (see *Aristeas* 301–302). Nevertheless it was widely understood in this way, and the view that the Septuagint was inspired became common in later Jewish and Christian tradition. Greek-speaking Alexandrian Jews do not appear to have read the Bible in Hebrew in their synagogues, nor to have made much effort to learn Hebrew. And their scholars, such as Philo, analysed the Greek text with the same manic attention to its linguistic detail as the later Rabbis bestowed on the original Hebrew. The unspoken assumption was that there is no need to bother with the Hebrew. The Greek text is fully sufficient, since it is equally inspired and authoritative.

Somewhat oddly one of the clearest statements of the inspiration of the Septuagint is found in Rabbinic literature—I say 'oddly', because the Rabbis were eager to assert the primacy of the Hebrew in order precisely to deny the authority of the Septuagint, which had become the Bible of the Greek-speaking Church. According to one Rabbinic retelling of the Aristeas Legend, King Ptolemy locked up the translators in separate rooms, and told them to translate the Torah incommunicado. When they emerged all their versions agreed precisely, word-for-word, to the extent that they had all made the same deliberate changes to the text! The reason for this miracle was because 'the Holy One, blessed be he, put wisdom into the heart of each of them, and they all agreed of one accord' (Babylonian Talmud, Meg. 9a–9b).[2]

Arguably the belief that the Greek is inspired is already implicit in the New Testament, which constantly cites the Greek Bible (though not always in its standard Septuagintal form), and draws fundamental teaching from it—a hazardous procedure, as later patristic writers fully realized, unless bolstered by a doctrine of the inspiration of the Septuagint. From dialogue with Jews some Church Fathers became aware that not only are certain Greek renderings suspect, but the Greek text differs substantially from that found in the Jews' Hebrew Torah scrolls. The standard defence of the Greek was that it was the *Hebrew* text that was corrupt: the Greek had preserved the original. This is an argument that Justin put to Trypho, when he claimed that the words,

[2] See further: Møgens Müller (1996); Martin Hengel (2004); A. Wasserstein and D.J. Wasserstein (2006); and more generally, Naomi Seidman (2006), and Tessa Rajak (2009).

'Tell among the nations that the Lord reigned from the wood' (i.e. the cross), found in some Greek manuscripts of Psalm 96(95) are original. The Jews removed 'from the wood' from the Hebrew to avoid a clear prophecy of the crucifixion.[3] The Christian claim that the synagogue Hebrew text is corrupt where it differs from the Greek figures regularly in Christian-Jewish debate, and it was adopted by Islam to explain the discrepancies between the Biblical and Qur'anic versions of Old Testament story. The argument is not quite as feeble and tendentious as it first sounds. Though 'from the wood' is certainly not the original Psalm text, there are cases where the text attested in the Septuagint may indeed be superior to that found in the standard Masoretic form of the Hebrew Bible. We now know that the Masoretic Text is only one of a number of Hebrew text-forms that circulated in antiquity, and that in places it most certainly *is* textually corrupt.

Christian reliance on inspired translation is evident in another, highly sensitive area. The Gospels were supposed to contain the *ipsissima verba* of Jesus, but Jesus, as Christian scholars have long realized, did not utter these words in Greek: he spoke Aramaic. Though his words have been preserved only in Greek in the Greek canonic Gospels, this was deemed sufficient, for those Gospels are inspired. If a collection of Jesus' sayings in Aramaic were to turn up, or the Hebrew original of the Gospel of Matthew, rumours of which circulated among Christian scholars in late antiquity, were to be found, it might cause some initial problems, could it be shown, as some modern scholars have argued, that the original words of Jesus have sometimes been mistranslated.[4] But the problem could be dealt with summarily by asserting the primacy of the inspired Greek version: whatever the Aramaic said, this was what Jesus meant. Christianity, unlike Judaism and Islam, has never shown the same concern to preserve and hear its Scriptures in the original: it has relied on translations right from the start.

The claim that inspiration could extend to translations gradually came to embrace the Latin versions in the West. One can see this idea beginning to germinate in Augustine. By the time he came to write the *City of God*, he had formed the settled opinion that it was necessary

[3] Justin, *Dialogue with Trypho* (lxxiii; see also lxxi–lxxii).

[4] Maurice Casey (1998, 2002). Older studies include: C.F. Burney (1922, 1925).

on theological grounds to assert the full inspiration of the Septuagint.[5] The translators had done their work under the influence of the Holy Spirit, and this meant that when they added things not in the Hebrew, or differed from it in other ways, they were still speaking the words of God. If the Septuagint could be faithfully rendered into Latin, then its divine authority would carry over to the new version.[6] Augustine had written earlier to Jerome to urge him to undertake this task, and forget about translating *iuxta Hebraeos*, because it was ecclesiastically dangerous and theologically unnecessary.[7] Certainly the Vulgate came to be treated *de facto* as in itself inspired Scripture in the Latin West, till it was finally formally proclaimed as such by the Council of Trent.[8] The inspiration of the Vulgate is implicit in some of the Reformation-period Catholic translations of the Bible, such as the Douai-Rheims. And the idea that translations can be inspired is alive and well in our own day. Some English-speaking Protestant fundamentalists assert that the King James' Version of the Bible is to all intents and purposes

---

[5] See Augustine, *City of God* (xviii, 42–45).

[6] There is an important point here, which is well put by Miles Smith, author of the preface to the King James Bible, 'The Translators to the Reader': '[W]e do not deny,' he writes, 'nay we affirm and avow, that the very meanest translation of the Bible in English, set forth by men of our profession...containeth the word of God, nay, is the word of God. As the King's speech which he uttered in Parliament, being translated into French, Dutch, Italian and Latin, is still the King's speech, though it be not interpreted by every translator with the like grace, nor peradventure so fitly for phrase, nor so expressly for sense, everywhere.' Implicit here is the claim that the Word of God is contained less in the *words* of the original text than in the *ideas* those words express, and if the same ideas can be expressed in other words, in another language, then the Word of God can be successfully transferred, and the translation, to the degree that it represents accurately the *ideas*, becomes the Word of God. This claim does not work, however, if, as in the Rabbinic doctrine of Scripture, the Word of God is seen as bound up inextricably with the physical words of the original, even with their graphic form. Scripture, on this view, becomes fundamentally untranslatable (see Tosefta Meg. 3.41 [Lieberman]; Babylonian Talmud, Qid. 49a–49b; Massekhet Soferim 1.7; Massekhet Sefer Torah 1.6).

[7] See Augustine, *Letters* 28, 71 and 82, and Jerome, *Letters* 112. The exchange of views between Augustine and Jerome on the matter of Bible translation is of great importance for our present theme. It shows vividly the tensions that can arise between theology and biblical scholarship.

[8] Council of Trent, Session IV, Decree concerning the Edition and the Use of the sacred Books: 'Moreover, the same sacred and holy Synod,—considering that no small utility may accrue to the Church of God, if it be made known which out of all the Latin editions, now in circulation, of the sacred books, is to be held as authentic,—ordains and declares, that the said old and vulgate edition, which, by the lengthened usage of so many years, has been approved of in the Church, be, in public lectures, disputations, sermons and expositions, held as authentic; and that no one is to dare, or presume to reject it under any pretext whatever.'

inspired, and to be preferred over all other translations. They even go so far as to argue that the marked preference which God has shown for this version, in using it providentially to minister to his people and spread his Gospel, proves, against modernist scholars, that the Greek and Hebrew texts which underlie it are the only true forms of the original Scriptures.

The problem, then, of which translation is authoritative is theologically speaking simply solved by declaring one version inspired. In fact, however, things were not quite so simple. Since the logical implication of an inspired translation is an inspired original, people will always be tempted to look at the original, if it is to hand, and it will be hard for them not to be troubled if they find discrepancies or apparent mistranslations in their translation. In polemical settings, either within the Church, or between Jews and Christians, opponents may be tempted to weaken a particular claim by arguing that it is based on a misunderstanding of the original or not actually supported there. Within the Church this appeal to the original has had notable champions. The most influential of these was Jerome. The movement *ad fontes*, began, however, a little before his time with Origen. Origen's great work of biblical scholarship, the Hexapla arranged in parallel columns a number of Greek translations of the Bible, Aquila, Symmachus, the standard Septuagint, Theodotion and so forth, and compared them with the original Hebrew, which was given in Hebrew characters in column 1 and in transcription in column 2. The Septuagint text was marked with signs to indicate plusses and minuses in comparison with the Hebrew. This is the first known attempt to compare the Septuagint systematically with the Hebrew. Origen's primary purpose was not to prioritize the Hebrew but to sort out the problems of the Septuagint, which was in considerable textual confusion in his day. He wrongly assumed that the Hebrew text of his day was the text from which the Septuagint had originally been translated, so any deviations from it must be due to corruption in the Greek. But an unintended consequence of his massive enterprise was to suggest that the Hebrew was the true Word of God. It had to be called in to solve the problems of the Greek, and the single, pure column of Hebrew must have contrasted eloquently with the conflict and confusion evinced by the multiple versions in Greek.

It was certainly no accident that Origen became interested in the Hebrew when he did. He lived in Caesarea Maritima, at a time when there was a flourishing and scholarly Jewish community in the town.

He almost certainly conversed, even debated, with some of the local Rabbis. He lived at a time when the Rabbinical movement in Palestine was attempting to impose its authority on the Greek-speaking Diaspora, and one of the ways they probably did this was by insisting that Jews in the Diaspora should read the Torah publicly in Hebrew, not in Greek. In other words the Rabbis were promoting strongly the primacy of the Hebrew as the Word of God. It is hard to see how Origen could have completed the Hexapla without Jewish help. He must surely have employed a Jewish scribe to write out the Hebrew column, and his transcription column may well have been based on a teaching-aid produced to help Greek speaking Jews to learn Hebrew, or to fulfil the duty of reading the Torah in Hebrew. It is incredible that he could have done both these columns on his own.

Jerome took the turn to the Hebrew further. Interestingly in the earlier part of his life he showed little interest in the Hebrew, and he produced Latin translations from the Greek. It was only when he moved to Bethlehem in the mid-390s that he discovered the Hebrew. Again the presence of a Jewish community which read the Bible in Hebrew was crucial. Jerome seems to have been a competent Hebraist—perhaps the only Church father of whom this can be said (Origen's knowledge of the language, despite Eusebius' eulogies, probably did not go very far). He had Jewish teachers, who passed on to him not only a knowledge of the language, but elements of Jewish tradition as well. It is in a letter dated 393 that he first provocatively refers to the Hebrew as the *Hebraica veritas*.[9] Jerome was a Biblical scholar to the finger-tips, but not much of a theologian. He seems blissfully unaware of the havoc he might be wreaking by appealing directly to the Hebrew. He says he turned to the Hebrew because he discovered there that the predictions of the coming of Christ were much clearer. This is curious, given that some of the classic prophecies, such as Isaiah 7:14, vanish when we turn to the original. Possibly the real reason he liked the Hebrew was that, under good Jewish tutelage, it yielded an awful lot more sense than the Greek.

Jerome became the great Bible teacher of the Western Church, and his advocacy of the Hebrew made it possible for others to follow in his steps. Study of Hebrew was still regarded as suspect by many church authorities, but more of it seems to have gone on than one might at

---

[9] See Stefan Rebenich (1993); Paul Decock (2008). Further, Adam Kamesar (1993).

first sight suppose. The Victorines and the Franciscans found the original Hebrew and the Jewish commentators useful allies in their struggle to promote the *sensus litteralis* of the Bible against allegorical readings. Nicholas of Lyra was a competent Hebraist, and his *postillae* are full of references to Hebrew and Jewish tradition.[10] This is well illustrated by his comments on the Song of Songs, where he follows Jewish tradition, represented by Rashi and the Targum, of interpreting the book as an historical allegory: for Rashi and the Targum it was an allegory of God's relationship to Israel, from the Exodus from Egypt till the coming of the Messiah; for Lyra it was an allegory of Christ's relationship to the Church, both under the old dispensation and the new, till the second coming. Lyra's dependency on Jewish tradition is evident on almost every page of his text, and it is confirmed by the curious little work entitled *Expositio hystorica in Canticum Canticorum secundum Salomonem* published by Sarah Kamin and Avrom Saltman (1989). The Salomon of the title is not, as one might first think, King Solomon, but Solomon Yitzḥaqi, better known as Rashi, the great north French Jewish commentator of the eleventh century. This work turns out to be Christianized Latin version of Rashi's commentary on Canticles.

An intriguing body of evidence for Christian Hebraism in the Middle Ages comes from England. A small but significant collection of bilingual Hebrew-Latin texts have survived in Corpus Christi College Library, Oxford, and elsewhere. It is now possible to say with a high degree of certainty that these were written in England, and not brought from Northern France. One of the Psalm texts graphically illustrates the co-operation between Jewish and Christian scholars needed to create the work. The Hebrew was done by a competent Jewish scribe who had obviously been commissioned to write the text with wide gaps between the lines, into which a Christian scholar has then inserted in a neat and practiced Latin hand a new Latin version of the Hebrew. A fragment of another bilingual Hebrew Latin text turned up a few years ago in the cartonage of the binding of a book in the University Library at Durham. The Hebrew text was a surprise: it was a fragment of the scurrilous mediaeval collection of Hebrew tales known as the Alphabet of ben Sira—a very rare manuscript fragment of this strange work. There also exists an impressive trilingual Hebrew-Latin-French dictionary of Biblical Hebrew, compiled or copied in the thirteenth

[10] Deeana Copeland Klepper (2007).

century in the Abbey of Ramsey in East Anglia.[11] Evidence for Christian Hebraism in the Middle Ages is steadily growing, and the more it grows, the more one realizes that the return to Scripture in its original languages at the time of the Reformation and Renaissance was less of a bolt from the blue than used to be thought.

However, prioritizing the Hebrew was fraught with theological danger, and it was to prove profoundly destabilizing. First, it opened the door to Jewish influence in the Church. That in itself, of course, was not necessarily a bad thing, but contacts with Jews were bound to raise disturbing and difficult questions. It was well-nigh impossible for Christians to learn Hebrew without a Jewish teacher, or to understand the original without consulting the great mediaeval Jewish commentators, especially Rashi and Qimḥi. Church authorities frowned on studying with Jews, and with some reason. The Dominican preacher Robert de Reddinge learned Hebrew with Jewish teachers in England around 1270 and shortly after caused a scandal by converting to Judaism. Jewish exegesis has played a highly significant, but still not fully documented role in Christian understanding of the Bible. The *Hebraica veritas* influenced the formation of the Church's canon. Jerome relegated to the category of Apocrypha any book in the Greek Old Testament, for which he could not find a Hebrew text among the synagogue scrolls. Though apocryphal and deuterocanonical books were preserved in the West, the Western Church tended to follow Jerome's lead in giving them a lower status, till the Council of Trent declared them unequivocally fully Scripture.

Second, and *much* more alarmingly, the appeal to the *Hebraica veritas* raised acutely questions of authority. The Old Testament of the early Church was Greek, not Hebrew, and it was the Greek text that shaped emerging Christian theology. New Testament writers largely quote the Septuagint. Resorting to the Hebrew runs the risk of problematizing the relationship between the two Testaments, even of cutting the umbilical cord that joins them. If, as Augustine wanted, Jerome had simply made a Latin version of the Septuagint, and if, in turn, only that had been rendered into the modern European languages, few problems would have arisen. But human nature being what it is, someone was bound in the end to want to look at the Hebrew.

[11] For details see Judith Olszowy-Schlanger (2003); Olszowy-Schlanger and A. Grondeux (2008).

Once the Hebrew was on the table the authority of the translations was inevitably impaired. It is hardly surprising that in the history of the Church, Christian Hebraism has generally been linked with liberalizing, radical movements, because the Hebrew provided a handy battering ram against the establishment. The Protestant Reformation offers the most striking case of its polemical use. The Reformers turned eagerly to the Hebrew, and some of them acquired a reasonable command of the language. They assumed, as it had been assumed since the time of Origen and Jerome, that the Hebrew text preserved by the Synagogue was authentic and highly accurate: certainly its uniformity across the world, and the Masoretic devices used to preserve it from corruption, were impressive and reassuring. Here the Reformers felt they had firm ground on which to stand, from which to launch an assault on Rome. At first they seemed to sweep all before them, but then a cloud appeared on the horizon: at first no bigger than a man's hand, it rapidly developed into a menacing thunderhead. It was all very well returning *ad fontes* but what were the *fontes*? Scholars rapidly discovered that there were significant variant readings in the original manuscripts. This, in principle, came as no surprise: they were philologically trained and well aware of the need to establish corrected texts of the Greek and Latin classics. But in the case of Holy Scripture this basic textual 'housekeeping' took on a theological dimension. The problem of textual variants was, at first, most obvious in the case of the New Testament. The early printed editions were done from late Byzantine codices, the inadequacy of which soon became apparent. It was widely known in scholarly circles that Théodore de Bèze had a Greek manuscript of the Gospels and Acts, the Codex Bezae, which differed strikingly in places from the *textus receptus*. In 1581 he presented it to the University of Cambridge where it still resides. The Codex Alexandrinus (now in the British Library) arrived in London in 1627 as a gift to King Charles I from the Patriarch of Constantinople, and was the subject of scholarly interest and inquiry. It was not just a question of the alarming amount of variation that the manuscripts displayed, giving the impression of a poorly preserved or uncertain text. Key doctrines could be involved, as in the famous *Comma Johanneum* (1 Jn 5.17), which in some manuscripts did not support the doctrine of the Trinity in the way that the traditional text did.

At first sight the Hebrew Bible was less problematic textually, because, as already noted, the codices of it showed an astonishingly uniform text. But here too problems soon surfaced. The sixteenth century witnessed not only a revival of interest in the Hebrew text, but in the ancient versions of the Hebrew as well. These were made readily accessible, side-by-side with the Hebrew, starting with the Genoa Psalter (1516), and running through the Complutensian, Antwerp, and Paris Polyglots to the London Polyglot. Scholars were perfectly aware that the Septuagint appeared to have been done from a Hebrew text which differed in places significantly from the standard Hebrew manuscripts. They also knew the Samaritan Pentateuch: it featured in some of the Polyglots. It is no accident that the interest in these ancient Bible versions was strong among Catholic Bible scholars: all the Polyglots, save the last, were done under Catholic auspices, and Catholic expertise in this area of Biblical Studies easily matched, if not surpassed, the best that could be mustered in the Protestant camp. One reason for this was theological: Catholic scholars were keen to establish the *uncertainty* of the originals, so that they could argue for the need for an external agent—the Church—to promulgate the authoritative text. Often regarded as products of progressive humanism, the great Catholic polyglot Bibles were actually important instruments of the Counter Reformation.

Even apart from the uncertainty injected into the text of the Hebrew Bible by the Septuagint and Samaritan Pentateuch, early Bible critics were aware of the possibility of conjectural emendation: changing *dalets* to *reshes* could in places create a more meaningful text. Conjectural emendation was rife in the study of the Classics (exemplified by the work of Richard Bentley), and some were happy to apply this approach to the Bible as well. The emendations proposed in the Hebrew Bible, were not numerous, but they contributed to the sense that the Hebrew was not quite as certain as one might hope. But perhaps most unsettling of all was the discovery that the pointing and accentuation were not original. Elijah Levita in his *Massoret ha-Massoret* (Venice, 1538) argued that the Tiberian vowels were added to the consonantal text in the fifth century by Jewish scholars. His suggestion was hotly disputed by many Protestants. The stakes were perceived to be high: the vowels carry a significant part of the sense of the Hebrew Bible, and Christian Hebraists were conscious of the fact that they would have found it difficult to learn Hebrew or read the Hebrew Bible without them. No-one was suggesting that the reading of the Hebrew Bible expressed in the vowels and accents was *invented* in the fifth century: the Tiberian Masoretes were recording and notating a traditional way of reading the text that had been passed down orally in synagogues for generations. But that was precisely the problem for Protestants: tradition was needed to 'complete' the Bible, tradition which depended on Jews, and indeed on 'Rabbins' (the Masoretes were assumed to be Rabbis), whom, in varying degrees, Protestant scholars to a man despised. This was not a problem within Judaism. Jews had always recognized that the Written Torah comprised only the consonantal text, minus the vowels and accents, and that is why Torah scrolls for liturgical use are purely consonantal. The vowels and accentuation, supplied from memory by the reader in synagogue, belong to the Oral Torah, which, of course, is deemed equally to go back to Moses on Sinai. But Protestants had no truck with Oral Torah, or with what they saw as its Christian analogue—the apostolic tradition claimed by the Church of Rome. Faced with barrage of uncertainty Protestant scholars found that what they had taken to be the firm ground of the *Hebraica veritas* was quaking beneath their feet.

This debate is neatly encapsulated in an exchange between two of the heavyweight Bible scholars in England in the seventeenth century—John Owen (1616–1683) and Brian Walton (1600–1661). In the late 1650s Owen, a leading Puritan divine, Vice-Chancellor of Oxford, and high in the counsels of the Commonwealth, started to write a book on the authority of the Bible, in which he attempted to expound a *Sola Scriptura* doctrine in an extreme form: the Scriptures in the divine original authenticate *themselves* as the Word of God, and are the standard by which all doctrine is to be judged.[12] They can themselves be judged by none, but stand in transcendent, self-authenticating majesty as the sole court of appeal on all matters of belief and practice. He then seems to have looked at the London Polyglot which had just come out under the editorship of Brian Walton, and he was thunderstruck by the degree of uncertainty which it seemed to imply was present in the copies of the Divine Original. He was particularly incensed by volume six which contained page after page of variant readings for both Testaments. He hastily added to his work a long section under the title, *A vindication of the purity and integrity of the Hebrew and Greek texts of the Old and New Testament, in some considerations of the prolegomena & appendix to the late Biblia polyglotta*, in which he ferociously attacked Walton. His argument is long and rambling, and the exact basis of his attack, voiced in the feisty rhetoric of the times, is

[12] John Owen (1659).

not entirely clear. On the surface he appears to accuse Walton primarily of shaking the faith of simple Christians by presenting them with an apparatus of variants of such a size as to leave them no option but to assume that the originals were corrupt and unreliable. Still worse Walton was affording Rome the chance—a chance he knew had been seized upon by Jean Morin[13] and others with both hands—to argue that Scripture has first to be authenticated by external ecclesiastical authority before it can be used as a rule of faith. 'We went from Rome,' he thundered, 'under the conduct of the purity of the Originals. I wish none have a mind to return thither again, under the pretence of their corruption.' He accused Walton of 'Mahometanism'—an allusion to the doctrine of *taḥrīf*, which Muslim scholars invoked to explain the discrepancies between the Qur'an and Scripture, a doctrine, as already noted, first invented by the early Christian apologists to defend the accuracy of the Septuagint against the Hebrew text by charging the Jews with deliberately corrupting Scripture.

Owen was not denying that there are variants in the copies of the Divine Original, but arguing that to trumpet them abroad ran the risk of unsettling the 'weaker brethren'. This is the argument on the surface, but, reading between the lines, it is obvious that Owen himself was rattled by the sheer scale of the variants, which, because the London Polyglot presented them *en masse*, may only have hit him for the first time. It clearly posed a problem for his claim about a self-authenticating original. Owen's *Considerations* is as much about reassuring himself as correcting any misimpression that Walton may have caused. He was particularly exercised by the question of the vowel points, and rashly made it almost an article of faith that they were prophetic in origin. He realized that to try and take them back to Moses was a lost cause, but he wanted to trace them at least to Ezra, that is to say to within the period when Jewish superintendence of Scripture was still under the guidance of the Holy Spirit. Walton answered Owen in kind in a little book entitled the *Considerator Considered*.[14] He agreed with Owen that no fundamental article of faith was imperilled by the

[13] See J. Morin (1631, 1660). On Morin see the note by Arjo Vanderjagt in Magne Sæbø (2008: 749). This whole volume provides the scholarly apparatus for this section of my essay, see, e.g., the chapter by Johann Anselm Steiger (154–190). Anthony Grafton and Joanna Weinberg (2011) open a new chapter in the history of the subject.

[14] Brian Walton (1659). The Owen-Walton debate is reviewed in Henry John Todd (1821), which shows how alive and contentious the issues it raised still were in the early nineteenth century.

textual variants—an oft-repeated claim, which was somewhat beside the point, and an assertion more of hope than of demonstrable fact. But for that reason he could see no point in concealing from ordinary Christians that variants exist. Above all he reiterated succinctly and with force the arguments for the post-biblical origins of the vowel points. Walton, who became Bishop of Chester after the Restoration, was a good Anglican, and doubtless happy with the classic Anglican doctrine of Scripture, tradition and reason as a three-fold *regula fidei*. He would not, in principle, have been fazed by the idea of authenticating Scripture either by tradition, or by the sanctified reason of scholars applying the methods of textual criticism.

This debate rumbled on through the eighteenth century. Once again we can illustrate it specifically from the study of the Bible in England. The editorial work of Francis Sawyer Parris at Cambridge and Benjamin Blayney at Oxford by modernizing the King James Bible gave it a new lease of life, and at the same time helped to entrench the Masoretic Text in the Old Testament and the *textus receptus* in the New as the authoritative originals.[15] But that the accuracy of these could be questioned was not forgotten. The King James Bible was challenged by a series of alternative translations done from different base-texts. For example, William Whiston, best known now for his translation of Josephus (1737), produced his *Primitive New Testament* (1745) which in the Gospels and Acts followed the Codex Bezae, with the 'imperfections' supplied from the 'vulgar Latin'; in the Pauline Epistles, the Codex Claromontanus; and in the rest of the New Testament, the Codex Alexandrinus.[16] William Newcome, who became Archbishop of Armagh, toiled for many years on a new version of the Bible. He

---

[15] Parris's editorial work began with the 1743 duodecimo (T.H. Darlow and H.F. Moule, *Historical Catalogue of Printed Editions of the English Bible 1525–1961*, rev. A.S. Herbert [British and Foreign Bible Society: London, 1968], hereafter = DM, no. 1963), and concluded with the 1760 octavo (DM 1131) Cambridge Bibles. The 1760 octavo was reprinted in Cambridge with additional corrections by H. Therold in 1762 both in folio (DM 1142) and in quarto (DM 1143). Blayney's work is enshrined in the 1769 Oxford folio (DM 1194). This became the textual standard for King James' Bibles down to the present day. Without this modernization it is doubtful the KJB would have survived. Blayney went as far as he dared in changing the text of the KJB, but that he thought a totally new translation was desirable is suggested by the fact that he spent the latter part of his life working on one: *Jeremiah and Lamentations* (Oxford, 1784) (DM 1297); *Zechariah* (Oxford, 1797) (DM 2429). On the work of Parris and Blayney see David Norton (2005).

[16] The Josephus translation has seldom been out of print since it appeared.

produced new translations of parts of the Old Testament, involving a significant amount of textual emendation, and a complete New Testament based on the new critical edition of the Greek by Johann Griesbach (1775–77)—the first seriously to challenge the dominance of the *textus receptus*.[17] Robert Lowth, one of the founders of the modern study of the Old Testament, and a significant influence on German biblical scholarship in the next century, made a pioneering translation of Isaiah in which he resorted freely to conjectural emendation.[18] Alexander Geddes followed in his wake: his rendering of the Old Testament consulted Kennicott and de Rossi's work on the Masoretic text, but since that involved few substantial changes, he turned to the Samaritan Pentateuch and to conjectural emendation to improve the text.[19] It is surely no accident that a number of these radical translators were not orthodox: Whiston was well known for his anti-Trinitarianism; Geddes, a Catholic, was regarded as a maverick by the Church authorities and suspended from holy orders. A close friend of Joseph Priestly, he was suspected of Unitarian sympathies. Lowth and Newcome were orthodox enough, but it is interesting that the latter's New Testament was used as the basis for the Unitarian New Testament of 1808, which was largely the work of Thomas Belsham (1808). This interest in challenging the hegemony of the King James Bible and the original texts it represented, cannot be divorced from the Deism, Rationalism, and Unitarianism which made such a deep impression on the intellectual life of the eighteenth century.[20]

The debate about the true text of the Bible burst out with renewed vigor in the nineteenth century under the impact of German critical

[17] William Newcome, *Minor Prophets* (Dublin, 1785) (DM 1309); *Ezekiel* (Dublin, 1788) (DM 1329); *An Attempt toward revising our English translation of the Greek Scriptures, or the New Covenant of Jesus Christ* (Dublin, 1796, but apparently not actually published till 1800) (DM 1415).

[18] Robert Lowth, *Isaiah. A New Translation, with a preliminary dissertation and notes* (London, 1788 and 1789) (DM 1269).

[19] Alexander Geddes, *The Holy Bible, or the Books accounted sacred by Jews and Christians, otherwise called the Books of the Old and New Covenants; faithfully translated from corrected texts of the originals. With various readings and explanatory notes.* First volume, Genesis to Joshua (London, 1792); second volume, Judges, 1 and 2 Samuel, 1 and 2 Kings, 1 and 2 Chronicles, Ruth, Prayer of Manasseh (London, 1797) (DM 1416); Psalms, ed. John Disney and Charles Butler (London, 1807) (DM 1505).

[20] It should be remembered that England, arguably, in the eighteenth century was the centre of radical Biblical scholarship, and that it was England, more than any other country, that gave birth to the critical movement in Germany in the nineteenth. See the classic essay by Henning Graf Reventlow (1980).

Biblical scholarship. This was in part a continuation of eighteenth century radicalism (particularly in its English manifestations), and indeed its genealogy can be traced back, in a way insufficiently acknowledged, to the sixteenth and seventeenth century tradition of sacred criticism. But it also marked important new departures. For the first time Higher Criticism began to be distinguished clearly from Lower Criticism, and to dominate the agenda. Lower Criticism was concerned with the text and philology of the Bible, and here the advances in Germany were less spectacular: German scholars often restated as their own linguistic and text-critical suggestions that had already been mooted by the *Critici Sacri* of the Reformation. Higher Criticism was concerned with going behind the Biblical text, dismantling it into its original sources, dating these, and rewriting Biblical history on the basis of this analysis.[21] And here huge strides were made. Discoveries in the fields of language, topography, and archaeology fuelled the developments. This new scholarship was increasingly registered in Bible translations. A flurry of these appeared in England in the nineteenth century (some conservative, some radical), culminating in the Revised Version New Testament of 1881, based effectively on the new edition of the Greek New Testament of Westcott and Hort, which set aside, for the first time in an 'official' version, the Textus Receptus.[22]

The textual basis of the Old Testament translations remained conservative for much longer, and did not admit significant textual changes till the second half of the twentieth century. Here the impact of the Dead Sea Scrolls can hardly be overestimated, because these dispelled forever any lingering possibility of arguing that the differences between the Septuagint and the Masoretic Text could be attributed purely to translational changes at the level of the Greek. Increasingly readings from the Dead Sea Scrolls Biblical manuscripts have found their way into the texts or footnotes of recent Bible versions.[23]

---

[21] For a readable survey see John Rogerson (1984).

[22] B.F. Westcott and F.J.A. Hort (1881–1882). This was not, of course, officially the textual basis of the Revised Version New Testament. That was published twice, by E. Palmer (1881), and F.H.A. Scrivener (1881, and reprints).

[23] First, to the best of my knowledge, in the New Revised Standard Version: see, e.g., its notes to Deuteronomy 32. The *Biblia Qumranica* Project aims to set out synoptically the differences between the Masoretic Text and the Dead Sea Bible manuscripts: see Beate Ego, Armin Lange, Hermann Lichtenberger, and Kristin de Toyer (eds.) (2004). Any English reader can gage the extent of these differences in Martin Abegg, Peter Flint, and Eugene Ulrich (translators) (1999).

Though this may seem sensible, in that these readings can demonstrably improve the intelligibility of the text, the debate which we have been tracing raises some questions. The theological issues, to which earlier generations were acutely sensitive, are still there, but perhaps now insufficiently appreciated. What is the intention of introducing new manuscript readings from the Dead Sea Scrolls or new conjectural emendations into Bibles for use in the churches? Was it to recover a truer form of the text, and because truer more religiously authoritative? The specter rises of some ultimate, perfect archetype, which, could it be recovered, would finally be the Archimedean textual *Pou stō* which the Church has been seeking since Jerome. But did such an archetype ever exist, and if it did is it recoverable, and if it is recoverable does it then automatically become the authoritative text-form of the Hebrew Bible for Christians? Or should it be acknowledged that the turn to the *Hebraica veritas*, from a religious standpoint, has run its course? The problem is that, in the case of the Hebrew Bible, it is now clear that the dividing line between text-criticism, on the one hand, and source- and redaction-criticism, on the other, is very thin, if, indeed, historically speaking, it ever existed: once we combine Higher and Lower Criticism, which German critical scholarship had been so careful to distinguish, the text of the Hebrew Bible goes into free-fall. A line may need to be drawn. Scholars will always want to trace any text they study back to its ultimate source or sources, and try to work out the phases of its literary evolution, but religious communities who hold that text to be Scripture are not obliged so to do, and the conclusions scholars reach about the history of the text have no automatic implications for them. Just as in the past various *translations* have been treated or declared as authoritative by religious communities, so it may be reasonable for them now to declare one form of *the original* authoritative for purposes of their doctrine, practice and worship, even if that form can be shown to be a recension of an older text and not historically the earliest text-form recoverable.[24] The

[24] This point has already been reached within Judaism, which, of course, since late antiquity has always followed the Hebrew. Maimonides endorsement of the Ben Asher form of the Masoretic Text has given the Masoretic Text an unassailable authority textually within Judaism. This is all the more surprising since it is possible the Ben Asher family were Karaites, a view I am still inclined to accept, despite the criticisms of Geoffrey Khan and other authorities (see Geoffrey Khan [2000: 52–55]). The counterclaim seems to be based on the existence of *baʿalei miqra* already in the Talmudic period, prior to the rise of Karaism, and the assumption that these must have been

turn *ad fontes* is always, in the short run, going to be a strong move, because an original will always, on the face of it, trump a translation in terms of intrinsic authority, but if the Church hoped by turning to the original Hebrew it would reach a natural point of textual rest then this hope has now been dashed. Any form of the Hebrew declared authoritative will always come under pressure from other and sometimes older forms of the text, but the safest course from the religious perspective may be to resist that pressure and not go off in pursuit of an ever-receding textual chimaera.[25]

References

Abegg, M., P. Flint, and E. Ulrich. 1999. *The Dead Sea Scrolls Bible* (Edinburgh: T & T Clark).

Belsham, T. 1808. *The New Testament, in an Improved Version, upon the Basis of Archbishop Newcome's New Translation: with a Corrected Text, and Notes Critical and Explanatory* (London: Richard Taylor and Co.).

Burney, C.F. 1922. *The Aramaic Origin of the Fourth Gospel* (Oxford: Clarendon Press).

——. 1925. *The Poetry of Our Lord: An Examination of the Formal Elements of Hebrew Poetry in the Discourses of Jesus Christ* (Oxford: Clarendon Press).

Casey, M. 1998. *Aramaic Sources of Mark's Gospel* (Cambridge: Cambridge University Press).

——. 2002. *An Aramaic Approach to Q: Sources for the Gospels of Matthew and Luke* (Cambridge: Cambridge University Press).

Darlow, T.H., and H.F. Moule. 1968. *Historical Catalogue of Printed Editions of the English Bible 1525–1961* (rev. A.S. Herbert; London: British and Foreign Bible Society).

Decock, P. 2008. 'Jerome's Turn to the "Hebraica veritas", and his Rejection of the Traditional View of the Septuagint', *Neotestamentica: Journal of the New Testament Society of South Africa* 42: 205–222.

Ego, B., A. Lange, H. Lichtenberger, and K. de Troyer (eds.). 2004. *Biblia Qumranica, Volume 3: The Minor Prophets* (Leiden: Brill).

Rabbis. But I cannot see any valid reason for supposing that they must have been members of the Rabbinic movement. We must not assume that the only scholarship in Hebrew in late antiquity was Rabbinic. I would argue that Judaism after 70 was more diverse then than is sometimes supposed, and that a priestly tradition of scholarship, distinct from the Rabbinic, survived. Expertise in the text of the Tanakh may have belonged specifically to this tradition. It is striking that when, as they occasionally do, the Rabbis of the Talmudic era note masoretic traditions, they seem to have little idea what they are about. This earlier essentially priestly textual expertise was taken up into later Karaism, which was not so innovatory as the Rabbanites tried to imply. But these arguments will have to wait for another day.

[25] The problem is illustrated by the Jesus Seminar's attempt to make Q a more authoritative Gospel than any of the canonic four.

Geddes, A. 1792. *The Holy Bible, or the Books Accounted Sacred by Jews and Christians, Otherwise Called the Books of the Old and New Covenants, Faithfully Translated from Corrected Texts of the Originals. With Various Readings and Explanatory Notes. First volume, Genesis to Joshua* (London: R. Faulder & J. Johnson).
——. 1797. *The Holy Bible... Second volume, Judges, 1 and 2 Samuel, 1 and 2 Kings, 1 and 2 Chronicles, Ruth, Prayer of Manasseh* (London: R. Faulder & J. Johnson).
——. 1807. *The Holy Bible...: Psalms* (ed. J. Disney and C. Butler; London: R. Faulder & J. Johnson).
Grafton, A., and J. Weinberg. 2011. *'I have always loved the Holy Tongue': Isaac Casaubon, the Jews and a Forgotten Chapter in Renaissance Scholarship* (Cambridge: Harvard University Press).
Hengel, M. 2004. *The Septuagint as Christian Scripture: Its Prehistory and the Problem of its Canon* (London: T & T Clark International).
Kamesar, A. 1993. *Jerome, Greek Scholarship and the Hebrew Bible* (Oxford: Clarendon Press).
Kamin, S., and A. Saltman (eds.) 1989. *Secundum Salomonem: A Thirteenth-Century Latin Commentary on the Song of Solomon* (Ramat Gan: Bar-Ilan University Press).
Khan, G. 2000. *Early Karaite Grammatical Texts* (Atlanta: Scholars Press).
Klepper, D.C. 2007. *The Insight of Unbelievers: Nicholas of Lyra and Christian Reading of Jewish Texts in the Later Middle Ages* (Philadelphia: University of Pennsylvania Press).
Lowth, R. 1788–89. *Isaiah. A New Translation, with a Preliminary Dissertation and Notes* (London: Dodsley & Cadell).
Morin, J. 1631. *Exercitationes Ecclesiasticae in utrumque Samaritanorum Pentateuchum* (Paris: Antonius Vitray).
——. 1660. *Exercitationes biblicae de hebraeici graecique textus sinceritate* (Paris: Gaspari Meturas).
Müller, M. 1996. *First Bible of the Church: A Plea for the Septuagint* (Sheffield: Sheffield Academic Press).
Newcome, W. 1785. *The Twelve Minor Prophets* (London: J. Johnson).
——. 1788. *Ezekiel* (Dublin: J. Johnson).
——. 1796 (1800). *An Attempt toward revising our English translation of the Greek Scriptures, or the New Covenant of Jesus Christ* (Dublin: J. Johnson).
Norton, D. 2005. *A Textual History of the King James Bible* (Cambridge: Cambridge University Press).
Olszowy-Schlanger, J. 2003. *Les manuscrits hébreux dans l'Angleterre médievale. Étude historique et paléographique* (Leuven: Peeters).
Olszowy-Schlanger, J., and Grondeux, A. (eds.). 2008. *Dictionnaire hébreu-latin-français de la Bible hébraique de l'abbaye de Ramsey (XIIIe siècle)* (Turnhout: Brepols).
Owen, J. 1659. *Of the Divine Originall, Authority, Self-evidencing Light, and Power of the Scriptures* (Oxford: T. Robinson).
Palmer, E. 1881. *The Greek New Testament, with the Readings Adopted by the Revisers of the Authorised Version* (Oxford: Clarendon Press).
Rajak, T. 2009. *Translation and Survival: The Greek Bible of the Ancient Jewish Diaspora* (Oxford: Oxford University Press).
Rebenich, S. 1993. 'Jerome, the "vir trilinguis" and the "hebraica veritas"', *Vigiliae Christianae* 47: 50–77.
Reventlow, H.G. 1980. *Bibelautorität und Geist der Moderne: Die Bedeutung des Bibelverständnisses für die Geistesgeschichte und politische Entwicklung in England von der Reformation bis zur Aufklärung* (Göttingen: Vandenhoeck & Ruprecht).
Rogerson, J. 1984. *Old Testament Criticism in the Nineteenth Century: England and Germany* (London: SPCK).
Sæbø, M. (ed.) 2008. *Hebrew Bible/Old Testament: The History of its Interpretation II, From the Renaissance to the Enlightenment* (Göttingen: Vandenhoeck & Ruprecht).

Scrivener, F.H.A. 1881. *The New Testament in the Original Greek According to the Text Followed by the Authorised Version, together with the Variations Adopted by the Revised Version* (Cambridge: Cambridge University Press).
Seidman, N. 2006. *Faithful Renderings: Jewish-Christian Difference and the Politics of Translation* (Chicago: Chicago University Press).
Steiger, J.A. 2008. '*Ad fontes!* The Early Humanist Concern for the *Hebraica veritas*', in Sæbø 2008: 154–90.
Todd, H.J. 1821. *Memoirs of the Life and Writings of the Rev. Brian Walton, D.D., Lord Bishop of Chester* (London: Rivington).
Walton, B. 1659. *The Considerator Considered: or, A Brief View of Certain Considerations upon the Biblia Polyglotta* (London: T. Roycrof).
Wasserstein, A., and D.J. Wasserstein. 2006. *The Legend of the Septuagint, from Classical Antiquity to Today* (Cambridge: Cambridge University Press).
Westcott, B.F., and F.J.A. Hort. 1881–82. *The New Testament in the Original Greek* (2 vols.; London: Macmillan).
Whiston, W. 1745. *Mr Whiston's Primitive New Testament* (Stamford and London).

A NINTH-CENTURY IRISH BOG PSALTER AND READING THE PSALMS AS 'THREE FIFTIES'

Susan E. Gillingham

In July 2006 the discovery of an early ninth century Psalter, still in its original binding, at Fadden More Bog, north Tipperary, was hailed by Patrick Wallace, Director of the National Museum of Ireland, as the greatest find ever to come from a European bog. The find has many parallels with the discovery of the Dead Sea Scrolls: the chance sighting by a worker digging up peat moss to create commercial potting soil, who 'saw something' beyond the bucket of his bulldozer; the Psalter's remarkable preservation, due to the low level of oxygen and to chemical substances in the soil which protected the vellum; its apparent deliberate concealment, perhaps to keep it safe from a Viking raid, indicated by the layer of camouflaging matting and a leather pouch; the recognition that this was a biblical text because of words exposed in the Latin (*ualle lacrimarum*, or 'valley of tears') which were quickly identified as coming from Ps. *83* (*HV* 84)[1] and may be compared with the recognition of Isaiah in the Dead Sea Scrolls; and the long-term international conservation project which has ensued, working on how to separate the congealed mess of some hundred vellum pages without ruining them. Some five years later, the initial view of the significance of this find has been confirmed: in 2010 a progress report detailed the difficulties but also successes of the preservation, and was followed by a television documentary on what is now known as the 'Faddon More Psalter'. Since June 2011 the Psalter has been on public display at the National Museum in Dublin.[2]

Although nowhere near as lavishly illustrated as its near contemporary the Book of Kells, the Bog Psalter's exposed first page nevertheless

[1] Two sets of abbreviations will be used throughout this paper. *HV* refers to the numbering of psalms in the Hebrew, and *PG* refers to the numbering in *Psalterium Gallicanum*, Jerome's translation preserved in the *Vulgate*. The numbers of psalms when taken from the *PG* will be offered in italics to prevent confusion.

[2] For the progress report see www.museum.ie/GetAttachment.aspx?id=432d9d81-909c-4921 and for information on the documentary, www.thurles.info/2010/09/07/faddan-more-psalter-on-rte-television.

reveals some illustration in its interlaced border and its figure of a bird (possibly an eagle). Similarly prominent decorations are evident after Pss. *50* (*HV* 51) and *100* (*HV* 101), as well as some discolored illustrations of initial letters to individual psalms. Such decorations suggest a provenance from a scriptorium, perhaps from one of the six monasteries within some ten miles of Fadden More. St. Brendan, Birr, near the holy well Toberbrandy, closest to the site of the Psalter's discovery, is a likely candidate. Bede, in his *Ecclesiastical History of the English Nation* (c. 731) describes how English monks travelled to Ireland to take advantage of the 'new learning' in Irish monastic schools, where the study of the Psalter was central. These monasteries near Fadden More would have been typical of such devotion to the Psalter, a topic which has been explored in detail and well documented by Martin McNamara.[3] Hence it is not impossible that the 'Fadden More Psalter' could eventually throw further light on the way in which Latin texts were read and used in Ireland.

One particular issue is the division of Psalters into 'Three Fifties', indicated in the Fadden More Psalter by the illuminations immediately before Pss. *1, 51* and *101.* It is well established that the 'Three Fifties' tradition, popularized in monastic rules such as those of Benedict and Columbanus, was a widespread Irish practice from as early as the fifth century.[4] The 'Rule of Ailbe', dating from the seventh century, which gives special attention to the devotional use of Ps. *118*, speaks, for example, of 'one hundred genuflections...at the "Beati" at the beginning of the day...[and] thrice fifty (psalms) dearer than [other works]....' (McNamara 2000: 357). Another rule, 'The Monastery of Tallaght', from the eighth century, which also emphasizes the importance of Ps. *118*, similarly highlights the chanting of the hundred and fifty psalms daily, in three fifties (McNamara 2000: 358–359). The 'Rule of Patrick', also from a Céli Dé background, refers to the singing of the 'Three Fifties' (mainly as an act of penitence) every canonical hour.[5] And in the *Liber Hymnorum,* an eleventh-century manuscript held at

[3] See McNamara (2000 and 2006). He also draws attention to the Springmount Bog Psalms (wax tablets including portions of Pss. 30–32) dating from about the seventh century CE, which appear to have been used as school exercises for reading and writing the psalms. The significance of just these two psalms is inevitably limited compared with the Fadden Psalter.

[4] For example McNamara (2000: 357–59); Jeffery (2000), especially the discussion in 'The Irish Office of the Three Fifites', pp. 102–108; and Henry (1960: 23–40).

[5] See O'Keefe, 'Rule of Patrick', p. 223, para. 12, quoted in Jeffery (2000: 105).

Trinity College Dublin, attributed to Pope Gregory, which contains the psalms from *3:7–144:11*, the division into 'Three Fifties' is created by the *Pater Noster* which occurs after Pss. *50* and *100*.[6] In other examples the 'Three Fifties' are divided by a selection of Canticles and by the Lord's Prayer; the penitential aspect of this rite is clear.[7]

Although primarily associated with Irish devotion, the tradition of 'Three Fifties' is not exclusively Irish. By the fourth century, Hilary of Poitiers writes of dividing the psalms into three groups of fifty, echoing the biblical years of Jubilee.[8] There is a reference to the practice of praying the psalms in 'Three Fifties' in Augustine's Commentary on Ps. 150.[9] Cassiodorus makes the same point in describing the Psalter as three stages of spiritual ascent towards the 'eternal Sabbath'.[10] This later became a common practice in both cathedral and monastic offices: a twelfth-century rite from Milan shows how the ritual of reading the psalms in three groups of fifties throughout the night was performed at liturgical occasions in the year, each 'fifty' divided by readings and singing of responsories (Jeffery 2000: 102). The tradition of subdividing the fifties into thirteen, twelve, twelve and thirteen psalms derives from the early Middle Ages, when many Orthodox churches adopted the practice of reciting portions of the 'Three Fifties' for the dead (a rite also evident in Irish devotion).[11]

There are several early illuminated examples of this tripartite division in Insular Psalters. One, from Mercia, contemporaneous with the Fadden More Psalter, is Aethelwald's Psalter in the Book of Cerne (Cambridge University Library, MS LI 1.10). The Vespasian Psalter, probably from the late eight century and possibly from Christ

[6] See McNamara (2006: 3).

[7] See Kenney (1968: 72–77): 'The three fifties every day, with their conclusion of the *Beati*, to the end of seven years, saves a soul out of hell' (quoted by Jeffery [2000: 104]).

[8] See Hilary, *Instr. Ps.* 10–11 (CCSL 61: 10), referred to in Daley (2004: 199).

[9] See Hegbin and Corrigan (1960). In his *Expositio Psalmorum,* Augustine makes much in his commentary on Ps. 150 of the significance of the number 150. He refers to different multiples of 7 + 8 and the Hebrew numbers 40 + 10, and observes that the 'three times fifty' division of the Psalter has Trinitarian significance.

[10] See Cassiodorus, *Exp. Ps., Praefatio* 12 (CCSL 97: 15). Interestingly Gregory of Nyssa (*Inscriptions* 1.5) and Jerome (*Comm Ps.* 40) adhere to the fivefold division, whilst Hilary, Augustine and Cassiodorus are more concerned with the 'Three Fifties'.

[11] The tradition of the repetition of the Lord's Prayer and the Hail Mary 150 times, for those who could not read the entire Psalter, and a similar tradition of dividing the 150 into three groups of fifty by way of knots on a prayer rope or beads on a rosary, is further evidence of the development of this practice.

Church Canterbury (British Library, Cotton Vespasian AI), has intricate zoomorphic and historiated initials, the major ones being before Pss. *1, 51* and *101* (others occuring between liturgical divisions). The mid ninth-century Douce Psalter (Bodleian Library, Oxford, MS 366) is made of purple parchment to create an 'imperial appeal', and has miniatures in silver and gold before Pss. *51* and *101* (Ps. 1 would almost certainly have had the same but it is missing). Illuminations of this nature continued well into the fourteenth century: David, Jerome, or emperors and kings were common subjects for Ps. 1, and by the eleventh century more Christological cycles emerged (including the Jesse Tree). For Ps. *51,* scenes from the life of David (and sometimes the saints) were more popular; and for Ps. *101,* as well as Davidic, hagiographic or Christological motifs, the portraits of patrons often appeared in illuminated borders or miniatures—probably because this was one of the pentitential psalms. It will be interesting to discover what is made of the initials for Pss. 1, *51* and *101* in the Fadden More Psalter.[12]

So overall, the 'Three Fifties' was a widespread tradition, and the Fadden More Psalter is potentially a good example of it. However, given the increasing interest in the fivefold division of the Psalter (*HV* 1–41, 42–72, 73–89, 90–106, 107–150) over the last thirty years or so, the dominance of a threefold division in earlier tradition raises some interesting questions about a variant reading of the Psalter in addition to the fivefold one.

The recent emphasis on the literary and theological shaping of the Psalter as a whole has developed in several ways. Sometimes it has focused on the way individual psalms with particular theological concerns have been placed within the Psalter—for example, Pss. 1, 19, 73, 90 and 119 are seen as placed at strategic points to indicate a didactic emphasis, and Pss. 2, 18, 72, 89 and 118 are seen to reflect a more royal emphasis. Sometimes the focus has been on the different theological agendas in each of the five books and the part each agenda plays in the theology of the Psalter as a whole. For example, Book III (Pss. 73–89) has been frequently noted for its emphasis on God's judgement upon the entire community, and for its increasing despair about any

[12] I am indebted to Dr. Elizabeth Solopova, Department of Special Collections and Western Manuscripts, Bodleian Library, for these observations and for fascinating insights on these features in fourteenth century manuscripts, many of which could not be included here.

protection offered by the Davidic covenant (Wilson 1993; Goulder 1996; Cole 2000). Book IV (Pss. 90–105), meanwhile, has been noted for emphasizing that the covenant with Moses will outlast the one with David, illustrated by its allusions to a hope beyond anything royal (Zenger 1991; Wallace 2007).

Another approach to the theological shaping of the Psalter has been to examine smaller collections within each of the five books. The Songs of Ascents (Pss. 120–134), within Book V, have been examined most in this respect (Seybold 1978; Seidel 1982; Viviers 1994; Crow 1996; Hunter 1999). Similarly the Kingship Psalms (Pss. 93–100) have been the focus of attention within Book IV (Howard 1997; Gerstenberger 2001), along with the so-called 'entrance liturgy' in Book I (Hossfeld and Zenger 1993b; Miller 1994). In none of these recent approaches has use been made of dividing the Psalms into 'Three Fifties'. An interesting exercise would be to consider what difference it makes to read the Psalter from the perspective of a threefold (equal) division rather than a fivefold (unequal) one. Immediately, of course, we are caught with incongruity: the Psalter used from the fifth century onwards was usually Jerome's *Psalterium Gallicanum*, and the numbering of the psalms here, because of its dependence on the LXX and hence its combining of Pss. 9 and 10, 114 and 115 and splitting of Pss. 116 and 147, is different both from the Hebrew and from most English versions. So should we conduct a survey of the Vulgate's threefold division, looking at what would be Pss. 1, 52, 102 and 150 in the Hebrew numbering, or should we take the Hebrew and English as normative and so focus on what would then be Pss. 1, 51, 101 and 150 instead? Given that this paper began with the Fadden More Psalter, and given that what has followed has affirmed the importance of the 'Three Fifties' in various Latin versions, I propose to look primarily at the threefold division using the numbering of the *Psalterium Gallicanum*.

In terms of the shaping of the Psalter overall, Ps. 1 remains constant in all the versions. A problem arises in deciding which psalm concludes the Psalter. Is it really Ps. *151*—the short victory song celebrating David's defeat of Goliath—or the hymn of praise, 150? The latter is most likely: the heading over Ps. 151, that it is 'supernumerary' (*hic psalmus proprie scriptus David et extra numerum*) rather confirms this. So, taking Pss. 1 and 150 as 'bookends' to the Psalter as a whole, in the first psalm we read of the importance of private reflection on the Torah as a guide for daily living and in the last (*sic*) psalm we hear a public paean of praise directed towards the God of all creation. Psalm 1 encapsulates the personal and reflective elements of the Psalter, and Ps. 150 its more communal and hymnic concerns.[13]

Looking at the first and last psalms not only within the Psalter as a whole but also within each of the 'Three Fifties' can similarly help us to assess the theological themes of the whole of that division, as Nancy de Claissé-Walford (1997) has demonstrated with respect to the fivefold division of the Psalter. I shall apply the same method to the threefold division. So, taking the 'First Fifty' within the *PG,* the contrast between the first and last psalms is most striking. Psalm *50*, attributed to King David, demonstrates by its title that the king was unable keep God's commands[14], apparently because of a natural inclination to sin.[15] If Ps. 1 emphasizes the gift of the Torah as a means of understanding how to live an ordered life, Ps. *50* emphasizes the need for God's gift of forgiveness as a means of achieving it.[16] Hence the anonymous paradigm of virtue in Ps. 1 becomes in Ps. *50* David, the forgiven sinner. Given the greater proportion of individual laments and complaint psalms within the 'First Fifty', Ps. *50* is an important summation of what has gone before. The ideal of keeping the Torah may be important, but the means of fulfilling it through God's good grace is even more so. Psalms 1 and *50* have another significant connection: the very end of the latter psalm stresses the importance of Jerusalem as the place where forgiveness is offered, so the two identity markers of the Jewish community, Torah and Temple, are each explicitly highlighted at the beginning and end of this 'First Fifty'.

Between these two psalms marked by personal piety—Ps. 1 of a more universal type, Ps. *50* being more specific—the prevailing mood of the collection in between is profoundly personal in its awareness of the

---

[13] Obviously if Ps. 151 is included, the first and last psalms would be about more personal concerns. Yet Pss. 1 and 150 are more effective in holding together the *complementary* themes in the Psalter as a whole. On reading Pss. 1 and 150 in this way, see Brueggemann (1991: 63–92).

[14] Part of the superscription reads: '...psalmus David cum venit ad eum Nathan propheta quando intravit ad Bethsabee'. The theme is continued in the following verses, for example, in v. 6: '...tibi soli peccavi et malum coram te feci ut iustificeris in sermonibus tuis et vincas cum iudicaris...'

[15] See v. 6: '...ecce enim in iniquitatibus conceptus sum et in peccatis concepit me mater mea...'

[16] Contrast Ps. 1.1–2 (NRSV) 'Happy are those who do not follow the advice of the wicked, or take the path that sinners tread, or sit in the seat of scoffers; / but their delight is in the law of the Lord, and on his law they meditate day and night' with 51.9–10 (NRSV): 'Hide your face from my sins, and blot out all my iniquities. / Create in me a clean heart, O God, and put a new and right spirit within me.'

vulnerability of the human condition. In Pss. 3–*13* the complaint form dominates, although the hymn about God's creation of humankind (Ps. 8) at the centre offers a brighter perspective. Psalms *14–23* are laments, psalms of confidence and royal psalms, and a further hymn about God's creative power (Ps. *18A*) at the mid-point again alleviates the overall mood. At the beginning and end are two liturgies about appropriate preparation for entering the Temple (Pss. *14* and *23*) and another psalm about the importance of the Torah (*18B*) is strategically placed in the middle. Psalms *24–33* again comprise mainly personal laments; Pss. *28* and *32*, further hymns to God as Creator, provide an important contrast. Psalms *34–40* are also personal, dealing with all aspects of sickness and impoverishment. By contrast, in Pss. *41–49* the more communal tenor which increasingly occurs in the 'Second Fifty' begins to surface: Pss. *41–2* and *48* are still more personal, but the communal lament (*43*), the wedding psalm (*44*), the hymns of Zion on each side of a hymn celebrating God's kingship (*45–47*), and the prophetic exhortation to the community (*49*) are all examples of the increasingly corporate concerns which make up most of the 'Second Fifty'. Psalm *50* is thus at the cusp of this change, belonging more to the personal laments which comprise the main part of the first division.

What then of the first and last psalms of the 'Second Fifty'? Psalm *51* is interesting because of the ways it mirrors Ps. 1. The most obvious correspondence is in the distinction between the righteous and the evildoer (epitomized in the Hebrew of both psalms as those who sin with their lips—the 'scoffers' (לֵ֫צִים) in Ps. 1.1, and those whose tongues are like sharp razors (לְשׁוֹנֶ֑ךָ כְּתַ֥עַר מְלֻטָּ֗שׁ) in Ps. 52.4 *HV (51.4 PG)*. Another clear association between both psalms is the belief that God will protect the godly. A specific link is in the image of the 'tree' which occurs in Pss. 1.3 and *51:10.* In Ps. *51* the comparison is of 'a fruitful olive tree' (וַאֲנִ֤י ׀ כְּזַ֣יִת רַ֭עֲנָן: *HV* 52.10) in the 'house of God' (בְּבֵ֣ית אֱלֹהִ֑ים).[17] In Ps. 1.3, the comparison is, less specifically, simply of 'a tree' (וְֽהָיָ֗ה כְּעֵץ֮) planted by 'streams of water' (עַֽל־פַּלְגֵ֫י מָ֥יִם), an image suggesting the life-giving waters of the Temple as in Ezek. 47.1–8 and Gen. 2.10–14.

What of Ps. *100*, which completes the 'Second Fifty'? This is the song of one who has been forgiven—the song which the suppliant in Ps. *50*, the final psalm of the 'First Fifty', yearns to sing once forgiveness has

[17] This is a cultic image, to which, for example, Zech. 4.3, 11–12 also allude.

been offered: 'exultabit lingua mea iustitiam tuam' (Ps. *50.16*) becomes 'misericordiam et iudicium cantabo tibi Domine psallam' (Ps. *100.1*). In Ps. *100*, the song is of the mercy and justice of God. These are almost the first words of the prayer in Ps. *51*, where the psalmist hopes to experience soon justice and mercy.[18] Both psalms speak of a heart made right with God and a life reflecting and teaching the wisdom of God. In Ps. *50.8* it is a future hope ('ecce enim veritatem dilexisti incerta et occulta sapientiae tuae manifestasti mihi'), whilst in Ps. *100.2* it has already been achieved ('intellegam in via inmaculata quando venies ad me perambulabam in innocentia cordis mei in medio domus meae'). Each psalmist speaks of the importance of witnessing to the community of faith: in Ps. *50.15* it is about teaching God's ways, once forgiven, to those who have sinned, whilst in Ps. *100.4–8* it is about exorcizing evil from the land and creating a purified community. Each psalmist ends with eyes fixed on Zion: in Ps. *50.20* the vision focuses on the physical restoration of the city ('benigne fac Domine in bona voluntate tua Sion et aedificentur muri Hierusalem') whilst Ps. *100.8* deals mainly with the city's spiritual renewal ('ut disperderem de civitate Domini omnes operantes iniquitatem').

So Ps. *51*, emulating Ps. 1 with its emphasis on God's protection of the righteous, and Ps. *100*, contrasting with Ps. *50* in its celebration of forgiveness already received, offer an appropriate beginning and ending for the 'Second Fifty', whose predominant theme has been God's judgement of the community. The darker psalms—and these are at the very heart of this division—are those of *Asaph* (*72–82*). On one side these psalms are bordered by personal laments 'of David' (*50–71*), and although they progress gradually into psalms with community concerns, almost all these psalms (with the exceptions of Pss. *64–67*, mainly thanksgiving psalms) have a pessimistic tenor. Bordering the *Asaphite* psalms on the other side are the (mainly) *Korahite* psalms, each displaying a wistful but increasingly gloomy mood (*83–87*). The darkest point of this whole collection is undoubtedly Ps. *88*, with its final lament on the end of the Davidic line. However, this failure having been publicly acknowledged, the mood brightens, as Pss. *89–99* offer an alternative hope in their assertion of a different covenant (with Moses) and an everlasting world rule (of God). Psalm *100* concludes with a note of optimism which fits well with the changing mood towards

[18] In theHebrew, the play is on חֶסֶד (Pss. 51.3 and 100.1).

the end of this collection. Just as Ps. *50* represented well the gradual change from personal to communal concerns at the end of the 'First Fifty', so Ps. *100* represents the transition to a more positive outlook at the end of the 'Second Fifty'.

What of Ps. *101,* which opens up the 'Third Fifty'? Here we may note some particular correspondences with Ps. *51.* The psalmist's suffering in Ps. *51* is apparently on account of a curse invoked by a 'worker of treachery' (עֹשֵׂה רְמִיָּה: *HV* 52:4) and a resolution is achieved by overpowering their destructive words with words purportedly from God. The suppliant's hope for restitution is based upon the belief that they are innocent and righteous before God. In Ps. *101* the suppliant suffers more general verbal taunts and curses ('tota die exprobrabant mihi inimici mei et qui laudabant me adversus me iurabant' [v. 9]), but here the resolution is achieved not by addressing the enemies but by addressing God himself in hymns of praise (*101.13–23, 26–29;* 102.12–22, 25–28). Furthermore, like the suppliant in Ps. *51,* the hope for restoration is based upon a sense of being innocent and righteous before God, and the two psalms note how the 'name' of God is particularly powerful in its effects.[19] What follows in the 'Third Fifty' is increasingly praise and thanksgiving, sometimes offered with personal concerns (as in Pss. *119–133*) and at other times offered with communal interests (as in the three Hallels of *103–105, 111–117* and *145–150*). Psalm *101* encapsulates these features in the one psalm: its personal interests are in the descriptions of pain and innocent suffering, its communal interests are in the affirmation (repeated three times) that God will rebuild Zion, and its praise and thanksgiving is expressed in the quotation of hymnic material in the middle and at the end.

What then of Ps. 150? Just as Ps. 1 opens up not only the 'First Fifty' but also the entire Psalter, so Ps. 150 closes not only the 'Third Fifty' but the Psalter as a whole. In effect it is an extended doxology—it becomes the song of praise promised in all the psalms which form the seams of the three divisions. It is the hope of the psalmist in Ps. *50.17* ('Domine labia mea aperies et os meum adnuntiabit laudem tuam') and it is expressed in Ps. *51.11* ('confitebor tibi in saeculum … quoniam bonum in conspectu sanctorum tuorum'); it is referred to in Ps. *100.1* ('misericordiam et iudicium cantabo tibi Domine psallam') and again

[19] Compare וַאֲקַוֶּה שִׁמְךָ כִּי־טוֹב נֶגֶד חֲסִידֶיךָ (52.11 [*51.11 PG*]) with the more Zion-focused expression לְסַפֵּר בְּצִיּוֹן שֵׁם יְהוָה (102.22 [*101.22 PG*]).

in *101.21* ('ut adnuntiet in Sion nomen Domini et laudem suam in Hierusalem').

So the theological shaping of the threefold division using the *Psalterium Gallicanum* allows for three distinct theological emphases. The 'First Fifty' is mainly about personal vulnerability, contrasting the need for obedience and trust (Ps. 1) with the difficulty of attaining it (Ps. *50*). The 'Second Fifty' also begins with this theme, but overall, is more about corporate suffering, with an increasing awareness of the effects of the judgement of God. This moves, gradually, into a different focus, upon God Himself (Ps. *100*). The 'Third Fifty' takes this theocentric emphasis further still: it is apparent in the personal hymnody of Ps. *101* and is fully displayed in the corporate paeon of praise in Ps. *150*. In brief, the wrestling with the apparent absence of God which dominates the personal and communal psalms of first two Fifties is gradually resolved in the Third Fifty, where God's presence within the restored community becomes increasingly apparent.[20]

What difference would it make if we were to look instead at the Hebrew version, following the numbers of the psalms used by most contemporary scholars? It would mean that the 'First Fifty' opened with reflections on obedience to the Torah and closed instead with a prophetic exhortation (50). The 'Second Fifty' would begin with the personal confession of guilt (51) and would end in a hymn of praise (100). The 'Third Fifty' would begin with a promise to reform the community (101) and end with the familiar paean of praise (150).

A few commentary series divide up the Psalter into three volumes, each of fifty psalms, but rarely do we find reflections on the theological shape of each independent volume and the contribution of each to the theology of the Psalter as a whole.[21] Yet what could have been noted is that the psalms at the beginnings and endings of each division have much in common, in language as well as theology. The most obvious examples are Pss. 1–2–3; but there are also common themes between

[20] In Christian tradition, the earlier use of the 'Three Fifties' as an act of penitence is thus most appropriate.

[21] The Anchor Bible Commentary makes no comment at all, being more concerned about the ancient Near Eastern correspondences in each individual psalm than any shape within the whole. The Word Bible Commentary Series, originally using three authors for all three divisions also fails to do this, trying to find instead some continuity with the next division by focussing on the five books which cut across the three divisions; similarly the Baker Academic Series by J. Goldingay. Hossfeld and Zenger (1993a; 2000; 2008) are exceptions in this respect.

Pss. 49–50–51–52, and between Pss. 99–100–101–102. For example, in Pss. 49–52 the shared issues include the importance of integrity of spirit before God, a conviction that God will protect his 'righteous ones' from evil, and (in Pss. 50–51–52, at least) the significance of Zion as the place where God can be found. Within Pss. 99–102 the shared characteristics are more theocentric, in the hymns of the kingship of God over the entire cosmos and the reminiscences about His commitment to His people. In all these psalms the importance of Zion as the place which brings together these complementary aspirations is evident.[22] So although the focus on the Hebrew and Latin numbering might change the emphasis in terms of the detail, the overall movement represented by these 'Three Fifties' remains the same—from personal to communal concerns between the first and second divisions, to an increasingly theocentric focus between the second and third divisions.

It will never be possible to know who once owned that Fadden More Psalter and how it came to be buried in the peat bog in what is now northern Tipperary. Clearly, someone sought to avoid its destruction, presumably in the hope that it might be of use to future generations. Whatever the intention, and whatever has emerged from the 'unfolding' of the vellum, I am fairly sure that the original owner would not have expected this Psalter to have elicited a response such as mine. Times have changed, both for prayerful and for intellectual reflections on the Psalms; nevertheless, the threads of continuity in the history of interpretation are still to be seen. And finally, just as I cannot help but think that the Fadden More Psalter's original owner would be bemused and amused by this paper, so I hope the present honorand will be too.

References

Brueggemann, W. 1991. 'Bounded by Obedience and Praise: The Psalms as Canon', *Journal for the Study of the Old Testament* 50: 63–92.

Cole, R. 2000. *The Shape and Message of Book III (Psalms 73–89)* (Journal for the Study of the Old Testament Supplement, 307; Sheffield: Sheffield Academic Press).

[22] The importance of the Zion tradition at the different 'seams' of the Psalter has been illustrated in Gillingham (2005: 308–341).

Crow, L.D. 1996. *The Songs of Ascents (Psalms 120–134): Their Place in Israelite History and Religion* (Society of Biblical Literature Dissertation Series, 148; Atlanta: Scholars Press).

Daley, B.E. 2004. 'Finding the Right Key: The Aims and Strategies of Early Christian Interpretation of the Psalms' in *Psalms in Community. Jewish and Christian Textual, Liturgical, and Artistic Traditions* (eds. H.W. Attridge and M.E. Fassler; Leiden/Boston: Brill) 189–206.

Gerstenberger, E.S. 2001. '"World Dominion" in Yahweh Kingship Psalms: Down to the Roots of Globalizing Concepts and Strategies', *Horizons of Biblical Theology* 23: 192–210.

Gillingham, S.E. 2005. 'The Zion Tradition and the Editing of the Hebrew Psalter' in *Temple and Worship. Proceedings of the Oxford Old Testament Seminar* (ed. J. Day; Sheffield: Sheffield Academic Press) 308–341.

Goulder, M.D. 1996. *The Psalms of Asaph and the Pentateuch. Studies in the Psalter III* (Journal for the Study of the Old Testament Supplement, 233; Sheffield: Sheffield Academic Press).

Hegbin, E.T.S., and E. Corrigan. 1960. *Augustine: Exposition on the Book of Psalms, Translated and Annotated* (Ancient Christian Writers, 30; Westminster: Newman Press).

Henry, P. 1960. 'Remarks on the Decoration of Three Irish Psalters', *Proceedings of the Royal Irish Academy* 61C: 23–40.

Hossfeld, F.L., and E. Zenger. 1993a. *Die Psalmen 1–50* (Neue Echter Bibel; Würzburg: Echter).

——. 1993b. '"Wer darf hinaufziehn zum Berg JHWHs?" Zur Redaktionsgeschichte und Theologie der Psalmengruppe 15–24', in *Biblische Theologie und gesellschaftlicher Wandel. Festschrift N. Lohfink* (eds. G. Braulik, W. Gross, and S. McEvenue; Freiburg/Basel/Wien: Herder) 166–182.

——. 2000. *Psalmen 51–100* (Herder Theologischer Kommentar zum Alten Testament; Freiburg/Basel/Wien: Herder).

——. 2008. *Psalmen 101–150* (Herder Theologischer Kommentar zum Alten Testament; Freiburg/Basel/Wien: Herder).

Howard, D.M. 1997. *The Structure of Psalms 93–100: Their Place in Israelite History* (Winona Lake: Eisenbrauns).

Hunter, A.G. 1999. 'Yahweh Comes Home to Zion: the Psalms of Ascents', in A.G. Hunter, *Psalms* (Old Testament Guides; London: Routledge) 173–258.

Jeffery, P. 2000. 'Eastern and Western Elements in the Irish Monastic Prayer of the Hours', in *The Divine Office of the Latin Middle Ages* (eds. R. Steiner, M.E. Fassler, and R.A. Baltzer; New York/Oxford: Oxford University Press) 99–146.

Kenny, J.F. 1968. *The Sources for the Early History of Ireland: Ecclesiastical* (Shannon: Irish University Press).

McNamara, M. 2000. *Psalms in the Early Irish Church* (Journal for the Study of the Old Testament Supplement, 165; Sheffield: Sheffield Academic Press).

——. 2006. Society of Biblical Literature Forum, http://www.sbl-site.org/publications/article.aspx?ArticleId=568.

Miller, P.D. 1994. 'Kingship, Torah, Obedience and Prayer: The Theology of Psalms 15–24' in *Neue Wege der Psalmenforschung* (eds. K. Seybold and E. Zenger, Freiburg/Basel/Wien: Herder) 127–142.

Seidel, H. 1982. 'Wallfahrtslieder' in *Das lebendige Wort. Beiträge zur kirchlichen Verkündigung. Festgabe für Gottfried Voigt* (eds. H. Seidel and K.-H. Bieritz; Berlin: Evangelische Verlagsanstalt) 26–40.

Seybold, K. 1978. *Die Wallfahrtspsalmen: Studien zur Entstehungsgeschichte von Psalmen 120–134* (Biblisch-Theologische Studien, 3; Neukirchen-Vluyn: Neukirchener).

Viviers, H. 1994. 'The Coherence of the ma'[a]lôt Psalms (Pss. 120–134)', *Zeitschrift für die Alttestamentliche Wissenschaft* 106: 275–289.

de Claissé-Walford, N.L. 1997. *Reading from the Beginning. The Shaping of the Hebrew Psalter* (Macon: Mercer University Press).
Wallace, R.E. 2007. *The Narrative Effect of Book IV of the Hebrew Psalter* (Studies in Biblical Literature, 112; New York: Peter Lang).
Walsh, P.G. 1990. *Cassiodurus: Exposition of the Psalms Translated and Annotated* (Ancient *Christian* Writers, 53; New York: Paulist Press).
Wilson, G.H. 1993. 'Understanding the Purposeful Arrangement of Psalms in the Psalter: Pitfalls and Promise', in *The Shape and Shaping of the Psalter* (ed. J.C. McCann; Journal for the Study of the Old Testament Supplement, 159; Sheffield: Sheffield Academic Press) 42–51.
Zenger, E. 1991. 'Israel und Kirche im gemeinsamen Gottesbund. Beobachtungen zum theologischen Programm des 4. Psalmenbuchs' in *Israel und Kirche heute. Beiträge zum christlich-jüdischen Dialog. FS E.L. Ehrlich* (eds. M. Marcus, E.W. Stegemann, and E. Zenger; Freiburg/Basel/Wien: Herder) 238–257.

THE GRAMMATICAL COMMENTARY ON HOSEA BY THE KARAITE YŪSUF IBN NŪḤ

Geoffrey Khan

The Karaite scholar ʾAbū Yaʿqūb Yūsuf ibn Nūḥ was active in Jerusalem in the second half of the tenth century CE. The surviving works that are explicitly attributed to him in the colophons of manuscripts all have the form of biblical commentaries. These include commentaries that are primarily exegetical in nature, a commentary that is concerned primarily with translation and a grammatical commentary.[1] Ibn Nūḥ was heir to a tradition of Hebrew grammar that had developed among the Karaites of Iraq and Iran. This was brought to Jerusalem in the migrations of Karaites from the East during the tenth century. Ibn Nūḥ himself was an immigrant from Iraq. During most of his adult life he resided in Palestine. According to Ibn al-Hītī, who wrote a chronicle of Karaite scholars, he had a college (*dār li-l-ʿilm*) in Jerusalem, which appears to have been established towards the end of the tenth century.[2]

One Hebrew grammatical text that is attributed to Yūsuf Ibn Nūḥ is extant. This work is referred to in the colophons either simply as the *Diqduq* or as *Nukat Diqduq* 'Points of Grammar'.[3] It is written in Arabic (in all extant manuscripts written in Hebrew script), though much of the technical terminology is Hebrew. The *Diqduq* is not a systematically arranged description of the Hebrew language with the various aspects of grammar presented in separate chapters but rather a series of grammatical notes on the Bible, together with sporadic exegetical comments. Occasionally a general principle of grammar is discussed, but in most cases grammatical concepts are not explained and their sense must be inferred from the context in which they are used.

---

[1] For further details see Khan (2000a: introduction).

[2] For the text of Ibn al-Hītī see Margoliouth (1897: 433, 438–39). Ibn al-Hītī was writing in the fifteenth century. For the background of Ibn Nūḥ's college, see Mann (1972: 33–34).

[3] A critical edition of Ibn Nūḥ's *Diqduq* to the Hagiographa with an analysis of its content is presented in Khan (2000a).

The work covers the entire Bible, selecting words and phrases that are deemed to require elucidation and analysis. It consists of a series of entries headed by a phrase from a biblical verse that constitutes the subject of the comment. The entries are arranged according to the order of verses in the biblical text. By no means all verses, however, are commented upon. The work was clearly intended to be used as an aid to the reading of the Bible. It does not offer instruction on the rudiments of Hebrew grammar but rather concentrates on points that Ibn Nūḥ believed may be problematic for the reader or concerning which there was controversy.

The main concern of the *Diqduq* is the analysis and explanation of word structure. On various occasions aspects of phonology and also the syntactic and rhetorical structure of a verse are taken into account, but this is generally done as a means of elucidating the form of a word. The *Diqduq*, therefore, is not a comprehensive grammar of Hebrew, either in its arrangement or in its content. It concentrates on what are regarded as problematic grammatical issues. These problematic issues are generally referred to as *masāʾil* (singular *masʾala* 'question') within the text of the *Diqduq*.

In his analysis of word structure, Ibn Nūḥ attempted to find consistent rules governing the formation of words. The ultimate purpose of his grammatical activity was the application of grammatical analysis in order to elucidate the precise meaning of the Biblical text and to demonstrate that there was nothing random or inconsistent about the language of the Bible. Differences in forms must be explained by positing differences in the process of derivation. The aim was to show that the language had a completely rational basis in its structure and differences in structure were in principle rationally motivated and intended to convey differences in meaning. A full description of the grammatical theory reflected by the text can be found in Khan (2000a). This is considerably different from that of the medieval 'western' tradition of Hebrew grammar that was developed in Spain by scholars such as Ḥayyūj and Ibn Janāḥ.

A few fragmentary texts are extant that are closely associated with Ibn Nūḥ's *Diqduq* and reflect a similar grammatical theory. These include the anonymous Karaite texts published in Khan (2000b). The Karaite tradition of Hebrew grammar was further developed by Ibn Nūḥ's pupil, ʾAbū al-Faraj Hārūn ibn al-Faraj, who wrote numerous works. The largest of these is a comprehensive work on Hebrew morphology and syntax consisting of eight parts entitled *al-Kitāb al-Muštamil ʿalā al-ʾUṣūl wa-l-Fuṣūl fī al-Luġa al-ʿIbrāniyya* ('The Comprehensive Book of General Principles and Particular Rules of the Hebrew Language'), which was completed in 1026 CE.[4] He composed a shorter version of the work called *al-Kitāb al-Kāfī fī al-Luġa al-ʿIbrāniyya* ('The Sufficient Book on the Hebrew Language').[5] A number of other medieval Karaite grammatical works are extant that are largely dependent on the writings of ʾAbū al-Faraj Hārūn and were written in the eleventh century. One such work is the grammatical treatise written in Hebrew known as *Meʾor ʿAyin* that was published by M.N. Zislin (1990) on the basis of a single surviving manuscript. An Arabic grammatical work that is closely related to *Meʾor ʿAyin* is *Kitāb al-ʿUqūd fī Taṣārīf al-Luġa al-ʿIbrāniyya* ('Book of Rules with regard to the Grammatical Inflections of the Hebrew Language'), the text of which has recently been established and studied by Nadezda Vidro (2009). In the tenth and eleventh centuries Karaite scholars also made important contributions to Hebrew lexicography. Of particular importance is the monumental dictionary of Biblical Hebrew and Aramaic known as *Kitāb Jāmiʿ al-ʾAlfāẓ* ('The Book of the Collection of Words') by ʾAbū Sulaymān Dāʾūd ibn ʾIbrāhīm al-Fāsī, which was published by Solomon Skoss (1936–45). Another significant Karaite lexicographical text from the later Middle Ages is *Kitāb al-Taysīr* ('The Book of Facilitation'), written by Solomon ibn Mubarrak ibn Ṣaʿīrat the end of the 13th or beginning of the 14th century, which has recently been published by José Martínez Delgado (2010).

In this paper I present the text of the *Diqduq* on the book of Hosea, which has hitherto remained unpublished. It has been preserved in the manuscript II Firkovitch Evr.-Arab. I 1756 (National Library of Russia, St. Petersburg). The Minor Prophets have been of particular interest to Robert Gordon, who has made important contributions to their exegesis and history of interpretation. The choice to focus on Ibn Nūḥ's *Diqduq* on Hosea is especially appropriate in the current state of research on medieval Karaite biblical exegesis, since there are now available a variety of Karaite exegetical texts on this book, which

---

[4] For a summary of the contents of the *al-Kitāb al-Muštamil* see Bacher (1895b: 232–256), who publishes a few short extracts. Recent studies of aspects of grammar in *al-Kitāb al-Muštamil* have been published by Maman (1996a, 1996b, 2007) and Basal (1998, 1999).

[5] A full edition and English translation of *al-Kitāb al-Kāfī* has been published G. Khan, M.A. Gallego and J. Olszowy-Schlanger (2003).

are of interest for comparative purposes. Of particular importance is the masterly edition of the commentary on Hosea by Yefet ben ʿEli recently published by Meira Polliack and Eliezer Schlossberg (2009).[6] Another key comparative source is an anonymous Karaite commentary on Hosea that was identified and prepared for publication from Genizah manuscript fragments by the late Friedrich Niessen. Extracts from this have appeared in Niessen (2001) and the full text will be published posthumously in Niessen (forthcoming). We also have the text of a commentary on the Minor Prophets by the Karaite Daniel al-Qumisi (ed. Markon 1957). The annotations on Ibn Nūḥ's *Diqduq* to Hosea that are offered here focus, for the most part, on the context of his comments in medieval Karaite biblical exegesis and the Karaite tradition of Hebrew grammatical thought.

Text

II Firkovitch Evr.-Arab. I 1756, fol. 92v

דבר ייי אשר היה אל הושע בן בארי וגֹ
תחלת דבר ייי בהושע: יקאל אול מא כאטב רב אלעאלמין להושע הו
אלדי קאל לה לך קח לך אשת זנונים וגֹ אלאן תחלת הי כלמה מצֹאפה
אלי דְבֶר אלתי הי לפטֹה עבר: ולנא גיר דלך לפטֹה מצֹאפה אלי לפטֹה
עבר נטֹיר בראשית בָּרָא ואן קאל קאיל אן לפטֹה ראשית קד תכון
מצֹאפה וקד תכון איצֹא מקטועה כּקֹ מגיד מראשית אחרית פהי כלמה
אלתי הי מצֹאפה פלאן ותכון מצֹאפה אלי כלמה הי לשון עבר יקאל לה
קד וגדנא קרִיַת חָנָה דוד והי מתל תְחִלַת דִבֶּר ויקאל אן דבֶר תפסירה
כטאב וליס הו לפטֹ עבר בל הו אסם אלכטאב נטֹיר והדבֵר אין בהם
ואלדי צאר דִבֶר ייי בהושע בגֹ נקט צאר כדלך מן גהה אלמקיף ואצלה
דִבֵּר בנקטתין בוזן קִטֵּר ועלי הדא אלתפסיר יכון תחלת דבר ייי בהושע
אבתדי כטאב רב אלעאלמין מע הושע ולא יכון דבֶר עבר: אשת זנו־
נים אעלם אן זנונים הי לפטֹה רבים ואליחיד יכון זְנוּן: ואלנון פי אכר
אלכלמה סבילה סביל אלנון אלדי פי אכר חָזון הָמוֹן אלדי ליס הו מן גוהר
אלכְּלַם אלתי הי מתצרפה: והדה אלאסמא אמרהא זְנֵה חֲזֵה הֲמֵה אעני
הי אסמא משתקה מן אללגה: ובקשָׁתַם ולא תמצא יקאל אן אלאמר
לזכר יכון בַּקֵּשׁ מדגוש ואלעבר יכון בִּקֵּשׁ ועבר אלנקבה יכון בִקְשָׁה וכאן
חקהא תכון ובִקְשָׁתַם וקד אכתצר פיה אלדגש: אֶתְנָה המה לי: אֶתְנָה

[6] An earlier edition was published by Birnbaum (1942).

הו אסם אלעטיה והו נט̇יר בִּנְיָה אלדי הו אסם אלבְּנֵי אעני הו נט̇ירה פי באב אלוזן כ̇ך והגזרה והבניה וקירותיה: ואדא זאד אלנון

Fol. 93r

פ[י אלא]סם יכון בִּנְיָן ויזול אלהי מן אלכלמה וכדלך יעמל אתנן: ואן קלנא אן בוגוד אלנון פי אתנן /זאל\ אלהֵי מן אכר אלכלמה יגוז יכון איצ̇א אן כמא זאל אלהי מן בִּנְיָה גא בדלה נון: ואלאקרב אן יכון בניָה אסם בראסה ובנין אסם בראסה וכדלך אתנה אסם בראסה ואתנן אסם בראסה ומעניהמא ואחד: ואיצ̇א חָרְבָּה וחָרְבָן מעניהמא מעני ואחד: נזמה וחליתה: אסם אלמדכר יכון חֲלִי: ואדא אכרג בלפט̇ה אלתאנית יכון חֶלְיָה נט̇יר שְׁבִי שִׁבְיָה ואלמצ̇אף מן שִׁבְיָה יכון שִׁבְיָתָה נט̇יר שִׁלְיָה שִׁלְיָתָה כ̇ך ובשליתה היוצת מבין רגליה: ותלך אחרי מאהביה אמרהא אֲהֵב מתל חַלֵּל יגי מנה מחלליה ולם יודגש אללמד פי מְחַלְלֶיהָ מן גהה אלגעיה וכדלך לם יודגש אלהי פי מְאַהֲבֶיהָ ולו כאן יקע פיה אלדגש כאן מְאַהְּבֶיה בוזן מְכַבְּדֶיהָ: לכן הנה אנכי מפתיה מְפַתֶּיהָ לשון רבים: ואליחיד יכון מְפַתֶּהָ בלא יוד ודלך אן אלאמר אלדי בוזן פַּתֵּה גַלֵּה אדא יכון אלפאעל לשון זכר מְפַתֶּה ואלמשאר אליה יכון מְפַתּוֹ ואלמשאר אלי נקבה יכון מְפַתֶּהָ או מפתה ואלרבים יכונו מְפַתִּים מְפַתֵּי מְפַתֶּיךָ מְפַתָּיו מְפַתֶּיהָ אלאן קולה מפתיה בלשון רבים יגוז יכון ישיר בה אלי אלקום אלדין ילטפו בישראל ויקוו קלובהם נט̇יר קולה חזקו ידים רפות וג̇ פסמיו האולי אלמחזקים מְפַתֶּיהָ במא יבשרוהם באלנחמות ויקוו קלובהם ואדא קלנא אנהם אלמבשרין אלדי יבשרו פי בלדאן אלגלות בט̇הור אליהו ע̇ אלס̇ פי אלבריה ליס יכון דלך בממתנע וקולה הנה אנכי מפתיה ונסב אלפעל אליה גל אסמה למעני אנה הו אלמסבב להדה אלבשאראת אלדין יבשרו בהא האולי אלמבשרין: אהבת רע ומנאפת תפסירה מחבובה אלזוג: וָאֶכְּרֶהָ לי אמרה נְכֹר נט̇יר נְצֹר יגי מנה וָאֶצְּרָה והו מכתצר אלנון אלאן קולה וָאֶכְּרֶהָ ולם יקל וָאֶכְרָהּ יקאל אנה יעמל לונין ואלמעני ואחד וליס הו מן גהה מצ̇אף ומכרת בל אלמצ̇אף ואלמכרת פי הדא אלבאב הו ואחד והו נט̇יר שְׂנָא מְצָא המא אמרין גא מן מְצָא וימצאָה מלאך ייי ולם יקל וַיִּמְצָאֶהָ נט̇יר וַיִּשְׂנָאֶהָ אמנון כ̇ך לאשה וַיִּשְׂנָאֶהָ:

Fol. 92v

וְדָמִיתִי אמך אמרהא דְמֵה ותפסירהא אֱבכּם: וקד [יעמל] הדא אללפט̇ תפסיר אכר ולאכן פי הדא אלמוצ̇ע יריד בה אלאנבכאם: ומקלו יגיד לו אלכלמה בלא אשארה תכון מֶקֶל נט̇יר רֶגֶל רַגְלוֹ חֶבֶל חַבְלוֹ חבור עצבים אפרָים: ולם יקל אפרַיִם למא קטע אלכלמה מן הנח לו וצאר הנח לו כלאם אכר ומעני אכר: אהבו הֵבוּ: תפסיר הֵבוּ אעטו לשון עבר ואמרה יכון הָבֵה ואלעבר יכון הֵבָה ואלרבים הֵבוּ בוזן זָרֵה זֵרָה זֵרוּ עבר אלרבים: כ̇ך אשר זֵרוּ את יהודה ולנא אואמר איצ̇א בוזן הָבֵה והו עָרֵה ויכון אלעבר /וקיר\ עֵרָה מגן: ומתלה המה קֵרוהו אמרה קָרֵה: ושחטה שטים העמיקו:

מן אלנאס מן קאל אן שַׁחֲטָה אסם פעל וליס הו מצדר: ואלאקרב אן יכון מצדר והו בוזן לְטַהֲרָה אלדי הו מצדר ואיצ̇א לְרִבְעָהּ אתה מצדר: ולו כאן אסם כאן לְרִבְעַת אתה ורסם אלמצדר אן לא יכון מצ̇אף בתו נט̇יר חָכְמַת יִרְאַת שַׁחֲטַת ואנמא הדה הי עלאמאת אלאסמא אלמצ̇אפה אעני אלתי הי מצ̇אפה פלאן פלדלך יקאל אן ושחטה הו מצדר: ולא יגהה מכם מזור יקאל ולא יְנַחִי מנכם אלעלה אלתי הי תחתאג̇ אן יְדַ֗ר עליהא: פצאר מזור אסם אלמוצ̇ע ויקאל אנה אסם אלערץ̇ בוזן מגור אלדי הו חדּר ומתלו מָשׁוֹשׂ הו פרח: יִגְהֶה אמרה גְהֵה נט̇יר נהה על המון מצרים: עֲקֻבָּה מדם: תפסירהא גרבזה ולשון זכר יכון עָקֹב בוזן נָקוֹד עָקֹד: כמו תנּור בֹּעֵרָה: אלהי פיה זאיד והו בֹּעֵר לשון זכר נט̇יר השפִּלה הגבה ואלהי אלאכיר פי השפָּלה זאיד נט̇יר בֹּעֵרָה: הֶחֱלוּ שרים: אמרה הַחֲלֵה ותפסיר החלו אמרצ̇ו יעני אמרצ̇ו אנפסהם: איסירם כשמע לעדתם אמרה הַיְסֵר נט̇יר הַיְצֵא: כי יְיֵלִילו על משכבותם קיל אן אמרה יְלֵיל נט̇יר ואלמנה לא יְיֵטִיב אמרה יֵטֵב וקד קיל אן יְיֵלִיל יְיֵטִיב אליוד אלאול אלדי תחתה שוא הו זאיד ואמרה הֵילֵל: ואלאינת יכון אֵילִיל יְלִיל נֵילִיל תֵּילִיל נט̇יר הֵיטֵיב יגי מנה אֵיטִיב יְיטִיב נֵיטִיב תֵיטִיב כי שבבים יהיה: שְׁבָבִים הי בוזן שְׁפָטִים ואליחיד יכון שֶׁבֶב

Fol. 97r

שֶׁפֶט נט̇יר בֶּגֶד בְּגָדִים ואיצ̇א יגוז יכון שָׁבָב שָׁפָט נט̇יר דֶבֶר[7] דְּבָרִים ותפסיר שְׁבָבִים יקאל אנהא שראראת מתל ולא יגה שביב אשו ולאכן אלאסמא וקעת מכתלפה אלואחד שְׁבִיב ואלאכר שֶׁבֶב ולנא מתל דלך והו פֶּסֶל בוזן שֶׁבֶב ולנא פְּסִיל בוזן שְׁבִיב כ̇ך פסילי אלהיהם ואליחיד יכון פְּסִיל או פָּסִיל: הִתְנוּ אהבים אמרהא הַתְנֵה בוזן הַרְבֵה הִרְבוּ: וַיָּחֵלּוּ מעט: אמרה הָחֵל בלא יוד: ולו כאן ביוד כאן וַיָּחִילוּ מתל וַיָּשִׁיבוּ: זבחי הַבְהָבַי: אליחיד יכון הַבְהָב ומעניה עטיה: נביא פח יקוש: יָקוֹש אסם אלפאעל בוזן עָשׁוֹק בָּחוֹן: יָקוּש הו אלמַוהוּק: מִלֵּדָה ומבטן ומהריון: יקאל אן תפסיר לֵדָה קד יכון ולֵאדה אעני אלערץ̇ בוזן עֵצָה: וקד יכון אסם אלמרה אלואלדה ופי הדא אלמוצ̇ע אדא פ֗סר אסם אלולאדה לא ימתנע מן קרינה ומחריון אלדי הו אסם אלחבל: ולנא מן אלאסמא מא תקע עלי אמראה: ואיצ̇א תקע עלי אלערץ̇ נט̇יר נְבָלָה יְשָׁרָה ומתלהמא כתיר: אלות שוא קיל אן אמרה אֲלֵה בלשון זכר ולשון נקבה יעמל אֱלִי כבתולה: אֲלֵה הו בוזן שְׁתֵה ואלמצדר שָׁתוֹת בוזן אָלוֹת אלדי הו מצדר: ולו כאן אָלוֹת אסם אלאימאן לכאן אֲלוֹת שוא וכאן אסם אליחיד אָלָה בוזן שָׁנָה אלדי אדא צארת רבים מצ̇אפה תכון שְׁנוֹת כ̇ך כי שנות מספר יאתיו פצארת אָלוֹת פי הדא אלמוצ̇ע מצדר ולא יקאל אנהא אסמא מן וגה אכר אן מהמא תמשי אלכלמה עלי באב אלתצריף לא נקול אנהא

[7] Sic MS, but the vocalization should clearly be דָּבָר.

אסם: בָּשְׁנָה אפרים יקח: מן אלנאס מן קאל אן בשנה אלנון פיה זאיד ואצלה בֹּשָׁה והדא אלנון הו אלנון אלזאיד מתל אלדי פי וקבנו לי משם ופי הֶדַּשְׁנָה מחלב ופי יעברֶנְהוּ: על בני עולה[8] יקאל אן מעני עַלְוָה הו עַוְלָה אעני אלגַור נטיר שַׂלְמָה שַׂמְלָה וקיל אן מעני בני עלוה הם אולאד אלרפעה יעני אלאגלי מן אלנאס וכאנו מעינין לבני בנימן אלדי כאנו טאלמין: עלוה יגוז יכון אסם משתק מן עֲלֵה מתל גַאֲוָה מן גְאֵה: באותי וְאֶסֳּרֵם יקאל אן אמרה הִסֹּר נטיר הִבֹּן וכאן חקה יכון וְאֶסֹרֵם ולאכן קד יעמל אוֹ אֱ כפיף

Fol. 97v

נטיר וְדָרְשׁוּ מחרבותיהם: ואפרים עגלה מלמדה לפטה מְלֻמָּדָה קד תקע עלי אלשכצה כֹּךְ האהנא ואיצֿא תקע עלי אלמצוה כֹּךְ ותהי יראתם אתי מצות אנשים מלמדה: אֹהַבְתִּי לדוש אליוד להא זאיד והי אֹהֶבֶת בוזן ותרא אֹיַבְתִּי אלתי הי אֹיֶבֶת ואליוד פיהא זאיד: וקאם שאון בעמיך אלאלף פי וקאם זאיד: כשד שלמן בית ארבאל יקאל אן שלמן הו שלמנאסר ויקאל אן שלמן הו אסם מלך מן אלמלוך וכדלך בית ארבאל הו אסם אלמכאן וכאן וקע פי הדא אלבלד נהב עטים ואן לם נערף פי אי זמאן כאן: ואנכי תִרְגַּלְתִּי לאפרים: אמרה תַּרְגֵּל בוזן פַּרְשֵׁז כַּלְכֵּל: כמרימֵי עֹל על לחיהם: יקאל אן לְחֵיהֶם אליחיד לה יכון לְחִי מתל אֲחִי אלדי הו אסם אלאך והי כלמה בראסהא והי גיר אָח: וגא מן לְחִי לְחֵיהֶם נטיר אֲחִי אֲחֵיהֶם ולו כאן אֲחֵיהֶם מן אָח כאן חקה אן יכון אָחֵיהֶם נטיר שָׂר שָׂרֵיהֶם: אעלם אידך אללה אן ואן כאן לְחֵיהֶם הו בוזן אֲחֵיהֶם פאלאקרב אן לא יכון מן לגה לחייו לאן מן רסם אלעֹל אן יגעל עלי אלבקר עלי ענקה לא עלי פכֵּה פישבה אן אליוד פי לְחֵיהֶם זאיד לאן לפטה אלרטב ואלרטובה מא וגדנא פיהא יוד ואלעגלה אדא געל עליהא אלניר עלי רקבתהא פאלמוצֿע יכון רטב והי תתאלם מן דלך פאלאקרב אן יפסר על לחיהם עלי ארטא־ בהם: ואט אליו אוכיל יקאל ורפק כאן אליה יעני כנת ארפק בה וכנת אקויה אי אעטיה אלטאקה כֹּךְ אוכיל אעלם אן אמרה הוֹכֵל והו פעל באלגיר נטיר הוֹרֵד ואלאמר פי אלנפס יכון הוּכֵל או הוּכַל ויגי מנה אוּכל יוּכַל נוּכַל תוּכַל: וחלה חרב בעריו יקאל ומבתדיה תכון אלסיף פי מְדִנה חָלָה הו בוזן שָׁבָה בָּאָה: ועמי תלואים אמרה תְּלָא מתל קְרָא קְרוּאִים תְּלוּאִים יחתמל אנהא מן לפטה תְּלָאָה והו אלעגז: ואל עַל יקראוה יקאל ואלי אלעאלי ידעוה יעני כאנו אלנביאים ידעו לישראל אלי טאעה אלרב אלעאלי גל תנאה ומא כאן יקבל מנהם וקיל אנהם כאנו ידעוה אלי אלנפע ומא כאנו יקבלו מנהם עַל מן לפט הוֹעיל פסרו
ואלתפסיר אלאול אקרב

[8] Sic MS, but read עלוה.

Fol. 38r

פי באב אללגה ולא אבוא בְעִיר ומא קאל בָעִיר יקאל אנה יחתמל כלמה
יצֹאף אליהא בְעִיר לאן בְעִיר הו מצֹאף: פאן קלנא ולא אגי פי מדינה
אחד גירך ימשי: ויהודה עד רד עם אל יקאל סבבוני בכחש אפֿ יעני
סָבבוּ על נביא ייי בכחש ובמרמה ויהודה איצֹא אלדי כאן טאיע מע
אלטאיק ומע אללה אלקדוס כאן נאמן הַם איצֹא סָבַב בכחש ובמרמה:
ובאונו שרה את אלהים: שָׂרָה אמרה שְׂרֵה בוזן עֲשֵׂה עָשָׂה וְדִבַּ֫רְתִּי על
הנביאים אלפרק בין וְדִבַּ֫רְתִּי אלי ודברתִּי על לבה הו אן ודבַּ֫רתי לשון
עבר ודברתִּי לשון עתיד: בגלגל שורים זבחו: יחתמל יכון שְׁוָרִים מן שֶׁוֶר
נטֹיר קֶבֶר קְבָרִים עֶבֶד עֲבָדִים ויחתמל איצֹא יכון מן שָׁוָר מתל דָּבָר
דְּבָרִים ואיצֹא מא ימתנע יכון מן שְׁוָר בוזן יְקָר יְקָרִים כְּתָב כְּתָבִים: מסכה
מכספם כתבונם: תְּבוּן אסם אלפטנה וגא מנה כתבונם ואיצֹא תְּבוּנָה
אסם אלפטנה: תְּבוּן הו בוזן גְּבוּל: בארץ תלאבות יחידה תכון תַּלְאוּבָה
יקאל אן תפסירה קפאר וקד יכון תלאוב לשון זכר בוזן תמרוּק: ואקרע
סגור לבם סְגוֹר הו בוזן חֲגוֹר שְׁחוֹק חֲלוֹם שחתך ישראל כי בי בעזרך:
הדא ישבה קול אנסאן יקול אֲהֶלַכְתִּךְ מעונתי ומדאדאתי לך: אי תוהמת
בכתרה מדאדאתי לך אני עאגז ען אדבך וקולה כי בי בעזרך ולם יקל כי
בי עזרך הו כמא יקול אלאנסאן פלאן בנפסה כרג פי ענאיה פלאן: אהי
מלכך אפוא יקאל אין הו אלדי כאן יקול אנא אכון מלכך אלאן חתי יגיתך
אן קדר עלי כלאצך: כי הוּא בין אחים יפריא הו באלף ותפסירה יתמר
נטֹיר יַפְרֶה אלדי הו בהֵי כל תשא עון: מעניה תשא /כל\ עון:

Translation

דְּבַר־יְהוָ֣ה ׀ אֲשֶׁ֣ר הָיָ֗ה אֶל־הוֹשֵׁ֙עַ֙ בֶּן־בְּאֵרִ֔י

תְּחִלַּ֥ת דִּבֶּר־יְהוָ֖ה בְּהוֹשֵׁ֑עַ (Hos. 1.2): The meaning is said to be 'The first thing that the Lord of the Universe spoke to Hosea was that he said to him לֵ֣ךְ קַח־לְךָ֞ אֵ֤שֶׁת זְנוּנִים֙ etc.' Now, תְּחִלַּ֥ת is a word that is conjoined to דִּבֶּר, which is a past form. We have other cases of a word conjoined to a past form, such as בְּרֵאשִׁ֖ית בָּרָ֣א (Gen. 1.1). If somebody says that the form רֵאשִׁית may be conjoined or may also be disjoined, as in מַגִּ֤יד מֵֽרֵאשִׁית֙ אַחֲרִ֔ית (Isa. 46.10), and it is a word that is conjoined to some (nominal) but (here) it would be conjoined to a word that is a past form, the response to him would be that we have found קִרְיַ֖ת חָנָ֣ה דָוִ֑ד (Isa. 29.1), which is (a word conjoined to a past form) like תְּחִלַּת דִּבֶּר. It is (also) said that דִּבֶּר should be translated 'speech' since it is not a past form but it is a noun meaning 'speech', like וְהַדִּבֵּ֖ר אֵ֣ין בָּהֶ֑ם (Jer. 5.13). The fact that דִּבֶּר־יְהוָ֖ה בְּהוֹשֵׁ֑עַ has *seghol* has arisen on account of the *maqqeph*, its original form being דִּבֵּר with *ṣere*, with the pattern קִטֵּר. According to this interpretation תְּחִלַּת דִּבֶּר־יְהוָה בְּהוֹשֵׁעַ should be (translated) 'the beginning of the speech of the Lord of the Universe with Hosea', and it would not be the past form דִּבֵּר.

אֵשֶׁת זְנוּנִים (Hos. 1.2): Take note that זְנוּנִים is a plural form and the singular would be זְנוּן. The *nun* at the end of the word is like the *nun* that occurs at the end of חָזוֹן and הָמוֹן, in that it does not belong to the substance of the words. Rather they are inflected (with the *nun*). These nouns have the imperative bases זְנֵה, חֲזֵה and הֲמֵה, I mean they are nouns derived from the lexical class.

וּבִקְשָׁתַם וְלֹא תִמְצָא (Hos. 2.9): It is said that the masculine imperative would be בַּקֵּשׁ with *dagesh* and the past form would be בִּקֵּשׁ. The feminine past form would be בִּקְשָׁה and so according to rule it should be וּבִקְשָׁתַם, but the *dagesh* in it has been contracted.

אֶתְנָה הֵמָּה לִי (Hos. 2.14): אֶתְנָה is a noun meaning 'gift/pay'. It is like בִּנְיָה, which is a noun meaning 'building', I mean it corresponds to it with regard to pattern, as in וְהַגִּזְרָה וְהַבִּנְיָה וְקִירוֹתֶיהָ (Ezek. 41:13). When a *nun* is added to the noun, it is בִּנְיָן and the *heh* is elided from the word. The noun אֶתְנַן is formed in the same way. If we say that when the *nun* is present in אֶתְנַן, the *heh* as been elided from the word, then it is possible that it is like when the *heh* of בִּנְיָה is elided, a *nun* takes its place. It is more likely that בִּנְיָה is a noun in its primary form and בִּנְיָן is a noun in its primary form, and likewise אֶתְנָה is a noun in its primary form and אֶתְנַן is a noun in its primary form and their meaning is the same. Also חָרְבָּה and חָרְבָּן have the same meaning.

נִזְמָהּ וְחֶלְיָתָהּ (Hos. 2.15): The masculine form of the noun is חֲלִי and when it is realized with a feminine form it is חֶלְיָה, like שְׁבִי, שִׁבְיָה. The conjoined form of שִׁבְיָה would be שִׁבְיָתָהּ like שִׁלְיָה, שִׁלְיָתָהּ, as in וּבְשִׁלְיָתָהּ הַיּוֹצֵת מִבֵּין רַגְלֶיהָ (Deut. 28:57).

וַתֵּלֶךְ אַחֲרֵי מְאַהֲבֶיהָ (Hos. 2.15): Its imperative is אַהֵב like הַלֵּל, from which is derived מְחַלְלֶיהָ (Exod. 31.14). The *lamed* in מְחַלְלֶיהָ does not have *dagesh* on account of the *gaʿya* and likewise the *heh* in מְאַהֲבֶיהָ does not have *dagesh*. If *dagesh* occurred in it, it would be מְאַהְּבֶיהָ with the pattern of מְכַבְּדֶיהָ (Lam. 1.8).

לָכֵן הִנֵּה אָנֹכִי מְפַתֶּיהָ (Hos. 2.16): מְפַתֶּיהָ is a plural form. The singular would be מְפַתָּהּ without *yod*. This is because the imperative of the pattern פַּתֵּה, גַּלֵּה—when the active participle is masculine singular (the form is) מְפַתֶּה, the form with a third person masculine singular suffix is מְפַתּוֹ, the form with a feminine suffix is מְפַתָּהּ or מְפַתָּהּ. The plural forms are מְפַתִּים, מְפַתַּי, מְפַתֶּיךָ, מְפַתָּיו, מְפַתֶּיהָ. Now, the plural form in the text מְפַתֶּיהָ may be referring to the people who show kindness to Israel and strengthen their hearts, as it says חַזְּקוּ יָדַיִם רָפוֹת etc. (Isa. 35.3). These 'strengtheners' were called מְפַתֶּיהָ on account of the words of comfort that they bring to them and so strengthen their heart. If we were to say that these were the missionaries who announced in the land of the exile the appearance of Elijah, peace be upon him, on the earth, that would not be unreasonable. The text says הִנֵּה אָנֹכִי מְפַתֶּיהָ in which the action is attributed to him of exalted name to express the meaning that he is the one causing the good tidings that these missionaries propagate.

אֲהֻבַת רֵעַ וּמְנָאָפֶת (Hos. 3.1): its translation is 'beloved of (her) spouse'.

וָאֶכְּרֶהָ לִּי (Hos. 3.2.): Its imperative is נְכֹר like נְצֹר, from which is derived וָאֶצְּרָה, its *nun* being contracted. Now, it says וָאֶכְּרֶהָ and not וָאֶכְּרָהּ. It is said that it can have two forms with the same meaning. It is not related to conjoined and disjoined status, rather conjoined and disjoined in this case are the same. It is like the two imperatives שְׂנָא and מְצָא. From מְצָא is derived וַיִּמְצָאָהּ מַלְאַךְ יְהוָה (Gen. 16.7), where it does not say וַיִּמְצָאֶהָ as in וַיִּשְׂנָאֶהָ אַמְנוֹן (2 Sam. 13.15) and likewise לְאִשָּׁה וַיִּשְׂנָאֶהָ (Deut. 22.16).

וְדָמִיתִי אִמֶּךָ (Hos. 4.5): Its imperative is דְּמֵה and its translation is 'I shall make dumb'. This form can have another sense but in this place 'becoming dumb' is what is intended.

וּמַקְלוֹ יַגִּיד לוֹ (Hos. 4.12): The word without a suffix would be מֶקֶל like חֶבֶל, רַגְלוֹ, רֶגֶל, חַבְלוֹ.

חֲבוּר עֲצַבִּים אֶפְרָיִם (Hos. 4.17): It did not say אֶפְרַיִם since the word is disjoined from הַנַּח־לוֹ and so הַנַּח־לוֹ is a different (unit of) speech and (with) a different sense.

אָהֲבוּ הֵבוּ (Hos. 4.18): The translation of הֵבוּ is 'they gave', a past form. Its imperative is הָבֵה and the past is הֵבָה, the plural being הֵבוּ, with the pattern of זְרֵה, זֵרָה, זֵרוּ, (the latter being) the plural past, as in אֲשֶׁר־זֵרוּ אֶת־יְהוּדָה (Zech. 2.4). We also have (other) imperatives with the pattern of הָבֵה, (one such) being עָרֵה, the past (of which is found in) וְקִיר עֵרָה מָגֵן (Isa. 22.6), and similarly הֵמָּה קֵרוּהוּ (Neh. 3.3), the imperative of which is קָרֵה.

וְשַׁחֲטָה שֵׂטִים הֶעְמִיקוּ (Hos. 5.2): Some people have said that שַׁחֲטָה is a verbal noun and not an infinitive. It is more likely, however, that it is an infinitive. It has the pattern of לְטַהֲרָה (Ezek. 39.14), which is an infintive. Also לְרִבְעָה אֹתָהּ (Lev. 20.16) is an infinitive. If it were a noun, it would be לְרִבְעַת אֹתָהּ. It is a feature of the infinitive that it is not conjoined by *taw*, like שַׁחֲטַת, יִרְאַת, חָכְמַת. This is a distinctive feature of conjoined nouns, I mean those that are conjoined to some (nominal). For this reason it is said that שַׁחֲטָה is an infinitive.

וְלֹא־יִגְהֶה מִכֶּם מָזוֹר (Hos. 5.13): This is said to mean 'and he will not remove from you the illness, which needs to be sprinkled upon'. The word מָזוֹר is a noun of place. It is also said that it is a noun denoting an abstraction, with the pattern of מָגוֹר, which means 'caution', and, likewise, מָשׂוֹשׂ, which means 'joy'. The imperative of יִגְהֶה is גְּהֵה, like נְהֵה עַל־הֲמוֹן מִצְרַיִם (Ezek. 32.18).

עֲקֻבָּה מִדָּם (Hos. 6.8): Its translation is 'deceptive'. The masculine form is עָקוֹב, with the pattern of נָקוֹד, עָקוֹד.

כְּמוֹ תַנּוּר בֹּעֵרָה (Hos. 7.4): The *heh* in this is added since it is the masculine form בֹּעֵר, as in הַשָּׁפָלָה הַגְבֵּהַ (Ezek. 21:31), where the *heh* in הַשָּׁפָלָה is added, as in בֹּעֵרָה.

הֶחֱלוּ שָׂרִים (Hos. 7.5): Its imperative is הַחֲלֵה and the translation of הֶחֱלוּ is 'they made ill', that is they made themselves ill.

אַיְסִרֵם כְּשֵׁמַע לַעֲדָתָם (Hos. 7.12): Its imperative is הַיְסֵר, like הַיְצֵא.

כִּי יְיֵלִילוּ עַל־מִשְׁכְּבוֹתָם (Hos. 7.14): It is said that its imperative is יֵלֵיל like וְאַלְמָנָה לֹא יְיֵטִיב (Job 24:21), the imperative of which is יֵטֵב. It is said also that the first *yod* under which there is *shewa* in יְיֵלִיל and יְיֵטִיב is added and the imperative is הֵילֵל. The forms with verbal prefixes (of הֵילֵל) are אֵילִיל, יֵלִיל, נֵילִיל, תֵּילִיל, like הֵיטִיב, from which are devired אֵיטִיב, נֵיטִיב, יֵיטִיב, תֵּיטִיב.

כִּי־שְׁבָבִים יִהְיֶה (Hos. 8.6): שְׁבָבִים has the pattern of שְׁפָטִים and the singular would be שֶׁבֶב, שֶׁפֶט, like בֶּגֶד, בְּגָדִים. It is also possible that it is שָׁבָב, שָׁפָט, like דָּבָר, דְּבָרִים. It is said that the translation of שְׁבָבִים is 'sparks', as in וְלֹא־יִגַּהּ שְׁבִיב אִשּׁוֹ (Job 18.5), but the nouns are different (in pattern), one is שְׁבִיב and the other is שֶׁבֶב. Similarly to this we have פֶּסֶל with the pattern of שֶׁבֶב and we have פְּסִיל with the pattern of שְׁבִיב, as in פְּסִילֵי אֱלֹהֵיהֶם (Deut. 7:25), the singular of which is פְּסִיל or פָּסִיל.

הִתְנוּ אֲהָבִים (Hos. 8.9): Its imperative is הַתְנֵה with the pattern of הַרְבֵּה, הִרְבּוּ.

וַיָּחֵלּוּ מְּעָט (Hos. 8.10): Its imperative is הָחֵל without *yod*. If it had *yod*, it would be וַיָּחִילוּ like וַיָּשִׁיבוּ.

זִבְחֵי הַבְהָבַי (Hos. 8.13): The singular would be הַבְהָב and its meaning is 'gift'.

נָבִיא פַּח יָקוֹשׁ (Hos. 9.8): יָקוֹשׁ is an active participle with the pattern of עָשׁוֹק, בָּחוֹן. The form יָקוּשׁ means 'the one that is caught'.

מִלֵּדָה וּמִבֶּטֶן וּמֵהֵרָיוֹן (Hos. 9.11): It is said that the translation of לֵדָה may be 'childbirth', that is the abstraction (process), with the pattern of עֵצָה, but may also be a noun denoting the woman giving birth. In this place, if it is interpreted as a noun meaning 'childbirth', this would be admissible from the contextual collocation with וּמֵהֵרָיוֹן, which is a noun meaning 'pregnancy'. We have nouns that refer to a woman and also to an abstraction, like נְבָלָה, יְשָׁרָה and many like these.

אָלוֹת שָׁוְא (Hos. 10.4): It is said that its imperative is אֲלֵה in the masculine. The feminine has the form אֱלִי כִּבְתוּלָה (Joel 1.8). The form אֲלֵה has the pattern of שְׁתֵה and the infinitive שְׁתוֹת has the pattern of אָלוֹת, which, therefore, is an infinitive. If אָלוֹת were a noun meaning 'belief', it would be אֲלוֹת שָׁוְא and the singular form of the noun would be אָלָה, with the pattern of שָׁנָה, which, when it is plural and conjoined, would be שְׁנוֹת, as in שְׁנוֹת מִסְפָּר יֶאֱתָיוּ (Job 16.22). So, in this place אָלוֹת is an infinitive. It cannot be said to be a noun for any other reason. Taking into account the behaviour of the word with regard to inflection, we cannot say that it is a noun.

בָּשְׁנָה אֶפְרַיִם יִקָּח (Hos. 10.6): Some people have said that the *nun* in בָּשְׁנָה is added and its original form is בֹּשָׁה and that this *nun* is like the added *nun* in וְקָבְנוֹ־לִי מִשָּׁם (Num. 23.13), in הֻדַּשְּׁנָה מֵחֵלֶב (Isa. 34.6) and in יַעַבְרֻנְהוּ (Jer. 5.22).

עַל־בְּנֵי עַלְוָה (Hos. 10.9): It is said that the meaning of עַלְוָה is עַוְלָה, that is 'wrongdoing', like שַׂלְמָה, שִׂמְלָה. It is said that the meaning of בְּנֵי עַלְוָה is 'the sons of exaltation', that is 'pre-eminent people' and that such people were helpers of the sons of Benjamin, who were evildoers. The form עַלְוָה may be a noun derived from עָלֶה as גַּאֲוָה is derived from גֵּאֶה.

בְּאַוָּתִ֖י וְאֶסֳּרֵ֑ם (Hos. 10.10): It is said that its imperative is הִסֹּר like הִבּוֹן. According to rule it should be וְאֶסֹּרֵם but the אוֹ been made into short אֳ, as in וְדָרְשׁ֗וּ מֵחָרְבוֹתֵיהֶֽם (Psa. 109.10).

וְאֶפְרַ֜יִם עֶגְלָ֤ה מְלֻמָּדָה֙ (Hos. 10.11): The form מְלֻמָּדָה֙ may relate to a person, as here, and may also relate to a commandment, as in וַתְּהִ֤י יִרְאָתָם֙ אֹתִ֔י מִצְוַ֥ת אֲנָשִׁ֖ים מְלֻמָּדָֽה (Isa. 29.13).

אֹהַ֣בְתִּי לָד֔וּשׁ (Hos. 10.11): The *yod* in it is added and it is (in origin) אֹהֶבֶת. It has the pattern of וְתֵרֶ֤א אֹיַבְתִּי֙ (Micah 7.10), which is (in origin) אֹיֶבֶת, the *yod* being added.

וְקָ֣אם שָׁא֣וֹן בְּעַמֶּ֔ךָ (Hos. 10.14): The *ʾaleph* in וְקָ֣אם is added.

כְּשֹׁ֤ד שַׁלְמַן֙ בֵּ֣ית אַרְבֵ֔אל (Hos. 10.14): It is said that שַׁלְמַן is Shalmaneser. It is also said that שַׁלְמַן is a name of a king. Likewise בֵּ֣ית אַרְבֵ֔אל is the name of a place. In this country there was great plundering although we do not know at what time it took place.

וְאָנֹכִ֤י תִרְגַּ֙לְתִּי֙ לְאֶפְרַ֔יִם (Hos. 11.3): Its imperative is תַּרְגֵּל with the pattern of כַּלְכֵּל, פַּרְשֵׁז.

כִּמְרִ֥ימֵי עֹ֖ל עַ֣ל לְחֵיהֶ֑ם (Hos. 11.4): It is said that the singular of לְחֵיהֶ֑ם is לְחִי like אֲחִי, which is a noun meaning 'brother' and a word in its primary form, which is different from אָח. From לְחִי is derived לְחֵיהֶ֑ם like אֲחִי, אֲחֵיהֶם. If אֲחֵיהֶם were derived from אָח it should be according to rule אָחֵיהֶם like שָׂר, שָׂרֵיהֶם. Take note, may God support you, that although לְחֵיהֶ֑ם has the pattern of אֲחֵיהֶם, it is more likely that it is not from the lexical class of לְחָיָו (cf. Cant. 5.13) because a yoke is customarily put on the neck of cattle not on their jaw and it seems that the *yod* in לְחֵיהֶ֑ם is added, since we have not found a *yod* in the words for 'moist' or 'moisture'. When a yoke is put on the neck of a heiffer, this place becomes moist and it becomes painful on account of this. So, it is preferable to translate עַ֣ל לְחֵיהֶ֑ם 'on their moist (places pl.)'.

וְאַ֥ט אֵלָ֖יו אוֹכִֽיל (Hos. 11.4): The sense of this is said to be 'and gentleness was for him', meaning I treated him gently and strengthened him, that is 'I gave him power', as it says אוֹכִֽיל. Take note that its imperative is הוֹכֵל. It is a transitive verb like הוֹרֵד. The intransitive imperative is הוּכֵל or הוּכַל, from which is derived אוּכַל, יוּכַל, נוּכַל, תּוּכַל.

וְחָלָ֤ה חֶ֙רֶב֙ בְּעָרָ֔יו (Hos. 11.6): This is said to mean 'and the sword will be beginning in his cities'. The form חָלָה has the pattern of שָׁבָה and בָּאָה.

וְעַמִּ֥י תְלוּאִ֖ים לִמְשׁוּבָתִ֑י (Hos. 11.7): Its imperative is תְּלָא like קְרוּאִים, קְרָא. It is possible that תְּלוּאִים is derived from the form תְּלָאָה, which is 'inability'.

וְאֶל־עַל֙ יִקְרָאֻ֔הוּ (Hos. 11.7): This is said to mean 'To the Exalted One they call him', that is the prophets were calling Israel to obedience of the Exalted Lord, who is worthy of the highest praise, but they do not give heed to them. It is also said that it means that they were calling Israel to benefit, but they did not give heed to them, עַל being derived from the word הוֹעִיל. It has been interpreted thus, but the first interpretation is the most satisfactory from a linguistic point of view.

וְלֹ֥א אָב֖וֹא בְּעִֽיר (Hos. 11.9): It does not say בָּעִיר. It is said that it is possible that בְּעִיר is conjoined to a word since בְּעִיר is a conjoined form. If we were to interpret it as 'and I shall not come into the town *of anybody other than you*', that would be acceptable.

וִיהוּדָ֗ה עֹ֥ד רָד֙ עִם־אֵ֔ל (Hos. 12.1): The words סְבָבֻ֤נִי בְכַ֙חַשׁ֙ אֶפְרַ֔יִם mean they surrounded the prophet of the Lord with lies and deceit and also Judah, who was obedient to the Almighty and was faithful to the Holy God, he also surrounded (the prophet) with lies and deceit.

וּבְאוֹנ֖וֹ שָׂרָ֥ה אֶת־אֱלֹהִֽים (Hos. 12.4): The imperative of שָׂרָה is שְׂרֵה with the pattern of עָשָׂה, עֲשֵׂה.

וְדִבַּ֙רְתִּי֙ עַל־הַנְּבִיאִ֔ים (Hos. 12.11): The difference between וְדִבַּ֙רְתִּי֙ and וְדִבַּרְתִּ֖י עַל־לִבָּֽהּ (Hos. 2.16) is that וְדִבַּ֙רְתִּי֙ is past and וְדִבַּרְתִּ֖י is future.

בַּגִּלְגָּ֖ל שְׁוָרִ֣ים זִבֵּ֑חוּ (Hos. 12.12): It is possible that שְׁוָרִים is derived from שֶׁוֶר, like קֶבֶר, קְבָרִים, עֶבֶד, עֲבָדִים. It is also possible that it is derived from שָׁוָר, like דָּבָר, דְּבָרִים. It is also not to be excluded that it is from שְׁוָר with the pattern of יְקָר, יְקָרִים, כְּתָב, כְּתָבִים.

מַסֵּכָ֨ה מִכַּסְפָּ֤ם כִּתְבוּנָם֙ (Hos. 13.2): תְּבוּן is a noun meaning 'intelligence', and from this is derived כִּתְבוּנָם. Also תְּבוּנָה is a noun meaning 'intelligence'. The form תְּבוּן has the pattern of גְּבוּל.

בְּאֶ֖רֶץ תַּלְאֻבֽוֹת (Hos. 13.5): The singular would be תַּלְאוּבָה. It is said that its translation is 'deserts'. (Its singular form) may also be the masculine form תַּלְאוּב, with the pattern of תַּמְרוּק.

וְאֶקְרַע סְגוֹר לִבָּם (Hos. 13.8): The form סְגוֹר has the pattern of חֲלוֹם, שְׁחוֹק, חֲגוֹר.

שִׁחֶתְךָ יִשְׂרָאֵל כִּי־בִי בְעֶזְרֶךָ (Hos. 13.9): This is like the speech of somebody saying 'My succour and aid to you has destroyed you', that is 'you imagined on account of the abundance of my aid to you that I was incapable of chastising you'. It says כִּי־בִי בְעֶזְרֶךָ and not כִּי־בִי עֶזְרֶךָ. It is like somebody saying 'somebody has gone out by himself (or: of his own accord) to care for somebody'.

אֱהִי מַלְכְּךָ אֵפוֹא (Hos. 13.10): This means 'Where now is the one who used to say "I shall be your king" to help you, if he is able to save you'.

כִּי הוּא בֵּן אַחִים יַפְרִיא (Hos. 13.15). This has *ʾaleph* and its translation is 'it bears fruit', like יַפְרֶה, which has *heh*.

כָּל־תִּשָּׂא עָוֹן (Hos. 14.3): Its meaning is תִּשָּׂא כָּל־עָוֹן.

Annotations

תְּחִלַּת דִּבֶּר־יְהוָה בְּהוֹשֵׁעַ (Hos. 1:2)
Ibn Nūḥ offers two alternative grammatical readings of this passage. According to one the form דִּבֶּר is interpreted as a verb and according to the other, introduced by the phrase 'and it is said' (*wa-yuqāl*), the form is a noun. When discussing grammatical issues, Ibn Nūḥ frequently cited various alternative opinions. Some of these may have reflected the differing opinions of scholars who were active in the Karaite grammatical circles in the tenth century. It is likely, however, that in most cases the primary purpose of the proposal of such alternatives is pedagogical, in that it was a method of inviting the reader to explore a variety of possibilities without them being necessarily attributable to any particular scholar. It encouraged enquiry and engagement rather than passive acceptance of authority. Indeed the text of Ibn Nūḥ's work appears to be closely associated with the oral teaching of grammar in the school-room rather than drawing on a preceding written source.

The terms translated 'conjoined' (*muḍāf*) and 'disjoined' (*maqṭūʿ*) correspond here to 'construct state' and 'absolute state' in modern terminology, but elsewhere in the *Diqduq* they are also used to express the distinction between what we now call a 'context form' and a 'pausal form' respectively (Khan 2000a: 112–115, Khan 2007c).

Yefet ben ʿEli interprets דִּבֶּר as a noun, as shown by his translation: אול מכֿאטבה אללה להושע 'the first speech of God to Hosea' (in all cases citations from Yefet are from the edition of Polliack and Schlossberg).

אֵ֣שֶׁת זְנוּנִ֔ים (Hos. 1.2)
The *jawhar* 'substance' of a word is broadly equivalent to the concept of abstract root. In Karaite grammatical theory, however, an abstract root did not serve as the base of morphological derivation. Rather the immediate morphological base of most derived words was an imperative form, in this case זְנֵה. Some nouns were considered to be in a morphologically primary form and not derived from any such base. A noun of this type is referred to as *ism bi-raʾsih* 'literally: a noun in its head'. Derivative words are related to their base and to other words derived from this base in what is known as a *luġa* 'lexical class'. The statement here that the nouns in question 'are nouns derived from the lexical class', therefore, refers to the fact that they are derivative and not in a morphologically primary form. For further details regarding Ibn Nūḥ's theory of derivational morphology see Khan (2000a: 39–90).

אֶתְנָ֤ה הֵ֙מָּה֙ לִ֔י (Hos. 2.14)
Ibn Nūḥ presents two opinions regarding the forms אֶתְנָה and אֶתְנָן. Either these are derived nouns ,the latter being derived from the former by the addition of *nun*, or, which he prefers, each is a noun in its primary form (*ism bi-raʾsihi*), without derivative affixes. Yefet in a list of difficult words at the end of his commentary expresses the opinion that the two forms are derived nouns: אֶתְנָה הֵמָּה תפסירהא מתֿל תפסיר אֶתְנָן ואלנון אלאול הוא גֹוהרי ואלנון אלאכיר הו מרכב ואמא אֶתְנָה פאלהֵי פיה מרכבה 'the sense of אֶתְנָ֤ה הֵ֙מָּה֙ is the same as that of אֶתְנָן, the first *nun* of which belongs to the substance (of the word) and the final *nun* is an affix. As for אֶתְנָה, the *heh* in it is an affix' (Polliack and Schlossberg 2009: 252).

As for the meaning of אֶתְנָה, other Karaite sources translate 'wages', e.g. the Anonymous Commentary on Hosea (ed. Niessen) געל הם לי 'they are wages for me', and Yefet אנהמא געלי (variant: געל לי) 'they are my wages/wages for me'.

נִזְמָהּ֙ וְחֶלְיָתָ֔הּ (Hos. 2.15)
The Anonymous Karaite Commentary has a slightly different grammatical analysis in that חֶלְיָה is said to be 'the feminine of חֲלִי

(vocalized חֶלְיֹ), because the absolute state of וַחֲלִי־כָתֶם (Prov. 25.12) is חֶלְיֹ' (מונת חֶלְיֹ לאן וַחֲלִי כָתֶם אלמפרד מנה חֶלְיֹ').

לָכֵן הִנֵּה אָנֹכִי מְפַתֶּיהָ (Hos. 2.16)
Ibn Nūḥ argues that the presence of the *yod* in מְפַתֶּיהָ requires it to be interpreted as a plural participle, since elsewhere forms with *yod* before the pronominal suffix are plural. Although this creates a syntactic difficulty with the singular subject אָנֹכִי, interpretation of meaning must be based strictly on the mophological form. This difficulty is overcome with the interpretation of the 1st person subject as the ultmate cause of the action of the group of people referred to by the form מְפַתֶּיהָ. Ibn Nūḥ interprets the verb as having a positive sense of 'showing kindness'. This is also the interpretation of Yefet, who translates האנא אלטף בהא 'Behold I shall treat her kindly'. Yefet regards the *yod* as pleonastic, as shown by his remark in the list of difficult words at the end of his commentary: מְפתֶיהָ אליוד פיה זאיד 'The *yod* in מְפַתֶּיהָ is added' (Polliack and Schlossberg 2009: 253). In his commentary Yefet states that this refers to a positive action, expressing closeness to her and acceptance of her repentance of sins, 'even though this was not complete repentance, but in accordance with what they had to do in the exile until the appearance of the Teacher of Righteousness' (ואן לם תכן תובה עלי אלכמאל כמא יגב ואנמא חסב מא יגב עליהם אן יפעלוה פי אלגלות אלי אן יטהר מורה צדק). They do not do their complete duty since they are not aware of what this duty is due to the fact that they do not have a Teacher of Righteousness and are unwittingly exposed to error in their understanding of duty. For Yefet and other Karaites the 'Teacher of Righteousness' was a messianic figure who at the end of days would solve difficulties and differences (Erder 2004: 366–368; Polliack and Schlossberg 2009: 282 n.27). This was similar to the concept of Elijah in Rabbinic sources as a messianic solver of difficulties and differences (מתרץ קושיות). Al-Qumisi makes a connection between מורה צדק and Elijah as solver of difficulties (Polliack and Schlossberg 2009: 39). According to Ibn Nūḥ מְפַתֶּיהָ is referring to events in the messianic age, in that it denotes the harbingers of the appearance of Elijah. He supports his construal of מְפַתֶּיהָ as plural by connecting it with the plural verbal form in חַזְּקוּ יָדַיִם רָפוֹת 'strengthen (pl.) weak hands' (Isa. 35.3), a passage that was associated with the messianic age in midrashic literature, e.g. *ʾOṣar Midrašim* (ed. Eisenstein, New York, 1915), 555, where it is interpreted as referring to the encouragement given by Elijah to the Israelites when he announces the arrival of the Messiah.

Al-Fāsī (ed. Skoss 1936–1945: II, 489) translates מְפַתֶּ֫יהָ ‘blandishing her’ (מתמלקהא) and comments that this means אלטף בהא עלי ידי מרשדיהא ‘I shall treat her kindly through her guides’, which appears to echo Ibn Nūḥ’s identification of plural agents of God’s kindness.

The Anonymous Karaite Commentary, by contrast, interprets מְפַתֶּ֫יהָ as having a negative meaning of ‘deceiving’: הודא אנא מוכְדִעְהא ‘Therefore behold I shall deceive her’, stating in the comments that ‘the term “deceiving” alludes to the signs, which he will reveal to them at the end of the exile so that they are deceived by them and go forth to the wilderness’.

אֲהֻ֫בַת רֵ֖עַ וּמְנָאָ֑פֶת (Hos. 3.1)
Yefet translates: זוׄגה מחבובה ענד צאחבהא ‘a wife beloved by her companion’, commenting ‘this companion is a husband’ (הו זוׄג), in accordance with the interpretation of Ibn Nūḥ. Al-Fāsī (ed. Skoss 1936–1945: I, 37) renders מחבובה לצאחבהא ‘beloved to her companion’. The Anonymous Karaite Commentary translates literally: מחבובה רפיק ‘beloved by a companion’.

וָאֶכְּרֶ֣הָ לִּ֔י (Hos. 3.2)
The issue addressed by Ibn Nūḥ here is that third person feminine singular suffixes on verbs can have two forms. He claims that they are used interchangeably without any distinction with regard to their contextual status (‘conjoined’ or ‘disjoined’, corresponding here to ‘context’ and ‘pausal’ forms). The reference to contextual status seems to be motivated by the fact that elsewhere in the *Diqduq* Ibn Nūḥ is exercised to explain the difference between the suffixes in וַֽיִּמְצָאָ֞הּ מַלְאַ֧ךְ יְהוָ֛ה (Gen. 16.7) and וַיִּשְׂנָאֶ֣הָ אַמְנ֗וֹן (2 Sam. 13.15) and opts for the explanation that the former is ‘disjoined’, necessitating the translation ‘he found her—that is to say the angel of the Lord’, whereas the latter is ‘conjoined’ (*Diqduq* to Ps. 105.10, ed. Khan 2000a). Here Ibn Nūḥ expresses a different opinion.

Yefet, the Anonymous Karaite Commentary and al-Fāsī (ed. Skoss 1936–1945: II, 128) agree with Ibn Nūḥ in their derivation of the verb and both translate אתבתתהא לי ‘I established/registered her for me’, i.e. I proved that she is my wife by the payments mentioned in the verse. A similar interpretation is followed by Ibn Ezra. This is contrary to the tradition of interpreting the verb as having the sense of ‘buying’, which can be traced to Rabbinic literature (Babylonian Talmud, Hul. 92a; see Polliack and Schlossberg 2009: 294 for further references).

וְדָמִיתִי אִמֶּךָ (Hos. 4.5)
Yefet and the Anonymous Karaite Commentary translate in the same way: אבכם 'I shall make dumb'.

וּמַקְלוֹ יַגִּיד לוֹ (Hos. 4.12)
Although the attested absolute form of מַקְלוֹ is מַקֵּל, the lack of *dagesh* in the form מַקְלוֹ makes its derivation from the attested form מַקֵּל problematic according to Ibn Nūḥ's system of derivational morphology. The identification of the morphological base of the word as the hypothetical form מֶקֶל is achieved by analogy with forms with suffixes such as רַגְלוֹ, which have the same pattern as מַקְלוֹ. Ibn Nūḥ applies a similar methodology to nouns with the feminine plural ending *-ōṯ* that lack the feminine ending in the attested singular, e.g. the plural form מִזְבְּחוֹת must have as its morphological base the hypothetical form מִזְבְּחָה rather than the attested form מִזְבֵּחַ (Khan 2000a: 64–66).

חֲבוּר עֲצַבִּים אֶפְרָיִם (Hos. 4.17)
According to Ibn Nūḥ a pausal form should always be taken into account in the interpretation of the meaning of a verse. In many cases it marks a discontinuity from one clause to the next due to a shift in what we would call nowadays discourse function (Khan 2000a: 116–127, Khan 2001). This is the point of Ibn Nūḥ's comment here that הַנַּח־לוֹ is a different (unit of) speech and (with) a different sense (כלאם אכר ומעני אכר), in that it marks a shift of function from assertion to command.

One interpretation offered by the Anonymous Karaite Commentary ignores the pausal form and accents and takes 'Ephraim' to be the subject of הַנַּח־לוֹ translating it: [א]פרים קד אקר לה 'Ephraim has established for him(self)'.

אָהֲבוּ הֵבוּ (Hos. 4.18)
The imperative הָבָה is identified elsewhere in the *Diqduq* as the base of יְהָבְךָ (Psa. 55.23) and הָבִי (Ruth 3.15), which, however, is said to have the meaning 'bring!' (האתי) rather than 'give' (Khan 2000a: 276–277, 452–453). Yefet in a list of difficult words at the end of his commentary states: אמרה הֵבָה יחיד הָבוּ אמר רבים הֵבָה עבר אליחיד הֵבוּ עבר רבים מתֿל זֵרוּ את יהודה 'Its imperative is הֵבָה (sic, read הָבָה) in the singular. The plural imperative is הָבוּ. הֵבָה is the past singular and הֵבוּ is the plural past form, like זֵרוּ אֶת־יְהוּדָה (Zech. 2.4)' (Polliack and Schlossberg 2009: 253).

Yefet translates חבו אעטו פגא אלסכ̇ף עלי אג̇לאהא 'they loved and gave, and stupidity came upon her honoured ones'. In his commentary he states that the meaning of 'they gave' is that 'they gave their offerings to foreign gods and gifts to foreign priests in the place that is intended for God's sanctuary'. A fragmentary passage in the Anonymous Karaite Commentary has ואעטו אנפסהם 'they gave themselves', which appears to be an interpretation of הֵבֽוּ.

וְשַׁחֲטָ֥ה שֵׂטִ֖ים הֶעְמִ֑יקוּ (Hos. 5.2)
Ibn Nūḥ interprets שֵׂטִים as the complement of וְשַׁחֲטָה, though does not offer a translation. The Anonymous Karaite Commentary interprets differently with שֵׂטִים the subject of the verb and וְשַׁחֲטָה the fronted object, translating ואלדַבְח האולי אלחאידין גַמַקו 'And the slaughter—these deviants have made deep', and commenting 'they did so frequently and excessively' (כתרו ובאלגו פי דלך). Yefet, on the other hand, interprets שֵׂטִים as the complement of וְשַׁחֲטָה, translating ודׄביחה אלחאידין גמקו 'They have made deep the slaughter of the deviants', but says nothing about its grammatical status. Al-Fāsī (ed. Skoss 1936–1945: II, 660) translates דביחה אלמחידין אלדי קד גמקו שנית 'The slaughter of the deviants that they have made deep I detest'. Al-Qumisi (ed. Markon 1957: 8) also glossed the word as דביחה. Several medieval Rabbanite commentators interpreted the word as infinitive (see Polliack and Schlossberg 2009: 320 for references).

וְלֹֽא־יִגְהֶ֥ה מִכֶּ֖ם מָזֽוֹר (Hos. 5.13)
Yefet translates ולא יברי מנכם אלסקם 'and he will not release the illness from you', using different vocabulary from Ibn Nūḥ. The modifying phrase 'which needs to be sprinkled upon' of Ibn Nūḥ reflects his grammatical analysis of the form as a noun of place or a noun denoting a verbal abstraction.

The Anonymous Karaite Commentary offers various interpretations of יִגְהֶה: (i) in place of יִכְהֶה, (ii) derived from יֵיטִ֣ב גֵּהָ֑ה (Prov. 17.22) and so meaning 'he will improve' (יוחַסִן), or (iii) derived from וְֽלֹא־יִ֝גַּ֗הּ (Job 18.5) and so meaning 'he illuminates, he shines' (יניר יצׄי).

עֲקֻבָּ֖ה מִדָּֽם (Hos. 6.8)
The Anonymous Karaite Commentary translates גרבזה מן גהה ספך אלדם 'deceptive on account of bloodshed' with the comment 'after they had reached the utmost degree of righteousness, these people of Gilead became corrupted…and they deceived the people, shed their

blood and took their properties' (אנהם בעד אן כאנו עלי נהאיה מא יכון מן אלצלאח האולי אהל אלגלעד אנפסדו...וצארו יחתאלוּ עלי אלנאס וג̇רבזה מן ספך פיספוכו דמאהם ויאכ̇דו אמואלהם). Yefet translates אלדמי 'and deceptive in the shedding of blood', commenting that this indicates that 'they shed innocent blood by deception and strategem' (יספכו דם אלברי באלג̇רבזה ואלחייל). Compare Targum בנכלין שאדין דם זכי 'They shed innocent blood with cunning' (Cathcart and Gordon 1989: 42).

כְּמ֣וֹ תַנּ֔וּר בֹּעֵ֖רָה (Hos. 7.4)

Most Karaites hold that בֹּעֵ֖רָה is masculine and the final *heh* is pleonastic. Yefet, in the list of difficult words at the end of his commentary, states that the word is masculine and the *heh* is 'added' (זאיד) since the stress is on the *ʿayin* (Polliack and Schlossberg 2009: 253). The Anonymous Karaite Commentary states that 'the *heh* in בֹּעֵרָה is added since תַנּ֔וּר is masculine'. Al-Fāsī (ed. Skoss 1936–1945: I, 253) comments: הו מדכר בתלחין אלעין מקאם בֹּעֵר ואלהי פהו תפכים 'It is mascline with stress on the *ʿayin* in place of בֹּעֵר, the *heh* being "expansive" (i.e. redundant).' Al-Qumisi (ed. Markon 1957: 10), on the other hand, interprets it as a feminine form referring to the feminine noun אֵשׁ, which he supplies in his paraphrase: כתנור אש אשר בערוה יתירה וחזקה מן מדת העצים אשר השיק בה האופה 'like an oven of fire which they made burn more intensely than the wood that the baker put on it'.

הֶחֱל֥וּ שָׂרִ֖ים (Hos. 7.5)

Ibn Nūḥ interprets the verb as causative. Since such a verb requires an object, he understands this to be an unexpressed reflexive object.

According to Yefet the object of the verb is 'our king': יום מלכנא אמרצ̇ו אלרוסא חמא אלכ̇מר 'the day when the chiefs made our king ill with the heat of wine'. Note also his remarks in the list of difficult words at the end of his commentary (Polliack and Schlossberg 2009: 253): אלאמר מנה הַחֲלֵה פלדלך פסרתה אמרצ̇ו ולם אפסרה מרצ̇ו ויריד בה אמרצ̇ו אלרוסא ללמלך 'Its imperative is הַחֲלֵה and so I have translated it "they made ill" and not "they became ill", the meaning being "the chiefs made the king ill"'. The lack of object marker on מלכנו may have been a grammatical difficulty for Ibn Nūḥ that prevented him from interpreting it as object.

The Anonymous Karaite Commentary offers two interpretations: 'they fell ill...from the great amount of drinking of wine' (מרצ̇ו פי... מן כתרה שורב אלכמר) or 'the chiefs made the king ill because they harmed him with the wine' (אמרצׄו אלמְלִך אלרווסא ממא חאפו עליה באלכמר).

אַיְסִרֵ֕ם כְּשֵׁ֖מַע לַעֲדָתָֽם (Hos. 7.12)
Both the Anonymous Karaite Commentary and Yefet (Polliack and Schlossberg 2009: 253) identify the imperative base of אַיְסִרֵ֕ם as הַיְסֵר. Yefet and al-Fāsī (ed. Skoss 1936–1945: II, 683) translate אודבהם 'I shall discipline them'. The Anonymous commentary states that the verb is derived from the lexical class of 'cessation' (לגה אלזיואל).

כִּֽי־שְׁבָבִ֥ים יִֽהְיֶ֖ה (Hos. 8.6)
Ibn Nūḥ interprets the meaning of שְׁבָבִ֥ים on the basis of וְֽלֹא־יִ֝גַּ֗הּ שְׁבִ֣יב אִשּֽׁוֹ (Job 18.5), justifying this by the morphological analogy of the synonymous pair פֶּסֶל and פְּסִיל. The Anonymous Karaite Commentary also translates 'sparks' (שְׁרַאר). This is, in fact, the interpretation found in the Targum: לנסרי לוחין יהי עגלא דשומרון 'The calf of Samaria will be reduced to bits of boards' (Cathcart and Gordon 1989: 46), which is followed by several western medieval exegetes and grammarians (see Polliack and Schlossberg 2009: 371–372 for references). Yefet, on the other hand, interprets it as 'captivity': פיציר עגֿל שמרון אלי אלסבי 'The calf of Samaria will go into captivity', so also al-Qumisi (ed. Markon 1957: 12): כי יאבדו עצביהם בעת אשר ילכו בגולה 'their idols will perish when they go into exile'.

הִתְנ֥וּ אֲהָבִֽים (Hos. 8.9)
For the imperative form הַתְנֵה see also *Diqduq* (Khan 2000a: 300) and the Anonymous Karaite Treatise on Verbs (Khan 2000b: 108).

וַיָּחֵ֣לּוּ מְּעָ֔ט (Hos. 8.10)
According to Ibn Nūḥ the imperative bases of the categories of verbs that we now call the *hif'il* of final geminate and middle weak verbs must have distinct imperative bases in order to account for their different inflection, although the attested imperatives may seem to have identical patterns, e.g. חָהֵל and הָשֵׁב. The middle weak verb is said to have *yod* in its imperative base. This is sometimes represented in the orthography of the imperative base in the *Diqduq*, e.g. the *Diqduq* to Job 20.15 (ed. Khan 2000a: 378–379): חַ֣יִל בָּ֭לַע וַיְקִאֶ֑נּוּ 'the imperative of וַיְקִאֶנּוּ is הָקֵיא with *yod*, like הָשֵׁיב.' Elsewhere the imperative base of middle weak verbs is written without a *yod* but it is stated that there is *yod* in the underlying substance (*jawhar*) of the verb, e.g. the

Diqduq to Jer. 1.17: 'the imperative הָקֵם has the same pattern as הָחֵת, but has *yod* in the underlying substance (*jawhar*)' (Khan 2000a: 77). A similar analysis is found the Karaite grammatical work *Kitāb al-ʿUqūd fī Taṣārīf al-Luġa al-ʿIbrāniyya* ('Book of Rules regarding the Grammatical Inflections of the Hebrew Language'), studied by Nadezda Vidro (2009: 88, 149–151).

זִבְחֵי הַבְהָבַי (Hos. 8.13)
The identification of the singular form as הַבְהָב implies that Ibn Nūḥ is interpreting the final *yod* as a pronominal suffix. The Anonymous Karaite Commentary translates דבאיח עטאיאי 'the sacrifices of my gifts', and so also interpets the *yod* as a pronominal suffix, but notes that some scholars interpret the final *yod* as pleonastic and so the allusion would be to 'the offerings they used make to the idols' (אלדבאיח אלדי ידבחוהא ללאותאן). Yefet regards the *yod* as pleonastic and translates דׄבאיח אלעטייה (variant: אלעטאיא) 'the sacrifice of the gift(s)'. Al-Fāsī (ed. Skoss 1936–1945: II, 5) analyses הַבְהָבַי as a compound: הבהבי הב הב הבי מן הב הב האת האת '(The form) הַבְהָבַי is הב הבי from הב הב "bring, bring"'.

נְבִ֖יא פַּח יָקוֹשׁ (Hos. 9.8)
Ibn Nūḥ interprets יָקוֹשׁ as an active participle by analogy with עָשׁוֹק, בָּחוֹן, which have the same pattern. Yefet translates with a verb which appears to be passive: אלמדעי מתׄל אלפך יוהק עלי כל טרקאתה 'The pretender (to prophecy) is like the trap that is set on all his roads', which is clarified in the commentary: אלפך אלמנצוב עלי אלטריק 'the trap that is set on the road'. According to al-Fāsī (ed. Skoss 1936–1945: II, 69) the form יוֹקֵשׁ is an active participle (*fāʿil*) and יָקוֹשׁ is a passive participle (*mafʿūl*), but the form יָקוֹשׁ, which occurs in our verse, is an infinitive (*maṣdar*).

מִלֵּדָה וּמִבֶּטֶן וּמֵהֵרָיוֹן (Hos. 9.11)
The Anonymous Karaite Commentary and Yefet translate 'childbirth' (ולאדה). Ibn Nūḥ does not cite any examples of the form לֵדָה being used with the sense of 'a woman in childbirth'. The purpose of his comment is that in principle feminine singular nouns can have both an abstract and a concrete reference. This principle is articulated in various places in the *Diqduq* (Khan 2000a: 103–104). The fact that לֵדָה may not be attested in the biblical corpus with the concrete meaning is no impediment to Ibn Nūḥ positing its existence in the language

due to this principle based on the analogy of feminine singular nouns such as יְשָׁרָה.

אָלוֹת שָׁוְא (Hos. 10.4)
On morphological grounds Ibn Nūḥ argues that אָלוֹת must be an infinitive, but does not offer a translation. Yefet in his commentary to the verse remarks as follows: אָלוֹת שוא יריד בה אנהם כאנו יחלפו באסמה באלכדב 'The meaning of אָלוֹת שָׁוְא is that they were swearing by his name falsely', which may suggest that he interprets אָלוֹת as having verbal force and so an infinitive, like Ibn Nūḥ. In the list of difficult words at the end of his commentary (Polliack and Schlossberg 2009: 254), however, Yefet states: תפסירה חֳרג̇ אסם רבים וְיחִידָהּ אָלָה מתֿל שנה שָׁנוֹת 'its translation is "oaths" (see Blau 2006: 117), it is a plural noun, the singular being אָלָה, like שָׁנָה, שָׁנוֹת,' which corresponds to his translation of the verse חרג̇ אלכדב. The Anonymous Karaite Commentary translates it as a noun: 'false oaths' (חֳורַג̇ גזאף). Note that the Targum renders with a verbal form: ימן לשקר 'they swear falsely' (Cathcart and Gordon 1989: 51).

בָּשְׁנָה אֶפְרַיִם יִקָּח (Hos. 10.6)
Anonymous Karaite Commentary: 'בָּשְׁנָה is a noun in place of בּוֹשָׁה' (בָשנה אסם מקאם בושָׁה). Yefet translates אלכ̇זי 'shame, contempt'; cf. Targum בהתא 'shame' and the medieval western exegetes. In the list of difficult words at the end of his commentary, Yefet offers two alternative morphological analyses: ואלנון פיה זאיד מתֿל שִׁבְעָנָה בנים ויג̇וז אנה אסם בראסה 'The *nun* in it is added, as in שִׁבְעָנָה בָּנִים (Job 42:13). It is also possible that it is a noun in its basic form' (Polliack and Schlossberg 2009: 254).

עַל־בְּנֵי עַלְוָה (Hos. 10.9)
The verse refers to the rising of the tribes to do battle with the tribe of Benjamin on account of the incident of the murder of the concubine (cf. Judg. 19.22ff.). Other Karaite sources, as most other exegetes, interpret עַלְוָה as being equivalent in meaning to עַוְלָה. The Anonymous Karaite Commentary, Yefet and al-Fāsī (ed. Skoss 1936–1945: I, 239) translate ג̇ור 'evildoing'. Yefet comments: והם בני בליעל אלד̇י אתלפו אלפילגש 'they are worthless men who abused the concubine'. Ibn Nūḥ offers a second alternative interpretation of עַלְוָה as an independent noun derived from the verb עלה meaning 'exaltedness' (אלרפעה), without assuming the transposition of letters. Compare al-Fāsī

(ed. Skoss 1936–1945: I, 240), who cites a second interpretation: ויקאל אן בני עלוה אלקריה אלעאליה והו קול מעתל 'It is said that בְּנֵי עַלְוָה means "the upper village", but this is a weak opinion'.

בְּאַוָּתִי וְאֶסֳּרֵם (Hos. 10.10)
The Anonymous Karaite Commentary has a different grammatical analysis: 'The imperative of וְאֶסֳּרֵם is סוֹר "bind!" Its imperative is not אֱסוֹר since then it would have been אֶאֱסְרֵם. It may also be from the lexical class of "chastising" (i.e. יסר), though according to rule it should be then אִסּוֹרֵם'.

אֹהַבְתִּי לָדוּשׁ (Hos. 10.11)
According to al-Fāsī (ed. Skoss 1936–1945: I, 37) אֹהַבְתִּי has a pleonastic final *yod* and has the grammatical pattern of אֹהַבְתְּ like וְיֹלַדְתְּ בֵּן (Gen. 16.11), not אֹהֶבֶת as maintained by Ibn Nūḥ.

וְקָאם שָׁאוֹן בְּעַמֶּךָ (Hos. 10.14)
Also ʾAbū al-Faraj Hārūn regards the *ʾaleph* in וְקָאם as 'added' (זאיד *zāʾid*) 'since it does not belong to the root of this lexical class' (אד ליסת מן אצל הדה אללגה) (Khan, Gallego, and Olszowy-Schlanger 2003d: 296–297). Yefet does not comment on this, but it was remarked on by western grammarians and exegetes. Ḥayyūj interpreted the *ʾaleph* in this word as a reflection of a 'soft' (*layyin*) letter that, according to his grammatical theory, was the middle radical of this verb; cf. *Kitāb al-ʾAfʿāl Ḏawāt Ḥurūf al-Līn* (ed. Jastrow 1897: 66), *Kitāb al-Nutaf* (ed. Basal 2001: 108–109).

כְּשֹׁד שַׁלְמַן בֵּית אַרְבֵאל (Hos. 10.14)
Yefet comments that Shalman could be Shalmaneser, in that it is 'half of the full name', אסר being a theophoric element referring to an idol of the Assyrians. He may also be another person who was an enemy of Israel. A similar analysis had already been expressed by Saadiah Gaon (see Polliack and Schlossberg 2009: 425 for references). The Anonymous Karaite Commentary remarks 'Some interpret the phrase as Shalmaneser; others, however, hold that it is the name of a king who plundered a city which is called Beth-Arbeland who was a famous (and) well-known king' (יוקאל אנה שלמנאסר וקיל אנה אסם מלך נְהַב קריה יוקאל להא בית ארבַל וכאן מלך משהור מערוף). Al-Fāsī likewise interprets the name as a shortened form (*muḵtaṣar*) of Shalmaser (ed. Skoss 1936–1945: II, 676).

כִּמְרִ֥ימֵי עֹ֖ל עַ֣ל לְחֵיהֶ֑ם (Hos. 11.4)
Yefet agrees with Ibn Nūḥ and translates מת̇ל מרפעי אלניר עלי טראו־תהם 'like those who lift the yoke on their moistness'. Note also his remark in the list of difficult words (Polliack and Schlossberg 2009: 254): תפסירה טראותהם מת̇ל עֵץ לַח ולו כאן תפסירה כ̇דיהם לכאן לֶחְיֵהֶם 'its translation is "their moisture" like עֵֽץ־לַ֙ח (Ezek. 21:3). If its translation were "their jaws", it would be לֶחְיֵהֶם.' Other Karaite sources translate the word as 'their jaws', e.g. the Anonymous Karaite Commentary (כַּ̇דיהם) and al-Fāsī (ed. Skoss 1936–1945: II, 105) (לחיהם).

וְאַ֥ט אֵלָ֖יו אוֹכִֽיל (Hos. 11.4)
Yefet translates: ואמיל אליה אוסע וקיל ואלטף בה אוסע 'I shall incline towards him and give power. It is said (it may also mean): I shall show gentleness to him and give power.' In his list of difficult words (Polliack and Schlossberg 2009: 254) he follows the first interpretation: וְאַט אמרה הַטֵה מת̇ל וָאַךְ אתך אמרה הַכֵה והו נאקץ הֵי 'The imperative of וְאַט is הַטֵה, like וָאַ֥ךְ אוֹתְךָ֛ (Exod. 9:15), in that it lacks *heh*.' The Anonymous Karaite Commentary translates מִלְ̇ת אליה ואנא אַ[טִי]ק 'I bent down to him, and I shall prevail' which is explained as meaning 'I have shown my benificence to them' (את̇הרת אחסאני עליהם) and 'all I have promised them, I shall be able to do' (גמיע מא וְעַדתהם בה אנא אקדר עליה). Al-Fāsī translates סאמייל אליה אלאפאת פאפניה 'I shall bring down (literally: cause to incline) misfortunes upon him and destroy him', interpreting אוֹכִיל as being related to כִּלָּה (ed. Skoss 1936–1945: II, 105).

וְחָלָ֥ה חֶ֙רֶב֙ בְּעָרָ֔יו (Hos. 11.6)
Ibn Nūḥ's translation of וְחָלָה with a participle and the verb 'to be' (ומבתדיה תכון אלסיף literally: 'one that begins will be the sword') rather than a finite verbal form reflects his analysis of the form as being derived from a noun base rather than a verbal imperative base. He says that it has the pattern of שָׁבָה and בָּאָה, which, according to modern parsing, are feminine singular participles. It is clear from elsewhere in the *Diqduq*, however, that Ibn Nūḥ believed that forms with unequivocably verbal inflection could be derived from noun bases. This applies, for example, to the form בֹּ֣ושׁוּ (Ps. 22.6) with a verbal inflectional ending. When verbs have a noun base, Ibn Nūḥ held that this should be reflected in their translation into Arabic by a nominal participle, e.g. בֹּ֣ושׁוּ (Ps. 22.6) should be translated *ṣārū ḵāziyīn* 'they

became ashamed'. Likewise the form תִּשְׁמוּרֵם (Prov. 14.3) is said to have a noun base and should be translated *takūn ḥāfiẓa lahum* 'it will be one that preserves them' rather than *taḥfuẓuhum* 'it will preserve them' (see Khan 2000a: 56–58 for further details).

The interpretation of the form as having the meaning of 'beginning' is found in other Karaite sources. Yefet translates ותבתדי אלסיף פי בלדאנה 'and the sword will begin in his cities', using a finite verb, and analyses the form as having an imperative base in his list of difficult words: אמרה חל מתל וְשָׁבָה לְאֶתְנַנָּה אמרה שוב 'its imperative is חל like וְשָׁבָה לְאֶתְנַנָּה (Isa. 23:17), the imperative of which is שׁוּב'. Al-Qumisi offers the Arabic gloss ויבתדי 'it will begin' (ed. Markon: 19). The Anonymous Karaite Commentary interprets this as meaning that 'the sword of the king of Assur began among them' (קד אבתדת סיף מלך אשור פיהם), but in the grammatical notes embedded in this text it is stated that the form is really a participle meaning (literally) 'it comes about beginning' (תחצול מובתדייה). Targum, on the other hand, interprets the form as meaning 'will occur/fall' (תחול), as also western medieval grammarians and exegetes (see Polliack and Schlossberg 2009: 434 for references).

וְעַמִּי תְלוּאִים לִמְשׁוּבָתִי. (Hos. 11.7)

The Anonymous Karaite Treatise on Verbs gives the imperative base of this as תְּלַא (sic vocalized with *pataḥ* in the manuscript) with the meaning 'be incapable' (אעגז), in accordance with the interpretation of Ibn Nūḥ (Khan 2000b: 76–77). Likewise al-Qumisi derives the form from תְּלָאָה. Targum has פליגין 'divided, undecided'. Yefet and the Anonymous Commentary, on the other hand, translate מעלקין 'suspended', as do western medeival grammarians and exegetes (see Polliack and Schlossberg 2009: 434 for references). In his list of difficult words Yefet states אמרה תְּלָא מתֹל קְרָא קְרוּאִים ואלתָו פיה גׄוהרי ולדלך עברתה מעלקין ולם אעברה עגׄזין 'Its imperative is תְּלָא like קְרוּאִים, קְרָא and the *taw* in it is a radical, so I have translated it "suspended" and not "incapable"', suggesting that he did not recognize the existence of an imperative form תְּלָא with a *taw* radical.

וְאֶל־עַל יִקְרָאֻהוּ (Hos. 11.7)

The interpretation of עַל as meaning' Exalted One 'is found in other Karaite sources. Yefet translates: ואלי אלעאלי ינאדוה 'and to the Exalted One they call him'. The Anonymous Karaite Commentary interprets 'He calls them through [his] prophets [...to] the Exalted One' (ויסתד-

אלעאלי [ה אלי]עיהם עלי אידי אנביא). ʾAbū al-Faraj Hārūn in *al-Kitāb al-Kāfī* interprets the form עַל as a 'noun' rather than a particle (Khan, Gallego, and Olszowy-Schlanger 2003d: 56–57). Ibn Nūḥ's alternative interpretation of the word as a noun meaning 'benefit' (*al-nafʿ*) is not found in other sources. Al-Fāsī (ed. Skoss 1936–1945: II, 396) interprets the word as a preposition with the sense of 'in the presence of' (*ʿinda*): ואלי ענד אלדי ידעונה גמיעא לא ישרף להם קדר אעני אלדאעי ואלמדעא 'and to the presence of the ones who call him—no power oversees any of them, I mean the caller or the called', comparing יֶעֱרַב עָלָיו שִׂיחִי (Ps. 104.34), where he claims the preposition also has the sense of *ʿinda*.

וְלֹא אָבוֹא בְּעִיר (Hos. 11.9)
According to Ibn Nūḥ a modifying phrase such as 'of anybody other than you' must be assumed to have been the complement of the conjoined form בְּעִיר and should be supplied in the translation, although this was elided. Elsewhere Ibn Nūḥ refers to this process explicitly as elision 'in the compilation (*fī al-tadwīn*)' of the text (see Khan 2000a: 128–131 for futher details). Yefet translates literally ולא אדכֹל פי מדינה 'I shall not enter a town', commenting יריד בה אני בעד אן אזלת כבודי מן ירושלים פליס אדכֹל בה אלי מדינה אכֹרי 'it means "After I have removed my honour from Jerusalem I shall not take it into another city"'. The translation in the Anonymous Karaite Commentary, although fragmentary, clearly supplies a phrase after עִיר and can be reconstructed 'I will not enter a cit[y other] th[an Jerusale]m' (וליס אדכול פי קרי[ה אוכרי] א[לא פי ירושל]ם). The commentary on this is 'he shows [that he will not choose] another land than the special land' (אור[א אנה ליס יכתא]ר בבלד גיר אלבלד אלכאץ). ʾAbū al-Faraj Hārūn in *al-Kitāb al-Kāfī* interprets בְּעִיר as a form that is 'not conjoined' (גיר מצׄאף), contrary to Ibn Nūḥ, (Khan, Gallego, and Olszowy-Schlanger 2003d: 664–665).

וִיהוּדָה עֹד רָד עִם־אֵל (Hos. 12.1)
Yefet translates ואיצׄא יהודה אלדׄי כאן טאיע ענד אלקאדר 'and also Judah who was obedient to the Almighty' (surrounded him with deceit)', which is close to the interpretation of Ibn Nūḥ. The Anonymous Karaite Commentary has ואל יהודה זאדה אסתולא מע אל[טאיק] ומע אלקו[דוס אלתא]ב[ת] 'And the people of Judah also became rulers with the Powerful One and the reliable Holy One', which is interpreted in the commentary thus 'It was not enough what Israel had

done, until also Judah had been established among them. The word רָד means “they made themselves masters”, “they became chiefs”, i.e. they had no need of me. Though I am powerful and though I am special and reliable, they had no need of me because of the manufactured idols who have no power and are not reliable’ (מא כפא מא פְעַלוה ישראל חתי יהודה איֿצא קד תאסא בהם וקו׳ רָדֿ יעני אסתַוולַו צארו ברוסא יעני אַסְתַגְנו עני מע מא אנא קאדר ומע מא אנא מכצוץ ותאבת אסתגנו עני באלאצנאם אלמוחדַתִה אלדי הי גַיר קאדרה וגַיר תאבתה). All interpret עוֹד as ‘also’. Note the use of the Persian particle הַם by Ibn Nūḥ, which is found elsewhere in his writings and in other Arabic texts written by his Karaite contemporaries (Khan 2000a: 157). Ibn Nūḥ and Yefet interpret רָד as an adjective ‘obedient’, but the Anonymous Commentary interprets this as a verb.

וְדִבַּ֙רְתִּי֙ עַל־הַנְּבִיאִ֔ים (Hos. 12.11)
The two different positions of the stress in the word וְדִבַּרְתִּי in Hos. 2.16 and Hos. 12.11 are cited by ʾAbū al-Faraj Hārūn in the introduction to *al-Kitāb al-Kāfī* as an example of the importance of paying attention to grammatical detail for the sake of the correct interpretation of the meaning of Scripture (Khan, Gallego, and Olszowy-Schlanger 2003d: 12–13).

בַּגִּלְגָּ֖ל שְׁוָרִ֣ים זִבֵּ֑חוּ (Hos. 12.12)
The Anonymous Karaite Commentary advocates one of these alternative morphological bases: ‘[The singular of] שְׁוָרִים is שְׁוָר, and it (is used) in the place of of שׁוֹר’ (שְׁוָרִים שְׁוָר והו מקאם שׁוֹר [ ]).

מַסֵּכָ֨ה מִכַּסְפָּ֤ם כִּתְבוּנָם֙ (Hos. 13.2)
Yefet translates כתמייזהם ‘in accordance with their discernment’ (variant: עלי קדר פהמהם ‘in accordance with their understanding’). The Anonymous Karaite Commentary, by contrast, renders כבנייתהם ‘according to their structure/shape’.

בְּאֶ֖רֶץ תַּלְאֻבֽוֹת (Hos. 13.5)
The word תַּלְאֻבוֹת is translated ‘deserts’ also by Yefet (אלקפאר) and the Anonymous Karaite Commentary (קִפָֿאר). Yefet in his list of difficult words (Polliack and Schlossberg 2009: 254) states הו אסם רבים ויחידה תלאובה והי פרדיה פי אלמקרא ‘It is a plural noun, its singular being תַּלְאוּבָה. It is unique in Scripture’.

שִׁחֶתְךָ֥ יִשְׂרָאֵ֖ל כִּֽי־בִ֥י בְעֶזְרֶֽךָ (Hos. 13.9)
The remarks of Ibn Nūḥ indicate that he interprets the phrase כִּֽי־בִ֥י בְעֶזְרֶֽךָ as meaning 'the fact that (I) by myself (have gone out) in your aid'. Yefet translates אפסדך יא ישראל אלד֗י בי נצרתך 'It destroyed you, oh Israel, that your help was through me' and comments אלד֗י בי כנת תצרך֗ אי באסמי כנת תדעי פי אוקאת שדאידך אנא כנת פי נצרתך 'that you cried to me, that is you called on my name, in times of trouble and I was your aid'. The Anonymous Karaite Commentary translates אנמא אפסדך יא אל אסראיל לִאַן בי כאנת תסתעין פצירת פי עַוְנך 'Indeed, it has destroyed you, oh people of Israel. For you turned to me for help, and I became your help', adding the comment מא אפסדכם ואהלככם אלא מא כונת אנתצר לכם ואגיתכם אבדא 'He would not have destroyed and annihilated you, if I had helped you and given you support'.

אֱהִ֤י מַלְכְּךָ֙ אֵפ֔וֹא (Hos. 13.10)
Yefet translates אכון מלכך אין הו ההנא חתי יגית֗ך פי כל בלדאנך '"I shall be your king"—where is he? Is he here to help you in all your cities?' The Anonymous Karaite Commentary translates אַין אלדי כאן יקול לך אנא אכון מליכך אלאן חתי יג̄יתך פי כל קוראך 'Where is the one who said to you, "I will now be your king", so that he may help you in all your cities?' Al-Fāsī (ed. Skoss 1936–1945: I, 428) has אלדי קאל לך אנא מלכך אכון אין הו פיגיתך 'The one who said to you "I shall be your king"—where is he that he may help you?'

כָּל־תִּשָּׂ֣א עָ֗וֹן (Hos. 14.3)
In the manuscript the scribe originally wrote מעניה כל תשא עון 'its meaning is כָּל־תִּשָּׂא עָוֹן', without any change in the order of the Biblical text, but this was corrected by a second hand by the deletion of the initial כָּל and its insertion between the final two words. In the *Diqduq* to Ps. 141.10 Ibn Nūḥ states that this arose by the process known as מקדם ומאוחר *muqdam 'u-me'uḥar* 'putting forward and putting back' and proposes that 'its meaning is כָּל־עָוֹן תִּשָּׂא' with a different word order from what we have in our text (Khan 2000a: 352–353). This interpretation is followed in the translations of Yefet (כל ד̇נב תגפר 'May you forgive all iniquity') and the Anonymous Karaite Commentary (כל דנב לנא תגפר 'May You forgive us all iniquity').

Concluding Remarks

The comparison of Ibn Nūḥ's grammatical and exegetical comments with other medieval Karaite works reveals numerous parallels but also a significant number of differences. Although many of the texts contain grammatical analyses that follow the same theoretical system as that of Ibn Nūḥ, it is clear that the authors of the texts are not dependent on Ibn Nūḥ's *Diqduq*. This is shown by the fact that their analyses are sometimes different from the ones presented by Ibn Nūḥ. Furthermore the comparative texts contain grammatical analyses of Hebrew words that are not included by Ibn Nūḥ. There is also a considerable diversity of exegesis across the Karaite corpus.

References

Basal, N. 1998. 'Part One of al-Kitāb al-Muštamil by Abū al-Faraj Harūn and Its Dependence on Ibn al-Sarrāj's Kitāb al-'Uṣūl fī al-Naḥw', *Lešonénu* 61: 191–209.

——. 1999. 'The Concept of ḥāl in al-Kitāb al-Muštamil of 'Abū al Faraj Hārūn in comparison with Ibn al Sarrāj', *Israel Oriental Studies* 19: 391–408.

——. 2001. *Kitāb al-Nutaf by Juda Ḥayyūj: A Critical Edition* (Tel Aviv: Tel Aviv University).

Birnbaum, P. 1942. *The Arabic Commentary of Yefet ben 'Ali the Karaite on the Book of Hosea* (Philadelphia: Dropsie College).

Blau, J. 2006. *A Dictionary of Mediaeval Judaeo-Arabic Texts* (Jerusalem: Academy of Hebrew Language, Israel Academy of Science and Humanities).

Cathcart, K.J., and R.P. Gordon. 1989. *The Targum of the Minor Prophets: Translated, with a Critical Introduction, Apparatus, and Notes* (The Aramaic Bible, 14; Edinburgh: T. & T. Clark).

Delgado, J.M. 2010. *Libro de la facilitación Kitab At-Taysir: diccionario judeo-árabe de hebreo bíblico* (Granada: Universidad de Granada).

Erder, Y. 2004. *The Karaite Mourners of Zion and the Qumran Scrolls* (Tel Aviv: Hakibbutz Hameuchad) [in Hebrew].

Jastrow, M. 1897. *The Weak and Geminative Verbs in Hebrew by Abu Zakariyyâ Yaḥyâ Ibn Dâwud of Fez known as Ḥayyûğ* (Leiden: Brill).

Khan, G. 2000a. *The Early Karaite Tradition of Hebrew Grammatical Thought: Including a Critical Edition, Translation and Analysis of the Diqduq of 'Abū Ya'qūb Yūsuf ibn Nūḥ on the Hagiographa* (Studies in Semitic Languages and Linguistics, 32; Leiden: Brill).

——. 2000b. *Early Karaite Grammatical Texts* (Masoretic Studies, 9; Atlanta: Society of Biblical Literature).

——. 2001. 'Biblical Exegesis and Grammatical Theory in the Karaite Tradition', in *Exegesis and Grammar in Medieval Karaite Texts* (ed. G. Khan; Journal of Semitic Studies Supplement, 13; Oxford: Oxford University Press) 127–149.

——. 2007. 'The Contextual Status of Words in the Early Karaite Tradition of Hebrew Grammar', in *Sha'arei Lashon. Studies in Hebrew, Aramaic, and Jewish Languages Presented to Moshe Bar-Asher* (ed. A. Maman, S.E. Fassberg, and Y. Breuer; Jerusalem: Bialik Institute) *117–*131.

Khan, G., M.A. Gallego, and J. Olszowy-Schlanger. 2003. *The Karaite Tradition of Hebrew Grammatical Thought in Its Classical Form: A Critical Edition and English Translation of Al-Kitāb Al-Kāfī Fī Al-Luġa Al-ʿIbrāniyya by ʾAbū Al-Faraj Hārūn Ibn Al-Faraj* (Studies in Semitic Languages and Linguistics, 37; Leiden: Brill).
Maman, A. 1996a. 'Ha-Maḥašava ha-Diqduqit b-Imey ha-Beynayim: Ben ha-Qaraim la-Rabbanim', *Language Studies* 7: 79–96.
——. 1996b. 'Ha-Maqor we-Šem ha-Peʿulla be-Tfisat ʾAbu al-Faraj Harun', in *Studies in Hebrew and Jewish Languages Presented to Shelomo Morag* (ed. M. Bar-Asher; Jerusalem: Bialik Institute) 119–149.
——. 2007. 'Karaite Hebrew Grammatical Thought: State of the Art', in *Maimónides y su Época* (ed. C. del Valle and S. García-Jalón; Madrid: Sociedad Estatal de Conmemoraciones Culturales) 429–438.
Mann, J. 1972. *Texts and Studies in Jewish History and Literature* (New York: Ktav).
Margoliouth, G. 1897. 'Ibn al-Hītī's Arabic Chronicle of Karaite Doctors', *Jewish Quarterly Review* 9 (3): 429–443.
Markon, I. 1957. *Daniel al-Qumisi: Pitron Šenem ʿAśar* (Jerusalem: Meqiṣe Nirdamim).
Niessen, F. 2001. 'An Anonymous Karaite Commentary on the Book of Hosea', in *Exegesis and Grammar in Medieval Karaite Texts* (ed. G. Khan; Journal of Semitic Studies Supplement, 13; Oxford: Oxford University Press) 77–126.
——. forthcoming. *A Karaite Commentary on Hosea* (Leiden-Boston: Brill).
Polliack, M., and E. Schlossberg. 2009. *Yefet Ben ʿEli's Commentary on Hosea. Annotated Edition, Hebrew Translation and Introduction* (Ramat Gan: Bar-Ilan University Press).
Skoss, S.L. 1936–1945. *The Hebrew-Arabic Dictionary of the Bible, Known as Kitāb Jāmiʿ Al-Alfāẓ (Agrōn) of David Ben Abraham Al-Fāsī the Karaite* (Yale Oriental Series Researches, 20–21; New Haven: Yale University Press).
Vidro, N. 2009. *Verbal Morphology in the Karaite Treatise on Hebrew Grammar Kitāb al-ʿUqūd fī Taṣārīf al-Luġa al-ʿIbrāniyya* (Ph.D. thesis; Cambridge: University of Cambridge).
Zislin, M.N. 1990. *Meʾor ʿAyin* (Moscow: Nauka).

GENERAL INDEX

BIBLICAL REFERENCES

RABBINIC REFERENCES